H A N D B O O K S

W9-DFO-547

DOMINICAN REPUBLIC

ANA CHAVIER CAAMAÑO

DOMINICAN REPUBLIC

SANTUARIO DE BALLENAS
JOROBADAS
DEL BANCO DE LA PLATA

A T L A N T I C   O C E A N

Playa Grande

Río San Juan

Parque Nacional Cabo Frances Viejo

Playa El Bretón

Playa Diamante

Bahía Escocesa

Playa Boza De Bojolo

Nagua

Las Terrenas

S a m a n á   P e n i n s u l a

Las Galeras

Playa Rincón

Cabo Samaná

5

Río Yuna

Sánchez

Santa Barbara de Samaná

Bahía de Samaná

Contuí

Parque Nacional Los Haitises

Sabana de la Mar

Reserva Científica Lagunas Redonda y Limón

Miches

El Cedro

C o r d i l l e r a   O r i e n t a l

Santo Domingo

103

107

Río Chavón

El Macao

Coastal Plain

Monte Plata

Hato Mayor

El Seíbo

Bávaro

Playa Cabeza de Toro

Río Ozama

Bayaguana

Río Magua

Río Soco

Higüey

1

SANTO DOMINGO

4

MELLA   HWY

Boca Chica

LAS AMÉRICAS   HWY

San Pedro de Macorís

4

3

La Romana

4

Punta Cana

Playa Punta Cana

San Cristóbal

Parque Nacional Submarino La Caleta

Playa Boca Chica

Playa Juan Dolio

Boca de Yuma

Playa Juanillo

Playa La Caleta

LAS AMÉRICAS INTERNATIONAL AIRPORT

Isla Catalina

Playa Bayahibe

Parque Nacional de Este

Playa Dominicus

S e a

Isla Saona

0   20 mi

0   20 km

Contents

Discover
the Dominican Republic

My memories of yearly visits to the Dominican Republic are dominated by my senses: the smell of the ocean while running through the waters of Boca Chica; the feel of the rough terrain of La Península de Samaná; the taste of afternoon espressos served in the backyard of our family home; and the impossible-to-ignore sound of merengue transcending the decades.

It can't go unnoticed that the Dominican Republic truly is a country of synchronized contrasts. It is a country of great antiquity and promising modernity but one deeply rooted in tradition and cultural pride. It is a land where lizard-inhabited deserts, coconut grove beaches, and mountainous peaks coexist. The Atlantic Ocean on the northern coast and the Caribbean Sea on the southern coast rock and sway as if dancing to the beat of a romantic *bachata*. Peaks and dales continue the curvaceous trend inland until the sultry heat and thick brine of the ocean air give way to the cool mountain breezes of the Cordillera Central – the mountain range home to the Caribbean's tallest peak, Pico Duarte. In the bustling capital city of Santo Domingo, 16th-century architecture sits alongside trendy bars and restaurants on the narrow cobblestone streets of Ciudad Colonial.

The Dominican Republic was the fountainhead for the New World and has given the western hemisphere many "firsts." The first paved road, the first hospital, and first university. But along with these

impressive beginnings, the Dominican Republic owns a tragic history with the genocide of the Taíno people, troubled Haitian/Dominican relations, and a brutal 20th-century dictatorship.

Most tourists flock to the country for its famous white-sand beaches, which teeter on the cliché of a postcard metaphor, but the Dominican Republic offers more. It is home to the world-renowned wind-surfing capital of Cabarete, white-water rafting on the Río Yaque del Norte, diving among some of the Caribbean's best-preserved reefs, a raucous Merengue Festival in Santo Domingo, and whale-watching in the Bahía de Samaná. In the underbelly of the island Taíno history is evident, with some of the best examples of rupestrian art in the Caribbean. The adventurous traveler has an abundance of opportunities, such as hiking the mountain ranges in Jarabacoa or canyoning down amazing waterfalls in Damajagua. Regardless of which region you choose, or what you seek, the Dominican Republic's recreational grab bag makes it a dynamic destination that offers something for every kind of traveler.

Planning Your Trip

▶ WHERE TO GO

Santo Domingo

Known as one of the Caribbean's most cosmopolitan cities, Santo Domingo offers fine dining, merengue-bumping dance clubs, cultural events with world-renowned acts, and top-notch accommodations. Rich with historical sights and restored colonial buildings, the central area of Ciudad Colonial is the bread and butter of Santo Domingo's tourism industry. History and metropolitan comforts like art and shopping are the perks of being in this bustling hive of activity.

The South-Central Coast

Running east from Santo Domingo to San Pedro de Macorís, this coastal area is perfect for a low-key beach vacation. The towns of Guayacanes and Juan Dolio offer quiet charm and beautiful beaches protected by offshore coral reefs. Vacationers who come here enjoy comfortable resort amenities without the clogged mass tourism of the Southeast and north.

The Southeast

The Southeast region—including the popular La Romana, Bayahibe, Bávaro, and Punta Cana areas—offers affordable Caribbean vacations with manicured beaches, exceptional golf courses, and both luxurious and all-inclusive accommodations. Ecotourism is alive and well in this region, home to two large national parks: arid Parque Nacional del Este and the mangrove-lined and cave-rich Parque Nacional Los Haitises. Just offshore, the most popular day trip of the region is to the powdery white-sand beaches of Isla Saona.

IF YOU HAVE...

Salto El Limón, La Península de Samaná

- **A LONG WEEKEND:** Visit Santo Domingo, the Ciudad Colonial, and the beaches of Guayacanes and Juan Dolio.
- **ONE WEEK:** See Puerto Plata, Damajagua, Cabarete, and Sosúa.
- **TWO WEEKS:** Travel to La Península de Samaná, Jarabacoa, and Constanza.

La Península de Samaná

This small sliver of land has become the Dominican Elysian fields of expats and independent travelers. The major communities—Las Terrenas, Las Galeras, and Samaná—have an individualistic feel and shun the "cookie cutter" vibe typical of other

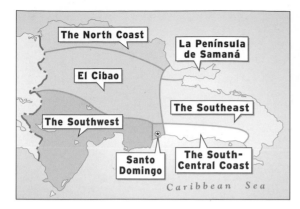

The North Coast

La Península de Samaná

El Cibao

The Southeast

The Southwest

Santo Domingo

The South-Central Coast

Caribbean Sea

regions. Humpback whales are the main draw to this region during winter months, when they come to the Bahía de Samaná to breed and give birth.

The North Coast

Stretching from the lowland lagoon in Río San Juan to the high cliffs and salt flats of Monte Cristi, the north coast's undulating topography is famous for the all-inclusive resort trend of the centrally located Puerto Plata and Playa Dorada area. The windsurfing

mecca of Cabarete and the snorkeling of Sosúa continue to draw tourists' attention eastward. West of Puerto Plata is tiny Luperón, whose pretty beaches are the gateway to the less tourist-trodden northwest section, including Parque Nacional Monte Cristi, a diving purist's dream.

El Cibao

The Cibao region has mountainous national parks, an eternal springtime climate, and scientific reserves that are home to endemic flora and fauna attracting nature lovers of all kinds. Outdoor activities abound, including parasailing, whitewater rafting, and canyoning in Jarabacoa and Constanza. Amid all this natural beauty is the nation's second largest city, Santiago, a vibrant metropolis rivaling Santo Domingo in cultural activity and nightlife.

The Southwest

Offering a diverse range of landscapes—desert

All-inclusive beach resorts can make the DR an easy stay.

the cliffs and crystalline waters of Bahía de las Águilas

terrain, verdant valleys, freshwater lagoons, saltwater lakes—this region is a perfect choice for visitors seeking a unique experience. At the largest park in the nation, Parque Nacional Jaragua, flamingo nesting grounds are just a boat ride away on the shores of Laguna de Oviedo. North of the park, the terrain turns to desert surrounding the salty Lago Enriquillo—where crocodiles and iguanas lounge about. At Bahía de Las Águilas, you will visit the most pristine beach in the country.

▶ WHEN TO GO

Most of the Dominican Republic enjoys balmy weather with average temperatures of 28–31°C (82–88°F) throughout the year. The exception to this climate is in the central mountains, where temperatures can sink to near freezing at night.

The heaviest tourist season is December–February, hiking up prices during these months. In La Península de Samaná the tourist season starts in December and tapers off in March due to prime humpback whale mating season. If you visit in February, try to attend Carnaval celebrations.

Dominicans usually take their vacations

street food in Santo Domingo

Carnaval is one of the DR's favorite festivals.

during Semana Santa (Holy Week), which is celebrated the week before Easter Sunday, making it difficult to book hotel rooms. It is like the Dominican spring break, and many beaches are closed due to the high incidence of drunken accidents. If you want to experience Santo Domingo without all the hectic ferocity that it normally has, Semana Santa is perfect timing.

While it may be tempting to take advantage of cheap airfare in the summer months, the trade-offs are mosquitoes, hurricanes, and extreme humidity. But the pluses are shorter lines and cheaper resort rates. The rainy season runs from May to October and sometimes through December in the northern half of the country. November is a good time because the big wave of tourists hasn't arrived yet.

▶ BEFORE YOU GO

Passports, Tourist Cards, and Visas

Every nationality needs a valid passport to enter the Dominican Republic. Most travelers don't need visas, just a tourist card. Check www.godominicanrepublic.com for a complete list of countries and requirements.

Tourist cards cost US$10 and are valid for up to 30 days. They can be purchased upon arrival. To stay longer than 30 days, you will need to pay about US$5 for each month you have overstayed.

Vaccinations

No vaccinations are required for entry into the Dominican Republic, but some are recommended for longer stays: hepatitis A, hepatitis B, tetanus-diphtheria, typhoid, chickenpox, and rabies.

Transportation

Many tourists take advantage of discounted packages available online that include airfare, all-inclusive hotel, and transportation. Crave a bit more independence? Try booking online

lush countryside of the Dominican Republic

for flights only, with sites like www.expedia.com or www.orbitz.com.

Once on the ground, taxis are easy to find at all airports. Agree on price before getting into the car. Santo Domingo's public taxi system is the *público*. These cheap public taxis have set routes and act as buses picking up other riders along their routes. *Motoconchos* are small moto-taxis. Although cost-effective, they can be dangerous and are recommended only for the adventurous.

Although car rental gives you freedom from the schedules of public transportation, fees and fuel costs run high, as do auto incidents.

The two major bus companies, Caribe Tours and Metro, have comfortable buses shuttling between major cities. Getting to smaller towns is done via the even cheaper guagua system. *Guaguas* are often crowded, and tourists can be overcharged.

What to Take

Consider anything drugstore-related a must-take to the Dominican Republic, especially if you are staying in a resort, as prices are highest there. Don't leave home without your prescription medications.

Lightweight fabric is a good choice for this warm climate, but take a warm layer for chilly nights near the ocean. Overall, the mountains are much cooler; pack warm and expect rain in the winter.

Diversity of landscape and activities signals diversity of footwear: sandals for beaches, boots for hiking, dress shoes for nighttime. Consider water shoes for wallowing in the surf to avoid cutting your feet on coral beds or stepping on sea critters.

Dominicans dress up to socialize. Jeans and T-shirts are sometimes too casual for evening, and many discos and restaurants have strict dress codes (especially in the cities). Daytime sightseeing calls for light clothing but never beachwear. Many historical sites and churches have strict rules about what is appropriate attire. For instance, going into the cathedral in the Ciudad Colonial wearing shorts, flip-flops, and a tank top is considered disrespectful.

Explore the Dominican Republic

▶ THE BEST OF THE DOMINICAN REPUBLIC

If you can swing it, 10–14 days in the Dominican Republic would give you sufficient time to dive into each of the various regions. With such biodiversity in one country, you may be surprised to discover just how wide the spectrum of activities ranges. This itinerary is for someone who is active and excited to dig into the nature and culture of the Dominican Republic. It is meant only as a "highlights to hit" itinerary. If you're traveling along and happen to fall in love with the surf scene in Cabarete, for instance, simply stop and keep surfing.

Day 1

Arrive at Aeropuerto Internacional Las Américas in Santo Domingo and settle into your hotel in the Ciudad Colonial. If you arrive during the day, set out on foot to explore the colonial sights and orient yourself. For dinner go to one of the restaurants on the Plaza de la Hispanidad.

Day 2

Spend the day exploring the Ciudad Colonial and all of its sights, including the New World's first street, Calle de las Damas, and ruins of the first hospital, Ruinas del Hospital San Nicolás de Barí. Leave time for the oldest cathedral in the western hemisphere, the Catedral Primada de América, and the Museo de las Casas Reales. Have

Ciudad Colonial, Santo Domingo

SEXIEST BEACHES

You: a bevy of swimsuits, sarongs, sunglasses, and trashy novels. The Dominican Republic: a plethora of dreamy beaches waiting for you to write your name in the sand, from manicured all-inclusive resort beaches to wild, remote hideaway coves. This is a winning combination.

Aura Beach House at Juan Dolio is, by far, the sexiest lounging spot for sophisticated beachgoers who want to simply pass the day at the beach but definitely don't want to rough it. Let's face it. All you want to do is get wet and then get hot in the sun, right? That makes Aura an ultra-sexy spot. Beds canopied with white fabric give optional shady spots (or privacy).

The beach at **Bahía Principe Clubs and Resorts** in Bávaro is a spot where you can mix with other sun-worshippers and order a cocktail in the sand.

Playa Limón on La Costa Esmeralda is popular with excursion tours because of its exquisitely beautiful coconut groves.

At **Cayo Levantado,** in the Bahía de Samaná, bathtub-warm waters await you after a catamaran ride with *Victoria Marine.*

Playa Rincón on the Samaná Peninsula is best reached by boat. This stunning sandy stretch is backed by a thick forest of palms. You can find boat captains at Playa Las Galeras in town willing to take you to the other secluded beaches on the tip of the peninsula, including **Playa Frontón** and **Playa Madama**.

The beaches of Cabarete: **Bozo Beach, Kite Beach,** and **Playa Encuentro** are wonderful

remote and pristine Bahía de Las Águilas

people-watching places even if you aren't into the water sports that have made them internationally famous – kiteboarding, surfing, and windsurfing. Lively nighttime entertainment can be found all along **Playa Cabarete.**

Bahía de Las Águilas is the country's most pristine beach, set in the most remote corner of the Southwest. Not many tourists make it out this way, making traffic low and the sexy beach quotient high.

dinner along the water at Adrian Tropical for a wonderful view of the stars and the surf while enjoying typical Dominican favorites like *mofongo* (mashed plantains). Afterward, stroll along the Malecón to the Renaissance Jaragua Hotel to dance the night away in its hot club, Jubilee.

Day 3

In Santo Domingo's Plaza de la Cultura, the Taíno artifact exhibit at the Museo del Hombre Dominicano is a first-rate way to learn about the pre-Columbian history of the nation. Catch a taxi to the peaceful Jardín Botánico Nacional to learn about the biodiversity of the Dominican Republic. Grab dinner in the Ciudad Colonial and save all your energy for dancing at Guácara Taína, located in the belly of an enormous cave. Make sure your rental-car reservations

BEST SMALL RESORTS

Paraíso Caño Hondo, on the fringe of the Parque Nacional Los Haitises

All of these resorts have something in common: Some are more off the grid than others, but all manage to spoil you. These are midpriced to high-priced options. If you are looking for a vacation of comfort but don't want to be in the mix of mass tourism, these are for you.

The resort **Paraíso Caño Hondo** (Sabana de la Mar) is set in Parque Nacional Los Haitises, giving nighttime an incredibly serene feeling. Disconnect from busy life and appreciate natural beauty. This is one of the best independent resorts in the nation.

Playa Esmeralda Beach Resort (Guayacanes) is a wonderful pick for a weekend stay. It offers all the things that the big resorts have but on a smaller scale.

Playa Las Galeras has great hotels, but independent **Villa Serena** steps out from the pack with a pool on the beach and excursion packages.

In El Cibao, the **Hotel Gran Jimenoa** (Jarabacoa) is an easy choice. Located directly on a river, it offers good food and all-inclusive options in the adventure capital of the country.

If **Casa Bonita** (Bahoruco) were in a beauty pageant, the rest of the contestants should be really nervous. Infinity pool, independently owned, amazing vistas, good food, elegant Caribbean-modern decor: It all means trouble for the rest of the small resorts. This hotel earns top kudos.

are in place for your drive to Barahona the next day.

Day 4

On your way to Barahona, in the arid region southwest of Santo Domingo on the Península de Pedernales, detour to see the Reserva Antropológica El Pomier north of San Cristóbal and marvel at hundreds of ancient Taíno drawings. Check into the Hotel Costa Larimar before heading out to dinner and dancing at Los Robles.

ADVENTURE SPORTS

The topographical landscape of the Dominican Republic is an extensive and intricate one – deserts, mountains, mangroves, forests, rainforests, rivers, waterfalls; short of an iceberg or two, the country's just about got it all covered. Because of this varied topography, the Dominican Republic has bloomed into a full-force adventure tourism destination.

CANYONING AND CASCADING

Canyoning uses equipment such as harnesses, helmets, ropes, and other climbing and rappelling tools to navigate up, down, across, under, and through waterfalls. Cascading is very similar to canyoning, but cascading does not use equipment other than the occasional rope and tends to cover shorter distances. Canyoning is more intensive and requires a greater level of physical fitness. **Damajagua,** a half hour outside Puerto Plata, is one of the best places to enjoy this sport.

HIKING

For serious hikers, the 47-kilometer climb to **Pico Duarte,** along the Cordillera Central in the **Parque Nacional Armando Bermúdez,** is the ultimate trek. At 3,087 meters, Duarte is the highest peak in the Caribbean, and it will take at least two days to ascend. Your reward is an amazing vista of the Cibao Valley. Shorter options would be to hike to the waterfalls of **Los Saltos de Jimenoa** and **Salto Baiguate** by Jarabacoa or in the high hills of **Constanza. La Península de Samaná** is also a wonderful place to trek.

MOUNTAIN BIKING

Adventure companies like **Iguana Mama** of **Cabarete** offer single-day mountain-bike tours as well as two-week-long bike trips; many incorporate other adventure activities. A favorite fat-tire ride is in the lush mountains of **Jarabacoa.** For a road-bike excursion, the **Lago Enriquillo Loop Road** has a good surface and not a lot of traffic.

QUAD RIDING OR ATVING

Four-wheel all-terrain vehicles can navigate terrain that is difficult to access with regular vehicles, such as tropical forest paths and mountain areas like the **Cordillera Septentrional** and **Cordillera Central.**

RIVER RAFTING

Río Yaque del Norte stretches over 290 kilometers in the Cordillera Central. The river reaches an impressive altitude of 2,580 meters, making it an exhilarating, raucous river-rafting route. The most respected outfitter in Jarabacoa is **Rancho Baiguate.**

ROCK CLIMBING

On the Península de Samaná, **Playa Frontón** is a popular area for climbing, with rocky cliffs overhanging a perfect sandy beach. Hire a boat from Playa Las Galeras or hike an hour to get there. The **Parque Mirador del Sur,** in Santo Domingo, has some free climb sites, but it can be quite crowded on the weekends.

WATER SPORTS

With its miles of coral reefs, diversity of underwater life and environment, and excellent

Península de Pedernales

kitesurfing in world-famous watersport town, Cabarete

visibility and temperature conditions, the Dominican Republic is one of the best places in the Caribbean for **scuba diving.** In the north, **Sosúa** is particularly popular for both beginning and advanced divers. Maximum depths of key diving sites range 8.5-36 meters. The southern shores – around **Bayahibe** and **Pedernales** – boast a vast sea of pristine coral reefs for the more adventurous diver. To get started, you must get certified. Classes are offered just about everywhere along the coast.

Good old-fashioned **surfing** remains the frontrunner of adventure sporting. **Playa Encuentro,** near Cabarete, is the ideal surfing spot. Wintertime offers up the best conditions, with consistent swells December-April. Although the swells vary the rest of the year, the water temperature (around 26°C, 79°F) makes for a good ride most any time. **Playa Preciosa,** by Río San Juan, has a good ride too, but the waters are a bit more dangerous (strong undertows).

Cabarete has the best beaches for **windsurfing** and **kiteboarding.** Wind conditions shift throughout the day – from light in the morning to heavier later in the day – allowing adventurers of all levels to find their niche. From mid-December to April consistent winds average 13-17 knots (24-32 kph, 15-20 mph). Wind speed picks up some June-September and can reach 13-22 knots (24-41 kph, 15-25 mph). During May and between October and December, the winds are less consistent.

Kiteboarding, sometimes called kitesurfing, is a combination of surfing, paragliding, windsurfing, wakeboarding, and kite flying. It is fairly easy to learn once you figure out how to control the kite and get the hang of a few board maneuvers. There are quite a few kiteboarding schools in Cabarete, most on **Kite Beach.**

Take a boat ride to Bahía de las Águilas – Eagles' Bay – and savor the beach's quiet and beauty.

Day 5

Get up very early for a day of beautiful scenery and a visit to a deserted beach. Drive to Las Cuevas, a small community of fishers who can also give you a boat ride to your ultimate destination, one of the last completely unspoiled and most remote beaches in the country, Bahía de las Águilas. If time permits, on your way back stop for a dip in the freshwater lagoons *(balnearios)* of San Rafael or Los Patos.

Day 6

Take Highway 46 toward Lago Enriquillo, making a quick stop at the Polo Magnético to witness first-hand the quirky phenomenon of your car rolling mysteriously uphill. Continue your drive around the Lago Enriquillo loop, stopping at the Parque Nacional Isla Cabritos to see crocodiles, flamingos, and iguanas lounging by the saltwater lake. Head back to Barahona by night and enjoy a more casual dinner at the locally popular Restaurante and Pizzería D'Lina.

Day 7

Return to Santo Domingo to return the rental car and catch a bus to the cooler mountainous village of Jarabacoa. Visit the waterfalls and swimming holes of the Saltos de Jimenoa and Salto de Baiguate. Stay at the Rancho Baiguate and make reservations with its excursion team to try an adventure sport such as canyoning or rafting on the Río Yaque del Norte. Rest up for your next day of adventure.

Day 8

While canyoning is indeed a thrilling and mind-boggling adventure, don't forget to enjoy the scenery as you navigate down waterfalls and across streams. Later go for a nice dinner on top of the hill at Jarabacoa's Jamaca de Dios just outside of town, overlooking the city lights.

Day 9

Catch an early bus north along Highway 5 and stop in Santiago to visit the Centro León cigar factory and art museum in the morning. Eat lunch in Puerto Plata at Aquaceros Bar & Grill, right along the Malecón, and then take a taxi to Fuerte San Felipe and the Museo del Ámbar Dominicano before heading to the snorkeler's favorite haunt, Sosúa (about 25 kilometers east of Puerto Plata) via bus or *guagua*.

Day 10

Dive or snorkel off the coast of Sosúa with a reputable outfitter like North Coast Diving. Have dinner at Sosúa's romantic La Puntilla de Piergiorgio for Italian food with an out-of-this-world view of the Atlantic.

Day 11

Early in the morning take off to the surfer-filled hot spot of Cabarete and settle in to your hotel. Explore the one main drag running parallel to the beach and then head over to Playa Cabarete and sign up with a windsurfing outfitter, like Vela, to teach you the ropes or rent you equipment. Cabarete's lively yet casual nightlife revolves around the bars along Playa Cabarete.

Day 12

Head over to Kite Beach to try out kitesurfing. Kite Club has lessons available, and you can join the club for weeks at a time. It's also a super-cool place to just chill by the surf and watch an international cast of surfers. Enjoy your last two days beach bumming in Cabarete before catching a *guagua* back to Santo Domingo for your flight out.

▶ NATURE LOVER'S TREK

The Dominican Republic has an astonishingly diverse ecosystem on two-thirds of the island of Hispaniola. Today, 25 percent of this area is protected and includes nine scientific reserves and sanctuaries and 16 national parks (three of which are submarine), covering over 12,000 square kilometers. If you don't have enough time to explore all of the country's mountainous highlands, pine savannas, mangroves, coastlines, sand dunes, rivers, and lagoons, following this itinerary will take you to the most diverse areas for a week of nature-loving fun.

Day 1

Fly into Santo Domingo and rent a four-wheel-drive vehicle; head 201 kilometers southwest to the coastal town of Barahona. Check into the Hotel Costa Larimar. Enjoy some fresh seafood at Brisas del Caribe right on Barahona's Malecón and some dancing at hot spot Los Robles.

Parque Nacional José del Carmen Ramírez

one of the hospitable iguanas of Lago Enriquillo

Day 2

Get an early start and drive along the very picturesque coastal Highway 44 to Parque Nacional Jaragua, the largest national park in the country, and hire a boat guide at the gate who'll take you to Laguna de Oviedo. There you can view the 130 bird species that live in the park (including flamingos), iguanas, and a cave that has Taíno drawings. Continue on to Las Cuevas village and hire a boat captain to take you to one of the last virgin beaches in the country, Bahía de las Águilas. The locals in Las Cuevas offer fresh seafood lunches prepared on the beachfront. Head back to your hotel in Barahona for the night.

Day 3

Take the arid and very hot Lago Enriquillo Loop Road to get to Parque Nacional Isla Cabritos. Stroll through the gardens at the entrance gate and mingle with the numerous ricord and rhinoceros iguanas. Purchase a tour that will take you to Lago Enriquillo to see American crocodiles and flamingos hang out by the mouth of the Río de la Descubierta. Continue the loop and head for the Taíno rock carvings at Las Caritas. After circling the lake on the loop road, stop for lunch in Neyba. Head back to Barahona for your last night in the southwestern region.

Day 4

From Barahona, travel to Constanza, in a beautiful circular valley surrounded by mountains 1,200 meters above sea level. Stay at Alto Cerro and enjoy the ranch's horseback-riding tour through the countryside. Dine at Lorenzo's, famous for its *chivo guisado* (goat stew) and other typical Dominican fare.

Day 5

Take a day trip to hike in the Parque

farmland in Constanza

Nacional Valle Nuevo (20 kilometers south of Constanza), where bird-watching reigns supreme. Afterward make the bumpy ride to a three-tiered waterfall, Salto de Aguas Blancas, and take a dip in its serene pool surrounded by the protected forest. If you still have energy you can take a drive to the Reserva Científica Ebano Verde, created to protect the 621 plant species, amphibians, reptiles, small mammal species (such as solenodons and bats), and 59 species of birds. Enjoy a six-kilometer hike here along a trail where trees are marked with information about their species. Back in Constanza, have a plate of *la bandera dominicana* (chicken, beans, rice, and fried plantains) at Aguas Blancas.

Day 6

Drive north to Jarabacoa, the gateway village to the central mountains and the national parks Armando Bermúdez and José del Carmen Ramírez. Stay at the Gran Jimenoa hotel, right on the bank of the Río de Jimenoa, and take short hikes to the waterfalls of Jimenoa and Baiguate, where you can dip into the pools.

Day 7

Take a tour of an organic coffee production plant at Café Monte Alto of Jarabacoa and enjoy a *cafecito* in their coffee shop before heading back to Santo Domingo to catch your flight the next day.

► HISTORICAL ROAD TRIP

Before Columbus, the indigenous Taíno people were a well-organized and peaceful society living on the island. Upon "discovery," their entire population was wiped out, but their influence on Dominican culture was not lost. Their history has come together like a puzzle put together from artifacts recovered at sites, cave drawings, and leftover cultural practices. The Taíno influence can still be heard in remnants of language that have been adopted into regular Spanish, and Dominicans still make a type of bread that has existed since Taíno days. A visitor could easily spend a week exploring just Taíno sites with some traditional beach fun along the way. But there is more to the history of the Dominican Republic than just the Taíno era. It encompasses Trujillo, Columbus, and many other influential moments. This itinerary is designed for travel with a rental car and can easily be tailored to fit your personal financial and scheduling needs.

Day 1

Fly into Punta Cana airport and rent a car. Drive to the burgeoning tourist destination of Bayahibe and check into one of the area's best all-inclusive resorts, the Iberostar Hacienda Dominicus. This resort maintains a beautiful beach strip for its guests to enjoy, and you can enjoy dinner within the hotel at one of its five restaurants and later learn how to merengue at the disco.

Day 2

At the tour package desk next to the lobby in the hotel, reserve a ride aboard a catamaran out to beautiful Isla Saona. Once on Isla Saona, walk to the Cueva Cotubanamá, a cave where Taíno families hid out from the Spanish. Spend the day at the beach soaking in the paradise they once lived in. Buffet lunch is served on the beach for all-inclusive guests. This can also be arranged through independent boat captains at the Bayahibe point.

Day 3

Just south of Bayahibe is Dominicus Americanus, where the entrance to the Parque Nacional del Este is located. Here,

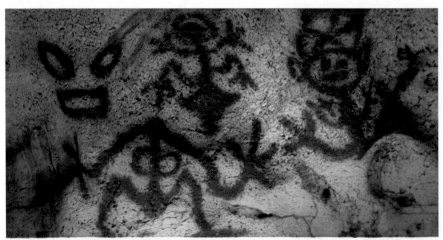

Taíno cave art has been pristinely preserved.

FOLKLORE, FARMING, AND FESTIVALS: DOMINICAN CULTURE TOUR

There is much to be seen in the Afro-Caribbean culture that is the Dominican Republic; the time of year you visit will determine where your focus should be. Here are some ideas to get you thinking about where to go to experience the art and culture of the Dominican Republic.

Santiago is a city that holds history in its hands and mixes the story of the folklore of the Dominican people with modern art. Start at the **Monumento a Los Héroes de la Restauración de la República** to learn of the history. Then go to **Museo des Artes Folklórico Tomás Morel** and on to the **Centro León** to get a good dose of Dominican art and its impact on modern-day society.

Take a drive through **Salcedo** and travel the **Ruta de Murales.** The entire town is painted with various artists' works. Some are heavy in political content and historical figures, and others are still lifes or portraits. Regardless of the theme, these murals have created a town-sized art museum.

A visit to **Higüerito de Moca** will show you the potters' studios that make the typical "face-less women" dolls. These dolls have become evocative of the Dominican race-less face. Our race and ethnicity cannot be pegged down to facial traits and is, therefore, in the imagination of the onlooker.

In **Yamasá,** visit an organization of organic cocoa farmers who have banded together in one production plant. Learn the entire process that makes the Dominican Republic the number one exporter of organic cocoa in the world. Cocoa has been an indigenous product since the Europeans began settling the island and has become an integral part of the Dominican diet. Farther down the road, at the **Cerámica Taína Hermanos Guillen,** see where the family Guillen keeps the Taíno pottery art alive in their studio. If you're here in June, go to the brothers' **Fiesta San Antonio** to experience the musical traditions of *gagá, gajumbe,* and *bambulá.* The Guillen brothers are generous and serve a typical *comida crilloa* with free drinks. Look for it on the first Sunday before June 13.

Festivals are perhaps the best way to feel the pulse of the Dominican culture, which is so tightly tied to dance and music. If you arrive during the **Merengue Festival** in Santo Domingo (July–August), make your way to the Malecón to feel the beat of the island all night long.

Plan your trip around **Carnaval** in February so that you can see the traditional masks and dances of Santo Domingo or La Vega.

Feel the beat of the Afro-Caribbean congo at the **Día de San Miguel** in the September festival of the patron saint of Villa Mella in Santo Domingo.

At the *fiesta patronal* of Baní from June 15 to June 24, you will see a flirtatious folkloric dance called *sarandunga* danced in celebration of San Juan Bautista. Its Afro-Caribbean rhythms use instruments like the *tamboreros* and *guireros*.

Experience Dominican culture during the Carnaval festival.

check out La Cueva de Berna and Cueva del Puente, caves with some easy and not-so-easy to spot Taíno drawings. Guides can be hired at the entrance to the park. Make sure to take a bottle of water on the journey into the park; it is a hot and arid place. This is a close day trip and you don't have to check out of your Bayahibe resort. Drive to San Rafael de Yuma and visit the Casa Ponce de León.

Day 4

On your way to Santo Domingo, stop and take a guided tour at the Cueva de las Maravillas, where you'll see some of the best examples of Taíno art in the Caribbean. Pictograms have been pristinely preserved and look as if they were drawn in recent years.

Day 5

While in Santo Domingo, check out the fantastic collection of Taíno artifacts at the Museo del Hombre Dominicano at the Plaza de la Cultura. At the front desk ask for a guide or some literature in your language. This is a wonderful mid-journey education on Taíno culture and rituals. Stroll through the Ciudad Colonial and visit some of the museums. An important piece of the native Taínos' story and the overall Dominican tale is the period of Spanish colonialism. Have dinner at El Conuco Restaurant to get a taste of *la bandera dominicana* and see some traditional merengue dancers.

Day 6

Take a day trip just north of San Cristóbal to the Reserva Antropológica El Pomier, the most significant collection of rock art found in the Caribbean. These finds are from not only the Taíno but the Igneri and Carib tribes as well, and are about 2,000 years old. Take a lunch break at Pastelería Chichita and then make your way up the hill to visit El Castillo del Cerro, the one-time home of Trujillo in San Cristóbal, before heading back to Santo Domingo.

Day 7

Get up early to return to Bayahibe to spend your last day soaking up the sun on Playa Bayahibe before your departure the next day. No trip to the Caribbean would be complete without a seafood dinner. Restaurante La Punta always offers the freshest of catches.

The DR's climate is ideal for orchids.

SANTO DOMINGO

Those who have never visited Santo Domingo sometimes believe the capital city to be a third-world town with nothing culturally significant to offer, but this perception could not be further from the truth. It's a city-slicker's undiscovered treasure, a Latin music lover's paradise, an in-love couple's metropolitan grab-bag of excitement, and a shopping addict's Pandora's box.

Santo Domingo offers a unique cultural experience for a variety of travelers: Couples will find romance in the quiet of the 500-year-old orchid- and bougainvillea-filled courtyards, singles will enjoy an unbeatable nightlife (with the best gay and lesbian scene in the country), museum-lovers will be satiated by the archaeological and arts and crafts exhibits, and the history buffs will find much to explore in the various colonial landmarks.

This frenetic metropolis is abuzz with the constant din of traffic and a wax and wane of action throughout the day. Activity rises with the morning sun: *Colmados* (small stores) sell their wares to the accompaniment of merengue soundtracks blaring from their radios, animated haggling takes place in marketplaces, business-people pile into *públicos* heading for work, and vendors roam residential neighborhoods shouting out their daily produce offerings in sing-song voices. When the sun hits its hottest temperature, the frenzy of the day reaches its liveliest, and the streets are choked beyond capacity with diesel trucks, *motoconchos,* and honking cars. Then around noon, the city suddenly, as if on cue, quiets down for an extended lunch hour. Many Dominicans retreat into the shade of their homes for a big meal, perhaps a nap and

HIGHLIGHTS

Ciudad Colonial: Stroll the same cobbled walkways and historical haunts where the Spanish plotted their conquests and pirates ravaged the city. Dine or even sleep in their former homes (page 30).

Parque Colón: Flanked by the oldest cathedral in the western hemisphere, colonial architecture, and pubs offering refreshing antidotes to the hot sun, Parque Colón is a perfect spot for relaxing after sightseeing (page 31).

Catedral Primada de América: Sit under the great arching ceiling of the oldest cathedral of the New World. Sir Francis Drake and his men captured and occupied it during their monthlong siege of the city (page 31).

Dance Clubs: You can't experience the Dominican Republic until you have danced to its rhythms. Whether you crave merengue, *bachata,* salsa, or techno music, you're bound to find the right mix. Santo Domingo has the biggest LGBT community on the island, where the clubs have some of the best DJs around (page 44).

Baseball: A trip to **Estadio Quisqueya** to watch baseball is a must in the country that produces Major League Baseball star players like a natural resource. These games are a ballgame and a party rolled into one (page 53).

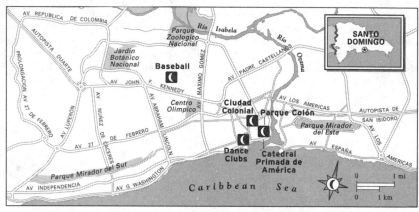

LOOK FOR **(** TO FIND RECOMMENDED SIGHTS, ACTIVITIES, DINING, AND LODGING.

a cold shower to battle the heat, and regroup for the afternoon when it's once again business as usual. Although still busy, afternoons in Santo Domingo are much more relaxed than the mornings. Calle El Conde is still alive with shoppers and tourists, as traffic picks up again, but the traditional espresso break around 4 P.M. allows worker bees to begin to wind down before the end of their work day, and around 6 P.M. most employees head home for dinner.

At nightfall, Santo Domingo's nightlife scene takes center stage and is sure to satisfy almost every need. You can dance in trendy clubs, eat in countless restaurants serving culinary favorites from around the world, or romance Lady Luck at the casinos along the Malecón. If you time your visit right, you can experience one of the exciting festivals that the city hosts: Carnaval, the Merengue Festival, or the Latin music festival, all of which go on until the wee hours of the morning.

A city of firsts, Santo Domingo boasts the

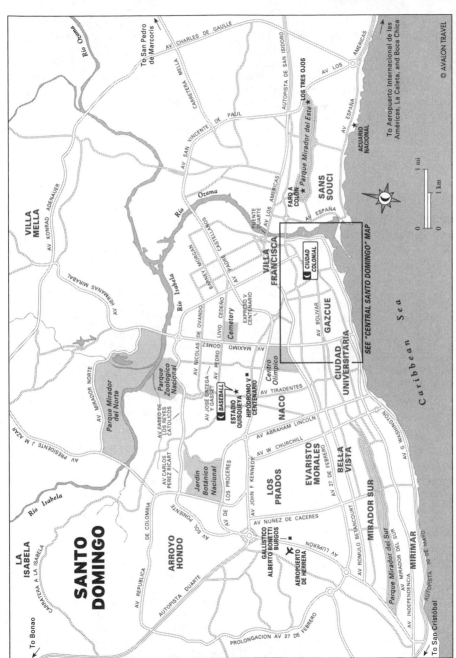

© AVALON TRAVEL

first hospital, paved street, and university of the New World, in addition to the oldest surviving cathedral and European fortress. Founded by Christopher Columbus's brother, Bartolomé, this city has survived the centuries; many buildings still stand and have been maintained or renovated within the Ciudad Colonial. Today, portions of the original walls of the city can still be seen, but greater Santo Domingo continues to expand in physical size and in population, which is nearing 2.5 million people.

History and modernity coexist here: Many hotels, restaurants, and bars in the Ciudad Colonial are restored from their original 16th-century buildings and homes and still offer the modern comforts that tourists have come to expect. The tourism industry has recognized the uniqueness of the Ciudad Colonial and has begun stringent efforts to maintain its historical significance along with supplying visitors with modern amenities. In January of 2009, the Minister of Tourism, Francisco Javier Garcia, announced a RD$10 billion restoration program to return the Ciudad Colonial and the Malecón area to "all their splendor and beauty and show the world that we are the owners of the most beautiful Colonial Zone in Latin America."

All major roads lead to Santo Domingo, which makes it a good choice for a base for your vacation, especially if you love city life and all it has to offer but need the beach or the mountains peppered into your visit. Transportation options are plentiful, and traveling to many beautiful destinations in the country can be done in a morning from Santo Domingo.

HISTORY

Santo Domingo was named a UNESCO World Cultural Heritage Site in 1990. Its history is both glorious and sad. While it has so many bragging rights as the City of Firsts, those firsts came at a very high price during different periods of time in this city's many centuries of existence. Many lives were lost (Taíno mostly) to pave the way for the city to be built and prosper.

Santo Domingo is the result of many failed attempts at settlement. Columbus couldn't catch a break. His first settlement at La Navidad was annihilated. When Christopher was away in Spain, the second try, La Isabela, which was just west of Puerto Plata, fell to yellow fever and mutiny while under the care of his brother, Bartolomé. Bartolomé then set up the third settlement, Nueva Isabela, on the eastern bank of the Río Ozama. Although it was thriving, it was eventually leveled by a hurricane. Finally, with the help of his governor, he founded Santo Domingo de Guzmán (the city's official name), an 11-block area on the western bank of the Río Ozama. And it began to thrive. At the same time, the brutalization of the Taíno natives raged on with forced labor.

Santo Domingo began to weaken, and pirates were catching wind of its vulnerability. In 1586, Sir Francis Drake, the English buccaneer, came to town and seized it for a month until he finally got the Spanish to pay him a ransom to get it back. He wasn't the last to try to take Santo Domingo, either. William Penn of England tried, and former slave François Dominique Toussaint L'Ouverture of Haiti succeeded until February 27, 1844, when Juan Pablo Duarte finally won independence for the Dominican Republic after a series of rapid-succession occupations by the French (1802 and 1804), the British (1803 and 1809), the Spanish (1809), and finally the Haitians in 1822—all of which happened in the Ciudad Colonial.

PLANNING YOUR TIME

Santo Domingo is a vibrant city with a lot to offer. Tourists can touch the same fortress walls where Columbus, Cortés, and Ponce de León once leaned. History buffs will need more than a couple of days to soak it all in and may want to hire a guide (the official tourism ones wear blue shirts and have Ministry of Tourism name tags) in order to fully appreciate the significance of all the sights. They are often very sure that you need them. This is debatable. Some are very knowledgeable (always agree on a price before commencing), but if you'd rather go it on your own, a simple *no gracias* should suffice. Many tourists can probably cover the **Ciudad Colonial** in a couple of days with a

DAY-TRIPPING IN MONTE PLATA

If you are vacationing in the city, you may come to the point of needing a break from the din of the metropolitan jungle. Those needing a refreshing change from the typical day trip to the beach should try going inland to the rich countryside of the province of Monte Plata.

The town of Bayaguana (25 km north of Carretera 4 on the Carretera 23) has a *fiesta patronal* on December 28, during which all the horses and several herds of livestock are paraded through town. The tradition began when a long drought caused cattle numbers to drop, and crops were suffering too. In a last-ditch effort, the townspeople offered a bull to their patron saint in the hopes that he would help it rain. After a few days, the rain came and the tradition stayed. The procession is anything but solemn. The parade is ushered through with loud music, songs, prayers, fireworks, and dancing, of course.

The **Cerámica Taína Hermanos Guillen** (Yamasá, Calle Duarte 9, tel. 809/525-0756) is a must-see for pottery fans or for those who want a taste of what is preserved of Taíno culture. The Guillen brothers create pottery replicas on their picturesque studio grounds in Yamasá. They will walk you through the whole artistic process. If you are there in June, don't miss the Fiesta San Antonio, which is held on the grounds of their studios.

Part of the Ruta del Cacao is available for touring in Yamasá as well, at **Bloque Cacaotero No. 2** (Yamasá, Calle Rafael de la Cruz 2, El Cercadillo, tel. 809/525-0641). Here you can learn all about the organic cacao process and even taste some of the product.

Balneario Comate (3 km from Bayaguana) is a popular spot for families on the weekends. This natural swimming pool has a small water fall fed by the Río Comate and is a wonderful place to spend the day. There is a thatched-roof covered dance floor with tables and chairs where they sometimes have live music. Light refreshments are sold.

Salto Alto is about 15 kilometers from Bayaguana and made up of three waterfalls that spill into a large azure pool.

Boya is a town that the mountains have made invisible to tourism. Here you can see the **Santa María de Boya**, a 16th-century church still standing. Nearby, the **Salto Socoa** waterfall will entice you into taking a swim in its crystalline waters.

All of these places are perfectly fine to visit on your own, but if you want a tour company that sets up day trips to all of these locations, look into **Tequia Experiences** (Av. Gustavo Mejia Ricart 69, tel. 809/563-0019, www.tequiaexperiences.com). This is a well-planned company dedicated to ecotourism, adventure, and sustainable tourism, based out of Santo Domingo, whose guides are knowledgeable in Dominican history, ecology, and culture and speak many languages. Their tour buses are modern and very comfortable.

---

self-guided tour, making sure to hit a couple of museums and save some time for shopping on El Conde.

For certain, the major tourism draw for Santo Domingo is the Ciudad Colonial, including sights like the **Catedral Primada de América** and the **Fortaleza Ozama**, but other sights elsewhere in the city are worth visiting as well, like the **Jardín Botánico Nacional,** the **Plaza de la Cultura,** and the **Faro a Colón.**

The Ciudad Colonial is easily walked in a comfortable pair of shoes. There are also plenty of *motoconchos* around for hiring a ride if walking isn't your thing—riding on the back of speedy little motorbikes can be a way to cover the small area quickly or if you need to leave the Ciudad Colonial.

Guided Tours

To get an *official* guide, go to the Parque Colón and look to the ones sitting near the cathedral or in the shade of the trees around the park. The key tip-off that they are official is the outfit—khaki pants and light blue dress shirt—and they have licenses (sometimes hanging around their necks) with the official state tourism logo on it. Ask to see it. These walking tours cost US$20–30 and last about 2.5 hours. The guides will take you to the major sights of the Ciudad Colonial. Always be sure to agree on the price before going with the guide. Some are notorious for trying to make an extra buck by the time the tour is over.

Another alternative is to join a large group for a tour. Major agencies include **Prieto Tours** (Av. Francia 125, tel. 809/685-0102, www.prieto-tours.com), **Omni Tours** (Roberto Pastoria 204, tel. 809/565-6591, www.omnitours.com.do), and **Metro Tours** (Av. 27 de Febrero, tel. 809/544-4580, www.metrotours.com.do).

Sights

Most historical sites in Santo Domingo are within the Ciudad Colonial (Colonial City). Churches, homes, the first European fortress in the western hemisphere, and other colonial-era buildings are all within walking distance of one another, although you could always flag down a horse-drawn carriage if you need a break from walking.

In the greater Santo Domingo area there are many other sights worth visiting, such as the expansive Jardín Botánico Nacional (National Botanical Garden); the Faro a Colón (Lighthouse of Columbus), where the remains of the explorer are said to be laid to rest; and the Plaza de la Cultura's Museo del Hombre Dominicano (Museum of the Dominican Man), which features an impressive display of Taíno artifacts.

CIUDAD COLONIAL

Along the western bank of the Río Ozama, where its waters meet the Caribbean Sea, lie 11 square blocks that make up the fountain-head of colonialism. Fortresses still stand guard

© ALICIA CHAVIER CAAMAÑO

flowering balconies in La Ciudad Colonial

over the harbor where Columbus's men finally docked their armada back in 1498.

Today the district offers tourists a walk back into history to when the conquistadors ambled along to the clinking of their armor and the gold in their pouches. Sixteenth-century architecture cohabits with the speeding mopeds of the new millennium. The smell of luscious Dominican cuisine curls through the air around the vendors and through the windows of museums.

With some buildings dating back to the early 1500s, efforts have been made to maintain the historical integrity or, in some cases, reincarnate them into hotels, pubs, cafés, and restaurants. But one thing is certain; you will find many authentic New World "firsts" here. Since it is the first European city in the New World, Santo Domingo boasts the first university, hospital, cathedral, and palace, to name a few.

Amid the historical surroundings is some of the best shopping in the city, on **Calle El Conde** and throughout the Ciudad Colonial. From cigar shops, small bookstores, and music stores to art, jewelry, and clothing, the Ciudad Colonial satisfies the interests and purchasing urges of even the hardest to please travelers.

After a long day of discovering the diversions available in the old city, finding a cozy spot amid the narrow cobblestone streets to relax and enjoy the lull that sets in with dusk is not a hard task to accomplish. Romantic courtyard restaurants and pubs offer the respite you'll need before setting out later in the evening should you decide to take advantage of the area's livelier nighttime entertainment choices. Once again, the Ciudad Colonial comes through for everyone. Karaoke singers, club-goers, and jazz enthusiasts have no worries; you will be satisfied.

The Ciudad Colonial of Santo Domingo is the most glorious of the highlights in the capital and should not be missed.

◖ Parque Colón

This park (Calle El Conde and Arzobispo Meriño) is a good place to start your tour of

Parque Colón

the New World's first city. It is a central meeting point for locals and tourists alike. It stands in front of the first cathedral in the hemisphere, Victorian and colonial buildings surround the square, it has a statue of Christopher Columbus by French sculptor Ernest Gilbert, and it's abuzz with activity. Pigeons flit about, as do gadget hawkers, tour guides, and shoeshine boys. This is by far the best spot for people-watching, and the sidewalk cafés are always full with people taking full advantage of the vantage point.

◖ Catedral Primada de América

The Catedral Primada de América or the **Holy Cathedral Church of Our Lady of Saint Mary of the Incarnation** (Calle Arzobispo Meriño, Parque Colón, 9 A.M.–4 P.M. daily, free) had its first stone placed by Diego Columbus himself in 1514. Construction went on until 1540, with many different architects adding to the combination of Gothic, Roman, and baroque styles. Unfortunately, it's hard to know exactly what it used to look like inside because when

© ANA CHAVIER CAAMAÑO

Sir Francis Drake came to town with his greedy band of pirates, they set up camp inside the cathedral and took everything, including what was nailed down, with them when they left. Dominicans are very proud of the fact that this cathedral is widely considered the first cathedral of the New World. Whether that is the historical truth or not is a source of contention that most Dominicans wave off with a patriotic flick of the wrist. Check out the great arching ceilings, sculptures, paintings, and 14 chapels inside. Make sure you're not wearing shorts or a tank top.

Fortaleza Ozama

Fortaleza Ozama (Calle de las Damas, tel. 809/686-0222, 9:30 A.M.–6:30 P.M. Mon.–Sat., 9 A.M.–4 P.M. Sun., US$1) was built in 1502 and underwent many changes and alterations over the next two centuries. From its prime position on a steep hill overlooking the mouth of the Ozama River, the Spanish launched conquests to Jamaica, Cuba, South America, and Mexico. It served as the first line of defense against attackers with its huge cannons, some of which are still aiming ominously at the waters below. Until the 1970s it served many functions, including as a military post and a prison, until it was opened to the public.

Inside the walls of the fort, the looming Torre del Homenaje (Tower of Homage), evoking classic Spanish castle design, is the oldest portion of the fort and has walls two meters thick. A climb to the top, up the narrow stairwells, is rewarded with a 360-degree view of the city. Also on-site is El Polvorín (The Powder House), which acted as the artillery and ammunition house. Standing in the middle of the walled yard is a bronze statue of Gonzalo Fernández de Oviedo, a famous historical chronicler who was put in charge of the fort; he lived and died there. His room was on the second floor of the fort and was turned into a prison cell after his death.

Optional and informative tours are offered by the guards at the front gate of the fort for about US$4 per person and given in Spanish, English, and French.

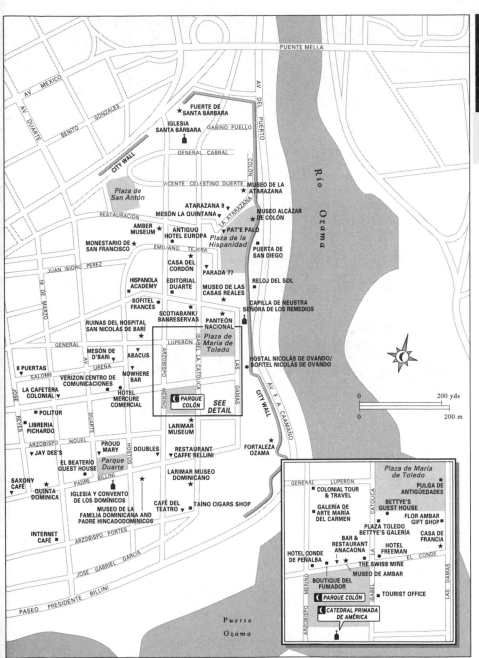

© ANA CHAVIER CAAMAÑO

Catedral Primada de América is the oldest cathedral in the New World – according to the Dominicans!

Calle de las Damas

In front of the Fortaleza Ozama and running north to the Plaza de la Hispanidad is Calle de las Damas (Street of the Ladies), the oldest paved street in the New World. It was constructed in 1502 for the wife of Diego Columbus so that she and her lady friends could go for afternoon strolls without mussing their dresses. **Plaza de María de Toledo** is a connecting passageway between Calle de las Damas and Calle Isabel La Católica; it was named for Diego Columbus's wife.

Along the Calle de las Damas is the *reloj del sol* (sundial) that was built for the royalty who lived in the Museo de las Casas Reales, which is directly in front of it. It's perfectly positioned so that a mere glance from the royal windows would reveal the time of day.

Panteón Nacional

Built in 1747 as a Jesuit church, the Panteón Nacional (Calle de las Damas and Mercedes, 9 A.M.–5 P.M. Tues.–Sun., free) served mostly as a warehouse and a theater until 1958, when Rafael Trujillo had it converted into a shrine for the country's most illustrious people. No doubt, he had selfish forethought of a memorial to himself, an idea that never materialized. Spanish dictator Francisco Franco donated the central chandelier. Today, some of the country's most influential people and political figures are honored here and entombed behind marble walls. The building is constructed entirely of massive limestone blocks with a neoclassical facade. Shorts, tank tops, and sneakers are discouraged.

Plaza de la Hispanidad

Much larger than Plaza Colón, the Plaza de la Hispanidad is another good spot for people-watching. Located in front of the Alcázar de Colón, this very sunny plaza's northwestern side is lined with buildings that were built in the 16th century and now have restaurants and bars in them. These establishments put their tables out on the sidewalk, making it a wonderful place to lounge with a beer at sunset, but it can be very hot during the day as there is virtually no shade.

Just down the hill, in back of the Alcázar

de Colón, is the **Puerto de San Diego.** It was built in 1571 and was the original main gate to the city. Some remnants can still be seen of the original wall that was erected to protect Santo Domingo from attackers rising from the river.

Monasterio de San Francisco

Sitting now in ruins is the Monasterio de San Francisco (Calle Hostos and Calle Emiliano Tejere), built in the early part of the 1500s for the first order of the Franciscan friars to come to the island. While it once was a glorious structure, originally with three connecting chapels, it underwent some disastrous events. First it was looted and then torched by Sir Francis Drake when he seized the city in 1586. It was restored but suffered earthquakes in 1673 and 1751; both times it was rebuilt. Its grisliest usage was when it served as an insane asylum from 1881 to the early 1930s (when a hurricane finally blew through). The chains used to hold the "patients" can still be seen. It was never restored. Now performances are staged amid the dramatically well-lit rubble in one of the oldest neighborhoods in Santo Domingo.

Ruinas del Hospital San Nicolás de Barí

A few blocks south of the Monasterio de San Francisco are the Ruinas del Hospital San Nicolás de Barí (Calle Hostos). They are the ruins of the first hospital built in the New World. The order to build came in 1503 by Governor Nicolás de Ovando. The design is in the classic form of a Latin cross, and it fared better than the monastery despite enduring the same catastrophes. Then in 1911 it suffered dire damage at the hands of a hurricane, forcing it to be felled as it was deemed a hazard to pedestrians.

Parque de Independencia

At the end of Calle El Conde, the Parque de Independencia (Independence Park) is the juncture of old and new Santo Domingo. It marks historical events and commemorates the long battle for independence. At the entrance to the Parque de Independencia is the **Puerto del Conde,** named for the Conde (Count) de Peñalba, who led the resistance to the British invasion in 1655. This is also the site of a march for independence that occurred in 1844 to overthrow the occupying forces from Haiti, thereby securing their independent republic and raising the Dominican flag for the first time. The **Altar de la Patria** (daily 8:30 A.M.–6 P.M., free) is the resting place of three of the Dominican Republic's most celebrated figures: Juan Pablo Duarte, Francisco del Rosario Sánchez, and Ramón Matías Mella. You should not wear shorts or short skirts to the Altar de la Patria. In the Parque de Independencia you will also find a marker from which all points in the city are measured.

Puerta de la Misericordia

The Gate of Mercy (Arzobispo Portes, near Palo Hincado) was erected as the western door to the city and is part of the original walls. It got its name because of the way some of the less fortunate locals would flock to it for protection during hurricanes and earthquakes. This is also where the first shot was fired on February 27, 1844, in the struggle for independence from neighboring Haiti.

Casa de Francia

The former home of Hernán Cortés, the Casa de Francia (Las Damas 42) is purportedly where he organized his brutal plans for conquering the Aztec nations of what is now modern Mexico. It served as a residence for nearly three centuries until it went through a series of government-owned incarnations and now houses the French Cultural Alliance and French Embassy. Although visitors cannot venture into the building (except for the lobby), walking past you cannot help but admire the facade. It is made of stone and is thought to be from the same designer as the Casa del Cordón.

Casa del Cordón

The House of the Cord (Calle Isabel La Católica at Emiliano Tejera, 8:15 A.M.–4 P.M. daily, free) is the first European residence in the western hemisphere, built in 1502 by an explorer, Francisco de Garay, who accompanied Columbus on his first voyage. It later belonged to Diego Columbus and his wife before he built the Alcázar de Columbus. It is named for the stonework on the facade of the house of a sash and cord. It is also the alleged spot where Drake went to a forced lineup of the women of Santo Domingo; he then collected all of their fine jewelry as part of the ransom for leaving Santo Domingo. The house is now home to the Banco Popular. The part that you can actually visit is the lobby and into the courtyard.

Hostal Nicolás de Ovando

Perhaps one of the most charming homes of colonial Santo Domingo, the Hostal Nicolás de Ovando (Las Damas at General Luperón) was built in 1509. It was the home of Governor Nicolás de Ovando, who is responsible for choosing the site on which Santo Domingo was built (after it had been destroyed by a hurricane in its original location). Christopher Columbus was often a guest of this home, and you can be too. It is now a luxurious Sofitel hotel (see *Accommodations*).

Iglesia de Nuestra Señora de las Mercedes

The Iglesia de Nuestra Señora de las Mercedes (Church of Our Lady of Mercy, Las Mercedes at José Reyes, free) is one of the most historic in all of Santo Domingo and one of the most frustrating to get in to see since its hours are notoriously irregular. It was built in the 1530s and was, of course, sacked by Sir Francis Drake. It was reconstructed afterward but it suffered hurricanes and earthquakes as well. Perhaps the most alluring aspect of the church (aside from the fact that it's still standing) is its elaborately carved mahogany altar and pulpit with a demon serpent. Note the cloister adjacent to the church; it is in its original condition. A Spanish monk and writer, Tirso de Molina, lived here from 1616 to 1618; he was in his late 20s or early 30s at this point in his life and was beginning to hone his skills with works for the stage in a form called *comedia nueva*.

Iglesia Santa Bárbara

Built in 1574, the Iglesia Santa Bárbara (Calle Isabel La Católica and Gabino Puello, 8:30 A.M.–7 P.M. daily, free) was constructed in honor of the patron saint of the military, so it's a little bit church and a little bit fortress. The white-washed, baroque structure is an amalgamation of pieces due to, yet again, the sacking that Drake gave it. The rebuilt church was put together like jammed puzzle pieces with three arches, two of which are windowless. Still, these additions are probably what kept it from toppling during some hefty hurricanes through the ages.

Just behind the church is the **Fuerte de Santa Bárbara** (Juan Parra at Av. Mella), which was erected in 1570 as a security defense for the city (and to keep the Taíno slaves in check). All that was to no avail when Drake blew through town. He easily captured it in 1586, and the rubble goes to show how quickly it went down.

El Convento de los Dominicos

Just south of El Conde is the El Convento de los Dominicos (Av. Duarte at Padre Billini, services held 7–9 A.M. and 5:30–7 P.M. Mon.–Fri., every hour 7 A.M.–noon and 7–8 P.M. Sun., free). It was built in 1510 and is the first convent of the Dominican order in the Americas. The outside of the building is an imposing structure, built of stone and brick with Spanish tile accents. Above the great wooden doors is a vine-like ornamentation leading up to the signature central round window at the top of the facade. Pope Paul III visited in 1538, granting the title of university after being impressed by the theology and teachings of the church. Hence, it became the first university of the New World. It was here that Father Bartolomé de las Casas did much of his famous writing about the Spanish atrocities committed against the Taíno people. Once inside the rosary chapel, don't forget to look up. The unique ceiling depicts classical gods and astrological figures on a zodiac wheel.

Capilla de Nuestra Señora de los Remedios

The chapel (Calle de las Damas at Las

Mercedes) was built in the 1500s in classic Gothic style, intended as a private chapel and mausoleum for the prominent families of Santo Domingo, like the Ovando and Davila families. This tiny church is unmistakable as you walk along Calle de las Damas, with its brick facade and triple-arched belfry. It was rebuilt in 1884 after being shut down for a short period because it was pronounced unsafe. Today, masses are held there.

Museo de las Casas Reales

Constructed in the 16th century in Renaissance style, the Museum of the Royal Houses (Calle de las Damas, tel. 809/682-4202, 9 A.M.–5 P.M. daily, RD$30) was the Palace of the Governor and the Audiencia Real (Royal Court), which was a panel of judges created to check the power of the governor. Just outside and opposite the museum a large sundial was positioned so that those inside could simply glance out the window and tell the time. The museum has an excellent re-creation of the colonial era using real colonial-period objects, including treasures recovered from sunken Spanish galleons, gilded furniture, art, and replicas of the *Niña,* the *Pinta,* and the *Santa María.* Each room has been re-created according to its original decor and usage. Taíno artifacts are on display as well. An impressive and varied collection of weaponry that was donated by Trujillo is on display on the second floor. If you only have time for one museum in the Ciudad Colonial, make this one it.

Museo Alcázar de Colón

Museo Alcázar de Colón (Plaza de la Hispanidad, tel. 809/682-4750, 9 A.M.–5 P.M. Tues.–Sat., 9 A.M.–4 P.M. Sun., RD$50) was a house that was originally used by Diego Columbus, Christopher's son, and his wife, María de Toledo. When they left the house in the early 1500s, they left it to friends who took good care of it for nearly 100 years. After that, it became a prison and a warehouse even until it was abandoned and actually became the city dump at one point. It is unbelievable when you walk through it today that at one

point only a couple of walls were left standing. The restoration took three turns from 1957 to 1992, and the building that stands today is a successful attempt at historical accuracy. This Isabelline-style, architectural restoration effort is a valiant one. The museum is decorated with the furniture, carpets, tapestries, ceramic pieces, Spanish manuscripts, musical instruments, beautiful Spanish-style woodwork (doors, beamed ceilings, desks, and gargoyles), and paintings that the Diego Columbus family home would have had in the time they lived in it. These are most likely 16th-century reproductions and not actual pieces that they owned like the guides of the museum tout. Nevertheless, this is a fine and important museum that represents a piece of Santo Domingo's history.

Larimar Museum

A remodeled 17th-century house holds the Larimar Museum (Calle Isabel La Católica 54, tel. 809/689-6605, www.larimarmuseum. com, 8 A.M.–6 P.M. Mon.–Sat., 8 A.M.–2 P.M. Sun., free). Larimar is an azure-blue stone that is mined only in the Dominican Republic. On the ground floor of this museum is a shop with a wonderful selection of good quality larimar and amber jewelry with a very friendly and helpful staff. Remember; all prices are negotiable. The museum is upstairs, and if you ask, one of the staff members can give you a guided tour for free; they are very knowledgeable. There are encased examples of the rare pectolite mined near Bahoruco on the Península de Pedernales. Exhibits explain everything from the mining procedure to how the jewelry is made. Signage is in Spanish and English.

Museo Mundo de Ámbar

In the Amber World Museum (Calle Arzobispo Meriño 452 and Restauración, tel. 809/682-3309, www.amberworldmuseum.com, 9 A.M.–6 P.M. Mon.–Sat., 9 A.M.–2 P.M. Sun., US$2), you'll see impressive examples of the ancient resin for which the Dominican Republic is famous. Along with an explanation of the formation of amber, which often trapped insects, leaves, and even some lizards, there is a beautiful display of some examples of such findings. You can watch an audiovisual tutorial on the mining process and on how amber jewelry is made. Signage is in English, German, and Spanish.

Museo de Ámbar

If you can't get enough of bugs in resin, head over to the Museum of Amber (Calle El Conde 107 and Parque Colón, tel. 809/221-1333, 9 A.M.–6 P.M. Mon.–Sat., free). Here you'll see another array of examples on the second floor above a well-stocked jewelry shop selling amber and larimar pieces.

Quinta Dominica

This very small museum (Padre Billini 202 at 19 de Marzo, www.quintadominica.com, tel. 809/687-5944, 9:30 A.M.–6 P.M. Mon.–Sat., 9 A.M.–2 P.M. Sun., free), which opened in 2004, doesn't have a permanent collection but has changing exhibits and events. Colonial art is the main focus but not always what is on the menu. Past exhibits have included modern metal sculptures and religious mosaic art. Past events include lectures on varied topics, readings with authors, and photography exhibits. The building is a renovated colonial home with a very pretty garden courtyard perfect for a rest from the bustle of the street. Signage is in Spanish only, and there is rarely literature available to accompany the art, but it doesn't impede the enjoyment.

Museo de la Atarazana

This museum (Calle Colón 4, tel. 809/682-5834, 9 A.M.–6 P.M. Thurs.–Tues., RD$50) is normally filled with the sunken treasures recovered from Spanish galleons that went down in the waters off the coast of the Dominican Republic, particularly the *Concepción,* which went down in the Bahía de Samaná. Coins, crucifixes, spoons, swords, plates, and silver bars, among other things, have all been found and are on display here. Signs are in Spanish and English. In 2009, the museum was temporarily closed for remodeling.

Museo Casa de Tostado

This Elizabethan-Gothic building was erected in 1503 as the house of Francisco Tostado, the clerk of the Spanish governor, Nicolas de Ovando. The double Gothic window on the exterior of the building above the front door is a sure sign you have found the right place. It is the only one of its kind in the western hemisphere. The Casa de Tostado now houses the **Museo de La Familia Dominicana** (Calle Arzobispo Meriño and Padre Billini, tel. 809/689-5000, 9 A.M.–4 P.M. Mon.–Sat., RD$50). This museum opened its doors in 1973, and most of the objects inside come from donations from families across the nation. The collection brings together articles such as furniture, paintings, photos, books, and personal items in an effort to highlight the traditions, culture, and history of the 19th-century Dominican family.

CENTRAL SANTO DOMINGO
Plaza de la Cultura

At the Plaza de la Cultura (Calle Pedro Henríquez Ureña) there are four museums, the national theater, and the national library.

Museo del Hombre Dominicano (Museum of the Dominican Man, tel. 809/687-3622, www.museodelhombredominicano.org.do, 10 A.M.–5 P.M. Tues.–Sun., RD$50) has an extensive and impressive collection ranging from Taíno artifacts (including tools, pottery, and other items from their daily lives) to items from the Spanish era and Dominican life today. Most of the Taíno artifacts can be found on the third floor. Spearheads, stone depictions of gods, pots, ceremonial pieces, and remnants of tools are all displayed in well-lit cases. The fourth floor is concerned with post-Columbus Dominican items. There is a section devoted to the Carnaval traditions as they relate to each region in the Dominican Republic, one for the African influence on Dominican culture, an exhibit on the effects slavery had on the history of the island, and an example of a typical rural Dominican home. Unfortunately, signage is all in Spanish. Make sure to ask for the English-speaking guides available at the front desk; you

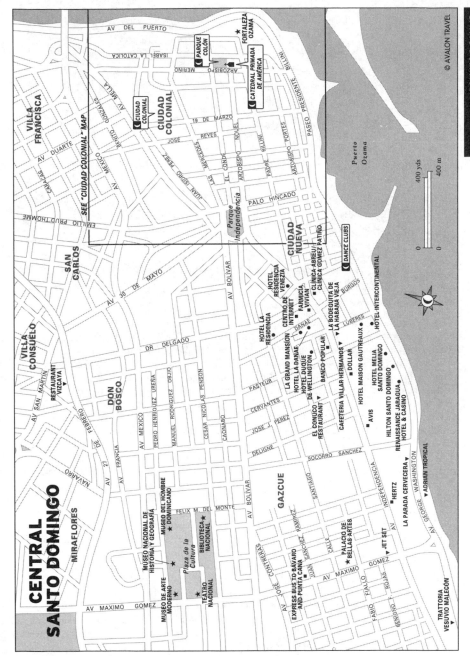

SANTO DOMINGO

© AVALON TRAVEL

CENTRAL SANTO DOMINGO

political rally near the Plaza de la Cultura

will pay an additional RD$50. Staff won't offer this service up freely, so be sure to request it. Many things are unmarked, so a guide would be very helpful. Tips are appreciated. There is a small café on the fourth floor, a gift shop on the first floor, and elevators make this an accessible museum.

The four-level **Museo de Arte Moderno** (tel. 809/685-2154, 10 A.M.–6 P.M. Tues.–Sun., RD$20), right next to the Museum of the Dominican Man, is an exciting step into the modern world after all that history. Modernist and postmodern paintings, installations, and sculptures by well-known and emerging Dominican artists are on display in a wonderful setting. As you enter, you're on the second level, so don't miss out on the bottom floor. Some of the well-known artists to look out for are: José Vela Zanetti, Adriana Billini, Cándido Bidó, and Celeste Woss y Gil. Save a good amount of time to wander and ponder.

The **Museo Nacional de Historia y Geografía** (tel. 809/686-6668, 9:30 A.M.–4 P.M. Tues.–Sun., RD$20) is conveniently organized in chronological order according to time periods and includes exhibits on Haitian/Dominican relations as well as the Trujillo years, with many of his personal effects, including one of the bullet-ridden cars that was involved in the shootout when he was assassinated (it is a little creepy). This is not the best of the museums in the bunch, but it's worth a stop if you're in the area. The American Occupation exhibition contains photos and items from American soldiers from those days.

The less striking **Museo de Historia Natural** (tel. 809/689-0106, 10 A.M.–5 P.M. Tues.–Sun., RD$50) has exhibits on the flora and fauna of the island and a collection of skeletons.

The **Teatro Nacional** (tel. 809/687-3191) is a venue for the national opera, ballet, and symphony. The venue has good acoustics and comfortable seating, and attracts an array of fantastic performers. The **Biblioteca Nacional** (National Library, tel. 809/688-4086, 8 A.M.–10 P.M. Mon.–Fri., Sat. and Sun. 8 A.M.–4 P.M.), although maybe not much of a vacation destination, might have some interest to those researching the culture of the

Dominican Republic. The library also has a children's section.

Palacio Nacional

The National Palace (Av. México at Av. 30 de Marzo, tel. 809/695-8000) is open to tours only by appointment and isn't a light visit. It takes persistence, but if you're granted a tour, dress your best. No shorts or flip-flops. Dominicans dress well for business appointments and expect you to do the same. This huge palace covers an entire block and is constructed of roseate marble from Samaná by Italian neoclassical design. It was inaugurated in 1947 and is ornately decorated inside with gilt mirrors, grand murals, and mahogany furniture. The most impressive area is the Room of Caryatids; 44 sculptures of draped women rise like columns, reminiscent of Versailles.

Palacio de Bellas Artes

The Palace of Fine Arts (Av. Máximo Gómez, www.bellasartes.gov.do, tel. 809/682-1325) is an impressively large theater that holds special performance events including the symphony, dance productions, and exhibits. Events are quite sporadic, so look in the local papers, consult with the concierge at your hotel, or call for a schedule.

Cándido Bidó Galería de Arte

In the heart of Gazcue, in a bright blue and orange renovated house (Dr. Báez 5, tel. 809/685-5310, www.galeriacandidobido.com, 9 A.M.–5 P.M. Mon.–Fri. and Sat. 9 A.M.–12:30 P.M.), is a gallery of art filled with the works of Cándido Bidó, one of the Dominican Republic's most celebrated contemporary artists. His works have been exhibited worldwide. But here, in this gallery in the middle of the Gazcue neighborhood, amidst the work of this native son from the Cibao region's small town of Bonao, you can study the paintings, which are like the sensation of the Caribbean sun in the middle of the country at *medio día* (noon). Bidó's depictions of a tropical land and the people in it have a curious shortage of the color green, but the brushstrokes come

in a multitude of other bright hues—orange and blue being his hallmark colors—and often overlaying the images with flowers and dots. The overall feeling of the paintings is similar to how magical realism reads in a García Márquez novel. Bright colors send the tropical humidity right off the canvas, while mask-like faces give you a sense of the magic of the land.

SOUTHWEST SANTO DOMINGO
Parque Mirador del Sur

The Southern Lookout Park (Av. Mirador del Sur) is a few blocks west of La Plaza de la Cultura and is popular with the yuppies of Santo Domingo. You'll find food vendors, shaded paths, and broad avenues, which are closed to traffic for three hours in the early morning and after dinner so that joggers, rollerbladers, and bicyclists can have free rein. The park has a wealth of limestone caves, some of which have been turned into restaurants and bars.

PARQUE MIRADOR DEL ESTE
Faro a Colón

Located in the Parque Mirador del Este (Eastern Lookout Park), the Lighthouse of Columbus (tel. 809/591-1492, 9:30 A.M.–5:30 P.M. Tues.–Sun., RD$100) cost a lot of money to build, was built in controversy, and houses controversy within as well. On the eastern bank of the Río Ozama, this gigantic structure stands 10 stories high and is in the shape of a cross. When there is sufficient power (almost never) or on special occasions, the high-powered lights along the top shine into the night, forming a white cross in the sky. With one flick of a switch, the *faro* can cause a blackout throughout Santo Domingo and has become a rather tired joke among the locals.

However, inside the structure is what is truly interesting. In the midsection of the cross is a tomb, guarded by soldiers in all-white uniforms, containing what is thought by many to be Columbus's remains. This is a controversial topic, as Spain and Italy both claim to have his remains elsewhere. Throughout the rest of the long structure are various displays of the indigenous people from many different nations—an ironic juxtaposition with the highly glorified and proudly displayed remains of Columbus.

Los Tres Ojos

The Three Eyes (Parque Mirador del Este, 9 A.M.–5 P.M. daily, US$1.75) have been a tourist draw for a very long time. Many tour groups stop here. Inside are caverns containing limestone sinkholes. A very steep staircase leads down to the underground caverns. Inside it is not a claustrophobia-inducing cave, but rather very tall and wide open. While it is called "The Three Eyes" there are actually four pools (sinkholes) with stalactites all around. The pools are filled with very clear and frigid water. In the deepest pool the "Dominican Tarzan" will do a demonstration, climbing to a high point and jumping off into the depths, for a tip of course. You can cross the third pool for an additional US$0.35 to the fourth hidden "eye." It is quite a tourist trap, but a rather pretty one at that. The Taínos are said to have used these caves as places for religious ceremonies.

Acuario Nacional

Just south of the Parque Mirador del Este is the National Aquarium (Av. España, 9 A.M.–5:30 P.M. Tues.–Sun., US$1.50), which is best visited if you have kids to entertain. There is a tank with a Plexiglas underwater walkway where kids love to see the rays, turtles, and huge fish "fly" above them. Also on-site is a shark tank and turtle-breeding project. Kids have fun; adults may find it unimpressive.

NORTHERN SANTO DOMINGO: ARROYO HONDO

Arroyo Hondo is a large and mainly residential area containing huge mansions with expansive manicured lawns, modest housing complexes, and some shanty towns toward the northern sector.

Jardín Botánico Nacional

The National Botanical Garden (Av. República de Colombia, 9 A.M.–6 P.M. daily, RD$30) is a lush and expansive display of many different kinds of plants—aquatics, orchids, bromeliads, a bamboo garden, many kinds of trees, and even a Japanese garden. This botanical garden is well taken care of, and there is a trolley (RD$15) that you can catch every 30 minutes. It drives you around and you hear explanations of the different areas in many languages. It is wonderful to enjoy the shady grounds and serenity, which you can't find in many places in the very frenetic Santo Domingo.

While there, visit the **Museo Ecológico** (9 A.M.–4 P.M. daily, US$0.35), which has encased displays of the many ecosystems of the Dominican Republic, including the deserts, mangroves, mountains, and beaches. This portion is air-conditioned. Children might enjoy this park, if only for the trolley (it looks like a little train) and the wide open spaces for running.

Parque Zoológico Nacional

The National Zoological Park (Av. los Reyes Católicos, 9 A.M.–6 P.M. Tues.–Sun., US$1) is your opportunity to see the extremely rare solenodon, if you missed seeing it in the wild. There is a rather impressive array of endemic and exotic animals. Watch the aquatic birds in their simulated lake or the crocodiles in a makeshift pond. Visitors without herpetophobia will enjoy the snake exhibit. There is even a bar-less tiger enclosure that makes animal lovers breathe a little easier. But many of the other animals are not so lucky and are in less-than-optimal cages. Taking a taxi (make sure to arrange for the return trip with the driver) is best as the zoo is in a remote corner of the city.

Museo Prehispánico

This museum (San Martín 176 and Lopé de Vega, 9 A.M.–5 P.M. Mon.–Fri., free) showcases a notable array of Taíno everyday artifacts, such as jewelry made of shell and teeth, pottery, and ceremonial pieces, like an intact *duho* (throne) for the cacique to use during religious ceremonies.

Museo Bellapart

Sure, this private art museum may be located

on top of a Honda dealership (Av. J.F. Kennedy and Dr. Lembert Peguero, 9 A.M.–6 P.M. Mon.–Fri., 9 A.M.–12:30 P.M. Sat., tel. 809/541-7721, www.museobellapart.com, free), but it holds in its permanent collection around 2,000 pieces, which give you a look of the Dominican artistic style from the 1890s through the 20th century within the media of paintings, sculptures, prints, and drawings. Be inspired by the work of key Dominican and foreign artists like Celeste Woss y Gil, Dario Suro, Gilberto Hernández Ortega, Eligio Pichardo, José Vela Zanetti, Jaime Colson, and Enrique García Godoy.

Entertainment and Events

NIGHTLIFE

Santo Domingo boasts a great nightlife scene, from casinos to pubs and karaoke bars to dance clubs. As of 2007, the Dominican Republic has had a curfew on establishments that serve alcohol. Bars and clubs now close at midnight Sunday through Thursday and 3 A.M. to 4 A.M. on Friday and Saturday. This does not apply to resorts and casinos. While the curfew law worked, the stringent closing time is overlooked by many establishments much of the time. You can expect that bars will remain open until around 2 A.M. almost every night.

Most dance clubs feature Latin music mixed in with American and European club-style house dance music. Women traveling solo or with other women should know that it is not uncommon to be asked to dance by a man you don't know. If you do not wish to dance with him simply say *"no gracias."* Even though Dominican men are very persistent and might not take your first answer, simply repeating it politely will probably work. Still, it is best for women to keep track of each other (as in any city). Many establishments have a dress code that doesn't allow you to wear jeans, T-shirts, or tennis shoes. If you don't abide by these dress codes, you run the risk of being turned away at the door.

The Ciudad Colonial in particular has a plethora of nighttime entertainment options worth visiting. Independently owned bars and restaurants are tucked into the centuries-old buildings all along the cobbled streets. Exploring these options is a major part of the charm.

It is a relatively safe area to walk around in the evening, provided you do not walk alone and you stay on the well-lighted streets. Take a taxi late at night, though (whether alone or with others). Taxi rates go up (not much) around midnight, but it's worth your safety; haggling for a price is harder at night.

One of the most long-standing Dominican establishments is the car wash, also called a *colmadon* or *parada.* These are essentially open-air beer joints; perhaps they have a *colmado* (store) attached, maybe a restaurant as well—sometimes they are literally car washes that sell beer. The point is, they are meeting places where people gather, socialize, listen to music, push tables aside, and even dance. They are a phenomenal way to get the true feel for the Dominican culture; flirt in the sultry night air, perhaps practice your Spanish with the locals (this is a slang hot spot after all), and try your hand at a game of dominoes. Often, *paradas* are the jumping-off point for the night, where plans for the evening are laid out, or where evenings wind down since most are open until the last person leaves (officially, they are supposed to adhere to the curfew law as well, but they are quite relaxed in that regard). You can find these *colmadones* and car washes scattered throughout every city and even along the highways. They are a Dominican tradition. Cute names make them memorable—like **El Dugout,** which is one block away from the baseball stadium on Avenida Tiradentes in Santo Domingo. Watch for signs along highways and along main roads in the cities; many times very famous Dominican singers will be booked for

MUSIC AND DANCE – DOMINICAN STYLE

MERENGUE

As the national music and dance of the Dominican Republic, the merengue has a colorful history. As with all Dominican stories, there are many versions. One story about the development of the merengue claims the dance was the result of a group of partying villagers who, out of sympathy for a war hero who had just returned home with a limp, danced as though they too had been wounded. Another, more likely story says that the dance was based upon the foot-dragging movement that resulted from slaves whose feet were chained together as they cut sugarcane in the fields. The idea is that these slaves, who observed the ballroom dances of their masters, adapted their own version set to the music of drumbeats to make it more enticing rhythmically. Where their masters' dances were on the stiff side, however, the slaves developed their movements to be more upbeat. And yet one more possibility is that merengue was spawned from a type of Cuban music called *upa upa*.

Today, merengue has several variants, including the more formal ballroom merengue and the contemporary club merengue, which incorporates the hips more in its movements. Famous merengue musicians include Sergio Vargas and Fernandito Villalona.

Few musical genres and dances have been so loaded with national significance as merengue has been. For a long time, it was the poster-child music and dance of the white-skinned, wealthy, and bourgeoisie of the nation and was the first music to be associated with Dominican nationalism. This concept was backed in large part by Trujillo himself using it at state functions, demanding that no one leave the dances until he himself had departed. He also went so far as to use the music as a propaganda tool, demanding that artists write songs about how great a leader he was. What Trujillo didn't count on was the built-in contradiction of merengue. The music and dance were derived from African roots, a suitable national symbol for a country loaded with racial and class contradictions.

Learning to dance merengue is fun and lessons are available poolside at all the big resorts. This partner dance has a hold where the

---

appearances at car washes and *paradas*. That is how beloved these establishments are.

Dance Clubs

The hotel bars along the Malecón have some of the hottest dance clubs in the city. Besides tourists, they are also frequented by a lot of the wealthy youth of Santo Domingo. Most clubs have a US$5–10 cover charge depending on whether it's live music or a DJ.

Of the hotel bars, **Jubilee** (Hotel Jaragua, Av. George Washington 367, tel. 809/221-2222, 9 P.M.–3 A.M. Tues.–Sat.) is the hottest and the swankiest. This is popular not only with tourists, but with many wealthy Dominicans dressed in their best "clubbing gear" and spending a lot on fancy drinks. Ladies, if you're looking for a place to wear all those hot new high-heeled shoes you just bought, Jubilee is

that place—just make sure you can dance in them. But don't expect a good crowd until late. An early evening start for a Dominican would be arriving to the club around 11 P.M., so don't expect the joint to jump until midnight.

Jet Set (Independencia 2253, tel. 809/535-4145, 10 P.M.–late, US$7) is a semi-casual place to hear good salsa and merengue. Sometimes the music is live. The dance floor fills after midnight.

Compared to the size of the other hotels along the Malecón, **El Napolitano** (Av. George Washington 101, tel. 809/687-1131, www.napolitanohotel.com, 9 P.M.–4 A.M. Thurs.–Sun.) is small. But its disco can still pack them in on the weekends. This is in part due to the fact that your drink bill won't be what you worry about all night. It's popular with 20–30-somethings and tourists.

follower is at a slight angle and slightly to the right of the leader. It isn't necessarily fancy patterns that generate the wows and raves from onlookers, but the motion of the movements. It is less booty wiggle than it is about contra-body movement between knee bending and upper body, resulting in the signature and sexy hip motion.

BACHATA

Bachata, another popular music and dance in the Dominican Republic, originated in the more rural areas of the country and has long been associated with the lower, working class and the dark-skinned people of the nation. It is a guitar-based music derived from the bolero. *Bachata* tends to be a bit more on the dramatic side, dealing with lost love, lost hope, and betrayal, all in a fog of heavy drinking and sex – filled with sexual double entendres. In general, the music is almost a kind of blues of the Caribbean. Juan Luis Guerra is a Dominican musician who has gained international popularity for *bachata*, as well as for merengue and for combining the two genres, but purists would argue that his music is

closer to a form of ballad or bolero than it is to *bachata*. Still, the international spotlight that shone on *bachata* as a result of his album titled *Bachata Rose* gave significant attention to other of the nation's beloved *bachateros*, like Antony Santos, Luis Vargas, Frank Reyes, and the duo Monchy y Alexandra, to name a few. It wasn't until the 1990s that *bachata* became socially acceptable in its own Dominican Republic. Before that, it was seen (by the upper class) as vulgar and the music of the lower barrios.

Lately, *bachata* has exploded into the ballrooms and clubs all over the world. *Bachata* dance festivals in Europe and North America are teaching people this four-beat dance. Three steps are taken and then a hip motion is made in the opposite direction in four beats. Repeat in the other direction. It is the signature hip motion that is perhaps the hardest for people learning the dance to master. But without it, whether subtle or sharp, the *bachata* is not being danced. With its increased popularity have come fusion dances like *bachatango*, which crosses *bachata* with Argentine tango moves.

At the **Maunaloa Club & Casino** (Calle Héroes de Luperón at Malecón, Centro de los Héroes, tel. 809/533-2151), the nightclub's two floors of tables overlooking a dance floor and a lush design give it a *Mambo Kings* feel. In fact, they have Cuban *son* night on Sundays. Other entertainment ranges from stand-up comedians to merengue orchestras, but you can expect live Latin music every night, starting around 11 P.M. By the end of the evening, your drink tab may be rather steep, but this venue is worth it.

Guácara Taína (Av. Mirador del Sur, tel. 809/533-2151, 9 P.M.–3 A.M.) is a very unique experience and was quite popular, although now it is more frequented by tourists and tour groups. It is in the belly of a massive cave—so massive that it can hold 2,000 people and has multiple dance floors. You should definitely

take a taxi here. Dance the salsa and merengue amidst stalactites and stalagmites.

Monte Cristo (Calle José Amador Soler and Abraham Lincoln, tel. 809/542-5000, 6 P.M.–5 A.M.) is a very popular spot. Named after the fictional Count of Monte Cristo, this English-style pub re-creates the story of this character through its decoration. There are different activities like video nights, wine-tastings, raffles, and of course, dancing to rock, merengue, and salsa. Appetizers are available. Dress nicely for this bar.

Bars and Pubs

La Parada Cervecera (Av. George Washington, no phone, 8 A.M.–midnight, free) has been around for a very long time and is a favorite on the Malecón. The beer is ice cold, the people-watching is fantastic, and the idea of a quiet conversation is downright laughable because the music is at top decibel, but that is also part of its charm. Music at speaker-distorting levels is a true Dominican institution. Merengue, *bachata,* salsa. Let it thump, baby! You're on vacation. You'll know it when you see the glowing frosty overflowing beer mug sign and hear the thumping music. This is a casual-dress outdoor joint with food as well, it's open all day long, and it has off-street parking and an adjacent car wash!

Atarazana 9 (Ciudad Colonial, Atarazana 9, tel. 809/688-0969, 9 P.M.–3 A.M., free) is just off Plaza de la Hispanidad in a very historic building and a safe area for tourist bar-hopping. It opens around 5 P.M., but live music doesn't get going until later (on the second floor). The drinks are great and the crowd is young and hip. Live emerging musicians like Pavel Nuñez have been known to play here. Dress is casual.

Abacus (Ciudad Colonial, Hostos 350 and Luperón, tel. 809/333-7272) is a good place for a stylish cocktail with your friends. The lounge has couches and soft lighting with DJ music.

Bio (Calle Sánchez and Padre Billini, no phone) is one of the newest and hippest bars in the Ciudad Colonial. The interior has a warm inviting glow that beckons you to approach and there's a great mix of music (house, techno, some Latin). However, there is an ooze of "cool" that can look a bit practiced. Nevertheless, this is a fun place to experience.

Parada 77 (Ciudad Colonial, Calle Isabel La Católica 225, tel. 809/221-7880, 9 P.M.–3 A.M. Mon.–Fri., 9 P.M.–"infinity" Sat.–Sun., www.parada77.com) is not a typical tourist bar at all. This small bar is at the far end of Isabela La Católica and is hot with the younger art crowd. It got its name from being bus stop *(parada)* number 77, so they never changed it. Not fancy in the least, it is almost completely devoid of furniture save for the bar stools and a few tables and chairs; management says this "encourages dancing." The only pictures allowed on the walls are of revolutionary thinkers (like Charlie Chaplin, Che Guevara, and Bob Marley), and the rest is decorated with the

graffiti, poetry, and artwork of patrons from all over the world clear up to the ceiling. Just ask for a pen from the very friendly bartender and leave your mark—I did. An eclectic variety of mostly alternative and world music is played, as well as merengue and salsa on occasion. The young-adult crowd is gay-friendly. There is an empty leg cast hanging on the wall that the manager said had "a long story" that would "go untold." It's that kind of odd Dominican humor that appeals. Coming here is a way to experience a different but very real part of Santo Domingo that tourists rarely see.

In stark contrast to Parada 77 (and at the opposite end of the same street), **K-ramba** (Ciudad Colonial, Calle Isabel La Católica 1, tel. 809/688-3587, 10 A.M.–3 A.M. Mon.–Sat.) is a very popular tourist bar owned by an Austrian expat. There is indoor and outdoor seating, and rock music is played. Many tourists feel safe going here late at night.

At **Café del Teatro** (Arzobispo Meriño 110, tel. 809/688-8173, www.casadeteatro.com), in the Casa de Teatro courtyard, nightly musicians playing classic jazz and Latin-jazz entertain an all-ages crowd with a sophisticated ear. Casual dress.

Walking past **Proud Mary** (Ciudad Colonial, Av. Duarte 55, tel. 809/689-6611, 8 P.M.–late, closed Mon.), you'll notice one thing right off the bat. There is no Latin beat pumping from inside. That might make some keep walking, but to many it's a magnetic pull. Maria, Spanish expat and owner of this 40-person-capacity bar, is indeed proud to say that she plays blues, jazz, and soft rock and that you will *never* hear Latin music coming from her stereo. Maria made the bar herself; literally every piece of decor was hand-crafted by her or a family member, and she enjoys talking to the expats and foreigners that hang out here (she has a few languages under her belt). It is a dimly lighted, wonderfully welcoming place with bar stools, some tall tables made of old cable spools, and a small couch area in the back. The music is uncommon in this merengue-or-die town, and played loud enough to enjoy but low enough to meet new friends. The full bar has good prices. Dress is casual.

Hard Rock Café Santo Domingo (Calle El Conde 103, tel. 809/686-7771, 11:30 A.M.–12:30 A.M. Sun.–Thurs., 11:30 A.M.–1 A.M. Fri. and Sat., www.hardrock.com) hardly needs any introduction, but many locals now regard this American joint as a good spot to see occasional live acoustic music and get a good burger.

Doubles (Arzobispo Meriño 154, tel. 809/258-2580, www.doublesbar.net) offers a very classy interior where you can have a drink on a plush couch with your sweetie or entertain some business clients at the classic long wooden bar. The music is a good mix of Latin and pop, but often it's too loud for a truly intimate conversation (clashing with the romantic couch setup). Still, this bar has been a favorite among locals and tourists for a long time.

Nowhere (Hostos 205, tel. 809/877-6258, 9 P.M.–4 A.M. Wed.–Sat., free) is a very popular bar for a late-night drink, mostly with the young crowd. House music, hip-hop, and Latin music are played in the different dance floors inside.

Cigarro Café (Lina Hotel, Av. Máximo Gomez, tel. 809/687-7685, 1 P.M.–1 A.M. Sun., 10 A.M.–1 A.M. Mon.–Thurs., 10 A.M.–3 A.M. Sat.), a small cigar lounge adjacent to the Barceló Lina Hotel (in the back parking lot), has a huge walk-in humidor that cigar aficionados will love and big comfy couches and chairs to disappear into. A full bar serves everything from quality whiskies and rums to rich espresso drinks. There are also outdoor sidewalk tables.

Gay and Lesbian Nightlife

Santo Domingo is a very metropolitan city. Entertainment options for the increasingly open gay community are becoming more stable. Sadly, gay establishments seem to have the life span of a bumblebee, but now, with an ever-growing out gay community, establishments are able to set up camp and keep their doors open for longer periods of time. The best resource for the gay nightlife in Santo Domingo is www.monaga.net.

Jay Dee's bar (Ciudad Colonial, José Reyes 10, tel. 809/333-5905, 8 P.M. to late Thurs.–Sat., US$4), owned by an American expat, is popular with locals and tourists alike. It has been in operation for over 10 years, a very long time in Santo Domingo gay bar years. Friday and Saturday nights the small dance floor can get very crowded (and really hot). Saturday is stripper night. The music is American pop, club, and Latin. The cover cost gets you a free *cuba libre* (rum and Coke) or Presidente (beer).

Cha (Malecón, Av. George Washington 165, no phone, Fri. 9P.M.–4A.M., Sat. 9P.M.–3A.M., Sun. 1P.M.–9P.M., US$1 cover) has hit the sweet spot as the new It bar, and it is ruling the Santo Domingo queer nightlife. Draws include good music, a great location right on the Malecón, drag shows, and strippers.

Amazonia (Gazcue, Dr. Delgado 71, 8 P.M. to late Fri.–Sat.) is a mostly lesbian bar, but all are welcome. It's a good place to go for a drink with friends.

Bar Friends (Polvorín 10 and Juan Isidro PÑrez, tel. 809/689-7572, 8 P.M. to late, closed Sun.) is frequented by tourists and locals alike. It was formerly Bar Phoenix but has changed ownership and been remodeled.

The bar **Esedeku** (Las Mercedes 341, tel. 809/869-6322, 8 P.M. to late Tues.–Sun.) derives its name from the way you pronounce the call letters for the Santo Domingo airport code (SDQ) in Spanish. The interior decor is sleek without being rigid, like a jetliner. You can get tapas-size dishes as well as drinks. This is a classy place and not for hustlers.

CASINOS

Most of the hotels along and near the Malecón have casinos in them. Casinos in the Dominican Republic are generally much smaller and have fewer games than the ones you find in the posh hotels of North America. Some major ones in Santo Domingo are the **Hotel InterContinental** (Av. George Washington 218, tel. 809/221-0000, www.intercontinental.com/santodomingo), **El Napolitano** (Av. George Washington 101, tel. 809/687-1131),

CARNAVAL AND ITS MASKS

Carnaval, generally observed throughout the Dominican Republic during the month of February (though for some areas, March), is steeped in tradition and historical significance. This Catholic-based, pre-Lenten festival was brought to the island by the Spanish and throughout the centuries has blended with the customs of Taíno and African cultures. It has become a celebration of life in a country whose people have such a rich culture and diverse heritage. Different regions tend to have their own customs and rituals pertaining to the occasion, but all exhibit a wealth of spirit and creativity, with local folklore coming alive in the form of masks and the characters adopted by those who don them.

La Vega is one of the most popular places to experience Carnaval, which it has been practicing for over 500 years. The celebration occurs every weekend during the month of February, culminating on the last Sunday of the month. Preparations – particularly the planning and crafting of costumes – begin months in advance. Registered groups of at least 10-15 people team up to create a theme for themselves and carry on together in the streets. La Vega's signature character is the *diablo cojuelo* (mischievous devil). Generally, the masks tend to be on the more grotesque side, with horns and elaborate facial features. People wearing these demon-esque masks run through the crowds walloping folks with inflated pig or cow bladders and whips. Other sub-events – like music and food and dancing – are often scheduled throughout the month, but the costumes and raucous, prankish behavior of the people sporting them truly make Carnaval a spectacular celebration.

Santiago is also host to a very popular Car-naval, one of the more traditional celebrations. Parades and mask-making competitions often get things started. Masks here tend to display a more animal-like theme, with two styles in particular: From the La Joya sector, masks sport horns aplenty, while the Los Pepines masks have a more duck-like appearance. The traditional *lechon* (pig) character originated in Santiago.

In Santiago, as well as in La Vega, the celebrations occur on two levels, the public and the private. While the street festivals with their dance troupes and parades are the main attractions, private businesses and clubs often conduct their own parties as well.

Most masks are derived from the theme of *el diablo* (the devil) but are known by different names and vary in depiction in different regions. The *diablo cojuelo* is the lame devil, named so because, having fallen when he was banished to earth, he walks with a limp. Those who wear the mask of this character must hobble about the streets. *Cachuas*, in **Cabral,** are horned devils. In **Monte Cristi,** the theme of *civiles* and *toros* presides, where the *toros* run about chasing down the *civiles*. In Santo Domingo and other areas men dressed as large-breasted women flirt with the crowds, who yell at them, *"Roba la gallina!"* which means, "Steal the hen!"

The largest and most spectacular Carnaval is celebrated in **Santo Domingo.** People from all over the country – and the world – commence to memorialize the day the Dominican Republic won its independence from Haiti. Costumes and celebrators of all regional backgrounds come together in the capital, where devils, duck-faced monsters, *toros*, transvestites, and horn-headed creatures run amok in the joyful spirit of their country.

and **Hotel Santo Domingo Casino** (Av. Independencia, tel. 809/221-1511).

They are generally open 4 P.M.–4 A.M. You can play with Dominican pesos or U.S. dollars (preferred). The odds are generally similar to Las Vegas odds, meaning profits kept by the casinos and winnings that walk away with the gamblers are similar in Santo Domingo.

Just like in Vegas, you'll find blackjack, craps, and slot machines. You'll find video poker, too, but often it is a Caribbean version of the kind you find in Vegas. Texas Hold 'em and Seven Card Stud are missing from the poker atmosphere and are replaced by a Caribbean version. Stay clear of Keno and Super Keno—the odds are horrendous.

While tipping the dealer may feel like a custom to you, it is not expected here as casinos have their dealers pool their tips to be evenly distributed among the other dealers (if at all). If you have questions, feel free to ask; most dealers speak English.

THEATER AND CINEMA

In the **Teatro Nacional** (National Theater, Plaza de la Cultura, tel. 809/687-3191, US$4–15) you can see performances for an amazingly affordable price. Ballet, symphony, drama, and opera performances are all held here. The ticket office is open 9:30 A.M.–12:30 P.M. and 3:30–6:30 P.M. For show information and times, call the box office, check the weekend edition of the newspaper, or ask the concierge at your hotel.

Palacio de Bellas Artes (Máximo Gomez and Independencia, tel. 809/682-1325, www.bellasartes.gov.do) has performances from the students of the National Conservatory. You can treat yourself to an evening of the orchestra, ballet, jazz, or theater.

Casa de Teatro (Arzobispo Meriño 110, tel. 809/688-8173, www.casateatro.com) has performances in jazz, Latin-jazz, dance, and other various showcases. It also has art shows and readings.

If sitting in a dark theater on your Caribbean vacation appeals, then **Cinemacentro Dominicano** (Av. George Washington, tel. 809/688-8710) and **Hollywood Diamond Cinemas** (Av. Abraham Lincoln, Diamond Mall, tel. 809/683-1189) both show Hollywood new releases as well as releases from around the world. It could be a good rainy-day option.

FESTIVALS AND FAIRS

New Year's Eve is a blast on the Malecón. You and about 200,000 of your closest Dominican friends will party and dance in the street together to dozens of different bandstands. This party goes until dawn. Plan your transportation to this festivity wisely. Craziness with taxis is a given. If you really want to be authentic, go and have a *sancocho* after your long night; you've earned it!

Carnaval is celebrated throughout the country during the month of February, having its swan song on the last weekend of February or first weekend in March in Santo Domingo. Representatives come from all the other towns with their town-specific costumes to take part in a long parade and street party along the Malecón with the Carnival King and professional dance groups. In some years the apex coincides with February 27, which is **Independence Day** in the Dominican Republic. The Malecón (Av. George Washington) is closed to traffic; stages, booths, and vendors set up camp for entertainment, and the party doesn't stop until well into the morning. Elaborately decorated floats and expertly designed costumes that won contests in their respective towns all come to be seen in the festivities. The scene along the waterfront explodes with color and jubilation.

Every June the Guillen brothers of Yamasá throw a huge bash for San Antonio. The **Fiesta San Antonio** attracts locals and tourists alike and is a wonderful opportunity to experience the musical traditions of *gagá, gajumbe,* and *bambulá.* The event is a generous one. Traditional *comida crilloa* and drinks are free. Look for it on the first Sunday before June 13.

The **Merengue Festival** of Santo Domingo is the largest one of its kind in the whole country, held for two weeks every year at the end of July and beginning of August. Events highlighting the country's signature music take place all over the city but center on the Malecón. The festival starts with a parade of dancers and musicians along the Malecón and includes food, drink, and arts.

The **Día de San Miguel** is the September festival of the patron saint of Villa Mella and Ciudad Colonial, celebrated by a procession and traditional music.

The **Chicharron and Folklore Fair** takes place at the end of November in Villa Mella Municipal Park. Visitors can enjoy the music and rhythms of congos, *palos,* and *priprí* and dance the *son.*

The annual **Feria Internacional del Libro Santo Domingo** (Santo Domingo International Book Fair) takes place from April to May at the Plaza de la Cultura and is a treat for bookworms.

Avenida Caracas, near Avenida Duarte, also called La Plaza del Libro ("The Reader's Walkway"), hosted **La Feria del Libro Nuevo y Viejo (New and Used Book Fair)** (last week of November), which was held for the first time in 2008 and rode on the success of **La Feria Internacional del Libro (International Book Fair)**, one of the nation's most successful festivals. Expect to see close to 70 vendors along the avenue, where you are sure to find bargains.

Shopping

Santo Domingo is a great place for all your shopping needs. If you're staying in the Ciudad Colonial, you will most likely find those must-haves in the shops on Calle El Conde or while you're walking around in the Ciudad Colonial. If you're willing to hunt for particular items or are looking for something specific, you can check out the shopping malls, flea markets, and high-end boutiques outside the Ciudad Colonial. Perishable items to buy in the Dominican Republic are Dominican rum, cigars, and coffee. If you're looking for longer-lasting mementos, Dominican-made larimar jewelry, amber, and original Dominican art are great choices.

ARTS AND CRAFTS

The paintings that are pushed in your face around all the tourist areas of the Dominican Republic are bright, colorful depictions of rural life duplicated ad nauseam; *most* of these are actually Haitian paintings, and mass produced. Most of the crafts available are the heavily duplicated faceless peasant woman dolls and anything made of shells. For the real Dominican deal, you'll need to search harder for the galleries and stores that carry the fine arts and crafts by established and emerging artists.

The Swiss Mine (Ciudad Colonial, Calle El Conde 101, tel. 809/221-1897, 9 A.M.–6 P.M. Mon.–Sat., 9:30 A.M.–3:30 P.M. Sun.) has a good collection of paintings in the back, in addition to the jewelry in the front of the store. Some are Dominican and quite good. If you're looking for guidance in what to buy, ask the Swiss owner for help. She has a good knowledge of what she's selling, many opinions, and advice on the topic.

What is a Tennessee expat doing in the Dominican Republic? Selling unique art, that's what. **Plaza Toledo Bettye's Galeria** (Ciudad Colonial, Calle Isabel La Católica 163, tel. 809/688-7649, 9 A.M.–6 P.M., closed Tues.) has colorful paintings (the good kind) donning the walls as well as jewelry and home furnishings like mirrors and interesting knickknacks.

Galería de Arte María del Carmen (Ciudad Colonial, Arzobispo Meriño 207, tel. 809/682-7609, 9 A.M.–7 P.M. daily) has been in operation for decades and has a good selection of original paintings. The staff is friendly, helpful, and very knowledgeable about the art pieces and the artists themselves.

Cándido Bidó Galería de Arte (Gazcue, Dr. Báez 5, tel. 809/544-5310) sells the works of this celebrated Dominican artist and other painters and sculptors. You can't miss it; it is the bright orange and blue house inspired by Bidó's signature colors.

BOOKS AND MAPS

Librería Pichardo (Ciudad Colonial, José Reyes at El Conde, 8 A.M.–7 P.M. Mon.–Fri., 8 A.M.–6 P.M. Sat.) has been around a long time. Located half a block off of El Conde, it looks like just a newsstand from the front, but if you go inside, you'll find stacks and stacks of mostly Spanish-language books.

If you're looking for foreign-language

dictionaries and maps, **Editorial Duarte** (Ciudad Colonial, Arzobispo Meriño at Mercedes, tel. 809/689-4832, 8 A.M.–7 P.M. Mon.–Fri., 8 A.M.–6 P.M. Sat.) is a good stop to make. It has a good selection of novels in Spanish as well.

Mapas Gaar (Ciudad Colonial, Espaillat at El Conde, tel. 809/688-8004, www.mapas-gaar.com.do, 8:30 A.M.–5:30 P.M. daily) is the best map maker in the Dominican Republic. Its store and offices are on the third floor of an office building just off of Calle El Conde. It has a good selection of regional, city, and road maps.

CLOTHING AND ACCESSORIES

All along El Conde, you'll find various shoe, clothing, and accessory shops—even some great fabric stores. The prices for fabric are very good. Should you want to explore the rest of the city's shopping, the options are endless. But there are a couple of malls and stores worth highlighting. **Plaza Central** (Av. 27 de Febrero and Av. Winston Churchill) has a great variety of services and stores, including clothing, music, jewelry, nail salons, and a food court. For higher-end shopping, head to **Plaza Acropolis** (Av. Winston Churchill and Rafael Augusto Sánchez, tel. 809/955-2020). It has haute couture Ferragamo heels and sensible Nine West pumps. The clothing runs the same gamut. Not quite a budget option, though.

For leather goods handmade in the Dominican Republic, head to **Fiori** on the second floor of Plaza Central (tel. 809/567-1298, 9:30 A.M.–7:30 P.M. Mon.–Sat.), which sells women's and men's bags, wallets, belts, and briefcases, all designed in and made from real Dominican leather.

Joyería Diquiabre Gift Shop (Plaza Central, first floor, tel. 809/563-4646) has all the typical gift shop items—jewelry, T-shirts, paintings, lacquered frames—but the prices are a bit lower. These are not rock-bottom prices on amber and larimar, but they are better than in the Ciudad Colonial.

Karla Reid (Plaza Central, first floor, tel. 809/732-6443) has a nice collection of good quality casual, dressy, and beach wear and fashionable accessories. The clothes are suitable for those who are more toward the hip side of the classic/hip scale of fashion.

Dominican-owned **Multi Centro La Sirena** (Av. Winston Churchill between Ángel S. Cabral and Gustavo Mejía Ricart, tel. 809/682-3107, 8 A.M.–10 P.M. Mon.–Sat., 9 A.M.–8 P.M. Sun.) is a multipurpose department store with everything you will need at great prices. It's an especially good option if you are visiting for an extended amount of time. Inside are household objects, clothing, personal hygiene items and other necessities, and a full-scale grocery store.

Ladies with a severe passion for shoes will have a ball in Santo Domingo. If there is one thing the women in Dominican culture know, it's how to build an outfit from the shoes up. You'll find a lot of shoe stores with great prices on El Conde, but if you're looking for something special and are willing to spend a little more time and money, go to **D'Bertha Shoes** (Av. Sarasota 19, Ensanche La Julia, tel. 809/482-0914 or 809/482-0924, www.dberthashoes.com). Yes, it is a special taxi ride, but those who love shoes understand the lengths one will go to for the perfect pair of strappy sandals. And chances are you'll find them here. This shoe store is the locals' little darling and has a fantastic selection of styles (mostly high heels, but you'll find some sandals and comfortable shoes), bags, and belts. This recently relocated store has upped the ante on shoe addiction by making the interior of their store pretty enough to hang out in, and the staff is very helpful once they've realized you're a serious shoe-aholic. Don't forget to check out the purses. Spanish and English are spoken here. D'Bertha's is so popular, they had to open a sister store, **Puntapie** (Gustavo Mejía Ricart 229, tel. 809/227-1088 or 809/683-6057), which kicked onto the scene with silvers and golds, playful fuschias, sequins, and oh so many other expressions of feminine elegance. More bags, clutches, and purses. Have fun!

JEWELRY

Flor Ámbar Gift Shop (Calle de las Damas 44, tel. 809/687-3793, 9 A.M.–6 P.M.) has a good selection of amber and larimar jewelry as well as other types. Other gift options include paintings, framed butterflies, coral, and fossils. Maps are for sale by the register.

Even if you don't end up buying a piece of larimar jewelry, visiting the **Larimar Museum** (Calle Isabel La Católica 55, tel. 809/689-6605, www.larimarmuseum.com, 9 A.M.–6 P.M.) will be worth your time. The store, located on the ground floor, has a wonderful selection of good quality pieces, and there's a very educational larimar museum upstairs. The very friendly staff members speak multiple languages and are very knowledgeable. The store also sells a lot of amber pieces.

Be mindful of purchasing jewelry and accessories made from tortoiseshell or coral. Certain species of turtles and coral (especially red coral) are endangered.

MARKETS

Get your haggling hat on! Whether you're just going to dig around or actually want to purchase something, the **Mercado Modelo** (Av. Mella between Tomás de la Concha and Del Monte y Tejada, 9 A.M.–5 P.M. daily) is a feast for your eyes and an overload of your senses. Located north of the Ciudad Colonial in a two-story building, this is a true litmus test of your bargaining skills. Wood carvings, Haitian paintings, music, cigars, and jewelry galore are only a small fraction of what you'll find at this market. Definitely dress down to come here, otherwise you'll be a target for high prices. The neighborhood isn't good after sunset.

The **Pulga de Antigüedades** (Ciudad Colonial, Plaza de María de Toledo, Calle General Luperón, 9 A.M.–4 P.M. Sun.) is a great flea market where prices are marked a lot higher with the expectation that you'll haggle.

CIGARS

Despite the preconception that Cubans are not to be competed with, many cigar aficionados would argue that Dominican cigars are the best in the world. Whatever the official word, they are readily available, and choosing some to take home can be a fun task. A full box can run up to US$120, but definitely shop around first. Calle El Conde has several stores.

Boutique del Fumador (Ciudad Colonial, El Conde 109, tel. 809/685-6425, 9 A.M.–7 P.M. Mon.–Sat., 10 A.M.–3:30 P.M. Sun.) is a factory outlet for Caoba, Montecristo, and Cohiba cigars located right on the Plaza Colón; you can watch the cigars being rolled.

To simply purchase cigars, **Taíno Cigars Shop** (Ciudad Colonial, Calle Isabel La Católica 52, tel. 809/221-5684, 9 A.M.–5 P.M. daily) offers fair prices on many cigar brands and accessories.

MUSIC

You will most definitely see men roaming the streets with stacks of merengue, *bachata*, and salsa CDs for purchase. These are pirated copies. To be on the safe side, head to El Conde, where you will find good, reputable music shops (and the CDs will actually have music on them!). **Musicalia Outlet** (Ciudad Colonial, El Conde, tel. 809/221-8445, 9 A.M.–12:30 P.M. and 2–5 P.M. Mon.–Sat.) has a good selection of many different genres.

Sports and Recreation

ⓒ BASEBALL

Baseball is not just the national sport; it's the national obsession. The country is famous for producing some of the world's best players. Many Dominicans follow the Dominican teams religiously from the end of October through January and in the off-season turn their attentions to the U.S. season. Many "hometown" boys who spent their lives playing stickball in the streets go on to hone their skills playing for the Dominican teams and then, with any luck, get snatched up by Major League Baseball teams from the United States, so watching American baseball can give a great sense of national pride.

If you are in town during the baseball season, it would be a shame to miss such a huge piece of Dominican culture and identity; see a game at the **Estadio Quisqueya** (Av. Tiradentes at San Cristóbal, tel. 809/540-5772, RD$300–800). Vendors roaming the stands sell snacks like empanadas, Presidente beer, and ice cream (other refreshments are sold inside). Experiencing a game in this stadium is a quick way to get to know complete strangers. Excited hugs often are exchanged with whomever is nearest when a good play is made. A lively marching band makes its way through the stadium, with a wake of dancing folks behind them. It is a great example of how happy and passionate Dominicans are in general.

There are six teams in the Dominican Republic, and two call Santo Domingo home base—the Tigres del Licey (Tigers of Licey) and Leones de Escogido (Lions of the Chosen One). The rivalry between the two is similar to that of the New York Yankees and Boston Red Sox. You can usually get tickets just by showing up before the game. Game times are 5 P.M. Sunday and 8 P.M. Tuesday, Wednesday, Friday, and Saturday.

HORSE RACING

Horse racing takes place in the **Hipódromo V Centenario** (Km 14.5 on the Autopista de las Américas, tel. 809/687-6060, free), which is halfway to Las Américas airport. Races start at 3 P.M. Tuesday, Thursday, and Saturday.

COCKFIGHTING

If you thought baseball was at the crux of Dominican culture then you've never seen cockfighting. It's been around longer and is taken very seriously. Admittedly, it is not for everyone. A cockfight can be over in the flap of a wing, or it can be a bloody battle lasting up to 15 minutes. The **Coliseo Gallístico Alberto Bonetti Burgos** (Av. Luperón, near the Herrera airport, tel. 809/565-3844, US$6–17) has matches held on Wednesday and Friday at 6:30 P.M. and Saturday at 3 P.M. This is the nicest *gallera* in the country, big and air-conditioned. Fighting cocks are treasured birds. Their owners have pampered them their entire lives, fed them with the best grains, and exercised them daily. The cocks are carried in the crook of the owner's arm like a crown being taken to a king, almost as if what is about to happen is all incredibly civilized. But fights are often to the death.

Accommodations

CIUDAD COLONIAL

Most visitors to Santo Domingo prefer to stay in the Ciudad Colonial because many of the accommodations here are filled with charm, history, and beauty. The enchanting courtyards and well-restored rooms within the converted colonial buildings brim with history and a romantic ambience that is impossible to resist. The typical Spanish brick archways and wrought-iron balconies decorated with flowers overlook cobblestone streets. There is the added bonus of being within walking distance of a majority of the city's historical sites, shopping along Calle El Conde, world-class dining options, and fun nightlife.

Under US$50

Hotel Aída (Espaillat 254, tel. 809/685-7692, fax 809/221-9393, US$45 in advance with fan only) has a convenient location near El Conde and is family run. Unfortunately, the rooms have no windows but are nice and clean. Some sleep three, and all rooms have private hot-water bathrooms. Given its low price and central location, it is popular and often full. There are no safety boxes in the rooms. They serve coffee and bread in the morning. There's a terrace overlooking foot traffic on Calle El Conde that's great for people-watching.

Hotel Freeman (Isabela La Católica, tel. 809/689-3961, US$30 d) has rather plain rooms, but they are clean. All have two queen-size beds and a private bathroom. The best thing this hotel has going for it is its location, just a half a block from Parque Colón.

The Dominican Republic doesn't have proper hostels like in Europe, but **Bettye's Guest House** (Isabela La Católica, tel. 809/688-7649, US$22–44) is as close as you'll get in Santo Domingo. You can choose between a bed in a dorm situation where you share a bathroom, or there are a couple of private rooms available for rental as well. The guest house doubles as an art gallery and is in an optimal location in the Ciudad Colonial. The price includes breakfast.

US$50-100

The charming **Antiguo Hotel Europa** (Arzobispo Meriño at Emiliano Tejera, www.antiguohoteleuropa.com, tel. 809/285-0005, US$75 d), built at the turn of the 20th century, has since been remodeled and has beautiful wrought-iron balconies. Most of the modern, standard rooms have a balcony (but make sure to request it), and all have a queen-size bed and tile floors. The Europa is a couple of blocks away from Plaza de la Hispanidad. Continental breakfast is included in the rate. Its Terraza Restaurant and Bar has Dominican cuisine and is on the roof, offering fantastic views of the ruins of the San Francisco monastery and the Ciudad Colonial. There is also a lobby bar.

El Beaterío Guest House (Av. Duarte 8, tel. 809/687-8657, www.elbeaterio.com, US$80 d with a/c) is a 16th-century abbey and has been renovated to have all modern conveniences without losing any historical charm. It is in the thick of the Ciudad Colonial. A stone-floored and plant-filled courtyard has wrought-iron balconies and terra-cotta rooftops with tiled stairways, making this an impressive sight. The rooms are small but comfortable and romantic with the exposed beam ceilings and colonial decor. Breakfast is included in the rate.

Hotel Conde de Peñalba (El Conde at Arzobispo Meriño, tel. 809/688-7121, www.condepenalba.com, US$75 with windows) has, without a doubt, the best location in the whole Ciudad Colonial, right in front of the Parque Colón. Try to get a room that has a balcony overlooking the park; room number 420 is the best with views of El Conde, Parque Colón, and all the way out to the sea. All of the rooms on the west side of the hotel have good views with flower-laden balconies—otherwise you will be in the back and have a *very* different view, but still a comfortable room. The trade-off: What you gain in view in this hotel, you will suffer in street noise. The restaurant on the first floor is a very popular spot for guests and nonguests alike. The rooms are comfortable and the bathrooms are quite small but have hair dryers and hot water. All rooms have air-conditioning, telephone, cable, and safety boxes. The hotel offers Internet service at the rate of US$2 for up to a half-hour.

At the 96-room **Hotel Mercure Comercial** (El Conde and Hostos, tel. 809/688-5500, www.accorhotels.com, US$94 d), all rooms have phones, TVs, fridges, and nice bathrooms. Tax, service, and breakfast are included in the rate. This is a favorite for business travelers; it has Internet service. Located right on the busy El Conde, the restaurant out front offers fantastic people-watching, definitely the best thing about the hotel; otherwise it is quite modest. It's no in the same category as the other colonial charmers. This has been renovated to be more of a Holiday Inn-type accommodation. You're paying for location with this one.

Hotel Discovery (Calle Arzobispo Nouel and Palo Hincado, www.discoverygranhotel.com, tel. 809/687-4048, US$65d), across the street from the Parque Independencia and at the start of Calle El Conde, puts you at the heart of the Ciudad Colonial. This is a good find. The hotel has clean, albeit simple, even bland rooms and a tastefully decorated rooftop terrace complete with a dipping pool to soak away the stress from a day of sightseeing.

US$100 and Up

◖ Doña Elvira (Padre Billini 207, tel. 809/221-7415, www.dona-elvira.com, US$90–130) is a 16th-century home that has been renovated into a 15-room hotel. The building retains its original beams in the 20-foot high ceiling. In the courtyard, you can take a dip in the pool or in the Jacuzzi, which is situated under an enormous 100-year-old mango tree that is still producing fruit. Rooms have cable TV, phones, wireless Internet, air-conditioning, fans, king- or queen-size (very comfortable) beds, and safety boxes upon request. Ask about tours and Spanish lessons at the front desk. All of the rooms are comfortable and charming. The unique Columbus room sleeps up to four people in one lofted bed and a couch in the main mezzanine; the

lofted bed situation is a bit difficult if you are over five feet seven inches, and you might need a mountain climbing kit for the treacherously steep staircase. The Antonetta is an elegant and spacious room.

Sofitel Nicolás de Ovando (Calle de las Damas, tel. 809/685-9955, www.sofitel.com, US$238–354 d) is easily the most luxurious hotel in the city, located in the renovated home of the first governor of the New World, Nicolás de Ovando. It is said that Christopher Columbus was once his guest here. The hotel has 107 elegant rooms and suites with stone walls and high dark wood ceilings. All rooms have marble bathrooms, TV, air-conditioning, safe boxes, phones, and Internet hookups. The pool overlooks the Río Ozama, and there is a well-equipped gym and a library. Buffet breakfast is included in the rate. The service is top-notch.

◖ Sofitel Francés (Las Mercedes at Arzobispo Meriño, tel. 809/685-9331, www.accorhotels.com, US$170 d), a restored colonial mansion, is the sister hotel to the Sofitel Nicolás de Ovando. Rooms have high ceilings, very comfortable beds, and dark wood furnishings. They surround the beautiful courtyard that holds the comfortable tables and chairs of the restaurant, which serves wonderful food. Breakfast is included in the rate.

A boutique hotel, **◖ Hodelpa Caribe Colonial** (Isabela La Católica 159, tel. 809/688-7799, www.hodelpa.com, US$100 d) has 54 rooms and is centrally located in the Ciudad Colonial, with many restaurants, bars, and shops right outside the front door. Rooms are modern but lack the charm that most hunger for when traveling to the Ciudad Colonial. The hotel and rooms are very clean and comfortable. All have air-conditioning, TV, and fridge. On-site amenities include a bar, restaurant, and Internet service.

MALECÓN

Hotels along the Malecón are more modern. They are mostly high-rise buildings and the antithesis to the old-world charm of the Ciudad Colonial and Gazcue neighborhoods. Even though some do offer phenomenal views of the Caribbean Sea (provided you get a room with a view), the ocean is not accessible in this area. These hotels do put you right in the thick of the hotel nightclubbing and casino scene. If that is your main focus, you're best off to stay here. However, it's a long walk to the Ciudad Colonial (or a short taxi ride).

US$50-100

The rooms in **Hotel Meliá Santo Domingo** (Av. George Washington 365, tel. 809/221-6666, www.solmelia.com, US$70 d) are comfortable and nicely appointed, though not unique. There are two good restaurants (one with lunch and dinner buffets and one that is a grill). The pool on the second-floor terrace is a nice escape from the busy world outside the hotel. The hotel offers a casino, health spa, tennis courts, and a disco. Service is good.

US$100 and Up

At the **Hotel Centenario Intercontinental** (Av. George Washington 218, tel. 809/221-0000, www.intercontinental.com/santodomingo, US$210 d), the simple elegance of the lobby is just a hint of what is to come. The rooms, although somewhat small, are very comfortable and tastefully decorated, with cable TV and pay-per-view plus a minibar. Tennis courts and a swimming pool with a Jacuzzi are on-site.

Although it is not the best hotel on the strip, **Renaissance Jaragua Hotel & Casino** (Av. George Washington 367, tel. 809/221-2222, www.marriott.com, US$100) is a massive one and you can't miss it. It's like being on the strip in Vegas. This hotel is known for its large casino and one of the most popular nightclubs, Jubilee. It is best to upgrade to a deluxe or suite; the rooms are dated a bit but comfortable, with all the amenities you would expect in a large hotel.

The 228-room, 21-floor **€ Hilton Santo Domingo** (Av. George Washington 500, tel. 809/685-0202, www.hiltoncaribbean.com/santodomingo, US$130 d) is the most recently renovated out of all those along the Malecón. It boasts the city's largest casino, and the rooms

almost all have a stunning ocean view from floor to ceiling windows. Duvets cover the stylishly decorated and very comfortable beds. Amenities include Internet hookup, electronic safety boxes, cable TV, and minibars. The pool is on the seventh floor and has a bar next to it. This is a full-service hotel.

GAZCUE

The historic neighborhood of Gazcue is a residential area just west of Parque Independencia. It was the neighborhood of Santo Domingo's upper class, and some of the buildings date back to the 1930s. The streets are shaded in a beautiful full canopy of trees. Today, restaurants have moved into the area, as well as some fashionable cafés. Gazcue is a possible alternative to the Ciudad Colonial because it has more budget options. You'll get more for your money if you're willing to walk to the Ciudad Colonial or take a very short taxi ride for your sightseeing.

Under US$50

Hotel Maison Gautreaux (Félix Mariano Lluberes 8, tel. 809/412-7837, fax 809/412-7840, www.maisongautreaux.net, US$32 d) is only one block off of the Malecón, but what a difference a block makes in price. All rooms have air-conditioning, hot-water bathrooms, cable TV, safe boxes, and hair dryers. The rooms are clean, simple, and nicely appointed. The on-site restaurant holds special nights like Monday Cigar Happy Hour and Steak House Friday.

At **Hotel La Residencia** (Calle Danae 62, tel. 809/412-7298, www.hotelresidencia.com, US$35–40), rooms have hot water and cable TV, and there's a kitchen on the third floor that guests can use, making it a good choice if you plan to stay in Santo Domingo for a while. There is a price difference in the rooms depending on whether you want to have air-conditioning or not. Regardless, all rooms have a fan. The rooms are very simple but they are clean. Laundry service, airport pickup, and tours are available for extra cost.

At **La Grand Mansíon** (Calle Danae 26,

tel. 809/689-8758, US$23), try to get one of the rooms with windows; the ones that don't have windows can feel cramped. Better yet, ask for the one with its own terrace. This hotel is good value for the money. Air-conditioning costs extra.

US$50–100

At **Hotel Duque de Wellington** (Av. Independencia 304, tel. 809/682-4525, www. hotelduque.com, US$60–70), it's kind of like you went home to visit family. The decor feels that way—comforting, like the guest room at your *tia* Sofia's house. Rooms have air-conditioning, TV, phones, fans, and security

boxes and are clean and comfortable. There is an on-site restaurant, Pasta & Algo Mas, which offers Italian food, and a travel agency. Room service is available. It's on a rather busy street. This is a gay-friendly hotel.

Hotel Residencia Venezia (Av. Independencia 45, tel. 809/682-5108, www. residence-venzia.com, US$50 d) is a very good choice just a few blocks away from Parque Independencia. The rooms are clean and have hot-water bathrooms, satellite TV, safety boxes, and a kitchenette. The hotel is also a good choice if you have more than two people. If you can swing a suite (which has a full kitchen), you'll have more space, including a balcony.

Food

Santo Domingo has an impressive array of historical sites, accommodation choices, and activities to keep you busy. It is perhaps no surprise, then, that the city has a bewildering array of restaurant choices as well. It is an epicure's paradise, with choices like Italian favorites, pub food, and French cuisine to seafood, Caribbean fusion, and sushi. If you're searching for a restaurant serving local cuisine, check the menu (typically posted outside of the front door or in the window of the establishment) for the words *comida criolla* and for dishes like *mofongo* (a plantain dish), *arroz con pollo* (rice and chicken), or any kind of meat served *guisado* (in a stew-like sauce).

CIUDAD COLONIAL

(**La Cafetera Colonial** (El Conde 253, tel. 809/682-7122, 7:30 A.M.–10 P.M. Mon.–Sat., US$2–5) has been around for decades, and locals say it has barely changed at all. Men who have been going to this café/diner for 25 years or more are still content to while away their afternoons perched on the stools at the counter talking about the old days. Sandwiches, fresh juices, and breakfasts are good, but the espresso and the pineapple cake will likely never be equaled elsewhere on the planet. This

is a top pick for its sentimental presence on El Conde.

The restaurant of **Restaurant & Hotel Conde de Peñalba** (El Conde at Arzobispo Meriño, tel. 809/688-7121, www.condepenalba.com, US$2–15) is in the best people-watching position, right across from Parque Colón. Sandwiches, omelets, and a good variety of international choices are on the menu, in addition to a good international beer selection. Try the Gallego sandwich for US$5. Just a few storefronts down is (**Bar & Restaurant Anacaona** (Calle El Conde 101 and Calle Isabel La Católica, tel. 809/682-8253). Anacaona has a relaxing atmosphere under a huge tree for shade on a hot day. The fish in coconut sauce is a tasty choice. Service is good, beer is cold, and the bathrooms are clean. These two restaurants are like "dueling banjos" for hungry tourists. They have perfect locations and similar prices.

The alluring (**Meson de D'Bari** (Hostos and Salomé Ureña, tel. 809/687-4091, noon–midnight daily, US$6–14) has been fashioned from what was once a private colonial home. Dominican art hangs on the walls and is for sale, making it like dining in an art gallery. The *cangrejos guisados* (crab stew) and *filet a la*

EAT LIKE A DOMINICAN

Want to try some local cuisine when you're in the Dominican Republic but don't know what to order while at the restaurant? Here are some key words to help make deciphering the menu a lot easier.

aguacate – avocado

arroz – rice

asopao – a thick soup made with rice and seafood or meat; very delicious and usually made for special occasions

ayuma – gem squash

bacalao – codfish

bandera dominicana – typical Dominican lunch of rice, beans, plantains, and meat

batata – sweet potato (often served fried at the beach)

casabe – cassava bread, a thick tortilla made with dried yucca

chicharrones – fried pork rind

chivo – goat (very popular in the Monte Cristi area where the goats are raised eating oregano, making for a spicier meat)

cocido – meaty stew

concón – the crunchy rice that sticks at the bottom of the pan (If you are a guest in someone's house, they will offer you the *concón* first because you are the guest. It is considered the best part. *Concón* means with-with! Little joke there.)

fría – cold; or it could mean beer! (If you see a sign that says *fría fría*, that means there is very cold beer for sale!)

frito – fried

garbanzos – chickpeas

guanábana – soursop

guandules – pigeon peas

guayaba – guava

guineo – banana

guisado/guisada – stewed (e.g., *pollo guisado* or chicken stew)

habas – faba beans

habichuelas blancas – white beans

habichuelas negras – black beans

habichuelas pintas – pinto beans

habichuelas rojas – red kidney beans

lambí – conch

lechosa – papaya (often blended into a delicious milkshake served at breakfast)

lentejas – lentils

limoncillo – Spanish lemon

locrio – a combination of rice, meat (or seafood), and vegetables

longaniza – spicy pork sausage (you will see this served in long strands on the side of the road)

mangú – mashed plantains (This is a very typical Dominican breakfast food, served with onions; it often has eggs or sausage on the side.)

maní – peanuts (These are also known as *cacahuate* and *cacahuete*, and are often sold between the cars at stoplights in Santo Domingo.)

mariscos – seafood

mofongo – plantains mashed with a mortar and pestle (not to be confused with *mondongo*)

mondongo – tripe (Feeling gutsy? Try this atypically typical dish.)

moro – dish made with rice and beans or pigeon peas

papa – potato (Not to be confused with the other *papa* – the Pope. It's all about context.)

picadera – appetizers or buffet

picante – spicy hot (Dominican cuisine is known to be more flavorful than spicy.)

pica pollo – breaded fried chicken

pincho – brochette/kebab

plátano – plantain

Presidente – leading brand of beer sold in the Dominican Republic

puerco en puya – spit-roasted pork

rabo encendido – an oxtail soup; literally, "tail on fire"

rés guisada – beef stew

salsa – sauce (unless you're in a disco – then someone is asking you to dance)

salsa de tomate – tomato paste

sancocho – a stew made with up to seven types of meat (This is a traditional and cherished Dominican culinary treasure. It is often served at special occasions or after a late night of partying. It's very good served with rice, avocado, and a *fría fría*.)

tayota – chayote

yuca – cassava, root of the yucca plant

Markets are great for produce.

criolla (filet of beef) are signature dishes. Or try the *lambí* stew (conch stew). Many more Dominican-style seafood and steak entrées are on the menu. The bar is quite a popular spot for nighttime entertainment, with live music on the weekends.

Café de las Flores (El Conde between Sánchez and José Reyes, tel. 809/689-1898, 9 A.M.–10 P.M. daily, US$4–10) has tables right on the walkway of El Conde; this is great for people-watching. The food is relatively cheap. Choices include breakfast sandwiches, *asopao* (soup), *mofongo,* meat, paella, and other typical Dominican dishes. The bright murals on the walls and the ceiling fans make it look achingly like a tourist trap; granted, there are better restaurants, but this location is tops for a quick lunch while shopping Calle El Conde.

Meson La Quintana (Calle La Atarazana 13, tel. 809/687-2646, 12:30 P.M.–1 A.M. Mon.–Sun., US$4–18), a Spanish restaurant, is appropriately located across from the Alcázar de Colón. Tapas are the specialty, served in a typical Spanish decor. Outdoor seating is available at night.

El Rey del Falafel (Padre Billini and Sánchez, tel. 809/412-2266, US$4–8) has Middle Eastern food for something different. Here in this newly remodeled restaurant, enjoy falafel sandwiches, shawarma, and hummus on the swanky new outdoor patio under the stars. They play a good mix of music and this is a popular place to have a drink on the weekends with the 30-somethings and up. It is a relaxing atmosphere.

Saxony CafÑ Galeria (Calle Padre Billini 205, tel. 809/221-6313) is a small, casual and inexpensive restaurant next door to the Doña Elvira Hotel. Here is the big shocker: It is a vegetarian restaurant. In the Dominican Republic, this is a major find. Enjoy fresh vegetable dishes over rice, eggplant parmesan, samosas, and many types of yogurt and natural juices.

Pat'e Palo (La Atarazana 25, tel. 809/687-8089, www.patepalo.com, opens at 4:30 P.M. Mon.–Thurs. and 1:30 P.M. Fri.–Sun., US$12–15) is off the Plaza de España. This restaurant serves some very delectable seafood in what was purportedly the first tavern of the New World back in 1505.

The open-air dining in **Ristorante La Briciola**'s courtyard (Arzobispo Meriño 152, www.labriciola.com.do, tel. 809/688-5055, lunch noon–3 P.M., dinner 7 P.M.–midnight Mon.–Sat., US$15–30) inspires romance, with candlelight and white tablecloths under the stars in the sky and elegance at every turn with fantastic service. The food is international and Italian with dishes like seafood gnocchi, tenderloin Angus with gorgonzola filling, and grilled lobster.

Pescadería Comedor Mora (Calle Profesor Gómez and Summerwells, open 24 hours), a budget seafood option, has a large open-air dining area with ceiling fans, but you order at a counter deli-style. It's rather a chaotic place; you just have to jump in and make yourself known—Dominicans don't really form orderly lines, not here anyway. Parking is available across the street. Options include *cangrejo guisado* (crab in sauce), fish in coconut sauce, *ensalada de pulpo* (octopus salad), fried seafood, paella, yucca, rice dishes, shrimp, and beer.

GAZCUE

El Conuco Restaurant (Gazcue, Calle Casimiro del Moya 152, tel. 809/686-0129, 11 A.M.–3 P.M. and 6 P.M.–12 A.M., daily, US$5–12) is unbelievably touristy, but the food is very good and the entertainment makes it a favorite for tourists. Through its corny veneer, its success is deserved because it serves very authentic and tasty Dominican fare, like *la bandera dominicana* by buffet or more exotic items like cow's-foot stew à la carte. The highlight of your visit (aside from the food) is when the entertainment dances the merengue and *bachata* with one performer dancing on top of a bottle.

Cafeteria Hermanos Villar (Gazcue, Av. Independencia at Pasteur, tel. 809/682-1433, 8 A.M.–10 P.M. daily, US$2–9) is a very popular place known mostly for its fantastic sandwiches, which are made on fresh bread in the traditional Dominican way, pressed flat with a hot iron. There are different kinds of meats to choose from and even some vegetarian ones. Some big ones can feed more than one person. This is a very economical way to eat.

La Bodeguita de la Habana Vieja (Gazcue, Av. Independencia 302, tel. 809/476-7626, noon–midnight daily, US$7–12) is a popular spot with the locals for its easy-going atmosphere and great food. The atmosphere is mixed. You won't want to wear shorts here (there are white tablecloths), but there is a TV playing, adding to its casual feel. There are a number of international dishes on the menu, but Cuban is the specialty, with favorites like *ropa vieja* (shredded beef served in a sauce).

SAN JUAN BOSCO

Restaurant Vizcaya (San Juan Bosco, Av. San Martin 42 and Dr. Delgado, tel. 809/686-2466, 10 A.M.–12 A.M. daily, US$2–15) is in the San Juan Bosco area (near the presidential palace), down the street from the government offices. This 45-year-old Spanish restaurant is a Santo Domingo institution. It is a favorite lunch spot of locals, government officials, and businesspeople. The entrance to the restaurant is lined with the memorabilia of the "good ol' days" when a filet mignon cost only 90 pesos (roughly US$2.50) and makes you long for the juke box to work again, but it is the food that has kept people coming back since the days of Trujillo. The menu is huge and the seafood is what they do very well, specifically the *cosido* and the octopus dish, *pulpo a la gallega*. They also serve tapas, grilled meats, rice dishes, pastas, sandwiches, and wonderful desserts.

MALECÓN

At **Adrian Tropical** (Malecón, Av. George Washington, 7 A.M.–2 A.M. daily, tel. 809/566-8373, US$11–20) the view alone is worth splurging on a meal like this. There are three Adrian Tropicals in town; make sure this is the one you go to. It is on the Malecón, built onto the cliffside over the water of the Caribbean Sea. The specialty is *mofongo* (the *camaronfongo* is the best), but other options are good as well, like the *pescado Boca Chica*, which is a big fried fish. Make sure to get a table on the patio, although there is indoor seating as well.

Trattoria Vesuvio Malecón (Malecón, Av. George Washington 521, tel. 809/221-1954, for pizza delivery tel. 809/221-3000, noon–11:30 P.M. daily, US$12–17) is a fixture in Santo Domingo, widely regarded as one of the top Italian restaurants since 1954. There are two Vesuvios, and they are right next to one another. The trattoria is the more casual (sleek and modern interior) of the two (Vesuvios on the Malecón is right next door). The specialty is gourmet pizza, but their art does not stop there: seafood, calzones, beef, veal, pasta, hamburgers, quesadillas—the list goes on. Vesuvios on the Malecón is well known for its seafood and is much more formal.

PLAZA UNIVERSITARIA LA JULIA

Peperoni (Plaza Universitaria La Julia, Av. Sarasota 23, tel. 809/508-1330, www.

peperoni.com.do, noon–midnight daily) is a trendy and popular spot with chic decor that serves international cuisine of all types. Try the sushi roll Dominican-style with tuna, avocado, and *plátano maduro* (ripe plantain); pasta; sandwiches; burgers; or polenta-crusted sea bass. The eclectic menu deserves to be explored.

Meson Cienfuegos (Plaza Universitaria La Julia, Av. Sarasota, tel. 809/532-1765, noon–midnight daily, US$10–25) is a Spanish restaurant serving traditional tapas and entrées amid a Spanish wine cellar decor with a very nice wine list. Try the paella for US$17 for two people.

LOS PRADOS

Restaurante Sully (Los Prados, Av. Charles Summer and Calle Las Caobas, Ensanche Carmelita, tel. 809/562-3389, 12–3:30 P.M. and 7 P.M.–midnight daily, US$3–7) is a casual restaurant specializing in seafood. Dishes range from Spanish paella to seafood stew. It has a large list of international and domestic drinks and fine wines. This is a very popular restaurant with the locals. You'll definitely need a taxi, and securing a ride back is best.

MIRADOR DEL SUR

Eating at **El Meson de la Cava** (Mirador del Sur, Av. Mirador Sur 1, tel. 809/533-2818, noon–midnight daily, US$10–20) is dining like you've probably never done before, inside the belly of a massive cave. Despite the stalactites, this is a formal restaurant with white tablecloths and waiters in tuxedos. Elegance and good food make for a dining experience, but it's not particularly fantastic cuisine. International choices include many fish dishes (like shrimp in a white wine sauce), veal cutlets, and lamb chops. Reservations are required.

Information and Services

Tourist Office

The most convenient Oficina de Turismo (Isabela la Católica 103, tel. 809/686-3858, 9 A.M.–3 P.M. Mon.–Fri.) is across from Parque Colón. You'll find many brochures and maps. The staff is helpful and speaks Spanish, English, and French.

Health and Emergency Services

Clínica Abreu and the adjacent **Clínica Gómez Patiño** (Av. Independencia at Burgos, tel. 809/688-4411, open 24 hours) are highly recommended as the best places in the city for foreigners needing medical care. Lots of different languages are spoken, and many of the doctors have been medically trained in the United States.

Padre Billini Hospital (Av. Sánchez between Arzobispo Nouel and Padre Billini, tel. 809/221-8272, open 24 hours) is closest to the Ciudad Colonial. The wait is long, but you'll get a free consultation.

Farmacia San Judas Tadeo (Independencia 57 at Bernardo Pichardo, tel. 809/685-8165) is open 24 hours and will deliver to the Ciudad Colonial and Gazcue. **Farmacia Vivian** (Independencia at Delgado, tel. 809/221-2000) will give you the same service.

The **Politur** (El Conde at José Reyes, tel. 809/689-6464, open 24 hours) can help you in most emergency situations, and most officers speak different languages. Dialing 911 will give you the regular police.

Money

For money in the Ciudad Colonial, you'll find ScotiaBank (tel. 809/689-5151) and BanReservas (tel. 809/960-2108), both located on Calle Isabel La Católica where it intersects with Las Mercedes. Both are open 8:30 A.M.–5 P.M. Monday through Saturday and have ATMs. It is best to get your cash during the day when there are a lot of people around.

In Gazcue, go to **Banco Popular** (Av. Independencia at Pasteur, tel. 809/685-3000,

9 A.M.–8 P.M. Mon.–Sat. and 9 A.M.–1 P.M. Sun.); it has an ATM, but since it is inside Farmacia Carmina, it is not available after hours.

Communications

Verizon Centro de Comunicaciones (El Conde 202, tel. 809/221-4249, fax 809/221-4167, 8 A.M.–9:30 P.M. daily) offers international calling services and Internet for about RD$1 per minute.

For Internet services in the Ciudad Colonial, go to **Internet Café** (José Reyes at Arzobispo Portes, 10:30 A.M.–10 P.M. Mon.–Sat., noon–10 P.M. Sun.) or **Cyber Red** (Sánchez 201, tel. 809/685-9267, 9 A.M.–9 P.M. daily), which is just off of El Conde. You can also make international calls at this location.

For Internet service in Gazcue, go to **Centro de Internet** (Av. Independencia 201, tel. 809/238-5149, 8:30 A.M.–9 P.M. Mon.–Sat., 8:30 A.M.–3 P.M. Sun.). It has decent service and offers international calling as well at very low rates (to the U.S. for US$0.17 per minute and to Europe for US$0.25).

Travel Agencies

If you should need additional plans within the Dominican Republic or help with travel changes, these are some reputable resources.

At well-established **Colonial Tour & Travel** (Arzobispo Meriño 209, tel. 809/688-5285, www.colonialtours.com, 8:30 A.M.–1 P.M. and 2:30–5:30 P.M. Mon.–Fri., 8:30 A.M.–noon Sat.), English, French, and Italian are spoken.

Giada Tours & Travel (Av. Independencia 304, tel. 809/686-6994, 8:30 A.M.–6 P.M.

Mon.–Fri., 9 A.M.–2 P.M. Sat.) can arrange for international and domestic travel as well as city tours. It's in the Hotel Duque de Wellington.

Spanish Lessons

If your goal is to have an immersion vacation and you need to learn some language skills to get that going, here are some options for Spanish language schools.

Hispaniola Academy (Calle Arzobispo Nouel 103, tel. 809/688-9192 or 809/689-8350, www.hispaniola.org) is in the Ciudad Colonial and offers a variety of packages. A week-long intensive course is the quickest. There are also accommodation options with a family or in a hotel. The academy also has Dominican culture classes like cooking and dance.

Instituto Intercultural del Caribe (Aristides Fiallo Cabral 456, tel. 809/571-3185, www.edase.com) offers packages ranging in intensity, length, and accommodation choices. This school operates on the intercultural exchange philosophy; there are opportunities to mix and mingle with language students from the Dominican Republic, and instructors often take the learning outside of the classroom to apply it in the real world.

Newspapers

To check out the local news or happenings in the city, pick up a newspaper. *Listín Diario* (www.listin.com.do) has the widest circulation. It and *El Caribe* (www.elcaribe.com.do), *Hoy* (www.hoy.com.do), and *Diario Libre* (www.diariolibre.com.do) are circulated in the morning.

Getting There

BY AIR

Santo Domingo is served by the **Aeropuerto Internacional Las Américas** (tel. 809/549-0328), which is 22 kilometers east of the metropolitan area.

Major carriers are: **Air Canada** (Av. Winston Churchill 63, tel. 809/541-5151), **Air France** (Av. Máximo Gómez 15, tel. 809/686-8432), **American Airlines** (El Conde, tel. 809/542-5151, airport tel. 809/549-0043), **Continental Airlines** (airport tel. 809/549-0757), **Iberia** (Av. Lope de Vega, tel. 809/686-9191, airport tel. 809/549-0205), **Jet Blue** (airport tel. 809/549-1793), **Lufthansa** (Av. George Washington, tel. 809/689-9625), and **US Airways** (Av. Gustavo Mejía Ricart 54, tel. 809/540-0505, airport tel. 809/549-0165).

BY FERRY

Only one connection exists: to and from Mayagüez, Puerto Rico, three times a week, run by **Ferries del Caribe** (tel. 809/688-4400, Mayagüez tel. 787/832-4400, www.ferriesdelcaribe.com, in Spanish). The ticket office and boarding port in Santo Domingo are at Avenida del Puerto, which is across from the Fortaleza Ozama. It is a 12-hour journey to Puerto Rico that you can do in an airplane-type seat (US$182) or in a private cabin with a window (US$295). From Santo Domingo, scheduled trips depart on Sunday, Tuesday, and Thursday at 8 P.M. and arrive in Mayagüez the next morning. From Mayagüez, ferries depart Monday, Wednesday, and Friday at 8 P.M. and arrive in Santo Domingo the next morning.

BY BUS

Caribe Tours (Av. 27 de Febrero at Av. Leopoldo Navarro, tel. 809/221-4422, www.caribetours.com.do, in Spanish) offers the most departure times and covers a wider area of the country than the **Metro** bus company (Av. Winston Churchill and Calle Francisco Prats Ramírez, behind Plaza Central, tel. 809/227-0101, www.metroserviciosturisticos.com) does. But both offer satisfactory service with big comfortable buses.

Most destinations in the Dominican Republic are within a four-hour ride. Ticket prices can fluctuate with the ever-changing economy but are usually quite low (under US$8). It is best to call or ask for a brochure and schedule at the station.

The express bus to **Bávaro/Punta Cana** (Juan Sánchez Ruiz at Máximo Gómez, US$10) is a direct service departing at 7 A.M., 10 A.M., 2 P.M., and 4 P.M. daily for a four-hour trip.

Although there is no official bus terminal, at the **Parque Enriquillo** near the Ciudad Colonial you can catch buses that aren't as nice as the luxury options from Caribe Tours and Metro (don't expect air-conditioning). They branch out all over the nation to places like Baní, Boca Chica, Higüey, Juan Dolio, La Romana, Puerto Plata, San Cristóbal, San Pedro de Macorís, Santiago, and Sosúa. These buses are not direct and make many stops in between. Expect prices for these to be under US$6. Read the signs in the front windows. You'll pay more for express buses, which only means they will stop less often.

BY CAR

Renting a car is easy at the airport. Many major companies have booths after you clear customs. Some companies are: **Avis** (airport tel. 809/549-0468; Av. Independencia at Socorro Sánchez, tel. 809/685-5095), **Budget** (airport tel. 809/549-0351; Av. John F. Kennedy at Av. Lope de Vega, tel. 809/566-6666), **Dollar** (airport tel. 809/549-0738; Av. Independencia 366, tel. 809/221-7368), **Hertz** (airport tel. 809/549-0454, Av. José Ma Heredia 1, tel. 809/221-5333). Shopping around on the Internet is always best for seasonal deals and special promotions.

Getting Around

BY CAR

Driving in Santo Domingo could be an exciting adventure for even Mario Andretti. You have to have nerves of steel and the calm of a monk while using the reflexes of a ninja. An alert copilot is always a great idea to read maps and warn of incoming street signs, *motoconchos,* and pedestrians.

Santo Domingo has three main highways running through it. When highways run through town, they are named by the avenues in the city, not by the highway names. Highway Sánchez, which runs east to west along the Caribbean coast, becomes Avenida George Washington (or the Malecón). Autopista Duarte, coming from the north and the Cibao region, transforms into the Avenida 27 de Febrero (a big corridor that facilitates the connection between the eastern and western sides of the city) and the Avenida John Fitzgerald Kennedy, which runs along the northern part of Santo Domingo. Both of these thoroughfares have elevated stretches and tunnels, making passage through the capital faster than along the smaller streets.

TAXIS

A taxi from Las Américas airport is around US$25–30 and takes about a half an hour. When you exit the airport, there will, most likely, be dozens of taxi scouts looking for passengers for the taxi drivers they represent. Do not let them take your bags or even walk you in the direction of a taxi until you've agreed on a price. This is the hook, and you will be expected to tip them. If you disagree on the price, chances are there will be another scout or driver that will outbid them. There is always room for haggling, but agree on the price before you let them help you with the bags or get in the car.

Santo Domingo is a very big city. If you plan to explore outside of the Ciudad Colonial, taxis are cheap and there are many of them. The taxis don't go by the meter system; it is usually just a quoted rate (around US$3). It is incredibly inexpensive, but you can haggle the price if you wish. Although it is not standard practice for the taxi drivers to just drive and wait for someone to flag them down, it isn't uncommon. More likely, though, they hang out at designated spots like along Parque Colón and Parque Duarte in the Ciudad Colonial.

Another way to get a cab is by calling, or having someone call for you. You tell them where you are and where you are going, and they let you know what car to look for and how long it will be. Not all taxis have air-conditioning, so if you want one that does, mention it; it may cost you a bit more. Agree on the price before you get in (with or without air-conditioning).

Taking a taxi at night is the best way to stay safe. Keep in mind that prices go up around midnight and haggling gets more difficult.

Techni Taxi (tel. 809/567-2010) has quick service, as do **Super Taxi** (tel. 809/536-7014) and **Apolo Taxi** (tel. 809/537-7771).

PUBLIC TRANSPORTATION
Públicos

Públicos are a very cheap option. You can get from one end of the city to the other for around US$0.25. Look for a sign that says *parada* (stop); they are found on major roads. In the Ciudad Colonial, you can find one at Parque Independencia where it meets Avenida Bolivar and Avenida Independencia.

Públicos are rough-looking cars and minivans that run the same major thoroughfares that buses do, but they stop anywhere you flag them down. Technically, they're supposed to have the word *público* on the license plate, but many don't, and even the ones who do want quicker results than waiting for you to be able to read the plates. Often, it comes down to the driver honking and waving at you to see if you want a ride. If you point like you'd like them to curb the car, they will. It costs about US$0.35, and sometimes the drivers will jam-pack their cars. If you're not comfortable with this, don't take a *público*. Beware: Although this is a safe means of transportation, pickpocketing is common, especially when the seats are jammed full.

Motoconchos

Motoconchos are the mopeds that buzz around and hang around parks. You can ride on the back of one of these, though you might feel like the drivers are maniacal demons. Don't expect a helmet to be offered up, but do expect a lot of weaving between tight traffic jams and scary turns. Agree on a price before hopping on, if you dare.

Metro

The Santo Domingo Metro system has had its share of critics. But after four years of waiting, in 2009 President Fernández was able to unveil the first line of his long-awaited Metro system. The US$700 million project takes passengers from the northern suburbs to downtown over 16 stops. He plans to start a second line shortly (another controversial promise). You can ride from Mamá Tingó in Villa Mella in the north all the way down to Centro de Héroes. You purchase a plastic card for RD$30 per passenger and it is rechargeable for RD$20 per ride.

Vicinity of Santo Domingo

The Monte Plata province has many opportunities for exciting day trips from your base of Santo Domingo. Accommodation options are very limited in this region, but things to do are varied and easily reached by a short distance from the capital on a good highway.

YAMASÁ

After traveling along the Máximo Gómez through the picturesque province of Monte Plata for 45 minutes (15 kilometers) to the northwest, you will come to the village of Yamasá. Here, you can visit the **Cerámica Taína Hermanos Guillen** of the Guillen brothers. Once you arrive, the energy of the Taíno gods takes over and you feel it all around you. These are the same brothers who host the **Fiesta San Antonio** for the community in June of every year. The factory is set amidst cocoa trees and the very palpable tranquility that the Monte Plata province exudes.

These brothers claim to have honed their own Taíno ancestral artistry of ceramics to perfect what are the closest replicas made. Most archaeologists agree this is true, save for the signature on each piece. When you come to their factory, they show you the steps that they take to mold their clay by hand, fire the pieces in huge ovens, and paint them by hand. You will then have the

opportunity to purchase pieces of their handiwork in the shop at a greatly reduced prices. For details, contact **Yamasá Tours** (Calle Duarte 9, tel. 809/525-0756, Yamasá), where English and Spanish are spoken.

© ANA CHAVIER CAAMAÑO

Monte Plata waterfall

You are in the land of cocoa! Over the past 20 years, CONACADO (Confederación Nacional de Cacaocultores Dominicanos or the National Confederation of Dominican Cacao Producers) has been building a strong web of *bloques,* or cocoa farmer associations, in the Dominican Republic. Over 40 percent of CANACADO's cocoa is sold in the Fair Trade market. Each year, the cooperative's Fair Trade premiums are distributed to the *bloques* for use in community projects like education, infrastructure, health, and development (like the development of cacao ecotourism!). You can visit one of the *bloques* and see how cocoa is fermented, dried, and processed: **Bloque Cacaotalero No. 2** (Calle Rafael de la Cruz 2, El Cercadillo, Yamasá, tel. 809/525-0641, blao.cacaotero@claro.net. do). At the end of the tour, they give you a cup of hot chocolate that is like none other in the world, totally organic and sustainable. Good for the karma, too.

THE SOUTH-CENTRAL COAST

East of Santo Domingo lie the city-dweller's quick-getaway towns—Boca Chica, Guayacanes, Juan Dolio, and San Pedro de Macorís—a slow-paced region complete with comfortable accommodation choices, local charm, beautiful beaches, and splendid golf courses. Here, Old World pastoral meets present-day tourism where the verdant, waving fields of sugarcane stand beside new golf courses and the turquoise waters of the Caribbean beaches are enjoyed without the super-heavy tourist traffic of other regions. This precarious balance between country life and international tourism makes this region an increasingly popular destination.

Historically devoted to the production of sugar and cattle raising, the South-Central Coast's popularity had not been on a consistent upswing until recently. While plantations and ranches still exist, the ever-expanding tourism industry is stretching its long arms to grapple plantation owners for their fertile inland acreage and the seaside locals for their white-sand properties along the Caribbean beachfront. Easy accessibility has aided in the growth of tourism in this region as well. For the most part, people arriving here fly into the Las Américas airport, but both Las Américas international airport and the airport at La Romana serve the resorts here. The proximity to Santo Domingo makes these towns easy day-trip options for those using the capital as home base.

Whether you are fleeing the heat of the city or arriving directly by airplane, you are sure to find a leisurely escape from your regular routine here. Spend your days in the shallow,

HIGHLIGHTS

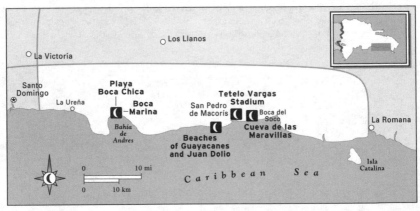 **Playa Boca Chica:** This beach is protected by a coral reef, which results in warm, shallow waters, making Playa Boca Chica safe for children. It is sometimes called the Dominican Republic's biggest swimming pool – a good day-at-the-beach destination since it's only a 15-minute drive from Santo Domingo (page 72).

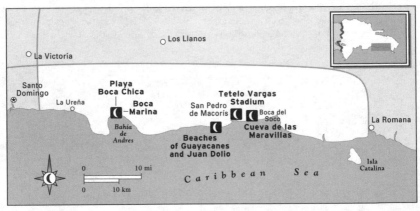 **Boca Marina:** Just 20 minutes away from Santo Domingo, you can dine on the water at Boca Chica's Boca Marina (or neighboring **Neptuno's Club Restaurant**). Lounge in the sun and swim by day – but nothing makes a vacation evening more romantic than dinner directly over the moonlit water (page 78).

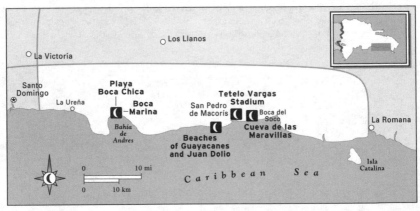 **Beaches of Guayacanes and Juan Dolio:** These *playas* are much more tranquil than Boca Chica – a laid-back lounger's paradise. Go during the week and make sure to pack your beach-read. This area is not as hectic as Boca Chica but has all the comforts of cuisine and service – the best of both worlds (page 79).

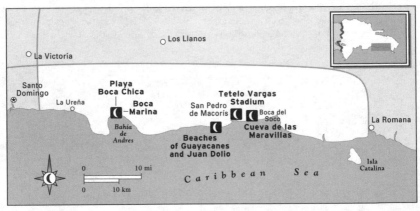 **Tetelo Vargas Stadium:** San Pedro de Macorís is known to diehard baseball fans as the baseball city or "land of the shortstops." In a country whose national passion is baseball, this is mecca. In this stadium, many Major League heroes, including Sammy Sosa, began their careers. Home to the local baseball team, Las Estrellas Orientales (The Eastern Stars), the large stadium becomes a major attraction between October and February for the nation's baseball season (page 87).

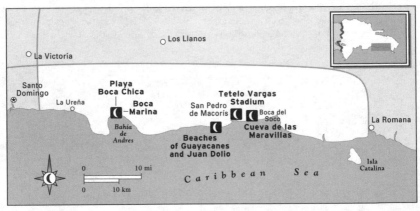 **Cueva de las Maravillas:** The beauty of this island runs deep. The award-winning **Cave of Wonders** is like a Taíno art gallery containing hundreds of rupestrian paintings, along with an impressive array of stalactites, stalagmites, and columns. Elevators and smooth walkways make it very wheelchair-accessible (page 87).

LOOK FOR TO FIND RECOMMENDED SIGHTS, ACTIVITIES, DINING, AND LODGING.

warm waters of Boca Chica, the all-inclusive resorts of Juan Dolio, or the picture-postcard beaches of Guayacanes. At night cheer on the baseball players in the world-famous Tetelo Vargas Stadium in San Pedro de Macorís or enjoy one of the many casinos in the all-inclusive resorts.

Sea lovers will find diving and snorkeling options along this stretch of coastline, in some of its coral reefs just offshore and shipwrecks where the clear, calm waters provide a perfect stage for viewing various creatures in their natural habitats. Land lovers can explore the limestone caves that litter the coastline and feature Taíno drawings.

If you're looking for the best of this stretch to spend a few days, head to Juan Dolio for a truly relaxing vacation. Boca Chica, even with its shallow and enticing bath-warm water, has become clogged with sex-tourism. Turning a blind eye to it for a few hours is one thing, but trying to spend your entire vacation in a vacuum of denial is impossible. To feel the buzz of a bustling Dominican city outside of the capital, head to a baseball game in San Pedro de Macorís.

PLANNING YOUR TIME

The South-Central Coast is a manageable area situated perfectly for lots of excursions within the region or to neighboring areas. The areas best suited for home base are Boca Chica (because of its lagoon-like waters and proximity to Santo Domingo) and Guayacanes and Juan Dolio (because of their beaches and numerous resorts).

All the towns listed in this chapter are, more or less, between Las Américas and San Pedro de Macorís, making arrivals and departures a breeze and keeping travel time within the area down to less than a couple of hours by car. In addition, Santo Domingo is within a convenient distance for a weekend of shopping, clubbing, cultural events, and sightseeing. No matter what you are calling home base, excursions can be arranged to Santo Domingo or other sites by your hotel.

Should you dare to drive on the highway (it can be a truly hair-raising experience), Highway 3 is well marked and is the spine from which these towns and sights emerge, making navigation uncomplicated.

Just 22 kilometers outside of Santo Domingo is **Parque Nacional Submarino La Caleta,** which is a protected coral reef where you can spend your time diving and exploring the purposely sunk shipwreck of the *Hickory*. Nearby, other shipwrecks include *El Limon,* a tugboat, and *The St. George,* a freighter that was sunk 100 feet below sea level. Divers can explore these wrecks and snorkelers can swim among reefs around the park's beach. Unfortunately,

© ALICIA CHAVIER CAAMAÑO

Carretera Las Américas, Santo Domingo to Boca Chica

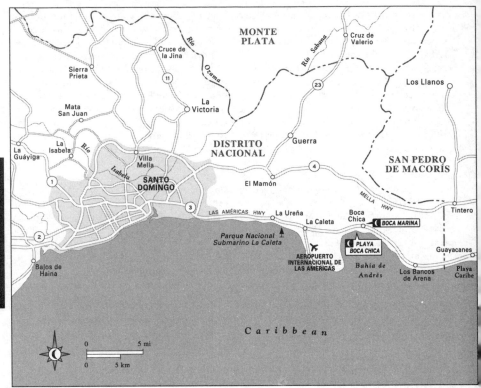

due to laid-back environmental attitudes and as the result of a hurricane in 2004, the fish sightings are somewhat minimal. However, the Ministry of the Environment is striving to change this through government funding for conservation. Dive shops in Boca Chica go to La Caleta regularly, and it's reachable by boat in about 17 minutes.

About 15 minutes farther east by car is Boca Chica, where the waters are shallow, warm, and clear like bathwater. Partying is a way of life in Boca Chica, but folks here also enjoy the long lazy days of basking in the sun and eating fried fish. It's a perfect afternoon getaway if you're staying in Santo Domingo or if a beach vacation with a little bit of city mixed in is for you.

Within a half an hour from Boca Chica, you will be in the areas of Guayacanes and Juan Dolio. Guayacanes was an old fishing village

that has a lovely beach where the locals tend to hang on Sundays, and Juan Dolio and Villas del Mar (a small area of Juan Dolio) are really a long strip of hotels and resorts. Picking a resort along here boils down to what you want your vacation to be like. If you require a lot of lying around on the beach time, then choose wisely, because getting to anything outside of what is offered in your hotel will require a small effort of travel and ingenuity on your part. If you want a little of both, be sure to pick a resort that offers lots of excursions. Many of them do.

San Pedro de Macorís is best left for the months of October through January when it is baseball season in the Dominican Republic. Games are mostly at night. Other than the stadium, tourism isn't developed in this town, unfortunately, but you will pass through to get to **Cueva de las Maravillas,** one of the best sights

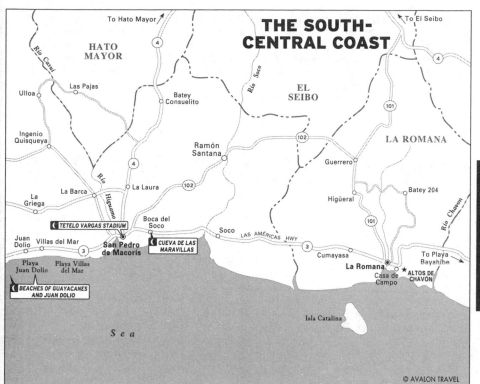

THE SOUTH-CENTRAL COAST

that this coast has to offer. Many of the resorts in this area offer excursions to the cave at an extra cost, and you will not be sorry you took the time away from sunbathing to go deep underground and see cave paintings that look as though they were drawn yesterday. About three hours are needed for a visit to the cave since a one-hour tour is given and travel time from either Juan Dolio or nearby La Romana (see the *Southeast* chapter) hotels can be around a half hour.

WEST OF BOCA CHICA
Parque Nacional Submarino La Caleta

This is among the smallest of the national parks. While it has a stretch of shoreline, the big attraction here is the underwater preserve. Parque Nacional Submarino La Caleta is just 20 kilometers east of Santo Domingo and has

a large coral reef, Taíno caves, and two shipwrecks in its underwater portion. The park was created in 1984 when the former treasure-hunting ship, the **Hickory,** was intentionally foundered to draw more divers to the area. This 44-meter-long ship, which sits about 18 meters below the surface of the water, was originally used to scour the Bahía de Samaná for treasures from the Spanish galleons that sank there in the 1700s. It is now home to sea creatures and sits in the warm, calm waters of the Caribbean Sea, making it an ideal spot for the diving newbie as well as for the experienced diver to explore. The *El Limón* tugboat, which was scuttled in 1998, is also a showplace for fish like trumpetfish, blue tangs, and squirrelfish, and other sea creatures. The *St. George* is a 60-meter freighter that was sunk in early 1999. It sits along a slope. Visibility is excellent.

Although the shipwrecks hog a lot of the publicity for the attraction to this park, don't forget to flipper over to the shallow coral gardens to navigate the spur-and-groove formations and take in the impressive varieties of hard and soft corals and fish.

La Caleta, as it is popularly known, is easily reached from a number of beach resorts and dive centers in Boca Chica. Best known is **Treasure Divers,** on the beach at the Don Juan Beach Resort, where travel and diving packages are offered for every skill level. Or take a half-day trip with **Neptuno Dive** out of Juan Dolio.

Unfortunately, damage to the coral reefs is a constant threat due to illegal fishing (sometimes chemicals such as bleach are used to fish!), artisanal fishing, and hurricanes. Nevertheless, La Caleta remains a popular dive site.

Boca Chica

A little farther east down Highway 3 from Parque Nacional Submarino La Caleta, only a five-minute drive east of Las Américas international airport, sits the former fishing village of Boca Chica. This was the hot spot for the rich in Trujillo's days. The wealthy from Santo Domingo would come to their Hamptons-esque getaways, wearing their best and using their posh seaside villas for their elaborate parties.

In the early 1950s, the first major hotel was opened due to the popularity of travel to this area, but by the 1970s, Boca Chica's reputation with tourists waned because of the development of tourism on the north coast.

However, the lagoon-like waters of the Bahía de Andrés could not be ignored for long, and international (mostly European) travelers started to return by the 1990s.

This financial flux has kept Boca Chica in constant economic doubt, and its reputation has been dragged through the mud by the severe prostitution and tourist scamming that evolved due to those hard times. Although these illicit activities are on a downward trend, they still exist and are being monitored by the local Politur (national tourism police) office. Nevertheless, a strange dichotomy exists between the larger hotel chains catering to families and some (but not all) of the small and cheaper hotels catering to the single male travelers looking for the debauchery side of Boca Chica. Many of the small hotels are doing their part in trying to clean up the act of Boca Chica.

Aside from this reputation, Boca Chica has benefited from the north and southeast coasts' infestation of all-inclusive resorts. Tourists who desired a less gentrified vacation destination and wanted to roam less-traveler-populated areas began to flock to Boca Chica and its smaller hotels once again, bringing their currency with them. Granted, big corporation hotel chains are following, but part of that road-less-traveled spirit still exists.

Boca Chica has a wide variety of restaurants, shops, and bars, many of which are owned by expats who couldn't end their vacations, left their homelands, and decided to open their own businesses. Most of these are along the street parallel to the beach, which gets closed to traffic at night to make way for a more laid-back but festive environment. Midweek visits are best if you want more tranquility, as this little town is a busy and lively place on the weekends.

SIGHTS

With very few sights in the area, scuba diving, water sports, sunbathing, and fishing are some of the main activities available in Boca Chica. Most of these recreational items center on and around the balmy waters of Playa Boca Chica.

Playa Boca Chica

Once you've spent a moment with your feet in the fine, powdery, white sand and waded in the clear blue waters of Playa Boca Chica, it is not

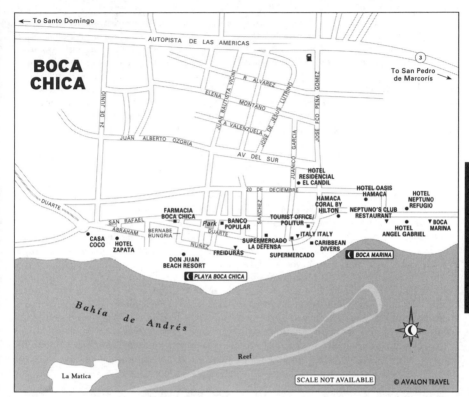

hard to understand why this beach is the town's main attraction. A coral reef at the mouth of the Bahía de Andrés (which you can wade out to) makes it impossible for big breakers and big fish to get through, resulting in calm water that is safe for children.

Playa Boca Chica is about five kilometers long, and on the far east side sits the **Hotel Oasis Hamaca.** Farther along is the **Don Juan Beach Resort** and its dive center, Treasure Divers; **Hotel Zapata** is toward the far western end. Between these locations are multiple restaurants and bars and booths serving fried foods.

Beachgoers can rent the tables and chairs spread all across the beach, for a price. But haggling is a must, and settling on a price before sitting down is essential. The same goes for ordering food and drinks to be brought to you by those offering service. It is easy to get taken

for a ride if you don't agree on price beforehand. After the price is negotiated, sit back, relax, and enjoy!

During low tide, it is possible to walk out to the islands of **La Matica** and **Los Pinos** (which used to be called La Piedra, "The Rock," before Australian pines were planted on it), just offshore, to do some bird-watching. The depth of the water averages only about 1.2 meters (in some spots it is only ankle deep), making it a pleasant journey either by foot or by shallow boat, which can be rented at the beach. La Matica (The Little Shrub) is more a mangrove than an island and a favorite spot for herons. Los Pinos (The Pines) has more hard ground to climb onto, and the mosquitoes can be aggressive. Reaching Los Pinos is a bit more difficult than getting to La Matica. Wear water shoes if you go walking.

During the weekdays mostly locals selling their wares and tourists enjoying the water and sun frequent the beach. Sunday at Playa Boca Chica is much more crowded—Dominicans from the city and surrounding areas come to the beach to cool off, especially a favorite for Christmas and New Year's Days.

Some of the larger all-inclusive hotels have built walls surrounding the beach space in front of their hotels in an effort to block the locals from entering. By Dominican law, this is illegal, but the law is not enforced and it is a common practice of big resort chains. Often they have armed guards to keep their guests quarantined from the rest of the beachgoers/locals. Anyone without the hotel's bracelet on will be stopped from entering. Sure, peddlers are kept at bay, but should you be a guest at one of these resorts, venturing beyond the resort walls to mingle with the Dominicans on their rightful beach means you can get your hair braided and have fried fish, *chicharrones* (fried pork skins), and *yaniqueques* (johnny-cakes) brought to you from the *freidurías* (frying establishments). At Playa Boca Chica you can also do your shopping for trinkets, souvenirs, and jewelry as you lie in the sun, thanks to the wandering peddlers. These vendors and hawkers can be aggressive, but a stern yet polite *"no gracias"* should do the trick when you've had enough.

ENTERTAINMENT AND EVENTS

Boca Chica is a beach town and not known for high cultural entertainment, but the bigger hotels tend to offer a wide variety of water sports and activities for daytime fun and have their own shows in the evenings. The **Hotel Oasis Hamaca** has a casino open to the public and one of the most formal discos in the area. Here you can find either live music or great salsa and merengue beats for a younger crowd. Those who are not guests of the hotel must pay a cover charge for the disco.

Keep in mind that while Boca Chica has one of the safest beaches for children to swim in and many family-friendly hotels, it also has

a long-standing sex tourism scene. The sex industry has sustained Boca Chica's bad reputation, and prostitution is big business here. After sundown, the atmosphere shifts from lazy beach town to a more debased one, and blatant offers for prostitution are not unheard of.

Many of the Boca Chica hotels (both all-inclusives and some smaller ones) that are trying to eradicate the smudge on their town's reputation have instituted a policy that anyone who isn't a guest of the hotel but wants to enter must purchase a pass. This cuts down on a lot of the prostitution because many of the sex-seeking travelers do not want this kind of bother and extra expense and, therefore, stay elsewhere.

The **Merengue Festival** (for information contact the tourism office in Santo Domingo, tel. 809/221-4660, fax 809/682-3806, www.dominicana.com.do) is held the third week of July. A spillover of the same festival that takes place along Malecón in Santo Domingo, this street festival is a lively expression of the merengue music and dance particular to the Dominican Republic. Dancing, exhibitions, food, drink, and games all take place along the main street, Calle Duarte.

SHOPPING

Boca Chica is not a choice place to do your shopping. Since the capital is so close, a day (or even an afternoon) in the Ciudad Colonial would give you the best opportunity for perusing a better variety of keepsakes, and you'll also find far better prices. Still, there are a few shops and stalls peppering the town along **Calle Duarte,** which runs directly parallel to the beach for about five or six blocks. Here you can find rum, cigars, artwork (but it is the typical Haitian kind and not authentic Dominican artwork), clothes, and crafts. The prices in these shops are very high compared to Santo Domingo. However, if you just stay on the beach, the shopping vendors will come to you (barrage you is more like it) with briefcases filled with jewelry, women ready to braid your hair, massages, and various local arts and crafts. Keep in mind that these vendors have hiked the prices way up expecting that there will be a healthy amount of haggling.

SPORTS AND RECREATION
Golf
The nearest golf course to Boca Chica is the 9-hole **San Andrés Caribe Golf Club** (Km 27 Las Américas Hwy., tel. 809/545-1278), open 8 A.M.–6:30 P.M. daily. The cost is US$17, and a caddy will cost you US$6 more. This par-36 course, which opened in 1993, is a good beginner's course and a great afternoon activity. Lessons are offered for US$10 per hour. Club and cart fees are extra. Don't expect a lot from this course if you're a serious golfer.

Diving and Snorkeling
Many of the all-inclusive hotels offer their guests beginning diving lessons in their pools and ocean dive excursions. PADI certification courses are often available. Look for offers for dives to the nearby *Hickory* and *El Limón* shipwrecks at **Parque Nacional Submarino La Caleta** and **Islas Catalina and Saona.** These islands can be reached from Boca Chica but are more accessible from the town of Bayahibe (see the *Southeast* chapter).

The Don Juan Beach Resort is home to **Treasure Divers** (Boca Chica Beach, tel. 809/687-9157, www.donjuanbeachresort.com). Located directly on the beach, it offers many diving and snorkeling excursions to beautiful reefs and the striking shipwrecks in the area, as well as combination packages including night dives. You can even rent an underwater camera. A unique venture is the thrilling cave diving at **La Sirena,** a freshwater cave filled with stalactites and stalagmites, limestone formations, and air spaces to dive up into. The water is crystal clear and warm. Certification courses are offered at Treasure Divers' dive school. All excursions are priced separately. Multiday packages start at US$209 per person. English, Spanish, and German are spoken.

Caribbean Divers (Calle Duarte 28, www.caribbeandivers.de, tel. 809/854-3483) has a number of different dive excursions for you to choose from depending on your experience level. They can take you to dive the *Hickory* shipwreck and even give you a PADI course. Dives average out to about US$45 each and are sold in packages. English, French, German, and Spanish are spoken.

The Don Juan Beach Resort also has public rentals of other sports gear and equipment, such as paddleboats (US$8), Jet Skis (US$22), and catamaran tours (US$23).

ACCOMMODATIONS
Under US$50
Boca Chica is filled with small, low-budget options. The **Hotel Angel Gabriel** (Calle Duarte 27, tel. 809/523-9299, www.hotelangelgabriel.com, US$50 d) has been in operation since November 2004, offering clean rooms, free breakfast, a pool, and proximity to the beach. If you're interested in something roomier, a two-bedroom suite with a kitchenette will cost you US$85. Another great low-budget option is the **Hotel Neptuno Refugio** (Calle Duarte, tel. 809/523-9934, fax 809/523-9863, www.dominicana.de/neptuno.htm, US$45 d). This quiet five-story hotel is across from Neptuno's Club Restaurant on the far eastern end of Boca Chica. If you have questions about the town, owner Rita Reyes is very knowledgeable. She has flyers and information in the office but speaks only Spanish. Small apartments are also available, and prices vary according to your view (US$50 for interior garden, US$55 for park, and US$60 for an ocean view). All rooms are equipped with cable TV, air-conditioning, permanent lights, hot water, a minibar, and security box, and there's daily cleaning service. The apartments are similar but with kitchenettes and private balconies. Discounts are given to those who stay longer than a week.

Casa Coco (Calle Dominguez 8, www.casacoco.net, tel. 809/523-4409, US$35). This eight-room hotel has basic rooms that are clean with cable TV. There are also two furnished apartments you can rent that have kitchenettes, TV, and air-conditioning. This is a good option if you decide to stay longer. Safety boxes are also available, as is laundry service (upon request). The hotel is about a three-minute walk away from the beach but has a nice quiet pool area. Spanish, English, French, and German are spoken.

US$50-100

Midrange hotels are more difficult to find in Boca Chica than budget or pricey ones. One of the best options is **Hotel Zapata** (Calle Abraham Núñez 27, tel. 809/523-4777, fax 809/523-5534, www.hotelzapata.com, US$70–75 s/d, US$140 apartments) because it is one of only a few hotels located directly on Playa Boca Chica and is the most affordable of all of them. In this family-owned, 22-room hotel, you can enjoy a standard room complete with air-conditioning, safety boxes, and cable TV. Some of the rooms have balconies. Two-bedroom apartments that fit up to four people are also available. The restaurant on-site cooks up both Creole and international favorites.

The **Hotel Residencial El Candil** (Calle Juanico Garcia #2 at 20 de Diciembre, tel. 809/523-4252, fax 809/523-4232, www.com-data.nl/hotel-boca-chica-candil, US$50/room) is slightly cheaper and has more security (all outside guests must leave identification at the front desk). Prices include taxes and airport transfer from Las Américas airport when staying a minimum of four nights. Studios and apartments are available as well. Apartments have air-conditioning, refrigerators, cable TV, equipped kitchenettes, hot water, safes, and telephones. This gay-friendly colonial-style, 24-room hotel is 150 meters from the beach and has a swimming pool and bar.

US$100 and Up

The **Hotel Oasis Hamaca** (Calle Duarte 26 and Av. Caracol, tel. 809/523-4611, www.oa-sishamaca.com, US$150 d high season) is the all-inclusive grande dame of the beach and was recently upgraded by the Hilton hotel chain. If you're looking for a worry-free Boca Chica vacation, this is it. It was the first hotel in town and is still considered by many the best. The Hamaca is the most posh, the biggest, and has the biggest portion of Playa Boca Chica blocked off for its own guests

(even though it is technically illegal to do so), thereby keeping the beach peddlers off the property. It offers oodles of activities, including water sports, tours and excursions, three tennis courts, spa services, and a fitness center for hotel guests. You will never go hungry with the multiple restaurants on-site. The casino and disco are some of the most popular nightlife spots in town. Outside guests have to pay a cover for entry into the disco, but the casino is free to the public. Prices do vary, so it is best to check the website for frequent deals.

The **Don Juan Beach Resort** (Calle Abraham Núñez, tel. 809/523-4511, U.S. tel. 800/820-1631, fax 809/688-5271, www.don-juanbeachresort.com, US$160 s high season) is an all-inclusive alternative to the Hamaca with three restaurants, four bars, and an ice cream parlor on-site. Try to book this when there are specials. There are nine connecting rooms, so ask for this type if you are traveling with friends or family. Cribs are available upon request. All rooms have air-conditioning, cable TV, phones, safety boxes, and private baths with tub and shower. For nighttime entertainment, there is also a small disco, but the main draw to this resort is its connection to **Treasure Divers** scuba school, where you can get certified and go on great diving excursions. Some wheelchair-accessible accommodations are available.

FOOD

Since Boca Chica was once a small fishing village, the seafood here is fresh and plentiful. Both Dominicans and foreigners own many of the restaurants here, so international choices such as Italian, Creole, American, and Swiss cuisine can be found. The most adventurous way to find food is to stroll down the beach or Calle Duarte and browse the many small restaurants and *freidurías* (stands where fish and other things are fried) until you find one that is appealing to you. The local dishes like *lambí criolla* (conch in a Creole-style sauce), *yaniqueques* (a type of fried bread), and the daily fried fish with fresh lime squeezed over

LA BANDERA DOMINICANA (THE DOMINICAN FLAG)

This national dish is a culinary symbol of the country, eaten by many Dominicans on a regular basis. The recipe consists of three parts: meat (in this case, chicken), rice and beans, and fried plantains.

BRAISED CHICKEN
Ingredients:
   1 whole chicken, cut up
   1 onion, chopped
   3–5 garlic cloves, minced
   1 green bell pepper, chopped
   1 tbsp. oregano
   1 dry hot red pepper
   2 tbsp. tomato paste diluted in water
   cilantro to taste
   1 tbsp. capers
   salt and pepper to taste
   a few splashes of lemon juice (either fresh or bottled)
   olive oil (enough to coat pan generously)

Combine all of the above ingredients except the olive oil. Cover and refrigerate for one hour. When chicken is done marinating, set aside. Heat oil in large frying pan or Dutch oven. Remove chicken from mixture and add to pan. Brown chicken on all sides. Add the rest of the mixture to pan, gradually adding up to 2 or 3 cups of water. (If the water is added in large amounts, the result is a stew-like consistency, which you don't want.) Continue cooking until chicken is heated all the way through. Set aside.

FRIED RIPE PLANTAINS
(PLÁTANO MADURO FRITO)
Ingredients:
   4 very ripe plantains
   oil to coat pan

Peel plaintains. Cut plantains in half across. Slice each half lengthwise into three pieces. Fry in oil (3-4 slices at a time) until brown. Drain on paper towel to remove excess oil.

RICE AND BEANS
Ingredients:
   1 cup dry white rice
   1-1½ cups water
   1 tbsp. olive oil
   1 tsp. salt

Rinse rice under cold water until water runs clear. Combine all ingredients and cook over medium-high to high heat until boiling. Reduce heat to medium and cover, cooking until all the water has been absorbed.
Ingredients:
   1 can red or pinto beans, rinsed, plus ½ can water
   ½ onion, chopped
   ½ green bell pepper, chopped
   2-3 garlic cloves, minced
   ½ tsp. oregano
   1 pinch dry red pepper (hot)
   1 pinch anise seed
   cilantro to taste
   1 tbsp. tomato paste diluted in water

Combine all ingredients and cook over medium heat until mixture thickens. Remove from heat. Add cooked rice and mix together. Serve the chicken, fried plantains, and the beans and rice together.

– Courtesy of Carmen Caamaño de Chavier

it are delectable choices for lunch. Don't rule out this choice for a quick lunch. They are fast, fresh, and traditional Dominican dishes. When buying food from the vendors or at the beachside restaurants, make sure the prices are solid before ordering or you could find yourself with an astronomical bill. It is an unfortunate but common scam to hike the bill up for the tourist who doesn't know the exchange rate beforehand.

Should you need provisions for your room or have a kitchen in your room and want to cook on your own, there is a **Supermarket** on the corner of Calle Duarte and Calle Juanico García (open 9 A.M.–8 P.M. Mon.–Sat., 9 A.M.–6 P.M. Sun.).

Italy Italy

This place (Calle Duarte 101, in the Plaza Turística, tel. 809/523-4001, morgantithomas@ yahoo.com, 8:30 A.M.–1 A.M. daily, US$14–17) has a casual atmosphere and specializes in, you guessed it, Italian food (and seafood).

◖ Boca Marina

Located in the tourist zone of Boca Chica and directly *on* the water (Calle Duarte 12A, tel. 809/523-6702 or 809/688-6810 reservations, bocamarina@hotmail.com/, 11 A.M.–midnight daily, US$9–24), this restaurant allows you to appreciate the natural beauty of Boca Chica while dining amid the seashell decor. It's definitely a hot spot that requires reservations during peak season. The 130-option menu features seafood. The food is prepared fresh with a distinctively Mediterranean influence. If you can swing it, try the grilled lobster for about US$24 per pound. One of the most popular dishes is shrimp in Thai sauce. During the day, Boca Marina poses as a beach club where people can swim, sunbathe, order food and drinks, and rack up a hefty-but-worth-it bill. It's a "be seen in the scene" place. Boca Marina is good for families as well since it has a special kids' swimming area and a special children's menu. At night the atmosphere is soaked in romance, and if you're fortunate enough to be in Boca Chica for a full moon, Boca Marina is a must for a late dinner. Secure and free parking is available.

Neptuno's Club Restaurant

Similar to Boca Marina but more affordable is this recently renovated restaurant (Calle Duarte 12, tel. 809/523-4703, fax 809/523-4251, 9 A.M.–10:30 P.M. Tues.–Sun., US$16–30). Specialties are seafood, including popular dishes like mahimahi ceviche and Spanish tapas to get your appetite going. Guests arrive by land and sea, anchoring boats just a bit clear of the shallow swimming space and walking in the water to get a table on the deck. This is a wonderful spot to spend your afternoon with the kids swimming and enjoying great and affordable food. Neptuno's boasts that it uses only organic food (such as the vegetables that are grown by local nuns and sweet-water shrimp free of chemicals) and never uses a microwave. There's a full bar, service for large groups, secure parking, and wheelchair-accessibility.

INFORMATION AND SERVICES

It wasn't until recently that the national tourism office took notice that there was a distinct need for a branch in Boca Chica. The **Oficina de Turismo** is on Calle Vicini and 20 de Diciembre.

For money transfer, banks with ATM machines, supermarkets, pharmaceuticals, Internet centers and money exchange, you will find almost everything you need along Calle Duarte, such as **Western Union** (Calle Duarte 65, tel. 809/523-4625, 8 A.M.–5 P.M. Mon.–Sat.) and **Banco Popular** (Calle Duarte 43, tel. 809/523-4300, 8 A.M.–3 P.M. Mon.–Fri., 8 A.M.–1 P.M. Sun.).

Health and Medical Care

Medical care is limited throughout the country and Boca Chica is no different. If you have a medical concern, most of the all-inclusive hotels have a medical center or a doctor on staff. The **Farmacia Boca Chica** (Calle Duarte #17, tel. 809/523-4708, 8:30 A.M.–9 P.M. Mon.–Sat., 8:30 A.M.–7 P.M. Sun.) is centrally located, and you can find most things you'll need. Of course, it is always best to bring any medication you take and anticipate needing in your carry-on baggage.

Call Center and Internet

Making a long-distance call can always be done through your hotel, but this is the most expensive option you have, and you (most likely) have to let the front desk know that you want to do so. Even though it's not as convenient as picking up your phone in your room, the most cost-effective way of making long-distance phone calls is to buy a pre-paid long-distance calling card. These are sold at any *colmado* or grocery store. Gift shops sometimes have them also. These calling cards can be used on any public phone.

Although using the **post office** (Calle Duarte, 8 A.M.–5 P.M. Mon.–Fri., 9 A.M.–noon

Sat.) isn't recommended (service is completely unreliable), it is located across from the Parque Central. If you need a call center, go to **Codetel Centro de Comunicaciones** (Av. San Rafael 1 and Av. Caracol, tel. 809/220-7911, 8 A.M.–10 P.M.).

For Internet you can walk along Calle Duarte to find an Internet service or go to **Centro de Internet JJ** (27 de Febrero 1, tel. 809/523-4120). Rates typically run around US$2–3 per hour at all of the establishments.

GETTING THERE
From Santo Domingo

If you're visiting for the day from Santo Domingo and you have chosen to drive, take Highway 3 east; there is a toll of RD$30. You will pass the exit for Las Américas international airport. Your trip will be about 31 kilometers (30 minutes). Should you leave the chaos to the local drivers' more-than-capable hands, a taxi should run you about US$25. You can also catch a Boca Chica express bus from the northern side of Parque Independencia. The bus runs until 9 P.M. and will cost you about US$2.50. Your other option to get to Boca Chica is to flag down a *guagua* (US$1) from Parque Enriquillo or Parque Independencia heading east. Just remember that the *guaguas* stop running after dark.

From the Airports

Aeropuerto Internacional Las Américas (tel. 809/549-0450) is accessible by many major international airlines. If you haven't arranged for pickup with your hotel prior to your arrival, you can hire a taxi for about US$15. Boca Chica is about a 10-minute ride east of the airport. As you exit customs and baggage claim, you will be faced with a throng of taxi drivers, all trying to offer you a ride. Don't let them take your bag until you've secured a price for the ride. From **Aeropuerto Internacional La Romana** (tel. 809/556-5565) you will have a 1.75-hour ride west, which will cost you about US$80.

GETTING AROUND

Walking is the easiest and best solution to getting around within Boca Chica. However, if you want to experience the motorcycle taxis called *motoconchos,* you can find them all over town. The young men who drive these scooters are found standing next to them or whizzing around honking at the tourists to see who needs a ride. Negotiate a cheap price before getting on one. Beware: These men drive erratically, the streets are filled with potholes, and the cars don't always see them, so a ride can be quite risky.

Guayacanes and Juan Dolio

If Boca Chica is too busy for your relaxing holiday, then head a few kilometers east to Guayacanes and Juan Dolio. These two small beach communities are considerably less touristy than Boca Chica and are smack-dab in the middle of the eastern south-central coastal region, making both Santo Domingo and La Romana good day-trip destinations.

Solitude is the number one reason that visitors return to these beach towns. This area is for the quiet vacationer, the independent traveler, who doesn't need too many choices but maybe wants to get in some golf, beach time, and even a little dancing and also wants great food choices,

without the long lines of the more popular resort areas of Punta Cana and Bávaro. There are all-inclusives here, but they aren't as heavily marketed as the ones in Punta Cana and Bávaro.

◖ BEACHES

Playa Caribe is in the small fishing community of Guayacanes. While this is a quieter destination than Boca Chica, it still is a rather popular beach when the weekend rolls around. Although most tourism has been funneled into the Puerto Plata and Punta Cana areas, in the last couple of decades hotels and resorts in this area have slowly begun sprouting up.

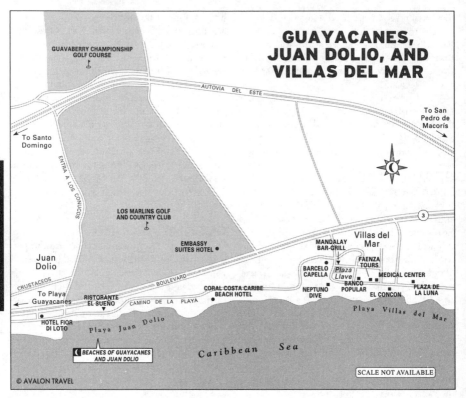

Playas Juan Dolio, with their small neighborhood of **Villas del Mar,** make up a stretch of beach that was developed, over decades, into a five-kilometer-long sprawling string of seaside hotels and resorts. Since there isn't much in the close vicinity of these towns, selection of your hotel becomes a more weighty decision. Villas del Mar is the stretch of Juan Dolio where you will find many shops, Internet services, and some hotels. Unless you invest in some excursions at extra cost, you should think of your vacation to Guayacanes and Juan Dolio (and Villas del Mar) in an "all I'm gonna do is lie on the beach" kind of way.

The water is rougher along this stretch than that of the placid Playa Boca Chica, and the beach does attract the usual souvenir hawkers but they're not as hard-core. While the beaches here are nice, they aren't as picturesque as others in the nation. Mainly, the advantage of this beach rests in its proximity (a one-hour ride) to the capital. It's a good place to get both tranquil beach time and lively city in one vacation.

ENTERTAINMENT

This area just isn't the place where the "partying kind" goes to vacation, but that doesn't mean there isn't a nightlife. Most of the entertainment is in the all-inclusive hotels. Some of the resorts will let outsiders into their discos for a cover charge or into their casinos for free. Outside of the hotels, you can visit some of the restaurants in the area and mingle with the other travelers and vacationing Dominicans.

El Batey Disco (Juan Dolio, Calle Principal 84, open Sat. until 2 A.M.) and **Chocolate Bar** (Juan Dolio, Calle Principal 127, open until

© ANA CHAVIER CAAMAÑO

Bring a book!

2 A.M.) are two options. The first is very popular a late-night dance spot with both locals and tourists. It plays mostly merengue and *bachata*. The latter is more of a hangout where you can belly up to the bar, order an ice-cold Presidente beer, and perhaps take your turn at the pool table. Both are open late (until they feel like closing).

One more diversion is gambling. The Sports Bar and Casino at the **Coral Costa Caribe** (Calle San Pedro de Macorís, Juan Dolio, tel. 809/562-6725, 8 P.M.–4 A.M.) is an American-style casino with music.

SPORTS AND RECREATION
Golf
The **Guavaberry Championship Golf Course** (Km 55, Nuevo Autovia del Este, Juan Dolio, tel. 809/333-4653, fax 809/333-3030, www.guavaberrygolf.com, greens fees US$99) has 7,156 yards and was designed by the South African–born professional golfer Gary Player. This course is a par-72, 18-hole course with rolling hills, wide fairways, and several sets of trees to challenge you. The amenities include a gourmet restaurant, pro shop, piano bar, meeting rooms, pool, and terraces. Reservations are recommended. Special packages can be arranged through the all-inclusive resorts or via the website for Guavaberry.

Diving and Snorkeling
Many dive sites are accessible from this area. The coral reefs offshore create a wonderful viewing spot for different types of coral and fish. If you have an underwater camera, take it! Most of these excursions can be booked with the resorts or through independent dive centers such as **Neptuno Dive** (on the Juan Dolio beach next to the Barceló Capella resort, tel. 809/526-2005, fax 809/526-1378, www.neptunodive.com, US$36 for one dive), which is one of the best. Everyone, from beginners (they will start you in the pool and work you up to the ocean) to those seeking instructor development courses, is welcome to take one of the many classes. If you want to brave the ocean after nightfall you'll need to pay an additional US$20. Excursions such as a day dive to **Isla Catalina,** which includes the bus and

© ANA CHAVIER CAAMAÑO

Guayacanes public beach

boat ride out to the island, lunch, and drinks, will cost US$69, or try cave diving at **Cueva Taína** (their most popular dive) for US$69 (for an additional fee, you can take a horseback ride around the cave site) and to some of the offshore reefs with depths ranging 10–30 meters. Paying in advance over the Internet will save you 20 percent. Prices listed here do not include the 16 percent tax.

Tours

If touring places like Isla Saona (US$65), Isla Catalina (US$65), or Santo Domingo (US$45) or going on a truck safari (US$65) is for you, then contact **Faenza Tours** (Juan Dolio, Villas del Mar, Calle Principal, tel. 809/526-1713, cell 829/340-0392, faenzarentacar@yahoo.com). They also rent four-wheel ATVs for US$55 for three hours. Other packages and rentals are available. It is best to secure a spot in your tour 2–3 days in advance as spots fill up.

ACCOMMODATIONS
Under US$50

Unique **Hotel Fior di Loto** (Calle Central 517, Juan Dolio, tel. 809/526-1146, fax 809/526-3332, www.fiordilotohotel.com, hotelfiordiloto@hotmail.com or hotelfiordiloto@yahoo.com, US$15–40 d depending on the season) is by far the best value in the area. It is gay-friendly and has been the little darling of Juan Dolio since 1996 when the very hospitable owner Mara Sandri opened it as a cultural center. Since then she has changed it into a 25-room hotel (13 have kitchenettes) with a noticeably Indian flare that caters to the independent traveler seeking solace. There are classes in women's hatha yoga (Monday, Wednesday, and Friday), meditation, psychology, and healing. The rooms are very simple but cozy; some have cooking facilities. Safety boxes are US$1 extra. Laundry service is available and there is a generator, plus a big deck for private sunbathing. The restaurant serves vegetarian food only to those staying in the hotel. Wireless Internet is free. There is a bar on-site. Staff can help organize tours for you via Faenza Tours at a special reduced rate for Fior di Loto guests. Transportation is close by, and staff can help you arrange some should you need it, even from

Las Américas airport. Banks and shopping are near and the beach is 50 meters away.

US$50-100

☪ Playa Esmeralda Beach Resort

(Guayacanes, Paseo Vicini, tel. 809/526-3434, fax 809/526-1744, www.hotel-playaesmeralda. com, playa.esmeralda@verizon.net.do, US$75 d). This small, 44-room all-inclusive hotel is popular with local and European tourists. The rooms are spacious and very comfortable with air-conditioning, ceiling fans, mini-fridge, TV, and terraces. There is no phone or Internet in the room, so you can really get that disconnected-from-the-world-on-vacation feel. There is a pool, a bar, and a restaurant serving Dominican and Italian dishes. Diving lessons are available in the pool, and the front desk can help with excursion offers. Massages are available in the spa, as are aerobics by the pool. This all-inclusive is a major bargain and very tranquil. The beach along this stretch is quite lovely, as is the hotel's poolside, with little competition for loungers.

Embassy Suites Hotel at Los Marlins Grand Resort

(Juan Dolio, tel. 809/688-9999, fax 809/526-1130, www.embassysuites.com, US$109 d) is a true golfer's hotel—greens fees to the Los Marlins golf course are included in your price, and although this hotel is not on the beach, it is overlooking the tropical golf course. All 126 rooms are two-room suites. This hotel is suited for the business traveler (complete with secretarial service, including translations) and is a good place for families since kids under 18 staying with an adult stay free (unless you want the all-inclusive option— then it is US$15 extra per child!). There are three restaurants and three bars. Every morning you can enjoy a complimentary breakfast, and complimentary cocktails are served nightly 5:30–7:30 P.M. Amenities include two pools (one with a swim-up bar), a Jacuzzi, a children's area, a pro shop, spa, fitness center, and beauty salon. Car rental on-site and to-and-from airport shuttles (available on request) make transportation a breeze. All rooms have private balconies, high-speed Internet access,

wet bars, cable TV, air-conditioning, and safety deposit boxes.

US$100 and Up

Coral Costa Caribe (Juan Dolio, tel. 809/540-2008, www.coralcostacaribe.com, starting at US$240 d) is a big all-inclusive near both Los Marlins and Guavaberry golf courses and has the best casino in the area. The 534-room resort is simply gigantic, filled with stuff to do for every type of visitor but mostly popular with the traveler who wants mostly to hang in the resort. There is guaranteed food 24 hours a day here, so gorge away. It's what vacations are for! You can work it off dancing in the disco. After all, there is a lively nightlife in this resort, with a disco that attracts people from other resorts, three pools, a kids' club, tennis, basketball, beach volleyball, minigolf, and various water sports, and you can get your PADI scuba certification. It's like a small town.

Barceló Capella (Villas del Mar, Juan Dolio, tel. 809/526-1080, www.barcelo.com, US$160 d) resort, with its Victorian-esque architecture, is a complete vacation package on its own. Again, this is a venue where many vacationers enjoy themselves without ever leaving the grounds. It boasts a great location, right on the beach, but bring some shoes; there is a great deal of coral, which makes it great for snorkeling but murder on your feet. As with most large all-inclusive resorts, the grounds are impeccably kept lush gardens, and the rooms are spacious and have all the regular amenities like minifridges, hair dryers, and irons. There is a disco, two pools, and a spa. It is a popular destination for honeymooners, who book special suites containing a Jacuzzi and king-size bed, as well as for families, whose children will be well occupied by the many child-specific activities available.

The best thing about all-inclusive **Barceló Talenquer** (Juan Dolio, Carretera Las Americas, www.barcelo.com, tel. 809/526-1510, US$60) is the seafood restaurant *L'Ecrevisse*. Otherwise, it is a rather standard all-inclusive that doesn't stand out as exceptional in service or design. On the weekend, the beach can get quite full with locals making

THE SOUTH-CENTRAL COAST

the hunt for lounge chairs and buffet lines a competitive sport.

FOOD

If you are staying at an all-inclusive hotel, the food there will be plentiful and somewhat varied. However, should you want to get out for a bit and treat yourself to a gourmet meal, **Deli Swiss** (Guayacanes, Calle Central 338, tel. 809/526-1226, 11 A.M.–9 P.M. daily) serves up some expensive but fresh and fantastic seafood. The prices vary dramatically as everything is cooked according to what is fresh. Suffice it to say that this won't be cheap, but it will be fantastic. The wine list is one of the best in the country. If you're not a wine connoisseur, let the waitstaff choose for you. Enjoy classical music while dining on the oceanfront terrace as garlic and the smell of the sea intermingle.

☪ Aura Beach House (Juan Dolio, tel. 809/526-2319, 11 A.M.–1 A.M. daily, US$10–27) is situated directly on the beach. This place is gorgeous, very tastefully decorated in white with natural woods and shells. This is more of a beach club by day, where you can sun yourself on chaise lounges in the sand, lunch at interspersed tables, or even contemplate life out on comfortable loungers in the shallow waters offshore. It's a place to spend the day in luxury on the beach. Swim a little, eat a lot, and spend a bunch. At night, aglow with candlelight, it transforms into a romantic must. Specialties include ceviche, salads, sushi, sashimi, seafood, pasta, crepes, and desserts. If you are a ceviche fan, get the Peruvian ceviche (*mero* marinated in lime and onions). In fact, get two. It's definitely a place to see and be seen yet relax at the same time. They have the ambience and pretty darn good cuisine, but lately, the service has suffered a bit due to the fact that they have at least three different servers per one table. Hopefully, they will rectify this misstep in their otherwise perfect recipe for success.

Playa del Pescador Bar & Restaurant (Guayacanes, tel. 809/526-2613, 8 A.M.–10:30 P.M. daily). This peaceful thatch-hut Dominican version of a tiki bar is sitting directly on the best sandy stretch of Guayacanes

beach. You can lie down on a lawn chair all day if you want, or sit under one of their *palapa* tables to be served from the restaurant. Seafood specialties like *camarones a la plancha, cazuela* (seafood stew), and paella are served fresh. Pick a crab or lobster from the tank and have them prepare it to your liking. Breakfast is available as well; there's a special VIP section on the second level. Don't get too dressed up—this is a casual and open air restaurant.

Ristorante El Sueño (Juan Dolio, Calle Principal 330, tel. 809/526-3903, 12 P.M.–3:30P.M. and 7P.M.–11 P.M. daily) is an Italian restaurant and pizzeria that is a nice respite, with its tablecloths and outdoor patio. The big menu includes soups, pastas, salads, meats, fish, seafood, and, of course, pizza. If you've never had pizza in the Dominican Republic, you're in for a treat here. Expect to spend about RD$300–500. Delivery is free.

El Concon (Juan Dolio, Calle Principal, tel. 809/526-2562, open 11 A.M.–11 P.M. Thurs.–Tues.) is a popular restaurant with locals that serves grilled seafood and fish, traditional dishes, pastas, and pizza. Delivery is available. It's on the beach but not facing the beach. Yeah, we wanted to know why, too.

☪ Mandalay Bar-Grill (Juan Dolio, Plaza Colonia Tropical, tel. 809/526-1108, noon–11 P.M. daily) is across the street from the Barceló Capella. The newest addition to the Juan Dolio scene is a sleek and swanky air-conditioned restaurant that has seating both inside and outside. Their generous menu offers Asian, seafood, pizza, Mexican, sushi, burgers, and sandwiches. There is no possible way you can't find something to eat here. In addition, it has one of the most impressive wine cellars around. Try the panko roll: cream cheese, plantains, and black tiger shrimp, which is then tempura fried. Once a month they have well-known Dominican musicians perform. Former acts have included Ramon Orlando and Anthony Rios.

INFORMATION AND SERVICES

Unfortunately, there isn't much in terms of services in Juan Dolio or Guayacanes, not even a tourism office, despite the growing number of tourists. Your best bet is to ask at your hotel (most have someone who will speak English) for anything you might need.

Plaza Llave (Juan Dolio) is across from the Barceló Capella and has gift shops, Internet access, money exchange, and a beauty shop. A few blocks down the main street is a **medical center** (tel. 809/526-1070).

If you desperately need to send something via mail, ask at your hotel's front desk. Do not send anything of any value through the postal service in the Dominican Republic.

Plaza de la Luna has a lot of gift shops where you can also buy small grocery items like cigarettes, coffee, and water. In addition you can get all of your vacation needs, like bathing suits, beach bags, throw-away cameras, and sunglasses. Located within this mini-mall is **ILSA Internet Café** (Juan Dolio, Plaza de la Luna, Calle Principal, www.ilsainterprisesa.info, inv.laurencio@codetel.net.do, tel. 809/526-2777), which serves as a phone center, Internet center, and bar/café. To call the United States it costs RD$15 per minute; local calls are RD$10 per minute, and calls to Europe are RD$25 per minute. Internet charges are: 1 hour, US$4; half hour, US$2; 15 minutes, US$1.

GETTING THERE

A taxi ride from Las Américas international airport takes you along Highway 3 and past Boca Chica. It will cost about US$30, and the ride to the Guayacanes/Juan Dolio area is about 30 minutes. From Santo Domingo, catch a bus from Parque Independencia (around US$2) and in about an hour you will arrive in the area. A taxi to Juan Dolio will run you about US$25 from Boca Chica.

There is no bus company serving the Juan Dolio and Guayacanes area, but if you are in a neighboring town, all you have to do is go out to Highway 3, stand on the side of the road with traffic going in the direction you want to travel, and flag down a *guagua*. They pass by about every 20 minutes. Before you get in, confirm the price (which is never very much—just be sure to have small bills), hop in, and enjoy traveling the way the locals do. It'll cost you around US$1 to go west to Boca Chica and US$2 to Santo Domingo. It is around US$1 to go east to San Pedro de Macorís.

If you are driving, as you travel from Boca Chica on Highway 3 you will come upon Guayacanes first and then Juan Dolio.

GETTING AROUND

There is no need for motorized anything in Guayacanes and Juan Dolio. There is so little traffic within town. *Motoconchos* are an option and they are all over the island. Just agree on a price before you get on. Many hotels have bikes to loan you or know where you can get one. Just ask at the front desk. Hotels can get you taxis, too, and they usually have rates posted or quickly available.

San Pedro de Macorís

At the junction where the Río Higuamo empties into the Caribbean Sea sits San Pedro de Macorís, a town that came to life as a major player in the production of sugar in the latter part of the 19th century. Many people from the Leeward and Windward Islands migrated or were "imported" to work here in the sugarcane fields. These people and their descendants are known today as *cocolos*. When they arrived they brought their distinctively African-influenced culture and traditions, with which they have added color and festivity to the town of San Pedro. This is most evident while enjoying the dances, music, and costumes of the **Cocolos Festival** (see *Events*).

By the time World War II came around, causing a worldwide sugar shortage and driving up the cost, San Pedro de Macorís began to

THE HISTORY OF SUGAR

© ANA CHAVIER CAAMAÑO

Sugar cane is one of the DR's most important exports.

Although sugar adds sweetness to our lives, its history is one of bitterness and slavery.

When the Moors invaded Europe in the 7th century, they brought their technology of sugar production with them. But it wasn't until the crusades in the 11th century that Europeans learned of the spice, as they reclaimed their land and grabbed the sugar plantations away from the Arabs.

On Columbus's second voyage to the New World, he brought with him some sugarcane to plant in the hope that he could start an industry on the island. The climate was perfect for it and it soon thrived. The first sugarcane mill began working in about 1516 in the Dominican Republic.

Columbus "recruited" the Taíno people to work the fields, as it was too arduous for his own men. But as the Taíno started dying off because of disease and abuse, the Spanish soon turned to Africa for more workers. That was when the sugar industry became married to African slavery and forever influenced the Caribbean and eventually the Americas. The slave trade began.

By the end of the 1800s, slavery was officially outlawed. But with the boom of the sugar industry in the late 19th century came an increasing economic need for more workers willing to do the back-breaking work of cutting cane. The African slaves were replaced by thousands of Haitian immigrants

who came to earn money. A 1920 census estimated that 28,000 Haitians were working in the cane fields. When the sugar refineries began shutting down a few years later and production waned, dictator Rafael Trujillo tersely requested that the immigrants leave the Dominican Republic; when they didn't, he slaughtered them.

Today there are over 500,000 Haitians working in the agricultural *bateyes* (small towns located near sugarcane fields where Haitians live and work), and they are brutally exploited. Often they are rounded up and deported (during 2000, the average was 10,000 per month). Many are beaten, robbed, or killed. These crimes have been called modern-day slavery by human-rights' advocates.

Despite the obvious bitter stains on the history of sugar's journey to the Dominican Republic, the industry has benefited the country as well. For years, the Dominican Republic was economically dependent on sugar, with most of the production in the Southeast region. In 2004, some 5.3 million metric tons of sugarcane were produced.

Tourism has now surpassed sugar in economic importance, but sugar remains one of the country's most important exports, and in 2008 the Dominican Republic started shipping sugar to the European Union under a new economic partnership in the hopes of tripling the country's sugar exports.

bulge with rich plantation owners and the town seemed to be on the right track to permanent prosperity. It was the "star" of the Caribbean, rife with money and cultural standing. But as the sugar prices dropped and people lost their jobs, San Pedro's economy slumped and the city began to deteriorate. People began leaving their homes in the desperate hope of finding jobs elsewhere. Since then it has never truly regained its former glory.

San Pedro de Macorís is also known for another resource that they seem determined to never stop producing—baseball players. Almost every Major League team has at least one Dominican on its roster. Some of the most famous players (Sammy Sosa, Pedro Guerrero, Pedro Gonzalez, and George Bell) have come from this town. It has become the main attraction here, especially since there is not much more to see or do within the city limits. Fans of the game who visit the area during the **baseball season** (Oct.–Jan.) should be sure to catch a game. In the off-season of American baseball, you can often find some of today's brightest big league baseball stars coming home to play for their former teams.

While at the stadium, you can purchase a bottle of rum to enjoy during the game. This land of sugarcane and baseball is also home to the distilleries of Brugal and Barceló, rum companies that produce millions of liters a year of what is arguably some of the best rum in the world.

Aside from sugar, rum, and baseball, in 1972 San Pedro gained a free trade zone, where native and foreign companies set up camp to manufacture their goods (such as textiles, shoes, electronic parts, etc.), offering jobs (albeit low-paying ones lacking many workers' rights) to the residents of San Pedro. In exchange, these companies are offered certain tax and customs incentives.

SIGHTS
◖ Tetelo Vargas Stadium
Home to **Las Estrellas Orientales** baseball team and some of the most elite players in the country, the Tetelo Vargas Stadium (Av. Circunvalación, www.estrellasorientales. com.do, tel. 809/246-4077) is the most well-known building in town. Boys who used to play stickball in the *campo,* with their makeshift milk-carton gloves, are now the graceful, competitive, and hungry-for-success Eastern Stars, as their name translates. Baseball season in the Dominican Republic is October–January. If you don't speak Spanish, ask at your hotel for tickets to a game and a taxi to take you. However, if you do speak Spanish, show up at the box office nice and early on the day of the game; you can get a ticket for about US$20 for front-row seats or about US$2 for bleacher seats. Games are usually at night. Schedules are available at the Estrellas Orientales website.

Catedral San Pedro Apóstol
This cathedral (Calle Charro near Av. Independencia, open daily 8 A.M.–8 P.M.) is not a major landmark, but it has a beauty all its own and has had a tumultuous struggle to stay standing. The church was constructed in 1850. In 1865, the church was leveled by a hurricane and later reconstructed. As if that weren't enough, it was devastated by fire in 1886. It was then that the present temple was erected. In 1996 it was elevated to a cathedral. In 2000, a five-year remodeling phase was set into motion. But as of 2005, no real progress had been made. The parishioners remain infuriated about this delay and have demanded that the government finally pay attention to the stained glass, marble floors, and carved wood, which could very well be ruined forever if ignored any longer.

◖ Cueva de las Maravillas
Located 15 kilometers east of San Pedro de Macorís at Boca del Soco on the San Pedro de Macorís–La Romana Highway, the Cave of Wonders (tel. 809/696-1797, www.cuevadelasmaravillas.com, 9 A.M.–6 P.M. Tues.–Sun., adults US$6, children under 12 US$3) is most certainly a highlight of the South-Central Coast region and should not be overlooked when you're in the area. Discovered in 1926, this cave has been the subject of many scientific

THE SOUTH-CENTRAL COAST

studies, because in its 840 meters, over 500 pictographs, petroglyphs, and engravings have been preserved as if drawn yesterday. It truly has the richest sample of rock art in the Antilles and also an impressive array of stalactites, stalagmites, and columns. The government took a great deal of care to make the cave accessible to visitors, and in 2003, the cave's team of architects won the Gold prize in the International Landscape Architecture Bienal Award. It has a 240-meter footpath and is equipped with museum-quality lighting. Ramps and elevators make it wheelchair-accessible. Also on-site is a museum, a shop, a place to buy snacks, and restrooms. You cannot explore the cave without a guide, but your entrance fee buys you a one-hour tour from a knowledgeable guide (some guides speak English). No photos are allowed inside the cave. The Cueva de las Maravillas is well-marked by a national park sign along the Carretera La Romana, east of San Pedro de Macorís. Getting here is easiest with your own car or by taxi. Simply arrange for the taxi to return for you in an hour.

EVENTS

The **Cocolos Festival,** held on June 29, is also the feast of St. Peter and St. Paul and is a perfect time to view the customs and traditions of the *cocolos* immigrants, the sugarcane field workers for the industry in the late part of the 19th century. Their African heritage is preserved through the vibrant, multicolored, mirrored costumes worn by the *guloyas* (dancers), who roam around the city streets performing the traditional dance to furious drumbeats—as the rum flows, of course.

ACCOMMODATIONS

Since San Pedro isn't a popular destination for tourists, there are few hotels and only one good one in the town itself. Many people who visit San Pedro do so on a day trip or just overnight to go to a baseball game. The **Hotel Macorix** (Av. Gaston Fernando Deligne, tel. 809/529-2100, fax 809/529-9239, www.hotelmacorix. com, US$50–75 d), built in 1969, is showing its age a little but has 170 clean rooms, a pool,

tennis court, restaurant, disco, business center, concierge service, and room service. The rooms are satisfactorily equipped with air-conditioning, a fridge, cable TV, and a balcony. Check-in is at 3 P.M.

Santana Beach Resort & Casino (Carretera San Pedro de Macorís, tel. 809/412-1010, fax 809/412-1818, h.santana@mail.cotursa-hotels. com, www.playasantanabeach.com, US$85 d) offers an all-inclusive resort experience. It has six restaurants, five bars (one of which is a swim-up bar in the gigantic pool), children's activities with a separate pool, nonmotorized water sports, a fitness center, a casino that has free entrance and drinks, tennis, and nightly entertainment. Amenities include a medical center, optional excursions, and the Dominican Village, which has a beauty shop and a minimarket. A standard room is called a junior suite and has two queen-size beds, air-conditioning and ceiling fan, cable TV, a stocked minibar, private terrace or balcony, full bathroom with shower and tub, and a safety box (at extra cost).

FOOD

Near the Catedral San Pedro Apóstal and on the waterfront, **Robby Mar** (Av. Francisco Dominguez Charro 35, tel. 809/529-4926, 10 A.M.–midnight daily, US$10–20) is the best restaurant in town; it has outdoor and indoor seating. The restaurant serves seafood, meats, salads, pastas, and other choices. The crab and lobster are fresh and sold by weight (without the shell)—try them grilled or with a garlic sauce. The owner, Tony, speaks English well and can help with any suggestions.

The Howard Johnson hotel is home to the **Bar Restaurant Apolo** (Av. Independencia 53, tel. 809/529-3749, 11 A.M.–11 P.M. daily), which serves Chinese food that is far from remarkable in a casual environment.

INFORMATION AND SERVICES

Despite the fact that San Pedro de Macorís is not a major tourist destination, an **Oficina de Turismo** (tel. 809/529-3644) serves the area.

For banking concerns, try **Banco Popular** (Calle 27 de Febrero 7, tel. 809/339-9005, 8 A.M.–3 P.M. Mon.–Fri, 8 A.M.–1 P.M. Sunday) or **Banco Progreso** (Av. Independencia 48, tel. 809/529-6933, 8 A.M.–4 P.M. Mon.–Fri, 8 A.M.–1 P.M. Sunday).

To make a long-distance call, go to the **Tricom** office (Av. Independencia 75, tel. 809/476-0688). Just down the block is **Farmacia Andreita** (Av. Independencia 55, tel. 809/529-3954) for any pharmaceutical needs.

GETTING THERE

From Santo Domingo and Las Américas international airport, San Pedro de Macorís is a little over an hour's drive east along Highway 3, 70 kilometers east of Santo Domingo.

If you're staying in the Juan Dolio resort area, catching a *guagua* or taxi will cost around US$1 or US$10 each way, respectively. Flag one down that is traveling in the right direction. Ask the driver to let you off as near to your destination as possible.

Public buses travel from San Pedro de Macorís's baseball stadium west to Santo Domingo's Parque Enriquillo (RD$70) and east to La Romana (RD$50) and Higüey (RD$70).

GETTING AROUND

San Pedro de Macorís is a congested town filled with trucks going to the industrial areas, sugarcane fields, and distilleries and has heavy clogs along the poorly marked streets and highways that run through. This leaves the traffic in a chaotic battle. Hire a taxi for your transportation rather than braving the back of a *motoconcho*.

THE SOUTH-CENTRAL COAST

THE SOUTHEAST

Opulent tourism and bucolic Dominican life strangely coexist in the Southeast region of the Dominican Republic. It is still not uncommon to see a motorcade of tour buses slowing down on the highway behind an oxen-driven cartload of sugarcane. It wasn't until the latter part of the 20th century that tourism really took off in this section of the republic, and the one-time rookie region quickly became the nation's leading economic powerhouse, overthrowing the incumbent Puerto Plata on the north coast as the favorite destination for travelers looking for paradise. The agricultural, livestock, and sugarcane industries that once ruled the area have had to bow down to the powerful allure of the pristine beaches, which have become the livelihood of the area and the country.

The Southeast region's main tourism areas—including La Romana and Bayahibe along the Caribbean coast and Punta Cana and Bávaro of the eastern coastline along the Atlantic—deliver what many visitors expect from a Caribbean vacation: exquisite beaches, catamaran rides, phenomenal golf courses, and luxurious accommodations. Their all-inclusive resorts are famous for being the best bargains in the Caribbean, and indeed, a good portion of the southeastern coastline is lined with these mega-complexes, boasting the largest number of hotel rooms in the country.

In addition to all of the tourist development, the Southeast is home to two of the nation's larger national parks, Parque Nacional del Este and Parque Nacional Los Haitises, and ecotourism is enjoying a steady rise in popularity. Visitors can hike miles of unspoiled beaches

© ANA CHAVIER CAAMAÑO

HIGHLIGHTS

◖ Altos de Chavón: This replica of a 16th-century Italian village is also home to a school of art and design. Shop in the many stores for original student art, souvenirs, and jewelry. Enjoy a show in the 7,000-seat amphitheater or dine in one of the many enticing restaurants (page 96).

◖ Isla Saona: This island is part of the **Parque Nacional del Este** and is the most popular day trip taken by tourists vacationing in the Southeast or Costa del Coco regions. After a boat trip through the crystalline waters where the Caribbean Sea meets the Atlantic Ocean, visitors can enjoy the powdery white-sand beaches of this picture-postcard island (page 104).

◖ La Piscina Natural: It doesn't seem right, but you can sit in the middle of the Caribbean Sea. La Piscina is a starfish-inhabited sandbar off the southwestern coast of the Parque Nacional del Este's peninsula. It's a hit with excursion boats taking visitors to Isla Saona. Although it can get quite congested with tourists, it is worth a short visit to bathe in the ultra-tranquil clear and balmy water (page 105).

◖ Parque Nacional del Este: This arid national park occupies almost the entire southeastern peninsula. It holds evidence of Taíno life; ruins, cave drawings, and burial sites have recently been discovered. This park is also home to some 539 species of flora, 144 types of birds, and the endangered bottle-nosed dolphins and manatees frolicking offshore (page 106).

◖ Punta Cana Beaches: Internationally famous for its plush white shores, tall coconut trees, turquoise waters, and myriad of all-inclusive hotels dotting the shores – be pampered as a guest of the resorts, or enjoy the afternoon with a day pass while relaxing in the Caribbean sun. Either way, this is vacationing (page 118).

◖ Parque Nacional Los Haitises: This is a treat for the ecocurious traveler. You enter the park by boat through the semi-spooky, mangrove-studded coastline. More than 750 species of plants, 110 species of birds, bats, and even the endangered manatee are at home in the extensive cave systems and lagoons throughout the park. A definite must for ecotravelers (page 133).

LOOK FOR ◖ TO FIND RECOMMENDED SIGHTS, ACTIVITIES, DINING, AND LODGING.

THE SOUTHEAST

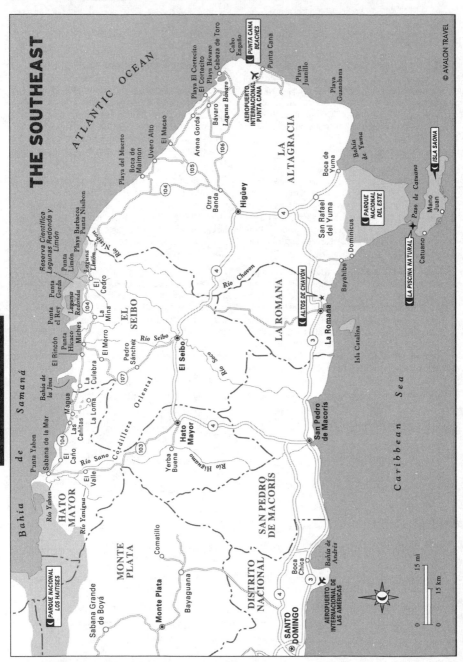

THE SOUTHEAST

© AVALON TRAVEL

and forests, paddle boats through mangroves in search of manatees, keep their eyes open for endemic and rare land animals (such as the rat-like solenodon), explore caves for Taíno drawings, and take bird-watching excursions. The Parque Nacional del Este, found where the waters of the Atlantic Ocean meet the Caribbean Sea, is an intensely hot and dry expanse, and the vastly different Los Haitises (as it is commonly referred to) is a mangrove-lined tropical sub-humid forest with a plush interior. Limestone caves dot both of these parks, protecting the ancient Taíno drawings found within many of them. A day of exploration to these caves is a trip back to a time when the Spanish conquistadors and native inhabitants of the islands were making their first impressions on each other, some of which is documented on the walls within.

The Dominican Republic's Ministry of Tourism is profoundly proud of the development of the tourism industry in this area, and it focuses much of its marketing attention on the maintenance and future of the area. Lately that has included the protection and development of ecofriendly tour options. Those looking for posh accommodations and isolation within the luxurious bubbles of all-inclusives will be perfectly satisfied with their choice to travel to the Southeast. While there are indeed other, more independent-traveler-friendly areas of the Dominican Republic, those who seek unique experiences will not be disappointed either.

PLANNING YOUR TIME

Most who visit the Southeast do so with the intention of never leaving the beach or their all-inclusive resort. There is a lot to be said about a vacation where you are pampered at a resort, all food and drink included, amid palm trees and some of the most beautiful and well-maintained beaches around.

But for those who tire of the same atmosphere, this region has much more to offer. Even if you are staying in a resort complex, one way to combat "resort fever" is to check out the excursions desk. They frequently offer exciting activities and day trips that can be added to your vacation for an extra charge. It is yet another worry-free way to vacation in an all-inclusive package

SPEAKING OF TAÍNO

Even though the Taíno people were nearly extinguished by Christopher Columbus and his men, their language has not completely disappeared. Over time, portions of it have appeared in the Spanish-speaking part of the Caribbean. More than 800 words are still used. Most of these words are for objects (for instance, *chichí* for baby), geographical places (like the city of Higüey), personal names, and flora and fauna. Often, the words are so widely used that they are mistaken for having Spanish origins, or the two languages can be interchangeable, as in the case of the Dominican slang *poquito* and the Taíno *chinchín*, both meaning "a little bit."

Just as the Taíno contributed to today's Dominican speech, so have some words found their way into regular English usage. The following are some examples:

- *barbacoa* – barbecue
- *caníbal* – cannibal
- *canoa* – canoe
- *casabe* – cassava
- *guayaba* – guava
- *hamaca* – hammock
- *huracán* – hurricane
- *iguana* – iguana
- *maíz* – maize
- *maraca* – maraca
- *sabana* – savanna
- *tabaco* – tobacco

and get some additional thrills; it won't even take a lot of planning on your part. But check what your options are soon after your arrival as reservations may be necessary, especially if the excursions require you to leave the Southeast. For instance, taking a day trip to the Ciudad Colonial in Santo Domingo requires a four-hour bus ride and could be done in one long day or overnight, with a stay in one of the charming hotels in the first city of the New World.

However, if resorts just aren't your cup of tea, *guaguas* are a very cheap and exciting way to travel. Keep in mind that they only run during daylight hours. The towns of **Bayahibe** on the southern coast, **El Cortecito** on the eastern Costa del Coco, and **Miches** or **Sabana de la Mar,** both on the Costa Esmeralda on the southern coast of the Bahía de Samaná, make great stop-offs for the independent traveler who seeks either rest and relaxation or action and adventure.

HISTORY

To the Taínos this area was known as the Higüey province and was the territory of a cacique named Cotubanamá (sometimes referred to as Cayacoa). But in 1503, Bartolomé de Las Casas destroyed much of the area, killing thousands of Taínos and their leader. By 1515 almost the entire population of Taínos was annihilated.

Researchers believe that this area (especially the Parque Nacional del Este) was the site of a major community of Taíno Caribbean civilization. Deep in the forest of the national park, scientists have discovered ruins, artifacts, and cave drawings pointing to the settlement of Taínos that had once called the Southeast home. And although there is Spanish documentation of these early events, the cave drawings discovered tell important stories of the first interactions and subsequent altercations between the Spanish and Taíno natives from the Taíno perspective. Additional pictographs were found in the caves of the Parque Nacional Los Haitises.

SPORTS AND RECREATION

Since most travelers come to the Southeast to hang out in all-inclusive resorts, there are countless opportunities to book an organized **tour** at the excursion desks located in resort lobbies. All have comparable prices, and many are not included in the cost of your all-inclusive vacation, so be very careful when booking your sport or excursion. As soon as you arrive to your resort, look through the offerings and book your choice, since these typically fill up quickly. Popular excursions include boat trips to Isla Saona or catamaran rides, adrenaline pumping zipline adventures, booze-infused safari excursions, boat trips through the mangroves, and cave exploring in the Parque Nacional Los Haitises, to name a few.

Golf is a massively popular sport that has enjoyed much success in this region, with courses designed by Pete Dye, Jack Nicklaus, and Nick Faldo. The Southeast has the widest variety of top-ranked and world-renowned courses in the country, making it the best destination for the golf aficionado. While you can certainly bring your own clubs on the airplane, renting equipment at the courses for an additional cost is also a possibility.

Diving and snorkeling trips are popular off the coasts of Islas Saona and Catalina. Independent diving outfitters (as well as hotel dive organizers) arrange transportation for visits to these locations, along with rental equipment (make sure of the cost), and sometimes provide lunch or snacks. You will see coral formations, drop-offs, schools of fish, and even wrecks like the *St. George* or the *Embassy.* Diving in the converging waters of the Atlantic and the Caribbean (near Punta Cana) can be a bit choppy with many currents and is not recommended for the beginner.

Deep-sea fishing, while not a top pick among visitors, can be arranged at most resort excursion desks. In the southern coastal town of Boca de Yuma, there are fishing boats lining the shore. Although there is nothing by way of a tourist infrastructure in this town, it is possible to hire a local fishing boat captain to take you out. Always ask about the experience of the captain and crew, and make sure that the charter has life vests, safety equipment, a working radio, and a license.

La Romana

Just like San Pedro de Macorís, La Romana was a sugar town. The town began to prosper in the 1960s when an American company, Gulf + Western Industries, became the owner of a sugar mill and began to invest heavily in other industries like cattle and cement. The company cleaned La Romana up and in the mid-1970s built the now world-famous **Casa de Campo** resort about 1.6 kilometers east of the town. Many wealthy and famous people, such as Bill Clinton, Julio Iglesias, and Michael Jackson, have come to spend their money at this luxurious resort while golfing on the world-class courses, buying or renting the lavish villas, or getting married in a whirlwind Dominican "quickie" wedding. In turn, the town was eventually able to afford a new state-of-the-art airport and bring in even more tourists than before.

La Romana is, to this day, a charming town with surprisingly little to offer tourists, but since it is geographically close to Casa de Campo it reaps the benefits of the foreign currency the resort brings to the region. If it weren't for the development of Casa de Campo and its adjacent tourist attraction, **Altos de Chavón,** this little town would still be a sleepy seaside village.

SIGHTS
Parque Central
Take an hour or two to hang out or wander around near La Romana's Parque Central. It is a central gathering point for townsfolk and bordered by the **Iglesia de Santa Rosa de Lima.** It is a good place to feel the vibe of this town that thrives on visitors, making it a phenomenal people-watching perch during the day and into early evening. The Parque Central is within walking distance to many restaurants and services as well as the town's outdoor market, where deals abound on veggies, handicrafts, housewares, and cheap trinkets.

Isla Catalina
Isla Catalina is the second largest island off the

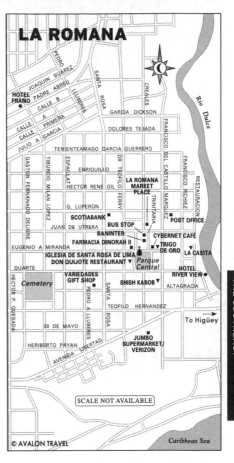

southeastern coast of the Dominican Republic. Named "Toeya" by the Taíno, it was renamed in honor of Saint Catalina by Columbus. Its beaches are powdery white and its waters are shallow and warm. The island itself is uninhabited, but the coral reef just offshore is populated by many sea creatures, which makes for a good afternoon of diving or snorkeling. The island is just two kilometers off the coast of La Romana and is mainly accessed via Casa de Campo's shuttle boats (about a 45-minute boat ride). This resort has set up a restaurant and bar on the island, making it all very civilized. Other excursion companies from Boca Chica, Juan Dolio, Bayahibe, Punta Cana, and the surrounding areas can arrange a trip for you as well. This has become a very popular day-trip destination.

This island is used by many cruise ships as a stopping point for their patrons to stretch their sea legs and get in a day of snorkeling and hiking. The highest elevation on the island is seven meters above sea level. Diving excursions are possible off the coast of Isla Catalina at the drop-off called *The Wall,* where scads of fish and coral can be seen along the vertical plunge, which starts at 5 meters and dips down to a depth of 40 meters.

Beaches

La Romana has three beautiful beaches: **El Caletón, La Minita,** and **La Caleta.** La Caleta is closest to the city and is the most visited during the summer. La Minita is walled into the Casa de Campo protective watch. It is a small but nice beach inaccessible to outsiders. To hang with the locals at the beach, visit El Caletón.

◖ Altos de Chavón

The most visited tourist spot in the Southeast is undoubtedly Altos de Chavón (Casa de Campo, tel. 809/523-8011, fax 809/523-8312, US$5). High above the Río Chavón sits this beautifully crafted mock 16th-century Mediterranean village. In the 1970s it was built to give guests of Casa de Campo and other tourists something to do, and it is now also home to an art school affiliated with the Parsons School of Design in New York.

Cobbled passages, plazas constructed of black river pebbles and sun-drenched coral, azalea-dripping stone archways, and wooden shutters on terra-cotta-roofed buildings create a time-warp sensation as you weave your way from café to boutique, shopping for original student artwork, jewelry, or souvenirs.

Attractions include top-notch restaurants, the Church of St. Stanislaus, and a 5,000-seat

open-air amphitheater where big-name concerts are regularly held. The Altos de Chavón **Regional Museum of Archaeology** (tel. 809/523-8554) houses more than 3,000 artifacts that document the island's pre-Columbian heritage from the pre-ceramic era to the Taíno people. In the three art galleries (call 809/523-8470 for more information), you can stroll among the showcased art of Dominican and international established and emerging artists.

Any amount of time spent at Altos de Chavón is a treat. Even though it seems a bit odd to have built a replica of a 16th-century Mediterranean village in the Caribbean and greatly removed from modern Dominican life, it is a rich addition to your island getaway vacation.

To drive to Altos de Chavón from La Romana, pass the Casa de Campo gates. Veer right at the fork in the road; it is marked with an Altos de Chavón sign.

A cab from La Romana should cost under US$10 each way. Ask for the taxi driver's card so that you can call for a return trip. A *motoconcho* would cost significantly less but they are not allowed inside the gates.

ENTERTAINMENT

Most travelers who come to the town of La Romana do so for the afternoon or just pass through, so the nightlife is almost completely limited to Casa de Campo and the other all-inclusive resorts, such as the **Santana Beach Resort** (tel. 809/412-1010, fax 809/412-1818, www.santanabeach.com), where you can buy a night pass that entitles you to dinner, drinks, and entrance into the discos. There are more nightlife options available in nearby Bayahibe.

Dinner at one of the many restaurants at Altos de Chavón is a romantic option that can be followed with dancing at the disco.

Michelin Baseball Stadium (tel. 809/556-6188, www.lostorosdeleste.com, tickets RD$50–250) holds baseball games during the winter. Baseball fans shouldn't miss an opportunity to catch a game at this stadium. Cheer loud and proud for the local team, La Romana Azucareros (La Romana Sugar Bowls), also known as Los Toros del Este.

SHOPPING

Altos de Chavón's **La Tienda** (Casa de Campo, tel. 809/523-3333, ext. 5398) is the perfect place to go for original art. Since it is the home of a school of design, many of the students' artworks and crafts are actually for sale. Handmade purses, clothing, paintings, and jewelry are a few of the choices. Other shops on the premises are filled with things like Dominican souvenirs and fine linen.

La Marina at Casa de Campo has lots of shops to keep you busy, selling everything from haute jewelry and clothing to chic beachwear.

SPORTS AND RECREATION

The sports and recreation choices are dominated by the offerings at Casa de Campo. Their menu of options is quite impressive and can keep you busy for days. If you're not a guest of the hotel, taking part in these sports may not be an option. However, for some things (e.g., the shooting range and golf) there are special prices making them open to all. All questions regarding booking can be directed to the main number (tel. 809/523-3333).

Golf

People travel from all over the world to golf on the Pete Dye–designed **Teeth of the Dog** course (Casa de Campo, tel. 809/523-8115, fax 809/523-8800, www.casadecampo.com.do, t.times@ccampo.com.do, golf@ccampo.com.do, 7:30 A.M.–5 P.M. daily, greens fees US$170 for hotel guests, US$225 non-hotel guests for 18 holes, caddies US$25). This 18-hole, par-72 course opened in 1971 and quickly shot up to the number one course in the Caribbean. It is currently ranked number 34 in the world by *Golf* magazine. Seven of the holes are along the ocean, and the terrain is challenging to even the best professionals around the globe. Reservations are *highly recommended* as space can sometimes be booked as far out as 12 months.

Another golf course in the Casa de Campo complex is **The Links** (tel. 809/523-8115, fax 809/523-8800, golf@ccampo.com.do, greens fees US$135 for hotel guests, US$150 non-hotel guests for 18 holes). It is more inland and opened in 1975. With its undulating hills, the layout resembles traditional British and Scottish courses, featuring small greens and several lagoons. Most golfers attest that it is equally as challenging as the Teeth of the Dog course. It too is an 18-hole, par-72 course. You can reserve a time 24 hours in advance.

Yet another option for golf at Casa de Campo, **Dye Fore** (tel. 809/523-8115, fax 809/523-8800, golf@ccampo.com.do, greens fees US$170 for hotel guests, US$225 non-hotel guests for 18 holes) is the newest of the resort's courses. It hugs the village of Altos de Chavón. Designed by Pete Dye as well, this spectacularly beautiful 18-hole golf course has breathtaking views of the village, the Río Chavón, and the Caribbean Sea. If you stray from the fairway, however, you will be punished in this terrain. This is a challenging course.

Fishing

Casa de Campo (tel. 809/523-3333, fax 809/523-8547, www.casadecampo.com.do) offers deep-sea and freshwater-river fishing trips from its private marina. The main catch in the sea is marlin, and you have the option of half-day (US$708) or full-day (US$836) charters. These prices are per boat and include fishing rods, bait, boat captain and mate, sodas, and bottled water.

In the river, championship snooker are waiting to be hooked. The river is a good excursion for photographers, too. The very scenic Río Chavón was the backdrop for the films *Apocalypse Now* and *Rambo*. A three-hour tour (including boat, guide, bait, tackle, and refreshments) will cost US$100 per person with a three-person limit per boat.

Snorkeling and Diving

Isla Catalina is the closest spot to snorkel off the coast of La Romana. Casa de Campo's **Circe Dive Shop** (tel. 809/246-3115, US$45

GOLFING THE DOMINICAN REPUBLIC

A golf vacation may be just what the doctor ordered – in fact, it has become one of the top tourist attractions of the country. The Dominican Republic has become a top contender in the race for the best golf vacation. Here are some of the best courses in the country.

SANTO DOMINGO
Las Lagunas Country Club
- Par: 72
- Holes: 18
- Length of course: 6,800 yards
- Fees and lessons: tel. 809/372-7441, www.laslagunas.com.do

SOUTH-CENTRAL COAST
Guavaberry Golf & Country Club
- Par: 72
- Holes: 18
- Length of course: 7,156 yards
- Fees and lessons: tel. 809/333-4653, www.guavaberrygolf.com

SOUTHEAST
Cocotal Golf and Country Club
- Par: 72
- Holes: 27
- Length of course: 7,183 yards
- Fees and lessons: tel. 809/687-4653, www.cocotalgolf.com

Dye Fore, Casa de Campo
- Par: 72
- Holes: 18
- Length of course: 7,770 yards
- Fees and lessons: No phone reservations. Tee-times in advance for hotel guests only, but course open to all. Tee-times made by request email to t.times@ccampo.com.do or by fax 305/858-4677. No advance tee-times needed for same-day arrival. www.casadecampo.com.do

La Hacienda
- Par: 72
- Holes: 18
- Length of course: 7,200 yards
- Fees and lessons: tel. 809/959-4653, www.puntacana.com

Las Iguanas Golf Course – opening late 2009
- www.capcana.com

The Links, Casa de Campo
- Par: 72
- Holes: 18
- Length of course: 6,461
- Fees and lessons: No phone reservations. Tee-times in advance for hotel guests only, but course open to all. Tee-times made by request email to t.times@ccampo.com.do or by fax 305/858-4677. No advance tee-

times needed for same-day arrival. www. casadecampo.com.do

Punta Cana Resort & Club's La Cana Golf Course
- Par: 72

- Holes: 18

- Length of course: 7,152 yards

- Fees and lessons: tel. 809/959-4653, www. puntacana.com

Punta Espada Golf Course
- Par: 72

- Holes: 18

- Length of course: 7,396yards

- Fees and lessons: tel. 809/955-9501, www. capcana.com

Roco Ki Golf Club
- Par: 72

- Holes: 18

- Length of course: 7,073 yards

- Fees and lessons: tel. 809/731-2824. www. rocoki.com

Teeth of the Dog, Casa de Campo
- Par: 72

- Holes: 18

- Length of course: 7,400

- Fees and lessons: No phone reservations.

Tee-times in advance for hotel guests only, but course open to all. Tee-times made by request email to t.times@ccampo.com.do or by fax 305/858-4677. No advance tee-times needed for same-day arrival. www. casadecampo.com.do

NORTH COAST
Playa Dorado Golf Club
- Par: 72

- Holes: 18

- Length of course: 6,730 yards

- Fees and lessons: tel. 809/320-3472, www. playadoradagolf.com

EL CIBAO
Jarabacoa Golf Club (a.k.a. Quintas de Primavera)
- Par: 36

- Holes: 9

- Length of course: White/2,911 yards; Red/2,900 yards

- Fees and lessons: tel. 809/782-9883

Las Aromas Golf Club
- Par: 70

- Holes: 18

- Length of course: 6,001

- Fees and lessons: 809/836-3064

THE SOUTHEAST

per person) is best equipped for snorkeling excursions. The cost includes the charter of the boat but not the rental of fins and a mask, which is US$11 per day. If you are on the all-inclusive plan at the resort, the gear fee is waived.

Isla Catalina can also be reached from the Bayahibe resorts and excursion companies.

Tennis

Casa de Campo's tennis center, **La Terraza** (tel. 809/523-3333, 7 A.M.–9 P.M., US$28 per hour during the day and US$35 at night) has been called the "Wimbledon of the Caribbean" by *Travel + Leisure* magazine. The center begins its day at dawn sweeping the courts and marking the lines on the 13 Har–Tru clay courts. At night, 10 of the courts are equipped with lights. This is a luxury tennis club complete with ball boys, a pro shop, and a spectator's deck. Lessons are available with a tennis pro at extra cost (US$69/hour). Rent racquets for US$10 per hour.

ACCOMMODATIONS

This region doesn't have many options outside of Casa de Campo, which is certainly the big kahuna of the La Romana area. There are a few small hotels in town, used mainly by traveling businesspeople or tourists just passing through town.

Under US$50

The 41-room **Hotel Frano** (Calle Padre Abreu 9, tel. 809/550-4744, US$45) is a good value for the money. Rooms are comfortable with a private bathroom, air-conditioning, TV, and hot water. A restaurant on-site serves excellent Dominican food. You can experience the town of La Romana itself, but you'll have to travel to see the beach.

Hotel River View (Calle Restauración 17, tel. 809/556-1181, hotelriverview@hotmail. com, US$35) has comfortable and clean rooms with TV, wireless Internet access, and private, hot water bathrooms. Located on the river. These are very basic rooms, so if you have to stay here, ask for a room with windows.

US$50-100

Santana Beach Resort & Casino (Carretera San Pedro de Macorís–La Romana, tel. 809/412-1010, www.playasantana.com, US$85 d) offers an all-inclusive resort experience for a lot less money than Casa de Campo. It has four à la carte restaurants and one buffet, five bars (one of which is a swim-up bar in the pool), children's activities with a separate pool, non-motorized water sports, a fitness center, a casino that has free entrance and drinks, tennis, and nightly entertainment. Amenities include a medical center, optional excursions, and the Dominican Village, which has a beauty shop and a minimarket. A standard room (simple in design and decor) has two queen-size beds, air-conditioning and ceiling fan, cable TV, a stocked minibar, private terrace or balcony, full bathroom with shower and tub, and a safety box (at extra cost).

US$100 and Up

◖ **Casa de Campo** (tel. 800/877-3643 or 809/523-3333, fax 809/523-8548, www.casa-decampo.com.do, US$178–375 per night and up in high season) is the crown jewel of La Romana without a doubt. Some argue that it is the best resort not only in the Dominican Republic, but in the entire Caribbean. After all, celebrities vacation here. Bill and Hillary have been known to vacation here. Michael Jackson married Lisa Marie Presley here. Julio Iglesias owned a villa here. Yes, it is the resort that appeals to the rich and famous, and it shows. The food is good, the reputation is better, and the amenities are the best of the best. It is more like a town than a resort. The property is huge—it has its own beach, marina, equestrian stables, shooting gallery, tennis courts, world-class golf courses, many restaurants and bars, spa, even a full-size grocery store. It's clean, walled off, and security is tight. All-inclusive packages include unlimited drinks, no menu restrictions, unlimited horseback riding, tennis, and nonmotorized water sports at Minitas Beach, and one round of 25 shots of skeet/trap shooting. Non-guests can buy a day pass at the information desk for

US$40 (includes access to beach and one meal at a beachside restaurant).

FOOD
Casa de Campo

Casa de Campo's **Marina & Yacht Club,** designed to look like Portofino, Italy, has many nice restaurants, international boutiques, galleries, jewelers, and even impromptu entertainment. The restaurants that are particularly notable are **La Casita** (6:30–11 P.M. daily; dress is casual elegance), which serves Spanish seafood amid views of yachts and the sea; and **Chinois** (tel. 809/523-2388, noon–3 P.M. and 6:30–11 P.M. daily; dress is casual for lunch), which has Cantonese-style lunch and dinner (a little overrated, but still better than most all-inclusive restaurants). Part of the charm of the restaurants in this area is their atmosphere. The Marina & Yacht Club is quite alluring as you sit back and watch the easy bobbing of the luxurious yachts. Reservations are recommended for all restaurants for dinner.

In the main area of Casa de Campo, restaurants include **Lago Grill** (tel. 809/523-3333, 7–11 A.M. and noon–3 P.M. Mon.–Sat., 6:30–11 A.M. and noon–4 P.M. Sun., US$6–14, breakfast buffet US$16) and **The Beach Club by Le Cirque** (tel. 809/523-3333, noon–4 P.M. and 7–11 P.M. daily, US$10–30). The first is a breakfast and lunch buffet with ample terraced space offering a view of the Teeth of the Dog golf course. The breakfast specialties are omelets prepared to your personal liking and a fresh-squeezed juice bar. Le Cirque has fresh salads, seafoods, and meats all prepared by Chef Alfio Longo, who was trained by New York's famous Le Cirque. Bathing suits are acceptable during lunchtime as it is on the beach.

Altos de Chavón

Dine amid the romantic scenery of the artists' village. **La Piazetta** (tel. 809/523-3333, 6–11 P.M. daily) is an à la carte Italian restaurant befitting its surroundings, complete with serenading musicians. There's a delicious antipasto bar, homemade pastas, seafood in varied sauces, meat, and poultry. And no Italian restaurant would be complete without succulent desserts and rich coffees. A children's menu is available. Don't forget to check out the humidor with cigars. Reservations are required.

La Romana Town

Trigo de Oro (Calle Eugenio A. Miranda, tel. 809/550-5650, US$2–14) is a wonderful French-owned café in a converted historical home. The chefs make all their own pastries. It is set apart from the street by a fence with lush greenery, making an inviting, shady courtyard and veranda where you can have a quiet cup of coffee and conversation. There's a full bar with wine and beer as well. Coffee and desserts are a specialty. Although it seems posh, the prices are cheap. The chocolate croissants are to die for.

At **Don Quijote** (Calle Diego Avila 44, tel. 809/556-2827, next to the Parque Central, closed Mon., US$7–15), savor a wonderful menu with items like filet mignon and seafood delicacies. Few places offer this kind of ambiance and service, so when you find it, you tend to want to stick around. Enjoy the tablecloths and candles and the view of the Parque Central for lunch or dinner. **La Casita** (Calle Francisco Doucadray 57, tel. 809/556-5932, 11 A.M.–11 P.M. daily, US$6–35) is decorated with hand-painted Italian porcelain to match the Italian menu, with good seafood such as lobster thermidor or salmon. Other menu choices worth consideration are the risottos and pastas.

Got a hankering for something other than the usual Dominican or Italian choices? Try **Shish Kabob** (Calle Francisco del Castillo Marquez 32, tel. 809/556-2737, Tues.–Sun. 10 A.M.–midnight, US$5–20) for some Middle Eastern food. Grilled kabobs, kabob pizza, and *dolmades* (stuffed grape leaves) are on the menu, along with a ton of other tasty choices, like *baba ghanoush.*

Tucked back into a very commercial area, on Calle Juan de Utrera, you will find **La Romana Market Place.** This is where the locals shop for fresh produce, housewares, and all kinds of everyday things.

INFORMATION AND SERVICES

Fortunately, La Romana has an **Oficina de Turismo** (Teniente Amado García, tel. 809/550-6922, 8 A.M.–2 P.M. Mon.–Fri.).

ScotiaBank (Calle Eugenio A Miranda, 8:30 A.M.–4:30 P.M. Mon.–Fri., 9 A.M.–1 P.M. Sat.) is across from the Parque Central and down the block from Trigo de Oro café.

Banco León (Calle Duarte, 8:30 A.M.–4:30 P.M. Mon.–Fri., 9 A.M.–1 P.M. Sat.) is another centrally located bank. Both have ATMs.

Jumbo Supermarket (Av. Libertad) has all the things you might need. It's more of a super center, selling food along with providing such services as a bank, American Air office, Verizon, Western Union, and Nestlé Ice Cream.

The post office (Calle Francisco del Castillo Marquéz, tel. 809/556-2265) is two blocks north of Parque Central.

High-speed Internet access and long-distance phone calls can be made at **Cybernet Café** (Calle Eugenio A. Miranda by the Parque Central, tel. 809/813-5514, cybernetcafe2000@hotmail.com, 8:30 A.M.–9 P.M. daily), across from ScotiaBank.

Farmacia Dinorah II is on the side of Parque Central (tel. 809/556-2225).

GETTING THERE

From Las Américas international airport you will have an 80-minute drive along Highway 3. As you enter La Romana from the east, Highway 3 turns into Avenida Padre Abreu in La Romana's city limits. Take a right onto Santa Rosa. This street will take you near the Parque Central, where you will find the bus stations and the Iglesia de Santa Rosa de Lima directly across from the park. You will also be in the general area for many of the communication centers, banks, cafés, and restaurants.

To make your way to Bayahibe and beyond, as you come into La Romana follow the signs to Casa de Campo—they will take you along Avenida La Liberta. This way, you can take a left on Avenida Santa Rosa and find yourself within a couple of blocks of the Parque Central if you want to stop off in La Romana for a quick bite to eat or to stretch your legs in the charming square. There are many one-way streets here, so be careful where you turn.

To take a bus from Santo Domingo, catch one on the southeast corner of Parque Enriquillo that says it is going to Higüey. This bus stops at the station across from Parque Central in La Romana. It costs about US$5.

From La Romana airport it is easiest to hail a taxi into town. It will cost very little and take only 10 minutes.

Aeropuerto La Romana (LRM, tel. 809/813-9000) is a three terminal airport (international, international private, and domestic) about eight kilometers east of La Romana. It receives flights from Puerto Rico and Miami. American Airlines (tel. 809/813-9080) and charter flights arranged by Canadian and European companies come through here. The airport has both short- and long-term parking available, and taxis and hotel shuttles wait in front of the building.

GETTING AROUND

There is not much in the town of La Romana to actually see. Exploring within the Parque Central and through the back streets is easiest on foot. What must-see sights there are require a mode of transportation as they are outside of city limits. To hire a taxi you can call **Santa Rosa Taxi** (tel. 809/550-1126, about RD$50) or hire a *motoconcho* by walking to the top of the Parque Central right in front of the church; they wait there. It will cost less than US$4 to go anywhere in town by *motoconcho* and US$7 for the taxi within the city. Don't forget to haggle and secure a price for either option before agreeing to an arrangement.

Dead set on car rental? La Romana airport has a branch of **Budget** (tel. 809/813-9111, www.budget.com). Another option is **Avis** (Calle Francisco del Castillo Márquez and Calle Duarte, tel. 809/550-0600, www.avis.com).

Bayahibe

Conveniently located near the La Romana airport and flanked to the south by the Parque Nacional del Este, the Bayahibe area is fast becoming a tourist destination. Traditionally, the area has been known as the doorway to the Parque Nacional del Este and the launching point to Isla Saona. But today, it is growing out of its "pit stop" reputation and becoming more of a hub for the resort-weary needing a change of scenery. Bayahibe's calm and low-key vibe provides a nice contrast to the sometimes over-stimulating poolside atmosphere of the all-inclusive resorts.

Until the late 1990s, this little seaside town was nearly untouched by tourism. Now, the resorts that populate the surrounding area are drawing tourists in record numbers. But the publicity has not turned this traditional fishing village into a cookie-cutter tourist trap yet. Bayahibe has been a favorite spot for independent travelers for many years and is still a good location for bargain hotels, cheap meals, and the quaint Caribbean experience that many are expecting when they book their trips to the Dominican Republic. Enjoying the slow pace of village life—hanging out in an open-air seafood restaurant and watching the fishermen haul in their day's catch—is a favorite way to spend time here. But action isn't too hard to find either. If you're not making use of the excursion desks at the mega-resorts, this is the place to find a local company to take you deep-sea fishing, scuba diving, or snorkeling. Some of the best diving in the country can be enjoyed at the offshore coral reefs and islands.

Despite the bulging tour industry waistline of the area, there is still no tourism office and very few services in the town of Bayahibe, but you will find small restaurants, cafés, a church, and some gift shops.

SIGHTS
Bayahibe and Dominicus Beaches
Playa Bayahibe (right in the town of

Bayahibe is a slow-paced fishing village.

© ANA CHAVIER CAAMAÑO

THE SOUTHEAST

Bayahibe), with its small sand stretch, has restaurants, services, boat captains, and food stands overlooking the beach, so you don't have to go far for anything. Sure, Playa Bayahibe isn't the postcard photo of a relaxing beach vacation you've traveled across the globe for, but if you go three miles east to **Playa Dominicus** you will find that photo-op. It is the first beach in the Dominican Republic to achieve the **Blue Flag Beach** status. This coveted eco-label gives high honors for a beach's commitment to sustainable development. It's the powdered sugar sand and crystal clear water you've been looking for. No heavy undertow makes it safer for swimming or snorkeling, too. The beach lies along the coast called Dominicus Americanus and has a free public parking lot; you can rent beach chairs. The easiest way to get between the two beaches is by taxi, which you can hail in the center of Bayahibe or outside the resorts of Dominicas Americanus (or call from your resort's front desk).

◖ Isla Saona

A trip to this island is the most popular excursion for those staying in Bayahibe, Punta Cana, and Bávaro hotels. Isla Saona, which is part of the Parque Nacional del Este just across the Bahía de Catalinita, attracts nearly 1,000 tourists a day.

Even back in the 16th and 17th centuries, Saona was used as a layover location. Spanish sailors struck a deal with Taíno chieftain Cotubanamá that allowed Isla Saona (originally named Adamanay by the Taínos) to be used as a minimart of sorts. The Spanish were allowed to stop and buy *casabe* bread made by the natives, gather firewood, and take a rest. It's not clear what the Taínos got out of the deal.

Today, the most exciting reason to go to Isla Saona is the "getting there." Through your resort or an independent company, you can book a catamaran, sailboat, or speedboat ride to the island for the day. The journey will show you the turquoise magnificence of the waters and the contrasting beauty of the limestone cliffs of the national park meeting the sea. Isla Saona sits in the crossing zone where the Caribbean and the Atlantic meet at the Canal de La Mona. Be on the lookout for dolphins; they've been known to follow the boats in this region!

The beaches of this 22-kilometer-long island are postcard worthy, with white sands and abundant palm trees. If you've booked through a resort, a barbecue-buffet lunch will most likely be provided on one of the beaches designated for the resort's use. The resorts also have open bars on "their" beaches for drinks. Ask a local to crack a coconut open for you for about US$2. Bring along a bottle of water.

A walk along the coast or on the inland trails of Saona is one way to escape the crowd

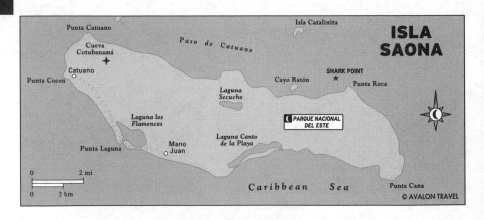

© ANA CHAVIER CAAMAÑO

the view from Isla Saona

on the beach (sort of) and add variety to your day. You'll need bug spray because the mosquitoes and sand flies can be more than bothersome. Saona's mangroves and lagoons are breeding grounds for many birds, including the Hispaniolan parrot, pelicans, and the red-footed booby. Flamingos can be found around the aptly named **Laguna de Los Flamencos** (Flamingo Lagoon) near the southwestern shore. Also on the western half of the island is the **Cueva Cotubanamá,** a cave where Chief Cotubanamá and his family hid out from the Spanish (they were eventually captured). It contains fine examples of rock art and can be reached by foot via a trail.

Mano Juan, a small, picturesque village on Isla Saona's southern shore, used to sustain itself with fishing but has now turned to the more lucrative (albeit less charming) hawking of trinkets to the tourists on the beach. Pastel homes line the beach so take your camera—this is the photo-op you've been waiting for.

Other than for lounging on the beach, Saona is known as a good spot for diving and snorkeling at the reefs just offshore. If you stay more toward shore, you'll see many shells and shrimp, but a little farther out await the giant sponges, coral, and colorful fish.

Unfortunately, the throngs of boats and hordes of tourists coming to spend the day on Isla Saona have done damage to its once serene underwater habitats and unspoiled beaches. Fuel in the water and noise levels of the boats add a congested feeling. With the popularity of this excursion growing, the problems are only increasing.

Reaching Isla Saona is easiest via Bayahibe, where there are a number of independent excursion vendors (see *Sports and Recreation*). Prices among them vary little.

◖ La Piscina Natural

La Piscina Natural, or Palmilla, as it's sometimes called, is a starfish-dotted sandbar in the waters between the Parque Nacional del Este and Isla Saona coastlines. Excursion boats whisking their customers to and from Isla Saona make a stopover in this spot where, more than a kilometer off the coast, one can wade around in clear water that never gets above the waist. It is a unique experience to be able to walk in the Caribbean Sea so far from land.

La Piscina, just like Isla Saona, is no longer a quiet paradise. It is heavily trodden by tourists, but it is easy to see why it's so popular. Under the warm water is a smooth blanket of white sand to walk upon. In some spots, you can sit with the water not even reaching your chin, and the ripples from approaching boats are the biggest waves you'll feel.

Although this site is a rare treat of striking beauty, the large number of boats dumping their fuel into the water here is taking its toll on the natural habitat for the starfish and other sea creatures. Unfortunately, some tour leaders and visitors are not careful when disturbing the red starfish whose home they are guests in; lifting them from the water for anything longer than just a few seconds kills them. If you want photos, get an underwater camera. During high tourist season, La Piscina can sometimes resemble freeway gridlock or a bar in the middle of the sea because of the numerous rum drinks and parties.

(Parque Nacional del Este

Declared a national park in 1975, Parque Nacional del Este is in the southeastern end of the country in the province of Altagracia between the towns of Bayahibe and Boca de Yuma. Its surface area includes the entire peninsula south of those two towns and is 808 square kilometers, of which 420 are land (including the islands of Catalina, Saona, and Catalinita), while 388 square kilometers are oceanic.

The peninsula is a combination of subtropical humid forest and dry forest with an average rainfall of about 120 centimeters a year. This region is notoriously hot. But if you can stand the heat and are interested in birdwatching, this park is a good location to spot 114 types of birds, including rare ones such as the white-crowned pigeon *(Columba leucocephala)*, the Hispaniolan parrot *(Amazona ventralis)*, the brown pelican *(Pelecanus occidentalis)*, the red-footed boobie *(Sula sula)*, the magnificent frigatebird *(Fregata magnificens)*,

the barn owl *(Tyto alba)*, and the herring gull *(Larus argentatus)*.

Topographically, the changing sea levels over the last million years created the peninsula out of limestone, resulting in a series of terraces and cliffs along the shoreline. Throughout the peninsula, traces of pre-Columbian Taíno life abound in subterranean tunnels and caves where many pictographs have been found. Although there are over 400 caves in the park, **Cueva del Puenta** is the easiest to visit by foot. It holds a small example of Taíno drawings depicting their culture, along with many stalactites and stalagmites. To access this cave, you will need to find a guide at the ranger post located about five kilometers past Dominicus Americanus. You will pay a small entrance fee to the park of about US$3 and you will get a guide who will accompany you to the site and show you some of the drawings. Make sure to take a flashlight and wear good walking shoes. The tour takes about a half an hour.

The park's coastline offers a variety of coral formations and is excellent for diving, especially along the western side. The eastern side of the peninsula has more limestone cliffs that drop off dramatically into the ocean. The southern tip has mangroves and saltwater lagoons and is a good spot to find birdlife. Many animals whose existence is threatened live in this protected area. Manatees *(Trichechus manatus)*, the bottle-nosed dolphin *(Turisops truncates)*, and various sea turtles swim the waters. The rat-like solenodon *(Solenodon paradoxus)*, the hutia *(Plagiodontia aedium)*, and the rhinoceros iguana *(Cyclura cornuta)* are found on land.

There is a **Park Office** (tel. 809/833-0022, 9 A.M.–1 P.M. daily) in the parking lot of Bayahibe where you can buy necessary permits (such as camping permits for Isla Catalinita), pay entrance into the park (RD$100), and ask questions about the park. If you have more in-depth questions regarding the Parque Nacional del Este contact **The Ecotourism Department of the National Parks Office** (tel. 809/472-3717), located next to Santo Domingo's zoological gardens. Camping is not permitted for tourists in the Parque Nacional del Este.

One of the most popular ways to gain access to the park is to hire a boat (and guide) in the Bayahibe harbor. Your guide will take you along the shore, and from there you can hike into the *parque*. These prices are negotiable and vary quite a bit. Always agree on a price before setting out. If you're coming via car, there are entrances at Bayahibe on the western edge and Boca de Yuma on the eastern side. Don't forget to get your entrance tickets at the ranger stations first. Hiring a guide for a hike will cost roughly RD$450 per group.

Isla Catalinita

Just off the eastern shore of the Parque Nacional del Este sits a tiny little uninhabited island very popular for diving and snorkeling excursions. Located where the Atlantic Ocean meets the Caribbean Sea, this is a spot to see bigger sharks, eagle rays, sea turtles, and more marine life. The coral reefs offer waters perfect for snorkeler's delights. Camping is possible on the island, but you'll need a permit. **Scubafun** (Calle Principal 28, Bayahibe, tel. 809/833-0003, fax 809/833-0005, www.scubafun.info, 7:30 A.M.–6 P.M. daily) will take you out to Isla Catalinita and Isla Saona in an all-day trip that includes a trip through mangroves, diving at **Shark Point,** snorkeling, lunch at Isla Saona, and splashing around at the Piscina Natural (US$70).

SPORTS AND RECREATION
Diving and Snorkeling

Located in the waters of Bayahibe are some of the country's best sites for diving and snorkeling. The warm Caribbean Sea offers perfect crystalline visibility and warm conditions for experienced and beginning divers. The calmness of these waters and the underwater terrain, compared to the rougher areas off the other coasts of the island, also make it easier for beginners.

The **St. George Wreck** was scuttled in 1999 as an artificial reef off the coast of the port of Bayahibe. It sits upright about 30–40 meters below the surface, and the currents can be rather strong down there, so this is a site for experienced divers only. You will see loads of marine life and have the chance to enter cabins and the cargo room. Another exciting dive site is **Padre Nuestro** cave. Well, it's more of a flooded 290-meter sweet-water tunnel. Again, only experienced divers will be able to explore the stalactites and stalagmites in this subterranean dive.

Excursions and Tours

At all-inclusive resorts, the activity desks offer many excursions, tours, and packages that can be added to your vacation. But for independent travelers, a few establishments in Bayahibe offer similar excursions.

Casa Daniel (Bayahibe, tel. 809/833-0050, www.casa-daniel.com, 8 A.M.–6 P.M. daily) is right on the waterfront at Bayahibe. Daniel and his wife, Susan, have put together a multilingual dive team that leads excursions in German, English, French, and Spanish. While beginners and experienced divers can both enjoy the colorful reef life in depths varying 10–25 meters, special excursions like night dives, wreck dives (*St. George*), cave trips (Padre Nuestro), and deeper dives are only offered to experienced divers. Without equipment rental, one-tank dives cost US$38. Packages of 6–10 dives are available (US$250–390). Equipment rental costs extra. A full-day snorkeling excursion to Saona and Catalinita costs US$76. In addition to snorkeling at the islands, you'll make stops to see some of the mangrove forest and La Piscina Natural. Inquire about family packages to Saona and Catalina Islands (price depends on the number of people in the party). PADI certification courses, refresher courses, and specialty courses are all available. Casa Daniel is perhaps the best choice, if only for its local reputation.

Scubafun (Calle Principal 28, Bayahibe, tel. 809/833-0003, fax 809/833-0005, www. scubafun.info, 7:30 A.M.–6 P.M. daily) is in the middle of Bayahibe. Want to do that cave diving at Padre Nuestro? Scubafun can take you there, including the tanks, weights, and a guide for US$69. Other excursions include a half-day boat trip to Isla Catalina that includes diving The Wall (US$45), as well as a full day at Isla Saona with drinks and a buffet lunch (US$59). A PADI certification beginner course is only US$235. Scubafun excursions are recommended for parties that have both divers and non-divers since they allow non-divers to join. This is a top-notch outfitter.

If you would like to try hiring a private boat, remember to always haggle the price before settling on the agreement. A reasonable price to expect for a ride from Bayahibe to Isla Saona is about RD$1,000–2,000 per person. Remember to ask if there are lifejackets in the vessel before boarding and ask to see them. Hint: If you agree to use the same boat for your return trip, secure the time and you may get a better price, but don't pay ahead of time for both ways, of course.

ACCOMMODATIONS

Bayahibe, try as it might, simply hasn't lifted itself up to the gold star status of Punta Cana's reputation in the tourism industry. A fair amount of construction and marketing went into the endeavor over the years to encourage visitor flow to this part of the country. Still, the deals in the all-inclusive resorts here remain better than those in the Punta Cana and Bávaro branches. That being said, choosing a hotel here could come down simply to where you get the best deal because they are all competing for your business. Don't count out the budget options in town either. If you don't plan on spending a lot of time in your room, they are perfectly viable solutions to an economical vacation since they are clean and well maintained. Be specific if you want air-conditioning or not; there is a few dollars difference in price at the budget hotels.

Under US$50

Within town, there are many options within walking distance of one another.

Hotel Bayahibe (Calle Principal, tel. 809/833-0159, www.hotelbayahibe.net, reservations@hotelbayahibe.net, US$40 d with breakfast) is the best bet in the budget category and has been a mainstay in Bayahibe for the independent traveler. Reservations are essential, particularly in peak season, as it tends to fill up quickly. There are 25 rooms, and all are equipped with hot-water bathrooms, air-conditioning, TV, phone, and refrigerator. Some have a kitchenette, which is great if you don't plan to dine out every meal. Rooms on the lower floor can be noisy, so if possible, request one on the top floor. Hotel Bayahibe is best for access to the sea and dive centers, and it offers free beach towels. They have their own restaurant, **Don Negro Restaurant,** which serves breakfast and dinner with a Creole and international menu. This hotel is the best of the budget options.

Cabañas Francisca (Calle Segunda, Bayahibe, tel. 809/556-2742, US$21 d) is next to the Hotel Bayahibe. You can get a very basic room for quite cheap. Request air-conditioning for a few dollars more. You will have cable TV, a refrigerator, and your own bathroom, but no hot water (time to hone your speedy shower skills).

Cabaña Trip Town (Calle Principal, no phone, US$24 d with air-conditioning, US$21 d without air-conditioning) is across from the Hotel Bayahibe. Parking is available for this pink and white 14-cabana hotel. All rooms have two beds (one double and one single). The maximum number of people allowed in a room is three, but you pay the same rate as you would if it were just two. Rooms have their own hot-water bathroom and TV. The ocean is a two-minute walk.

Villa Iguana (Bayahibe, tel. 809/833-0203, cell 809/757-1059, www.villaiguana.de, US$39 d) is a German-owned hotel associated with the scuba excursion company Scubafun. Together, they offer dive and accommodation packages. In the hotel, there are seven standard rooms (with private bath, air-conditioning, fridge, and safe) and three apartments (with kitchenette, private bath, one bedroom, an extra bed for a third person in the living room, and a safe; some have balconies). There is one penthouse suite available, which occupies the entire fourth floor; you can enjoy your ocean view, air-conditioning, fridge, private bath, private pool, outdoor living room, and sun deck for only US$69! All rooms are very clean and a good value.

US$50-100

If neither low-budget options nor mega-complex resorts appeal to you, **Cabaña Elke** (Av. Eladia, Dominicus Americanus, tel. 809/689-8249, www.viwi.it, room US$65 d, apartment US$80 d) might be perfect. Although not in the town of Bayahibe, it is near the beach of Dominicus, just south of town. Guests enjoy clean accommodations (either standard rooms or apartment style), a pool, bar, and restaurant (for lunch and dinner only). Apartments have a sitting area, kitchenette, and a loft bedroom and face the garden and pool area. This is a hotel to escape to since there are no phones or televisions in the rooms. A plus to Cabaña Elke is that it is directly behind the Viva Wyndham Dominicus Beach resort, so Elke guests can purchase a day pass to the swanky Wyndham grounds for US$40 a day, thereby enjoying the best beach in the area without having to commit to the giant all-inclusive style or price.

US$100 and Up

In the last 10 years, all-inclusive resorts have begun to sprout up near the town of Bayahibe; prior to that, most all-inclusives in this region were relegated to the Punta Cana/Bávaro area. But with the popularity of this type of vacation package, coupled with the pristine beauty of the beaches near Bayahibe, these plush resorts can't help but be manicured, luxurious, and pampering. After all, they are all fighting for your business and the competition is stiff. The surreal part of it is that in this all-inclusive rat race, they can end up like cookie-cutter replicas offering accommodations and amenities similar to one another. Most resorts' rooms have two double beds or a king-size bed, minibar, air-conditioning, fan, hair dryer, iron, cable TV, phone, hot-water bathrooms, and terrace. In-room security boxes are available, but usually for an extra charge. And as with most things in the Dominican Republic, if you tip your chambermaid you're likely to get better service such as more towels in your bathroom or a fully stocked minibar refrigerator.

Prices for all-inclusives in this section are based on double occupancy of a standard room per night in high season. Traveling in low season will reduce the cost. If wheelchair accessibility is a priority for your room, make reservations far in advance as many only have a few rooms specifically designed to suit your needs.

Iberostar Hacienda Dominicus (Playa Dominicus, Dominicus Americanus, tel. 809/688-3600 or 888/923-2722, fax 809/221-0921, www.iberostar.com, US$150 d), about five kilometers south of Bayahibe, has one of the best beaches around, complete with a lively lighthouse bar right on the sand. The impressively luxurious lobby is the tip-off for the extreme comfort of the entire resort. The grounds are perfectly maintained, where flamingos and peacocks wander around the many fountains and tropical foliage. There are five restaurants (one buffet and four à la carte) to choose from, a variety of bars (including a disco for nighttime entertainment), three swimming pools (plus one kiddie pool), various shops, and nightly entertainment in the resort's theater. Amenities include Internet access, health care, massage (extra charge), fitness room, water sports (kayaking, snorkeling, and windsurfing are available with free equipment), and daytime poolside entertainment. Hacienda Dominicus has almost 500 rooms, all of which are very comfortable (huge showers, too!) and meet the high demands of their growing American clientele. It claims five-star hotel quality, and indeed gives you most everything you need. However, the food is where the five-star claim gets only *a bit* exaggerated. Despite the number of restaurants to choose from, the choices can get a bit repetitious if you are there for longer than a week.

Dreams La Romana Resort & Spa (Playa Bayahibe, tel. 809/221-8880, www. dreamsresorts.com, starting at US$189 d) is a confusing name for the location, but this is situated on Playa Bayahibe. This is the recently upgraded Sunscape Casa del Mar Resort. With the changing of the guard came significant changes in style. The rooms are wonderfully appointed, huge, clean, and modern with flat-screen TVs, wireless Internet, luxurious bathrooms, and electronic safety box. The rooms are kept very clean and have turn-down service. There are nine restaurants on-site, including the casual World Café, serving international fare, and the restaurant Bordeaux, for adults only, which is a candlelit romance-inspiring French venue.

There are three spas on-site for added relaxation, and they offer a full range of body treatments as well as cedar saunas, indoor and outdoor hydrotherapy pools, steam rooms, reflexology therapies, and a spa boutique. Can't stand the idea of missing football while you're away? American football fans will be pleased to know that Dreams has a Monday Night Football beach party. Tailgating never felt like this. A 10-meter screen is set up on the Caribbean sand, and you're in a beach lounger (ice-cold beer in hand, of course) with all the American-favorite football foods, like wings, popcorn, burgers, and pizza—it's definitely a unique way to watch football. The folks back home will be jealous! The resort has a full activity list for kids and teens too. Kids can play on the ocean trampoline, take part in a treasure hunt, have storytelling time, arts and crafts, and video games. The Core Zone Teen Club has late-night discos, weekly bonfires on the beach, snack bars that serve non-alcoholic drinks, and a rock climbing wall for starters. It truly is a place for the whole family.

In the 532-room **Oasis Canoa** (Playa Dominicus, tel. 809/682-2662, www.hotelesoasis.com, from US$150 d), you will find spacious rooms with all the comfortable amenities of an all-inclusive resort. This is a popular resort with the European traveler, so expect the food in the buffet to be more suited to their tastes and traditions. There are six restaurants (Italian and Tex Mex are among the specialties) and five bars, including a disco, where the music seems to pack more punch than the drinks. But it's the beach that puts a happy smile on the guests' faces. The water is a magnificently clear blue, and oddly enough, there's

not much of a fight for beach chairs. Other on-site amenities include tennis, scuba lessons, a full-service spa at extra charge, baby-sitting service, fitness center, and all nonmotorized water sports, which are included in the cost of your stay. There is also a spa. Children under the age of five stay free.

The 《 **Viva Wyndham Dominicus Beach** (Playa Dominicus, Dominicus Americanus, tel. 809/686-5658, www.vivaresorts.com, starting at US$190 d) and its sister resort, the **Viva Wyndham Dominicus Palace** (Playa Dominicus, Dominicus Americanus, tel. 809/686-5658, www.vivaresorts.com, starting at US$230 d), share a glorious three-kilometer expanse of Bayahibe beach, perhaps the best of the area. It is big enough so that the lively events (volleyball, beach aerobics, and merengue) happening at one end of the beach won't disturb your hard-earned afternoon siesta under the hundreds of palm trees.

The bigger of the two, Dominicus Beach, has a whopping 530 rooms available as standard, superior, or bungalows. Aside from the fantastic beach, there are three pools and four diverse restaurants, four bars, daily and nightly entertainment, a supervised kids' club, dive center, and many sports (four tennis courts, a basketball court, and even a soccer field) and activities to squelch any boredom that might occur. Guests of Dominicus Beach can use the spa at Dominicus Palace for an additional fee. Take your own snorkel gear, though; the hotel doesn't rent the equipment out because there aren't any sections of water blocked off for snorkelers and boats tend to speed by carelessly. The reef is beautiful nonetheless, and worth the effort if you play it safe. The Dominicus Beach is very popular with the Italian travelers, so it has a livelier atmosphere, and dressing up at night is common.

Dominicus Palace is the smaller of the two sister properties, with just 330 rooms within several colonial-style buildings and one pool. Seven restaurants offer many choices, including the open-air, oceanfront buffet where the cuisine is served up accompanied by a refreshing breeze rolling in from the Caribbean Sea.

Not a bad way to wake up in the morning. Also on-site are two bars, a disco, a spa, dive center, tour desk, a kids' club, and entertainment programs.

Dominicus Palace offers a full-service spa. You have full access to facilities at Viva Wyndham Dominicus Beach and its amenities, such as the lighted tennis courts and multiple pools, just a stroll in the sand away.

FOOD AND NIGHTLIFE

With a view of the bay of Bayahibe, **Restaurante Mare Nostrum** (Calle Principal, tel. 809/833-0055, Mon.–Sat. for lunch and dinner, US$15–25) offers a first-rate Italian dinner in a chic setting. Homemade pasta, risotto, seafood, and a tasty wine selection are begging to be enjoyed.

Restaurante La Punta (Calle Principal 20, tel. 809/833-0082, 11:30 A.M.–9 P.M. daily, US$10–25) is a long-time favorite with tourists. The seafood is the best in town, very fresh, and a great break from the all-inclusive food, which can be bland and repetitious. It is right on the beachfront and serves seafood dishes and Caribbean-style cocktails. Grilled lobster is tops here.

Casual **Bamboo Beach Bar Restaurant and Grill** (US$7–20), right on the point of Bayahibe, has a wide variety of pizzas and seafood.

Café Restaurante Leidy (right on the point, US$5–15) serves breakfast, lunch, and dinner on the eastern side of Playa Bayahibe. Seafood, pasta, chicken, pork, and beef choices are numerous, all to be enjoyed in a breezy atmosphere.

Lively **Big Sur** (Playa Bayahibe, open nightly) disco is popular with tourists and locals alike. It is a casual, open-air (that means no air conditioner), thatch-roofed disco that really gets hopping with *bachata* and merengue when the locals arrive after their workweek is over. Big Sur is right on the point of Bayahibe.

Restaurante Yssamar (right on the point, no phone, US$10–20) is the definition of unpretentious dining. Renowned for its seafood, casual atmosphere, and location right on the point in Bayahibe, Restaurante Yssamar places its tables directly on the sand under a thatched roof. Especially good is the lobster or squid in typical Dominican sauces.

Colmado Billy (Bayahibe, no phone, 7:30 A.M.–10 P.M. Mon.–Sat., 7:30 A.M.–7 P.M. Sun.) is a typical Dominican *colmado* (small grocer). Standard staples include canned and dried goods, rum, bread, and cheese. But even more typical is how this *colmado* doubles as the get-ready-to-roll meeting point for the evening's events. Have an ice-cold Presidente with the locals and chill out to the tunes of the tinkling *bachata* that is sure to be pouring out over the radio, because this is not just a grocery store; it's a hangout joint.

INFORMATION AND SERVICES

While Bayahibe is definitely the sort of town where an independent traveler can lounge around feeling the vibe of being immersed in the culture of Dominican life and lose track of time, one can also become acutely aware of the lack of information and services that are available in Bayahibe. In 2009, there was no Internet communication service and still no tourism office. If you are staying in an all-inclusive resort, you will likely have Internet services there (most likely slow).

Money

To change U.S. dollars, euros, or traveler's checks, you can go to **Agencia de Cambio Sánchez** (Calle Principal, Bayahibe, tel. 809/833-0201, 8 A.M.–10 P.M. Mon.–Sat., 8 A.M.–6 P.M. Sun.), the only exchange center in Bayahibe. It's right next to Hotel Llave del Mar. **Western Union** (Bayahibe, 8 A.M.–6 P.M. daily) is another place where you can change money. You can also make long-distance calls. Try to get small bills. Dominicans hate receiving large bills for anything and will try to refuse to make change. In part it is because it makes haggling for lower prices a lot more difficult. They will argue that they "don't have change." You will be forced to give the bigger bill up.

THE SOUTHEAST

There are **ATMs** in many of the big resorts; they dispense pesos only. It is best to bring cash with you if you need small bills for tipping since the dollar is more appreciated in today's economy than the Dominican peso.

For a bank in Bayahibe, try **BanReservas,** which may have a small branch with no ATM next to Hotel Bayahibe.

Banco Popular (Dominicus Americanus, open 24 hours) is by the Wyndham Dominicus Beach Hotel and has an ATM.

GETTING THERE

Bayahibe is only 25 minutes east of La Romana, two hours east of Santo Domingo, one hour and 45 minutes west of Punta Cana, and 40 minutes south of Higüey. La Romana international airport is the most convenient arrival port for Bayahibe and Dominicus Americanus. Highway 3 will lead you to a southbound road about two kilometers long that forks off leading you to the two beaches. Go right and you'll get the dirt road to Bayahibe. Choose left and you'll get the paved road to Dominicus Americanus.

A *público* from La Romana to Bayahibe will cost you US$2.50. A *guagua* to and from La Romana (every 20 minutes all day long until 7 P.M.) is US$1.50, and to or from Higüey (every 40 minutes) will run you US$2. To catch a *guagua,* check across from the Super

Colmado Bayahibe in the town center. Try to have small bills or exact change.

Taking a taxi is a more expensive option, but perhaps the most reliable form of transport: From La Romana Airport it's US$45; Higüey, US$65; Las Américas international airport, US$90; Punta Cana airport, US$90. Prices can vary from taxi to taxi, so definitely haggle and settle on the rate and if you'll be paying in dollars or pesos before getting into the car. It is best to have correct change. Taxis tend to stop outside the major resort area of Dominicus Americanus (outside Viva Wyndham Dominicus Beach) or in the center of Bayahibe.

If you are staying at one of the big resorts, arranging transportation with their shuttle services is a breeze, and the cost is usually included in your package. Ask while booking your trip.

GETTING AROUND

Bayahibe is a very manageable town to walk. Your feet are free transportation, and everything is within a *plátano*'s throw. A few *motoconchos* that hang out in the center of town can take you where you need to go for about US$1. Most people only use them for transport to the main highway, where they can flag down a *guagua* to La Romana or Higüey. Car-rental agencies are congregated in Dominicus Americanus around the big hotels.

Higüey

A bustling town with a population of nearly 150,000, Higüey is best known for the Basilica de Nuestra Señora de la Altagracia, which contains a shrine to the Virgin Mary that draws religious pilgrims from all over the country seeking forgiveness and miracles. Although Higüey doesn't have much to offer tourists, the basilica is indeed worth a visit if you happen to be passing through.

Higüey is the hub town for the southeastern corner of the Dominican Republic. In the heart of La Altagracia province, Higüey is a

nucleus for agriculture. Sugar, coffee, tobacco, cacao, rice, and corn are significant contributors to local economy, as are the cattle and pork industries. Transportation converges here as well. If you are taking any bus within the eastern half of the country, you are likely to catch a connection in this dusty town. Buses coming from Sabana de la Mar, Bávaro, La Romana, and Santo Domingo all join here to swap passengers.

The Taínos referred to this region as the "land where the sun was born." And indeed

THE MYSTERIES OF LA ALETA

In 1997, scientists were wandering around in the Parque Nacional del Este and stumbled upon a subterranean chamber more than 30 meters deep and filled with water. Diving in temperatures of roughly 24°C (74°F), the scientists encountered three layers of water, two clear and one middle sulfuric layer. Below this sulfur layer, many Taíno artifacts were found on a mound, perfectly preserved because of the lack of ambient light (thanks to the sulfur layer) and because of a lack of oxygen in the environment. Wooden artifacts, *higüeros* (gourds), baskets, war clubs, bowls, hatchet handles, and ceramic vessels were found. It is possible that looters made off with highly decorated items. Carbon dating of what the scientists were able to hold on to dated the artifacts to A.D. 1035-1420. Because of the level of preservation, the Manantial de La Aleta (Spring of the Fin) is one of the most important archaeological sites in the Caribbean.

But what were these things doing that far underground? Analysis of the items indicates that the well at La Aleta was ceremonial. Some of the decorated pottery may have held offerings of food, and some had images of bats on them. The Taínos considered bats sacred. A very rare *dujo*, which is a wooden stool made solely for a Taíno chief to sit on during ceremo-

nies, was also found. It is quite literally a "seat of power." Another artifact was a wooden vomiting spatula, which was an item used in the *cohoba* ceremonies and ritual feasts. (*Cohoba* is a powerful hallucinogenic made from the seeds of a *Piptadenia peregrina*.) The idea behind its usage was to pass successfully through a stage of a ritual meant to purify the body by vomiting before communing with the *zemis* (spiritual beings).

The province of Higüey seemed to be an important ceremonial center for the easternmost of the five provinces of the island at the time. Also near the well are four plazas used for public ceremonies, ritual dances, and ball games. That this many ritual places were found concentrated in one area (the greatest number grouped together on the island of Hispaniola) marks La Aleta as a prominent place in the province of Higüey and indicates that its importance was primarily religious. It seems to have been a largely ceremonial center, not a place that people called home on a permanent basis.

Taínos threw the objects (spiritual gifts) in the well, which seemed from the surface to be a bottomless portal into the underworld. Items dropped down the well would disappear from view the moment they hit the sulfuric layer of water, adding to the mystery.

the sun's rays feel ultra-strong here—sunscreen is a must-have when visiting this town.

SIGHTS
La Basilica de Nuestra Señora de la Altagracia

The basilica (8 A.M.–6 P.M. Mon.–Sat., 8 A.M.–8 P.M. Sun.) is definitely the focal point of Higüey and an important structure in the predominantly Catholic Dominican Republic. It is the house of the patron saint of all Dominicans, Our Lady of Altagracia, the Virgin Mary. Construction began during Trujillo's dictatorship in 1954, was inaugurated by Pope John Paul in 1971, but wasn't actually completed until Balaguer's presidency in 1972. The basilica sits on 40,000 square meters, and

the basilica itself is about 4,600 square meters. Its signature, enormous concrete arches loom 80 meters into the Higüey sky, signifying the shape of praying hands, and were designed by the French team of Pierre Dupré and Dovnoyer de Segonzac. The eclectic design allows a harmonious mixture of the traditional Catholic footprint shape of a cross, coupled with a modern rising form. Inside, parishioners hear mass under multiple arches that lead to the altar and frame a magnificent stained glass wall behind it.

Even more famous than the celebrated architecture of the basilica itself is the encased, framed painting of the Virgen de La Altagracia (Virgin of the Higher Grace). This depiction of the Holy Mother draws pilgrims from all over the country, who form a line to one by one

THE SOUTHEAST

THE PAINTING OF THE VIRGIN MARY

The painting of the Virgin Mary on the altar in the Basilica de Nuestra Señora de la Altagracia is encased not only in glass but also in a fog of legend and folklore. There are many tales of how the painting came to be depending on whom you ask. How did the painting make it to the basilica? Who brought it? Renditions and versions swirl around in the oral-tradition mixer of Dominican culture.

In one version, a merchant was asked by his daughter to get a portrait of Our Lady of Altagracia on his next trip to Santo Domingo. He'd never heard the title and was discussing it while staying overnight at a friend's house just as an old bearded man happened by. The old man pulled a painting out of his satchel and said that it was what the merchant had been searching for, the Virgin of Altagracia. The merchant and his friend gave the old man a place to stay for the night, but by morning he was gone and they never saw him again. The merchant took the painting to his elated

daughter. They placed it on the mantel in their home, but it kept disappearing, whereupon they would find it again outside. They finally placed it in a church.

Another legend says a sick child from Higüey gave an old man (thought to be an apostle) a meal and a place to stay, so the man healed her and in the morning left the portrait for her.

Perhaps the most popular story is the one where a sick little girl was visited by the Virgin Mary, who appeared to her in an orange tree that once stood in the place of the original basilica. (In yet another version, it was three children!) A portrait of the Virgin Mary appeared under the tree, so the child/children took it home; by morning, the portrait had disappeared and was found back under the tree. The painting is now built into the basilica.

To this day, orange trees are a major theme in the artwork throughout the basilica, and on January 21 oranges are prominent, sold in piles for the Día de la Altagracia festival.

worship and ask for healing miracles. Prepare to stand in line as some have much to say to her.

The basilica also has artwork on either side of the altar by the Spanish muralist José Vela Zanetti. On the edges of the massive parking lot and across the street from the basilica are various memorabilia stands and shops where you can purchase a wide assortment of trinkets such as candles, plastic rosaries, and photos of the Pope. Wear clothing that respectfully covers your knees and shoulders or you won't be allowed to enter the basilica.

Mercado de Higüey

Higüey is the center of the Southeast's very fertile agricultural region. Why go to a grocery store when this is the place to shop for avocados the size of a toddler's head? The produce of this outdoor market (Av. La Libertad, between Guerrero del Rosario and Las Carreras, Mon.–Sat. 8 A.M.–5 P.M.) is overflowing and the crowd is buzzing with life. This is a great way to experience zippy Higüey life with the

locals and buy fresh fruit and vegetables at very low cost, all while supporting the local farmers and economy.

There are many snack and lunch stands at the major intersections. You can get treats like *pastelitos* (a fried, meat-filled puff pastry), sweets, freshly squeezed fruit juices, sandwiches, and cold beverages.

FESTIVALS

On January 21, **Día de la Altagracia,** thousands of devoted pilgrims from all over the Dominican Republic come to La Basilica de Nuestra Señora de la Altagracia to fulfill promises made in prayer to the Virgin Mary, the Dominican patron saint, and touch the painting of her that hangs behind the altar.

But it's not only Catholicism that draws people to Higüey for Altagracia Day. As with anything in the Dominican Republic, where there is a gathering, there is dancing in the streets to blaring merengue music and flowing rum. Oranges, conveniently in season this time of year, are abundantly for sale in honor of the legend that the Virgin Mary appeared in an orange tree to a sick little girl, miraculously healing her.

ACCOMMODATIONS

While not a destination city, Higüey has a couple of options for a good night's sleep. **Hotel Santa Clara** (Lic Felix Servio Ducoudray 9, tel. 809/554-2040, US$15 d with fan only) has 31 very clean and comfortable, albeit small and simple, rooms (US$22 d with air-conditioning—in Higüey it is a good investment). All rooms have TV and private baths with hot water. There is a small kitchenette on the main floor off the central courtyard where you can make coffee or heat up food. Parking is available across the street.

Hotel Restaurant Don Carlos (Calle Juan Ponce de León at Sánchez, tel. 809/554-2344, US$26–35 d, front desk open 24 hours) has 62 rooms. Although it's older and, therefore, not as well kept as the Hotel Santa Clara, it is a good bet for availability and has a startlingly splendid restaurant. All rooms have air-conditioning, hot water bathrooms, and cable TV. The hotel consists of two buildings; one is older than the other, and the price difference depends on which side you get. Request a room in the "newer" of the two wings. It is cleaner and definitely less run-down. The Don Carlos has a bar that stays open until 2:30 A.M. and offers light *picaderas* (appetizers).

FOOD

Hotel Restaurant Don Carlos (Calle Juan Ponce de León at Sánchez, tel. 809/554-2344, 7 A.M.–11:30 P.M. daily, US$2–18), two blocks behind the basilica, serves traditional Dominican and foreign dishes in a casual environment and has long been popular with travelers and locals alike. Breakfast, lunch, and dinner are all available. For lunch and dinner, the plate of the day is only US$2, which usually consists of chicken, rice, and beans, or *la bandera dominicana* (chicken, rice and beans, and fried plantains).

The Dominican fast-food chicken joint **Pollo Victorina** (Plaza El Naranjo, Av. La Altagracia, tel. 809/554-5616) is not a culinary marvel, but it is an option for a quick, cheap meal on the go. It is conveniently located near Plaza El Naranjo and the basilica.

For a nice meal close to the basilica, try **El Meson de Cervantes** (Arzobispo Nouel 79, tel. 809/554-2754, 10 A.M.–midnight daily, US$7–15) for some traditional Dominican dishes (their specialty is meat, like beefsteak with onions), but they also have seafood and vegetable dishes. Service is good too.

INFORMATION AND SERVICES

Avenida La Libertad is the main commercial street in Higüey. Driving or walking along it, you will come across markets, restaurants, and shops. If you're passing through, visiting the basilica, and only need a few provisions, **Plaza Barcelona** (Av. La Altagracia at Av. Juan XXIII) is a strip mall near the basilica where you can find fast food at **Pollo Victorina,** gas and snacks at **Esso,** Internet access at **Tropical Internet Access Center** (tel. 809/554-3576, 9 A.M.–10 P.M. Mon.–Sat., 9 A.M.–5 P.M. Sun.), and an ATM at **Banco Popular** (8:15 A.M.–4 P.M. Mon.–Fri., 9 A.M.–1 P.M. Sun.).

Banco León (Av. La Altagracia 51, tel. 809/554-5301, www.leon.com.do, 8:15 A.M.–4 P.M. Mon.–Fri., 9 A.M.–1 P.M. Sun.) also has an ATM.

The Higüey **post office** is on Calle Agustín Guerrero (8 A.M.–3 P.M. Mon.–Fri.), but use the services at a resort instead since postal services in the Dominican Republic are generally poor to horrible.

GETTING THERE AND AROUND

The Higüey bus station is located right across from the basilica, which is very convenient in order to see it in between transfers. The *guagua* station, on the other hand, is farther east of the basilica. This is a very inconvenient transfer if you have lots of luggage. So if you want to see the basilica, stick with a simple bus transfer.

From Santo Domingo, you can catch a 2.25-hour bus ride at the **Sichoprola** bus station

(J. Ravelo 92, by Parque Enriquillo, tel. 809/686-0637, 6 A.M.–6 P.M. daily, US$5.10) to Higüey, making stops along the way. Once in Higüey, it makes various stops including in front of the basilica and at other bus stations where you can transfer to another bus if your final destination is not Higüey. Buses from Sabana de la Mar, Miches, Punta Cana/Bávaro, La Romana, and Santo Domingo all connect here. Tell the bus driver where you need to go and you'll be taken to the right spot. When boarding and purchasing your ticket, ask where the bus is going; some have signs displaying their destinations, but not always. The connecting buses have frequent departures during the day, but after sunset it is very limited. Start out early if traveling by bus.

Guaguas bound for Punta Cana, Bávaro (RD$100), and Miches can be found at the *guagua* terminal located on Calle Luperón and Avenida Libertad.

The Mella Highway connects Santo Domingo and Higüey. Once in Higüey, eastbound Avenida La Libertad becomes Highway 105, which leads to a connection to Bávaro and the rest of the Costa del Coco. Southbound Avenida Hermanos Trejo becomes Highway 4, which leads you to Boca de Yuma and the La Romana turnoff. Alternatively, west-running Avenida La Altagracia becomes Highway 4 outside of town and will take you to El Seibo and Hato Mayor.

To get around town, simply flag down a taxi. Higüey is filled with them during all hours.

AROUND HIGÜEY
La Otra Banda

A few kilometers north of Higüey is the eccentric town of La Otra Banda, known for maintaining its gingerbread architecture, which the founding fathers brought from the Canary Islands. This is a photographer's opportunity to get photos of the pretty little houses you see on postcards. After the concrete and lusterless town of Higüey, La Otra Banda is a welcome pass-through point.

As if not to appear "too cute," though, La Otra Banda is also known for its butchers and meat since the livestock industry supports this area. It is common to see cuts of meat and freshly made strings of *longaniza* (sausages) hanging in market windows; this can be an odd sight. Exercise caution in buying these meats; they've often been sitting out for quite some time and (unfortunately) might not be entirely safe for the fragile stomachs of foreigners.

While you are there, check out the Dominican jewelry store **Harrison's** (Carretera Otra Banda, tel. 809/552-1997) and its high-quality amber, larimar, and Dominican black jade pieces.

Coming from Higüey on Highway 105, you'll reach a fork in the road where you can choose to stay the course on Highway 105 toward El Macao or take a right onto Avenida Macao, which becomes Highway 106 toward the Bávaro/Punta Cana resort area on the Costa del Coco.

Boca de Yuma

Farther south along Highway 4, at the mouth of the Bahía de Yuma and near the entrance to Parque Nacional del Este, is the town of Boca de Yuma. Before Hurricane Georges blasted through in 1998, leaving hotels in ruins and seafood restaurants upturned in its wake, Boca de Yuma was a quaint fishing village that annually hosted an international deep-sea fishing tournament. Even though those days are gone, you can still get some great seafood here.

Now, unfortunately, there is only one hotel in town, and a few places to eat, but don't expect any services. This is a tiny Dominican town. Travelers wanting to flee from the hordes of tourists in the more trodden areas of Punta Cana and even Bayahibe will find solace in a nice day trip at Boca de Yuma's rocky shoreline to watch the colorful wooden fishing boats bob in the surf. The best way to get here is in your own vehicle.

SIGHTS

Playa Borinquen is a pretty beach that is reachable by boat. You will need to hire a fishing boat captain to row you across the Río Yuma for RD$30 each way. The trip takes about 10 minutes. After you arrive, there are steps and a short hike to the actual beach.

The limestone cave **Cueva de Berna** (8 A.M.–2 P.M. daily), just southwest of Boca de Yuma, has an impressive deposit of Taíno rupestrian art. Unfortunately, there is some graffiti mixed in at the mouth of the cave, but the cave is now under protection to preserve the historic pictograms within. Set aside about a half hour to explore the drawings. Although you don't have to have a guide to enter, one can be hired for about US$0.50 so that you can be sure to not miss any of the artwork—a tip is appreciated.

Just west of Boca de Yuma is the northeastern gateway of **Parque Nacional del Este** (admission US$3.50), marked by a small cabin, which leads to a long scenic trail where you can enjoy views of the ocean and Isla Saona, birdwatching, and various flora and fauna.

San Rafael and Casa Ponce de León

South of Higüey along Highway 4 is San Rafael de Yuma. This dusty and simple little town is the site of the home-turned-museum of Spanish conquistador Ponce de León. This museum is the only attraction, making the town a poor choice for overnight stays. The **Casa Ponce de León** (7 A.M.–5 P.M. Mon.–Sat., US$1.50) is an important historical landmark containing many artifacts that were previously owned by Ponce de León and his family, including some of their furniture, household wares, and even a suit of armor said to be his.

The home was built in 1505–1508 by Taíno slaves for de León when he was lieutenant governor of Higüey. The home has been brought back to nearly its original glory and is in good condition.

No signs lead you to the museum, but if you're coming from the west, once in town turn left onto the dirt road right before the town cemetery. After a kilometer, you'll see the entrance on the right-hand side with the rectangular, two-story, stone museum at the end. A bus will drop you off at the station near the cemetery. You can either walk the rest of the way (a little over one kilometer) or hire a *motoconcho*. All tours and signage in the museum are in Spanish only.

ACCOMMODATIONS AND FOOD

The only hotel in town is **El Viejo Pirata** (Calle Duarte 1, tel. 809/780-3236, www.hotelviejopirata.com, US$33 without breakfast) and is like a buried treasure. Its six neatly decorated rooms are welcoming even if they are simple. The tiled and charming poolside is set on the dramatic cliffs overlooking the sea for a perfect place to wind down your day with a sunset cocktail. The seafood restaurant on-site serves great Italian and international dishes like *mero* (grouper) Mediterranean style.

There are many small restaurants and small *freidurías* (fish fryers) lining the main road and the water where you can enjoy the catch of the day. The *freidurías* are the most cost-effective way to enjoy the bounty of the ocean. You will spend about RD$50–100 on a piece of fish and some *tostones*. You can't beat that price or the taste!

THE SOUTHEAST

Punta Cana, Bávaro, and Around

The extreme eastern coast is best known for its all-inclusive resorts. It used to be that Punta Cana and Bávaro were two distinctively different areas (towns even!) with Punta Cana to the south and Bávaro farther north, separated by a long, winding road with little in between. Now, due to the tourism marketing, after trying on many different titles (like the Coconut Coast) the entire area is most commonly referred to as "Punta Cana."

The all-inclusive resorts of the Punta Cana and Bávaro areas have spent much time and money to portray their venues as the only choices along the coast. This is not the case. While there is indeed an overwhelming number of luxurious and affordable all-inclusive choices, there are also a few independent and less tourist-packed options (mostly farther north).

The Bávaro and Punta Cana resorts are especially popular with spring breakers, who raise the volume around the pools and party all night long at the big resort complexes, which offer many nighttime entertainment options. On the other hand, the all-inclusives are especially targeted toward families looking to satisfy their myriad needs for less cost than other Caribbean vacations. These resorts are like mini cities. Child care and kid-friendly activities give parents worry-free vacations and perhaps even some alone time for unwinding from a life otherwise consumed with car pools, PTA meetings, and laundry.

Some resorts cater to those who want child-free surroundings. This is especially popular with couples seeking the one-stop wedding and honeymoon vacation, where the ceremony, accommodations, food, flowers, cake, and honeymoon are bundled in one convenient package simple to arrange. Just bring your dress (or white bikini), tuxedo (or Speedo), willing-to-travel wedding party, and say "I do."

The independent traveler might be happier in another part of the country. Since the big resorts have taken up so much of the area, driving through can be somewhat surreal. These walled cities seem to swallow up their "citizens," many of whom will gladly disappear into their confines, emerging only to make their way to the airport at the end of their vacation.

Still, while the all-inclusives stretch for many kilometers along the coast, it is a long coastline that still has plenty to offer beyond the walls of the resorts if one desires a good search. Farther north, along the coastlines of the El Seibo and Hato Mayor provinces, await virgin beaches (think El Macao and Uvero Alto), wetlands, Taíno cave drawings, and the sky-combing coconut groves.

A vast majority of travelers to this coast are visiting the all-inclusive resorts and arrive via the Punta Cana airport. Most resorts have shuttle services that take guests directly from the airport to their compounds, making it a very worry-free arrival.

Combined, the Punta Cana and Bávaro areas are the gem of the southeastern tip of the Dominican Republic, mainly known for their fantastic beaches. While Punta Cana does have some resorts and is the name that is tossed about as the major resort area, in reality, there are many more choices for all-inclusives and other accommodations nearer to Bávaro.

Europeans have been traveling to the Punta Cana area for decades, and most resorts try to make them comfortable by offering European comforts in the tropics (such as food choices in the buffets), but with the American influx, resorts have folded American tastes and needs to their accommodations.

For any services, there are plazas near Bávaro, but the only real town in the area is a small beach town called **El Cortecito;** it's a great place for a break from the all-inclusive resort.

SIGHTS
◖ Beaches

Beaches in the Dominican Republic are, in theory, open to the public. Of course, that hasn't stopped the mega-resorts from trying

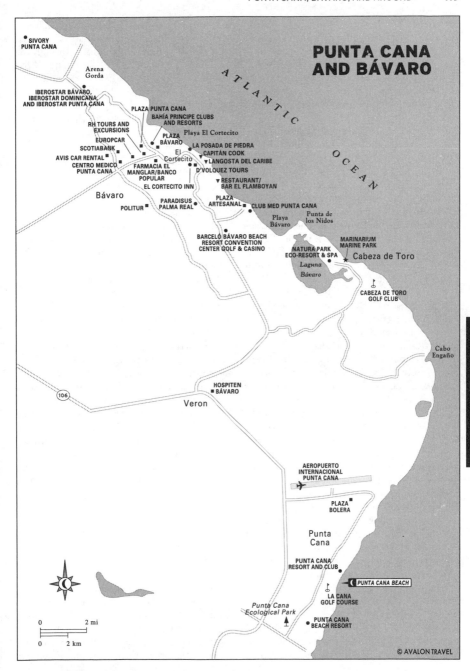

PUNTA CANA
AND BÁVARO

ATLANTIC

OCEAN

- SIVORY
  PUNTA CANA
- Arena
  Gorda
- IBEROSTAR BÁVARO,
  IBEROSTAR DOMINICANA,
  AND IBEROSTAR PUNTA CANA
- PLAZA PUNTA CANA
- BAHÍA PRINCIPE CLUBS
  AND RESORTS
- RH TOURS AND
  EXCURSIONS
- PLAZA
  BÁVARO
- Playa El Cortecito
- EUROPCAR
- SCOTIABANK
- El
  Cortecito
- LA POSADA DE PIEDRA
- CAPITÁN COOK
- LANGOSTA DEL CARIBE
- AVIS CAR RENTAL
- CENTRO MEDICO
  PUNTA CANA
- FARMACIA EL
  MANGLAR/BANCO
  POPULAR
- D'VOLQUEZ TOURS
- EL CORTECITO INN
- RESTAURANT/
  BAR EL FLAMBOYAN
- Bávaro
- PARADISUS
  PALMA REAL
- PLAZA
  ARTESANAL
- CLUB MED PUNTA CANA
- POLITUR
- Playa
  Bávaro
- Punta de
  los Nidos
- BARCELÓ BÁVARO BEACH
  RESORT CONVENTION
  CENTER GOLF & CASINO
- MARINARIUM
  MARINE PARK
- NATURA PARK
  ECO-RESORT & SPA
- Cabeza de Toro
- Laguna
  Bávaro
- CABEZA DE TORO
  GOLF CLUB
- Cabo
  Engaño
- HOSPITEN
  BÁVARO
- (106)
- Veron
- AEROPUERTO
  INTERNACIONAL
  PUNTA CANA
- PLAZA
  BOLERA
- Punta
  Cana
- PUNTA CANA
  RESORT AND CLUB
- PUNTA CANA BEACH
- LA CANA
  GOLF COURSE
- Punta Cana
  Ecological Park
- PUNTA CANA
  BEACH RESORT

0   2 mi

0   2 km

© AVALON TRAVEL

to restrict their beaches to just their paying guests. Many of them offer day passes for about US$40 if you would like to freely enjoy their grounds, including "their" portion of beach. By law, though, everyone has the right to be on any stretch of beach they want; if you're not a guest of the hotel, you may have to just park yourself on the sand.

The beaches along the southeastern shoreline are arguably the best in the country. **Playa Punta Cana** has about 30 miles of swaying palms and very fine white sand. It is one of the finest stretches of beach in the nation and is the reason why it is such a prime resort location. **Playa Bávaro** is another of the wide, white-sand beauties lined with tall coconut trees and laced with resorts; it is just north of Playa Punta Cana on the eastern shoreline. They appear as one extended strip. The beach at **Cabo Engaño,** between the beaches of Punta Cana and Bávaro, offers near idyllic conditions for surfing and windsurfing. But be warned; the wind can be rather rough.

Playa El Cortecito is an often-crowded public beach where local fishers still bring in their boats, but more on the mark, it is a haven for souvenir shops and wandering vendors. It is a good access spot for a nice long walk along the coastline.

The beaches north of El Cortecito have shabby roads that are best traversed by trucks or SUVs. **Playa El Macao** is about 15 kilometers up the coastline. It is a sandy-bottomed spectacular beach that has a drastic drop-off, not the best for children. Since it is so beautiful, though, it has become a popular stop-off for four-wheeler excursions coming from the nearby resorts, taking away a lot of the peaceful charm. The beaches at **Boca de Maímon** and **Playa del Muerto** are deserted stretches that offer seclusion at its best and are well worth the effort even if the roads are terrible.

Punta Cana Ecological Park

About a kilometer from the Punta Cana Resort and Club, Punta Cana Ecological Park (tel. 809/959-8483, www.puntacana.org, 8 A.M.–4 P.M. daily) is a natural refuge

for local flora and fauna, including many rare plants and endangered animals. A guided tour (US$10 adult, US$5 child) through the portion of the park called the **Parque Ojos Indígenas** (Indigenous Eyes Park) takes you through thickly vegetated trails of natural and cultivated gardens. You'll pass natural freshwater lagoons, and kids especially will like the petting farm, where Dominican domesticated animals are available to touch and feed. The iguana habitat has examples of the rhinoceros iguana, which is a species endemic to the island of Hispaniola. Agricultural exhibits have Dominican crops like the cacao bean, coffee, and tobacco, including a display of a traditional Dominican farm or *conuco*. Guided tours are given in English, Spanish, German, and French. Self-guided tours are possible by purchasing a booklet at the visitor's center.

Horseback tours (US$20 for one hour, US$30 for two hours) are a fun way to see the park and all it has to offer, along with an extended ride along the coast. They must be arranged ahead of time.

Supporting this park is a great way not only to have fun and learn something about the country you are visiting, but also to give back through sustainable tourism. The Punta Cana Resort and Club created the Punta Cana Ecological Foundation and the Coastal Marine Project. They are nonprofit organizations that work to protect the ecosystem and sustain the health of the coastal zone and coral reefs. It has made significant headway in promoting the growing sustainable tourism industry in the Dominican Republic.

Marinarium Marine Park

This is another simultaneously fun, educational, and ecotourism-minded activity. A half-day cruise with the Marinarium (Cabeza de Toro/Bávaro, tel. 809/689-5183, www.marinarium.com, US$72/adult and US$36/ages 2–12) starts with your Safari Express from your hotel to the launching point along the coast at Cabeza de Toro. After boarding what looks like a giant pontoon boat with a viewing chamber on the bottom (watch the fish and coral go by!), you'll take a short ride to the controlled section in the ocean, which stretches for some 40,000 square meters and reaches depths of three meters. You'll snorkel with sharks, rays, and much more tropical marine life. Even though it is a little spendy, it is a good excursion for families. Cost includes drinks, snacks, and snorkel gear. Kids also enjoy the educational trip back to shore with a chance to win a free T-shirt. English, Spanish, and French are spoken. Reservations are necessary and can only be made through hotel excursion desks. Adults and teens (over 13) can go on the half-day Reef Explorer excursion (US$89) to a floating island where you can have a snorkeling tour on the reef, have a close encounter with stingrays, take a kayak, or lounge in the water on floating mats. You can even get a relaxing massage. There is a health bar with fruit juices and snacks.

SHOPPING

Most of the huge all-inclusive resorts have their own gift shops, sometimes many, as at **Bahía Principe Clubs and Resorts.** Outside of the mega-resorts, the other plazas are somewhat limited. Expect trinket shops, not high fashion.

Plaza Artesanal Bibijagua

This plaza (8 A.M.–midnight daily) is a collection of stalls positioned directly on the sandy shore between Bávaro and Cabeza de Toro. Here you'll find all the standard Dominican gift-shop trinkets: sarongs, T-shirts, jewelry, bottles of Mamajuana, rum, and cigars. The atmosphere is rife with the sounds of haggling and the not-so-distant roar of the ocean. Parking is available.

Plaza Bávaro

This shopping complex comprises a few plazas: Plaza Punta Cana, Plaza Bávaro (across the street), and Bávaro Shopping Center (on the south side of Plaza Punta Cana). They are mainly tourist-oriented with trinket shops, cigar shops, a pharmacy, a photo shop, a bank, and other services.

SPORTS AND RECREATION
Tours and Excursions

Excursion tours are easy to set up at all-inclusive resorts. Every resort has an excursion desk set up in the lobby with books filled with information on the types of activities, complete with prices. You will want to look at this book as soon as you arrive at your resort since excursions fill up quickly. Here is a list of outfitters in case you want or need to book it solo.

Bavaro Runners Safari Adventures (tel. 809/466-1135, www.bavarorunners.com, US$60–80) organizes half-day trips to La Romana and Altos de Chavón, horseback riding, a look at sugarcane plantations, jeep excursions, and other excursions. Price includes lunch and drinks.

RH Tours and Excursions (El Cortecito, tel. 809/552-1425, www.rhtours.com, 9 A.M.–7 P.M. daily) is a one-stop paradise for choices in excursions. It's in El Cortecito near the Capitán Cook restaurant. This long-established and trusted company offers excursions such as a half-day quad trip (US$55), caving expeditions (US$105), a Santo Domingo day trip (US$65), Parque Nacional Los Haitises tours (US$105), deep-sea fishing (US$85), a zipline adventure (US$89), reef explorer with equipment and snacks (US$89), even trips into the country to meet the people (US$75), and many more. Languages spoken are English, Spanish, German, and French. Ask about kids' prices!

Walk down toward the north end of El Cortecito to find other independent excursion companies. Kiosks offer a bevy of choices from catamaran rides, snorkeling, and flying boats to windsurfing, sailing, and banana boat rides.

The **Punta Cana Express Bus Bar** (Punta Cana, tel. 809/686-9290, cell 809/481-1469) is an all-day excursion package. You are picked up at your hotel at 8 A.M. in a large "party bus," and the tour passes sugarcane fields and coffee and cacao plantations. You'll see a cockfight, then move on to a ranch for some horse riding along the beach. Lunch is provided at the ranch. You are returned to your hotel around 4:30 P.M. Two vehicle choices are available depending on the size of your party. The jeep for four people is US$80 per person, whereas booking a truck to hold 18–20 people is US$75 per person. Everything is included.

D'Volquez Tours (El Cortecito, tel. 809/552-1861, www.dvolquez.com) offers a variety of excursions much like the ones offered by RH Tours (including quad bikes and truck safaris).

Deep-Sea Fishing

Anglers will be happy to know that deep-sea fishing is possible and an exciting reality here in the Southeast. It's as easy as chartering a boat to feel the thrill of the big blue deep waters. Some fish you can try to wrangle into the boat are: Atlantic blue marlin, Atlantic sailfish, yellowfin tuna, mahimahi, and wahoo.

Booking a trip with your resort is the easiest way to arrange an excursion. If you are on your own, though, contact **First Class Fishing** (El Cortecito, tel. 809/867-0381, www.firstclass-fishing.com, starting at US$99 for one angler walk-on), a truly first-rate outfitter of deep-sea fishing excursions with over 15 years experience. A four-hour VIP charter for up to seven anglers will run you US$640 on a boat that is 40–42 feet and is equipped with all the appropriate safety equipment. Cost includes fishing gear, snacks, beers, soft drinks, ice, and transfer from any Punta Cana area resort for up to seven people and two watchers. Reservations with a deposit are required.

Golf

La Cana Golf Course (Punta Cana Resort and Club, tel. 809/959-2262, fax 809/959-4653, www.puntacana.com, tee times 7 A.M.–4 P.M.) is both challenging and beautiful. Designed by Pete B. Dye, this 18-hole, par-72 course opened in 2001 and has 14 holes with views of the Caribbean Sea and 4 that run alongside it. If you are going to go all out and splurge for a round, this is the best in the area. This course is part of one of the best hotels in the area, and the beauty, service, and prices indicate this. Greens fees for 18 holes are US$165 for nonguests of the hotel, US$102 for 9 holes.

Catalonia Cabeza de Toro Golf Club (Bávaro Catalonia Resort, tel. 809/412-0000, fax 809/412-2001, tee times 7 A.M.–4 P.M.) has two 9-hole courses; one is a regular 9-hole course (par 35) and the other is a 9-hole executive course (par 3) that opened in 2000. While they are short courses, it's a stimulating and enjoyable play for both novice and experienced golfers, with its five lakes (adding water obstacles), numerous shade trees, and wide fairways. Greens fees are considerably less than at the La Cana course. Greens fees are US$45 for a round on the 9-hole course (cart US$20 extra) and US$65 for two rounds (cart US$25 extra).

The **Cocotal Golf and Country Club** (El Cortecito, tel. 809/687-4653, www.cocotalgolf.com) has been carved out of what used to be a coconut plantation. Spanish golf champion José "Pepe" Gancedo designed two courses (18 and 9 holes) by using what nature already afforded the lush and rolling landscape. Lakes, tactical placement of trees and bunkers, generous fairways and greens, and the peaceful surroundings can fool a golfer. This is a challenging course. Winds run opposite of play direction, waters wrap greens, and just when you thought you had the wind figured out, it is at your back. Greens fees plus cart rental for the 18-hole course are US$112. Fees for the 9-hole plus a cart are US$65. Lessons are offered through the Cocotal Golf Academy for US$80 per hour.

The new **Faldo Legacy Course at Roco Ki** (Punta Cana, tel. 888/476-2654 or 809/731-2824, www.rocoki.com) has golf enthusiasts falling all over themselves. In 2008, it was named as one of the world's best new golf courses. It is a par 72 course with 18 holes surrounded by dunes, marsh, and woodland that opens to the sea. The course billows and folds over the cliffs and canyons along with the waves of the ocean. Not only is it beautiful but it is strategically challenging. If the winds and crooked topography don't get you, the beauty might bewitch you completely. Cost for play is US$220–400 (depending on season).

Other golf courses in the area include **Punta Blanca** (Punta Cana Beach Resort, Carretera

Arena Gorda–Macao, Bávaro, tel. 809/468-4734, www.punta-blanca.com), **Golf de Bávaro** (Barceló Bávaro Beach Resort, Punta Cana, www.barcelogolf.com), **La Hacienda** (Punta Cana Resort and Club, www.puntacana.com), and **Las Lagunas** and **Punta Espada** Golf Courses (Cap Cana, www.capcana.com).

ACCOMMODATIONS
Under US$100

If the all-inclusive scene doesn't appeal to you, here are some options for independent accommodations under US$100.

El Cortecito Inn (Av. Melia Fiesta, El Cortecito, tel. 809/552-0639, fax 809/552-0639, US$60 d per room w/breakfast), a 70-unit hotel right on the main strip of El Cortecito and only 40 meters from the beach, offers very basic rooms, each with its own private bath. Don't expect pampering. The location is convenient, just paces from shops, restaurants, the beach, and excursion offices. Children up to seven years old stay free. This hotel has seen better days, and has dated decor and poor maintenance, but it has a pool and a bar/restaurant where the food portions are generous. Some rooms have balconies. Free parking is available.

At **La Posada de Piedra** (Playa El Cortecito, Bávaro, tel. 809/221-0754, www.laposadadepiedra.com, US$35–45 d) it's all about location, location, location (for an extremely low price). This very small (five rooms, to be exact) family-owned hotel offers low-maintenance, independent travelers the accommodations they've been looking for. Two of the rooms are actually in the owner's home, where you'll have your own private bath, a ceiling fan, and a shared balcony overlooking an amazing view of the ocean. The other three rooms are in very basic cabanas on the beach. Meals and drinks are available in a family-style atmosphere. It's a short walk to the shops and restaurants of El Cortecito.

US$100-200
Natura Park Eco-Resort & Spa (Cabeza de Toro, Punta Cana, tel. 809/221-2626, fax 809/221-6060, www.blau-hotels.com, US$150 d) sits next to Laguna Bávaro along a beautiful estuary and a spectacular stretch of white-sand beach great for long walks. This is a good choice if you are an ecoconscious traveler who wants to be pampered at the same time. It is known for its efforts to minimize impact on the environment, such as using only reusable cups and biodegradable soap in your bathroom. There are 510 rooms and 20 suites; the pool has a swim-up bar and a children's area, and there is a luxurious spa with massage and beauty treatments available. If you don't speak a word of Spanish, communication might be a challenge since much of the staff does not speak English. Rooms are not luxurious but are more than comfortable, and all have a terrace or balcony.

Barceló Dominican Beach (Bávaro, tel. 809/221-0714, www.barcelodominicanbeach.com, US$110–210) is situated on the gorgeous Playa Bávaro and offers 731 comfortable and nicely decorated rooms with regular amenities. There are over 65 suites that are very pleasing upgrades—including 12 honeymoon suites. The resort as a whole is kept very clean, from the gardens to the restaurants to the rooms. There are six à la carte restaurants, three buffets, and two snack bars (serving snacks 24 hours a day), as well as eight (yes, eight) bars (counting one coffee bar).

It's a long name—**Barceló Bávaro Beach Resort Convention Center Golf & Casino** (Playa Bávaro, Punta Cana, tel. 809/686-5797, fax 809/686-5797, www.barcelo.com, from US$110 d)—but for a complex of five all-inclusive resorts (Bávaro Palace, Bávaro Beach, Bávaro Caribe, Bávaro Golf, and Bávaro Casino) within its almost 13-square-kilometer confines, it is only fitting. All but the Bávaro Casino are situated along the ocean. This complex is best for those who want a great number of choices for entertainment in addition to their beloved beach time. It can be a rather lively party scene, especially during spring break. As a guest, you have access to most of the rest of the complex's amenities as well, including some restaurants, the casino, discos, the Tropicalissimo show, and golf. Make no mistake, though; this is an excellent location for families. The myriad food choices within the entire complex are reason enough; there are water sports galore, kids' clubs, minigolf, sporting courts (basketball, soccer, tennis), and baby-sitting as well.

The Bávaro Palace (from US$300) recently upgraded its junior suites, which will make your stay truly more luxurious with a hot tub on your balcony. All of the buildings have elevators, making accessibility easier. It has a buffet, five à la carte restaurants, and five bars (one in the pool). If you plan on exploring the rest of the grounds, make sure to ask for a map and catch one of the free shuttles that make frequent tours and stops.

When it comes to all-inclusive affordable luxury, the Iberostar hotels—**Iberostar Bávaro, Iberostar Dominicana,** and **Iberostar Punta Cana** (Playa Bávaro, tel. 809/221-6500, fax 809/688-6186, www.iberostar.com, US$150–195)—hit a home run. Located right next to one another, all have ingredients for a tasty cocktail of relaxation and entertainment, offering huge pools, excursion options, open-air buffets as well as à la carte international-themed restaurants, very comfortable rooms, and some of the best beach stretches around.

The Iberostar Bávaro is an all-suite resort. Each junior suite has a sunken living room and balcony or patio; with the cost of your stay, you have access to the other Iberostar hotels. It has nine restaurants and a lake-like pool surrounded by palms with a swim-up bar and separate area for the kids. Also available are children's programs, a casino, billiards, archery, and even a teen disco among the so many other amenities.

The main attraction at **Club Med Punta Cana** (Playa Punta Cana, Punta Cana, tel. 809/687-2767, www.clubmed.com, US$125–240) is its variety of activities: many water sports, aerobics, horseback riding, flying trapeze, kickboxing, yoga, tennis, and much more. Children will be kept quite happy with the myriad kid-geared activities, like

rollerblading, educational fun, circus lessons, and dancing. Guests are international, mostly from Europe.

For the utmost in tranquility for your vacation, **(Punta Cana Resort and Club** (Playa Punta Cana, Punta Cana, tel. 809/959-2262, fax 809/959-3951, www.puntacana.com, US$150–200 d depending on season) is a welcome oasis, even if traveling with the entire family. Although there are some things to keep you busy, it is definitely not a party scene. Families and older couples are happiest here. Enjoy a daytime tennis match (night tennis costs US$10/hour). If getting out into the "big blue" is your idea of paradise, you can rent a boat, scuba dive, or go deep-sea fishing at the resort's full-service marina. Booking these activities ahead of time is highly advised.

Just a quick jaunt to the right of the beach area, by the hotel's marina, is Punta Cana Resort and Club's 240-hectare private ecological reserve. Fighting the heat of the Caribbean midday is a joy while taking a dip in the Manantial Yauya natural spring. Guided tours, bird-watching tours, and educational workshops are available at the Parque Ojos Indígenas.

The resort accommodations themselves are set on more than a hectare of lush gardens along five kilometers of powdery coastline. Rooms are very nicely decorated, but lunch and drinks are not included in the price. There are many excursions to choose from, at extra charge, and they can be arranged in the hotel's own travel agency.

US$200 and Up

A surge in upscale all-inclusives skyrocketed in the last five years. When you compare what these rooms would go for in other parts of the Caribbean, these resorts are still a considerable deal. The travel industry is in the process of wooing travelers in search of a Shangri-La vacation. Not only are they paying close attention to design in these newer resorts, but they are adding amenities such as butler service, non-buffet eateries, VIP areas with their own pools and restaurants, and family freebies.

Many resorts that have been around for a while have renovated to add these features and give facelifts.

Bahía Principe Clubs and Resorts (Arena Gorda–Macao, Bávaro, tel. 809/552-1444, www.bahia-principe.com) is a complex home to the **Gran Bahía Principe Punta Cana** (US$268) and the **Gran Bahía Principe Bávaro** (US$260). Don't let the names fool you; they are side by side along the same amazing pearl-white beach of Playa Bávaro. The grounds are very well tended, lush, and vast enough to offer frequent-running shuttle services to take you from one end to another. Down by the beach, there is one large pool that can get quite lively, but in the middle of the complex there are two other pools reserved for quieter sun worship. The rooms are spacious with very nice bathrooms. Nightly entertainment is abundant at the Principe resorts. Cabaret-style shows, a piano bar, and karaoke night (it's fun to hear singers from many nations) are relaxing ways to pass the evening. For more lively nights, head over to the Pueblo Principe (the resort's "small town") and listen to live music, watch a dance contest, groove the night away in the disco, or test your luck in the casino. The excursion office offers many attractive ways to spice up your vacation. But, for those who would rather stay put, this complex has everything you need. You'll find a pharmacy, along with shops (albeit quite overpriced) with trinkets, jewelry, clothing, and anything else you want in the Pueblo Principe.

If you've been on a search for a hotel that doesn't have a kids' club as a major selling point, here it is: **Excellence Punta Cana** (Playas Uvero Alto, Punta Cana, tel. 809/685-9880, fax 809/685-9990, www.excellence-resorts.com, US$450 and up d depending on season). This is an adults-only (18 or older) resort, making it extremely popular as a honeymoon resort. There are two huge pools, with the biggest one stretching longer than a football field and containing a swim-up bar. At the beach, you'll find perfectly powdery sand for kilometers, great for long walks with your honey. The waves are strong, which makes it great for boogie boarding, but the strong undertow doesn't make it a peaceful swimming spot. If you walk to the right of the resort and around the bend, the water can be calmer. At Excellence's spa you can enjoy many soothing treatments, including a couple's massage. There are eight different restaurants, one of which includes a seaside candlelight dinner. Another, The Lobster House, is devoted entirely to the yummy crustacean! At night you can enjoy the martini bar, take in nightly stage performances, go dancing in the disco (Alegria), gamble in the casino, or (and this is the best part) take a moonlit horseback ride along the ocean! Romance is in the air at Excellence. All 446 rooms have a four-poster bed and Jacuzzi for two. Couples celebrating honeymoons or anniversaries receive complimentary special treatment (you must mention when booking and show proof when you arrive). Special honeymoon and anniversary packages are available for US$600 per couple and include items like arrival fruit basket, breakfast in bed, private beachfront dinner, and a spa treatment. There is even a complimentary wedding package, but wedding packages that offer services above and beyond start at US$850.

◖ Paradisus Palma Real (Playa Bávaro/Punta Cana, tel. 809/688-5000, www.solmelia.com, US$400 and up) is a 554-suite luxury resort. Among its amenities are six restaurants serving international cuisine, a kids' club, three more-than-generous-in-size pools, tennis, and a fitness center including trainers and yoga, tai chi, and pilates classes. Each guest gets unlimited greens fees at the Cocotal Golf and Country Club, and there is a casino and live shows for nightly entertainment. Each beautifully appointed suite boasts a Jacuzzi for two, a private terrace, flat-screen TV, 24-hour room service, and minibar. The Paradisus Palma Real, realizing the market for the luxury-seeking travelers flocking to the Dominican Republic, raised the stakes in the game of tourism with their 2007 addition (a resort-within-a-resort), **The Reserve,** complete with sparkling new pools, a private lounge, and 190 luxury suites. Eighty of those include family

THE SOUTHEAST

concierge service with parental dreamy additions like private family check-in, kid's beach kit, specially appointed suites, walkie-talkies for easy communication with family, and more to make your family vacation stress free.

Sivory Punta Cana (Uvero Alto, www.sivorypuntacana.com, tel. 809/333-0500, US$300 and up) is located about 60 minutes from the Punta Cana airport. Sure, that is far, but the distance adds to the feeling of being removed from the hustle and bustle. The hotel can arrange for airport pickup. Once you arrive, you've found that paradise you've been looking for. Sit back and chill out. The huge rooms are so beautifully appointed (flat-screen TVs, couple's showers, fine linens, high speed Internet, etc.) you may be tempted to spend all your time inside, but try not to succumb to the allure of it because the beach is immaculate and the infinity pool area will melt away any memory of stresses you had back at home. Want to duck the paparazzi and have your own private pool? Look for a suite on the ground floor. Gourmands and especially wine lovers will be happy here.

At **NH Real Arena** (Bávaro, tel. 809/221-4646, www.edenh-realarena.com, US$200 and up) the 642 regular rooms are spacious, clean, and modern with incredibly comfortable beds. Not only are the rooms decorated with natural and green tones, but they are taking on a "go green" quality as well. For instance, you need to put your room key into a slot in order to operate the lights and air-conditioning in your room, and if you want a change of towels, you'll need to place them in the more-than-generously-sized Jacuzzi tub (of course the simple fact that there is one in each room negates the water conservation effort). The beach and the pool, where it seems they spent a great deal of effort in their design, are particularly lovely, extremely peaceful, and well kept. One of the bragging points of this resort is that you don't need to make reservations for their four specialty restaurants. It is a complete fabrication and an utter frustration among most travelers there. Don't let that dissuade you; just make your reservations upon arrival. The food,

although not stellar, is quite good. The buffet has a suitable variety for everyday choices, especially breakfast. Also available on-site: business center, kids' club, seven bars, spa, tennis. One strange thing about the rooms that can't go unnoticed: The bathroom is exposed to the bedroom save for the toilet and shower, each in their separate rooms with frosted-over glass doors. This could make for a very uncomfortable roommate situation. Really, it's only appropriate for couples or, well, exhibitionists.

FOOD AND DRINK

Eating in the all-inclusive resorts is fun at first with the buffet lines serving up a fairly good variety of dishes, trying hard to cater to all nationalities from Europe, Canada, and the United States. Generally, you can expect a well-balanced buffet of breads, fruits, egg dishes, and cereals for breakfast. Pizza, pastas, soups, salads, hamburgers and hot dogs fill the spread for lunch. And for dinner, you can expect Italian dishes, seafood specialties, more pizza (always pizza), Dominican fare, vegetables, grilled meats, pastas, salad bars, and delectable desserts to chose from. The choices can seem downright staggering the first couple of days. But, save for the specialty restaurants (which aren't always included in your all-inclusive rate and sometimes come at a hefty additional cost), the romance of the buffet line can fade after a few days, and foodies will start to feel like they're dining in captivity. One solution is to dine at another resort's specialty restaurant. Check to make sure your restaurant choice allows outside guests. Making a reservation is critical as most resorts' specialty restaurants fill up with their own guests, making room for outside guests challenging. You'll want to call with as much notice as you can and take a taxi between resorts. The maze of Puerto Plata/Bávaro resorts can be confusing at night.

Most people who vacation in this part of the Dominican Republic do so in the all-inclusive resorts and will stay in those compounds for the duration of their trip. Therefore, independent restaurants that last are rare. But there are a few and if you find yourself feeling the itch for a different venue or menu, venture into El Cortecito for a meal.

Capitán Cook (El Cortecito, tel. 809/552-1061, noon–midnight daily, US$11–45) is well known for its freshly grilled seafood, ambience, and amazing location right on the main drag of El Cortecito and directly on the beach. Super-fresh fish is grilled to order in the outdoor kitchen. The chefs bounce around one another, adding to the already vibrant atmosphere of this (mostly) outdoor restaurant. At tables under thatch-roofed gazebos, food and drinks are served in front of the azure ocean to the tune of wandering *bachata* musicians. Should you choose to sit inside, there is a more formal indoor dining area overlooking the ocean. Grilled fish and other meats come served with salad, potatoes, or fries. Other delights include entrées like seafood spaghetti or an appetizer mix for the table to share. A meal plan that comes complete with transportation from your hotel can even be arranged. For US$40 per person during the day, you'll be picked up by boat. At night, for US$45 per person, you'll receive a taxi ride. They will travel the entire coastline to get you, but reservations are required.

The much less exciting but reliable **Restaurant/Bar El Flamboyan** (El Cortecito Inn, Av. Melia Fiesta, El Cortecito, tel. 809/552-0639, fax 809/552-0639, 11 A.M.–2 A.M. daily, US$5–22) is just across the street from Capitán Cook's in El Cortecito Inn. The restaurant serves international and Dominican food in generous portions, including lobster for US$22. Dress is casual.

On the beach in the town of El Cortecito, at **Langosta del Caribe** (El Cortecito, tel. 809/552-0774, US$11–20) you'll sit under umbrellas with your feet directly in the sand. Langosta del Caribe has a complimentary boat pickup service from wherever you are staying in the Bávaro area. Its specialty is grilled seafood. You can choose your own lobster, and cooks will prepare it on the barbecue or however you desire. After you eat, you can swim at the beach or rest on some of their beach loungers. This is a great way to enjoy a lazy afternoon on the beach.

Nightlife in El Cortecito tends to suffer in choices even more since most people tend to stick around their resorts at night after long days in the sun. Try **La Sirenita,** right where the main street fades away, for a local favorite hangout.

INFORMATION AND SERVICES

When you are staying in an all-inclusive resort, many services are located within the walls of the complex. Otherwise, the best places to go for most services are the small town of El Cortecito and the plazas making up the **Plaza Bávaro** area.

Communications

In El Cortecito, the only public Internet connection is at **Tri Com** (9 A.M.–11 P.M. daily, US$3/hour). It is also a call center. Calls to the U.S. run US$0.42 per minute; calls to Europe are US$0.70 a minute.

Cone Xion.com (Plaza Punta Cana, 8 A.M.–11 P.M. Mon.–Sat., 9 A.M.–11 P.M. Sun.) has a call center and Internet connection.

Banks and Money Exchange

All of these banks will exchange U.S. dollars, euros, and traveler's checks and have ATMs.

Banco Popular is in Plaza Bávaro (tel. 809/552-0613, 9 A.M.–4 P.M. Mon.–Fri.).

Banco del Progreso has a couple of locations: inside El Cortecito Supermarket (El Cortecito, 9 A.M.–9 P.M. Mon.–Sat.) and in Plaza Bolera (Bávaro, 9 A.M.–4 P.M. Mon.–Fri.).

ScotiaBank is in Plaza Brisas (Bávaro, tel. 809/552-1500, fax 809/552-1504, 9 A.M.–5 P.M. Mon.–Fri., 9 A.M.–1 P.M. Sat.).

For money transfers, there is a **Western Union** (Plaza Bávaro, tel. 809/532-7381, 8 A.M.–5 P.M. Mon.–Sat.).

Health and Emergencies

All-inclusive resorts have small clinics that can treat you for minor ailments and concerns for an extra cost, but if you have other more serious concerns, there are some rather nice choices available in this heavy tourist area.

Hospiten Bávaro (Carretera Higüey–Punta Cana, tel. 809/686-1414) is the best bet for care should you need it. Doctors here speak English, French, and German, and the emergency room is open 24 hours. This 70-bed hospital opened in 2000 and has the latest medical and surgical technology, an intensive care unit, a blood bank, and X-ray machines. Hospiten Bávaro is on the highway in between Punta Cana and Bávaro, just before you turn to Bávaro.

Centro Médico Punta Cana (Bávaro, tel. 809/552-1506) is another reliable and good choice for medical care in the area. The name is a bit confusing since it is actually in Bávaro about a kilometer before the turn off to El Cortecito, near the bus station. The ER is open 24 hours.

It is absolutely best to take medications with you from home as they can be overpriced in the resort pharmacies, even over-the-counter medications. However, there are pharmacies in El Cortecito and the plazas of Plaza Bávaro. **Farmacia El Manglar** (Plaza Punta Cana, Bávaro, tel. 809/552-1533, 8 A.M.–midnight daily) will even deliver what you need to your hotel.

Politur (Tourist Police, tel. 809/686-8227) has two locations serving the area, both open 24 hours: next to the bus terminal in Bávaro and in the Plaza Bolera in Punta Cana near the airport.

GETTING THERE
By Air
The entire southeastern region is best served by the **Aeropuerto Internacional Punta Cana.** Catching a taxi to your hotel is no problem and can be quite inexpensive, costing under US$30–60. This range reflects the Punta Cana area prices and up to Uvero Alto. Make sure to agree on the price before getting in the cab or letting them help you with baggage. Most people staying in all-inclusive resorts arrange for a ride on one of their resort's free shuttles. Inquire about it when booking your vacation.

Although the country is easy to drive around and few fly between destinations within the Dominican Republic, air travel is a growing

trend. **Takeoff Destination Service S.A.** (Plaza Brisas de Bávaro 8, Bávaro, tel. 809/552-1333, fax 809/552-1113, www.takeoffweb.com) has flights between Punta Cana and Santo Domingo (US$89), Puerto Plata (US$119), and Samaná (US$99). It can also arrange excursions, charter flights, shuttle transfers, and hotel pickups; it has a flight school.

By Bus
Guaguas are an option for independent travelers who arrive during the day. Once the sun disappears, so does this mode of transportation. Just stand on the side of the road for the direction you want to travel and flag one down. Let them know where you are going before getting aboard; they won't let you on if they're not going in your direction. A ride on one of these small public "buses" is about US$1.50 but could be more depending on how far you're going.

Coming from Santo Domingo, you can catch an **express bus** in the Gazcue neighborhood bus station at the Plaza Los Girasols (Juan Sánchez Ramírez 31, tel. 809/682-9670, US$7) to the major resorts of the Punta Cana/Bávaro area. They all pass through Higüey two times a day (7 A.M. and 4 P.M.).

Buses also leave from Santo Domingo's Parque Enriquillo for a two-leg trip connecting in Higüey. In Higüey, you must transfer to another bus. Most have signs in them displaying their destinations, but it is best to ask which one you should board. For each leg of the trip, you'll pay on board the bus (US$5 from Santo Domingo to Higüey and US$2 from Higüey to Bávaro).

By Car
From Higüey, travel northeast along Highway 105 to the town of La Otra Banda, where you turn off onto Highway 106 to get to the Bávaro/Punta Cana area.

GETTING AROUND
Taxis are easy to get through your hotel. Many resorts post the cost in menu form at the front desk or at their front gates. You can also call

the **Siuratural** (tel. 809/221-2741) company for 24-hour service.

Car Rental

Most visitors who come to the Southeast don't rent cars because they are staying in resort complexes and don't consider leaving them. Still, one would think it would be relatively easy to rent a car right at the airport in this high-tourist area. That's not the case, but, never fear, there are car-rental places scattered throughout the Punta Cana area. It is a wonderful way to break out of the mold and see the less touristy Dominican Republic. Book a rental online if you can; prices can be more reasonable that way (they are rather pricey in this part of the Dominican Republic). Cost fluctuates here in a very haphazard manner in all seasons. Expect to pay anywhere from US$35 to over US$100 a day for an economy car. **Avis Car Rental** (Arena Gorda, Carretera Friusa-Riu, tel. 809/688-1354), **Budget Rental Car** (Bávaro, tel. 809/985-2830, www.budget.com. do), and **Europcar** (Calle Gustavo Mejía, near Plaza Punta Cana, tel. 809/686-2861) all rent cars in the area.

La Costa Esmeralda

MICHES AND SURROUNDING AREA

The seaside town of Miches is tucked into a small bay at the southern mouth of the Bahía de Samaná. The town itself doesn't offer a lot to a traveler and is mainly a stop-off point for transfer to Sabana de la Mar, a town located west along the same shore. This coastline, which stretches from the easternmost edge of El Seibo province and across the coast of Hato Mayor to Sabana de la Mar in the west at the junction to the National Park Los Haitises, is sometimes referred to as La Costa Esmeralda and is home to two lagoons, Redonda and Limón. The beaches near here are less manicured and more on the wild side.

Highway 104 leads you away from Bávaro to the absolutely stunning **Playa Limón** (turn off in the town of El Cedro in a northerly direction) and **Punta El Rey** (turn off in the town of La Mina). Playa Limón is three kilometers of unparalleled beauty that draws tour groups occasionally but, for the most part, is not over-crowded. In fact, near Playa Limón is the scientific reserve at **Laguna Limón,** a freshwater reserve that meets up with Playa Limón at the coast and is well known for the fantastic bird-watching within its wetlands and mangroves. Just around the curve of the coastline, into what becomes the southern edge of the mouth of the **Bahía de Samaná,** is Punta El Rey, truly a breathtaking beach.

Playa Limón, Lagunas Redonda and Limón, and Punta El Rey

If you rented a car in Puerto Plata, this is a great drive to take, a truly wonderful opportunity to see some unspoiled countryside before it gets swallowed up by the encroachment of mass tourism. Enjoy it while it lasts.

First, take Highway 105 to El Macao and meet up with Highway 104. Don't expect perfect road conditions (the whole time); having a sturdy car would be ideal. Playa Limón is about 20 kilometers east of Miches. The beach is a spectacular beauty lined with coconut groves. Turtles lay their eggs here in the springtime. Taking a walk here along the three-kilometer-long golden and unspoiled beach will be quite peaceful—that is, until the tours arrive on horseback in the early afternoon.

Bird watchers will enjoy Laguna Redonda and **Laguna Limón,** although the former is especially difficult to reach. Mostly, at Laguna Redondo, there are fishing boats whose captains you can convince to take you out onto the water for about RD$120, but there are no real outposts for tourists or nature enthusiasts.

Laguna Limón is the more accessible of the two freshwater lagoons and is surrounded by

THE SOUTHEAST

a wetland and coastal mangrove. The national park station is on the highway. Entrance fee is RD$100. For the full effect, you should hire a boat and a guide to take you onto the water for about RD$250 per person. Tours are also arranged by **Hotel La Cueva** (tel. 809/470-0870, www.lacuevalimon.com).

Northwest of Laguna Redonda and just east of Miches is Punta El Rey. Tour groups stop near here to enjoy the splendor of this gorgeous spot on horseback. But if you're not with a tour, you might have a difficult time finding it. From El Cedro, on Carretera 104, traveling west toward Miches, take the turnoff at La Mina de Miches marked "La Costa Esmeralda." At the next fork in the road veer left, and at the next intersection (three kilometers farther) take a right. This is where the road gets rough, making your spirits wither, but do not despair—just four kilometers down the road you will find your beach nirvana.

Accommodations and Food

Although there aren't a lot of choices in the area since tourism is still quite relegated to the Bávaro area, this could be good news for the independent traveler. It means there are smaller hotels where you can stay for a fraction of the cost of the mega-complexes in the Punta Cana and Bávaro area. The two listed are in or around Miches and are run by the same Swiss group.

Coco Loco Beach Club (Playa Miches, Miches, tel. 809/553-5920, www.abatrex.com/cocoloco, US$35 d) is a 10-cabin hotel right on the beach that offers simple but clean accommodations, each with two double beds, bathroom (no hot water), fan, table with chairs, and a private porch. Cabins do not have a TV, phone, or air-conditioning. This area is particularly good for kids; there is no traffic and the plush grass is great to jump, play volleyball, or run around on. The main building is a two-story structure with an open-air lounge and restaurant serving fish, shrimp, pasta, salads, and sandwiches. It's directly on Playa Miches just across the river from the town.

The main selling point of **Hotel La Loma** (Miches, tel. 809/553-5562, www.hotel-laloma.com, US$50 d) is its view, without a doubt. You can enjoy the panorama of the breathtaking Bahía de Samaná, where sunsets are amazing. The rooms are simple and quite comfortable, each with one king-size and one twin bed, air-conditioning, TV, a private bath, and balconies looking down over the small pool and the vista. The hotel's restaurant is open for all meals, and breakfast is only US$5 per person, served with the same amazing view as a backdrop. Hotel La Loma is in the hills overlooking the Bahía de Miches.

The hotel at **Hotel-Restaurant La Cueva** (El Cedro, tel. 809/470-0876, http://miches.ifp3.com/, US$40–50 per day) is nice enough for a couple of nights. It is clean with electricity all the time (that's big news here!) and a seafood restaurant. The real gem of it is the setting. Hotel La Cueva is in one of the most gorgeous areas in the Southeast and can arrange for a multitude of ecotours, such as horseback riding or a visit to a local coffee and cocoa plantation. La Cueva is near the village of El Cedro (on Carretera 104, 24 km east of Miches), 300 meters to Playa Limón.

Services

If you are looking to find all the comforts of home during your vacation, this is not the spot. Despite the beautiful beaches and breathtaking vistas, Miches is not set up to receive tourists. There is no hospital or Internet access. Street signs aren't always in place, but one to keep in mind is Calle Mella.

BanReservas (Miches, 9:30 A.M.–3 P.M. Mon., Wed., and Fri.) has an ATM, and you can exchange money. It's in the center of town about a block south of Calle Mella.

Codetel Centro de Comunicaciones (Miches, Calle Mella, Mon.–Sat. 8 A.M.–10 P.M.) offers international calls to the U.S. (US$0.40/minute) and Europe (US$1.30/minute).

Getting There

Taking a *guagua* to or from Miches is relatively easy. They leave Higüey on the half hour all day until 5 P.M. (US$4) and will drop you at the gas station on the eastern edge of Miches. *Guaguas* headed for Sabana de la Mar (US$2.50) leave every 25 minutes from the western end of town.

Motoconchos will be around the gas station for you to hire if you need to get around town, or to some of the area's beaches. Expect to pay around RD$100, but you can haggle prices and secure the price before hopping on.

SABANA DE LA MAR

Although it's not a tourist attraction town, most travelers pass through Sabana de la Mar to get to the Parque Nacional Los Haitises or to catch a ferry to Samaná. There are very few services, accommodations, or places to eat in Sabana de la Mar.

Accommodations and Food

The resort 【 **Paraíso Caño Hondo** (Sabana de la Mar, tel. 809/248-5995, cell 809/889-9454, www.paraisocanohondo.com, website in Spanish only, US$40 d with all meals included) wins top honors. It truly is one of the most special places to stay in the entire Dominican Republic for so many reasons. One, savory authentic Dominican food at the restaurant, El Cayuco. Two, green design while maintaining their own unique style without sacrificing comfort. Three, the pastoral view over the rice fields, clearing the Parque Nacional Los Haitises, all the way to the Bahía de Samaná. Four, management, staff, and tour guides who are all passionate about the environment and maintaining the natural resources in the Dominican Republic. And five, it is Dominican-owned, making it a sustainable tourism option.

Located right at the foot of the Parque Nacional Los Haitises, it is a fantastic choice as a base to explore the park. This small hotel offers very comfortable rooms decorated with rustic elements of the area, containing two or three full-size beds, a ceiling fan, and private hot water bath. In the quiet surroundings, you can hear the sounds of the nearby river and the native birds from the park. Nature lovers will

© ANA CHAVIER CAAMAÑO

sleepy market in Sabana de la Mar

THE SOUTHEAST

fall hard for this place. Rates are less expensive in low season and less expensive if you choose to not include all meals in your plan, although keep in mind that food choices outside the hotel are sparse. Stone pathways lead to various river-fed pools where, amid the waterfalls and thick vegetation, you can take a dip in the heat of the day. If you're looking for the ultimate privacy, try to book for midweek; most excursions and student groups pass through on the weekends. If you're just in the area for the day, ask about a pass so that you can enjoy a swim in the pools without staying the night. One of the best views is from the Carpintero room in what is the newer of the two buildings. It's quite a hike up a hill—not for someone not able to walk steep hills—especially at night. Boat and hiking excursions are available.

Besides being a great hotel choice, the Paraíso offers ecological excursions ranging from walking tours (US$18), camping, horseback riding, and moonlight and other boat rides (US$15–33) to excursions to the park's caves. During humpback whale season you can go on a whale-watching tour in the Bahía de Samaná (US$57 per person).

Hotel Riverside (tel. 809//556-7465, US$15 with a/c, US$10 without) is a very basic but clean seven-room hotel on the main road into Sabana de la Mar from Hato Mayor. All rooms have a refrigerator and tile floors. Since it is on such a busy road, ask for a room on the second floor in the back. You will have a better night's sleep and a breeze. Coffee is offered up in the morning (included in the price of your room), and you can buy soda and beer at the front desk. The accommodating staff will even make grocery store or pharmacy runs for you. This is a good location if you want to remain in the town of Sabana de la Mar.

Hotel Lomas Lindas (Carretera Miches, tel. 809/520-2387, www.lomaslindas.piczo.com, US$17) is a four-room hotel five kilometers outside of Sabana de la Mar as you are driving toward Miches and is a last choice for places to stay overnight. However, coming here to enjoy a traditional Dominican and European meal in the low-key, open-air eatery amidst acres of rolling greenery, as geese stroll by, is another matter. As for the three rooms available, when the electricity works they have air-conditioning and TV but no windows. Every room does have its own bathroom, and they are rather clean despite their small size. Let it be known—this hotel is for the adventurer and the thrifty traveler. At night, there's have a small dance floor. Internet access is available on-site but there are no phones in the rooms. There are many hiking trails around and they will arrange for horseback riding, tropical nature walks in Los Haitises, boat trips, and day trips to Santo Domingo at negotiable prices. French, German, English, and Spanish spoken.

Services
As in Miches, don't expect a lot of variety or services in Sabana de la Mar.

BanReservas (Calle Duarte, 9 A.M.–5 P.M. Mon.–Fri., 9 A.M.–1 P.M. Sat.) has an ATM. **Codetel Centro de Comunicaciones** (Calle Duarte, 8 A.M.–10 P.M. Mon.–Sat.).

Open-air **Sabana de la Mar Market** (Duberay St. at 27 de Febrero) has overflowing fresh produce like different varieties of peppers and fruit if you are looking for some "real" food for your lunch baskets.

Getting There
There is a *guagua* stop at the convergence of Highways 103 and 104 in Sabana de la Mar. A ticket to Santo Domingo (via Hato Mayor) will cost you about US$4; buses leave every half hour 6 A.M.–4 P.M. A ticket to Miches will cost US$2.50, and buses leave every half hour.

Transportation Maritimo (tel. 809/538-2556, US$3.50) is the only choice to get across the bay to Samaná and, surprisingly, is the most direct way to get to the Costa Ámbar (via Samaná). The ride takes about an hour, leaving at 9 A.M., 11 A.M., 3 P.M., and 5 P.M. daily.

You may want to rent a sturdy car for this journey if you plan on going it on your own. Driving from Santo Domingo, go east on Carretera 3 (past the airport) and transfer to Carretera 4 east and then north so that you bypass San Pedro de Macorís. If you end up in that city, you will end up in a maelstrom of traffic. Head to the town of Hato Mayor and switch to Carretera 103 north toward Sabana de la Mar. Prepare for a bumpy ride. Try to make this trip in daylight since this last stretch of highway can be curvy and at times try your nerves. Dominican drivers swerve like young stockcar racers trying to prove themselves to miss potholes. The road from Miches to Sabana de la Mar is notoriously horrendous. You will need an SUV and a strong stomach. If you still insist on driving it on your own, just don't drive at night since drivers tend to swerve to avoid potholes, sometimes without headlights!

Going to Paraíso Caño Hondo? Once in Sabana de la Mar, you take a left off the main road in town that is well-marked with a sign to the hotel. To head to the ferry docks, just drive straight to the water after entering town.

Getting Around
Walking is easiest in Sabana de la Mar because it is so small. *Motoconchos* tool around the area,

and it will run you US$2–3 for a ride to the park. The best place to look for a taxi is the bus stop or the ferry dock. Secure a price before getting in. You can catch a *motoconcho* from here to Paraíso Caño Hondo (about 12 km) for about US$3 one way.

◀ PARQUE NACIONAL LOS HAITISES

The Dominican Republic is blessed to have a great deal of ecodiversity for such a small country, and the Parque Nacional Los Haitises (Land of the Mountains National Park) is one of the most distinctive of its national reserves, comprising nearly 160 kilometers of mangroves, estuaries, coves, and bays that together embrace the southwestern curve of the Bahía de Samaná.

Over 700 species of flora (17 are endemic to the area) thrive in the subhumid tropical forest due to its great amount of annual rainfall. Roughly 110 species of birds nest here, including the blue heron, the great white egret, the brown pelican, the roseate tern, and the rare Hispaniolan parakeet. The park's fauna includes scores of bats, tortoises, and manatees, which reside in the mangrove systems along the coast and various caves throughout.

The extensive limestone cave system is a major attraction for its examples of stalactites, stalagmites, and Taíno pictographs and petroglyphs depicting animals, rituals, faces, and divine beings.

Considering the rugged topography and its remoteness, the park is best conquered by boat excursions. They will take you through mangroves, rivers, and islets, and include walking through forest area and caves along the coast.

Coming from Highway 103 or 104, you'll see a park service sign in the south end of Sabana de la Mar. Excursions for the Parque Nacional Los Haitises are best done through various companies in Sabana de la Mar, Samaná, and Sánchez. If you want to explore on your own, you will need to pay RD$100 to enter the park.

Tours

Touring Los Haitises by boat is easy in a half-day excursion, and most places will offer this

© SAMUEL KRUCKER

hikers in Los Haitises

THE SOUTHEAST

in a package along with lunch; the price will also include the entrance to the park.

Paraíso Caño Hondo (Sabana de la Mar, tel. 809/248-5995, cell 809/889-9454, www.paraisocanohondo.com, website in Spanish only) offers tours that include a walk through the countryside and sub-humid forests, a boat trip through the mangroves, and the option to tour a few different caves. Signs from the center of Sabana de la Mar will direct you to Paraíso Caño Hondo (which is the same way to the Parque Los Haitises). The tour guides for this outfitter are particularly knowledgeable and passionate about the subject matter. I highly recommend this company. Tours start around US$45 (including guide, lunch, and entrance fee).

Sabana Tours Excursion Company (Av. de los Héroes 43, Sabana de la Mar, tel. 809/974-1753), on the water in Sabana de la Mar, claims to be the best in town. Certainly, they have a good variety of trips and packages, some of which include lunch and drinks (all prices are per person): whale watching in the Bahia de Samaná (US$99 with lunch/US$85 without lunch), afternoon at Cayo Levantado (US$85), Los Haitises walking tour (US$70 with lunch/US$49 without lunch), Samana (US$49), Las Galeras (US$56), Las Terrenas (US$70).

Amilka Tours (Calle Colón 15, Sánchez, tel. 809/552-7664 or 809/552-7922), located across the bay, will bring you by boat to Los Haitises.

Victoria Marine (Calle Mella and Av. Malecón, tel. 809/538-2494, www.whalesamana.com) is a popular and highly respected whale excursion outfitter in Samaná, but they also offer excursions to Los Haitises for US$55.

LA PENÍNSULA DE SAMANÁ

Dominicans refer to La Península de Samaná as the Land of Eternal Spring. Its bright sunshine and life-giving rains overflow the peninsula's mountainsides with vibrant green foliage and flowering plants. The peninsula, roughly 40 kilometers long and 15 kilometers wide, is also home to some of the country's most beloved beaches and has been a long-time favorite destination for the independent and backpacking tourist. In general, the Dominican Republic has a laid-back vibe, but on La Península de Samaná that mentality is encouraged. Mom-and-pop businesses and budget accommodations thrive on the peninsula, whereas in other parts of the country they are being drowned out by commercialism and big business. La Península de Samaná is easily the prettiest area in the country and the one that will get you to come back to the Dominican Republic time and again.

Las Terrenas, Las Galeras, and Samaná are the three small towns worth visiting. Along the northern Atlantic coast, the town of Las Terrenas is the busiest, offers the most variety for accommodations and restaurants, has long sandy stretches of beach, and has the best nightlife of the three towns. Las Galeras, on the eastern tip of the arm, is by far the most quiet and remote, and the beaches are, without doubt, the most beautiful on the peninsula—especially the famous Playa Rincón, with its gently curved white-sand beach backed by a thick coconut grove. Santa Bárbara de Samaná (commonly called "Samaná"), the capital of the province

HIGHLIGHTS

◖ **Cayo Levantado:** Sweep over the turquoise waters of the Bahía de Samaná aboard a catamaran to this island. Enjoy a light lunch served right on the beach and float in the warm, shallow water. During whale season, this is a great way to wind down after the excitement of visiting the huge mammals in their natural habitat (page 139).

◖ **Salto El Limón:** The trek to this waterfall is an ecotourist's dream. Ride a horse through some of the country's most beautifully rainforested mountains, climb down the heavily vegetated trail, and take a dip in the pool that the 52-meter-high waterfall empties into (page 140).

◖ **Whale-Watching:** Humpback whales put on an exhilarating display in the Bahía de Samaná. These 30- to 50-ton creatures travel

from as far away as Iceland every year to the waters just off the northern shore and proceed into the Bahía de Samaná for breeding and calving rituals. See them crest and splash just meters from your boat (page 141).

◖ **Playa Rincón:** Enjoy the striking beauty of this remote beach, known as one of the top 10 beaches in the Caribbean. With the clear water of the Bahía de Rincón on one side and a thick palm grove on the other, it feels like a level of heaven (page 149).

◖ **Nightlife in Las Terrenas:** Whether you want a gourmet meal or to go out dancing, Las Terrenas is the pulse of the peninsula. The international mix of expat business owners has given this town a unique and exciting vibe (page 161).

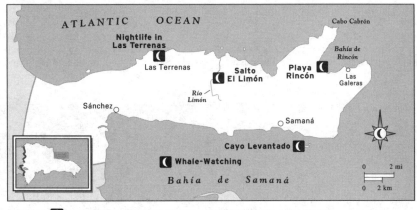

LOOK FOR ◖ TO FIND RECOMMENDED SIGHTS, ACTIVITIES, DINING, AND LODGING.

of Samaná, is on the Bahía de Samaná and is best known for its excursions to see the humpback whales in their natural habitat in the waters right offshore. The humpback whales arrive every winter to give birth and mate in the waters of the Bahía de Samaná. Samaná has also become a busy port for the arrival of cruise ships.

PLANNING YOUR TIME

La Península de Samaná is a major destination for the tourist who doesn't want to be confined behind the walls of an all-inclusive resort. It is chock-full of independent hotels, mom-and-pop restaurants, and small tour operators. Since it is a small sliver of land that is relatively easily traversed in a doable amount

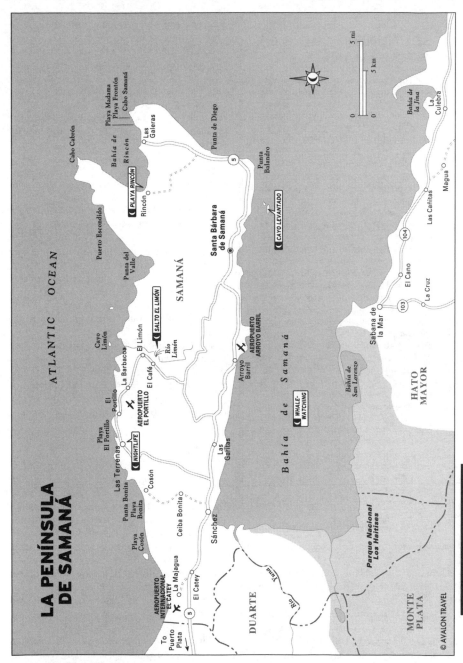

LA PENÍNSULA DE SAMANÁ

© AVALON TRAVEL

SETTLING INTO SAMANÁ

When Christopher Columbus attempted to settle the peninsula, the Ciguayo natives began to defend themselves with arrows; he immediately retreated (after having killed and enslaved many), naming the bay the Golfo de las Flechas (Gulf of the Arrows). The Spanish eventually ran the Ciguayos off the peninsula.

After that, with the exception of a motley assortment of pirates, the peninsula was nearly uninhabited until the 18th century, when settlers from the Canary Islands began to populate the area. In 1820, while this portion of the island was under Haitian control and together with U.S. abolitionists, land was gifted to 2,500 former slaves of the United States. Still visible today are their contributions to the culture of the area. The descendants of the former slaves – "Los Ingleses" (The English), as they were called – still speak a sort of English/Spanish mixture. There is an ever-present sizzle of frying *yaniqueques* (johnnycakes), which the settlers introduced to the present-day Dominican culinary fare. And the Methodist religion is still practiced.

In 1946, Santa Bárbara de Samaná was destroyed by a major fire. Most of its original wooden houses and buildings fell to the destruction, rising in a puff of black smoke, while one building stood in the midst of the ashes: the Methodist church or **La Churcha.** It was originally donated to the ex-slaves by the Methodist church and imported from England. To this day, "La Churcha" stands as a beloved heirloom of the family history of the region.

Flights arrive here every day from Puerto Rico and Europe. Other airports are Aeropuerto Internacional El Portillo (by Las Terrenas) and the Aeropuerto Internacional Arroyo Barril near Samaná. These latter two airports are small and have domestic flights despite their names. If you're flying into Puerto Plata or any other airport in the Dominican Republic, plan on using your first day for travel and getting settled in.

The three major towns on the peninsula—Samaná, Las Galeras, and Las Terrenas—while close to one another on the peninsula, are remote compared to the rest of the country. You'll need four hours of travel time from Puerto Plata, and the other airports are farther away than that. However, if you are traveling from Santo Domingo, there is a new highway to take you as far as the turnoff to Sánchez. This cuts travel time in half and makes this route easy. Once you've gotten to your hotel, though, especially if you're staying in one of the towns, walking around is the easiest way to get your bearings and explore.

Next up, decide if you're going to do any excursions. For instance, if you're going to go whale-watching in the Bahía de Samaná or take a horseback ride to **Salto El Limón,** but you're staying in Las Terrenas, arrange for reservations and transportation right away since tour spots could fill up.

HISTORY

Certainly when Christopher Columbus landed on Playa Las Flechas (Arrows Beach) back in the 1400s he didn't expect to be welcomed by a fusillade of arrows from the Taínos living along the southern coast of the Península de Samaná, but that is exactly what happened. Unfortunately, the Taínos made a grave mistake by helping Columbus to subjugate their fellow tribesmen, and it set the tone for many centuries of a turbulent history. Everyone wanted the peninsula. Pirates would hide out here, ex-slaves and African refugees settled here, various nations eyed it for outposts and bases.

The Samaná Peninsula, on very old maps, is sometimes shown as an island. The Río Yuna's

of time, it is possible to spend your entire vacation on just the peninsula and find plenty to keep you occupied.

Airports that serve La Península de Samaná make it more accessible than ever. The newest is the Aeropuerto Internacional El Catey on the highway between Nagua and Sánchez.

estuary now flows into the Bahía de Samaná, but there once was a channel that reached all the way up to the northern coast, creating a marshy waterway across the stretched neck of the peninsula.

Crafty pirates used this channel as an escape route to evade the Spanish. Back then, buccaneers loved Samaná for just the sort of escapist vibe the channel evoked. It seems that to this day, Samaná acts more like an island unto itself because of this history. It has a tradition of being the adopted home of invaders, violators, expatriates, and those with wanderlust.

Hundreds of years later, the former marshy waterway is now a fertile stretch of land on which rice grows easily (near the town of Sánchez), the pirate ships have all buried themselves in the waters offshore, and the expats have opened businesses.

In 1756 Spain established Santa Bárbara de Samaná and populated it with settlers from the Canary Islands. The land was then given up to Napoleon Bonaparte in an agreement that he give up some French-controlled land back in Spain. Even though Napoleon loved the area,

he was later forced to give it up by separate British and Haitian invasions.

The United States brought freed slaves to Samaná in the 1820s. The United States had its eye on the Península de Samaná as a potential naval base in the latter part of the 1800s. President Buenaventura Báez was all for it. It meant money and weapons and power for him. But the U.S. Senate rejected the deal. Báez, desperate for any deal, offered a 99-year lease up to a private company, giving them total political rule over Samaná, but, fortunately (as Dominicans see it) the deal fell through and Samaná stayed a part of the Dominican Republic. The Americans, for the time being, seemed otherwise occupied with Cuba's Guantanamo Bay, until World War I when they again occupied the area in an effort to keep Germany out and from establishing a base on the island.

Today, evidence of the mix of cultures that have settled here over the centuries can be seen in the last names of residents (left over from freed American slaves) as well as a language that developed as a result of the English, French, and German immigrants.

Santa Bárbara de Samaná

For the majority of the year, the seaside town of Santa Bárbara de Samaná (commonly referred to as Samaná) is mainly quiet. Then in January, Samaná's population dramatically skyrockets with tourists from all over the world who have come to see the humpback whales that migrate to the waters of the Bahía de Samaná. A fresh energy fills the area. In the bay, the huge beasts lob their tails and breach just meters from the tourist-filled boats. In the town, the normal tranquility is replaced with the drone of *motoconchos,* tour buses, and vendors.

Since 2005, Samaná has evolved into a cruise-ship stopover port. This new identity has caused an explosion in the local tourism industry there, multiplying the amount of visitors and services offered in Samaná.

The popularity of Samaná during whale-

watching season cannot be denied. It is truly a remarkable natural event that must not be missed.

Samaná has, until recently, been able to claim independence from the all-inclusive crunch. But since the Bahía Principe chain has opened a couple of its hotels and with their "Pueblo Principe" in downtown Samaná, they have given the seaside town both a more commercial feel and a major tourism boost.

SIGHTS AND RECREATION
◖ Cayo Levantado

This island, also known as Bacardi Island, though choked with tourists, has a beautiful white-sand beach. Due to the island's protected positioning in the bay, the waters are calm, shallow with a plush sandy bottom, and

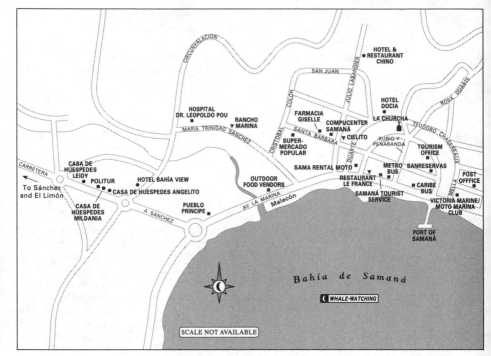

warm. This is an enjoyable place to take the family. The **Gran Bahía Principe Levantado** hotel occupies two-thirds of the island. Cruise ships dock here as well.

It's easiest to obtain a ride to Cayo Levantado by going directly to the Port of Samaná, where boats will take you there for US$10–15 per person, round-trip. Always try to work a better deal if you have more people in your party, and agree on a price before boarding the vessel.

Alternatively, about eight kilometers east of Samaná is a beach called **Playa Carenero** in a village of the same name. Here you will find multiple boat captains who can ferry you to Cayo Levantado for RD$1,500 for a boatload of 1–5 people round-trip. If you have more than that in your party, it is RD$300 each person. Another option is to go to the Gran Bahía Principe check-in dock. This is where guests of the Bahía Principe resorts are ferried back and forth to Cayo Levantado. It is one kilometer farther down

the Samaná–Las Galeras Road. Pay US$9 to board one of their boats.

After disembarking on Cayo Levantado, follow the crowd and you'll eventually see dozens of booths selling crafts; past there is a beach where you can rent loungers for about US$3. Food vendors sell ice-cold beers and plates of freshly fried fish with rice and salad for US$9. Beware: The trinket-hawkers are *everywhere* and rather persistent.

It is possible to **camp** on the remote side of Cayo Levantado. You will need to get a permit from the authorities at the port, which costs US$5, but to cut to the chase, go directly to **Victoria Marine** (Calle Mella at Av. La Marina, www.whalesamana.com, tel. 809/538-2494), since they are the ones that set up transportation and are allowed to sell you a permit as well.

(Salto El Limón

Nestled in a thickly forested area in the middle

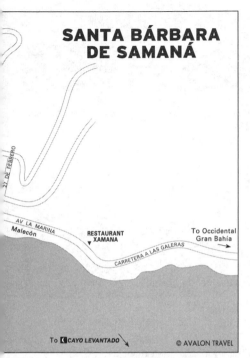

SANTA BÁRBARA DE SAMANÁ

27 DE FEBRERO

AV. LA MARINA
Malecón

RESTAURANT
▼ XAMANA

To Occidental
Gran Bahía →

CARRETERA A LAS GALERAS

To ◖CAYO LEVANTADO ↘

© AVALON TRAVEL

of the Samaná Peninsula, northwest of the town of Samaná, is Salto El Limón (Lemon Waterfall). This 52-meter-high cascade falls into a swimming hole, giving a most refreshing end to the somewhat difficult, and at times hair-raising, trek it takes to get there. Most people go to the waterfall by horseback. *Paradas* (literally "stops," but in this instance it means a horseback-riding tour operator) line the highway that cuts across the peninsula from El Limón to Samaná. These outfitters' routes vary, but most will provide your party with a horse, a guide who will walk beside you up the mountain, and the option of a lunch prepared for you upon your return. It is an awesome experience that shouldn't be missed when you visit the peninsula. Although the horses take you most of the way, you will need to make a descent to the Salto's pool from a lookout point—about a 15-minute jaunt by foot and it is rather steep in spots. Only those who are in good physical condition should do this hike.

Since you will be riding horses, wearing long pants is a great idea. But don't forget your bathing suit; the dip in the pool is a refreshing reward after this hike.

One operator is **Parada Ramona y Basilio** (El Café, Carretera Samaná–El Limón, Km 23, tel. 809/282-6309, US$22). While the trail that this *parada* follows is one of the longer ones, it is a very enjoyable and scenic ride. Ramona and Basilio are the two very hospitable hosts of this well-organized operation, and you'll find them along the road from El Limón to Samaná, marked with a big sign in front of the thatch-roofed pink house. While Ramona is the head chef for your savory meal, Basilio will give you an education on cacao and coffee production. The horse ride portion of your trek takes you through the small village of El Café, over the Río Limón in two different spots, and up mountainous passes where you'll see clear over to Cayo Limón on the northern shore of the Bahía de Samaná. You take a break at a small hilltop rest stop. It is a wonderful place to take photos of the waterfall from a distance, and you can also purchase refreshments before you continue on to the falls on foot. The hike down can be rather steep in spots (don't forget—you have to climb back up!) and it's not easy after a rain has come through. Your guide will wait at the top of the hill to return you to the *parada* on horseback again. The guides walking your party up and down the mountain depend heavily on your tips.

◖ Whale-Watching

One of the major reasons the town of Samaná is on the tourism map is because it is one of the best places in the world to observe dozens of humpback whales in their natural environment. This awe-inspiring activity will take you near Cayo Levantado on the turquoise waters of the Bahía de Samaná, where the giant, white-finned humpbacks practice their mating rituals. Every year, thousands of these huge mammals come from the faraway waters of Greenland and Iceland to the Bahía de Samaná.

Victoria Marine (Calle Mella at Av. La

© ANA CHAVIER CAAMAÑO

Bahía de Samaná, Santa Bárbara de Samaná

Marina, tel. 809/538-2494, www.whalesa-mana.com, US$55/adult, US$30/ages 5–10, free age 4 and under) tours leave at 9 A.M. and 1:30 P.M. Canadian marine mammal specialist Kim Beddall was the first to offer whale-watching tours in Samaná back in 1985, and through the years she has been sharing her considerable knowledge with a vast majority of the tourists that come to Samaná. Experience and respect for the whales results in a highly recommendable tour group. Victoria Marine adheres strictly to the whale-watching regulations set in place to minimize the impact on the whales, such as the number of boats observing the whales at one time, distance to the whales, time limits, and speeds in the bay and around the animals. Kim keeps a record of the whales that pass through the bay and asks that anyone who snaps a photo of the tail markings, which are like a whale fingerprint, to email them to her.

Free refreshments are provided on the boat, and information about the whales is given over a speaker. Tours are given in French, English, German, and Spanish. Be sure to ask about the optional stop at Cayo Levantado after observing the whales. This option gives you a couple of hours to swim at the beach and then enjoy a catamaran ride back to Samaná.

Also offering whale-watching excursions is the **Samaná Tourist Service** (Av. La Marina 6, tel. 809/538-2848, samanatour@codetel.net.do, US$65, tours 8:30 A.M.–12:30 P.M. and 2:30–6:30 P.M. Mon.–Fri., 8:30 A.M.–12:30 P.M. Sat.).

Moto Marina Club (Av. Malecón 3, tel. 809/538-2302, motomarina@yahoo.com, 8 A.M.–6 P.M.) has whale-watching coupled with a visit to Cayo Levantado excursion. Reserve two days in advance to make sure there is space available. When whale season is over, there are other excursions offered.

Amilka Tours (Calle Colón, Sánchez, tel. 809/552-7664, www.amilkatoursdominican.com, US$50) out of the town of Sánchez, offers whale excursions among their many other choices.

La Churcha

This small Evangelical church (Calle Duarte, 9 A.M.–6 P.M. daily) is a few blocks from the

TWO-TON DOMINICAN BABIES

Most humpback whales that live in the northern Atlantic Ocean are Dominicans. It is here that female humpback whales are courted by males, where they mate, and where the babies are born 12 very long months later. The balmy waters of the Bahía de Samaná are the perfect "delivery room" for baby humpback whales. Shallow waters create warmer temperatures and therefore cause less shock to the calf upon delivery.

Each female will have only one baby every 2-3 years, a baby that can measure 3-5 meters in length and weigh up to two metric tons. "¡Que grande!"

Within 2-3 months the calves must be ready to accompany their mothers on the long migration back to the northern Atlantic Ocean, where humpbacks feed for the summer before they return to the Caribbean to start the process all over again. For that journey, the baby swims below its mom to suckle her nutrient-rich milk, thereby building up its own blubber. Calves can be dependent on their mothers for food for a whole year, until the next time they return to the Caribbean. In that time, the baby will have doubled in size. But this year is treacherous. If something should happen to the mom, the calf is doomed. No other female whale can nurse it since they only have enough milk for their own calves.

Every year, around December, the humpbacks start coming back, tourists get their cameras out, and the boats circle, hoping to catch a glimpse of mom and baby practicing the acrobatics that humpbacks are famous for. Seeing a 40-ton adult whale leap high into the air and land with a enormous splash is an amazing display of grace and power. But seeing a baby attempt to mimic what mom has just done is a stunning illustration of nature and the circle of life.

The Bahía de Samaná is an important sanctuary for the humpback whale's survival, and it is one of the largest estuaries in the Dominican Republic and the Caribbean. Threats to the system include fishing, deforestation, whale-watching tourism, and cruise ship encroachment. Most smaller boats (those of the whale-watching excursion boats) follow strict rules for getting close to the whales. However, cruise ships push close to them with their vessel noises and pollutants, displacing them further out to sea every year.

water. The materials were originally shipped all the way from England for the then recent immigrants of the Canary Islands. The wooden interior, red tin roof, and zinc siding were assembled back in 1823 in Santa Bárbara de Samaná and was barely restored until 2007, when various donors got together, hired architects, and began to save the church from damage sustained over the years. Overall, La Churcha remains as it came to Samaná back in 1823 but for a few replaced pieces of siding that had to be shipped from Germany to keep it historically correct, and the original floor had been changed from the wood to ceramic back in the 1930s. Some services are held in English.

ACCOMMODATIONS

Despite the huge burst of tourism during the whale-watching season, accommodation choices within the town of Samaná remain surprisingly limited, no doubt in part due to the fact that most people visiting the area do so only to take part in a whale-watching cruise for a few hours. If you don't need all the frills of the all-inclusives, there are a few *pensiones* in town that offer relatively good deals for a satisfying night's sleep directly in town.

Under US$50

Ask for a balcony at **Hotel Bahía View** (Av. Circunvalación 4, near the middle traffic circle along Francisco del Rosario Sánchez, tel. 809/538-2186, US$27 d with a/c, US$24 d without a/c). Even though all 10 rooms have ceiling fans and hot water and are kept clean (there's no TV), the rooms with a balcony are more comfortable, if only for that extra little bit of space. The restaurant below is good, but not included in the rate. This hotel is a good value, but keep in mind that the strict check-out time is at 11 A.M. or they charge you for another day. It is a great value and a long-time favorite.

Just a few blocks from the seafront, in a quiet part of town, is **Hotel Docia** (Teodoro Chasereaux at Rosa Duarte, tel. 809/538-2041, fax 809/538-2458, US$17 d), perfect for the backpacker who doesn't expect bells and whistles. You do get a very clean room with a private bathroom and free coffee in the morning. With the town center just a short walk away, there are plenty of options for food, but there is a small kitchen in the hotel available for guests to do light cooking.

These three guesthouses are all in a row on Calle Francisco del Rosario Sánchez and cost roughly the same amount (RD$1,000–1,500) per room: **Casa de Huespedes Angelito** (33, tel. 809/538-3338) is a suitable establishment for one night, but be prepared for power outages. It has incredibly basic rooms with TV, somewhat shaky ceiling fans, and private baths. **Casa de Huespedes Leidy** (50, tel. 809/538-3315) is another inexpensive option. There are nine rooms and one "suite"; air-conditioning is an option. Perhaps the best option of the three is **Casa de Huespedes Mildania** (41, tel. 809/538-2151). It is clean and offers air-conditioning and TV, and has a lovely seating area in the front of the building where you can watch the foot traffic go by and enjoy the night air. In all of these options, ask for a room away from the front of the building. The street can be quite noisy.

Hotel & Restaurant Chino (Calle San Juan 1, tel. 809/538-2215, RD$1,600 d), high up on the hill, is the restaurant with the fantastic views and now a hotel! Unfortunately, although the rooms are remarkably clean and new, and have air-conditioning, hot water, and great views, you had better make sure to request a room with a window or balcony. If you don't, you will be paying a high price for a dark, albeit clean room that is not within walking distance to the beach. Rooms 7 and 8 have balconies with breathtaking views all the way down to the Bahía de Samaná for RD$2,000 per night.

US$100 and Up

Gran Bahía Principe Cayacoa (Loma Puerto Escondido, tel. 809/538-3131, www.bahia-principe.com, US$140) rests, like a jewel on a crown, shining over Santa Bárbara de Samaná and the bay. It is the result of a glamorous remake of a hotel that has ushered in a new era of class to the tourism industry in Samaná. This Caribbean-style all-inclusive offers 209 standard rooms and 86 junior suites. From the hotel at the top of the cliff, where the pool is located, you can take one of two panoramic elevators down to the beach area and enjoy the day by the sea. Pueblo Principe was built as the entertainment provider for this resort since resort nightlife here is rather quiet. Pueblo Principe has the discos and bars and is located in the town of Samaná, to which you must take a shuttle. Some may find that (and the elevator to the beach) a hassle. Still, this is a good midrange all-inclusive option.

The beach on Cayo Levantado is pristine and **Gran Bahía Principe Cayo Levantado** (Cayo Levantado, tel. 809/538-3232, www.bahia-principe.com, US$200) will give you that paradise vacation you've been wanting. But beware; being on an island off the coast of an island might give those who like nightlife the feeling of being trapped. You are at the mercy of Bahía Principe's boat service to get you to Samaná if you want to experience life outside the hotel. Then again, if you're looking for a spot for isolation and relaxation, you've found it. The rooms are large and attractive.

Rivaling the Cayacoa's views is the **Gran Bahía Principe** (Carretera Samaná–Las Galeras, tel. 809/538-34343, www.bahia-principe.com, US$330 d). This Victorian-style all-inclusive is situated on a point overlooking the Bahía de Samaná and Cayo Levantado and was recently remodeled and reopened in a new and striking way. It has 110 rooms with one buffet and two specialty restaurants, two smallish swimming pools, A solarium with hammocks, tennis courts, and a gym. The rooms are new with a plantation-style update and complete with all the proper all-inclusive trimmings, like satellite TV, Jacuzzi tubs, air-conditioning, minibars, and safety boxes (at extra cost). There is a spa on-site as well as a beauty salon. The hotel's private beach is down the dramatic staircase, but you can also take a golf cart ride to the beach from the front desk. It is the kind of place where even the staff is well-dressed. Your all-inclusive rate will cover some fun things like water sports, tennis court fees, on-site scuba lessons, and dance lessons. A free daily shuttle will take you to Samaná. Take note: Activities for kids are rather limited.

FOOD

Many of Samaná's restaurants are along the Malecón (Avenida La Marina). Since Samaná has been a favorite expat residential area, there is a good assortment of cuisine, including French, American, Italian, Chinese, and of course Dominican. In a region surrounded by the sea and teeming with coconut groves, one must simply try a typical regional dish with any kind of fish in coconut sauce.

La Hacienda (Av. La Marina, tel. 809/538-2383, 5–11:30 P.M. Thurs.–Tues. for dinner, grill and bar open at noon, US$8–15) has a great reputation and for good reason. The food varies from international choices to specialty French cuisine dishes and is wonderful. The menu is in three languages, making ordering easier. For dinner try the steak in peppercorn sauce, experiment with seafood like octopus, or go for some traditional Dominican chicken.

Restaurant El Bambu (Av. La Marina, tel. 809/538-2661, noon–3 P.M. and 7 P.M.–midnight, , US$3–10) is directly in front of the Victoria Marine excursion office. While it is not a culinary delight like La Hacienda, it is a suitable choice for a quick lunch after your whale-watching excursion. It serves international favorites like sandwiches and pasta.

Bianchimani Franco, the restaurateur who made Santo Domingo's former Caffe Bellini one of the most successful restaurants in the nation, is back at it. At **Restaurant Xamana** (Av. La Marina, tel. 809/538-2129, US$10–30) you can enjoy top grade Italian and international dishes. Fish is always fresh, so try the *pescado carpaccio* or the *spaghetti mare*.

© ANA CHAVIER CAAMAÑO

Samaná market

There are also many beef choices and a phenomenal lamb lineup. For dessert, we recommend the house favorites tiramisu and *dulce de coco Samaná*. The atmosphere, in classic Franco style, is stylish and sleek without being stuffy. At the end of your meal, you'll receive a complimentary *chinolacello* or *mangolacello* liquor made with seasonal passionfruit or mango just for the restaurant. This dining experience far surpasses any other in Samaná. Franco has done it again.

Rancho Marina (Av. Maria Trinidad Sánchez 13, tel. 809/538-2057, ranchomarina@hotmail.com, 8 A.M.–midnight, Fridays no dinner, Saturdays only dinner) is a major local seafood favorite. Tucked into the neighborhood of Samaná, this smallish restaurant can get pretty busy due to their very reasonable prices. At the front of the establishment there is a buffet line (seating in the back), but there is more available even though there is no menu. If you speak Spanish, ask what else is available that day. Try the fish in coconut sauce or, if you like tripe, try the *mondongo*. The *mofongo* (mashed plantain) is great here.

Chino's (Calle San Juan 1, tel. 809/538-2215, 11 A.M.–11 P.M. daily, US$5–15) is on the top of a hill (just behind the Hotel Docia) with a fantastic view. The thing about the food in Samaná is that it reflects the number of expats that live there. Here you can get everything from French crepes to Italian pizzas to American burgers and now Chinese food. Stir-fry, egg rolls, wonton soup, it's all here. Dominican dishes are served too. Indoor and outdoor seating available.

Restaurant Le France (Av. La Marina, tel. 809/538-2257, 10 A.M.–11 P.M. Tues.–Sun., US$5–15), right next to Le Café de Paris, despite its name offers Dominican fare along with French dishes in a relaxed atmosphere. Have a meal in the fresh breeze and watch Samaná go by.

Need something sweet? Try a local favorite. The English cakes at **D'Vieja Pan Ingles** (Carretera Samaná–Las Galeras, tel. 809/435-6634) are a Samaná tradition and are made best right here at this tiny stand popular with locals. Although the English cakes put it on the map, try the *dulce de coco,* served in a cup with a spoon and made with sweet potatoes and coconut; its unique tastiness is incomparable to anything, anywhere. English spoken here.

Around dinnertime, small food stands along the waterfront serve cheap eats and ice-cold beers. It's a good place to grab a casual meal, watch the boats, and ask the locals where the best place for merengue dancing is, since it seems to change constantly.

ENTERTAINMENT AND EVENTS
Nightlife
Tourists in Samaná tend to make a night of their dining experience and then plant themselves wherever the lively atmosphere is on that particular night. Samaná does not have the same hopping nightlife scene of Las Terrenas, but fun can usually be found at the numerous open-air stalls that are set up at dusk on the weekends along the Malecón. A couple have even have laid out makeshift dance floors so that customers can enjoy a good merengue or *bachata* in the night air.

Naomi's (Av. La Marina, 9 P.M.–4 A.M. Fri.–Sun., US$2), on the waterfront above the Restaurant Le France, is the local favorite for merengue and *bachata* dancing. It can get pretty packed.

Cielito (Calle Lebantiel, free admission) is the current merengue, *bachata* and salsa dancing hot spot. You can feel the beat pumping in your chest the music is loud and good. The crowd is mostly locals but tourists are peppered in lightly. The dance floor gets crowded as this is a very small club.

The **Piano Bar** (Av. La Marina, Pueblo Principe) disco is new and has nice lights and is on the main tourist drag. It doesn't fill up like Cielito and is, somehow, less authentic. But, it is a nice facility and has a nice dance floor.

Festivals
There are few times that Dominicans stray from their loyalty to dancing the merengue or the *bachata,* but if you're in the area on

October 24 for the **Festival of San Rafael** or on December 4 for the **Patron Saint Day,** you'll see the traditional dances *bambulá* and *chivo florete* being performed in the streets. Their roots are from the African slaves and the immigrating American freed slaves who populated the area. Processions, open-air music, dancing in the streets, and stalls selling food, beverages, and local crafts are all part of these festivals.

The town holds a series of annual **Harvest Festivals** on Fridays from late August through the end of October with traditions dating back to the yam and rice festivals of the Canary Islands of west Africa. Each one is in a different church with the biggest at La Churcha on the last Friday in October.

INFORMATION
AND SERVICES
Tourist Information

At the **Oficina de Turismo** (Av. Santa Bárbara, tel. 809/538-2332, 8:30 A.M.–3 P.M. Mon.–Fri.), you can get maps and some information about the peninsula. It's not the most efficient office, but with tourism booming in Samaná, that will hopefully change.

Communications

CompuCenter Samaná (Calle Lavandier, tel. 809/538-3146, 9 A.M.–12:30 P.M. and 3–6 P.M. Mon.–Fri.) offers Internet service for RD$50 per half hour.

Centro de Comunicaciones (Calle Santa Bárbara, tel. 809/536-2133, 8 A.M.–10 P.M. daily) is sometimes closed 1–2 P.M. for a lunch hour. It is both an Internet and international call center. The Internet connection costs US$1.75, and long-distance calls are US$0.35 per minute to the U.S., US$0.75 per minute to Europe.

The **post office** (Calle Santa Bárbara, 8:30 A.M.–5 P.M. Mon.–Fri.) is not the most reliable way to communicate with the rest of the world.

Health and Emergencies

Hospital Dr. Leopoldo Pou (Av. María Trinidad Sánchez 15, tel. 809/538-2597) offers emergency medical care 24 hours a day and dental care.

Farmacia Giselle (Calle Santa Bárbara 2, tel. 809/538-2303, 8 A.M.–10 P.M. Mon.–Sat., 8 A.M.–noon Sun.) is the most reliable pharmacy in town, with a bigger selection of meds and other potential needs. It's one block past Duarte at Calle Julio Labandier.

Most **Politur** (Francisco del Rosario Sánchez, tel. 809/754-3066, 24 hours) employees speak another language, but if you have a Spanish dictionary, take it with you, just in case.

Money

Banco Popular (Av. La Marina 4, tel. 809/538-3666, 8 A.M.–4 P.M. Mon.–Fri., 9 A.M.–1 P.M. Sat.) is the bank with the best location, right in the thick of it all, across from the Port of Samaná. It has an ATM.

One block off the Malecón is **BanReservas** (Calle Santa Bárbara, tel. 809/538-2255, 8 A.M.–5 P.M. Mon.–Fri., 9 A.M.–1 P.M. Sat.) and also **ScotiaBank** (Calle Francisco del Rosario Sánchez 111, tel. 809/538-3474, 8 A.M.–4 P.M. Mon.–Fri.).

GETTING THERE
By Car

From Puerto Plata, after the town of Cabarete, Carretera (Highway) 5 starts its southward bend toward the town of Sánchez, where it continues along the southern coast of the Samaná Peninsula. After Carretera 5 runs east through the town of Samaná, it curves upward along the eastern coast of the peninsula to end in Las Galeras.

In January 2008, the Santo Domingo–Samaná (officially named Juan Pablo II) Carretera opened. The motorway is only 110 kilometers long, but it cuts travel time in half. This highway leads directly to Carretera 5. Once you exit the new highway onto Carretera 5, turn right toward Samaná. What was a smooth ride will no longer be as luxurious. This road takes you past the town of El Catey and the International Airport El Catey.

Continue along the same route and you will find yourself in Santa Bárbara de Samaná.

By Air

There are three airports on the peninsula: **Aeropuerto Internacional El Catey** (tel. 809/338-5888) in the town of El Catey, near Sánchez; **Aeropuerto Internacional Arroyo Barril** (tel. 809/248-2718), on the southern coast; and **Aeropuerto Internacional El Portillo** (tel. 809/248-2289), just outside of Las Terrenas on the northern coast. The first is the newest and began operation in 2006 with flights daily from Puerto Rico, Canada, and Europe. The second and third are more for private charters.

For now, the airport at El Portillo has a few companies that have regularly scheduled flights departing and arriving every day.

Takeoff Destination Service S.A. (Plaza Brisas de Bávaro 8, Bávaro, tel. 809/552-1333, www.takeoffweb.com), located in the Southeast, has flights Monday, Wednesday, and Friday between Punta Cana and Las Terrenas for US$149.

Aerodomca (Aeropuerto Internacional de Herrera, Santo Domingo tel. 809/826-4141, Las Terrenas tel. 809/240-6571, www.aerodomca.com) offers flights from the airport at El Portillo to Santo Domingo (US$80). Reservations are required with a 24-hour advance notice.

Both of these companies also offer taxi services.

By Bus and *Guagua*

The station of **Caribe Tours** (Av. La Marina, tel. 809/538-2229) is directly across from the Port of Samaná. Rides (4.5 hours) are offered to and from Santo Domingo at 7 A.M., 8:30 A.M., 10 A.M., 1 P.M., 2:30 P.M., and 4 P.M. (US$8.50) daily.

Another bus company, **Metro** (Av. La Marina, tel. 809/538-2851), just a block away, offers the same ride to Santo Domingo for US$8 but only twice a day (8 A.M.and 3 P.M.). Both of these companies' routes stop in Sánchez, Nagua, and San Pedro de Macorís along the way.

The Samaná *guaguas* stop at the *mercado* (a block north of Av. La Marina, no phone), and you can catch rides to Las Galeras (US$2), El Limón (US$2), and Sánchez (US$2) nearly every 15 minutes 6 A.M.–6 P.M. *Guaguas* to Sánchez stop at 4:30 P.M. If you want to get off at any point along the way, just tell them and they will let you out. Similarly, you can flag down *guaguas* on the main roads, but it is usually best to go to a *guagua* stop to ensure getting a seat.

By Ferry

Traveling from Samaná to Sabana de la Mar is possible via the Bahía de Samaná. At the **Transporte Maritimo** (Av. La Marina, tel. 809/538-2556, US$3.50), you can catch a ferry for a one-hour ride across the water. They leave at 7 A.M., 9 A.M., 11 A.M., and 3 P.M. If you have arrived into Samaná from a ferry departing from Sabana de la Mar, you will be left at Playa de las Flechas. From there you will need to catch a *motoconcho* or a *guagua* into town (US$1).

GETTING AROUND

Samaná is easiest on foot. It is small and most of the restaurants and other locations are just a stroll away. Like in other towns in the Dominican Republic, though, *motoconchos* and motorized rickshaws are everywhere. They hang out around the entrance to the Port of Samaná and can be hired for US$1–3 depending on distance to be traveled.

If you plan on doing any driving throughout the rest of the peninsula and want to rent a car, there are rental places in town. Consider spending the extra money for a four-wheel-drive as many of the roads can be rough and uneven.

If you plan on doing some driving, go to the long-standing local car rental company **Xamaná Rent Moto** (Av. La Marina 5, tel. 809/538-2380, 8 A.M.–noon and 2–6 P.M.).

Las Galeras

While La Península de Samaná is a magnet for independent travelers seeking the uncommon track in the Dominican Republic, Las Galeras is for those who seek an even more potent version of that. Those who like small village life as an alternative to their regular hectic lives at home will fall in love with the coconut plantations, numerous secluded and private beaches, and the tropical lushness of the undulating hills throughout this region. Las Galeras went virtually unnoticed until the early 1990s. Its remarkable beaches (some that you'll have to reach by boat or hike to in order to enjoy), remote location on the Samaná Peninsula, and the slow-paced tranquility of the village have created a following among independent travelers from Europe and Canada over the past two decades.

Whether you drive from Samaná or Las Terrenas on your way to Las Galeras, it is a gorgeous trip. Turn up the *bachata,* maybe some Anthony Santos, roll the windows down, and enjoy your trip to the tip of paradise. But when you arrive, don't expect supermarkets, huge resorts, travel agencies, and night-bumping discos. Your choices may be more limited, but your satisfaction will be deeper if you are looking for calmness.

BEACHES

Las Galeras is known for its untouched beaches. Walking the white sands, you might find yourself on a secluded beach, surrounded by tall palms. These beaches have been hailed by many Dominicans as the most gorgeous in all of the Dominican Republic. Certainly, if you are not staying overnight in Las Galeras, their splendor alone is reason for a day trip.

◖ Playa Rincón

If the beaches of Las Galeras are the jewels of the beaches in the Dominican Republic, then Playa Rincón goes even beyond that. As if on a stage, it is surrounded by the 600-meter cliffs of Cape Cabrón and a thick curtain of palm trees that run into the plush white sand and clear sapphire water. Sound too perfect for reality? It is not: Playa Rincón is one of those beaches that you thought you'd never find. It is not perfect in the manicured, raked-sand way, but in the wild and deserted-in-paradise way with fallen coconuts and twigs from trees scattering the ground. And, there is plenty of sand space for all who go there. There are even several spots to buy freshly caught seafood and rent beach chairs.

Playa Rincón's remoteness and terrible roads are probably keeping it from being overcrowded. To reach Playa Rincón by car, a four-wheel-drive (like a jeep) is strongly recommended. The eight-kilometer trip from Las Galeras to the town of Rincón takes 40 minutes, and then you turn off for a two-kilometer, very rough ride to the beach. But the best way to reach Playa Rincón is by boat. At the main beach in Las Galeras you can find local boat captains with whom you can make arrangements for a departure and pickup time to Playa Rincón or any of the other beaches in the area (about US$12 per person). If you decide to take a taxi, you'll pay about US$50 round-trip.

The **Río Frío** is a freshwater river that flows along the western end of Playa Rincón. It is a popular place to take a dip, despite the frigid temperature of the water, and grab something to eat at the fresh fish shacks set up there.

Playa Las Galeras, Playa Cala Blanca, and Playita

At the north end of Highway 5 is Playa Las Galeras, a perfectly good beach where you can catch boats to other beaches or simply while away the afternoon enjoying the white sands and calm waters, with lunch from a small fish stand.

Adjacent Playa Cala Blanca, a short walking distance away, is a tranquil beach perfect for families with small children. The coral reef offshore prevents big waves from making it to the beach, creating a shallow, warm, and tranquil pool.

© ANA CHAVIER CAAMAÑO

the tranquil Playa Las Galeras

Playita can be reached by foot or from the main road just south of Las Galeras; turn west onto a dirt road that is marked for the beach and the Hotel La Playita. The beach itself has tranquil surf, a wide sandy area, and a coconut grove. You can get some fresh fish and a cool drink from the stands here.

Playas Madama and Frontón

These adjoining beaches are a bit harder to get to, but their beauty will give a huge payoff to those who make the effort. East of Las Galeras are the rocky shores and high bluffs surrounding Playas Madama and Frontón. Playa Madama is wonderful for snorkeling, and it is not unheard of to find these beaches with few to no other people on them. These beaches are best reached by boat. Negotiate a price with the Playa Las Galeras local boat captains.

SPORTS AND RECREATION
Diving and Snorkeling

Experienced divers will enjoy the sites at **Cabo Cabrón,** one of the best dive sites on the northern coast; it's known for its walls.

In the reefs, you'll see many creatures, including turtles, barracudas, tuna, and dolphins. Special highlights are The Cathedral, a colossal underwater cave, and The Tower, which is a deep 24-meter diameter underwater summit rising from 50 meters to within 5 meters of the water's surface. This pinnacle is covered in gorgonian fans, sponges, and corals and is home to a wonderful array of marine life. In the fissures of the wall you'll encounter spider crabs and lobster, while swarms of colorful tropical fish swirl around you in search of food.

The diving along the eastern coast of La Península de Samaná is an exciting adventure, especially at Cabo Cabrón. Water visibility ranges 30–45 meters, and January–March whales migrate to the Bahía de Samaná for the yearly mating season.

Dive Samaná (Playa Las Galeras, tel. 809/538-0210, 7 A.M.–6 P.M. daily) offers dive excursions to some remarkable drop-offs where you'll see eels, rays, barracudas, and sea turtles. Dive Samaná is at the end of Casa Marina Bay's stretch of beach. Dives run US$60 for a one-

© ANA CHAVIER CAAMAÑO

Boat captains wait on Playa Las Galeras to take you to other beaches.

tank dive (includes all equipment), and other packages are also available for up to four tanks. PADI certifications are available. Reservations are recommended.

Grand Paradise Samaná Dive Center (Casa Marina Bay Resort, 7 A.M.–6 P.M. daily) can take you on a two-tank dive for US$114, including the rental of the equipment, or a snorkeling trip for US$12.

Horseback Riding

A great way to experience the countryside and get to the secluded beaches of the area is to go on horseback. Discover beautiful vistas looking down to the country's most beautiful beaches or wind you way through coconut groves and the Dominican countryside.

La Rancheta (tel. 809/878-0637, www. larancheta.com, US$35–US$65) offers a variety of horse riding trips ranging from a half-day trip to Playa Madama, where you can swim and explore a cave; a full-day trip to Playa Frontón (if you're lucky enough to be there in whale season, you will see some just off shore);

to an overnight trip to Playa Frontón with all meals and tent provided (US$205). The owners of the establishment, Karin and Ronald, are multilingual and make great efforts to put together personalized trips.

Hiking

If being bipedal is more your speed, then there are some nature trails that should satisfy your urge to see flora and scenery of the Dominican Republic. You can go to the **Tourist Service Office** (tel. 809/538-2740) right in the center of town and ask for a guide. But you can also head over to a lookout that is five kilometers outside of town. Walk past the turnoffs for Playas Madama and Frontón and climb up the hillside. It'll be a long and steep climb. La Rancheta can also arrange for a guided hike.

Tours and Excursions

Aventura Tropical (Calle Principal, tel. 809/538-0249, 8 A.M.–7 P.M. Mon.–Sat., 8 A.M.–1 P.M. Sun.) has excursions including hikes to secluded beaches, whale-watching, boat trips through Los Haitises, and even a tour that will take you through a village where you'll get an in-depth glimpse at rural Dominican life.

At **Dario Perez Servic Travel** (Plaza Lucitania, tel. 809/924-6081 or 809/538-0110) you can rent quad bikes (US$50), take a horseback riding tour to Playa Rincón (US$60) that will last 5–6 hours and include lunch, and arrange dive excursions (US$50 for one dive including equipment; negotiate for more dives).

Nightlife

Las Galeras is not known for its nightlife. If you're looking for wild nights of spirited dancing and mingling, head to Las Terrenas. There is, however, a place to get in a little *bachata* or merengue dancing in Las Galeras. **V.I.P.** (Calle Principal, 9 P.M.–late, free) is a popular club that draws locals from all over the surrounding area to dance on the weekends, and dancing is one of the best and most authentic ways to explore the Dominican culture.

LA PENÍNSULA DE SAMANÁ

ACCOMMODATIONS
Under US$50

Casa ¿Por Qué No? (just north of the main intersection in town, tel. 809/712-5631, US$50 d) is a small bed-and-breakfast with only two rooms; it is only open November–April but is a lovely choice. The owners, Pierre and Monick, come from a long line of hoteliers so they know what they are doing. Each room is clean and nicely appointed, just like you are in the guest room of a family member's home. Each has a private soft-water bathroom and includes a patio overlooking the flourishing and well-tended garden. Rates include a home-cooked breakfast served on your patio or in the garden itself with menu items like crepes, sensational French toast, and for a treat, homemade ice cream or cake.

Villa Casa Lotus (Playa Las Galeras, tel. 809/538-0119, www.casalotus.ch.vu/, US$40 per person and up) is a quaint guesthouse next to the sea, moments from the center of Las Galeras. It sits under a canopy of palm trees and has three double bedrooms and one single-bedroom apartment. All of the rooms have a private hot-water bathroom, and the apartment has a kitchen and can accommodate up to four people. Decor includes wood furnishings, mosquito-net canopies over the beds, exposed beam ceilings, and French doors to the lush tropical garden. The owner will prepare vegetarian meals for those who request them.

The seven clean and simple cabins of **Paradiso Bungalow** (Calle Principal, tel. 809/967-7295, US$27 d) each have their own cold-water bathroom, small porch with patio furniture, double bed, and ceiling fans. The bungalows are all in a plush garden 60 meters from the beach.

US$50-100

Apart Hotel La Isleta (tel. 809/538-0016, www.la-isleta.com, US$65), 100 meters from the center of Las Galeras, has six very captivating apartments, each with its own complete kitchen, private hot-water bathroom, and porch with a magnificent ocean view. Tastefully decorated with tropical colors, these cabin-like apartments with loft bedrooms offer a spaciousness that you just can't get in a standard hotel room, making them particularly well suited to families. Each unit has a water cooler and TV. Weekly and monthly rates are available. Amenities include a barbecue, Jacuzzi, and bar.

There are 10 apartments of varying size in **Apart-Hotel Plaza Lusitania** (Calle Principal, tel. 809/538-0093, www.plazalusitania.com, US$60–100 per apartment). The smallest is a one-room flat with two beds, and the largest is a two-room flat with six beds. All apartments have small kitchenettes, private baths, and tile floors throughout, and are decorated with island furniture and art. All have balconies and are kept very clean. This hotel is on the second level of a shopping area that includes a grocery store and a restaurant that serves Dominican and Italian. Rates include breakfast. Parking is free.

Juan y Lolo Bungalows (Calle A 313, tel. 809/538-0208, www.juanylolo.com, US$40–120) is one of the best bungalow rental companies in Las Galeras. All bungalows are tastefully decorated and have kitchens, bathrooms, and patios. The style of the bungalows varies considerably, from Caribbean thatch-roofed simplicity to a Columbus-era bungalow complete with Queen Isabella–inspired furniture. All have incredible rates for what you get.

Romi Caraibes (1 km inland from the beach, tel. 809/538-0193, romicaraibes.free. fr, US$70 d) is hidden from the road behind a large iron gate. If you speak French or Spanish, you're in luck, because this is a wonderful place to disappear from the world. The four rooms at this bed and breakfast, owned by a hospitable French couple, are very clean, modern, and spacious. Enjoy quiet afternoons taking a dip in the pool or lazing about in the garden. Also available are wireless Internet and a pool table. All rooms have air-conditioning, cable TV, refrigerators, safes, and soft hot water. Family-style breakfast is included in the price of your room.

A few paces west, you'll find **C Sol Azul** (1 km inland from the beach, tel. 809/882-

8790, www.elsolazul.com, US$52 d). This delightful thatched-roof bed and breakfast has four rooms and a swimming pool. It's run by a friendly Swiss couple, who have truly made this a romantic getaway. From the white mosquito netting draped over all the beds in the warm glow of the terra-cotta walls to the private patios that lead to a garden with a fantastic pool where you can wash off the heat of the day or take a nap in one of the hammocks, this place will caress you with tranquility. But you won't be too disconnected if you don't want to be since they have wireless Internet too. Breakfast is included, and sometimes a barbecue dinner is cooked alfresco by the pool. They'll let you know—it's all very relaxed here. French, German, English, and Spanish are spoken here.

US$100 and Up

◖ **Todo Blanco** (Beach Road East, tel. 809/538-0201, www.hoteltodoblanco.com, US$100 d) is set back in a leafy garden from the main road that leads from Las Galeras along the beach, which makes it a very quiet oasis for a peaceful vacation. The rooms are large and have balconies (request an ocean view and air-conditioning if you prefer). All have hot water and a safety box. A restaurant on-site serves breakfast only at an additional rate.

On the curved bay of Playa Las Galeras is the plush oasis at ◖ **Villa Serena** (tel. 809/538-0000, fax 809/538-0009, www.villaserena.com, US$160 d w/air-conditioning in peak season), a white, two-story, Victorian-inspired hotel. One of the most charming things about the hotel is that all 21 rooms are decorated differently, adding to the unique experience. All rooms have private balconies and face the ocean. Not all the rooms have air-conditioning, but those on the second floor receive a very refreshing sea breeze. This hotel is a very romantic honeymoon spot (ask about the free honeymoon package when staying a minimum of five nights) and is great for those wishing for tranquility. A small pool surrounded by natural stones sits between the hotel and the sea among the garden's color-bursting tropical plants and palm trees. The other fantastic reason to spend the rather hefty rate on this hotel is the restaurant. Guests can enjoy Dominican and French cuisine at one of the best restaurants in the town of Las Galeras. Rates include breakfast. Tours can be organized, and free bicycles and snorkel gear are available for guests.

FOOD

Many great meals can be had at the shacks found at the entrance to Playa Las Galeras. Fish and shellfish are caught daily and cooked right on the beach. It is a great, low-cost way to go.

Expats who've settled here have turned Las Galeras (much like the rest of the Samaná peninsula) into a culinary pleasure. And although many hotels have their own restaurants, there are good choices in town as well. Just a stroll down the main drag will reveal many options.

◖ **Chez Denise** (Calle Principal near the main intersection, tel. 809/538-0219, 9 A.M.–11 P.M. Mon.–Sat., US$5–15) has been a darling of the expats and tourists. In this casual and open-air restaurant, both French and Dominican dishes are served. Crepes are a delectable specialty, as is the fresh fish in coconut sauce.

El Pescador (Calle Principal, tel. 809/538-0052, 4 P.M.–midnight Tues.–Sun. in the winter high season only, US$7–17) is often called the best seafood restaurant in town by locals. When in the Caribbean on vacation, seeking the freshest seafood can become an obsession. Just as the name would suggest, "The Fisherman" specializes in the freshest catches of the day. The grilled fish is always a good bet, but more experimental dishes like stewed crab, paella, and *lambí* beg to be tried.

◖ **Patisserie Boulangerie Français** (Calle Principal, 7 A.M.–7 P.M. Tues.–Sun., US$2–5) is the place to come for a perfect espresso drink, French pastry, or loaf of bread made from scratch. This is a sweet-tooth's dream. Breakfast options are available.

I'm not sure if it's the sauce, the cheese, the many ingredients, or the fact that vacations bring taste buds alive, but the pizza is fabulous at **Pizzeria** (Calle Principal, 11 A.M.–3 P.M. and 6 P.M.–midnight Wed.–Sun., US$6.50–9)—crispy-crusted slices of paradise.

At **L'Aventura Pizzeria** (Calle Las Galeras, US$5–10), not only does this place serve up some tasty eats like pizza, pasta, and grilled meats and seafood, but it also does double duty as a popular nightlife spot with a bar and disco in the back where you can dance to merengue and *bachata*.

For a seriously great spot to sit and chill with a plate of good seafood and a cool drink, head to **Gri Gri** (Calle Las Galeras). It is open for breakfast, lunch, and dinner serving everything from pasta to crepes and fish to meat.

INFORMATION AND SERVICES

The services are offered in Las Galeras are mostly near the main intersection in town. While there is no tourism office in Las Galeras, there are many expat business owners and English-speaking visitors who can direct you if you need help.

Las Galeras Tourist Service (Calle Principal, tel. 809/538-2740) in the center of Las Galeras is a one-stop service center offering money exchange, safety deposit box rental, a gift shop (with cigars, souvenirs, and art), Internet access, and motorbike and car rental. The **Farmacia Joven** (Calle Principal, tel. 809/538-0103, Mon.–Sat. 8 A.M.–9:30 P.M.) is centrally located and has a good variety of general medications.

Communications

Internet Las Galeras (Calle Principal, 8:30 A.M.–8 P.M. Mon.–Sat., 9 A.M.–12:30 P.M. and 2:30–8 P.M. Sun., US$6.25/hour) offers Internet connection, although it's expensive. They also sell stamps and will mail letters for you.

Located on the first level of the **Plaza**

Lusitania is **Centro de Comunicaciones** (Calle Principal, 8 A.M.–noon and 1–10 P.M. daily), the best bet in town for long-distance calls.

GETTING THERE

Las Galeras enjoys its remote location on the peninsula, and therefore transportation options are limited. From Samaná, the best way to go about this is by car or *guagua* since there is no bus service. Where Highway 5 intersects with Calle Principal, right at the entrance to the beach, is where all *guaguas* stop to pick up passengers traveling to and from Samaná. A one-way trip between Las Galeras and Samaná costs US$2 for the 45-minute ride. You can expect to find one leaving every 15 minutes 7 A.M.–5 P.M.

You can take a taxi from the Aeropuerto Internacional El Catey for about US$90 one-way.

GETTING AROUND

Las Galeras is very walkable, with all services near or around the main Calle Principal and where that intersects with Highway 5 coming from Samaná. But with so many beaches in the area, renting a car is an option worth considering. The roads can be pothole-ridden nightmares, so a four-wheel-drive is optimal. Make sure to ask for a map. Most rental places have staff that speak English.

Xamaná Rent Moto (Calle Principal, tel. 809/538-0208, 9 A.M.–noon and 3–6 P.M. Mon.–Fri., 9 A.M.–noon Sat. and Sun., starting at US$25/day) has cars and also rents motorcycles for a more adventurous way to traverse the countryside.

Caribe Fun Rentals (Calle Principal, tel. 809/538-0109, 9 A.M.–6 P.M. Mon.–Sat., 9 A.M.–noon Sun.), across the street from Xamaná, rents motorcycles (US$25) and vehicles (US$70–100) by the day.

Las Terrenas

Las Terrenas is a humming hive of activity. Slow-strolling tourists and speeding *motoconchos* coexist somehow. The flaxen-colored sand and indigo waters of the beach, fringed by palm trees, stretch for kilometers and remind us that Las Terrenas is still a place to relax and enjoy paradise despite the frenzy that swirls around, even into the early morning hours. This is the best place to come on the peninsula if you're wanting a vacation of both slow days in the sun and a fun-filled nightlife. The other towns on the peninsula just don't have the same vibe.

In the late 1970s, tourists traveling to the small town began falling in love with it and started staying for good. These expats, mostly from European countries like France, Italy, and Switzerland, have opened many hotels, restaurants, and other businesses that continue to thrive and give new tourists plenty of appealing options.

© ALICIA CHAVIER CAAMAÑO

The streets hum with activity in Las Terrenas.

BEACHES

Las Terrenas is known for its beaches. The road from Samaná to Las Terrenas turns into the main drag, Avenida Duarte, in town. Once it runs into the town's cemetery, a sharp left turn will take you to Avenida Francisco Alberto Caamaño, which leads you to **Playa Las Terrenas,** where you'll find many restaurants and bars in the **Pueblo de Los Pescadores.**

Continuing west, some of the area's best beaches can be reached either by *motoconcho* (about a 10-minute ride) or by foot along the coastal road or on the shore itself. If you decide to walk along the shore, a pair of water shoes is a good idea, since you have to cross a rather marshy area.

Playa Las Ballenas and **Isla Las Ballenas** offer good snorkeling and diving opportunities. Advanced divers head to the offshore shipwreck and the underwater cave of Isla Las Ballenas, as do snorkelers for the tiny island's coral reefs.

Playa Bonita, or Pretty Beach, is a nice alternative to Playa Las Terrenas, not because it is more beautiful but because this stretch of golden sand is consistently less crowded. Some of the hotels that reside along the shore of Playa Bonita manicure the strips of beach near them, but the rest of Playa Bonita, although nice, tends to be scattered with natural debris. Farther west along the coast, the delightful and untouched **Playa Cosón** appears thick with vegetation over six kilometers of golden sand.

SHOPPING

Compared to Las Galeras and Samaná, Las Terrenas has more to offer to those who want to spend their money on things to take home. Three shopping plazas all have the same hours of operation (9 A.M.–8 P.M. Mon.–Sat., 9 A.M.–3 P.M. Sun.) and are very close to one another along Avenida Duarte. **Plaza Taína** holds a *cambio*, **Mini-Market Ray,** a newsstand, and clothing and other stores. The shops of **El Paseo** include a film store, **Farmacia**

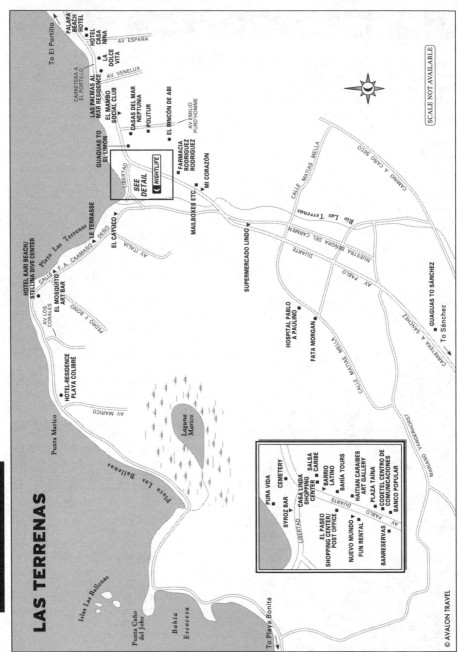

LAS TERRENAS

SCALE NOT AVAILABLE

To El Portillo

PALAPA BEACH HOTEL
HOTEL CASA NINA
AV ESPAÑA
LA DOLCE VITA
AV VENELUX
CARRETERA A EL PORTILLO
LAS PALMAS AL MAR RESIDENCE
EL MAMBO SOCIAL CLUB
CASAS DEL MAR NEPTUNIA
POLITUR
EL RINCÓN DE ABI
AV EMILLIO PURO-HOMME

GUAGUAS TO EL LIMÓN
LIBERTAD
FARMACIA RODRIGUEZ RODRIGUEZ
MI CORAZON
SEE DETAIL
NIGHTLIFE
MAILBOXES ETC.

HOTEL KARI BEACH/ STELLINA DIVE CENTER
Playa Las Terrenas
LE TERRASSE
CALLE E.A. CAAMAÑO
DEÑO
EL CAYUCO
AV ITALIA

CALLE MATIAS MELLA
Río Las Terrenas
CAMINO A CAÑO SECO

SUPERMERCADO LINDO

AV LOS CORALES
EL MOSQUITO ART BAR
PEDRO F. BONO
NUESTRA SEÑORA DEL CARMEN
DUARTE
AV PABLO

HOTEL-RESIDENCE PLAYA COLIBRÉ
AV MARICO
Punta Marico

HOSPITAL PABLO A PAULINO
FATA MORGAN
CALLE MATIAS MELLA
GUAGUAS TO SÁNCHEZ
To Sánchez
CARRETERA A SÁNCHEZ

Playa Las Ballenas

Laguna Marico

Bahía Escocesa
Islas Las Ballenas
Punta Caño del Joho

To Playa Bonita

MARIANA VANDERHORST

© AVALON TRAVEL

Detail

PURA VIDA
SYROZ BAR
CASA LINDA SHOPPING CENTER
SALSA CARIBE
BARRIO LATINO
CEMETERY
BAHÍA TOURS
HAITIAN CARAIBES ART GALLERY
PLAZA TAINA
CODETEL CENTRO DE COMUNICACIONES
BANCO POPULAR
EL PASEO SHOPPING CENTER/ POST OFFICE
NUEVO MUNDO FUN RENTAL
BANRESERVAS
LIBERTAD
DUARTE
AV PABLO

Hemaopatia (for sunscreen and medications), **Deci's** (shoes and clothing), an ATM, **Terrenas En Plata** (a high quality jewelry store filled with works by Dominican artisans), and an Internet access center. **Casa Linda** has yet more souvenir and clothing shops.

Haitian Caraibes Art Gallery (Av. Duarte 159, tel. 809/240-6250, 9 A.M.–1 P.M. and 4–8 P.M. Mon.–Sat.) offers a fantastic selection of good quality Haitian paintings, cigars, art, clothing, and jewelry.

La Cueva de Los Indios (Plaza Taína, tel. 809/240-5168) has typical artwork from the island as well as a nice array of amber, larimar, and black coral jewelry. Visa and Mastercard are accepted. English, French, German, and Italian are spoken.

Along Calle Libertad, on the water's side toward Calle Francisco Caamaño Deño there are many secondhand and knockoff clothing vendors tucked into small buildings and in alleys. Haggling is expected. You can buy everything from sandals and purses to blazers and bathing suits. It is surprising the deals you can get.

SPORTS AND RECREATION
Diving and Snorkeling
A number of diving centers are located in Las Terrenas, and two of the best are **Stellina Dive Center** (Kari Beach Hotel, Calle Francisco Alberto Caamaño Deño, tel. 809/868-4415, 9 A.M.–1 P.M. and 3–5 P.M. daily, www.stellinadiving.com), which offers dive packages starting at a one-tank dive for US$30 (with equipment), and **Las Terrenas Divers** (Hotel Bahía Las Ballenas, Playa Bonita, tel. 809/889-2422, www.lt-divers.com), which offers PADI courses and excursions such as cave diving (US$38–390). Purchase one dive for US$38 or packages of up to 10 dives for US$320. If you need to rent equipment, add US$10 to each dive.

Dance Lessons
Learning about a culture through its cuisine, art, and history can be fun, but few things teach you more about the people that you are visiting and their attitude toward life than learning to dance with them. At ◀ **Salsa Caribe** (Plaza Casa Linda, tel. 809/880-4609 or 809/977-1795, www.salsacaribevent.com) you can take lessons in salsa, merengue, *bachata,* Dominican *son,* reggaeton, cha-cha, and mambo. Other fitness classes are also available. Classes run US$10 for 55 minutes, but packages can be tailored to your level and according to your length of stay. Packages of private lessons can be arranged in any combination of dances. Dominicans rarely hear music and sit still. Learning to dance to merengue, *bachata,* or even salsa will give you great insight into the culture you are visiting.

Water Sport Rentals
Pura Vida (Calle Libertad 2, tel. 809/862-0485, www.puravidaplanet.com/repdom, 10 A.M.–5:30 P.M. daily) started in 1995 and is the premier and first IKO certified water sport school and rental hookup in Las Terrenas. Three surf-crazed buddies started the business and now offer lessons, rentals, and excursions in surfing, kite surfing, wakeboarding, and mountain biking. There are two locations: one in the center of town (in front of El Paseo) and the second at Playa Bonita, where their surfing school is. Also opening soon are spots in El Portillo and Playa Las Ballenas. Group lessons will run you US$100 for two hours of kitesurfing and US$30 for a one-hour group surfing lesson. Mountain biking, kitesurfing, and windsurfing expeditions can be arranged.

Tours and Excursions
Although there are many water sports and things to do in Las Terrenas, you have even more exciting options. Las Terrenas excursion operators offer a good variety of activities from which to choose.

Bahia Tours (Av. Duarte 237, tel. 809/240-6088, www.bahia-tours.com, 9 A.M.–1 P.M. and 3:30–7 P.M.) offers day trips and local excursions throughout the peninsula as well as overnight excursions to other locales in the Dominican Republic. Local excursion prices are per person and include transportation, like whale-watching in the Bahía de Samaná

(US$70), a horseback ride to the waterfall of El Limón (US$25), lunch and a catamaran ride to Cayo Levantado (US$78 per adult, US$38 per child), an excursion to Los Haitises National Park (US$60), or a jeep ride to beautiful Playa Rincón (US$70).

Safari Quad Excursions (Av. Duarte, tel. 809/240-6056, cell 809/869-8031, www.safari-quads.com), across from Plaza Taína, rents quads for exploring the region's countryside and beaches. They'll lead you on an all-day expedition, leaving at 9 A.M. and returning at 4:30 P.M., through enchanted hills and landscapes, along deserted beaches, and to a typical Dominican household of El Limón.

ACCOMMODATIONS

Las Terrenas has a wider assortment of hotel options than Samaná but is not nearly as inundated with the big company all-inclusives like on the Southeast or Northern coasts.

Under US$50

Hotel Casa Nina (Av. 27 de Febrero, tel. 809/240-5490, www.hotel-casanina.com, US$59 with breakfast) is embraced by a lovely tropical garden on Playa Punta Popy. The resort consists of 15 clean, simple bungalows with hot-water bathrooms, all arranged around a quiet pool.

Casas del Mar Neptunia (Av. Emilio Prud'Homme, tel. 809/240-6617, fax 809/240-6070, www.casas-del-mar-neptunia.com, US$40 d) is half a block from the ocean, on a street perpendicular to the highway leading to El Portillo. It offers a serene atmosphere even though it is close to the center of town. The spacious and charming bungalows are set in a garden around a thatched-roof cabana where breakfast is served every day. Since all bungalows have large doors that swing open onto their own private terrace, you have the option of enjoying your breakfast there as well. All units have a fan, private bathrooms, daily maid service, and a refrigerator. Cabanas sleep up to four people. Two apartments can sleep up to six people and offer air-conditioning-optional bedrooms (starting at US$55/night). English, French, and Spanish are spoken.

The bungalows at **Fata Morgana** (La Ceiba, tel. 809/836-5541, www.samana.net/fatamorgana, US$15) may be just the budget accommodation for those travelers who enjoy sinking into the rural culture of their surroundings. Fata Morgana is about five minutes from the town center and beach. With the distance comes peacefulness. Enjoy a quiet read in the rocking chair of your own bungalow. You can even borrow a book from the library. The cheerfully decorated bungalows are clean and have fans and private bathrooms. The owner, Edit Dejong, can give you tours of the area, and you can even borrow a bicycle if you need transportation, although *motoconchos* are easy to find.

El Rincón de Abi (Av. Emilio Prud'Homme, tel. 809/240-6639, www.el-rincon-de-abi.com, US$32 d) has six rooms and one two-bedroom apartment (US$45) in a quiet neighborhood. Rooms are straightforward but colorful, clean and a good value. There is a pool to hang out by as well as a bar, and you'll remain connected with wireless Internet. Breakfast is included in your rate.

US$50-100

This 24-room **Hotel Acaya** (Playa Bonita, tel. 809/240-6111, www.atlantis-hotel.com.do, US$65 for 2 beds, US$90 for double bed) rests on a prime stretch of Playa Bonita location, giving it a tranquil feeling. Although this is a casual hotel, there is a stylish air to it. The rooms do not have a phone or TV in them for that added feeling of vacation, but do have wireless Internet. It has a restaurant and bar. You can rent kite boards. Pay only US$15 for children over eight and US$30 for a third adult in your room.

Casa Grande Beach Resort (Playa Bonita, Calle F Peña Gomez, tel. 809/240-6349, www.casagrandebeachresort.com, US$60 d in high season) is a charmer. Located directly on Playa Bonita, this small 13-room hotel has gone to great lengths to make your vacation memorable. Each room is decorated uniquely with brightly painted accents, throw pillows, gauze curtains, and other touches to remind you that you're not vacationing inside of a machine-made hotel. The restaurant appeals to the same idea that ambience is half the fun. Presentation is superb, as is the taste of their unique mixture of Mediterranean, Asian, and Creole cooking.

Palapa Beach Hotel (Carretera El Portillo, tel. 809/240-6797, www.palapabeach.com, US$65) is a stylishly designed small hotel with 16 bungalows, all of which are uniquely and tastefully decorated with natural appointments. The multilingual staff is very accommodating and willing to work with many special requests. The bungalows are two levels with a loft bedroom, and more beds are available. Below the bedroom is a seating area, which is also kitchenette-capable upon request. The Palapa's excursion office offers exciting packages like fishing cruises, sunset drink cruises, catamaran rides, diving, wind- and kitesurfing (Pura Vida, the water sport company, is right next to them on the beach), and Jet Ski rental. While the hotel itself is across the highway from the beach, the Palapa Beach Hotel has an area of the beach quartered off where they serve breakfast, lunch, and drinks on the sand. On the second level of the hotel is a trendy lounge with an amazing view of the ocean; Japanese delights like sushi and other international favorites are served. The hotel has an Internet café and can arrange for transfer from area airports. The pool is small but located in a tropical garden brimming with vegetation.

La Dolce Vita (Carretera a El Portillo, tel. 809/240-5069, fax 809/240-5072, www.ladolcevitaresidence.com, US$100 per night per one-bedroom apartment) has apartments with ocean views, and all come with a fully equipped kitchen, TV, DSL Internet connection, and safe. This is a good residence for many travelers staying together or for families. One-, two-, and three-bedroom apartments are available, all very nicely appointed, clean and comfortably sized, with their own porch. The three-bedroom apartments have three bathrooms, one of which has a Jacuzzi in it! Air-conditioning is extra. There is a restaurant next

to the medium-sized pool. The beach is just across the highway to El Portillo.

Hotel-Residence Playa Colibrí (Calle Francisco Alberto Caamaño Deño, tel. 809/240-6434, www.playacolibri.com, US$81–150) has 45 apartments in four different layouts (priced accordingly), all offering fully equipped kitchenettes, TV, ceiling fans, terraces, in-room safe boxes, and daily cleaning service. Layouts go from a two-person studio to a very spacious split-level apartment with two bedrooms and two baths. Colibrí is less than two kilometers from the center of Las Terrenas and right on the beach with countless palm trees on white sand and a coral reef offshore. The pool has a Jacuzzi, and there is a restaurant/bar. This is a great find for families and traveling groups looking to settle into a comfortable place for a longer stay.

The rooms in the **Hotel Kari Beach** (Calle Francisco Alberto Caamaño Deño, tel. 809/240-6187, www.karibeach.com, US$58 d) are brightly decorated, clean, have vaulted ceilings, and are well ventilated. Only 3 of the 24 rooms have air-conditioning, but all have private bathrooms and TV and wireless Internet is available. Hotel Kari has one of Las Terrenas's dive shops, which makes the hotel a good base for divers. Good Italian and international fare is served in the restaurant. Rates include breakfast.

Hotel Atlantis (Playa Bonita, tel. 809/240-6111, www.atlantis-hotel.com.do, US$70–160 per room in high season), located on a gorgeous stretch of Playa Bonita, is not a luxurious hotel, but a study in quiet simplicity and phenomenal French cuisine. The restaurant is one sure reason why foodies will choose to stay here. Meals are prepared by Chef Gerard Prystaz, former chef of the French Presidential Palace. The rooms, although simple in their decor, are stylish, some sleeping up to four people. The only bungalow, the Damascus, has a garden view and two separate rooms to accommodate four people with a marble bathroom (US$160/night). Wireless Internet is available throughout the hotel, and there is a children's playground between the hotel and the beach.

LA PENÍNSULA DE SAMANÁ

US$100 and Up

Hotel Bahia Las Ballenas (Playa Bonita, tel. 809/240-6066, www.bahia-las-ballenas. net, US$105 d, breakfast included) is spread over one of the best tropical gardens on Playa Bonita. The 32 rooms are generous in size (big enough to add an extra bed) and colorful with high, vaulted thatch roofed ceilings (adding more outside air and sounds from the ocean) and have patios overlooking the garden. While the unique open-air bathrooms might be thrilling to some, it might be too much nature to others. The pool area is inviting with loungers aplenty.

Las Palmas al Mar Residence (Carretera a El Portillo, tel. 809/240-6292, fax 809/240-6089, www.laspalmasalmar.com, US$73–148 per cottage per night in high season) has a collection of 12 two-level cottages placed in a neatly manicured setting. The pool is small, but the beach is just across the street. The cottages have a kitchenette, seating area with a fold out couch, one bedroom with a double bed, one with two single beds, two bathrooms, and lovely wraparound porches with barbecues. This is a wonderful place to stay if you want comfortable and clean accommodations but are willing to stock up the refrigerator and dine out because Las Palmas doesn't have a restaurant. No matter though, it is within walking distance to a great many choices. Other amenities include: purified water, cable TV with DVD player, safe, and DSL Internet hookup. Price doesn't include air-conditioning, and discounts are given for longer stays.

The best thing about **Hotel Gran Bahía Principe El Portillo** (Carretera a El Portillo–El Limón, tel. 809/240-6100, www.bahia-princ-ipe.com, US$240 d) is its surroundings. This all-inclusive is four kilometers away from Las Terrenas, placed on lush grounds on a marvelous beach. It has 204 rooms and 192 junior suites and has all that can be expected from any all-inclusive chain resort in terms of comfort needs and things to occupy your time (tennis, water sports, aerobics, dancing, etc.). Although the surroundings make it beautiful, it can also give the resort a feeling of isolation.

As it stands, this resort is not a "throw-down party," despite their efforts with the nightly entertainment. No, instead what you will find is a relaxing environment where on the porch of your room you can hear the busy sounds of the tropical nights. The rooms are spacious and comfortable. Request one that is in a block closer to the beach. The higher the block number, the farther from the beach.

FOOD

Where the Río Las Terrenas meets the Atlantic Ocean is a cluster of fishing shacks known as **El Pueblo de Los Pescadores** that have become the most popular dining spot in town. Most open to the road and have waterfront seating.

El Cayuco (Pueblo de Los Pescadores, noon–11 P.M. daily, US$5–15) is a Spanish restaurant that will serve you an eye-catching paella filled with fresh seafood and tantalizing tapas. It is a casual restaurant and a good value for the prices.

A French restaurant right in front of the sea, **La Salsa** (Pueblo de Los Pescadores, tel. 809/240-6805, cell 809/816-2970, 7 P.M.–midnight daily, US$11–20) transforms local products like lobster and fresh fish into tasty dishes. There is a good selection of red meat dishes as well.

◖ **Le Terrasse** (Pueblo de Los Pescadores, tel. 809/240-6351, noon–2:30 P.M. and 7 P.M.–11 P.M., RD$350–700) is a cozy and romantic upscale restaurant that sets itself apart from the rest along the row of dining choices in the Pueblo de Los Pescadores. The whitewashed cottage is appointed with white linen tablecloths and red tropical flowers and candles on the tables. Fresh seafood is bought right off the beach and prepared every day in the restaurant with a Mediterranean flair. Try the tuna carpaccio salad (RD$320). There is also a wide variety of meats and pastas and a good wine list.

◖ **El Mambo Social Club** (Av. 27 de Febrero, tel. 809/240-5312 or 809/877-8374, 7 P.M.–1 A.M. daily) doubles as a luxurious lounge bar filled with stylish couches, billiard and card tables, and a bevy of good whiskies. It is also a top-rate restaurant whose chef, Willy (a former Michelin-starred chef), concocts recipes with rich Caribbean flavors and savory sauces like crab in a coconut Creole sauce. Feel the need for something in the raw like sushi and sashimi? You can make reservations for that here. The music is superb and rounds out the whole evening. If a restaurant can be sexy, this is it.

Barrio Latino (Calle Francisco Alberto Caamaño Deño, tel. 809/240-6367, 7:30 A.M.–midnight daily, US$2–13) is a great place to go if you need to please a lot of different tastes, as it's popular with both Europeans and Americans for breakfast. Other satisfying dishes include burgers, pizzas, salads, and sandwiches. Häagen-Dazs ice cream for dessert or a fresh fruit juice might help cool you down. The restaurant is open-sided and a great place for people-watching.

La Yuca Caliente (Calle Libertad 6, tel. 809/240-6634, noon–midnight, US$10–25) is a Spanish restaurant located right on the beach serving tapas, pizzas, and wine.

If you didn't expect to find a fine dining experience on your beach vacation, you will be pleasantly surprised at **(Mi Corazon** (Calle Duarte 7 and Carretera Cosón, tel. 809/240-5329, www.micorazon.com, 7:30 P.M.–late, closed Sundays and Mondays May–July, closed Mondays November–April, closed all of October, US$8–25). This French- and Swiss-owned and -operated restaurant has a stylish interior set in an open-air courtyard with a bar/lounge on the second level perfect for pre-dinner cocktails and stargazing on plush sofas. Terra-cotta floors and iron railings give the whole place a colonial feel. On the first level, the courtyard is luxurious and glowing with candles and white tablecloths, but the food is the real star here. The menu changes often, with dishes like crayfish carpaccio and a tomato caviar with truffled olive oil ice cream, or ceviche made with mahimahi, swordfish with wasabi caviar and soy sauce jelly, or beef tenderloin with a red wine jus. Mouth watering yet?

You've had your seafood, your Italian pizzas, your steak and cocktails, now what? Craving something sweet? **Heladería Bruno** (Plaza El Paseo, Calle Francisco Alberto Caamaño Deño) has that glorious Dominican coffee that can't be duplicated when you get home as well as sweet cooling ice cream—good opposites that go well together on a hot day.

Super Mercado Rey (Av. Duarte 57, tel. 809/240-6010, 8 A.M.–10 P.M. Mon.–Sat., 8 A.M.–2 P.M. Sun.) has basic provisions like canned goods, bread, and water. It's a good place to buy long-distance phone cards. There may be a small fresh fruit vendor on the other side of the grocer's parking lot.

Supermercado Lindo (Plaza Rosado, Av. Duarte, tel. 809/240-6003, 8 A.M.–9 P.M. Mon.–Sat., 8 A.M.–6 P.M. Sun.) is yet another market with canned goods, produce, and more.

But if you are here for a long time, **Supermercado Ignacio** (Av. Nuestra Señora Del Carmen 146, tel. 809/240-6243) is a good bet since it is the biggest and busiest in town with the best variety.

(NIGHTLIFE

Roaming from one bar to the next is effortless when sticking to **Pueblo de Los Pescadores.** After the dinner hours, most restaurants turn into bars and lounges, and they're lined up like dominoes. Here are a few outside of that area that are worthy of exploration as well.

Swanky **Syroz Bar** (Pueblo de Los Pescadores, Calle Libertad, tel. 809/866-5577, 5 P.M.–4 A.M. Mon.–Sat.) sends you into a reality melt-down as you listen to live jazz on the beach. Really, what could be better for jazz lovers outside of a corner booth at the Blue Note in New York? Okay, that might be taking it a bit far. But, swaying to the tunes under the stars with a cocktail on the deck facing the ocean or inside in the candlelit ambience doesn't sound too shabby. Syroz hosts regular DJ nights with soul, jazz, and other music theme nights, some with professional dancers.

El Mosquito Art Bar (Pueblo de Los Pescadores, tel. 809/857-4684, 6 P.M.–midnight daily), at the entrance of the Pueblo de Los Pescadores, is the perfect place to enjoy a cocktail from the gigantic drink menu or a plate of tapas. You can sit and listen to the great music on couches on the patio overlooking the ocean. The bar hosts live music and art exhibits that go well with their much-touted piña coladas.

Guia (Pueblo de Los Pescadores, tel. 809/240-5133, 8 P.M.–late) has three floors of nighttime entertainment packed into one sleek new club. The first floor is a disco with merengue and *bachata* beats, the second floor has a techno club, and on the top is a terrace with a relaxing lounge.

Nuevo Mundo (Av. Duarte, 9 P.M.–4 A.M. Wed.–Sun.) is a disco popular with Dominicans because it plays mostly merengue and *bachata*. It has turned into a spot for the tourists wanting to experience more of the culture's music and dance.

INFORMATION AND SERVICES
Health and Emergencies
Farmacia Rodriguez Rodriguez (Av. Duarte 208, tel. 809/240-6084, 8 A.M.–8 P.M. daily) is a good pharmacy on the main drag, right near the Banco Popular. It offers a good selection of meds and other necessities.

Hospital Pablo A. Paulino (Calle Matias Mella, tel. 809/274-6474) has an emergency room open 24 hours.

Politur (Av. Emilio Prud'Homme, tel. 809/240-6595, open 24 hours) officers are there to help you with emergencies. Most tourism police speak another language, but a Spanish dictionary would be helpful just in case.

Communications
For long-distance calls in Las Terrenas, head to **Codetel Centro de Comunicaciones** (Av. Duarte, 8 A.M.–10 P.M. daily), on the main drag near Plaza Taína.

Don't need to communicate but just want word that the outside world still exists? Head over to the **Newsstand of Plaza Taína** (Av. Duarte, 9 A.M.–8 P.M. daily) and grab a paper. The newsstand has a good (albeit very expensive) selection of newspapers from all over the world.

The **post office** (El Paseo shopping center, Calle Francisco Alberto Caamaño Deño, 9 A.M.–1 P.M. and 3–5 P.M. Mon.–Fri.) is not the best, fastest, or most trusted way to communicate from the Dominican Republic, but it is acceptable for those postcards to send home.

For sending something faster and more reliably, go to **Mailboxes Etc.** (Av. Duarte 39, tel. 809/240-6347), where they have FedEx, UPS, DHL, and USPS services (as well as Internet services).

Internet Access
The nice thing about vacationing in Las Terrenas is that you can escape your daily life without falling off the planet. Many of the hotels are jumping on the cyber bandwagon by offering Internet hookups as an amenity. Additionally, in town there are a number of options.

Conveniently located **Cyber Heladería** (El Paseo shopping center, Calle Francisco Alberto Caamaño Deño, 8 A.M.–9 P.M. Mon.–Sat., 8 A.M.–3 P.M. Sun.) offers connections and ice cream. You can get about the same rate at **Mailboxes Etc.** (Av. Duarte 39, tel. 809/240-6347).

Codetel Centro de Comunicaciones (Av. Duarte, 8 A.M.–10 P.M. daily), in addition to being a telephone call center, offers cheap connection fees.

Money
Fort Knox Money Exchange (El Paseo shopping center, Av. Duarte, tel. 809/240-6719, 8 A.M.–1 P.M. and 4–8 P.M. Mon.–Sat., 10 A.M.–1 P.M. Sun.) exchanges euros and American dollars. There are many other *cambios* along Av. Duarte, or you can exchange money in the banks.

Banco Popular (Av. Duarte, 9 A.M.–5 P.M. Mon.–Fri., 9 A.M.–1 P.M. Sat.), just next to the Farmacia Rodriguez Rodriguez, has a 24-hour ATM.

BanReservas (Av. Duarte, 9 A.M.–6 P.M. Mon.–Fri., 9 A.M.–1 P.M. Sat.), right across the street from the Banco Popular, also has a 24-hour ATM.

Banco del Progreso (Av. Duarte, tel. 809/240-6409, 9 A.M.–3:30 P.M. Mon.–Fri., 9 A.M.–1 P.M. Sat.) is in the El Paseo shopping center.

GETTING THERE
By Air

Las Terrenas is only a few kilometers from **Aeropuerto Internacional El Portillo** (tel. 809/248-2289), which receives some flights from Europe but mostly inter-Dominican flights. It is a very small operation. A couple of companies serve the Samaná Peninsula: **Takeoff Destination Service S.A.** (Plaza Brisas de Bávaro 8, Bávaro, tel. 809/552-1333, fax 809/552-1113, www.takeoffweb.com), in the Southeast, has a flight between Punta Cana and Samaná for US$149 with regular flights every Monday, Wednesday, and Friday. They offer a flight between Santo Domingo and Samaná for US$250.

Aerodomca (Aeropuerto Arroyo Barril Samaná, tel. 809/248-2566, or Santo Domingo tel. 809/567-1195, www.aerodomca.com) offers flights from the airport at El Portillo to Santo Domingo (US$85) and Punta Cana (US$85) as well as other airports in the Dominican Republic and throughout the Caribbean. Reservations are required with a 24-hour advance notice.

Catching a taxi into town is no problem from the airport at El Portillo. When flights arrive, taxis wait around (usually they are the minivan type to accommodate luggage) and will run you around US$8–10.

You can take a taxi from the El Catey airport for about US$90 one-way.

By Bus

Guaguas make stops in Las Terrenas along Avenida Duarte. To catch one going to Sánchez, go to the stop along the highway to Sánchez (US$1.50 leaving every 20–25 minutes 7 A.M.–6 P.M.). The stop for a *guagua* going toward El Limón (US$1.75 leaving every 15 minutes 7 A.M.–5 P.M.) is more centrally located

near the intersection of Avenida Duarte and the highway to El Portillo.

By Car

If arriving from the west, make a left turn outside the town of Sánchez for a beautiful drive up over the Cordillera Samaná, *la loma* (the hill) between Las Terrenas and Sánchez. It is a curvy, steep road that gives spectacular views of the Bahía de Samaná and the Parque Nacional Los Haitises. Watch out for fallen branches, coconuts, and palm debris, especially after a strong rainstorm. Las Terrenas is 17 kilometers northeast of Sánchez. Traveling along this road, if you would like a rest and a bite to eat, stop halfway between Sánchez and Las Terrenas at the Tex Mex restaurant **El Vaquero** (Carretera Sánchez–Las Terrenas), where not only is the food killer, but the view is to die for, overlooking the mountains of the Samaná Peninsula from a perch in the village of El Naranjito.

If you are approaching Las Terrenas from the east, perhaps from Las Galeras, you must first go through Samaná, then turn right on the road toward El Limón and El Portillo. It is another 30–45 minutes to reach Las Terrenas.

GETTING AROUND

You will never come up empty trying to flag down a *motoconcho* in Las Terrenas. There seem to be hundreds buzzing throughout the town. But really, walking is incredibly easy, a lot safer, and completely free.

To get to the area's other beaches (like Playa Bonita and Cosón), either a *motoconcho* (US$2–7 respectively) or taxi (US$10–20) can get you there. Secure the price before hopping on or in.

Car and Motor Rental

ADA Rental Car (Plaza Taína, tel. 809/704-3232, 9 A.M.–1 P.M. and 2:30–7 P.M. Mon.–Sat.) rents cars.

Fun Rental (Av. Duarte 258, tel. 809/240-6784) rents quads and scooters, which can be a fun way to get around town and keep your dependence on public transport down. Expect to spend at least US$15 a day for a scooter.

SÁNCHEZ

Back in the 1800s, Sánchez was a major fishing village. To this day, there is a lot of shrimping here, catching some of the biggest and best in the country. Now, however, what Higüey is to the Southeast, Sánchez is to the Samaná Peninsula: a transportation hub. Those who stop in Sánchez are mainly doing so to get to other places on the peninsula or to catch a boat to Los Haitises (Sánchez is the closest launching point to the national park). If you find yourself in Sánchez and have some time, take a stroll through town and notice the brightly colored Victorian homes or wander down by the sea where the ruins of the old port (leftover from the early 20th century) are lying in their rusty state, jutting out into the water.

Getting to La Península de Samaná

This is where buses from Santo Domingo and Puerto Plata stop to exchange and pick up passengers whose final destination is to either Samaná or Las Terrenas. Two bus companies serve this area. The trip to Santo Domingo takes four hours.

Caribe Tours (tel. 809/552-7434, www.caribetours.com, US$7.50) has buses to and from Santo Domingo at 7:30 A.M., 9 A.M., 10:30 A.M., 1:30 P.M., 3 P.M. and 4:30 P.M.

Metro (tel. 809/552-7332, US$7.50) has service twice a day at 9 A.M. and 5 P.M. to Santo Domingo.

Getting to Parque Nacional Los Haitises

Most who visit the *parque* are doing so through tour agencies from other towns. However, local boats in Sánchez can take you as well.

One reputable company has been running tours out of Sánchez for over 10 years. **Amilka Tours** (Calle Colón 15, tel. 809/552-7664, www.amilkatoursdominican.com) will take you to Los Haitises for US$50 per person (minimum four people). Fee includes lunch, drinks, and entrance into park. You'll pay extra for a tour guide (RD$200). They will take you through mangroves and you'll see the Taíno drawings on the cave walls. It is worth the cost to get the guide. Amilka can also take you whale-watching during whale season (US$50). Calling a day ahead to reserve a spot is a good idea, but you can just show up. Buffet lunches of fish, rice, pasta, and salad for the tours are served at the beach, where there are bathrooms available as well.

THE NORTH COAST

Those who visit the North Coast, also known as La Costa Ámbar (The Amber Coast) will find that its menu of activities is as varied as its topography. At the northwestern corner of the country lagoons rest peacefully amidst mangroves and thick vegetation, mountainous tropical forests reach to blue skies, and arid cliffs fall steeply into the ocean's breakers. And whether you are an adventure junkie, a history buff, or a sun-seeking beachcomber, there is something in this region to satisfy your needs.

When Christopher Columbus made his second journey to the New World in 1493 he founded the second European settlement in the New World on this stretch of coastline at La Isabela in the northwest. All that now remains of that settlement are the ruins of their destroyed encampment, which can be seen in the Parque Nacional La Isabela. After the miserable failure of La Isabela, Columbus and his men moved to Santo Domingo and the north coast became mainly an import-and-export shipping yard for hundreds of years. But the mountainous tropical forests with no real passageways caused the area to be secluded from the rest of the country and unsettled for many years. Tourists didn't even start visiting this region until the late 1900s.

Although much of this region still has wide expanses of undeveloped land, many people associate the North Coast with the all-inclusive resorts of the Playa Dorada region. But there is so much more here to experience along the north coast: Windsurfers and kitesurfers recognize Cabarete's prowess as a major port of call for water sport lovers,

© ANA CHAVIER CAAMAÑO

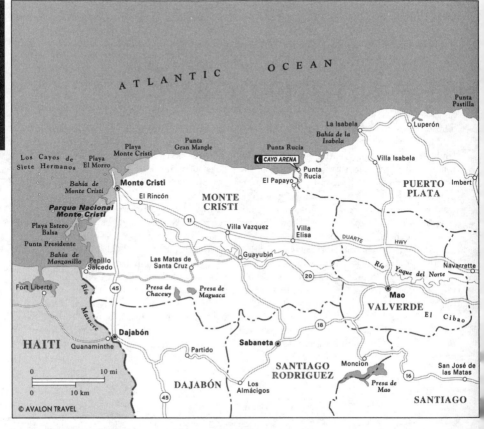

Sosúa has emerged as a scuba diver's dream, and untouched beaches are scattered all along the curvaceous coastline.

There is more buzzing in the air than just the din of *motoconchos* that clog the city streets of Puerto Plata. In recent years, there has been massive motivation from the Ministry of Tourism to funnel pesos into the region once again in an effort to activate the economy of the region so it can compete with the nation's bread and butter provider, Punta Cana/ Bávaro. Puerto Plata's central park was given a facelift, newly constructed and hoping-to-be-filled luxury condos line the highways and beaches, even Sosúa's notorious sex-tourism was somewhat eradicated (it unfortunately didn't take) all in an effort to revitalize the north coast.

The farther west from Puerto Plata you travel, the less desperate for attention the tourism industry seems to be. If you are looking for relaxed independence, go west. But if action and entertainment are your goal, then the Cabarete, Sosúa, and Puerto Plata regions are for you.

PLANNING YOUR TIME

It is said that 95 percent of travelers who visit this coast fly in to Puerto Plata, find their resort shuttles, and spend the rest of their vacation within the confines of its walls. If you are prone to "resort fever" or have adventure on your mind, then you will want to budget your

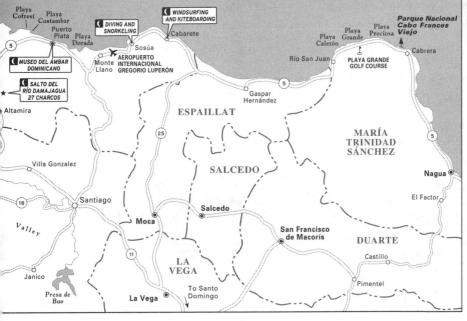

time for the many things to see and do along the Amber Coast. Deciding how and where to concentrate your time is a daunting task with so many options available. Choosing your main focus before arrival is essential. For instance, if you want to spend most of your time kiteboarding, then Cabarete is the place to focus your vacation. Will you be taking a *guagua,* renting a car, or depending on the bus schedules to get you from location to location? If you are at the mercy of public transportation, leave time in your itinerary for missed connections.

Days on the beach are a given. It's what the northern coast does best. But an afternoon saved for visiting the Museo del Ámbar Dominicano and the Fuerte San Felipe in

Puerto Plata or getting a tour of the first settlement of the New World in La Isabela is all you need for a break from the sand.

If you fly in to Puerto Plata and drive east toward Río San Juan, save at least a day for snorkeling in Sosúa and a couple of days for water sports in Cabarete.

Choosing to go west from Puerto Plata is a decision that requires more time. Perhaps that is why tourism wanes the farther west you travel. Not that there isn't a lot to see and do, but there is a lot of ground to cover between stops. Driving from Puerto Plata to Monte Cristi, there is an opportunity for an afternoon in historic Puerto Plata, or to spend the night and visit Ocean World the next day.

HIGHLIGHTS

◖ **Windsurfing and Kiteboarding in Cabarete:** Glide across the water at top speed where world champions ride. All, from beginner to pro, agree that Cabarete has some of the premier conditions for water sports in the entire world (pages 173 and 174).

◖ **Diving and Snorkeling in Sosúa:** Explore the coral gardens, walls, wrecks, and reefs off the coast of Sosúa in supreme diving conditions (page 185).

◖ **Museo del Ámbar Dominicano:** This museum has the most impressive display of ancient resin in the country. Here, 40-million-year-old bugs lie frozen forever in a golden casing (page 192).

◖ **Salto del Río Damajagua 27 Charcos:** Slip, slide, jump, and leap your way through a series of tunnels, caves, and pools. It's an exhilarating test of your endurance and level of adrenaline addiction (page 206).

◖ **Cayo Arena:** Just off the coast of Punta Rucia, this picturesque sandbar fits no more than 100 people at a time and offers up fantastic snorkeling. The constantly shrinking and expanding ultra-white sand of this tiny sandbar can be your Paradise Island for the afternoon (page 209).

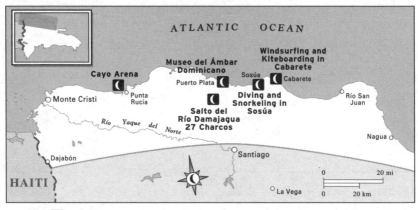

LOOK FOR ◖ TO FIND RECOMMENDED SIGHTS, ACTIVITIES, DINING, AND LODGING.

In Luperón, spend the night mixing and mingling over beers with expats and in the morning take an early swim at Playa Grande before heading off to see the ruins of La Isabela and the Templo de Las Américas. Continuing west, you'll have to budget a few days for a full visit to Monte Cristi and even more if you choose to detour to Punta Rucia.

All in all, the north coast offers a great variety of activities in many different locales. No matter which direction you go, or if you stay put in one locale, book tours and excursions either prior to arrival or in the first days of your stay to avoid the disappointment of not getting a spot.

While traveling according to an itinerary, you may find paradise along the way and can't bring yourself to move onward. If you truly want to experience the Dominican way of life, then do as the Dominicans do and wing it. If you suddenly feel like scrapping your plans to stay at one beach, then spread out your towel and relax.

Río San Juan

This is one of only a few towns along the North Coast that maintain their small-town peacefulness. There isn't much in the way of nightlife and there aren't many choices for hotels. What Río San Juan is blessed with, though, are some spectacular beaches that make for fun diving and snorkeling.

SIGHTS AND BEACHES
Laguna Gri-Gri

This mangrove-blanketed area with its marine caverns is what put Río San Juan on the tourism map to begin with, but since the huge media push of Playa Grande, it has fallen from its previous glory and suffers from lack of upkeep. However, tours are still given and can be quite a relaxing excursion.

Look for the **Laguna Gri-Gri Tour Booth** (tel. 809/589-2277) at the entrance to the lagoon, which is at the end of Calle Duarte. There you can arrange for a boat to take you for the two-hour ride through a kilometer of mangroves to Swallows Cave, where hundreds of the birds nest, onward for a swim in the

Natural Swimming Pool. If you like, you can extend your trip for a two-hour layover at Playa Caletón. For a boatload of 3–7 people the trip will run you about US$30.

Playa Caletón

Known locally as La Playita, this beach is a petite slice of paradise. Golden sand meets clear blue water, and palm trees give shelter from the sun. It's the perfect place to spend an afternoon, quietly reading, swimming, and enjoying lunch at one of the food stands. The turnoff is marked from the main road, and if you take a *guagua* or *motoconcho,* it will most likely drop you off there and you'll have to hoof it the rest of the way; no worries, it's not even a kilometer to the water.

Playa Grande

This is a gorgeous and gigantic beach. "Big Beach" is aptly named in that everything about it dwarfs you. Tall cliffs surround the area and its band of golden sand is wide, backed by a thick coconut grove that continues for miles. If you walk east, you'll keep finding more hidden spots where you can get more privacy than on the main stretch. Even the water seems bigger here—it is definitely stronger. The wind whips into this area and creates a robust surf with a strong undertow. It's not the beach for children or people who aren't strong swimmers.

There are quite a few food stands where you can get lunch and drinks, and various stalls with bathing suits, jewelry, and trinkets. Vendors proffer beach chairs (US$2/day), snorkeling gear, bodyboards (US$5/hour), and surfboards (US$25/day).

The entrance from the main road is clearly marked. It leads down to a parking lot in the trees at Playa Grande. To get there, you have to pass through a gate that's been put up by hotel developers. If it is closed, it doesn't mean the beach is closed. The beach is open to the public by law. If the gate is open and you take a *guagua* or *motoconcho,* ask the driver to take you all the way down to the parking lot. It is about a 1.5-kilometer walk from the turnoff to the beach.

Playa Preciosa

Although this beach, whose name translates as "Beautiful Beach," is truly that, it is also a scary display of strong water—not a place for a leisurely swim. If you want to sit and watch some daring and very experienced surfers brave the waters, this could be entertaining. It is less than a kilometer east of Playa Grande and can be accessed by the same entrance road from the main highway.

SPORTS AND RECREATION
Diving and Snorkeling

For snorkelers that are new to the sport, the **Natural Swimming Pool** is perfect in that many fish can be seen in shallow clear waters. For more experienced divers, there are many coral reefs and canyons with caves and swim-through holes. Exploring **Crab Canyon,** you will dive underwater 26 meters through colorful stone arches. **Seven Hills** has a wall of coral dropping more than 50 meters and **Cave Du-Du** is a freshwater cave best for advanced divers.

Unfortunately, there is no dive outfitter in Río San Juan. It is best to organize a dive excursion with companies from Sosúa.

ACCOMMODATIONS

There are no accommodations in the town of Río San Juan. Instead, the choices listed here are nearby at Playa Grande or just east of town.

Hotel La Catalina (Los Farallones, Catalina, tel. 809/589-7700, fax 809/589-7550, www. lacatalina.com, US$98 d) is east of Río San Juan, near the town of Cabrera. This hotel has 30 rooms and apartments, all of which are very comfortable with tropical floral decoration and cool tile floors, and every room has a great view of the ocean and the lush countryside. Tennis court, billiard room, library, and two swimming pools are some of the other amenities. A free shuttle to Playa Grande and breakfast are included in the rate. Wedding packages for up to 20 people include photographer, ceremony on the beach (or in the hotel), fees for the judge, decorations, bouquet and boutonniere, reception, breakfast in bed for the bride and groom, and one complimentary night's stay for US$3,000. Similar honeymoon packages are available.

Bahía Principe San Juan (Carretera Gaspar Hernández Km 18, Playa Grande, tel. 809/226-1590, fax 809/226-1994, www.bahia-principe.com, US$188 d) is a massive all-inclusive. Its 1,000-plus rooms are spread out over a large, well-manicured area expansive enough to warrant a trolley service to take guests from spot to spot. There are six restaurants, 11 bars, three pools, tennis courts, minigolf, a soccer field, spa, gym, supermarket, bank, excursion desk—the list goes on from there and you get the idea. It is a town. And a nice one. All rooms come with two double beds or one king-size, air-conditioning, private bath, satellite TV, safe, minibar, and balcony or terrace. Water sports are available also, although some cost extra.

FOOD

Just as the accommodations are limited, so too is the restaurant selection.

Le Café Paris (Calle Sánchez, tel. 809/844-4899, 8 A.M.–9 P.M. daily, US$5–18) is a nice place to have a slow meal or a drink outside. The food is okay but there is plenty to look at since it is right across from where the boats to Laguna Gri-Gri dock. The area has a charming atmosphere with the shade-filled lagoon. The menu has French food, pizza, and some grilled seafood.

El Corral del Pollo (Calle 16 de Agosto, tel. 809/963-8269, 8 A.M.–6 P.M. daily, US$8–20) serves Spanish cuisine like paella in a casual atmosphere.

Locals love to recommend **Cheo's Café** (Calle Padre Billini, tel. 809/589-2290, US$7–17) and the tourists love to eat here. International favorites are available, but so are rabbit in coconut sauce and grilled catch of the day.

INFORMATION AND SERVICES

For such a small town, services are plentiful, and most are along the main drag of Calle Duarte. All are within walking distance.

Banco Progreso (Calle Duarte 38, 8:30 A.M.–4 P.M. Mon.–Fri., 9 A.M.–1 P.M. Sat., tel. 809/589-2393) has a 24-hour ATM at the corner of Duarte and Alvarado. The **post office** is farther toward the Laguna between Mella and Bulbuena.

For an Internet communication option **Solana.com** (Calle 30 de Marzo 32, 8 A.M.–8:30 P.M. Mon.–Sat., 8 A.M.–noon Sun., tel. 809/549-2498) offers connections for US$1.80 per hour.

The **Oficina de Turismo** (Tourism Office, Calle Mella at Calle 16 de Agosto, tel. 809/589-2831, 8 A.M.–4 P.M. Mon.–Fri.) is available if you have any more questions or want brochures and maps of the area.

Health and Emergencies

If you travel west on Highway 5, the tourist police office, **Politur** (Carretera a Cabarete, tel. 809/754-3241), is on the lefthand side after you've passed Calle Duarte.

Farmacia Reyes (Calle Duarte, tel. 809/589-2234, 8 A.M.–noon and 2–6 P.M. Mon.–Fri., 8 A.M.–noon Sat.) has necessary meds and necessities.

Getting There and Around

At the intersection of Highway 5 and Calle Duarte, buses, *motoconchos,* and *guaguas* all stop to pick up passengers.

Caribe Tours (Hwy. 5, tel. 809/589-2644) has a bus leaving for a 4.5-hour trip to Santo Domingo for US$8.50 at 6:30 A.M., 7:45 A.M., 9:30 A.M., 2 P.M., and 3:30 P.M. every day.

There are usually a few people waiting on *guaguas* at this intersection so you can ask questions, but the ones headed for Cabarete (US$2.25), Sosúa (US$2.15), and Puerto Plata (US$2.50) leave every 15 minutes 6 A.M.–5 P.M. daily. The *guaguas* going east leave every 10 minutes. To take one to Playa Grande it only costs US$1, and to Nagua it is US$2, where you can then catch transportation to Samaná.

Two blocks up Duarte at Calle Dr. Virgilio Garcia there is a **taxi stand** where you can hail one to take you to the area beaches or your hotel.

Renting a car is always a great way to see the countryside, and this stretch of Highway 5, all the way to Puerto Plata, is relatively well-maintained. **Playa Grande Rent-a-Car** (Calle Duarte 15, tel. 809/589-2391, 8 A.M.–6 P.M.) has cars for rent starting around US$45 for the day.

Nagua sits quietly on coastal Highway 5, 36 kilometers northwest of Sánchez. It doesn't have anything to offer a tourist (it's rather uninteresting) except that it serves as a gateway and transportation hub between the North Coast and La Península de Samaná.

Guaguas converge here and can take you to many cities, including: Sánchez, San Francisco de Macorís, Moca, Santiago, and the north coast towns.

Guaguas heading for the northern coastal towns can be hailed on the main highway. Just stand on the side of the road for the direction you need to go and wave one down. They pass quite frequently, about every 15–20 minutes.

Guaguas heading inland need to be hailed just where they turn off of Highway 5 and onto Highway 132. If you are coming via a *guagua* and need to transfer, tell the driver your final destination so you can be let off at the appropriate spot to flag down the next one. These connections aren't as frequent as the northbound *guaguas,* arriving once an hour.

Caribe Tours (Calle Mella, tel. 809/589-2644, US$6) has a bus that goes from Nagua to Santo Domingo every day at 7:30 A.M., 8 A.M., 8:30 A.M., 10 A.M., 10:30 A.M., 11 A.M., 2 P.M., 3 P.M., 4:30 P.M., and 5:30 P.M.

Cabarete

Known internationally as a top windsurfing and kitesurfing spot, Cabarete has been a choice location for adventure-sport enthusiasts. The area has also appealed to young and young-at-heart travelers, with its many low-budget accommodation options and easygoing nightlife. Charming, hip, and low-key, Cabarete was the sort of place that you'd purposely miss your flight home for so that you could deny that the rest of the world existed for just a little while longer.

But when Cabarete stepped into the world's windsurfing spotlight, people and businesses suddenly started coming in droves. Now the once-small fishing town is a jam-packed, horn-beeping hotbed of tourist activity. There are still budget accommodations and places to eat, but now there are amenities to please every type of traveler.

BEACHES
Playa Cabarete
This is the main beach in town, and it is windsurfing and kiteboarding central. The Bahía de Cabarete is a gradual semicircular stretch that is great for people-watching. On the sand

are countless bars, restaurants, and hotels from which to set up camp and witness the acrobatics of the hot shots and bless-their-hearts-for-trying beginners. It isn't an easy surf, but it is close to ideal. All the natural conditions that form this bay play a part in the perfection of the area for water sports. The temperature of the water is always balmy so forget the wetsuit. There is an offshore reef at the entrance to the two-kilometer-wide bay where the more experienced surfers ride, but the majority of the sea floor becomes sandy once you are in the bay itself. Combine these things with the direction of the eastern trade winds, which start blowing in around noon, and the low-lying hills behind Cabarete and you've got outstanding wave and beach conditions.

The western, downwind portion of Playa Cabarete is called **Bozo Beach,** which is named for the beginning windsurfers and kiteboarders still getting the hang of the sport who get pulled by the wind to this end of the beach.

Kite Beach
This beach is about two kilometers west of

Playa Cabarete, just past Bozo Beach, and clearly is named for the sport that it is ideally suited for. The wind is stable here, perfect for kitesurfing, since you need to have good control of your sail as the wind picks you up high into the air above the ocean. This beach can be much more populated on the days when there is a good wind. Everyone—from beginners to training professionals—finds Kite Beach the best. In fact, the conditions are so perfect that many world kitesurfing competitions have been held on this beach.

Playa Encuentro

What the other beaches are to wind and kite surfers, Playa Encuentro is to regular wave surfers. Big waves, strong tides, and deep water draw crowds of surfers, especially in the morning when the water and wind conditions are prime. It's best if you start before 7 A.M.— it gets blown out fast here. In the beginning, hang back and watch the regulars and locals for a bit to learn the etiquette of the water. After the surfers' prime hours are gone, the windsurfers and kiteboarders join in. The beach break at Playa Encuentro has a strong current, so watch where the locals paddle out. There are quality reef breaks to challenge you, like The Destroyer, which is fast and shallow (good for short boards); the Coco Pipe; and La Preciosa (The Precious One).

SPORTS AND RECREATION

Cabarete is, without a doubt, the water-sports capital of the Dominican Republic. It could even be why you chose to vacation here. Cabarete is chock-full of outfitters, schools where beginner lessons are given, and places to rent the equipment you will need.

◖ Windsurfing

The sport that started the entire hullabaloo about Cabarete is still, despite the rise in popularity of kiteboarding, very popular and big business here. Playa Cabarete is a good beach for beginners and experienced windsurfers alike due to the strong winds necessary for the sport and the sandy sea floor of the inner bay.

The conditions in the morning are usually good for beginners and children since the wind isn't as strong and the water is flatter, which gives you more time to pull the sail up and get your balance. By about noon, the wind usually starts to pick up and blows parallel to the shore at up to 25–45 kilometers per hour. Additionally, it's calmer toward shore and rougher out where the coral reef breaks the waves. This is where the hotshots go to jump, do their 360-degree spins, and do flips.

You'll find lots of places that offer lessons and equipment rental right on the shore of Playa Cabarete. Generally, boards rent for US$50 per day or US$200–270 per week. Ask about package deals where you can pay a lump sum and you get a set amount of days, but you don't have to use them all in a row. Also ask about damage insurance, which can run you about US$45 for a week. Lessons are a great way to get into the sport. Beginners can expect to pay US$40 an hour for private instruction.

Vela/Spinout/Dare2Fly (Playa Cabarete, tel. 809/571-0805, www.velacabarete.com), on the upwind end of the beach, is a reliable, highly regarded, well-stocked outfitter who has some of the most high-tech and fancy equipment for rent. You'll look like a pro even if you end up doing a face plant. Vela offers a beginner windsurfer program (US$140 for 4–6 hours), private lessons (US$55 per hour with equipment), and advanced packages. Kiteboarding instruction is also available with their Dare2Fly school.

Club Nathalie Simon (Playa Cabarete, tel. 809/571-0848, www.cabaretewindsurf.com, 9 A.M.–6 P.M. daily) is on the west end of the beach. It has very nice equipment for rent for all skill levels. The instructors will only teach 1–3 people maximum, which allows you to progress more quickly. Kids as young as five can learn the sport with lessons on the lagoon behind the beach. CNS also rents kayaks and boogie boards.

Fanatic Windsurf Center (Playa Cabarete, tel. 809/571-0861, www.fanatic-cabarete.com) offers rental of equipment at good rates by using older equipment, which is a good deal if you're doing it for the first time. A family package includes lessons for the parents and child care while you're on the water. Or, if your children are ready to learn windsurfing, they can take lessons also. Ten hours will only run you US$280, private lessons are US$60 per hour (for US$90 your lesson will be two hours). Some of the best locations for windsurfing in the world are located in Spanish-speaking countries, so why not include Spanish language lessons for an extra US$5 per hour? Fanatic Windsurf Center can arrange for your lessons at a nearby language school.

◖ Kiteboarding

While windsurfing put Cabarete on the map, kiteboarding is gaining in popularity quickly. It is impressive to watch from the shore, let alone try. One moment you're skimming along the surface of the waves, then you suddenly swoop into the air for a hang time above the ocean.

Both Kite Beach and Bozo Beach are good spots for learning, but Bozo seems to be less crowded. This exhilarating sport is best when you have lots of hours of instruction (6–12 is standard), and it is best to choose a quality school. It is a dangerous sport that you'd be wise to learn from the best.

Kiteboarding is more expensive to learn, and beginners should expect to pay around US$250 for six hours of lessons. Try to shop around, though; there are so many instructors around that you should get your money's worth by having an instructor with whom you have a good rapport and who makes you feel safe.

Super-cool **Kite Club** (Kite Beach, tel. 809/571-9748, www.kiteclubcabarete.com), at the upwind tip of Kite Beach, offers beginners a three-day beginner course (US$459), including gear and insurance. Lessons are available in English, French, German, and Spanish. If you buy a membership (starting at US$20/week) for the duration of your trip you get special incentives, like use of a locker, use of Kite Club facilities, and access to a rescue boat (could come in handy). An on-site restaurant specializes in tasty food that perks you up after a good run but won't weigh you down so you can get

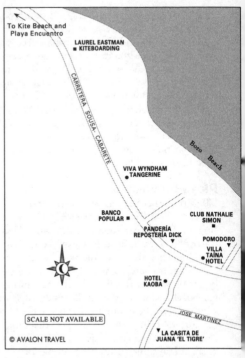

back out there. Inquire about the accommodation choices: cottages (US$30 includes breakfast and dinner, shared bath), studios (US$66), and apartments (starting at US$77).

Laurel Eastman Kiteboarding (ApartHotel Caracol, tel. 809/571-0564, www.laureleastman.com) offers lessons in many different alluring packages like one called Transformation into Kiteboarder, which is a four-day package for those new to the sport for US$460. Other packages include kids' classes and women-only classes.

Club Mistral (Playa Cabarete, tel. 809/571-0770, www.club-mistral.com) has the credibility of having many operations worldwide. This German company offers many kitesurfing (US$240/six hours, private lesson is US$193/two hours), windsurfing (US$65/two hours), surfing (US$45/two hours), and combo packages. Prices are for beginner lessons only and increase for skill level.

Dare2Fly (Cabarete, tel. 809/571-0805,

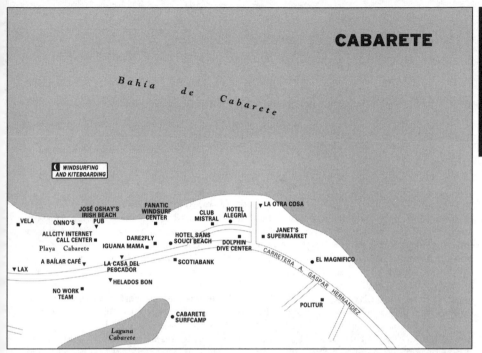

CABARETE

Bahía de Cabarete

WINDSURFING AND KITEBOARDING

VELA
ONNO'S
JOSÉ OSHAY'S IRISH BEACH PUB
FANATIC WINDSURF CENTER
CLUB MISTRAL
HOTEL ALEGRÍA
LA OTRA COSA
JANET'S SUPERMARKET
ALLCITY INTERNET CALL CENTER
DARE2FLY
IGUANA MAMA
HOTEL SANS SOUCI BEACH
DOLPHIN DIVE CENTER
Playa Cabarete
A BAÍLAR CAFÉ
LA CASA DEL PESCADOR
SCOTIABANK
EL MAGNIFICO
LAX
HELADOS BON
NO WORK TEAM
CABARETE SURFCAMP
CARRETERA A. GASPAR HERNANDEZ
POLITUR
Laguna Cabarete

www.velacabarete.com), owned and operated by Vela Windsurf Center, is a full-service IKO-affiliated (International Kiteboarding Organization, www.ikointl.com) outfitter offering lessons and gear rental. All beginners get board, kite, harness, helmet, and vest included in their lesson rates (maximum three students to a lesson). The beginner group course is three days long for nine hours a day (US$390).

Surfing

The surfing on Playa Encuentro is some of the best on the island. Although kitesurfing has stolen the global spotlight, good old retro surfing is making a big comeback in Cabarete. Reef breaks include Coco Pipe, Encuentro, and The Destroyer. Surfboard rental is quite inexpensive compared to wind- and kitesurfing. Board rental is typically around US$15 for a half day. Beginners and experienced surfers alike might enjoy the surf camps that some outfitters offer. A five-day camp can cost US$150.

No Work Team (Calle Principal, tel. 809/571-0820, www.noworkteamcabarete. com) offers a mini course where you'll learn about the sport and how to handle the equipment, paddle across waves, and catch them (US$40/day, includes board rental). Perhaps the best deal is the US$210 saver for five days of lessons and two days of rental (one week total). Get a ride from Cabarete to Encuentro and back on the No Work Team shuttle for US$5. Rides run every day at 6:30 A.M. or 8:30 A.M. and take you back to Cabarete at 8:15 P.M.

Take Off (Playa Encuentro, tel. 809/963-7873, www.321takeoff.com) is another outfitter right at the beach.

Cabarete Surf Camp (Calle Bahia 11, Playa Encuentro, office hours 9 A.M.–1 P.M. and 2–6 P.M. Mon.–Sat., tel. 809/571-0733, www. cabaretesurfcamp.com) belongs to the hotel of the same name. The surf camp offers to teach students of the ocean to evaluate the sea and wave conditions, body position and paddling, wave selection, and, of course, the rules of riding the waves. The intensive surf course includes daily transport to beach, surf lessons, board rental, leash, wax, and even sunblock for one week (US$299). If you don't need the lessons then you'll pay only US$140 a week. Only need the ride to the beach? Pay only US$35 for the week. Packages exist for accommodations and surfing.

Diving

While this is clearly not the big sport of this area, **Dolphin Dive Center** (tel. 809/571-0842, www.dolphindivecenter.com, 9 A.M.–1 P.M. and 2–6 P.M. Mon.–Sat.) can arrange for transfer to the nearly 20 dive sites within a 20-minute boat ride, including underwater tunnels and canyons 25 meters under the surface. It is a popular place to see eels and angelfish. Experienced divers will be able to dive the freshwater caves near Cabrera. One dive is US$46 with full equipment provided. Dive packages start with a Discover Scuba Diving package for US$50 (minimum age is 10) that will take place in a pool or pool-like condition. Next up is the PADI certification course for US$219 and all the way up to instructor courses.

Tours and Excursions

Iguana Mama (Calle Principal, tel. 809/571-0908, www.iguanamama.com) is the best eco-tour operator in the Dominican Republic. It has been around for a while and has a great selection of exhilarating tours and excursions, like hiking, trekking, canyoning, and cascading, as well as some more laid-back choices like catamaran rides. But Iguana Mama is best known for its mountain-biking trips (starting at US$65), from one-day to multiday biking excursions that take you deep into the Dominican Republic that few other tourists see. Some trips even go across the entire country! *¡Muy Difícil!* Hiking and mule trips to Pico Duarte are a good choice through this company as well (US$450). Waterfall tours are all the rage in extreme tourism, and Iguana Mama has set up a spectrum of options from the 27 Waterfalls (US$79) to

the aptly named Super Big Bastard (US$149), where you will need some prior knowledge of canyoning and some swimming prowess (and a reasonable amount of *cojones*). Browse the website or stop by the office to look at brochures to get a feel for the limitless possibilities available to you; if you don't see just the right excursion, they will customize one for you. Among the top 10 reasons to choose Iguana Mama as your tour operator is that they run a truly sustainable and responsible tourism company by keeping an eye on the community they are in and not running rampant over it without giving back. We love that.

Tours, Trips, Treks & Travel (Cabarete, tel. 809/867-8884, www.4tdomrep.com) offers excursions that are adventure based and educational, ranging from photography safaris throughout the country to Santo Domingo museum tours to deep-sea fishing or golf excursions.

Cabarete Nature Park & Caves (Callejon de la Loma, tel. 829/201-4363, 9 A.M.–4 P.M. daily, US$15/ adults, kids half price). Take your bathing suit when you take a 90-minute tour with an expert guide through a protected area where you will learn about trees and medicinal plants, fauna, and the Taíno Indians and explore the Crystal Cave, because you will be able to swim in the frigid water of the cave 25 meters below the surface. Tours are given in English, Spanish, German, or French. You cannot visit this site without a tour guide. Although the walk is a pleasant and easy one for elderly and children, the cave swim is a different story because of the frigid temperature, about 23°C (73°F).

ENTERTAINMENT AND EVENTS
Nightlife

Cabarete's surfers and youthful visitors have given the small town a laid-back nightlife. But don't mistake laid-back for dead. Many of the restaurants lining the shore transform into spirited bars after dinner hours, where music and drinks flow, but they close fairly early (around 1 or 2 A.M. on the weekend).

C **LAX** (Playa Cabarete, www.lax-cabarete. com, 9 A.M.–1 A.M. daily) is certainly the hot spot and favorite happy hour (4–6 P.M.) restaurant that also serves a wide variety of items for breakfast, lunch, and dinner, but it is the popular starter venue mainly because of its *re-LAX-ed* atmosphere. Cash only.

Two dueling hot spots right next to one another are **Bambú** (Playa Cabarete, tel. 809/982-4549, 6 P.M.–1 A.M. daily), a large club with comfy sofas, and **Onno's** (tel. 809/571-0461, 9 A.M.–1 A.M. daily), which gets crazy-packed at night. Both offer outrageous drink specials and hours of music-pumping zaniness.

If you can't help but crave a little American bar food, **José Oshay's Irish Beach Pub** (Playa Cabarete, tel. 809/571-0775, 8 A.M.–11 P.M. daily) is the place for you. The owners are an Irish-American father and son team who opened this bar back in 2002. Since then they have been serving fish and chips, bangers and mash, and shepherd's pie right on the beach in Cabarete. An annual St. Patrick's Day bash complete with bagpipes and Irish dancers sends this stretch of beach into a frenzy with upwards of 2,000 in attendance. Other popular dishes are a plate of nachos big enough to feed four, freshly caught seafood, cocktails, and tropical frozen drinks. A live rock band plays five nights a week.

C **A Baílar Cafe** (Calle Principal, tel. 809/916-4551, 10 A.M.–11 P.M. daily, www.a-bailar.net) is both a restaurant and a Latin dance school located in the center of Cabarete. The casual restaurant serves sandwiches, empanadas, hamburgers, and pastas. But taking a dance lesson is another way to spend your evening. Tony Vargas, the charming *el professor de baile,* will set your merengue into motion, put the spice in your salsa, and make your *bachata* blush. The dance floor is in the back of the restaurant and is sufficient for a small party. Lessons are US$14 per person or US$45 for three one-hour lessons. Classes are available seven days a week 11 A.M.–6 P.M. All levels are available. There is no better way to discover the culture of the Dominican Republic than to get dancing! This is our celebration of life. *¡Eso!*

Festivals and Events

Fourteen years ago, Cabarete became home to the annual Dominican Republic Jazz Festival due to organizer Lorenzo Sancassani's love of music. As Cabarete moved further into the forefront as one of the world's prime locations for water sports, his team has developed the Master of the Ocean competition, the Kitesurfing World Cup, and, for fun, the International Sand Castle Competition.

Festivals here are the perfect mix of events, wonderful dining, fun nightlife, and great accommodations. Visit www.cabareteevents.com for more information.

The **Master of the Ocean** competition (www.masteroftheocean.com), which celebrated its seventh year in 2009, challenges individuals in their mastery of kitesurfing, windsurfing, and surfing. While they are judged in individual categories, the winner is the one who can prove that they've got the chops to master all three categories. International as well as national competitors compete to become crowned master of the waves. The rounds are held at various area beaches, but the final heat is at Playa Encuentro with its big, intimidating waves so as to ensure challenge for the participants and theatrics for the spectators. It is a thrilling event.

Held in November, the **Dominican Republic Jazz Festival** (www.drjazzfestival. com) is one of the most important jazz festivals of the Caribbean. It celebrates jazz with artists that visit from many countries of the world in addition to Dominican talent. Every night there are 2–3 bands (making sure that one is Dominican), a kids' concert, and a concentration of Latin jazz.

Caribbean Laser Midwinter Regatta, held in January, is a race for one design class of boats. It kicks off a world calendar of regattas. Some of the top sailors come for this event since the winds of Cabarete are legendary and appreciated by water sport enthusiasts of all kinds. The event brings together past and present Olympic champions as well as master sailors of all levels.

The **International Sand Castle**

VILLA RENTALS

Travelers looking for accommodations outside the walls of the ever-popular all-inclusive resorts have quite a few alternatives, and excellent ones at that.

Renting a villa is a great option for the independent-minded tourist. Whether one is seeking exclusivity, privacy, and/or affordability, villas offer an opportunity to personalize your vacation in ways that all-inclusive resorts cannot. Luxury villas are available for those who want to live like a rock star and are therefore willing to pay like a rock star.

The **Sea Horse Ranch** (Carretera Sosúa–Cabarete, tel. 809/571-3880, fax 809/571-2374, www.sea-horse-ranch.com, US$1,000–3,000 per night) is a 100-hectare development on the north coast between Sosúa and Cabarete. Many villas, all of which have private swimming pools, are available seaside or with private gardens. Particularly of interest is the Sea Horse Ranch Equestrian Center, which offers riding lessons and wilderness and beach tours.

Bea Location (La Ceiba, Las Terrenas, tel. 809/885-4074, www.bealocation.com, US$200–4,000 per week) offers rental villas and new beachfront apartments, including a luxurious penthouse with rooftop Jacuzzi that sleeps up to eight. All have maid service. All located in Las Terrenas along Samaná Peninsula, each villa is of a unique design – from romantic bungalows ideal for a couple to the Casa Lila, which sleeps up to six people and features a garden with a swimming pool, to the Villa Loma Bonita, with its second-floor infinity pool, outdoor living room, and accommodations for up to 16 people. Bea Location also offers for rent Caribbean-style seaside apartments with an ocean view and terrace. With so many options to choose from, you really can't go wrong.

If you are feeling on the fence in terms of whether to choose a villa or a resort, the **Excel Villas at Casa de Campo** (La Romana, tel. 305/856-5405, http://casadcampo. net/villa_microsite/excel_club_villa_index. htm#, US$600–1,800) offers the best of both worlds. You get the privacy of a villa but access to resort amenities. In La Romana on the Caribbean coast, the villas range from three to six bedrooms and have either a whirlpool or a swimming pool. With fully equipped kitchens and comfortable furnishings, the Excel Villas truly can be your "home away from home." Plus, you can tell all your friends you stayed at the resort where Michael Jackson married Lisa Marie Presley, where the Clintons have vacationed, and where Oscar de la Renta once lived and Julio Iglesias keeps a home.

If more moderately priced accommodations are more your speed, but comfort and quality are still high on your list of priorities (as well they should be!), the Dominican Republic does not lack for housing options.

With swinging hammocks for napping and large beds for a good night's sleep, **Natura Cabanas** (Paseo del Sol 5, Perla Marina, Sosúa, tel. 809/571-1507, www.naturacabana.com, US$90 d) truly is a one-of-a-kind alternative to your typical hotel. First of all, the rooms are individual bungalows. Second, each is designed for maximum comfort and minimal effect on the environment. Overhead fan petals (in lieu of air-conditioning) and hand-crafted bamboo furniture make these ecologically sensitive accommodations accommodating to you and the environment.

Also check out the following for more villa rental information: www.puerto-plata.com, www.a1vacations.com, and www.dominican-holiday.com.

For choosing a villa in a specific area of the Dominican Republic, go to www.vrbo.com.

Competition is an event that both kids and adults will enjoy. Forget the plastic bucket and shovel kit; these competitors are serious! It's held in Cabarete in the end of February every year with adult and kid competitions.

Cabarete Race Week and the **Kitesurfing World Cup** are held in the month of June when the winds are prime. During this time Cabarete is overcome with international windsurfers and kiteboarders ready to compete in the tournaments. These events are fun to witness, but if you plan on traveling here during this time, book your hotel well in advance.

ACCOMMODATIONS

There are plenty of accommodations and a good assortment for all income levels. Cabarete is unique in that there are two peak travel seasons: December to April and mid-June to mid-September, when the winds give good surfing conditions.

Under US$50

Cabarete Surf Camp (tel. 809/571-0733, www.cabaretesurfcamp.com, US$25–US$77 per night per person) belongs to the surf camp of the same name. The lodging choices include rooms in cottages, bungalows, studios, and one- or two-bedroom apartments. It just can't get any sweeter than this for the money. The cottage options are clean and come with a *mosquiterro* (mosquito net, necessary for keeping the pesky buggers away at night), sink, maid service, and breakfast and dinner. The most economical option is room 51. For a group of up to six people, choose the Tarzan House, a thatched roof hut raised high off the ground and surrounded by palms with its own terrace and kitchen. The grounds are well kept with a quiet garden and pool area. Perhaps it is so quiet because everyone is surfing with the surf school on-site. You can catch a ride to the beach or take lessons from their pros. The restaurant has a set menu served in the open-air picnic tables that includes a wide assortment of choices for breakfast and international barbecue for dinner, paying special attention to vegetarian choices.

Caribica Sanssouci Aparthotels (Cabarete, tel. 809/571-0755, www.caribica.com, US$12–26 per person) is a chain of very affordable rooms and apartments. **Beach Hotel Caribica, Casa Caribica, Surf Caribica, Playa Caribica, Villa Caribica, Plaza Caribica,** and **Park Caribica** are all located in Cabarete and starting at a mindboggling US$12 per person. The Hotel Sans Souci Beach is at the far eastern end of Playa Cabarete, directly on the beach, and is the nicest of the bunch. The rest of them are nothing fancy and are showing their age, but their rooms are clean and spacious with cable TV, safe, and refrigerator; best of all, most have a panoramic ocean view. Parking is free. Chances are, if you came to spend your time in the water and not the hotel room and don't mind a place that is incredibly basic but clean, then these rooms will be fine.

Hotel Alegría (Callejón 2, tel. 809/571-0455, www.hotel-alegria.com, US$40 d and up), tucked into a side road, has cheap accommodations and is relatively comfortable and acceptable for those on a budget. One three-bedroom, three-bathroom apartment would be good for friends traveling together. This is a good value if you are staying for an extended amount of time. Features include a rooftop gym and Jacuzzi.

The 28 bungalows at **Hotel Kaoba** (Calle Principal, tel. 809/571-0300, www.kaoba.com, US$45 d and up) enjoy close proximity to the beach but without being in all the craziness. It is quieter than some of the other hotels that are directly on the beach, and this one is actually closer to the lagoon. There are also 15 rooms and 10 deluxe rooms available. All rooms have TV and minibars, and some have kitchenettes. There is a pool and a restaurant/bar.

The name alone sets a hotel up for high expectations: What **Extreme** (Carretera Sosúa 5, tel. 809/571-0880, www.extremehotels.com, US$45 d, minimum two-night stay) offers (not that other places don't) is an in-house kiteboarding school, a surf school, and a skate park (at extra cost to you) called Six Feet Under (named after the reef breaker Six Feet Over, which is just in front of the hotel). The rooms are nice and comfortable, but if you're staying in a hotel that caters to action sport enthusiasts, you probably won't spend a lot of time in there anyway. Free wireless Internet is available so that you can check surf and wind conditions. Plenty of day excursions are available if there's not enough wind. Extreme prides itself on an exercise-hard-all-day, party-all-night atmosphere. The bar is actually a distillery for crying out loud. That being said, they are working on going green by solar heating the hot water and hanging dry the laundry. Their power is run on "street service" and therefore can go out occasionally. But when it does, happy hour is on! Definitely for the sporty, thrill-seeking crowd.

US$50-100

Kite Beach Hotel (Carretera Sosúa, tel. 809/571-0878, www.kitebeachhotel.com, US$66 d) offers comfortable and very clean rooms with nice and roomy bathrooms, remote control air-conditioning, phone, cable TV, ceiling fan, and safe. Unfortunately, only the suites and apartments have balconies with ocean views (US$108–130 d), and both of those have kitchenettes. The pool area has good views of the goings-on of Kite Beach. A breakfast buffet is included in the rate. It's a good value for kiteboarders because you can get a package deal including lessons.

All rooms at **Villa Taína Hotel** (Calle Principal, tel. 809/571-0722, www.villataina. com, standard room US$95 d, standard oceanside US$115 d) are equipped with air-conditioning, Internet connection, minibar, balcony or terrace, and nice bathrooms. The pool is small but attractive, there is direct access to the beach, and the restaurant and bar overlook the ocean. A generous buffet breakfast is included with the rate and half-board rate options are available.

US$100 and Up

Viva Wyndham Tangerine (Calle Principal, tel. 809/571-0420, fax 809/571-9550, www. vivaresorts.com, US$290 d) is a good all-inclusive option. The 223 rooms are very comfortable (especially the bed) with large spacious bathrooms—a little plain, but kept ultra-clean. The buffet, while trying to cater to all nationalities, does reasonably well. All the regular all-inclusive amenities are present: nighttime entertainment, large pool, direct access to beach, and disco to name a few. Do try to get a room in the building closest to the ocean; although your view to the water is not completely unobstructed (the restaurant and pool come first), you can get that fresh ocean breeze to come through your windows.

Natura Cabanas (Paseo del Sol 5, Cabarete, tel. 809/571-1507, www.naturacabana.com, US$120 d and up), between Cabarete and Sosúa, offers 10 charming bungalows as an alternative to the staid room you get at other hotels. This family-owned unique hideaway is a treat. Each separately named (not numbered) bungalow (such as Cabana India, Mexicali, or Caracol) has a rustic interior of bamboo, caoba wood, and stone coral. The environmentally sensitive use of materials (like eucalyptus, which scares away insects naturally) and the design blend this hotel into the environment without disrupting the natural beauty of the area. Some bungalows have kitchenettes and all have minifridges. A vacation spent in this hotel is one of lazy days in one of the numerous hammocks, healthy meals in the restaurant, sunning yourself by the pool, taking a yoga or pilates (or a fusion of the two: yogalates!) class by the ocean, and indulging in a spa treatment on-site. Rates include airport transfer, breakfast, and maid service. This is truly a good find.

Velero Beach Resort (Carretera Sosúa, tel. 809/571-9727, www.velerobeach.com, US$122 d) is easily the best hotel in Cabarete, with spacious rooms that are kept mercilessly clean, as are the grounds. The Velero is positioned at the eastern end of Cabarete beach, giving it a more placid feel than if you were in the thick of the business, especially when you lounge around on one of the covered beach beds. The service is superb. A regular double room has one queen bed and one double bed, satellite TV, Internet, small refrigerator, a safe, and a small private balcony with ocean view. The penthouse will spoil you and your entourage with three bedrooms and three bathrooms over 2,100 square feet and a panoramic view of the ocean on the top floor (US$342).

If you scoff at the idea of staying in an all-inclusive hotel and want the freedom of a well-designed condominium or apartment with your own kitchen, then **(El Magnifico** (Carretera Sosúa, tel. 809/571-0868, www.hotelmagnifico.com, US$101 and up) is the place for you. All are stylish with modern appointments (even the older Caribbean-themed building is more modern than some of the other hotel choices in town). There are size options from studio to "Presidential Penthouse." This is not the place to go if you want amenities galore; the only one you will find is the pool in the lush tropical garden. Some of the best restaurants and bars are a couple minutes' walk away in downtown Cabarete. Building 6 is a new contemporary structure whose units come equipped with dishwashers, coffeemakers, air-conditioning, Internet, and flat screen TVs. Ask about renting a cell phone, because you won't find phones in your rooms.

FOOD

Playa Cabarete is a romantic and charming area, and many of the restaurants here provide that sort of atmosphere as well. Many offer beachfront dining, but be prepared to pay higher prices than at the venues farther from the beach. Some of the restaurants also turn into lively nightlife spots after dinner.

Pandería Repostería Dick (on the west end of town, tel. 809/571-0612, 7 A.M.–3 P.M. Thurs.–Tues., US$3–6) is a great breakfast spot very popular with the locals and tourists alike. It serves international breakfast favorites and freshly baked bread. The coffee is phenomenal and just the kick in the pants you need. Breakfast is served until 1 P.M., so that those late-rising kiteboarders can get some before they go out on the water.

La Casa del Pescador (Playa Cabarete, tel. 809/571-0760, 8 A.M.–11 P.M. daily, US$6–17) might not be much to look at, but the seafood

and fish are excellent. This is a celebrated mainstay in Cabarete. Specialties include seafood spaghetti and paella.

Reservations are essential at **Blue Moon Retreat** (Los Brazos, tel. 809/223-0614, noon–midnight, US$18), best known for its East Indian/Caribbean restaurant, which requires a minimum of eight people per party. Enjoy your dinner served in the traditional manner on comfy cushions on the floor. Tandoori chicken, curried goat, vegetable curries, and homemade chutneys arrive on banana leaves as plates. Blue Moon is east of Cabarete on the highway to Sabaneta. Turn right toward Jamao al Norte and go through Los Brazos, where you'll see a sign directing you to take a left up a hill.

La Casita de Juana "El Tigre" (Callejón de la Loma, tel. 809/801-1338, open 2 P.M.–1 A.M. Wed.–Mon., US$1–8) is a favorite with the locals, serving famous seafood stews, a killer fish in garlic sauce, savory *sancocho,* and a phenomenal *chivo* in *salsa picante.* All dishes come with rice and salad with fried plantain. The owner, Juana, is so welcoming she just may sit at your table or dance with you (even though there is no designated dance floor) in this lively and friendly establishment she has created.

The owners of **(La Otra Cosa** (La Punta, tel. 809/571-0607, 8:30 A.M.–11 P.M., closed Tues., US$15–35) have created the perfect recipe for romance. The menu has French-Caribbean influences with a smattering of other international touches. The mahimahi on a bed of saffron rice is spectacular. A full bar is able to make any favorite drinks you have (with all the *good* Dominican rums in stock), and there is a generous wine list. If dinner didn't woo you, then dessert will make you fall further in love. But it's the view and the ambience that push it all over the edge, and isn't that half the dining experience anyway? The open-air restaurant is in full frontal of the sea, and at night, with the candles lit, there is no more romantic place on the beach since this place is on the quiet end of Playa Cabarete.

Pomodoro (Calle Principal, tel. 809/571-0085, US$7–14) is a casual pizza joint that serves up the best pies on the beach using quality toppings. Try one with fresh seafood on top or one of the many calzones. Since the owner is a music-loving Cabarete festival organizer, there is often live music here.

Centrally located **Helados Bon** (Calle Principal, 11:30 A.M.–11 P.M. daily, starting at US$1.50) is open late. Somehow ice cream just tastes better here. Maybe it's the heat or maybe it's the ingredients. One thing is for sure; it is the stuff that Dominican childhoods are made of, with flavors like *bizcocho* (cake) and *mantecado,* which is a rich buttery vanilla.

At **Janet's Supermarket** (Carretera Gaspar Hernández, 8 A.M.–8 P.M. Mon.–Sat., 8 A.M.–1 P.M. Sun.) you can find almost all of your grocery needs, including dry goods, produce, and sundries.

INFORMATION AND SERVICES
Health and Emergencies
The **Politur** (Carretera Gaspar Hernández, tel. 809/571-0713, 24 hours) office is at the eastern outside end of town.

Servi-Med Medical Office (tel. 809/571-0964, 24-hour service) is right in the middle of town across from Sky Internet Access, and they'll come to you. English and German are spoken. On staff are four doctors, a dentist, and a chiropractor.

Money
ScotiaBank (Calle Principal 1, tel. 809/571-0292, 8:30 A.M.–4:30 P.M. Mon.–Fri., 9 A.M.–1 P.M. Sat.) has a 24-hour ATM on the east end of town, and **Banco Popular** (Carretera Sosúa 1, tel. 809/571-0903, 9 A.M.–5 P.M. Mon.–Fri., 9 A.M.–1 P.M. Sat.) has a 24-hour ATM on the western end of town.

Money exchange offices are along the main drag and will all change euros, U.S. currency, and traveler's checks.

Communications
Allcity Internet Call Center (Calle Principal 1, second floor, tel. 809/571-0112, 9 A.M.–9 P.M. Mon.–Sat., closed Sun.) offers wireless Internet connection for US$1 per minute as well as long-distance call service.

There is no post office in Cabarete, but you can ask your hotel's front desk to post mail for you.

Getting There and Around
Guaguas can be hailed anywhere along the main road that skewers Cabarete. Remember to stand on the side of the road for the direction in which you want to travel; that way you'll be certain to catch the right one. When in doubt, say the name of the town you wish to go to and they either will or will not let you on, depending. Trips to Río San Juan (US$2.25) take an hour, Sosúa (US$0.50) is a 30-minute ride, and to Puerto Plata (US$1.75) it's a one-hour ride. No major bus company comes to Cabarete, but you can catch one to Sosúa and then hop a *guagua* to Cabarete

There are taxi stands along the main drag and *motoconchos* can always be waved down if you feel like taking part in a more dangerous activity than kitesurfing. It is always standard practice to haggle for taxis and *motoconchos* before agreeing on a price. Don't be shy, this town is crawling with them. You can take a *motoconcho* to all the area beaches for under US$3.

Sosúa

Sosúa sits in the curve of the Bahía de Sosúa, laying out a pretty golden beach for tourists who come to the northern town to take advantage of the peaceful waters for swimming, snorkeling and nearby diving. It also offers visitors wonderful hotel accommodations and a bevy of restaurant choices, all of which are cheaper than nearby Puerto Plata and Cabarete.

Sosúa is a town with a sad history. In 1937, Trujillo ordered a massacre of over 20,000 Haitians. He realized that he needed to clean up his tarnished image, and he was eager for

the incident to be overlooked. Since World War II was underway, Trujillo, under the guise of altruism, offered political asylum to Jewish refugees escaping Hitler's Nazi Germany. Thus, in 1939, Sosúa was founded by nearly 600 European Jewish immigrants. In true Trujillo form, there was yet another ulterior motive. He was also trying to "whiten" the race of the Dominican Republic, one of his constant obsessions. While some of the Jewish families integrated and stayed in the Dominican Republic, many of them left. About 20 families remain in

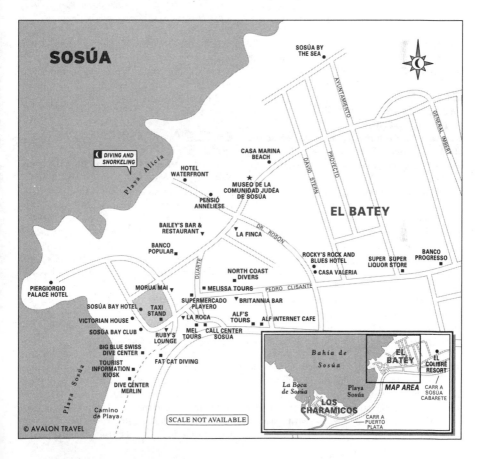

© AVALON TRAVEL

Sosúa today, and the legacy of their relatives, in the myriad skills they brought with them, still lives on in the community. A strong dairy and cured meat industry was formed when the first refugees came during World War II. And the synagogue that was built still holds services.

The beauty of a place like Sosúa naturally generates a strong tourism industry. But, when the sex tourism industry took over, that's when things really began to boom. Since then, the government has gone to various measures in an effort to squelch the activities, and for more than two decades the economy of the town has been trying to recover. Sosúa still suffers from a somewhat tarnished reputation. But if you can choose to look the other way for the rather obvious happenings and enjoy the plethora that Sosúa has to offer, this town is one of the best towns to use as a home base for exploring the rest of the northern coast, both for its location and for its lower prices.

SIGHTS
Museo de la Comunidad Judía de Sosúa

The **Jewish Community Museum of Sosúa** (Calle Dr. Alejo Martínez, tel. 809/571-1386, 9 A.M.–1 P.M. and 2–4 P.M., US$3) stands next to the synagogue of Sosúa. Inside you'll see exhibits on the story of the Jewish immigration and influence on the Dominican Republic. Trujillo had hoped that by inviting the Jewish families to immigrate and work on a plantation (few were actually farmers) he could convince the world he was not the anti-Semitic, ruthless dictator he truly was. Trujillo was a self-promoter and the act was simply a marketing ploy. Few Jewish families stayed more than a few years, but in the time that they were here they began a successful meat and dairy industry that survives to this day and is collectively referred to as Productos Sosúa. It is known to be the finest in the country. In the museum you'll see a chronology of the lives of the Jewish settlers during their time in the Dominican Republic. It is a well-maintained museum whose signs are in English and Spanish, and it's worth a stop to learn about the unique history of Sosúa.

Playa Sosúa

Playa Sosúa is the main beach; it lies in the middle of two neighborhoods (El Batey and Los Charamicos). The beach's tawny, fine sand is the point where the two worlds combine. Dominicans from Los Charamicos and the tourists from El Batey come together, making for a rather crowded but fun beach. This public space is lined with restaurants, vendors, bars, and excursion desks, all vying for the attention of the tourists. It's a busy place. You can rent beach loungers for about US$2.

Playa Alicia

To the east of Playa Sosúa is a smaller and definitely less crowded beach called Playa Alicia, most commonly referred to as Playita (Little Beach). It is at the end of Calle Dr. Rosen by the Hotel Sosúa by the Sea, and a staircase leads down the rocky cliff. Since it's harder to get to, you won't find as many vendors of trinkets, food, or drink, but you'll find peace and quiet compared to the overly populated Playa Sosúa.

ENTERTAINMENT AND EVENTS

Easy-going **Rocky's Rock and Blues Bar and Hotel** (Calle Dr. Rosen 22, El Batey, tel. 809/571-2951, www.rockysbar.com, 7 A.M.–2 A.M. daily) admittedly caters to expats and tourists, but it is popular with locals as well. You can grab an ice-cold Presidente or try a Mamajuana shooter to some rock and blues music (obviously). The Canadian-American menu has dishes like fried chicken and homemade pies. Rocky's has very basic rooms for rent.

Britannia Bar (Calle Pedro Clisante and Calle Libre, tel. 809/571-1959, www.britanniasosua.com, 10 A.M.–late), a long-standing expat favorite, is clean and popular with tourists. Local beers like Presidente and Bohemia are in abundance, but they also have imports like Guinness, Beck's and Bud. A long list of liquors behind the bar create some of the specialty drinks. Don't forget to create a good food base to soak up the liquid fun with some truly yummy bar food. Try a Hungry Man Burger or some appetizers like the shrimp sizzler served with plenty of bread.

At **Ruby's Lounge** (Pedro Clisante and Calle Arzeno, 1 P.M.–1 A.M. daily), a cool expat-owned bar, you can listen to live music (Fridays), do a little dancing, or belt out a tune during karaoke (Sundays) in the bar, which is located on the first floor. Upstairs, you can settle down for a drink in the lounge. There's an amazing all-day happy "hour" that lasts from 1 P.M. to 8:30 P.M. The international clientele is friendly. With prostitution glaringly apparent almost everywhere in Sosúa, in this bar it's not as prominent as in other nightclubs.

SHOPPING

There are many trinket shops in Sosúa, but for a nice art shop go to **Viva** (Calle Dr. Alejo Martínez, tel. 809/571-2581). It has a wonderful selection of local art and Dominican paintings. It is a good place to buy a traditional Dominican craft gift for someone back home.

Patrick's Silversmithy (Calle Pedro Clisante 9, tel. 809/571-2121) has interesting larimar, amber, and coral jewelry pieces that are affordable and unique.

Shopping along **Playa Sosúa,** you'll be able to find all the regular trinkets in a long line of booths. Haggle your head off for T-shirts, sunglasses, jewelry, and paintings and you'll hopefully get a good deal. Shopping like this might get a little tiresome, while being hounded by all the hawkers trying to get you to buy their lookalike wares, but it is an adventure, and you don't have to leave the beach.

SPORTS AND RECREATION
◖ Diving and Snorkeling

Sosúa is considered one of the premium dive sites along the North Coast. With the quality comes the popularity and therefore your choices are immense. Numerous dive shops exist, and most are along the Calle Arzeno where it meets the beach entrance.

There are many interesting and exciting dive locations near Sosúa. The *Zíngara* wreck, a 148-foot sunken cargo ship, has a maximum depth of 36 meters. You may run into moray eels here. Adjacent to the ship is a reef wall giving you the option to explore in shallower waters. Here you will see numerous kinds of corals and sponges. Airport Wall is about a 20-minute boat ride from Sosúa and is for advanced divers. Its maximum depth is 24 meters, and it's considered one of the best dive spots in the region. An 18-meter coral wall and maze of tunnels are home to large elkhorn coral, lobster, and schools of fish. The Coral Gardens (maximum depth 18 meters) and West Wall (maximum depth 30 meters) dive sites both offer various multicolored soft and large types of coral as well as sea urchins and angelfish. Sadly, chronic over-fishing has stripped many Sosúa dive sites of the opportunities to see the multitudes of sea life of yesteryear.

Select other dive sites are reachable from Sosúa via diving outfitters based in town. Cayo Arena (or Paradise Island), located off the coast of Luperón, is a circle of colorful coral reefs with an inner sandbank. This is a snorkeler's heaven. Many outfitters have speedboats that will whisk you away to this remote location. It can take up to three hours each way. It can get quite clogged with tours.

In nearby Río San Juan, you can dive the very popular Laguna Gri-Gri. Here you will see the tiny sea creatures and move up to the big ones like moray eels, barracudas, and stingrays. Also present are multicolored fan corals and sponges. Cave Du-Du is a freshwater cave with crystal-clear visibility about 90 minutes east of Sosúa. Seasoned cave divers will love this dive; those being introduced to the sport will be hooked forever.

Dives vary between companies but usually start around US$35 for a one-tank dive. Dive packages are always a way to ensure saving money if you plan to go more than once. Snorkeling is a lower-cost alternative with some excursions as low as US$10. Prices usually include equipment and are always subject to how much equipment you need and how many locations or tanks you choose. All of the dive outfitters offer certification courses and special excursions. One piece of advice: Find one that speaks your language of choice.

Near the entrance to Sosúa beach, **Fat Cat Diving** (Calle Gregorio Luperón, Caseta 32, tel. 809/586-1392, www.fatcat-diving.com, 9 A.M.–5 P.M. daily) has great deals on courses for beginners and advanced divers. The regular dive site is just offshore and costs US$35 for a one-tank dive. The more tanks you purchase, the more you save per dive. Fat Cat offers many excursions. If you have multiple skill levels in your party, an all-day excursion to Cayo Arena is an excellent choice. It runs US$35 if you are only going to snorkel, US$75 if you choose to dive there. For advanced divers only, there is a dive at the freshwater cave near Cabarete, Cave Du-Du. Here you pay US$95 and you get lunch, transportation, and beverages. Snorkeling with Fat Cat is the most cost effective. For only US$10 they will take you out to the reefs, and that includes the gear you'll need. Transportation from your accommodations at Playa Dorada and Cabarete are possible for extra cost. Victoria, the head instructor, is very nice and speaks English and German fluently.

Located on the same street are **Big Blue Swiss Dive Center** (tel. 809/571-2916, 9 A.M.–5 P.M. daily) and **Dive Center Merlin** (tel. 809/571-4309, 9 A.M.–5 P.M. daily), offering similar packages and courses.

North Coast Divers (Calle Pedro Clisante 8, tel. 809/571-1028, www.northcoastdiving.com, 8 A.M.–6 P.M. daily) is one of the most reputable diving outfitters on the northern coast and perhaps the entire island. They will take you on excursions to all the scuba hot spots like Cave Du-Du and Airport Wall. Starting price for diving adventures is US$60. Snorkeling trips and individual packages can be arranged as well.

Dolphin Dive Center (tel. 809/571-0842, www.dolphindivecenter.com, 9 A.M.–1 P.M. and 2–6 P.M. Mon.–Sat.) has on menu about 20 dive sites, including the tunnels and El Muro, a reef wall up to 24 meters deep where you will see barrel sponges. One dive is US$46 with full equipment provided. Dive packages start with a Discover Scuba Diving package for US$50 (minimum age is 10),

which will take place in a pool or pool-like condition. Next up is the PADI certification course for US$219 and all the way up to instructor courses.

Tours and Excursions

There are many tour and excursion companies in Sosúa. Do a little shopping around and ask a lot of questions about what you'll get for your money. Many tour operators offer local excursions as well as ones that take you as far away as the mountains of the Cordillera Central or the capital city. It is important to find out how long the trip will take, including transportation and activity time at your destination. Choose a different company if the other allows you more or less time (whichever you prefer) at your destination.

As you enter Playa Sosúa, there is a **tourist information kiosk** (tel. 809/571-1868, cell 809/223-5068) that offers glass-bottom boat excursions that take you for a 40-minute tour of Sosúa Bay to show you the colorful and varied coral formations and sea life for which Sosúa Bay is famous (US$12). Tours leave every 45 minutes. The kiosk offers many other excursions.

Melissa Tours (Calle Duarte 2, tel. 809/571-2567, 8 A.M.–5:30 P.M. Mon.–Fri., 8 A.M.–noon Sat.) is a locally owned tour company that offers excursions and tours to various places throughout the country, such as Samaná (US$30), and even one to Haiti (US$65).

Alf's Tours (Calle Padre Clisante 12, tel. 809/571-1734, www.alftour.com, 9 A.M.–6 P.M. daily) has many trips to choose from, including one all the way to Santo Domingo for US$58. It's next to an Internet café owned by the same company.

Mel Tours (Beachway Plaza, tel. 809/571-2057, www.mel-tour.com, 8:30 A.M.–5 P.M. Mon.–Sat., 9 A.M.–2 P.M. Sun.) has tours that include exciting vacation options like Paradise Island (US$60), deep-sea fishing (starting at US$67), horseback riding (US$45/half day), and jeep safari excursions (US$42 adults, US$29 children). Many more options are available.

ACCOMMODATIONS

Even though Sosúa is very popular, it is still an affordable vacation destination offering both budget and luxurious accommodation options. There are only a few all-inclusive hotels in town, and even those are considerably smaller when compared their counterparts in other areas of the country, adding a more personal feel to the facilities.

US$50 and Under

Rocky's Rock and Blues Bar and Hotel (Calle Dr. Rosen 22, tel. 809/571-2951, www.rockysbar.com, US$25/night) is comfortable but not fancy by any stretch. This five-room, Canadian-owned hotel offers private bathrooms, TV in each room, wireless Internet throughout, and 24-hour electricity, and is adjacent to the bar and restaurant, which is quite a popular hangout with expats, locals, and tourists. That said, don't count on it being very quiet. Rocky's also rents condos starting at US$225 per week in a building with a pool, laundry, and maid service. It's a great value with either choice.

Dutch-owned **El Colibrí Resort** (Calle Pedro Clisante 141, tel. 809/571-1847, www.elcolibri.net, US$25 d w/fan only) has very clean and modest rooms. Air-conditioning costs extra, as does a view of the pool, which is a good idea since there is a sliding glass door to the patio that aids air circulation. Although it is showing its age a bit, there is a nice pool with the restaurant right next to it, a laundry, and maid service, and airport transfers are offered. English, German, and Dutch are spoken.

Pensión Anneliese (Dr. Rosen, tel. 809/571-2208, US$25–40) is right near the better, less crowded beach in Sosúa. The rooms are clean and have a small refrigerator and private bath, and there's a pool. It's nothing too special, but the short walk to the beach could make up for it.

◖ **Hotel Waterfront** (Calle Dr. Rosen, tel. 809/571-2670, www.hotelwaterfrontdr.com, US$50 d), on a six-meter cliff facing the Atlantic Ocean, offers comfort in a simple way. Yes, the 27 rooms are a little plain, but the view

from the pool, restaurant (one of the best in town), and patio will all quickly win you over. All rooms have a terrace or balcony looking out over the lush tropical gardens. Cabanas are also available. The hotel is in front of Sosúa's best beach, Playa Alicia. If you don't like the limitations of all-inclusives, this hotel is a good match.

US$50-100

Piergiorgio Palace Hotel (Calle La Puntilla, tel. 809/571-2626, www.piergiorgiopalace.com, US$95 d in high season for first floor, US$125 d in high season with an ocean view), in a quiet neighborhood and atop dramatic cliffs overlooking the ocean, has some of the best views in Sosúa. The building is of a Victorian style, and rooms are spacious with good light, private baths, and balconies. They're kept very clean and are reasonably comfortable despite the darn chintzy decor. Of course, you could make up for the chintziness by insisting on an ocean-view room (you'll pay extra for this, but it's worth it). The hotel is a little aged but is a good choice for that view, a very romantic setting especially at sunset, and a good restaurant. Staff can help you arrange excursions and activities. There's no beach at this hotel, but steps lead you down to the rocks where you can snorkel. Rates include breakfast. Did we mention the view?

Sosúa by the Sea (Calle B Phillips and Martinez, tel. 809/571-3222, www.sosuabythesea.com, US$75 d) is on a beautiful stretch of beach with magnificent views, just a short walk from town. The 91-room hotel is small enough that it doesn't feel like you're just a number but large enough to offer amenities that you will want such as a restaurant (and a great one at that), two bars, gift shop, beauty salon, massage center, and a good-sized pool. The rooms have been remodeled, making them more than clean and comfortable in a sleek tropical design.

Casa Valeria (Calle Dr. Rosen 28, tel. 809/571-3565, www.hotelcasavaleria.com, US$50). Here is your chance to spend your vacation in a quiet little unpretentious hotel and appreciate why you are not at work, but are instead in a small town in the Caribbean, thousands of miles away. Surrounding the relaxing tropical garden are nine very clean hotel rooms and studios, six of which have direct access to the pool. All rooms have cable TV, fans, lockboxes, air-conditioning, and simple but cheery decor. The restaurant and bar directly next door serves breakfast (American, European, and Dominican) and dinner with both Dominican and international dishes, including tapas. This hotel is an exceptional value.

US$100 and Up

One of Sosúa's nicest hotels, **Sosúa Bay Hotel** (Calle Pedro Clisante, tel. 809/571-4000, www.starzresorts.com, US$100–150) offers optimum service and accommodations with a killer view of Sosúa Bay. This resort can rival the Playa Dorada all-inclusives in that the rooms are just as comfortable (however, that can be a bit humdrum). On the cliffs overlooking the bay, two pools are built on two different levels of terraces with ample space and loungers in which to sun yourself. Beach access is limited, so instead a ladder leads from the wooden deck down to the clear teal water, a unique and strikingly beautiful solution. There is a casino on-site.

(Victorian House (Calle Pedro Clisante, tel. 809/571-4000, www.starzresorts.com, US$150 and up d) is adjacent to the Sosúa Bay Club and run by the same parent company, Starz Resorts. The difference is that this one is considered in its "Boutique Collection" and is therefore much more lavish and expensive. Perched high on the cliffs overlooking Sosúa Bay, this hotel is constructed to mimic the Caribbean plantation-style home from the outside. The rooms are luxuriously decorated compared to other all-inclusives. Also available are split-level penthouses in case you didn't feel pampered enough. Make sure to ask for a room with a sea view.

Casa Marina Beach (Calle Dr. Alejo Martínez, tel. 809/571-3690, www.amhsamarina.com, US$150 d) is on Playa Alicia, one of its only positive aspects—not that anything is particularly bad, just not striking. It offers

the same things that most all-inclusives do. Standard rooms are equipped with two beds, air-conditioning, TV, telephone, and private bath, along with garden, pool, or ocean views. It is comfortable and clean and a good value if you plan on dining in the hotel most nights. Cuisine is Mexican, seafood, and Italian.

FOOD

Many of the restaurants can be found on Calle Pedro Clisante and are quite varied. **La Roca** (Calle Pedro Clisante 1, tel. 809/571-3893, 8 A.M.–11 P.M. daily, US$7–15) serves fresh seafood that is quite good. If you like barbecue, you'll enjoy the Friday all-you-can-eat special for US$8, or try one of the shrimp dishes sold by the pound, sandwiches, pastas, or select Mexican dishes. There's both indoor and outdoor seating on a patio.

(**La Puntilla de Piergiorgio** (Calle La Puntilla 1, tel. 809/571-2215, noon–11 P.M. daily, US$9–25), the restaurant on the roomy, multi-leveled terraces of the Hotel Piergiorgio, cooks up Italian cuisine. Under the stars and high above the Atlantic, you will enjoy such dishes as freshly caught fish, cannelloni, steak in peppercorn sauce, and wood-fired pizzas. The food is good, but the view is amazing. It is a powerfully romantic place at sunset with the orange, red, and yellow sky burning over the immense ocean. Exercise caution when choosing your dining partner—you might be engaged to each other by dessert.

Piergiorgio doesn't have the market cornered on sunset dinners. (**On the Waterfront** (Calle Dr. Rosen 1, tel. 809/571-2670, 7 A.M.–10 P.M. daily, US$8–30) does it very well and with even better food. Popular dishes include filet of sole in orange sauce, sea bass meunière, conch, or a hefty filet mignon flambéed in pepper sauce. The ambience (aside from the sunset) is casual elegance under an open-beam thatched roof and open to the breeze.

Bailey's Bar & Restaurant (Calle Alejo Martínez, tel. 809/571-3085, www.baileys-sosua.com, US$8–20) is open for breakfast, lunch, and dinner serving Dominican (like *sancocho*) and international (omelets, burgers, pastas) favorites to expats and tourists alike. This is the perfect resolution to the dreaded resort-buffet meltdown that can occur after a few days in an all-inclusive. Head over to Bailey's buffet in the garden for something new with better choices than in the hotels.

Britannia Bar (Calle Pedro Clisante and Calle Libre, tel. 809/571-1959, www.britannia-sosua.com, 10 A.M.–late daily) is a long-standing expat favorite that's clean and is popular with tourists. If you have had a hankering for some bangers and mash, or maybe some good ol' bar food, you've come to the right joint.

One of the more expensive places to dine in Sosúa is (**Morua Mai** (Calle Pedro Clisante, tel. 809/571-2966, 8 A.M.–midnight, US$7–25). The international cuisine includes steaks, seafood, and pork. Try the linguini with clams in a white wine sauce or the generous seafood paella, and real homemade cheesecake or the "anything flambéed" for dessert. Dine inside with white tablecloths or out on the sidewalk café under the palm trees. Morua Mai has a nice collection of wines, cigars, and cocktails, too.

Restaurante Pizzería Bolonga (Calle A. Martínez 33 and Ayuntamiental, noon–11 P.M. daily, tel. 809/571-1454) serves wood-fired pizzas, antipasti, a long list of very good pastas, and other Italian specialties.

No epicurean's trek through Sosúa would be complete without a visit to (**La Finca** (Alejo Martinez 18, tel. 809/571-3825, www.restaurantelafinca.net, open 5–11 P.M. daily, US$12–50). If your restaurant's name translates to "the farm," you'd better be serving pure and good food. On La Finca's menu, you will find stewed goat in rum sauce, chateaubriand, various pasta dishes, a mixed seafood platter for two, and some truly wonderful desserts, not to mention a generous wine list.

Supermercado Playero (Calle Pedro Clisante, tel. 809/571-1821, 8 A.M.–10 P.M. daily) offers a good selection of necessities and is centrally located near Calle Duarte.

At **Super Super Liquor Store** (Calle Pedro Clisante 77, tel. 809/571-3862, 8 A.M.–8 P.M. Mon.–Sat.) you'll find the requisite Brugal and Presidente, some wine, and cigars, but not a huge selection.

INFORMATION AND SERVICES

Near the intersection of Calles Duarte and Pedro Clisante you'll most likely find everything you need. It is the main commercial sector of El Batey (the tourist neighborhood of Sosúa).

Health and Emergencies

On the road to Cabarete, **Centro Médico Bella Vista** (Carretera Sosúa–Cabarete, tel. 809/571-3429, 24 hours) is the best place to go for medical attention. For emergencies, though, dial 911 like you would in the United States.

Farmacia Sosúa (Calle Pedro Clisante 10, tel. 809/571-2350, 8 A.M.–7 P.M. Mon.–Sat.) is conveniently located near the supermarkets and other storefronts, offering a good selection.

Money

Banking options are **Banco Popular** (Calle Dr. Alejo Martinez, tel. 809/571-2555, 8:15 A.M.–4 P.M. Mon.–Fri., 9 A.M.–1 P.M. Sat.) and **Banco Progreso** (Calle Dr. Alejo Martinez, tel. 809/571-2815, 8:30 A.M.–4 P.M. Mon.–Fri., 9 A.M.–1 P.M. Sat.). Both have ATM machines.

Communications

Rocky's Bar (Calle Dr. Rosen 22, tel. 809/571-2951, www.rockysbar.com) has free wireless Internet and cable hookups. You can't beat that. There is also an **Internet Café** (Calle Pedro Clisante 12, tel. 809/571-1734, 9 A.M.–10 P.M.).

At **Call Center Sosúa** (Beachway Plaza, tel. 809/571-3464, 8 A.M.–7 P.M. Mon.–Fri. and 8 A.M.–6 P.M. Sat.) you can make a call to the U.S. for US$0.32 per minute and to Europe for US$0.75 per minute.

GETTING THERE

Most people fly in to Puerto Plata (Aeropuerto Internacional Gregorio Luperón) and then take a cab, *guagua,* or hotel shuttle to their accommodations in Sosúa. Expect to pay around US$20 for a cab and US$1 for a *guagua*.

Caribe Tours (Carretera a Puerto Plata, tel. 809/571-3808) is in the Los Charamicos neighborhood. From Sosúa you can catch a bus to Santo Domingo (US$8.50) leaving every hour 5:15 A.M.–7 P.M. daily.

For around the same cost, **Metro Tours** (Av. Luperón, tel. 809/571-3480) has lines that run

to and from Puerto Plata, Santiago, and Santo Domingo at 8:20 A.M., 10:20 A.M., 1:20 P.M., and 5:50 P.M.

GETTING AROUND

Walking is easiest in Sosúa. If you need a ride to some farther away spot, you can either flag down a *motoconcho* (US$3 on average) or catch a taxi at the taxi stand (tel. 809/571-3027) on Calle Pedro Clisante at Calle Dr. Rosen.

Puerto Plata and Playa Dorada

The town of Puerto Plata was named, in 1493, by Columbus because of the way the sun shone on the water, creating the illusion of a mass of silver coins *(plata)*. This port was originally used as a stopover for ships carrying loads of silver on their way to Spain from Mexico. But of course in those days, where there were riches, there were pirates. Things got so bad that the Spanish crown insisted that the port be

abandoned, only to revisit and move in again 100 years later. The town remained a trading port until it built up its tourism industry beginning in the 1960s. The area experienced its most lucrative years in the 1990s when the economy swelled from the revenue that tourism created, far surpassing the tobacco, sugar, and cattle industries that had sustained it for so long. However, with the more recent birth

© ANA CHAVIER CAAMAÑO

Puerto Plata has been spruced up in recent years.

of a lucrative tourism industry in the Southeast of the country, the economy here is once again slightly declining.

Even though the name Puerto Plata and the term all-inclusive are still synonymous, the real seedbed of the resort scene in the area is east of Puerto Plata on Playa Dorada. Playa Dorada is a resort complex just east of the town of Puerto Plata where long stretches of golden sand lure tourists to these worry-free sanctuaries where all their needs are met in one place. When booking a vacation, resorts will often use the names Puerto Plata and Playa Dorada interchangeably.

Aside from the beautiful beach here, Puerto Plata's charming town square lined with restored Victorian homes offers plenty of reasons to wander outside of the resort complex. The town features a reputable amber museum, a colonial fortress, and a cable-car ride up the verdant and plush mountainside of Pico Isabel de Torres. Puerto Plata also presents an annual jazz festival and Carnaval celebration.

Today, Puerto Plata is a very clean town due to the efforts the government has put into sprucing up the town.

SIGHTS

Finding sights in Puerto Plata is easy if you remember certain streets for directional purposes if you're walking or driving around on your own. Puerto Plata's **Malecón** (the street that runs along the sea) is called Avenida Circunvalación Norte and Avenida General Luperón as it gets closer to the end where it meets up with the Fuerte San Felipe. Six blocks to the southwest (inland) is the **Parque Central** (actually called Parque Independencia), which is sandwiched between Calle José del Carmen Ariza and Calle Separación. A main street to keep in mind is **Avenida Beller.** It is the road immediately to the north of the Parque Central and runs east–west. Following Avenida Beller to the east will take you toward Playa Dorada and then the airport.

Playa Dorada is the gated resort complex containing many all-inclusive resorts located 2.5 kilometers east of Puerto Plata.

© ANA CHAVIER CAAMAÑO

downtown Puerto Plata

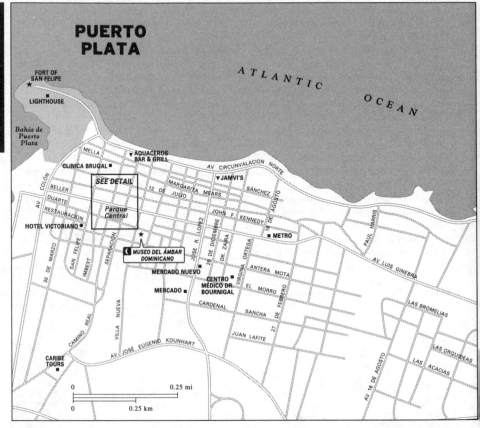

Playa Dorada

If you've booked a vacation at a resort in Puerto Plata, chances are very good that it is located just one kilometer away from the old city of Puerto Plata, in the mega-resort complex of Playa Dorada. Developed in the 1970s, it has enjoyed swells and dips in its success. Massive success came with the rise of tourism to the Dominican Republic but receded when tourists discovered (and a great deal of tourism pesos were poured into the marketing of) the southeastern region at Punta Cana and Bávaro.

◖ Museo del Ámbar Dominicano

The Dominican Amber Museum (Calle Duarte 61, tel. 809/586-2848, www. ambermuseum.com, 9 A.M.–6 P.M. Mon.–Sat., US$1.75), in an old Victorian mansion, houses a stunning array of amber pieces; some of them are quite rare. The most celebrated find is that of a 40-centimeter lizard perfectly conserved, dating back 30–40 million years. There are many other impressive pieces in the collection, which is well displayed with good signage and can be described to you personally by a guide in English or Spanish. Unfortunately, they have closed the gift shop associated with this museum. In order to take home a piece of amber jewelry, you'll have to head over to the Fine Gift Center, which also has an amber museum (the Galería de Ámbar).

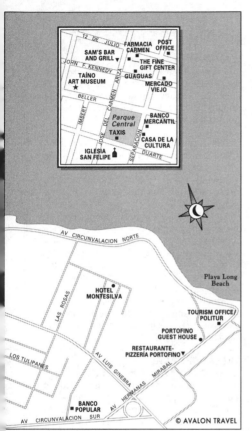

English and Spanish. The Fine Gift Center jewelry store is on the first floor and is a wonderful place to purchase keepsakes for your friends and relatives back home.

Casa de La Cultura

This **Cultural Center** (Calle Separación, tel. 809/261-2731, 9 A.M.–noon and 3–5 P.M. Mon.–Fri., free), on the first floor of one of the renovated homes that sit around Parque Central, often hosts cultural and literary events as well as exhibitions of Dominican artists.

Iglesia San Felipe

The Iglesia San Felipe (Puerto Plata, Calle Duarte, 8 A.M.–noon Mon.–Sat., 7 A.M.–8 P.M. Sun.) was devastated by Hurricane Georges in 1998. The uniquely two-steepled church is a picturesque sight just off the Parque Central. In 2005 the church finally underwent a facelift to repair the damage from the storm. In addition, various Puerto Plata families donated beautiful Italian stained-glass windows to further beautify the church.

Museo de Arte Taíno

The Taíno Art Museum (Puerto Plata, Calle Beller, Plaza Arawak, tel. 809/586-7601, free) is an odd little museum that houses *replicas* of Taíno artifacts. To make things weirder, it has incredibly erratic hours of operation, and signage is in Spanish only. This is worthy of a stop only if you are completely enraptured by Taíno history, no matter how inauthentic the exhibit may be. Some reproductions are sold.

Fuerte San Felipe

The Fort of San Felipe (Puerto Plata, Av. Circunvalación, 9 A.M.–5 P.M. daily, US$0.50), unlike the very visible ruins in the Ciudad Colonial of Santo Domingo, is sadly the only remaining structure from Puerto Plata's colonial days. Built between 1564 and 1577 as a line of defense from invasion by sea, for much of its life its hulking walls and deep moat were put to use as a prison instead. Today, it houses a slightly disappointing museum. The building itself is remarkable, but the contents within

Galeria de Ámbar

The Amber Gallery (Calle 12 de Julio and Jose del Carmen Ariza, tel. 809/586-6467, www.ambercollection.itgo.com, 9 A.M.–6 P.M. Mon.–Fri., 9 A.M.–2 P.M. Sat., closed Sun., US$1), not to be eclipsed by its competitor, has an impressive collection of amber pieces but also adds a very important and educational exhibit of Dominican products. After you've seen the amber, you'll be led by a guide through rum, mamajuana, sugar, tobacco, coffee, and Taíno artifacts exhibits—an excellent way to learn about the history of these products and the way they have shaped Dominican culture through the ages. Guides speak English, French, German, and Spanish. Signage is in

DOMINICAN AMBER: NOT JUST A PRETTY FACE

A substantial amount of the world's amber comes from the Dominican Republic. Formed over millions upon millions of years (we're talking anywhere from 30 to 80 million), Dominican amber is among the most pure and widely sought due to its translucent quality, making it one of the most valuable in the world. In fact, in terms of commercial availability, Dominican amber is second only to that from the Baltic region of Europe.

FORMATION IS
A STICKY SITUATION

Amber is a fossilized resin, formed when the sap from trees – produced as a protection against potentially invading insects – was carried away by streams and re-deposited into the earth, polymerizing the substance over millions of years. In the Dominican Republic, this tree was the locust, genus *Hymenaea*. Occasionally, living creatures, like insects, were picked up along the way by the oozing sap, resulting in the fossilization of these animals inside the amber.

Although amber was discovered thousands of years ago, it really only became popular starting in the 1960s. The industry of mining amber can be a dangerous one, as most deposits are found buried deeply in mountains and hillsides.

VALUE: IT'S WHAT'S
ON THE OUTSIDE AND
INSIDE THAT COUNTS

While amber is not a mineral, it is widely considered to be a gemstone – in fact, it's one of the few non-mineral gemstones allowed to be called such. Even prehistoric people valued it; it is believed that amber was one of the first substances used for ornamentation. To this day, amber is a highly sought jewelry material.

Called amber because of its golden color, the gemstone can come in many different colors ranging from yellow to orange to red, to syrupy brown, to blues and blacks. The more rare the color, the more valuable the stone.

An "inclusion" – the suspension of a tiny fossilized animal in the nugget – also adds value to amber. Though it is quite rare, occasionally the preserved bodies of flies, ants, small termites, or beetles are found embedded in the amber. Most difficult to find, and therefore the most valuable, are inclusions of large spiders, scorpions, and even small frogs and lizards. Contrary to the ideas made popular in the film *Jurassic Park*, mosquitoes, too, are an uncommon find.

JURASSIC PARK:
COULD IT REALLY HAPPEN?

Speaking of the rarity of finding a mosquito buried in a nugget of amber, the chance of a real-life Jurassic Park happening is close to zilch, but, well, never say never. It won't be from any mosquito buried in amber found in the Dominican Republic, though, as the fossil resin here is not old enough to contain one that might have fed on a dinosaur.

---

are rather uneventful. Cannonballs and bayonets make up a majority of the artifacts. The views of the **Bahía de Puerto Plata** and the Atlantic from on top where a couple of cannons still stand guard and the surrounding grounds are very nice and provide for some attractive photo-ops. Tours are given in English, French, German, and Spanish.

Also on-site is a **lighthouse,** which was built in 1879 and restored a few years ago. It originally employed a unique revolving light and shadow system of illumination, fueled by kerosene. *El faro* was a beacon to ships and a symbol of the then industrial progress of Puerto Plata. An octagonal cupola sits high upon the yellow I-beams but is no longer in service.

Pico Isabel de Torres
and the Teleférico

Rising nearly 800 meters above Puerto Plata is Isabel de Torres Peak, which Christopher Columbus named for the queen who helped fund his expeditions. You can ride to the top of the mountain via the Teleférico (Camino a los Dominguez, tel. 809/970-0501, 8:30 A.M.–5 P.M. Thurs.–Tues., closed Wed., round-trip RD$350 per person), which you board at the base of the mountain; it takes you up to the flat top and to the Christ the Redeemer statue (a smaller version of the one in Brazil), where you can enjoy a very beautiful view of the Bahía de Puerto Plata and surrounding area. While you're there, amble about in the 13.5-hectare **botanical garden** and its multiple trails. The subtropical vegetation is home to 15 brooks and streams and is especially beautiful in the morning when the sun isn't as hot and the air is cooler. Appreciating the vegetation on the entire mountainside can be done by guided nature walk all the way up to the top of the mountain. This nature walk takes two hours and you'll be shown 594 plants and flowers, including fruit such as mango, guayaba, and passion fruit. Tours start in the morning and early afternoon (RD$35–50 for 1–5 people). A less natural but perhaps more thrill-seeking way to go up the mountainside is by motorbike. There are seven different difficult paths to bump and speed over as you make your way to the top of Pico Isabel de Torres. Renting a motorbike for only RD$1,300 yields not only the bike but also the guide who drives the motorbike (with you on the back) and shows you all the nature highlights. Although this might disappoint the motocross-lovers, this terrain can be rather persnickety and nothing beats local knowledge when it comes to safety. Take your binoculars!

Brugal Rum Bottling Plant

This bottling plant (Carretera a Playa Dorada, tel. 809/586-2531, 8 A.M.–4 P.M. Mon.–Fri., free) has an important role in the lives of many Dominicans. Rum is ingrained into all social events and festivities, and the industry employs many. Its product is one of the few uniformly appreciated and utilized items bridging a very wide gap between all Dominican walks of life. And yet what could be a potentially very interesting and culturally significant topic and tour instead is a woeful swing and a miss. Upon arrival with throngs of other tourists pouring off of buses, you are led into a standing-room-only theater where you watch a very short film about rum and the Brugal company that fills you with anticipation of what is to come. Then, you are given a few moments to watch the bottling process. And then it's over. It's short and uneventful. Afterward, you're given a drink and the opportunity to buy the product and other articles bearing the Brugal insignia.

SPORTS AND RECREATION

All the Playa Dorada resorts offer countless excursions like diving, snorkeling, fishing, and even some farther-reaching tours that will take you all the way to Santo Domingo. It is best to check with the excursion desk at your resort for these options.

The main sporting attraction off the beach is the 18-hole championship, par-72 **Playa Dorada Golf Club** (Playa Dorada, tel. 809/320-3472, www.playadoradagolf.com, 7 A.M.–7 P.M.). Designed by Robert Trent Jones Jr., it wraps around the entire Playa Dorada resort complex and along the coast. Anyone can enjoy the on-site restaurant and bar, golfer or not. Greens fees are US$50 for 9 holes and US$75 for 18 holes. Caddies (US$8 for 9 and US$15 for 18 holes) are obligatory, whereas carts (US$18 for 9 holes and US$24 for 18 holes) are optional. It is best to book your tee time through your resort since many of them offer special rates.

Fun City Action Park (Carretera Puerto Plata–Sosúa Km 8, tel. 809/320-1031, www. funcity-gokarts.com, 10 A.M.–6 P.M. Mon.–Fri., 10 A.M.–9 P.M.Sat. and Sun.) is only 10 minutes from Puerto Plata. Most kids can get fussy with resort life if there isn't much diversion; if that is the case with yours, take them to this multiple-track go-cart racing complex. There are bumper cars also and a playground for the younger children (2–8 years old). Fun City has a free taxi service from your hotel. Day passes cost US$15 for adults and US$10 for kids 12 and under. Price includes unlimited rides, but food and drinks are not included.

RUM AND BEER

RUM

If merengue is the national music and dance of the Dominican Republic, rum is the country's national drink. Dominican rum, or *ron*, is widely considered one of the smoothest, most distinguished rums in the world. More than four million cases of rum are produced in the Dominican Republic each year.

The rum industry has its beginnings in the 18th century, when sugarcane brought over from Africa found a place in the Dominican (and world) market. Sugarcane juice is extracted from the stalks and heated to boiling until it takes on the thicker consistency of syrup. Mixed with water and left to ferment, a rum is born. Of course, with modern technology, the refining processes have become a little more complex. Rum producers in the Dominican Republic are known for their particularly natural processes of distillation, and the liquor is often left to age in imported American white oak kegs.

There are three types of basic rum: light (*blanco*), amber (*amarillo*), and dark (*anejo*). Light rum has the highest alcohol proof and tends to be more popular for use in mixed drinks. Amber rum has been aged for at least a year, during which its distinct flavor develops. Dark rum is the smoothest and is often consumed on its own or on the rocks.

There are many locally produced rums in the Dominican Republic, but the most popular brands are Barceló & Co., Brugal, and Bermúdez.

The favorite way to serve rum is straight up or on the rocks with a squeeze of lime. As for popular rum drinks, perhaps the most well known is the *Cuba libre* or rum and coke.

BEER

You'll see the adds everywhere, and even the mildest of beer aficionados will end up with a Pavlovian response to seeing the color green by the end of their vacations. Presidente, the pilsner in the green bottle, is by far the number one selling beer on the island and the number one way to battle the strong Caribbean heat. It is not a heavy beer, very light bodied and refreshing, crisp and blonde and kept ice cold in the green *colmado* freezers. Say *"Dame una fria"* ("give me a cold one") and you will get a Presidente; pulling it from the freezer into the hot air blanches the glass white, making the *vestida de novia* or "wedding dress." Is it love? Your endorphins soar. Yes, it just might be.

Let us not forget the other brands. You ask for a *fria* and the assumption is made for you. If you want something else, you'd better be specific. Bohemia is a pilsner and cheaper than Presidente and slightly fruitier. Presidente Light has the same good qualities as the regular but is not as full bodied. Rather a letdown after tasting the real thing. Quisqueya comes from the Taíno word meaning "Mother Earth" and is a pilsner-type. You will find this most often in your mini-refrigerators in the all-inclusive hotels. It'll do in a pinch.

ENTERTAINMENT AND EVENTS
Bars and Dance Clubs

Hemingway's Café (Playa Dorada Plaza, tel. 809/320-2230, noon–2 A.M. daily, US$4–19) is a popular hangout right in the middle of the Playa Dorada resorts. It looks unlike any other venue in the complex, decorated like Papa Hemingway just cleaned out his boathouse, with nautical equipment everywhere. The good variety of food includes bar food favorites like burgers and quesadillas. It's air-conditioned to

the max and has a lively atmosphere at night with live rock and karaoke nights.

Spice (Playa Dorada, tel. 809/320-1046, www.occidentalhotels.com, 8 P.M.–2 A.M. daily, RD$100), although not the hot spot it once was, has undergone a makeover and is making a comeback hoping to become a popular dance club with tourists again on the grounds of Golden Beach Holiday Village. Music is a mix of Latin and international pop. The dance floor starts to crowd between 11 P.M. and midnight. The management hopes to resurrect the former (and at one time very popular) Mangú disco from the dead. Playing the same mix of music is the **Crazy Moon** (Playa Dorada, tel. 809/320-3663, 10 P.M.–4 A.M. daily, US$4 cover charge), at the Paradise Beach Resort. It's popular.

In recent years, the resort dance scene has become hotter at **CocoBongo** (Playa Dorada Plaza, tel. 809/320-2259, 6 P.M.–2 A.M. weekdays, 6 P.M.–4 A.M. weekends), which can get a bit crowded. It plays Euro and hip-hop music (no cover). Eat dinner outside and dance inside. The **Roadways Steak House** (Plaza Playa Dorada 1, tel. 809/320-2259) is a popular chill-out bar with a disco inside that is perfect for getting your evening started.

It is advisable to take a taxi between these venues.

Festivals
Festivals are what Dominicans do best. In Puerto Plata three festivals are held annually.

The Cultural Festival is held in the third week of June. It is a celebration of Dominican customs and arts with performances held at the Fuerte de San Felipe of folk music, traditional African dances, salsa, and merengue. Art exhibits are displayed in the Parque Central.

Perhaps the most beloved festival of all is the **Merengue Festival.** Though the festival is not yet even 10 years old, merengue has been the dance and a way of life in the Dominican Republic for generations. It is the soundtrack to which your vacation will most likely take place. It blares out of car windows, on the corners of *colmados,* on the beaches, or is simply carried through the air on the voices of the Dominicans, who always seem to be singing. The festival is a four-day extravaganza held the first week of October. The Merengue Festival is celebrated in many locations throughout the country. In Puerto Plata, the entire length of the three-kilometer Malecón (Puerto Plata and Avenida Circunvalación) is shut down to make way for food stalls.

SHOPPING
The Fine Gift Center
Located on the ground floor, just beneath the Amber Gallery, the Fine Gift Center (Calle 12 de Julio and Jose del Carmen Ariza, tel. 809/586-6467, www.ambercollection.itgo.com, 9 A.M.–6 P.M. Mon.–Fri., 9 A.M.–2 P.M. Sat., closed Sun.) has a wide assortment of amber, larimar, and shell jewelry. You can also buy postcards and T-shirts, coffee, vanilla, mamajuana, and many other souvenirs.

Two worlds, two markets. Goods at the **Mercado Nuevo** (Puerto Plata, Av. Isabel de Torres and Villanueva, 8 A.M.–9 P.M. Mon.–Sat.) are not as plentiful as at the Mercado in Santo Domingo, but it has a great selection of Dominican and Haitian art, the usual trinkets along with rums and cigars, and some fresh produce. The vendors inflate prices expecting that you'll haggle or in the hopes that you'll actually pay them. The **Mercado Viejo** Puerto Plata, Calle Ureña and Separación, 8 A.M.–6:30 P.M. Mon.–Sat.) is another matter. The Old Market is where you will find the *botanicos,* the everyday items that Dominicans need for their homes, more produce, and better prices, but fewer trinkets.

Playa Dorada Plaza (Playa Dorada, Calle Duarte at Avenida 30 de Marzo, tel. 809/320-6645, fax 809/320-8243) is a good bet for anything you might need, services or shopping, in the area. Here you'll find a variety of (frequently changing) bars and restaurants, jewelry stores, tour operators, Internet access, and gift shops galore. From the main road, take the western entrance into the Playa Dorada complex.

ACCOMMODATIONS
Under US$50
Not many options exist in the area as far as satisfactory low-budget accommodations. These moderately priced alternatives could work, though.

Portofino Guest House (Puerto Plata, Av. Hermanas Mirabal 12, tel. 809/586-2858, fax 809/586-5050, US$28 d) has 20 comfortable rooms that are kept very clean and come with a private hot-water bathroom, cable TV, and

A SPA FOR THE SPIRIT

This Dominican-owned business is not only good for you, but good for the community. **Jasmine Spa and Wellness Center** (Tubagua, Carretera Turística Luperón Km 12, tel. 829/252-5272, www.jasmine-spa-wellness.com, US$249 per person d high season) is located on 16 hectares of the tropical Cordillera Septentrional.

This holistic health retreat has one- to three-week on-site wellness programs including meals and accommodations. If you have been needing a place to recharge your fast-moving new millennium batteries, this skilled staff will help you. People from all walks of life come here to manage weight, improve diet, stop smoking, get over caffeine intake, or just take in the beauty of the natural environment and detox their systems of emotional and physical stresses of life.

Leave your computer and iPod at home, though. Forget about bringing alcohol and tobacco, and even newspapers and magazines, as all of these items are expressly forbidden. Check the website for what you can and cannot bring.

Spa treatments include: mud treatments, facials (US$20), full body massages (US$50-80), beach treatment (complete with seaweed wrap and sand scrub with dip in the ocean), hot stone massages, shiatsu, reflexology, and more. **Day passes** to the spa (US$125 per person) come complete with fresh juice, a one-hour massage, lunch, a tour of the whole grounds, and your choice between facial, manicure, or pedicure. You can also take a dip in the freshwater dipping pool. They can arrange for transportation from your hotel or resort for an additional fee.

For a more invigorating experience, take a *bachata*, merengue, or yoga class. Go horseback riding (US$25), hiking (US$10-20), or on an excursion to the Sosúa flea market.

There are four comfortable rooms, each with one queen-size bed. There is no air-conditioning, but you won't need it because of the perpetual spring-like mountain air. If you want a fan, the staff will happily supply one for you, but for the most part, they try to keep things as natural to the environment as they can – but never fear, you will have hot water.

They offer a mix of Dominican, Indian, Italian, and Thai choices for food and even cater to those who chose vegetarian, raw food, fat free, or fresh fruit juice diets. All the food is grown on-site and they try to use mostly organic products.

By the time you leave the Jasmine Spa and Wellness Center, you will be addicted to it and it only.

air-conditioning. The pleasant garden is shady and has a refreshing pool. You are a short walk from the beach.

Hotel Montesilva (Puerto Plata, Calle La Estancia, tel. 809/320-0205, US$35 d) is a good value. It's on a quiet street and offers clean rooms with comfortable beds. All have a private hot-water bathroom, fan, and cable TV. Not all have balconies.

Centrally located **Hotel Victoriano** (Puerto Plata, Calle San Felipe 33 at Restauración, tel. 809/586-9752, US$28 d) gives clean rooms and is within walking distance of many restaurants. It's a backpacker's favorite. Rooms have fan or air-conditioning and cable TV.

Playa Dorada
All-Inclusive Resorts

The Playa Dorada beach is a very pretty golden sand stretch of heaven. The water tends to get deeper quicker here than on the southern coast of the country and tends to be colder. Children should be monitored.

While beaches in the Dominican Republic are technically public property, resorts do everything they can to try to keep "outsiders" away. All-inclusive guests are tagged with colored plastic bracelets that have their hotel's insignia on them. If you are a nonguest and have somehow found your way onto Playa Dorada, hide your wrist and act normal; it is not uncommon for resorts to employ security guards to patrol the beach.

For the most part, all-inclusive accommodations and resorts tend to be similar to each other no matter how much they try to distinguish themselves from one another either in bragging rights or in how many stars they give themselves. It is regular all-inclusive practice to have available in a standard room the following amenities: either two doubles or one king-size bed, air-conditioning, cable TV, telephone, private balcony or terrace, full private hot-water bath, optional safety box (usually at extra cost to you), and often a small refrigerator or mini-bar. Any variations on the regular theme will be pointed out. Strange hidden cost: Sometimes you have to pay a deposit for a remote control for your television. Make sure to keep your receipt or you will not be given that deposit back.

The resorts usually have a buffet for breakfast, lunch, and dinner, but you have optional specialty restaurants to choose from for dinner. Make sure these are included in your all-inclusive package before you book a reservation (which you have to do at the guest services desk), or you will end up with an unexpected cost at the end of your trip.

If you want something truly standout sensational (as far as resorts go that is), go for the boutique classification. These tend to go the extra mile in decor, cuisine, service, and comfort. Of course, your bill goes skyward as well, but if you can swing it, you'll be happier. Because of the price tag, these boutique hotels tend to be less crowded and quieter than their all-inclusive counterparts.

When booking an all-inclusive (or boutique hotel) vacation, it is highly advisable to shop around for the best deal. There are many ways to do this. One popular way is to research on travel websites like www.orbitz.com, www.travelocity.com, www.expedia.com, or www.tripadvisor.com. The prices given here are general guidelines for high season based on double occupancy.

Viva Wyndham Playa Dorada Resort (Playa Dorada, tel. 809/686-5658, www.vivaresorts.com, US$150) is a short but very pretty walk from the beach, and the landscaping overall is especially pretty with a waterfall by the pool. Rooms are spacious and clean, and all have nice balconies. While it is a smaller three-star resort, it is one of the nicer and gets many rave reviews. Specialty restaurants include Asian (Bambu) and Mediterranean (Ibiza Beach) ones that are especially good; both require special reservations and fill up fast. It is a good idea to plan that on your arrival. The resort has a kids' club that can help you keep the little ones active for the duration of your vacation.

The 386-room **Puerto Plata Village Caribbean Resort** (Playa Dorada, tel. 809/320-4012, www.puertoplatavillage.com, US$130 d) is the furthest resort from the beach. To make up for it, though, a shuttle goes from hotel to beach every 15 minutes and it is only a five-minute ride. On the sand, in the section set aside for this resort, are a bar and a grill. The resort is done in a faux-Victorian-style design in pastel colors, and the rooms are clean and comfortable. This is a good resort for kids since they have lots of activities and there are two pools. It's a wheelchair-friendly environment. The food is basic but good.

Holiday Village Golden Beach (Playa Dorada, tel. 809/320-3800, fax 809/320-4161, www.occidentalhotels.com, US$115–140 d) was the first resort to open in Playa Dorada back in 1983 (formerly known as the Occidental Allegro Jack Tar Village). It sits directly adjacent to the Playa Dorada golf course, and the beach, which is well-maintained, is just a few short steps from the pool area. There are two pools, one for adults only that has a waterfall and swim-up bar, and the grounds are lush and beautiful. The standard rooms, dubbed "superior" here, all have a garden or golf course view, but if you opt for the "superior premium" room, you'll be placed closer to the ocean and swimming pools. The Holiday Village is home to the new Spice discotheque and a very nice casino. The cuisine at this resort is well known to be some of the best in all of the Playa Dorada resorts.

Bluebay Villas Doradas (Playa Dorada, tel. 809/320-3000, www.bluebayresorts.com, US$75–100 d), geared toward those over 18, is located on a wonderful stretch of beach and is an ideal choice for couples wanting a romantic getaway without the kids. All rooms come equipped with the comforts you would expect from an all-inclusive, plus they are stylishly decorated and up to date since the hotel was recently renovated in a chic if not minimalist and modern style. The grounds have three pools and three tennis courts and boast an 18-hole golf course designed by Robert Trent Jones. Four restaurants will keep your culinary tastes busy with choices in international, seafood, Asian fusion, and grilled meat menus.

By far the most luxurious and elegant resort in Playa Dorada, **⟨⟨ Casa Colonial Beach and Spa** (Playa Dorada, tel. 809/320-2111, www.casacolonialhotel.com, US$350–and up d) is designed in the architectural style of a colonial mansion and decorated with contemporary and colonial accents. Built in 2004, its 52 rooms, junior suites, and deluxe suites are all gloriously chic with marble floors, plush linens, and canopy beds. Amenities include Roman-style tubs and separate showers, wireless Internet in the lobby and by the pools (cable access in the rooms), flat-screen cable TV, bathrobes and slippers, and very good-sized balconies. The spa has 13 treatment rooms, including a couple's treatment room, outdoor spa treatments, and pilates and yoga classes. A rooftop infinity pool and four (yes, four) Jacuzzis overlook the Atlantic in a dramatic sweeping panorama. The cuisine is top rate and served in two exquisite dining rooms. Although all eight suites are named after the Garcia family, who own the hotel, to book that extra special room ask for the Don Francisco Deluxe Suite. This suite will spoil you in every way possible with its plush pillows, claw-foot tub facing the ocean, and four-poster bed fit for a queen. The Casa Colonial is handicapped accessible to every part of the resort *except* the pools. To those who need accessibility in their lives, this is a huge and unfortunate oversight. However, the beach is still accessible. Casa Colonial is not an all-inclusive hotel. In its upscale way, it has taken on a quiet, cocktails-before-dinner refined mood despite its location in the thick of all-inclusive central. Still, one person's "too

sedate and boring" is another person's "paradise and tranquility."

FOOD
Puerto Plata
Restaurante-Pizzería Portofino (Calle Hermanas Mirabal 12, tel. 809/261-2423, US$5–12) offers some of the best pizza and pasta in town, along with other Italian favorites like eggplant parmesan. Next to the Portofino Guest House, it's a good choice for a casual night out in the open air.

Tex Mex is the specialty at **⟨⟨ Aquaceros Bar & Grill** (Malecón 32, tel. 809/586-2796, 10 A.M.–2 A.M., US$7–14), but dishes also include fresh barbecued fish, lobster, and burgers. The distinctive Dominican ambience along the Malecón, with the fresh sea breeze and merengue music, makes it a favorite.

Sam's Bar and Grill (Calle José del Carmen Ariza 34, tel. 809/586-7267, 8 A.M.–11 P.M. daily, US$4–12) is an institution with the local expats for dishes like meatloaf, chili, Philly cheesesteaks, pancakes, chicken cordon bleu, and a great many other American diner favorites. You'll often find a sporting event of some kind on the televisions, and it is a lively place for drinks around dinnertime. Sam's has free Internet access.

Jamvi's (Malecón 18 and Calle Lopez, tel. 809/320-7265, open 11 A.M.–midnight daily) serves national and international dishes like pizza, burgers, and steak. The location on the Malecón and directly on the beach is a perfect place to enjoy the view and a glass of wine.

Playa Dorada
Hemingway's Café (Playa Dorada Plaza, tel. 809/320-2230, noon–2 A.M. daily, US$4–19) is a good hangout and a good restaurant. This maritime-decorated bar in the plaza serves mostly American and Mexican food. It's air-conditioned inside with umbrella tables out front for alfresco dining.

Canadian-owned **Café Cito** (Carretera Sosúa–Puerto Plata Km 4, tel. 809/586-7923, www.cafecito.info, 10:30 A.M.–midnight daily, US$4–17) is a favorite for expats and a nice respite away from all-inclusive buffet doldrums. Menu items include international items like filet mignon, burgers, nachos, and moussaka. Jazz music and a good cigar can be thoroughly enjoyed on the open-air terrace. With great service, you can't beat a great meal in such a relaxing and fun atmosphere.

(El Manguito (Carretera a Playa Dorada, tel. 809/586-4392, open 1 P.M.–1 A.M. daily, US$5–20) serves traditional and outstanding Dominican cuisine with excellent service and gets great reviews. Try a plate of *pollo* in a wine sauce, very fresh seafood like *cangrejo asado*, or, if you're feeling adventurous, some tripe stew. For dessert, the coconut milk flan is a must. It is about a 10- to 15-minute walk from the Playa Dorada resorts. It's across the street from Café Cito and hard to see from the road—worth the hunt. *Cuba libres* cost only RD$60, and the beers are equally inexpensive, so make sure to ask the staff to call you a taxi to return to your resort if you need it.

Lucia (Casa Colonial, Playa Dorada, tel. 809/320-2111, www.casacolonialhotel.com, 6 P.M.–midnight, US$14–35), the upscale and signature restaurant of the boutique hotel Casa Colonial, was the designed by Dominican designer Sarah Garcia, whose inspiration was born from memories of her family's vacations in Tuscany, Italy. Incorporating Dominican materials into the design with French, Spanish, and Italian influences on her style, she came up with her restaurant, Lucia. Executive Chef Angel Mejia trained in Washington D.C.'s Gordon Center. Suffice it to say, the new Lucia has an impressive menu that offers items like fresh foie gras served with a rum mango sauce and a mashed pumpkin potato or Tres-Viche (a tuna, lobster, and Chilean sea bass ceviche). For the ultimate culinary dining, call ahead and reserve the private dining room in the wine cellar with the extensive selection of fine wines.

INFORMATION AND SERVICES

When staying in a resort in Playa Dorada, any services you may need can be found at **Playa Dorada Plaza** (Calle Duarte and Avenida 30 de Marzo, tel. 809/320-6645), which is in the middle of the entire complex. Services include Internet and a call center, medical service, pharmacy, and banks.

Health and Emergencies

Fortunately, Puerto Plata has some of the best medical services around. **Clínica Brugal** (Puerto Plata, José del Carmen Ariza 15, tel. 809/586-2519) has 24-hour emergency service and a doctor who speaks English, German, and Spanish. **Centro Médico Dr. Bournigal** (Puerto Plata, Antera Mota, tel. 809/586-2342) is a highly recommended hospital and has a pharmacy (tel. 809/586-8821) on the premises. Staff speak many languages and there is 24-hour service in the clinic.

There are many pharmacies all over Puerto Plata. For a centrally located one, try **Farmacia Carmen** (Calle 12 de Julio 39, tel. 809/586-2525). For a 24-hour pharmacy, you'll need to go to **Farmacia Deleyte** (Av. Kennedy 89, tel. 809/586-2583). It is in front of the Parque Luperón.

The tourism police office, **Politur** (Puerto Plata, Hermanas Mirabal, tel. 809/582-2331), is open 24 hours a day near Long Beach. This agency was set up to help tourists with their concerns.

Communications

For Internet connections in Puerto Plata, your best choice, other than the free wireless Internet in your room if you have that in your all-inclusive, is **Compudotcom** (12 de Julio 68, tel. 809/261-6165), where you can get online for US$0.70 per hour, or **Internet Flash** (Separación and Margarita, 8 A.M.–9 P.M. Mon.–Sat., 10 A.M.–2 P.M. Sun.), which has a friendly and knowledgeable staff and good facilities.

Money

Banco Popular (Av. Circunvalación Sur, 9 A.M.–5 P.M. Mon.–Fri., 9 A.M.–1 P.M. Sat.) is near Avenida Hermanas Mirabal and has a 24-hour ATM. If you're downtown near the Parque Central, go to the more conveniently located **Banco Mercantil** (Separación, 8:30 A.M.–5 P.M. Mon.–Fri., 9 A.M.–1 P.M. Sat.); it has an ATM as well.

Tourist Information

The **Oficina de Turismo** (809/586-5059, 9 A.M.–3 P.M.) is above the Politur office on Calle Hermanas Mirabal at the Malecón. The very friendly staff speak English, Spanish, and German and have lots of maps and brochures.

Post Office

The Puerto Plata **post office** (7 A.M.–5 P.M. Mon.–Fri., 7 A.M.–noon Sat.) is on Calle 12 de Julio where it meets Separación, but don't rely on Dominican postal services for communication.

GETTING THERE
By Air

The **Aeropuerto Internacional Gregorio Luperón** (tel. 809/586-0107) is about 18 kilometers east of Puerto Plata and Playa Dorada. A **taxi** to or from the airport to this area costs US$20.

This is the airport that most travelers fly into if they are visiting Cofresí, Maimón, Luperón, Puerto Plata, Playa Dorada, Sosúa, Cabarete, Playa Grande, and Cabrera hotels. Some of the airlines that serve the airport are: **American Airlines** (tel. 800/200-5151, www.aa.com), **Continental** (tel. 809/200-1062, www.continental.com), **Air Canada** (tel. 809/541-5151, www.aircanada.com), **AirEuropa** (www.air-europa.com), **JetBlue Airways** (www.jetblue.com) and **Delta** (tel. 809/585-0973, www.delta.com).

By Car

Coming from the south, take Autopista Duarte 1 northward to Via Santiago, then take Exit 5 to the right, which is the route to Puerto Plata.

Driving from the east simply take the coastal and very scenic Highway 5, which runs all the way from Las Galeras on the Península de Samaná to Puerto Plata and then curves south.

By Bus

Caribe Tours (Puerto Plata, Calle Camino Real at Eugenio Kunhardt, by the Parque Central, tel. 809/586-4544 or 576-0790) has service to Santo Domingo (US$8) with stops in Santiago (US$7) and La Vega (US$5). A bus leaves every hour for the four-hour ride from Puerto Plata to Santo Domingo, daily.

Metro (Calle 16 de Agosto, tel. 809/586-6062, www.metroserviciosturisticos.com) offers service to Santo Domingo (US$8.50), and with just one stop in Santiago (US$7), you'll shave half an hour off your travel time. Buses leave at 6 A.M., 7 A.M., 9 A.M., 11 A.M., 2 P.M., 3 P.M., 4 P.M., and 6:30 P.M.

Guaguas are a low-budget option. Eastbound ones line up on the northern end of the Parque Central; they'll stop at the gate to Playa Dorada and then continue onward along Highway 5 with stops in Sosúa, Cabarete, and finally Río San Juan. If you're heading to Nagua you'll have to transfer and then in Nagua transfer again for Samaná. You can be dropped off anywhere and flag them down anywhere. It really is a very efficient mode of transportation.

GETTING AROUND
Car Rental

Should you choose to rent a car to do some exploration on your own, you can find them via kiosks in the airport, along the highway between Playa Dorada and Puerto Plata, or along the Malecón in Puerto Plata. Rates start around US$50 a day and of course depend on the type of car you get. You can also ask your hotel's front desk if they can help you secure one.

Companies include **Avis** (Carretera a Puerto Plata tel. 809/586-4436, airport tel. 809/586-7007; Playa Dorada Plaza tel. 809/320-4888, www.avis.com), **Budget** (tel. 809/586-0284 or 800/527-0700, www.budget.com), and **Hertz** (Carretera a Puerto Plata Sosúa Km 12, tel. 809/586-0200 or 800/654-3001, www.hertz.com). All have offices at the airport.

Taxis

Beware the inflated tourist price. Cabs are not metered here, and if you don't speak any Spanish and don't agree on a price before you get in, you'll get taken for a ride in more ways than one. A good rule to go with is, just don't pay more than US$10 to go a distance that is about the length of Playa Dorada to Cofresí. You can find taxis around Parque Central. If you need a taxi for a two-way trip, consider reserving the driver to return and pick you up at an agreed upon time for the return.

Motoconchos

This is your cheapest option by far. You can expect to pay about US$1 for a short ride. But be mindful that these are not safe by any means. Consider other forms of transportation.

Costambar and Playa Cofresí

Adjacent to Puerto Plata are the two very small communities of Costambar and Cofresí. Costambar is an open beach protected by coral reefs abundant with almond trees, very pretty and way less tourist-ridden than Playa Dorada. For the most part, Costambar consists of time shares, villas, townhouses, and not much else.

Playa Cofresí, five kilometers from Costambar, is named after the Puerto Rican pirate Roberto Cofresí, known to many as the "Robin Hood of the Caribbean," who is said to have buried his treasures either in the waters or somewhere between Cofresí and the Bahía de Samaná. Although the beach here isn't as pretty as that of Costambar or Playa Dorada, it does have a couple of resorts and many villas and homes.

SIGHTS
Ocean World

Playa Cofresí is also home to the large and very commercial Ocean World (Playa Cofresí, tel. 809/291-1000, www.oceanworldmarina.com, 9 A.M.–5 P.M. daily, ages 13 and up US$55, ages 4–12 US$40, under 4 free). You can snorkel in a tank with tropical fish and a faux (although done quite well) coral reef, visit two aviaries with native and nonnative species of tropical birds, swim in the same pool as a tiger shark (with a glass wall partition), and view stingray and shark feedings. But for additional cost, you can take a step closer to interact with some of the animals. Swim with the dolphins (US$185 per person), have a dolphin "encounter" that involves getting "kisses" and "dancing" with our frisky friends (US$98 per person), or enjoy a sea lion encounter (US$80). Also onsite are lockers for your personal belongings,

a restaurant, and a big Ocean World souvenir shop, of course. You can arrange for pickup and drop-off from your hotel; don't forget your sunscreen. Reservations (3–6 months in advance) are necessary for the special programs, especially the dolphin swim. Kids who love animals have a lot of fun at Ocean World.

The **Ocean World Casino** (www.oceanworldcasino.com) has a full range of table games like blackjack, craps, American roulette, and Caribbean poker and a slew of slot machines, as well as a sports bar. If you're in the area at night and have a sudden desire for a Vegas-like show, catch the **Bravissimo** (tel. 809/291-2000) show for a tropical dance show with unique and fabulous costumes that you would expect from a Vegas show but won't get in your all-inclusive nighttime entertainment.

ACCOMMODATIONS

For a regular hotel, stay in Cofresí. Costambar is made up of short-term rentals, condos, and time shares (see the sidebar *Villa Rentals*).

Chris and Mady's (Playa Cofresí, tel. 809/970-7502, www.chrisandmadys.com, 7:30 A.M.–10 P.M., US$40–80) is an independent traveler's dream. It's next to a restaurant of the same name where both locals and tourists come to hang out and above a small supermarket and gift shop. This three-unit building has one two-bedroom unit with a kitchen, a one-bedroom unit with a kitchen, and a studio with a kitchenette. All units have full baths and are very tastefully decorated and clean. You can also rent a guest house one block away.

Lifestyle Hacienda Resorts (Playa Cofresí, tel. 809/586-1227, www.hacienda-resorts.com, US$150 d) is a complex of four all-inclusive hotels. Of the four, the Crown Villas is the best with the biggest price tag (US$2,275 and up per 1–6 people, per night). It offers 90 private three- and four-bedroom villas in Mediterranean style with private pools. All of the other hotels offer spacious rooms with balconies. The Lifestyle Tropical Beach Resort & Spa is directly on the beach and has 282 rooms, a kids' club, lots of sports offerings, and of course, the spa. The location of this hotel, directly on Cofresí Beach, is reason enough to book here. Make sure to ask for a room with a balcony overlooking the beach.

FOOD
Playa Cofresí
Restaurant Los Dos (Villa Cofresí, tel. 809/970-7638, open from 6 P.M. Tues.–Sun., US$9–15) serves classic and fusion dishes and hosts special nights like Country Grill Night where they play country music galore and grill everything in sight. Or the All American Night, when the menu includes chicken wings, chili, and potato skins and American beers are

on special. It's a casual atmosphere and very friendly environment.

The open-air thatched-roof seaside restaurant **Chris and Mady's** (Playa Cofresí, tel. 809/970-7502, www.chrisandmadys.com, US$4–30) is a popular hangout. Seafood is the best thing going here—it's super fresh and cheap. Combine it with the equally good steak in a surf-and-turf, and you're in meaty heaven. There are sandwiches and a good selection of international options like pizza and burgers. The vibe is low-key and welcoming, and it is no wonder this open-air restaurant has remained a favorite among locals and travelers alike. Oh, and take your laptop and take advantage of the free wireless! There is a barbecue every Sunday at 6 P.M.

Le Papillon (Villas Cofresí, 8 A.M.–11 P.M. Tues.–Sun., tel. 809/970-7640, www.lepapillon-puertoplata.com, US$15–30) is at Villas Cofresí, five kilometers south of the center of Puerto Plata. The German owner, Thomas, has mixed cultures into a culinary joy, with plates like chicken-stuffed shrimp. Here in this airy

© ANA CHAVIER CAAMAÑO

fish fry, Playa Cofresí

restaurant, fresh seafood prepared with local spices is a specialty, but they also serve steaks, chicken, and pork as well as some vegetarian entrées. If you are a turtle lover, and not as the main dish, then you will appreciate Thomas's Turtle Rescue and Release Program. Eating here supports his efforts to save the turtles of the Dominican Republic.

At **Los Tres Cocos** (Las Rocas, tel. 809/993-4503, open for dinner Wed.–Mon., US$8–20), try something different from the Austrian-owned chef, Mickey, who has built himself quite the following in the area. Specialties include rack of lamb and duck breast in orange sauce. It is a romantic setting in an open-air restaurant.

Costambar

Jenny's Market (Costambar, Calle Principal 4, tel. 809/970-7503, 8 A.M.–9:30 P.M. daily) is a good place to get a surprising array of supplies if you're doing a short-term rental. It has a delivery service and an Internet café, postal service, call center, and fast food quick fix eatery adjacent to the market.

El Carey Beach Bar (Playa Costambar) is a phenomenal place to grab a burger or some grilled seafood and enjoy the *vida de la playa*— and that "life on the beach" is especially great when they host their very tasty barbecue Friday nights!

Bieke's Bar (Costambar, Calle Principal, across from Jenny's Market, open noon–10 P.M. daily) is famous for it's Bieke Burger and fries combo (RD$160). Special of the day is always a good way to go.

INFORMATION AND SERVICES

There's no need to go all the way to Puerto Plata, although the services are better there; for medical services head to **Sun Village Resort and Bungalows** (Playa Cofresí, tel. 866/970-3377 or 888/970-3364) or on the grounds of the **Lifestyle Hacienda Resorts** (Playa Cofresí, tel. 809/586-1227, www.hacienda-resorts.com) to the **Tourist Medical Services,** where you will also find a **pharmacy** (9 A.M.–noon and 1 P.M.–6 P.M.). Both facilities are 24 hours and have multilingual staffs.

For Internet services check out **Dot Com Internet Café** (Costambar, Calle 12 de Julio, tel. 809/261-6165, 8:30 A.M.–9 P.M. daily). **Jenny's Cyber Café** (Costambar, Calle Central, tel. 809/970-3028, 8 A.M.–9:30 P.M. daily) is a great find because not only can you get on the Internet, you can order Mexican food and other favorites. Jenny's Market is directly adjacent. **Internet Costambar** (Calle Principal) not only has wireless Internet, it also serves cold drinks, full-scale meals for breakfast, lunch, and dinner, and appetizers like nachos or onion rings. Once a week they have two hours of free Internet.

GETTING THERE AND AROUND

To get to this area from Puerto Plata a taxi will cost US$5–7. Agree on the price before getting in. Unfortunately, *guaguas* don't go to either Costambar or Playa Cofresí. They exit onto the highway toward Santiago before Costambar. Once there, walking is the best option for getting around within the villages themselves. To go to a neighboring community, you'll need a *motoconcho,* or call the Costambar taxi stand (tel. 809/970-7318).

Car Rental

Within Costambar or Cofresí, you won't need a car, but to get out beyond town limits you might want to rent one. **Costambar Rent Car** (Costambar, Calle Central 4, tel. 809/970-7005, cell 809/757-3744, 8 A.M.–6 P.M. Mon.–Sat., 8 A.M.–10 P.M. Sun.) rents regular and four-wheel-drive vehicles.

West of Puerto Plata

As the North Coast stretches past Puerto Plata to the west, the concentration of tourist areas and visitors declines enormously. It is partially because of the popularity of the all-inclusive resort vacationing trend, which keeps people grounded in Playa Dorada; partially because there is a lot to do east of Puerto Plata; and partially because visitors have not been made aware of the offerings of the western half of the northern coast. Those who do venture over visit a few select places for a short amount of time, perhaps on a guided tour for the day with a tour package from their all-inclusive resort.

Whatever the case may be, it is well worth the effort to check out this half of the North Coast. Whether checking out the beautiful beach at Luperón, doing some world-class diving in Monte Cristi, canyoning in Damajagua, or going to the Haitian market in the border town of Dajabón, excitement and individuality await but crowds and mass tourism do not.

DAMAJAGUA
◖ Salto del Río Damajagua 27 Charcos

In the forested hills near the town of Imbert about 22 kilometers southwest of Puerto Plata, 27 waterfalls or Salto del Río Damajagua 27 Charcos (info@27charcos.com, www.27charcos.com, 8:30 A.M.–4 P.M. daily, waterfalls 1–7 RD$250, waterfalls 1–12 RD$310, waterfalls 1–27 RD$460) connect through a series of canyons, tunnels, caves, and natural pools. In this area you can take heart-pumping leaps off cliffs, slip and slide through naturally formed water slides, and dunk into waterfall pools. The hike to get to these waterfalls can be demanding, from the aptly named first waterfall, La Virgen, to the last, The Last One. Visitors interested in seeing this set of cascades should be able to swim and should have good upper-body strength. You can either go it on your own or with an organized tour company. If you choose to go it alone, the price includes a life vest and helmet. Wear

your swimsuit and closed toe shoes that can get wet, bring a waterproof camera, and take some small bills for tipping and refreshments. Since the waterfalls have absolutely exploded onto the ecotourism scene in the last 10 years, the visitors center has become quite nice. It has a restaurant, very clean bathrooms, and a gift shop.

Many hotels arrange excursions available for booking at their excursion desks. However, one of the drawbacks of using a tour company is that they tend to take you only through the first seven waterfalls. With twenty-one left to go, you have missed out on a vast majority of Los Charcos. But the most reputable adventure-tour company in the country, **Iguana Mama** (Cabarete, tel. 809/571-0908, www.iguanamama.com, 8 A.M.–5 P.M. daily, US$79 per person), leads regular trips to Damajagua and will take you all the way to the top. Iguana Mama also provides transportation to the area, breakfast, and lunch.

To get to Damajagua from Puerto Plata by car, travel the Puerto Plata–Navarrete Highway (Highway 5) heading towards Santiago. After 20 minutes, you'll pass through the town of Imbert. Continue on the main highway; you will see a sign that reads Ingenio Amistad on your left and then cross a bridge. The road veers left by a sugarcane field. You will see a large Brugal billboard; this is directly next to the entrance to the Damajagua waterfalls.

To reach Damajagua by *guagua,* board a Santiago-bound *guagua* and tell the *cobrador* that you want off at "27 Charcos" or "*la cascada.*" The trip should cost you around RD$50 one-way.

LUPERÓN

Luperón is a quiet and inviting little town with a lot of expats, yet it's still steeped in traditional Dominican small-town ways. Example: Once when I was there, a road was closed down to traffic and a man was redirecting cars; upon being asked why, the man replied, "because there is a sick woman who lives on this street." Traffic had been prevented from passing her house out of respect for the dying. It is the kind of town where people still know their neighbors and still watch out for one another.

Luperón is on the Bahía de Luperón, which is about 50 kilometers west of Puerto Plata. In this town of 20,000, inhabitants still make their living through fishing. It is well-known for its marina, Marina Puerto Blanca, one of the few safe harbors in the Dominican Republic, where many boats moor themselves in order to stock up on supplies or simply take a break from the sea. Yachts from all over the world stop here because the natural shape of the bay makes it a shelter from hurricanes. Still, there are not a lot of services and, thus, not a lot of tourists despite a rather sizable expat community.

Sights

After discovering La Navidad, Columbus returned to Spain, leaving about 40 of his men in charge of the settlement, thinking that it would all be under control. But upon his return a year later, he found all of his men dead and La Navidad completely obliterated. Columbus then sailed 110 kilometers east, founded a new settlement, and named it after Spain's Queen Isabela. The new settlement, La Isabela, would not survive long either. Life was hard on the settlers. Lawlessness became a way of life, hurricanes blew through, and disease ran rampant, all claiming the lives of many. Some simply gave up the search for gold (their main reason for being there in the first place) and returned to Spain. Eventually, anyone remaining gave up entirely and went to the thriving new town, Santo Domingo.

Today, only ruins and a general layout of the original settlement can be seen at **Parque Nacional La Isabela** (9 A.M.–5 P.M. daily, US$3), which once included Christopher Columbus's original house, a cemetery with both Spanish and Taíno graves, and what is thought to have been the first City Hall of the New World. The archaeological remains used to be more plentiful, but Trujillo asked a local

official to "clean up" the area so that he could bring visiting dignitaries to visit. The local official then made a grave mistake by misunderstanding El Jefe and had a majority of La Isabela bulldozed and shoved into the water of the Atlantic Ocean, losing copious amounts of archaeological and historical grandeur, not something Trujillo could forgive. It was a mistake that cost the official his life.

Many Dominicans refer to La Isabela, now a national park, as the first settlement of the New World. Perhaps the reason they consider it the "first," practically ignoring that La Navidad even existed, is that more of a community was built in La Isabela. Most importantly, though, the first Catholic mass was said by Fray Bernardo Boil in 1494, thereby blessing the settlement.

A museum houses some artifacts uncovered in the area. The entrance fee affords you a personal guide to take you through the site and the museum. It is customary to tip. Getting to La Isabela is easiest if you drive (just follow Carretera La Isabela from Luperón) or take a taxi. From Luperón, a taxi will cost about US$30.

Templo de Las Américas (9 A.M.–6 P.M. daily, free) was built as a replica of the church where Fray Bernardo Boil said the first mass on January 6, 1494. It was built using some of the rubble from Columbus's first home, the original church, and the first City Hall. On January 6, 1994, a mass was said to commemorate the 500-year anniversary of that historic mass. Inside you'll see pieces of art donated by every Latin American country and a statue from Genoa, Italy (Columbus's home town), of Columbus praying to the Virgin Mary to protect his sailors.

Recreation

In a bay as popular as Bahía de Luperón, there are bound to be **sailing** opportunities. Unfortunately, it is not quite as prevalent as one might hope. If you go down to the **Marina Puerto Blanco** (tel. 809/571-8644) or any of the restaurants and bars in town, and ask around, you can find someone who is willing to take you out on the water. Prices vary greatly. Agree on a price before committing. Whenever you secure a boat captain to take you out, make it good practice to check that they have functioning radio and radar, adequate number of life jackets for the amount of people in your party, and an emergency life raft. Another chance to look for a boat captain is at the **Luperón Marina Yacht Club** (tel. 809/571-8606) just east of the Marina Puerto Blanco.

If you thought that beautiful beaches of the north stop at Playa Dorada, you'll be pleasantly surprised to find **Playa Grande,** with its beautiful long stretch of golden sand and blue water. The sea bottom is sandy in spots and rocky in other parts farther offshore. A majority of the beach is lined by an all-inclusive, but beaches are public property by law, and there are a couple of public entrances so you can enjoy it even if you're not staying at the resort. One entrance is next to the **Luperón Beach Resort** and another is marked by a sign along the highway about 700 meters from the resort.

Accommodations

Hotel Dally (Luperón, Calle Duarte, tel. 809/571-8034, US$18 d), in the middle of Luperón, has clean rooms with fans and hot-water bathrooms. It has an adjacent seafood restaurant.

Luperón Beach Resort (Carretera de Las Américas, tel. 809/571-8303, www.besthotels.es, US$90–125 d) and **Tropical Luperón** (Carretera de Las Américas, tel. 809/571-8303, www.besthotels.es, US$100–150 d) are two spacious resorts next to one another on the same beach. They are very similar in amenities. Accommodations are roomy and comfortable with balconies. Suites have a big seating area. The pool is nice and the beach is long and not overcrowded, with plenty of shady areas. While the food at the regular buffet is good and varied, the food at the beachside grill is substandard. At night there is entertainment either in the poolside open-air dance floor with live music, or in the amphitheater for shows. All in all, don't expect the luxury accommodations

that you'd find elsewhere, but they're a good value.

La Casa del Sol (Luperón, Calle 27 de Febrero, tel. 809/571-8403, US$30) has five good rooms to rent and is a laid-back, comfortable, and welcoming hotel, but don't expect frills. It is about 1.5 kilometers outside of Luperón along the Carretera Las Américas.

Miamar (El Castillo, Calle Vista Mar, tel. 809/471-9157, US$25–50, breakfast included) is located on a scenic hill with a swimming pool and more-than-generous-sized rooms with king-sized beds.

Food and Nightlife

Luperón is not a party town in the disco-hopping sense, like in Playa Dorada. However, it wouldn't be the Dominican Republic if you didn't find someone playing music out of a stereo at top volume from a *colmado*, a car, or just a radio with friends gathered around.

Captain Steve's Restaurant and Bar (Luperón, Calle Duarte at 27 de Febrero, US$4–12) serves a few favorites like pizzas, burgers, fish sticks, onion rings, and also sells provisions. It's a popular and laid-back thatch-roofed, open-air restaurant popular with the growing expat crowd. If you have a meal there, you can use their Internet for free. Keep Steve's place in mind for laundry service, swimming in the pool (US$3 per person), and even showers.

La Yola Bar Restaurant (Luperón, Calle 27 de Febrero, tel. 809/571-8511, closed Tues., US$4–9) serves good international and Dominican fare in an open-air thatched-roof venue. While the seafood is famous here, the other items shouldn't be overlooked. Every Wednesday night they have a movie night where people wine and dine and watch a movie alfresco for less than US$10 per person.

Information and Services

Any services you may need, you're bound to find along Calle Duarte. **Politur** (Luperón, Calle Duarte at 16 de Agosto, Bldg. 53, first floor, tel. 809/581-8045) is open 24 hours. **Farmacia Danessa** (Luperón, Av.

Independencia 10, tel. 809/571-8855) is across from the Parque Independencia, which is a good place to look for many other services.

Mini Super López (Luperón, Av. Duarte 36, tel. 809/571-8175, 9 A.M.–5 P.M.) is located at the stoplight (the only one) in Luperón and has necessities you may need.

Getting There and Around

Entering Luperón from the south, the highway becomes Calle Duarte, which leads you to Avenida 27 de Febrero; this is the main drag, where you'll find Luperón's commercial district. From here, the port is east. To get to Playa Grande and Parque Nacional La Isabela, stay on 27 de Febrero; this will turn into the Carretera de La Isabela, which you will follow for 19 kilometers to reach the national park. Walking is the best option for getting around this small town.

PUNTA RUCIA

Punta Rucia is a small fishing village that is a very quiet place, no raucous party-town here. But when the tour groups come, they descend in droves. Most people who visit here do so on a day excursion from any number of all-inclusive resorts along the North Coast to visit Cayo Arena (Paradise Island). There are no services in Punta Rucia, so if you plan on staying a night or so, come very prepared. You are now in one of the most remote and disconnected areas of the Dominican Republic. Don't expect a cell phone to have a signal here.

Playa Ensenada

Beaches here are mostly utilized by Dominican families and have, for the most part, remained a well-kept secret from regular tourism. All along this stretch of the northern coastline, the further you get from Puerto, the cheaper and more bountiful the seafood seems to get. Feast your eyes and your bellies. There are many food stalls lining the beach. Walk around and pick the freshest looking and ask for the best price. They will prepare it for you and direct you to a table on the beach. Options might

include fresh king crab, cooked over an open fire (RD$200), and lobster (RD$250). Playa Ensenada is a one-kilometer-long stretch of nearly white sand surrounded within the embrace of a mountain range. Its waters have gentle waves due to offshore coral reefs keeping breakers out, making it a great spot for kids to play.

Cayo Arena

Cayo Arena is a beautiful sandbar 10 kilometers into the middle of the Atlantic off the coast of Punta Rucia. It's often called **Paradise Island** by tour guides, and it is easy to understand why. Ultra-white sand gently slopes into the mind-bendingly clear turquoise water, where snorkeling is good due to coral reefs making a home for schools of fish that could quite possibly eat out of your hand. It is difficult to say how big the "island" is because it shrinks and expands depending on the season and the ocean's currents.

On the island there are small food shacks and that's it—there is no room for anything

Pick your feast on Playa Ensenada.

else. In fact, tour operators have to alternate times to be there in order to have enough space on the island for their guests. If you're an independent traveler and you speak Spanish, ask around Punta Rucia or talk with the fishermen to see if anyone else can take you.

Getting to Cayo Arena takes a 45-minute boat ride over choppy waters, making it not suitable for small children. Booking a trip to Cayo Arena is easy through most all-inclusive hotels along the northern shore and even into the Samaná Península. Consider, though, that travel time takes a large portion of the day. Typically, an excursion to Cayo Arena allows about 2.5 hours on the actual "island"; on the way back, depending on how far you have to travel, you may be shown the area's coastal mangroves as part of the package deal. Consult your hotel excursion desk for details.

Accommodations, Food, and Tours

El Paraíso Tours (tel. 809/320-7606, www. cayoparaiso.com) offers very basic rooms (US$35) that are situated across from the tour operation of the same name. El Paraíso Tours works in conjunction with north coast hotels, which makes it a practiced excursion operation. Independent travelers arriving in Punta Rucia can reserve a spot on a boat to Cayo Arena just one day in advance. A speedboat adventure (US$40) will take you to the sandbar for snorkeling and through mangroves to see a completely different environment, including lunch and snacks. But the luxurious VIP yacht tour is the crème de la crème. Cruising along the coast like a movie star on the *Sir Francis Drake* ship, you'll visit La Isabela, share a snack of oysters and champagne, go for a swim at Punta Rucia with lunch served on the beach, then head out to Cayo Arena for an afternoon of snorkeling and return through the mangroves, all for US$170.

Villa Nadine (Punta Rucia, U.S. tel. 215/850-4155, D.R. tel. 809/757-2252, www. villanadine.com, US$100–250 per night) is by far the nicest place to stay in Punta Rucia. This villa is yards from the beach, with beautiful landscaping. The expansive master suite on the top floor is the way to spend your vacation. Wake up with your queen-size bed directly across from a huge verandah view of the Atlantic Ocean. It has a unique circular bathroom and shower and private dressing area; otherwise, the room is open. Sit and enjoy cocktails on the rooftop deck at sunset or in the Jacuzzi. In the gourmet kitchen, owners will prepare meals for you that will be served on another balcony that overlooks the beach. Excursions can be arranged with Villa Nadine, like horseback riding (US$70), a visit to Monte Cristi and the Haitian market in Dajabón (US$70), or scuba diving (two dives US$80) in the unspoiled waters of the Parque Nacional Monte Cristi.

Getting There and Around

Since there is no bus service of any kind to this area the only way to get here independently is by driving. To be perfectly frank, reaching Punta Rucia is a veritable nightmare. There are two routes from which to choose. There is the "longer but semi-comfortable" route, or the "shorter but horrifically uncomfortable" route. The first is a 25-kilometer road from Villa Isabella that is paved for part of the way, and there are two rivers over which you will need to cross. A four-wheel-drive vehicle is best for this journey. You can usually drive right through them, but locals will usually help if you need them. Tipping is customary. Head toward the town Estero Hondo. Playa Ensenada and Punta Rucia are just beyond that. The second route is from the Santiago–Monte Cristi Highway (Carretera 1). Turn off at Villa Elisa; this is where reality seems to end and it feels more like traveling on an amusement park ride for 14 kilometers. Please hold on to the bar!

MONTE CRISTI

Monte Cristi is about 135 kilometers west of Puerto Plata and is the capital of the arid and desert-like province of the same name. There isn't a lot of tourism here, but those who do come enjoy beaches and diving. It is said that the surrounding waters have about 180 sunken galleons whose treasures still quietly rest in the sea. Others come to see the Parque Nacional Monte Cristi and its subtropical dry forest, its lagoons, and the 274-meter-high mesa. Off the coast is a collection of islands where sea turtles lay their eggs. Most of the residents of Monte Cristi still make their living farming the land, fishing, or from the salt flats in the north.

The town was founded in the early part of the 16th century and for many years was an important trading port for cattle and manufactured goods. But in 1606, the Spanish crown ordered the northwest corner of the country to be evacuated and moved to Santo Domingo, when it had become clear that pirates were gaining control of trading with the colonists after having bullied the Spanish galleons from the shores.

And for 150 years, Monte Cristi was a ghost town. That is, until the French began moving into the territory. Concerned about losing control of the land, the Spanish moved 100 farming families from the Canary Islands and settled them into the area. Once again, it became an important port with its perfect positioning at the mouth of the Yaque del Norte river basin. Timber and tobacco were floated down from such towns as Santiago and La Vega to be exported from Monte Cristi. The timber industry began to attract Europeans, who settled the area, and the economy flourished.

But the prosperous time came to an end when, in 1860, the four-year Restoration War, in which the Dominicans fought the Spanish for their independence, ruined the city. But the European influence was still present as they rebuilt in their Victorian architecture, some of which survives to this day.

On Avenida Mella is the former house where Máximo Gómez (Cuban military commander) and José Martí (leader of the Cuban independence movement) signed the Montecristi Manifesto for Cuba's independence on March 25, 1895.

Sights

The town of Monte Cristi is hugged on three sides by the **Parque Nacional Monte Cristi,**

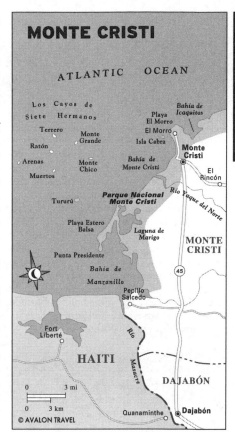

which is made up of lagoons on either side of the town, beaches, a cluster of islands called Los Cayos de los Siete Hermanos, and one hill (El Morro) rising 239 meters above sea level and shaped like a camel's back. Living in the mangroves are more than 160 species of birds and more than 10 species of reptiles; both the ever-elusive manatee and rare solenodon call this national park home.

At Monte Cristi's main beach, **Playa Juan de Bolaños** (located at the end of Avenida San Fernando where it meets the sea), you can find some hotel accommodations and restaurants, but the beach itself is not grand.

The beach affectionately called **Playa Detras del Morro** is behind the hill that looks like a camel's back. It's worth seeking it out, because it is the best in the area. It's a beautiful half moon of sand surrounded by the rocky cliffs. Following Avenida San Fernando to the national park will take you right to the beach. The steps leading up the hillside were closed when we passed through in 2009, but hopefully they will be repaired when you visit because it is a marvelous view from the top, although it's incredibly windy.

If you're up for a short boat ride, catch one out to **Isla Cabra,** where there is a nice and very private beach. Just ask one of the boat captains at Playa Juan de Bolaños and negotiate for a round-trip boat ride. Make sure to get a flat rate for the entire boatload of you, rather than per person, and have it agreed upon before you get in. Here you can also find a boat to take you snorkeling.

Los Cayos de los Siete Hermanos are about a kilometer from shore and are part of the national park. The white beaches of these uninhabited islands are beautiful, and there are many dive spots in the offshore reefs.

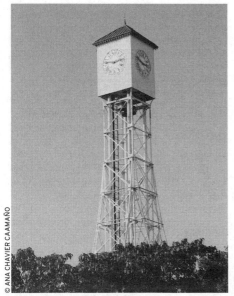

© ANA CHAVIER CAAMAÑO

clock tower, Monte Cristi

La Casa de Máximo Gómez (Av. Mella, 9 A.M.–noon and 2:30–5:30 P.M., free) was once the home of the Dominican who was instrumental in Cuba's independence and the Dominican restoration, Máximo Gómez. Inside are photos and mementos. If you speak Spanish, you can ask for a historical tour of the museum. Tipping is greatly appreciated.

Parque Central or, as it's sometimes called, Parque Reloj, is at the corner of Calle Duarte and San Fernando. The clock tower here is notable. Remind you of anything? It has an Eiffel Tower quality to it. In the late 1990s it was restored. Lining the park are some run-down Victorian homes, some of which have been restored (a little). They all stand in testament to the European influence that the third wave of settlers had on Monte Cristi.

Festivals

On January 21, the **Día de la Virgen de la Altagracia** (the protector of the hearts of all Dominicans), nearly 2,000 pilgrims climb up to the top of El Morro to pray and camp out overnight. Simultaneously, many pilgrims are on their way to Higüey to pray.

Carnaval in Monte Cristi is a particularly legendary one. It is one of the oldest Carnaval celebrations in the country, having started 471 years ago. On Sundays during the entire month of February, spectators have the opportunity to witness a competition between the *toros* (the bulls) and the *civiles* (the civilians). It is an aggressive spectacle but popular nonetheless. Around two in the afternoon the Monte Cristi streets fill up with music, costumes, and the colorful crowds of Carnaval. The *toros* wear costumes with elaborate bull masks and wield whips. The *civiles* are undisguised and unprotected, and yet, they taunt the *toros,* which the *toros* gladly take on. What happens then seems a strange custom to visitors: The *civiles* voluntarily accept furious whip lashes from the *toros.* If you want to see the tradition, don't step into the street—it is sometimes seen as a challenge. Stay clear but enjoy this very old and exciting festival's tradition.

Sports and Recreation

Divers can explore the colonial galleons off-shore or go diving around Los Cayos de los Siete Hermanos. If you're not planning on staying in the Monte Cristi area but are still interested in diving here, many of the dive companies along the north coast offer day trips to Monte Cristi, so you won't miss out on the opportunity to see its coral reefs and sunken ships.

Other sporting options, like **deep-sea fishing** and excursions to Haiti, can be booked through the **Restaurant El Bistrot** (Calle San Fernando 26, tel. 809/579-2091, www.elbistrot.com), a hotel and restaurant that has rental equipment and excursion options like a trip through old Monte Cristi, to the salt mines, to the mangroves, or out to Los Siete Hermanos. Starting price for all excursions is US$45.

It is possible to ask any boat captain on the beach of Playa Juan de Bolaños if they are willing to take you out in their vessels, but at **Club Nautico** (road to El Morro, tel. 809/579-2530) you can talk to the men at the entrance and they will help you find a boat captain with a more seaworthy craft, complete with life vests and working radar, to arrange a **deep-sea fishing** excursion. The price will depend on the owner of the boat as these are all independent captains docked in the marina. You are sure to catch something in these waters since tourism hasn't quite caught up with Monte Cristi. Expect to pay about RD$1,200 for a deep-sea fishing excursion. These captains are also willing to take you out for diving, but as a ride only; you have to provide your own equipment. It is best to arrange with a captain one day in advance so that they have time to ready their boat for the trip. Club Nautico has a cafeteria where they serve simple meals. Always ask to see the life vests before getting into the boat, and agree on the price before commencing with the trip. Tipping guides is customary.

Hostal San Fernando (road to El Morro, tel. 809/579-2249, hostalsanfernando@hotmail.com, ecomarinamontecristi.com, website in Spanish only) offers snorkeling, diving, and city tours. Their diving package is US$150 per day and includes equipment, transportation to Los Siete Hermanos, and room and board at their hotel. In the snorkeling trips you'll be taken to all seven of the islands at Los Cayos de los Siete Hermanos, where you can snorkel at a couple of spots (US$320 per group of up to 12 people). Their city tour takes you to the cemetery, shows you the Victorian architecture and the salt mines, lets you sample some of the gastronomy that Monte Cristi is known for, and takes you to the La Casa de Máximo Gómez.

Accommodations

Aparta-Hotel Cayo Arena (Playa Juan de Bolaños, tel. 809/579-3145, US$40–50) is a great value. Two-bedroom apartments (one queen bed and two single beds) have attractive balconies, fully equipped kitchens, living rooms, cable TV, and bathrooms with hot water. Amenities include a small pool and bar. They also offer half- and full-day fishing excursions; prices start at US$70 and depend on length and if you go in the bay or out to deep sea.

For those who want a great place to stay within walking distance of the national park, **Hostal San Fernando** (Carretera El Morro Km 2, tel. 809/579-2249, US$45 d) is a wonderful choice. Situated near El Morro, these spacious and simple but nicely decorated bungalows are comfortable and clean, each with its own patio, air-conditioning, fan, phone, hot water, and TV. The decor is nautical with natural tones, which is quite calming. At the center of the resort is a nice garden and pool to unwind in on a day when you are not busy taking advantage of their many excursion options or diving packages. Hostal San Fernando has a restaurant and bar on-site with gorgeous views of the spanning countryside. It's one of the best choices of the area.

The 33-room **Hotel Montechico** (Playa Juan de Bolaño, tel. 809/579-2565, US$20 with fan) was built 70 years ago as Club Ramfis by Trujillo himself for his beloved son Ramfis. Although it must have been quite the beach club back in the day, it is sad to see that this hotel, with so very much potential, is desperately in need of some TLC. However, it is conveniently located on the beach and has clean and pleasant rooms with balconies. Those that have ocean views have the most spectacular ones you can get in Monte Cristi, hands down. In fact, it is said that this is one of the best sunset views in the world. The rooms to request are: room 33 (has two beds), room 27 (one bed) and suite 9 (has a Jacuzzi). Other rooms with ocean views: 31, 32, 26, 25, 10, and 8. If you want air-conditioning, request it; the price is higher although not by much (about US$10 more). The breeze off the water should be sufficient, though. The restaurant is a little misleading. Tables are set as if they are ready to receive guests, but no food exists; however, food can be brought to your room if you request it. Sadly, in typical Dominican style, customer service is in deficit. But man oh man, that view!

Los Jardines (tel. 809/579-2091, www.elbistro.com) is next door to the Aparta-Hotel Cayo Arena. Choose between two basic bungalows, each with two rooms and bathrooms. Keep in mind they don't have kitchen facilities, so they are better for just a night or two. Los Jardines arranges for excursions to various places in the national park at additional cost.

If you want a hotel that is going to be clean and quiet perhaps you want one that is not a misnomer. There is nothing chic about **Chic Hotel** (Benito Monción 44, tel. 809/579-2316, US$25 d fan, US$30 d a/c). The price is great, though, for a rather comfortable bed in a very small room cluttered with furniture (why two TVs?). If you are looking for very inexpensive, this hotel has a few things going for it: a middle-of-town location, a restaurant (not that it is anything to brag about), a bar, and an Internet café (giving you a very strong wireless Internet signal even in your room). Whatever you do, get a room with a window. Otherwise, you might be put on the ground floor with no window and the air will be stagnant, which makes for a very long night.

Food and Entertainment

If you really want to try a regional culinary tradition, you need to order *chivo liniero;* it is a spicy goat dish that achieves its exquisite taste because the goats of this region feed on wild oregano, so the meat has been naturally seasoned. Most restaurants serve a dish containing some type of *chivo* in this area.

The restaurant of **Hostal San Fernando** (road to El Morro, tel. 809/964-0248, 8 A.M.–late daily, US$5–20) has traditional chicken, beef, and fish choices as well as good breakfasts. This enjoyable spot is on the road out to El Morro.

Comedor Adela (Juan de la Cruz Alvarez 41, tel. 809/579-2254, 8 A.M.–6 P.M. daily, US$10 and under) offers an inviting, casual atmosphere, and you can order good renditions of traditional Dominican favorites, like *la bandera dominicana*. Sit outside in the courtyard or inside in what could easily be your *abuela* Carmen's dining room, complete with pink and white tablecloths covered in plastic and *mecedoras* (rocking chairs) in the corner. If you're going to try regional goat, try it here. The plate of the day (rice and beans, meat and salad) is only US$3.50. Someone should talk to *abuela* and tell her she's being too kind.

Not only is the seafood a great reason to come to **El Bistrot** (Calle San Fernando 26, tel. 809/579-2091, www.elbistrot.com, 11 A.M.–2:30 P.M. and 6 P.M.–midnight Mon.–Fri., 10 A.M.–midnight Sat. and Sun., US$5–20), but the ambience is worth it as well. You can sit either in the open air of a courtyard or inside. Other dishes include regional goat, sandwiches, and various pastas. It's a very welcoming establishment.

The party at **Double Via** (Calle Duarte and Calle Colón) doesn't get going here on Fridays and Saturdays until after 10:30 or 11 at night even though they are open earlier, and things don't wind down until about 2 A.M. On Sundays expect things to get started around 3 P.M. and end around midnight. You will be able to dance to a good variety of merengue and *bachata* music. Guys, it has become standard practice for some women to ask you to buy them a beer if you have asked them to dance, so don't be surprised by this. If this happens, don't be surprised if you end up buying a round for her girlfriends, too. Of course, you don't have to do any of this, but it is a polite thing to do. Don't flash money around, though. This will make you the biggest target around, both for beer buying and potential pick-pocketing. Ladies, it is best not to take purses to discos.

Information and Services

Calle Duarte is the main commercial area of Monte Cristi. Everything is either on or very near there. The **Politur** (Playa Juan de Bolaños, tel. 809/579-3980) is open 24 hours for any emergencies, and **Hospital Padre Fantino** (Av. 27 de Febrero, tel. 809/579-2401, 24 hours) is a basic hospital facility, but it does have a 24-hour emergency room.

To access money, **BanReservas** (Calle Duarte, tel. 809/579-2392, 8 A.M.–5 P.M. Mon.–Fri., 9 A.M.–1 P.M. Sat.) has a 24-hour ATM.

Getting There and Around

Highway 1 (Autopista Duarte) coming into Monte Cristi from the Southeast becomes Calle Duarte (the main drag) in town. Highway 45 into town from Dajabón becomes Avenida Mella. Incidentally, this is a notoriously dangerous highway to drive at night. Many Dominicans advise highly against it as robberies are very common.

Caribe Tours (Av. Mella and Rodriguez Camargo, tel. 809/579-2129) is a block north from Calle Duarte. You can catch a bus to Santo Domingo (US$8.50) leaving at 7 A.M., 9 A.M., 1:45 P.M., 2:45 P.M., and 4 P.M. This same bus makes a stop in Santiago (US$3.65).

There is a *guagua* terminal on Calle Duarte between 27 de Febrero and Benito Monción. They go to Dajabón and Santiago (US$1–4) and generally depart every 20 minutes.

Walking is best in Monte Cristi, but as usual, *motoconchos* are readily available if you're feeling adventurous.

DAJABÓN

A trip to Dajabón is not on the itinerary of many tourists. This Dominican–Haitian border town is a trading post, just as it has been for centuries. Back in the 17th century, most of the northwest, including Dajabón, was evacuated when the Spanish crown regarded its colonists' trading practices with foreigners to be treasonous behavior. After over 100 years, those foreigners began settling the evacuated land, so the Spanish, in fear of losing the areas they had found so hard to conquer, resettled their land. To this day, Dajabón remains a center for trade between Haiti and the Dominican Republic.

Dajabón is best saved for a day visit since there are no services and the only activity there is to go to the Haitian Market. But since the highways around Dajabón are too dangerous to drive at night, should you get caught losing track of time, there is one hotel worth mentioning.

Hotel Juan Calvo (Calle Presidente Henríquez 48, tel. 809/579-8285, US$10 d with fan only), next to the Parque Central, offers comfortable clean rooms.

Haitian Market

Every day Dajabón is a bustling center of trade as Haitians come over to the Dominican side of the border to sell an unbelievable variety of objects like pots and pans, shoes, perfumes, clothing, and tools. They spread their wares on blankets on the ground, on tables under the shade of a tarp. Dominicans come to the town to purchase these items at rock-bottom prices. The scene is one of a great amount of haggling, lively conversation, and frenzied negotiations. You won't find typical souvenirs, but the experience of rich cultural traditions between the two nations and the photos you'll gather might be all the memento you'll need.

Getting There and Around

Crossing over into Haiti can be a bit confusing. It's hard to say just how much you will pay since it seems to be up to the discretion of whomever you ask at the time. For the most part, though, you'll pay US$20 to the **Dominican immigration office** (8 A.M.–5 P.M. daily) and US$10 to the **Haitian immigration**

office on the other side. You shouldn't have to pay a return fee, but sometimes that proves otherwise for tourists.

Caribe Tours (Calle Marcelo Carrasco, tel. 809/579-8554) is at Marcelo Carrasco and Presidente Henríquez. A trip to Santo Domingo (US$7.50) stops in Monte Cristi and Santiago and leaves at 6:45 A.M., 8:30 A.M., 10:15 A.M., 1 P.M., 2:25 P.M., and 3:15 P.M. Buses leave Santo Domingo for Dajabón at 6:30 A.M., 8 A.M., 9:30 A.M., 1 P.M., 2 P.M., and 3:45 P.M., stopping in Monte Cristi and Santiago.

Catch a *guagua* to Monte Cristi at the station by the entrance to town. *Guaguas* leave Monte Cristi for Dajabón every 20 minutes from the terminal on Calle Duarte.

Getting around within Dajabón is best on foot as it is so small. But taxis and *motoconchos* tend to hang out around the border crossing and on the main street in town.

EL CIBAO

The Cordillera Central (Central Mountains) and the Valle del Cibao make up the fertile backbone of the Dominican Republic, referred to by Dominicans as El Cibao. Removed from the lazy beach towns and all-inclusive resorts, this lush region highlights the biodiversity of the country, featuring ranches, vegetable and fruit farms, twisting mountain roads, crashing waterfalls, rushing rivers, and crisp, fresh air. The area is abundant with produce ranging from potatoes, coffee, tobacco, and vegetables to some not-so-typical fruits such as strawberries and apples.

Most tourists who come to the tropics typically head to the beaches. But the adventure-minded independent travelers seeking the antithesis of plastic-bracelet all-inclusive resorts come here to enjoy the backyard garden of the Dominican Republic—it's a getaway favorite for the Dominicans themselves. The area offers a visitor not only a taste of mountain culture but also an insider's view of the Dominican city-folk relaxing and at play, taking a break from their own hectic lives.

Ecotourism and adventure travel have gained substantial momentum in the tourism industry of the Dominican Republic. Every year more tourists become aware of the richness and diversity of the Dominican Republic's topography, and many choose El Cibao to create a fun, more adventure-focused vacation. Abundant outdoor activities include rafting, canyoning, and treks to Pico Duarte. Whether you ride a mule or do a five-day hike on foot, the climb to the summit of Pico Duarte is one of the most popular activities here, where the reward is a

© ANA CHAVIER CAAMAÑO

HIGHLIGHTS

◖ Centro León: This is easily the best museum in the country. See Dominican culture, art, and history in the state-of-the-art facility. While you're there, watch and learn how cigars are made (page 221).

◖ Carnaval in La Vega: Join in the fun during the pre-Lenten Carnaval celebration often touted as the best in the country. Dance in the streets at one of the best parties thrown in the Dominican Republic (page 229).

◖ Pico Duarte: Hike 3,087 meters to the top of the highest peak in the Caribbean. This challenging trek takes you to the summit, where on a clear day you can see all the way to the Atlantic Ocean and Caribbean Sea (page 237).

◖ Parque Nacional Valle Nuevo: Take in the phenomenal bird-watching opportunity in this protected forest and then head over to the **Salto de Aguas Blancas** for a dip in the pool of the three-tiered waterfall (page 241).

◖ Ruta de Murales: Take **The Mural Route** through **Salcedo** – the town is its own art gallery. From the water tower on the edge of town with the likenesses of the Mirabal sisters, all the way to the **Museo de Hermanas Mirabal,** you will find murals on fences, banks, hotels, and anything with a smooth surface (page 246).

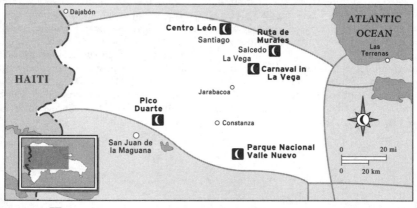

LOOK FOR ◖ TO FIND RECOMMENDED SIGHTS, ACTIVITIES, DINING, AND LODGING.

panoramic view of the Caribbean Sea and the Atlantic Ocean.

PLANNING YOUR TIME

If you are looking to have an action-filled vacation but don't want to move around a lot, Jarabacoa is a fantastic place to make a base camp. Many adventure activities are local, and you can get a lot of action packed into even a three- or four-day vacation. From Jarabacoa you can also book farther-away excursions with local tour companies who will provide transportation. However, if you want to be more mobile, this part of the country is a bit more challenging to get around in via public transportation—it's not impossible, just allow for more time for waiting for buses and *guaguas*. Renting a car is a better idea, but a four-wheel-drive is highly recommended for the power needed to get over mountain passes and often rough and rugged terrain.

To hike Pico Duarte, consider going with a tour group. It will alleviate a lot of planning and logistic complications for you, especially

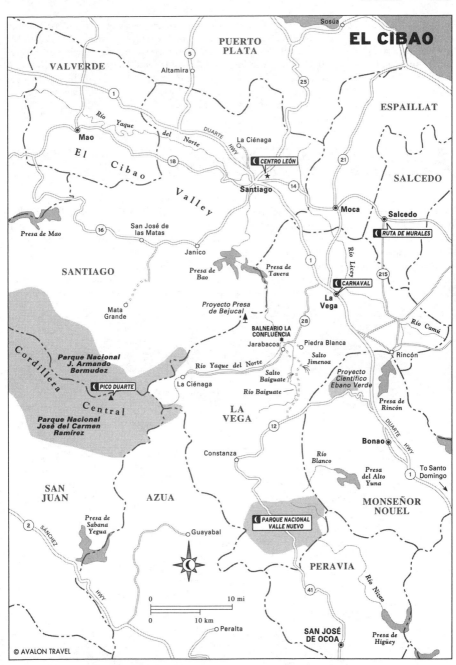

EL CIBAO

if you don't speak Spanish. But if you want to wing it on your own, decide ahead of time which route you'd like to take. That way, you know how many days of travel time and hike time you'll need. For instance, if flying into Santiago (which is best for this area), you should have a day for getting from the airport to your base camp and settling in, booking your trek in the first day or two of arrival with an independent guide. It is best to give your guides a day or two for their own preparations and for yours (you'll need to buy provisions). A minimum of three days should be saved for the actual hike (some can do it in two, but it's best to be safe). After that you'll need your travel time back to the airport.

Santiago

The second-largest city of the Dominican Republic, Santiago de Los Treinte Caballeros (more commonly referred to as Santiago) is an important commercial center in the Valle del Cibao as well as in the Dominican Republic as a whole. The fertile land yields bananas, cocoa, and coffee. Most importantly, the tobacco and sugarcane grown here are turned into rum and cigars, making Santiago a very important and lucrative city for the republic.

It is a bustling city but not as frenetic as Santo Domingo, and it somehow seems more ordered, perhaps because it is steeped in a culture of business and not so much in travel. Therefore, accommodations cater to the international businesspeople who frequent the area.

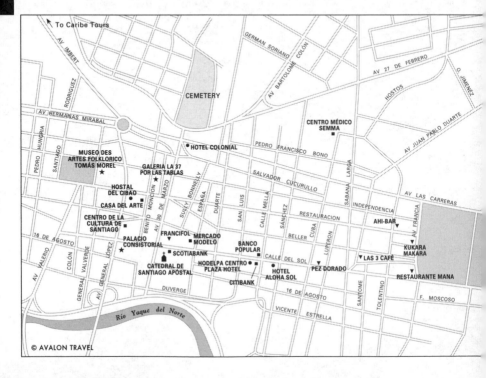

Although there is a good nightlife and arts scene, there are not many sights. As it is the gateway to the surrounding ecotourism of the Cordillera Central, with an international airport just 24 kilometers away and the Autopista Duarte connecting to Santo Domingo, tourists often swing through Santiago for an afternoon or for a night before they head to the mountains where adventure sports await.

Bartolomé Columbus, Christopher's older brother, first founded Santiago in 1495, in the hopes of finding gold. In 1562, it was ravaged and destroyed by a catastrophic earthquake. Eventually the townspeople rebuilt onto what is the modern-day site of Santiago, along the eastern banks of the Río Yaque del Norte. Unfortunately, that was just the beginning of Santiago's long string of difficult times. Pirate attacks, French invasions, three more earthquakes, and a major fire during the Restoration War challenged and all but extinguished

Santiago. But it was after that war that the city truly began to thrive. As World War I raged in the rest of the world, prices for products grown in the area so easily (sugar, tobacco, and coffee) rose dramatically, and the city got steadily richer until the 1920s. Today, Santiago's economy has leveled off, but there are still quite a few very wealthy families because of the agriculture and tobacco industries.

SIGHTS
◖ Centro León

If you can choose only one thing to do in Santiago, make this it. The Centro León (Av. 27 de Febrero 146, Villa Progreso, tel. 809/582-2315, fax 809/724-7644, www.centroleon.org.do, 10 A.M.–7 P.M. Tues.–Sun., US$2, free Tues.) is the country's finest museum, housing art, anthropological, and cultural exhibitions. It also hosts artistic seminars, workshops, film festivals, and music performances. Centro León has an impressive collection devoted to the anthropology and ethnological collections of the Dominican peoples over 5,000 years, from pre-Columbian times to contemporary days. Another section is devoted to visual art and the evolution of Dominican art (and its influences) that is filled with paintings, sculptures, drawings, photographs, and installation art by both national and international artists. Section three is devoted to the folklore of the Dominican Republic and the rest of Latin America. It often has film screenings, concerts, or temporary exhibits.

The museum was founded by the León Jimenes family, one of the most successful families in the Dominican Republic. They built their fortune in the tobacco, beer, and banking industries, and their story is told in the fourth exhibit, on the second floor of a stand-alone building on the well-manicured grounds of the center. On the first floor of the same small museum is a small mock-cigar workshop where you can watch the talented cigar rollers work their magic and a store where you can purchase the highly ranked Aurora cigars. Tours require reservations two days in advance and are given in English, German, French (US$5.50), and Spanish (US$3.50), lasting 1–2 hours.

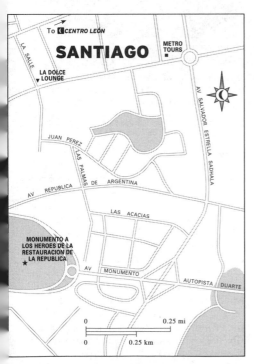

EL CIBAO

CIGARS: THE LONG AND SHORT OF IT

Some of the best cigars in the world come from Santiago and its surrounding areas. The Valle de Cibao, where Santiago is located, is particularly fertile, with just the right combination of rich soil, sunshine, and the cool temperature rolling off the surrounding mountains. Though today machines do a lot of the work of creating a cigar, it is – and will always be – the hand-rolled cigar that reigns supreme.

The process starts, of course, with tobacco seeds, many of which are actually derived from Cuban varieties. Once the seeds have been germinated and the plants are harvested (all of which takes approximately six weeks), the leaves are housed in a drying room, where the dehydration results in lowered nicotine levels and eliminates ammonia. Here, the dried leaves are bundled and aged for anywhere from 2 to 10 years. Once the aging process is complete, the hand-rolling begins.

There are three parts to a cigar: the wrapper, the filler, and the binder. A long filler has been produced from whole leaves, whereas as a short filler comes from whatever clippings are left behind after the long fillers have been rolled, or from ground leaves. The long filler (perhaps accompanied by some short filler) is bound by several leaves, and the binder and filler together form a cylindrical shape – the

© ALICIA CHAVIER CAAMAÑO

Dominican cigars top the charts with cigar aficionados the world over.

cigar shape – at which point the wrapper is applied. After another aging process, the cut and shaped cigar is ready for consumption.

Monumento a Los Héroes de la Restauración de la República (Puerto del Sol)

The Monument to the Heroes of the Restoration of the Republic (Av. Monumental, 9 a.m.–5:30 p.m. Tues.–Sun., closed Mon., RD$60) is hard to miss. Not because it has such interesting features inside or because it has a good exhibit. No, it is literally hard to miss. It is an eight-story tower, five of which are devoted to the museum, perched on top of a tall hill overlooking all of Santiago. Trujillo had commissioned that it be built in honor of himself (in classic Trujillo egoism), but when the dictator was assassinated, it was rededicated to honor those who died

in the Restoration War. The museum and grounds were completely renovated in 2007, giving it a more welcoming feel than the previously grungy and unfinished one. Outside in the plaza are collections of bronze statues depicting noteworthy Dominicans like artists and ball players, along with palm trees and a gorgeous sprawling lawn (and lots of wandering treat vendors). The museum is dedicated to Dominican history and the history of the restoration. At dusk this is a wonderful spot to come and watch the sunset and have a beer, which you can buy from the vendors. From here you can see the entire city and surrounding mountains, a truly spectacular view.

© ANA CHAVIER CAAMAÑO

Monumento a Los Héroes de la Restauración de la República

Museo des Artes Folklórico Tomás Morel

This folklore museum (Av. Restauración 174, tel. 809/582-6787, 9 A.M.–noon and 3:30–6 P.M. Mon.–Fri., free) was the brain-child of Tomás Morel, a celebrated Dominican poet and cultural critic. In its somewhat dusty walls is a great abundance of traditional Santiago Carnaval memorabilia, including a collection of ornate handmade masks from the region's celebration of the annual event. This museum provides one of the better key-hole observations into the traditions of the country's beloved event. Here you will learn about all of the different costumed characters of the tradition, like the *lechones* who wear elaborate costumes and were originally meant to keep order by marching ahead of the parade and creating a path through the crowds. They had, at one time, carried small staffs to shoo the onlookers, but they were eventually replaced by sisal rope whips, and later an inflated pig's bladder was attached to the end of the sisal rope.

Palacio Consistorial

In this museum (Calle del Sol, Parque Duarte, 9 A.M.–6 P.M. Mon.–Fri., 9 A.M.–2 P.M. Sat., free) you can learn all about the history of Santiago. It is in an attractive Victorian building that once housed city hall. It now contains a highly regarded collection of old and recent works by local artists. As part of the annual Carnaval celebration, colorful masks from all over the country are on display.

Parque Duarte and the Catedral de Santiago Apóstol

If you follow the Calle del Sol (named so for the way the sun shines on it) from the Monumento a Los Héroes de la Restauración de la República, south, you will run into downtown Santiago and, eventually, Parque Duarte, which is a lovely tree-lined square, and the Catedral de Santiago Apóstol (Calle 16 de Agosto, Parque Central, 7 A.M.–9 P.M. Mon.–Sat., 7 A.M.–8 P.M. Sun.). The cathedral, with its combination neoclassical and Gothic architecture, was built in the latter part of the 1800s. It holds an ornately carved mahogany altar and beautiful stained-glass windows created by artist José Rincón-Morá in the 1980s.

SHOPPING

The central and most popular shopping district for Santiago is along Calle del Sol. It is a great way to feel the commerce-culture of Santiago and get a feel for this city. Simply strolling along this busy street, you'll find many small stores, vendors, and hawkers.

Much like the Mercado Modelo in Santo Domingo, there is a lot to pick from at **Mercado Modelo** (Calle del Sol, 9 A.M.–5 P.M. Mon.–Sat.): knickknacks, souvenirs, Haitian paintings, jewelry, and all sort of other things to set yourself to haggling over. That is half the fun anyway.

Since you're in the region of serious tobacco production, it would be wise to make your cigar purchases here. At **Centro León** (Av. 27 de Febrero 146, Villa Progreso, tel. 809/582-2315, fax 809/724-7644, 10 A.M.–7 P.M. Tues.–Sun.)

EL CIBAO

you can not only watch the rollers at work, you can buy some of the world's best cigars.

ENTERTAINMENT AND EVENTS
Art Exhibits, Performances, and Classes

If you are visiting Santiago for more than a day, perhaps taking in an art or music class or going to some performances will bring you closer to the culture of the area. Call or stop by and check the schedule of events at each locale since they change often. The **Casa del Arte** (Benito Monción, tel. 809/471-7839, 9 A.M.–7 P.M. Mon.–Sat., free) shows exhibits by local artists and holds cultural events in an outdoor gallery space.

Across the street from Casa del Arte is **Galería La 37 por Las Tablas** (Benito Monción, tel. 809/587-3033). Here you can enjoy music, dance, and theater performances (also in an outdoor theater), take dance and other kinds of classes, participate in cultural talks, and attend lectures. Admission depends upon the activity or event.

The **Centro de la Cultura de Santiago** (Calle del Sol, tel. 809/226-5222, 9 A.M.–6 P.M. daily) has music and theater performances and classes.

Nightlife

A good place to set out on foot in search of your type of watering hole is around the Monumento a la Restauración. Since it is a busy area, it is a safe area to walk.

Ahi-Bar Café and Grill (Calle Tolentino and Restauraciñn, tel. 809/581-6779, 4 P.M.–3 A.M.) is a good bar to start out the night because it serves food, but it is most popular as a drinking spot, especially on Friday nights. The large patio is good for open-air conversation, and the bar is quite popular with the blue-blooded youth of Santiago. The karaoke on Sundays starts at 8 P.M. Now, at **Ahi-Bar Dance** you can groove to merengue, *bachata* and salsa in Ahi's dance club directly adjacent to the Café and Grill. The club is small but they've dressed it with modern furniture and swank lighting.

The crowd tends to be younger than that of the Café and Grill crowd. A small stage allows for live music every Friday night starting at 9 P.M.

The contemporary crowd at **Francifol** (Calle del Sol 127, tel. 809/971-5558) doesn't even get going until midnight or 1 A.M., but it is a popular place with the youth of Santiago.

While a hotel bar doesn't exactly scream adventure, if what you're after is a before dinner or night-starter cocktail with friends, **Cosmopolitan** (Hodelpa Gran Almirante Hotel, Estrella Sadhalá and Calle 10, tel. 809/580-1992) is a perfectly acceptable place to have it. It is a comfortable and classy-looking place. But have no illusions, it is a hotel bar after all, so the later the hours get, the seedier the clientele becomes. But if you can overlook that, have a nightcap.

La Dolce Lounge (Plaza Zona Rosa, Av. Duarte and Calle La Salle, tel. 809/971-0415) attracts the youth of Santiago in droves. It can be a bumping party with flashing lights and a mad-mixing DJ spinning everything from reggaeton to techno or a live band gigging merengue to salsa. It is a loud party atmosphere not for conversation.

At **Tipico Monte Bar** (Av. 27 de Febrero, tel. 809/575-0300, www.tipicomontebar.com) there is plenty going on. If what you're after is to hear "real" Dominican merengue and see some great dancers, then this is the spot. Live music happens often, so admission varies with these acts (about RD$100–RD$300). Plans are in development to offer dance classes in merengue, *bachata,* and salsa. Dress is casual. The club is located in the Las Colinas neighborhood, which is north of Santiago. You'll need to take a taxi, which will run you about US$3 one way.

Festivals

The *caretas* (masks) of Santiago's **Carnaval** are especially ornate, making this city's Carnaval celebration a particularly special one to take part in. Competitions for the best mask are held annually in the days leading up to Carnaval.

At the Carnaval parade in Santiago you'll

see two character masks that are specific to Santiago, the *lechŏn* (piglet) and the *pepin* (a make-believe animal that looks like a duck with spiked horns). Santiago's celebration is special in that you will see a fantastic variety of costumes and cultures represented here that have affected the overall Carnaval celebration of the whole country and throughout history. All of the characters carry the *vejigas* (inflated animal bladders) and hit onlookers with them. If you don't want to be bruised, stay off the street; better yet, try to watch the Carnaval parade from a balcony.

While the most lively and best-known Carnaval celebration in the country is in nearby La Vega (perhaps because it is the most well-organized), Santiago is trying to increase the visibility and popularity of its celebration. Festivities begin around four in the afternoon and go late into the night with live merengue and *bachata* music. At the monument, there is art on exhibit and groups doing folkloric and cultural performances. Making your base camp in Santiago (provided you arrange accommodations well in advance) is a great idea so that you can go to both towns' celebrations. All Carnaval celebrations in the country happen every Sunday during the month of February.

Sports and Recreation

Las Aromas Golf Course (Santiago, tel. 809/626-1288, www.hodelpa.com/golf, 6 a.m.–dusk, greens fees: RD$800 (non-members) and RD$600 (members), discounts for hotel guests) was designed by Pete Dye in the early 1980s and has 18 moderately challenging holes in the Cibao's hilly terrain. Those who love the heartland will appreciate the panoramic views of the Cibao Valley located just five minutes from Santiago. Be sure to wear a shirt with a collar and no denim pants.

ACCOMMODATIONS

Although Santiago is the second-largest city in the country, there are very few choices for accommodations.

Under US$50

Hostal del Cibao (Calle Benito Monción 40,

tel. 809/581-7775, US$12 d) is the place to rest the heads of the weary backpackers and budget travelers. Located just a short walk from the Parque Central, there are 14 rooms available. All are spacious with private bath (no hot water), cable TV, and fan. Enjoy early evenings watching Santiago on your private balcony.

Hotel Colonial (Salvador Cucurullo 115, tel. 809/247-3122, US$13 d) is between Calle 30 de Marzo and España. It offers clean rooms that are a bit small and simple with cable TV, fan, and private bathroom. The staff here is very hospitable and friendly. Next to Hotel Colonial is the **Colonial Deluxe,** which charges a little more since the building and its rooms are newer.

Camp David (Carretera Luperón Km 7 ½, tel. 809/276-6400, www.campdavidranch. com, US$41–US$50 d) is located along the Carretera Turística on a mountainside filled with huge homes, overlooking a breathtaking view of the valley. It was opened in 1987 by a Trujillo fan and is decorated with some of the dictator's personal belongings, like books, photos, and license plates, and a few of his old cars are parked in the lobby. The immortalization of a brutal dictator seems a bit strange for a hotel theme. Nevertheless, the rest of the decor is tastefully sparse throughout the hotel's bar and restaurant (which is also quite good), making it a suitable choice for accommodation, especially if you want to get out of the city. The rooms are big and have hot water. Room number 5 (sleeps two) has the best view, but the whole place is starting to show its age. You don't come here for modernity; you come for the wide sweeping view of the Cibao Valley. When booking a room, make sure to mention "room with a view" because all rooms cost the same amount.

US$50-100

Hotel Aloha Sol (Calle del Sol 50, tel. 809/583-0090, www.alohasol.com, US$55–75 d) is close to shopping and other services. There is Internet service, a restaurant, and a piano bar (4 p.m.–midnight). The rooms are very clean and have air-conditioning, cable TV, and a minibar, but you'll be billed if you use anything from it. You can request a room with a fax machine in it if you are here on business. The rooms are all a bit cramped, even the suites.

Hodelpa Centro Plaza Hotel (Calle Mella 54 and Calle del Sol, tel. 809/581-7000, www. hodelpa.com, US$75) was recently renovated, and that is great news because now it not only has a phenomenal location, but also it has very comfortable carpeted rooms with air-conditioning, goose down pillows, cable TV, mini-bars, a gym, and a great restaurant on the top floor that will give you panoramic views of the city as you dine.

US$100 and Up

Hodelpa Gran Almirante (Av. Estrella Sadhalá and Calle 10, tel. 809/580-1992, www.hodelpa.com, US$200–290) is Vegas in Santiago, baby! Complete with casino till the wee hours and rooms with all the trimmings (air-conditioning, hair dryers, wireless Internet access, minibar, cable TV, etc.), four restaurants, pool and Jacuzzi, and fitness center. It's only 15 minutes from the airport.

FOOD

There are many restaurants around the monument and on Calle del Sol. **(** **Pez Dorado** (Calle del Sol 43, tel. 809/582-2518, noon–12 P.M. daily, US$11–40) is a surprisingly nice change from the regular cuisine found in the Dominican Republic; it serves *comida criolla* (traditional Dominican fare), Chinese, and other international dishes. They don't let you go hungry and it's a popular place on the weekends. It has been popular in Santiago since the 1950s.

Kukara Makara (Av. Francia 7, tel. 809/241-3143, 8 A.M.–late, US$5–20) is a Tex Mex, cowboy-inspired restaurant serving thick meals like steak, burritos (including a veggie one), and grilled food. It also has seafood, sandwiches, and burgers. Sure, the cheesy quality of the theme may be a bit touristy, but the food is actually quite good, and if you've just spent a while combing through the museum at the

monument and are dying of hunger, this is very near there.

Restaurante Mana (Av. Francia and Calle del Sol, US$3–7) is a small, very casual, cafeteria-style restaurant down the hill from the monument. It's very affordable; for US$3, you can get rice and beans, meat, a side order, and a drink. What a value for the budget traveler! The food is good, too. Just get in line and point to what you want. Dining is on picnic tables under a roof, but open-air.

Las 3 Café (Calle Tolentino 38, tel. 809/276-5909, noon–late, US$6–12) is a very good choice for Dominican *criolla* fare. It's within the bar district and serves wonderful midpriced meals.

When dining at **Camp David** (Carretera Luperón Km 7 ½, tel. 809/276-6400, US$10–25), the first thing you'll notice is the spectacular panoramic view. Next is the almost overwhelming size of the menu, with seafood dishes like *mero en salsa de cerveza* (grouper in beer sauce), numerous meat choices, pastas, and rice dishes. Make your meal a well-rounded one with a wine picked from their generous wine cellar. If you find yourself romanced by the view, just book a room for the night.

INFORMATION AND SERVICES

Calle del Sol is the main drag, where you'll find many vendors, hotels, banks, and other services. It intersects with Avenida 30 de Marzo at the Parque Central, which is a commercial street also.

For a 24-hour emergency room, go to **Centro Médico Semma** (Pedro Francisco Bonó, tel. 809/226-1053). Also good to know about is a specialty women's care facility, **Hospital de la Mujer** (Av. Imbert, tel. 809/575-8963), which has a 24-hour emergency room; they will treat anyone.

But if you have time to get to **Hospital Metropolitano de Santiago** (Autopista Duarte Km 2.8, tel. 829/947-2222, ext. 5060, www.homshospital.com), it is a newer hospital with specialists of every variety—an emergency and trauma unit, lab, cardiology, pharmacy, gynecology—you name it, they have it.

Banco Popular is near the intersection of Sánchez and Calle del Sol. **ScotiaBank** (Calle del Sol at 30 de Marzo) has one as well. They have the same hours (8 A.M.–5 P.M. Mon.–Fri., 8 A.M.–12:30 P.M. Sat.).

GETTING THERE
By Air
The **Aeropuerto Internacional del Cibao** (tel. 809/233-8000, www.aeropuertocibao. com.do) is 20 minutes out of town. Airlines that service it are: **American** (tel. 809/233-8403, www.aa.com), **Continental** (tel. 809/233-8161, www.continental.com), **Delta** (tel. 809/233-8487, www.delta.com), and **Jet Blue** (tel. 809/233-8212, www.jetblue.com). Taking a taxi from the airport to Santiago costs US$15–20.

By Bus
There are two bus stations in town. **Caribe Tours** (27 de Febrero at Las Américas, tel. 809/576-0790, www.caribetours.com.do) is in the Las Colinas neighborhood and has bus service going to many cities. There are 26 Santo Domingo (US$6.70) buses every day leaving 6 A.M.–8:15 P.M. and stopping in La Vega. For Puerto Plata (US$2.75), with a stop in Sosúa, buses leave every hour on the half hour 8:30 A.M.–9:30 P.M., and Monte Cristi (US$3.65) has six buses 9:15 A.M.–6:15 P.M., stopping in Dajabón along the way.

Metro Tours (Av. Juan Pablo Duarte and Calle Maímon, tel. 809/587-3837, www.metroservicioturisticos.com) is a second choice that has service to Santo Domingo (US$7) every two hours and Puerto Plata (US$2.75) six times a day (starting at 9 A.M. and ending at 9 P.M.).

By Car
The Carretera 1 cuts through the nation from Santo Domingo and after 164 kilometers reaches Santiago, where it bends west for 120 kilometers to Monte Cristi—making a trip from either of these directions very direct.

From Puerto Plata one only needs to take the Carretera 5 to the Carretera 1 for the easiest-to-map route.

The airport at Santiago has a bevy of car rental agencies to choose from. Booking online ahead of arrival is always the best way to ensure both a good rate and availability: **Alamo** (tel. 809/233-8163, www.alamo.com); **Avis** (tel. 809/582-7007, www.avis.com); **Dollar** (tel. 809/233-8108, www.dollar.com); **Eurocar** (tel. 809/233-8150, www.europcar.com); **Honda Rent-a-car** (tel. 809/233-8179, www. hondarentcar.com); **National Rent-A-Car** (tel. 809/233-8163, www.nationalcar.com).

GETTING AROUND
If you're driving through, the street to keep in mind is Calle del Sol (the main commercial drag), which runs east into the Monumento a Los Héroes de la Restauración. The main streets that lead in and out of town are Avenida 27 de Febrero, which will take you north, and Avenida Las Carreras, which goes south toward Santo Domingo. All highways (*carreteras* or *autopistas*) into town—Autopista Duarte, Carretera Duarte, and Carretera Turística (which is another name for the Carretera Luperón)—lead to the city center. The infuriating way that Dominican highways have multiple names has never been more aggravating.

Taxis (US$3–5) are relatively inexpensive, especially if you're just taking them from a restaurant or bar to your hotel. They're a lot safer than *motoconchos* or walking at night.

AROUND SANTIAGO
Surrounding Santiago are mostly tobacco farmlands and other farms. This doesn't exactly make for a tourist hopping place. To some, that is music to their traveling ears.

La Cumbre
Traveling along the scenic Carretera Turística north through the countryside, snaking up curvaceous mountainous passages, no doubt marveling at the tree-plush landscape being laid out below, you will come to La Cumbre, which translates to "The Summit." This area

EL CIBAO

© ANA CHAVIER CAAMAÑO

faceless dolls in Higüerito de Moca

is famous for its amber mines and was used as the setting for a scene in *Jurassic Park*. You will know you have found La Cumbre when you start seeing roadside stalls selling souvenirs. There will be a marked turnoff for La Cumbre de Juan Vegas, which you will need to follow for about three kilometers. From there you will need to walk up and over the hill to where the mines are found. The company **Tours Trips Treks & Travel** (tel. 809/867-8884, www.4domrep.com) leads expeditions to these mountains for a visit to the amber mines.

If you just want to enjoy a good meal and one of the country's great mountain views, go to either **Rancho La Cumbre Bar & Restaurant** for a steak or **El Caffeto Bar & Restaurant** (Carretera Moca–Jamao, La Cumbre, tel. 809/471-0015, caffeto@hotmail.com), where they have live jazz music on the fourth Friday of every month (possibly more nights in the works). Even without the music, the view of the Cibao that these restaurants offer is breathtaking and worth a stop.

Higüerito de Moca

Many of the country's typical "faceless women" dolls, vases, and other forms of pottery sold to tourists in resorts and gift shops have been thrown and painted by hand in the backyard studios of artisans in the tiny village of Higüerito de Moca (commonly referred to as Higüerito). The village is eight kilometers south of Santiago just off the Autopista Duarte, or if you are approaching from La Vega, you will turn right off the highway at the 14.5 kilometer marker. At the fork in the road, turn left. Look for (or ask the townspeople for directions to) the shack made of wooden slats, **Artesania Mery** (tel. 809/783-3259, 9 A.M.–5 P.M. Mon.–Fri.). Here you can watch the artists make the dolls that have come to represent the fusion of cultures and races that have made up the Dominican face. Where one person may imagine a mulatto face, another may see a European image or an African one. Sadly, these artists, who sell their pieces to large corporate hotels or stores, rarely see profit returns, so it is customary that you purchase something if you visit the studios.

La Vega

La Concepción de La Vega (commonly referred to as La Vega) sits in the middle of the Valle del Cibao (Cibao Valley). The countryside is plush with vegetation and is an area that is rich in production of tobacco, rice, fruit, and vegetables. La Vega has so very little to offer tourists, it ranks low on the priority list for most. That is, until February, when the small town's streets overflow with hundreds of thousands of Dominicans and tourists for its Carnaval celebration. It is the one thing that keeps La Vega on the map.

SIGHTS
Catedral de la Concepción
This architectural oddity is on the Parque Central and is impossible to miss. The "trainwreck" design was a sincere try at a contemporary version of Spanish Imperial style, complete with castle details. It ended up looking something like a concrete power plant. For those who are admirers of modern architecture, this building does not evoke the genius of Niemeyer sculptural beauty, but rather raises curiosity. So in the spirit of "This I gotta see!" the cathedral is on Avenida Antonio Guzmán at Padre Adolfo. One of the great things about a trip to the cathedral is visiting the *pastelito* vendors that can be found out front. These meat-filled pastries are absolutely great for a quick snack and an excuse to take a break from sightseeing.

Santo Cerro
Holy Hill is along a road stemming from Autopista Duarte, about five kilometers north of La Vega. Up on the hill with a magnificent view of the Cibao Valley sits **Iglesia Las Mercedes** (9 A.M.–noon and 2–6 P.M. daily), a popular pilgrimage site that contains a hole into which Christopher Columbus is said to have placed a cross given to him by Queen Isabela. The cross that was placed there (and is now "missing") is said to have been involved in a miracle during a Spanish versus Taíno battle. The natives tried to burn the religious

symbol, but when it wouldn't catch fire, the Virgin Mary is said to have appeared on it and scared off the Taínos. The Spanish rejoiced and the Dominicans now venerate the spot where the faithful believe it took place on pilgrimage days like September 24 (the patron saint day of Our Lady of the Mercies).

Going to Santo Cerro for the view is a nice side trip. Look for the *níspero* tree near the church. A plaque says it is a descendant of one planted in the late 1400s that was used to build the original wooden church that stood there. Around the church are many stores selling religious items and souvenirs.

La Vega Vieja
"Old La Vega," a few kilometers northeast of present-day La Vega, was founded in 1494 by Christopher Columbus to act as a stronghold for all the gold he assumed he'd find in the region. The settlement gained prosperity, but it was not due to gold. It was the fertility of the valley and the sugarcane industry that began here. But the prosperity ended when, in 1562, a massive earthquake destroyed the town. The **ruins of La Vega Vieja** (9 A.M.–noon and 2–5 P.M. daily, US$1) contain the overgrown remains of the fort, church, and some houses that stood where the original settlement had been, or what was left after the earthquake and a few hundred years.

◖ Carnaval
Although situated in the picturesque and serene valley of La Vega Real, 125 kilometers north of Santo Domingo, La Vega lacks significant tourist sights, and for 11 months out of a year there really isn't a reason to visit. But for that one month, February, the best reason to come here emerges during the pre-Lenten celebration of Carnaval, when La Vega explodes with energy and activity. Most Dominicans agree that the Carnaval of La Vega is the best, rowdiest, and most fun in the whole country and that no other can rival it.

Every Sunday in the six weeks before Lent, La Vega virtually doubles in size when almost 100,000 visitors pack the town dancing in the streets, and it seems that all hell breaks loose. La Vega's mask (each town has its own) is an ornately decorated and colorful devil with bulging wrathful eyes and teeth. These costumes alone are reason enough to come to Carnaval. These magnificently gruesome devils march along the parade in jingle-bell covered costumes wielding *vejigas* (traditionally, inflated cow or pig bladders) that they use to thwack bystanders on the backside. To stay clear of this tradition, stay on the bleachers set up along the parade route, find a balcony to watch from above, or don't step off the curb into the street—that is a sign that you are fair game.

ACCOMMODATIONS AND FOOD

La Vega is best reserved for a day trip. It is more desirable to stay in nearby Jarabacoa where the accommodation choices are more plentiful. Unfortunately, the accommodations and food options in this town leave much to be desired with some truly dismal choices. But should you get stranded or simply decide to stay, the **Hotel El Rey** (Calle Restauración 3, tel. 809/573-9797, US$49 d) is the best choice. Rooms are clean with cable TV and a fan but showing their age. There is free parking and a restaurant serving good *comida criolla* (Dominican food). The staff is attentive and friendly.

INFORMATION AND SERVICES

There are very limited services in La Vega. There is a **BanReservas** (Padre Adolfo 24, tel. 809/573-2989, 9 A.M.–5 P.M. Mon.–Fri., 9 A.M.–1 P.M. Sat.); it has an ATM, or try **Banco León** (Av. Independencia, tel. 809/277-0060).

If you need a pharmacy, **Farmacia Ferreira** (Av. P. Garcia 20, tel. 809/573-2102) should be able to give you what you need, but you'll have to make the trip to Santiago for any medical attention.

GETTING THERE AND AROUND

The odd thing about La Vega is that it is highly accessible by both car and bus, from many directions, and still there are so very few services available.

Caribe Tours (Av. Pedro A. Rivera 37, tel. 809/573-6806, www.caribetours.com, 6:30 A.M.–9 P.M.) has a very steady stream of buses coming through its station. Santo Domingo–bound (US$4.50) buses leave every half hour or so. Northern-bound buses make stops in Santiago (US$1.85), Puerto Plata (US$4.50), and Sosúa (US$5) and leave every hour. A bus for Jarabacoa (US$2.40) leaves at scattered times throughout the day as it is a transfer bus from Santo Domingo.

The north–south-running Autopista Duarte files right past La Vega, making it a major stopover for traffic coming from major destinations on either coast. The main drag, Avenida Antonio Guzmán Fernández, parallels Autopista Duarte in town and then comes to meet it just north of town. Look for the main plaza near Avenida Guzmán Fernández and Padre Adolfo; that's where you'll also find the cathedral and the bank. It's an easy 40 kilometers along the Autopista Duarte (Carretera 1) from Santiago to La Vega and 118 kilometers from Santo Domingo northbound on the same highway. Getting around within the town of La Vega is as easy as strolling around, since it is relatively small. If you need a taxi, call **Taxi Del Valle** (Av. Rivas 27, tel. 809/573-1313).

Jarabacoa

In the heart of the **Cordillera Central** mountains, often referred to as the "Dominican Alps," is the town of Jarabacoa, whose name is the Taíno word for "place of abundant waters." Its abundance is seen not only in the fertility of its land, but also in what it has to offer visitors.

Thick vegetation surrounds the rich agricultural region, and products such as vegetables, coffee, flowers, and strawberries seem to grow without effort. The delectable red fruit can be seen in brimming-over baskets for sale along the curving road up the mountainside, and the marketplace of Jarabacoa is abundant with produce.

Jarabacoa has long been a popular spot for Dominicans as a summer getaway from their life in the city and the muggy heat of the coastal lowlands. The 500 meters above sea level impart constant spring-like mild days and cool evenings. Foreign visitors come because Jarabacoa presents promises of adventure. It is the launching point for treks to Pico Duarte (the highest peak in the Caribbean), white-water rafting, and canyoning in the waterfalls and rivers (Jimenoa, Baiguate, and Yaque del Norte converge nearby). It is the Dominican Republic that is relatively new to the scene of tourism and the new darling of ecotravel.

There are many popular Dominican adages regarding this town. Although it is modest in size, its reputation is larger than life with sayings like, "Jarabacoa, where the most handsome Dominican men are born" and "God may be everywhere, but he sleeps in Jarabacoa."

SIGHTS

The waterfalls listed here are a fair distance away, so either rent your own transportation or get a taxi to take you. Consider asking your driver to be a round-trip driver for you and establish your time for return. Also, asking a driver to take you around to all three waterfalls for a flat rate is a good idea. Secure prices before beginning your trip.

El Salto de Baiguate

Coming from Jarabacoa, follow Calle El Carmen east; it becomes the Carretera Constanza outside of town. There will be a sign for this waterfall in roughly three kilometers; follow the turnoff, which will take you through a very small village until you reach a parking lot. Walk along a path in a gorge until you come to some steps that lead to the waterfall. There is no charge to come here on your own. Swimming is nice (albeit cold) here, and lots of excursions stop either on foot or horseback.

Los Saltos de Jimenoa

The two Jimenoa waterfalls are more stunning than the one at Baiguate. The first, and most dramatic, is **Salto Jimenoa Uno.**

JARABACOA

To Jarabacoa Golf Club, Salto Jimenoa Dos, and Gran Jimenoa Hotel

POST OFFICE
CARIBE TOURS
RESTAURANTE EL RANCHO
POLITUR
CEMETERY
JOSÉ DURAN
CLÍNICA DR. TERRERA
ENTRE AMIGOS CAFÉ
HOTEL BRISAS DEL YAQUE
TRICOM
COLON
FARMACIA INDEPENDENCIA
A&G SERVICIOS MÚLTIPLES
SUPERMERCADO JARABACOA
FARMACIA MIGUELINA
MELLA
SÁNCHEZ
DUARTE
CENTRO DE COPIADO Y PAPELERÍA
HOTEL PLAZA CENTRAL-MARIO N GALAN
TOURIST OFFICE
D'Parque Galería
OBDULIO JIMÉNEZ
CALLE EL CARMEN
To Salto Jimenoa Uno, Rancho Baiguate, and Constanza
16 DE AGOSTO
To La Ciénaga

PELEGRINA HERRERA
NORBERTO TIBURTO
AV INDEPENDENCIA
LUPERON
MARIO NELSON GALAN
MIRABAL

SCALE NOT AVAILABLE

© AVALON TRAVEL

Follow the road out of Jarabacoa via the road to Constanza. It turns to a dirt road after a bit, so don't be surprised. Seven kilometers outside of Jarabacoa, you'll pass through a tiny village and then see a small turnoff on your left—this will quickly turn into more of a trail. Follow this path down to the pool at the base of the falls. Salto Jimenoa Uno is about 60 meters high and is fed from a hidden lake above that sends its water crashing in a huge pool at the bottom. It looks like something from the movies. In fact it was. It was a chosen location for a scene in *Jurassic Park.*

The second is called **Salto Jimenoa Dos** (admittance RD$100). This is perhaps the most frequently visited of the falls. Coming from Jarabacoa, you'll drive northeast for three kilometers on the road to Highway Duarte. Follow the signs that lead you to the falls at a fork in the road. After another five kilometers or so, there is a parking lot. Once you've paid the ranger, walk along a trail between canyon walls that includes suspension bridges. These falls are about 40 meters high and splash down into a deep turquoise pool. The water is absolutely frigid, but great for a swim.

Café Monte Alto

One of the true treats of visiting this region is tasting the rich product of its land. The coffee grown in this region is the best in the country. Café Monte Alto (Altos del Yaque, tel. 809/574-2618, www.gbr.com.do) was founded in 1943 by Belarminio Ramírez, as a small coffee production farm. Over the years it has grown and been passed down over three family generations. It now occupies over 350 hectares of the Cordillera Central. They have both Café Monte Alto brand and the Café Monte Alto Orgánico brand, which is 100 percent chemical free. Café Monte Alto gives tours for free and tours of the processing plant. You will also have a chance to enjoy a phenomenal (and strong) cup of espresso or other coffee drink in their café on-site. They will explain the full process from plant to bean, to wet mill, dry mill, sorting, roasting, packaging, and then, finally, into your cup. Purchase some of their product to take home. This makes an excellent gift for friends. Tours are given in Spanish, English, French, and German.

SPORTS AND RECREATION

While Cabarete is the extreme sport capital of the north, Jarabacoa is that of the Cordillera Central. Travelers who are not content with a vacation of being sand-potatoes with a drink in their hand and doing nothing but gathering UV rays come here, to the central highlands, for excitement and adventure in sports such as mountain biking, river rafting, cascading, canyoning, and quad riding.

These are conquer-your-fears sports. They get your adrenaline pumping maniacally through your bloodstream and push you in ways you weren't expecting. The exhilaration of rushing rapids while rafting on the Río Yaque del Norte, the concentration and agility needed for a top-speed bicycle spin down a mountain trail, the "don't look down" butterflies of stepping over that first edge during canyoning—these are only a few of the emotions spawned while taking advantage of all the sports that Jarabacoa has to offer.

Hiking

Day hikes are fun for an afternoon of rigorous activity but without the commitment you need to do the hike to Pico Duarte.

El Mogote is the best choice for a same day trek. Take the Carretera Jarabacoa–Manobao (a road that also leads you to the La Ciénega setting-off point for the trek to Pico Duarte) to get there. Two kilometers outside of town, you will turn up a steep hill on the left (there is no sign). Allow yourself 5–6 hours round-trip for this hike. Take food, wear some hiking boots if you have them, and remember your water. Pace yourself; it is incredibly steep in some points. At the base of this hike, you'll find the Selesian monastery **Centro Selesiano,** whose monks have taken the vow of silence and support themselves with their pasta factory.

Although there are other day hikes (very poorly marked) that can be done independently, you can also go with **Rancho Baiguate.**

Give a day or two warning that you're coming so you can reserve your spot and find out the appropriate time of departure.

White-Water Rafting

The Río Yaque del Norte is a fast-flowing river that rises up from the northern slopes of the Cordillera Central and runs northwest until it spills into the Bahía de Monte Cristi. Its waters are used as irrigation for farms growing rice, sugarcane, and tobacco, and in most recent years for carrying the rafts of white-water-rafting adventure seekers like you. Conquering this bad boy can be an exhilarating activity for a day trip.

Rafting outfitters will provide helmets as well as a wetsuit, lifejacket, and a lesson in rafting technique and safety. This trip takes a fair amount of strength as there is a lot of paddling to be done, and it is not a suitable trip for kids under the age of 12. Outfitters will most likely provide meals and a snack as well. These are Class III rapids on a scale of I–VI. Getting wet is the idea as you carve your way through the canyons of the Dominican Alps, so dress accordingly: shorts, T-shirt, and rubber-soled shoes. Bring a change of clothes with you or you will have a soggy, itchy trip home.

Adventure Sport Tours

Rancho Baiguate (Jarabacoa, Carretera a Constanza, tel. 809/574-6890, www.ranchobaiguate.com) offers an extensive list of excursions, such as local activities like canyoning (US$50), mountain biking, trekking (US$17.50 for two hours or US$25 for four hours), river rafting (US$50), and horseback and jeep tours to the waterfalls (US$9–21). Or conquer your fear of heights on the Maroma's Parcour ropes course (US$16). Treks to Pico Duarte come in 3- to 5-day packages and vary in price (starting at US$255) depending on how many people are in the group. Price quotes and reservations can be made via phone or email.

Iguana Mama (Cabarete, tel. 809/571-0908, www.iguanamama.com, 8 A.M.–5 P.M. daily) is one of the most reputable and highly recommended adventure tour companies in the country. Although it based in Cabarete, they do many tour excursions in Jarabacoa. Programs include guided mountain-biking tours, whitewater rafting (US$80), and multiday treks to Pico Duarte (US$450), among many other excursions and trip packages throughout the country.

Golf

Jarabacoa Golf Club (tel. 809/782-9883, 7:30 A.M.–7 P.M. daily) is a 9-hole uneventful golf course nestled in the pine woods just outside of Jarabacoa. Greens fees are US$30 to go twice around and play a full 18 holes. Caddies and carts are optional. This course is well marked by a sign on the road to Jarabacoa about one kilometer before reaching the town.

ACCOMMODATIONS
Under US$50

Hotel Plaza Central (Mario N. Galan, tel. 809/524-7768, US$35 d) offers clean but very basic rooms with ceiling fans and private bathrooms. There are no screens on the big windows, so the mosquitoes can be a bit bothersome, but the air flows freely, as does the noise from the rather busy location (about a half block from Parque Central). The management will let you lock your bags in the office when you're out.

Hotel Brisas del Yaque (Luperón at Peregrina Herrera, tel. 809/574-4490, US$33) is the best deal in town. It doesn't have a restaurant but is close to many in town. The rooms are a little cramped but new and very clean, with brick and wood decor, private bathroom, TV, air-conditioning, and a cool tile floor. Some have magnificent views of the mountains, a big plus!

US$50-100

Rancho Baiguate (Carretera Constanza Km 5, tel. 809/574-6890, www.ranchobaiguate.com.do, US$70–100 d) is an adventure ranch and hotel rolled into one. It is still a good place to bring kids. The ranch is five kilometers east of Jarabacoa and removed from the noise of the town. This is not "roughing it" at camp, but it is not a luxury dude ranch either. Nature lovers will be comfortable here. The rooms vary in style from standard to luxury (ranch-style). The rooms are spacious and clean. The mood is rustic with vaulted ceilings (complete with a quiet ceiling fan!), a porch with chairs, and private, clean hot-water bathrooms. There is no air-conditioning (you won't need it); windows have screens but the mosquitoes are relentless in the country when dusk sets in, so bring some sort of bug repellent. There's no TV or phone in the room. At night the silence is wonderful, but when the electricity goes out, it is very dark. If you don't find candles in your room, ask for them at the front desk. The ranch is next to a river and has a restaurant, pool, sporting courts, and tons of adventure sport opportunities. The staff is very friendly and speak English well. This is the best place to stay in Jarabacoa if you plan on doing lots of adventure excursions. Many groups and independent travelers come to the ranch in the day to take part in their sporting menu.

(Hotel Gran Jimenoa (Av. La Confluenza, tel. 809/574-6304, superior room US$57–US$75 d) is a phenomenal option. Located along the banks of the Río Jimenoa, this hotel offers very clean, spacious, and comfortable rooms private baths and private balconies. Besides a large pool and a Jacuzzi on-site there is a separate open-air, thatch-roofed party hut overlooking the river where they hold events such as karaoke and dances. The restaurant overlooks the river as well and serves very good food. If there was such an award, they would win the Moon Dominican Republic's "Best Night's Sleep Award." A combination of the comfort of the beds and the roaring surf of the river and you will be sawing logs in no time. Hands down, the best hotel in town.

FOOD

Most people who visit Jarabacoa do so because they want to play hard and be adventurous all day long. By the time dusk sets in, they are ready for dinner and a relaxing evening.

D'Parque Galería Pizzeria (Calle Duarte 37 and Calle Hermanas Mirabal, tel. 809/574-

Coffee grown in Jarabacoa is the country's best.

© ANA CHAVIER CAAMAÑO

6749, 9 A.M.–midnight daily, US$3–17) sits on prime people-watching real estate in Jarabacoa, directly across from the Parque Central. And the menu has great variety: It's as if they were afraid to be labeled a "really great pizza joint," so they threw in a wonderful variety of other tasty dishes like grilled steak, fillet of grouper, *mofongo,* and various sandwiches and salads. Not only do they specialize in fantastic pizzas cooked in a special oven, but also in *comida criolla,* which is the national cuisine: characteristically flavorful without being spicy. The Creole food is mirrored by paintings depicting the pastoral countryside scene and *pilones*— mortar and pestles used for grinding spices in Dominican homes. The restaurant has a family-friendly and relaxed atmosphere.

Restaurante El Rancho (Av. Independencia 1, tel. 809/574-4557, 9 A.M.–11 P.M., US$8–15) is one of the oldest restaurants in Jarabacoa and is also part of the Rancho Baiguate family. It has a good assortment of international food and *comida criolla.* Locals and tourists have been praising this as the best place in town. Try the goat *mofongo* or a Dominican favorite, *asopao.* Food is made from locally grown products.

C Aroma de la Montaña (Independencia 43, tel. 829/452-6879, www.jamacadedios. com, Mon.–Thurs. 11 A.M.–10 P.M., Fri.–Sun. 11 A.M.–11 P.M., US$3–15). Whether you sit inside or out on the patio, you will realize why they say that "While God may be everywhere, He sleeps in Jarabacoa" when you see your view. Aroma de la Montaña is situated on the crest of a mountain within the gated community Jamaca de Dios, overlooking the valley and all of Jarabacoa. Michael and Lisa Ballentine, the very hospitable American expat owners, have created quite a stir in El Cibao with their country-club-meets-thatched-roof, *bohio*-style restaurant with the awesome view. House specialties are from the grill with Asian sea bass, steak Italian style, and eggplant tortini with red sauce. Salad portions are served with generosity using organic-grown products grown on the Jamaca de Dios land whenever possible. Culinary presentation is stellar, as is

the attentive service (a rarity in the Dominican Republic). Nights can be chilly in this open-air restaurant, so take an extra layer and make sure to drive a car capable of maneuvering up steep hills. Entrance to Jamaca de Dios is on the Carretera de Palo Blanco. Tell the guard you are going to the restaurant and follow the main road all the way up the mountain until you reach it.

Maybe dining in the restaurant of a hotel doesn't sound very adventurous, but **Hotel Gran Jimenoa** (Av. La Confluencia, tel. 809/574-6304, www.granjimenoa.com, 7 A.M.– 11 P.M. daily, US$12–35) is one of Jarabacoa's best bets. Its best feature is a fantastic view, as it's situated right alongside the Río Jimenoa's roaring waters. The food is not as good as the view, but it's not bad either. International choices include some very good fish dishes.

At the **Jarabacoa River Club** (Carretera Jarabacoa–Manabao Km 4, tel. 809/574-2456, www.jarabacoariverclub.com) you can purchase a day pass (RD$700) to swim in the five pools and eat at the buffet restaurant. You can eat in the à la carte restaurant, **El Bambú,** for extra cost. Every Monday night dance to live merengue or *bachata* music. When finished, this resort will be a beauty as it is built around the Río Yaque del Norte with a panoramic view of the mountains. The rooms were not yet complete.

Supermercado Jarabacoa (Av. Independencia 39, tel. 809/574-2780, 8 A.M.– 10 P.M. Mon.–Sat., 9 A.M.–1 P.M. Sun.) is a good all-purpose grocery store where you can get provisions for an independent hike or day at the waterfalls.

NIGHTLIFE

The Parque Central, as with many small towns in the Dominican Republic, is a major gathering point for social activity. It is a great place for people-watching during the day, and at night, the restaurants that abut it are a great place to go for a meal and a drink. As always, keep your eye on the *colmados,* as those too are the social centers of Dominican culture. Oftentimes, people hang out there and have a beer, listening to loud merengue or *bachata* talking and laughing the night away.

Start the evening off with karaoke at **Entre Amigos Café** (Calle Colón 182, tel. 809/574-7979, www.entreamigosbar.com, 9 P.M.–late Fri.–Sun.). The party really starts when the merengue and *bachata* start going.

INFORMATION AND SERVICES

Jarabacoa has an **Oficina de Turismo** (tel. 809/574-7287) in Plaza Ramírez on the second floor. They are very friendly but only speak Spanish.

Health and Emergencies

Politur (José Duran, tel. 809/754-3216) is open 24 hours.

Clínica Dr. Terrera (Av. Independencia 2-A, tel. 809/574-4597) offers 24-hour medical care.

Farmacia Miguelina (Mario N. Galan 13, tel. 809/574-2750, 7:30 A.M.–9:30 P.M. Mon.–Sat., 7:30 A.M.–4 P.M. Sun.) has a good variety of different medications, and they deliver, too, or try **Farmacia Independencia** (Independencia 44, tel. 809/574-4264, 8 A.M.–12:30 P.M. and 2–7:30 P.M. Mon.–Sat.).

Communications

For communication options, try the **TriCom** office on Avenida Independencia to make long-distance calls, the **post office** on the same stretch, or **A&G Servicios Múltiples** (Calle Independencia 43, tel. 809/574-4065).

The **Centro de Copiado y Papelería** (Calle Duarte 53, tel. 809/574-2902) is available for Internet services.

GETTING THERE

Flying in to Santiago is best as it is only an hour's drive to Jarabacoa. The town is equidistant from both Puerto Plata and Santo Domingo at roughly 130 kilometers from each.

Caribe Tours (Calle José Duran 3, tel. 809/574-6299) has regular service to Jarabacoa from Santo Domingo (US$5.50) at 7 A.M., 10 A.M., 1:30 P.M., and 4:30 P.M. with a stop in La Vega (US$2.30). However, right next door to this terminal is a *guagua* stop where for about US$1 less there is a *guagua* that leaves for La Vega every 20 minutes or so.

GETTING AROUND

Walking is easy within the city of Jarabacoa. But if you are staying out of the town, you'll need some transportation, whether renting a car or hiring a ride of some sort, especially if you plan to be out at night. Taxis usually hang around near the intersection of Duran and Independencia. *Motoconchos* should only be hired during the day.

Car-rental agencies are numerous for such a small town. It is best to rent an SUV for this area since roads can be rough and *certainly,* the best idea is to rent it in nearby Santiago from a trustworthy company that you know. However, here in town **Francis Luna Rent a Car** (Carretera a Salto Jimenoa, tel. 809/574-2981, 8 A.M.–noon and 2–6 P.M. Mon.–Sat., 8 A.M.–noon and 2–5 P.M. Sun.) is a standard choice.

Parques Nacionales Bermúdez y Ramírez

Together the national parks of Armando Bermúdez and José del Carmen Ramírez occupy a whopping 1,530 square kilometers of the central mountainous area, which includes the highest point in the Antilles, Pico Duarte, and neighboring peaks La Pelona, La Rucilla, and Pico Yaque. The parks were established in the late 1950s in an effort to salvage what was left of the virgin forest of the island. Since Columbus and his men arrived, it's estimated that nearly two-thirds of the island's forests were destroyed due to fire and development.

The northern **Parque Nacional Armando Bermúdez** is the larger of the two, with 766 square kilometers of protected area. It has both subtropical humid forest and subtropical rainforest temperate zones, giving it a perpetual spring-like climate with temperatures sometimes dipping to a chilly 18°F (-8°C) during December and January nights, leaving a thin layer of frost over the foliage. Flora of the park is varied and depends upon the elevation but mainly consists of local pine trees like the Creole pine *(Pinus occidentalis)*, a tree endemic to the island.

The park is home to many birds and other fauna like the Hispaniolan parrot, Hispaniolan trogon, the palm chat (the Dominican national bird), the Hispaniolan woodpecker, the hutia (a rodent), and a wild boar species. In the lower elevations, small snakes are found.

Directly south of Bermúdez is the **Parque Nacional José del Carmen Ramírez,** covering 764 square kilometers of the Cordillera Central. Inside its region are the Yaque del Sur, San Juan, and Mijo Rivers, and its climate is subtropical humid mountain forest. This park is also home to the Valle del Tétero, where you'll find pre-Columbian rock art.

Combined, the two parks have lavish amounts of water running through the region. More than 10 of the country's main river systems flow through them, making them some of the most fertile regions in the nation, irrigating almost 5,000 hectares of land.

Planning a vacation within the national parks alone is a way to experience the Dominican Republic in a way that most tourists do not. If you are hiking, plan on having a couple of days of preparation and at the very least 2–5 days of hiking time, depending on which trail you decide to take. Everyone entering the park must have a guide accompanying them.

If your time in the parks is only a leg of your trip within the greater Dominican Republic, save a couple of days for exploration at least. Spending a cool night in the mountain air is a refreshing break from the humidity and sticky heat of the coastal areas. Plus, you'll want a couple of afternoons for exploration of waterfalls, bird-watching, or whatever catches your attention.

◖ PICO DUARTE

The "Dominican Alps" are home to the highest peak in the Caribbean. While Pico Duarte is not the Matterhorn of Switzerland, it does stand tall at 3,087 meters. Surprisingly, while the Matterhorn weighs in at 4,478 meters and was conquered for the first time in 1865, no attempts to climb Pico Duarte occurred until 1944.

Not so surprisingly, the peak used to be named Pico Trujillo, when the dictator predictably named it after himself during his tenure. But when he was assassinated, the peak was renamed for founding father Pablo Duarte.

This challenging climb has been made a little easier since the 1980s, when cutting of trails was begun in an effort to increase ecotourism. Currently, nearly 3,000 people hike Pico Duarte and the surrounding peaks every year.

HIKING TRAILS

When choosing a route to take to the top of Pico Duarte, consider how long you've got to spend and honestly ask yourself what sort of stamina or at what athletic level are you able to hike. There are five different routes with varying degrees of stamina needed.

EL CIBAO

DON'T FORGET YOUR CAMERA: WHAT TO TAKE ON YOUR HIKE TO PICO DUARTE

Many hikers prepare for so long about the logistics of how to get to the top of the mountain that they lose sight of what to put (or what not to put) in their packs. Here are some suggestions from head to toe and beyond.

Head: Hat, sunglasses, and eyeglasses (or contacts).

Body: Two to three inner layer shirts, one pullover long sleeve sweatshirt type (middle layer), swimsuit, underwear, and one waterproof rain jacket.

Hands: You may want to consider gloves. It can get very cold at night.

Legs: One pair of shorts, one pair of pants.

Feet: Hiking boots or good walking shoes. But, for the sake of your feet and your mood, don't take shoes that you haven't broken in yet. These should be well-worn shoes. Extra laces might be a good idea. If you don't use them someone will. Take three pairs of socks. Bring sandals for around camp.

Equipment and Gear: Binoculars, camera, sunblock, bug repellent, personal water bottle, bandana, medium-sized towel, flashlight or headlamp, personal first aid kit, toiletries, hand sanitizer, pocketknife, sleeping bag, and mat.

Other: Prescription medication, a smaller pack (e.g., a fanny pack) if you are having a mule carry your larger bag.

Remember to pack the garbage out that you have brought in and leave no footprint behind.

The five routes differ in that the first two routes (La Ciénaga and Mata Grande) leave the Cibao Valley rising upward via the northern slope of the Cordillera Central within the Parque Nacional Armando Bermúdez. Trade winds in this area bring greater amounts of rain, and there are many natural freshwater sources for a large extent of the way. The latter three routes rise via the southern slope of the Cordillera Central within the Parque Nacional José del Carmen Ramírez, where rain is less prevalent, and therefore have a drier climate with fewer potable water sources.

La Ciénaga to Pico Duarte

This route starts in the small town of La Ciénaga just west of Jarabacoa. It is the most popular route to Pico Duarte because it is the shortest and easiest, at 23.1 kilometers one way. Hiring an independent guide is easier in La Ciénaga than in other launching points. The park guides recommend to reserve three days and two nights for this hike. Beginning a final ascent to the peak well before dawn will reward you with the astonishing sunrise while on top. This route's vertical ascent is about 2,280 meters.

Getting to La Ciénaga from Jarabacoa is as easy as flagging down a *público,* a regular car (usually rather worn down) used as an inexpensive taxi. Or catch a *guagua* for about US$3.

Mata Grande to Pico Duarte

This is the second most difficult route and a popular alternative to the La Ciénaga route. It comes recommended as the most beautiful route of the five. It is a hike of 90 kilometers round-trip that takes three days and has a 3,800-meter ascent, leaving from Mata Grande near San José de las Matas. You'll go over the second-highest peak, La Pelona, too, finally summiting Pico Duarte on the third day. Hiring mules and guides in Mata Grande is similar to in La Ciénaga; secure them two days ahead, and strongly consider hiring a pack mule (the guide may insist) and even a cook (US$10 per day). Your guide and/or cook can help you decide how much food to bring and what to buy.

If you are looking for a more challenging climb than the La Ciénaga one, this is a good choice. Making the trip with organized tours is possible and often easier on you, especially if you don't speak Spanish. The trailhead at Mata

© ANA CHAVIER CAAMAÑO

More than 10 of the DR's main rivers flow through Parques Nacionales Bermúdez y Ramírez.

Grande is located about 13 miles south east of San José de las Matas; take the marked turnoff at Pedregal toward Mata Grande, 15 kilometers down the road to the ranger station.

Sabaneta to Pico Duarte

Sabaneta to Pico Duarte (the Sabaneta just north of San Juan de la Maguana—not the one near Dajabón) is the most arduous of the direct routes and takes three days. The vertical ascent is 3,800, just like the Mata Grande trek, but 96 kilometers round-trip. There are two campsites along the way: Alto de la Rosa and Macutico, where you'll stop on the first and second nights. Again, a guide is obligatory and pack mules are highly recommended. The positive aspect about this trek is that since it is the longest, there will be less overcrowding. Take the highway to Sabaneta north for 20 kilometers from San Juan de la Maguana.

Constanza to Pico Duarte

This route is 86 kilometers round-trip and has a 1,600-meter vertical ascent that takes

3–5 days to navigate depending on your ability level. Constanza is the easternmost departure point. On the first day of your hike via this route, you'll see the impact that humans have had on the area as you will traverse farmland and small towns and onward into more densely vegetated areas on the second day that are recovering from previous human encroachment. The turnoff for Constanza is between La Vega and Bonao on the Carretera Duarte. The only tour company offering this route is **Mountain Expedition** out of Constanza; otherwise this is a very difficult route to navigate on your own.

Las Lagunas to Pico Duarte

This route is 72 kilometers round-trip and has a vertical ascent of 2,000 meters. It's a six-day trip leaving from Las Lagunas outside of Padre Las Casas in the Azua Province. After about 20 kilometers, it unites with the Constanza route.

To get to the Las Lagunas liftoff spot, you'll leave San Juan de la Maguana, traveling east along the Carretera Sánchez; turn left (north) at the sign for the Cruce de las Yayas and go nine kilometers to Padre Las Casas. Take a left at the town's main intersection and travel about 100 meters farther to the ranger station. No tour companies offer this trek, so you will need to hire a guide and mules here.

Organized Tours and Guides

There are tour companies that provide worry-free packages of treks to Pico Duarte, or you can wing it on your own by hiring a guide at the park entrances. The advantage of booking through a tour company is that everything will be taken care of: where you'll sleep, what you'll eat, transportation to the launch point. It is a convenient solution for those who don't have time to plan prior to arrival or are not experienced multiday hikers. If you've never done it before, there is a lot you could forget, so it is best to leave the details to the professionals so you can concentrate on just having fun.

Rancho Baiguate (Jarabacoa, Carretera a Constanza, tel. 809/574-6890, www.ranchobaiguate.com) has treks in 3- to 5-day packages

EL CIBAO

that vary in price depending on how many people are in the group. Call or email to reserve your spot and get a price quote. Prices start at US$255.

Although located in Cabarete, **Iguana Mama** (Cabarete, tel. 809/571-0908, www.iguanamama.com, 8 A.M.–5 P.M. daily) is one of the best trekking companies in the country. For US$450, they'll do all the prep, and you'll just enjoy yourself for three days and two nights riding mules, spotting rare birds, traversing rivers and creeks, and of course, hiking to the top of the highest peak in the Caribbean.

Mountain Expedition (tel.829/801-7199 or 809/674-1596, erivanbittar@hotmail.com) is a company based in Constanza that will arrange for lots of different mountain excursions, whether on foot, horseback, or four-wheeler. As far as trekking to Pico Duarte goes, this is the only outfitter that will take you from Constanza, preferably in February (when the heavy rain season is usually done). It's a three-day trip (prices start at US$150).

If you would rather be independent of a tour company, the national park fee is RD$100 per person. Guides typically cost around US$10–20 per day and can be found by asking at the park entrances' ranger stations. You can't be completely independent, though; hiring a guide is mandatory. The parks require that for overnight hikes, there is at least one guide for every three trekkers. Most guides take along a mule to carry their equipment, but it is generally a good idea to hire additional mules to assist in carrying your own loads; they cost about US$10 per day. Something else to consider when contemplating the necessity of renting a mule—many hikers find that partway through their journey to the summit, the road gets a little too rough, and that they are not as physically up to the challenge as they thought they were. In cases like these—not all that uncommon, actually—people find that spending part of the journey on the back of a mule is a welcome relief. Have your hands free for photo taking! For a mule to ride (RD$350/day) or to carry your packs (RD$300/day) you'll need to contact Alex Corona of the Ecotour Department (tel. 809/604-4862) to make reservations.

Custom dictates that you buy all provisions for the whole journey, for yourself and the guides, and tip them at the end. In making arrangements for your trek independently, it is best to find the guide a couple of days in advance so that preparations can be made with adequate time. They will help you figure out how much food to buy, too. You'll need to bring bottled water or some sort of purification system. Just remember to pack out what you take in. Guides are usually willing to tailor trips to your needs and desires (although the cost will vary accordingly).

ACCOMMODATIONS AND FOOD

Most people who come to hike Pico Duarte stay in Jarabacoa or Constanza hotels—that is, until they are on the actual hike. There are about a dozen campgrounds along the way providing very basic shelter. These cabins are basically an empty wooden box and do not have beds (you sleep on the floor). It is not possible to reserve a cabin and they are not tended to by the parks on a regular basis. There are kitchenettes outside of the cabins to cook your meals.

INFORMATION AND SERVICES

Admission to the park is RD$100 and you must be accompanied by a guide at all times. The **ranger stations** (8 A.M.–5 P.M.) are at the start of each of the La Ciénaga, Sabaneta, Mata Grande, Las Lagunas, and Constanza trails. Here you can ask for maps (but it's rare that they are stocked with them) and ask about guides if you are not hiking with an organized tour group.

Preparation

Climbing Pico Duarte is no small feat. Preparing, both mentally and physically, for the (at minimum) two-day hike to its apex can be something of a task in itself. Before you throw on your boots and strap on your backpack, there are quite a few details to consider.

Generally, a trip up Pico Duarte requires a good deal of packing. First off, proper attire is key to enjoying your journey. A variety of clothing will help ensure your comfort through the temperamental climate. The temperature typically ranges 12–21°C (54–70°F) but can dip below freezing, especially in the winter months. Yearly rainfall is between 1,000 and 4,000 millimeters, so waterproof gear is invaluable. Toiletries like sunscreen, toilet paper, and bug repellent will also help make your trip more comfortable and safer. Hiking boots are a must! (Keep in mind, even the top-of-the-line hiking boots will be of little use to you if they are not thoroughly broken in.) Some of the route can be tough going, ranging from dry, rocky terrain to muddy paths to slippery stone, so protect your feet, ankles, and joints as much as possible. A walking stick might also come in handy and make navigating the uneven topography a little easier. Simpler shoes, like sneakers or sandals, are good to wear once you've reached the campsite. If the idea of sharing a cabin with a bunch of strangers is not appealing, some camping items you may need are sleeping bags, flashlights, cookware, and tents.

Constanza

Constanza is in a circular valley surrounded by mountains 1,200 meters above sea level. The pastoral scenery offers some of the best views in the country and is what makes it a favorite getaway spot for Dominicans and foreigners. Although it is not a destination filled with as many activities as Jarabacoa, it is a peaceful respite and a jumping off point to one of the routes to Pico Duarte.

The fertile grounds are the livelihood for many families in the region. In the 1950s, Trujillo invited 200 Japanese families to the area to farm the land. His hope was to convert the land into a highly productive agricultural center. Today, many Japanese families remain and the area cultivates a great deal of the country's produce for local consumption and exportation. Although winter temperatures can sometimes dip down to freezing at night, the marvelously fertile ground and pleasant daytime temperatures stimulate the growth of strawberries, cabbage, potatoes, onions, cauliflower, and a great deal of garlic as well as flowers.

Constanza is a wonderful choice for those looking for ecotourism options like mountain biking, four wheeling, motorcycling, hang-gliding, trekking, jeep safari trips, and horseback riding. Even just taking a dip in the cool crystalline waters of the natural spa at El Arroyazo is an adventure unlike the standard beach-bum Caribbean vacation.

SIGHTS

Since most of the sights worth seeing near Constanza are quite far from the town itself, you'll need a good four-wheel-drive to get around and to reach many of the sights and activities.

Santuario de La Virgen de Altagracia

Driving on the Carretera Santo Domingo–Constanza, you will reach a curve at a very high point where you will find this small church. This popular stopping point offers devout Catholics an opportunity to light a candle and offer prayers to La Virgen de la Altagracia or buy one of the rosaries that will no doubt be sold outside by a vendor. Others can marvel at the valley that lies beyond this mountainside. Constanza is 38 kilometers away, but you can easily see it from this vantage point.

◖ Parque Nacional Valle Nuevo

Located 16 kilometers south of Constanza is Valle Nuevo National Park. The road to it is horrific, but beautiful views make it worth the work. The park covers an area of 657 square kilometers. This protected forest is 2,640 meters

EL CIBAO

EL CIBAO

© ANA CHAVIER CAAMAÑO

Constanza's fertile grounds support many farmers and their families.

above sea level and the climate can be cool and wet with an annual average rainfall over 2,500 millimeters. It is excellent for bird-watching, with 65 species of birds in the park, including the blue-hooded euphonia, the pine warbler, and the white-winged warbler, which is endemic to Hispaniola.

The three-tiered waterfall **Salto de Aguas Blancas** is in the Valle Nuevo park. It is 135 meters high and falls into a gorgeous pool whose average temperature is 10° C (50°F). You'll definitely need a tough four-wheel-drive to make the two-hour round-trip venture to this park.

On the higher plains of the Valle Nuevo, you'll encounter a monument built in 1957 by the communities of Constanza and San Juan de Ocoa. **Las Pirámides** mark the geographic center of the Dominican Republic. This is also very close to the area where Colonel Francisco Caamaño Deño, former guerilla leader, general, and president, was murdered while fighting the regime of President Joaquín Balaguer. A monument is placed in his honor.

Reserva Científica Ebano Verde

At one time, the endangered native green ebony *(ébano verde)* tree faced extinction. It was threatened due to its coveted precious wood. But in 1989, a 23-square-kilometer scientific reserve was created by a nonprofit foundation to preserve it, and now 621 plant species are protected in its boundaries. This reserve is meant to represent the ecosystem that exists in the entire zone. It is made up of a central mountain range between La Vega, Jarabacoa, and Constanza. There are also amphibious, reptilian, and mammalian species (like solenodons and bats), plus 59 species of birds including the *cotorra* and *el zumbadorcito* (which is the second smallest bird in the world), 17 of which are endemic to the island. The reserve is 30 kilometers northeast along the road from Constanza. Once inside you'll find a six-kilometer trail and information posted on trees.

To do a seven-kilometer-long nature walk in the Ebano Verde, you must first call the office of **Fundación PROGRESSIO** (tel. 809/565-1422) in Santo Domingo to arrange opening of the gates. You'll definitely want to drive a four-wheel-drive vehicle and wear some good hiking boots and take plenty of water. The climate in this part of the country is significantly cooler, so take some layers you can wear and peel off if you get warm. The temperature can certainly drop both in the early morning and at night.

The first entrance point is 15 kilometers from the crossroad of El Abanico on the Carretera Duarte at the hermitage of Casabito. Six kilometers farther at El Arroyazo, another entrance can be found. Here you will also find the Ebano Verde Science Reserve. If the museum is open (irregular hours) you can go in and see some photos and drawings of flora and fauna (in Spanish only).

This entrance will also lead you to the **Balneario El Arroyazo,** a natural pool created from a waterfall in the El Arroyazo river. Anyone can swim there for free. This entrance, museum, and balneario are three kilometers off the main road to Constanza.

ACCOMMODATIONS

It may feel awkward to pack warm pajamas for a trip to the Caribbean, but if you're sleeping in the cool Dominican Alps climate, you might need them. **Mi Casa** (Luperón at Sánchez, tel. 809/539-2764, US$15 d) has 11 very basic yet clean rooms with private bathrooms; one is a suite that can sleep four people. There's a restaurant on-site.

◖ **Alto Cerro** (two kilometers east of town, tel. 809/539-1553, www.altocerro.com, US$30 d, camping US$10) is on a bluff outside of Constanza. This tourist complex has two- and three-bedroom villas, rooms, and camping facilities, and all have panoramic views of the fertile valley below. The villas are equipped for two, four, five, or seven people with balconies, TV, phone, fireplace, and safe. The rooms are spacious and comfortable and operate on a bed-and-breakfast plan, whereas the suites and villas have kitchens and there is a small market for provisions. But if you don't feel like cooking, there is a restaurant that beats going all the way into town for the next available dining choice. It is a wonderful place for families that offers horseback riding, quad rental, and a large play area for kids. This complex is an excellent value, no matter which accommodation you choose. Meal plans can be arranged.

Hotel Vista del Valle (Antonio María García 41 and Matilde Viñas, tel. 809/539-2071, US$22 d Mon.–Fri., US$36 Fri.–Mon.) is kitty-corner from the baseball field. You'll have hot water and a TV. Room 9 has a skylight and double doors that open out the front of the hotel, tile floors, and high ceilings. Rooms without exterior windows have a mystery smell and don't have the same vaulted ceilings. Ventilation is key here. This hotel is in town, so you can walk to do things, a plus if you want to be in the middle of happenings.

Rooms on the second floor of **Mi Cabaña** (Carretera General Antonio Duvergé, tel. 809/539-2930, www.micabana.net, US$20 d Mon.–Fri., US$25 Fri.–Mon.) have balconies off the front and back of the room with phenomenal views out the back. The bad news: The walls are thin. Like rice paper. The light is dim and there's no bedside lamp, and with the lights going out anyway, regardless if they have a generator or not, things get very dark when you're this removed from city lights. There's no hot water in the sink and no phone in the room. Remember, it's cold in Constanza. These rooms are completely devoid of warmth both in temperature and character. However, you will get a mini refrigerator and TV (non-cable), good size room, and a vaulted ceiling on the second floor. The resort has a pool, basketball court, and outdoor eating area. They do have a good breakfast buffet.

At **Hotel Bohio** (Calle Rufino Espinosa 15, tel. 809/539-2696, www.hotelbohio.com, RD$800 d Mon.–Thurs., RD$1,400 d Fri.–Sun.) the very friendly staff welcome you warmly as you enter into the living room-like entrance of this small 20-room hotel. It's not a fancy place but the rooms are clean, and some have small sunny terraces with mini-fridge. Otherwise, it's very basic.

Rancho Constanza (Calle Duarte, tel. 809/539-3268, www.ranchoconstanza.tripod. com) has cabins with full kitchens and all utensils you'll need. There is a playground on site for kids, and the cabins are clean and spacious with basic furniture. Staff can arrange for a

EL CIBAO

variety of excursions like treks to Arroyo Frio or Aguas Blancas or an agricultural tour.

Hotel Valle Nuevo (Calle Gratereaux, tel. 809/539-1144) is a new three-level hotel located in town and behind a large security gate. The rooms are kept simple but very clean. Each room has a private hot-water bathroom, and each floor has a nice balcony to share.

At **Villa Pajon** (Reserva Científica Valle Nuevo, tel. 809/412-5210 or 809/412-5209, www.villapajon.com, US$55–140) seven cabins are surrounded by lush forest (nine kilometers south of Aguas Blancas) and built on the site of an old sawmill. It does get cold out here, so each cabin has its own fireplace and beds are fitted with adequate bedding for chilly nights. They all have private baths, kitchens, outdoor barbecues, and multiple bedrooms. Bring your own food or, at an additional cost, you can arrange for all cooking and cleaning to be done for you. Villa Pajon can also arrange for hiking, agrotourism, and horseback riding adventures. If you are looking for a gorgeous place in the country very removed from the hubbub of regular society, this ecolodge is tops.

FOOD

In the Dominican Republic's garden, Constanza offers fresh local produce not typically found elsewhere on the island in such abundance.

Lorenzo's (Luperón 83, tel. 809/539-2008, 8 A.M.–11 P.M. daily, US$5–11) serves fantastic Dominican down-home cooking like *chivo guisado* (goat sautéed and served in a sauce), guinea fowl, or rabbit cooked in wine. Lorenzo's also has an assortment of pastas, pizzas, and sandwiches.

At ◖ **Aguas Blancas** (Rufino Espinosa 54, tel. 809/539-1561, 10 A.M.–late daily, US$4–10), they like to say that they'll close when everyone goes home. And it is a popular place that comes highly recommended as the best in town. It serves great typical Dominican *comida* for low prices. *La bandera dominicana,* which is a plate of rice and beans with salad and your choice of meat, is always a good choice.

Rancho Macajo (Carretera Duvergé, tel. 809/707-3805), a restaurant and zoo (no, really!) is a popular stop-off for excursioners before heading out in the afternoon. On the

produce aplenty in El Cibao

© ANA CHAVIER CAAMAÑO

menu are international dishes like tacos and pizza. But you should really try some of the Dominican dishes, like *sancocho*.

Go to **Mercado Municipal** (Gratereaux at 14 de Julio, 7 A.M.–6 P.M. Mon.–Sat., 7 A.M.–noon Sun.) if you need some fresh produce or to see the splendid variety that grows in this very fertile region.

INFORMATION AND SERVICES

For tourist information there is the **Cluster Ecoturistico Constanza** (Calle Viña near Abreu, tel. 809/539-1022, www.constanza.com.do), which is actually a lot more useful (with tons of information) than the **Oficina de Turismo** (Calle Matilde Viña, tel. 809/539-2900, 9 A.M.–1 P.M. and 2–6 P.M. Mon.–Fri.) in town, where they have limited information and an occasional brochure to give out.

Health and Emergencies

For health care, you have to go to Santiago since there is no health care at all in Constanza. The **Farmacia Constanza** (Luperón 76 at Libertad, tel. 809/539-2880, 8 A.M.–11 P.M. Mon.–Sat., 8 A.M.–9 P.M. Sun.) has a decent selection of medications and is at the west end of town.

Money and Communications

Banco León (Luperón 19, tel. 809/539-2603, www.leon.com.do, 8 A.M.–5 P.M. Mon.–Fri., 9 A.M.–1 P.M. Sat.) is centrally located, has an ATM, and exchanges money.

There is a call center, **Plaza de Servicios y Telecomunicaciones** (Luperón 11, tel. 809/539-2337) that offers international phone service.

GETTING THERE AND AROUND

If you're driving to Constanza, you'll need a four-wheel-drive vehicle for the hills. Going on a clear day is best. Drivers tend to drive in the middle of the road. A quick honk around the blind corners is wise; open your window and listen for others doing the same. Fog or

low clouds can make your trip a huge mistake or nerve-wracking and make your morning *mangú* come right back up. You'll need to remain quite alert on these roads. You'll pay a RD$30 toll getting out of Santo Domingo and the rest of the highway is a nice new road.

The Carretera Duarte (from Santo Domingo) is the safest way into Constanza. At the summit of a mountain pass, you will pass the Santuario de La Virgen de Altagracia, and at that point you will start your descent into Constanza.

Arriving from Jarabacoa, you will take the Carretera Jarabacoa–El Río–Constanza, 48 kilometers of pure jostling nightmare. There are plans to rebuild this road, but no real progress yet.

The main drag of Constanza is Calle Luperón. On this street is a gas station that doubles as a bus stop at the eastern end. You can catch buses going to Santo Domingo (US$5.50), Santiago (US$5.50), and La Vega (US$2.75).

Guaguas also take off from the same stop (*la parada* to the locals). You can catch one going to Jarabacoa (US$2.80) and El Abanico. From these two stops you can connect to other cities.

La parada (the stop) is also the place to find *motoconchos* and taxis to take you around locally, although Constanza is very easily walked. As with all forms of transportation, make sure you agree on the price before getting on board.

MOCA

Moca is the Taíno word meaning "tree that grows at the edge of rivers." Lying just west of Salcedo, Moca is the capital of the Espaillat province located 16 kilometers east of Santiago. It has been an important agricultural base in the country since it was founded in 1780. Coffee, cocoa, and tobacco are produced here in abundance. It has been said that the best yucca in the country is grown here.

Moca has played an important role in two periods in Dominican history. First, it was the birthplace of the short-lived Moca Constitution of 1842 that set democratic standards for government. Secondly, it was the site of the assassination of Ulises Heureaux, the tyrannical Dominican president who led his people into great economic decline.

Although there is no monument to commemorate the Moca Constitution, there is a monument dedicated to the men who assassinated Heureaux in downtown Moca, in a small park where Heureaux died on Calle Vásquez.

La Sacrada Corazón de Jesús (Calle Sánchez and Calle Corazón) has a pretty array of stained glass windows, a remarkable clock tower, and an impressive pipe organ.

There are very few choices for accommodations in Moca, but one decent one is **Hotel Oasis** (Calle Córdova 121, tel. 8095/578-5994, US$30), with comfortable rooms featuring air-conditioning, TV in each.

Try not to miss **El Caffeto Bar & Restaurant** (Carretera Moca–Jamao, La Cumbre, tel. 809/471-0015, caffeto@hotmail.com) on your way into town. They have live jazz music on the fourth Friday of every month (possibly more nights in the works). More importantly, the magnificent view of the Cibao from this restaurant is spellbinding and the food is good too. In town, try **D'Gala de la Maza Café and Restaurant** (Av. De La Maza 7, tel. 809/578-2756, US$8–15) specializing in seafood and *comida criolla*.

SALCEDO

Salcedo is a town for painters to love, Dominican historians to make a pilgrimage to, and for women of any nationality to come and pay homage to, and it will all be apparent by the first sight of the water tower on the Carretera Moca–Salcedo.

Salcedo, home of the famous Mirabal family, is 14 kilometers east of the town of Moca and 22 kilometers west of San Francisco de Macorís. The water tower has a hand-painted mural of the three Mirabal sisters, who are revered in Dominican history and became martyrs for Dominican liberty and women's rights. The day of their murder, November 25, has been declared as the International Day Against Violence Towards Women. Dedé Mirabal, the last surviving sister, still lives in Salcedo.

Accommodation choices are slim in Salcedo. It is best saved for a day trip to visit the sights. However, if you must stay, an option is **Hotel La Casona Gran Imperial** (Calle Doroteo Tapia 51, tel. 809/577-4468, RD$350–1,000). Be careful what you book; if you don't mind sharing a bathroom (five or six of the rooms share a bathroom), then go for the lower price. But if you want your own, then you need to specify and pay the higher price. The rooms are clean, but the "Gran Imperial" title is stretching it. The hotel is centrally located and will do if you get stuck in Salcedo. Not many windows.

❰ Ruta de Murales

Throughout the town, you will see countless colorful murals along the **Mural Route,** which travels throughout the town of Salcedo and onward to Tenares. The bulk of its murals are in Salcedo. One theme that is represented in the murals throughout is the presence of butterflies in many of the paintings. This is in reference to the Mirabal women's codename in their fight against Trujillo. Murals are painted on fences, on government buildings, houses, and on banks. Murals are absolutely everywhere and they have become a sense of pride for Salcedo and a defining character for the town. Meander through the streets by car, hire a *motoconcho* (you can find one by the Plaza Central), or just walk, but certainly take your camera.

Museo de Hermanas Mirabal

This museum (9 A.M.–9 P.M. daily, RD$30) is the house that the Mirabal sisters grew up in. The house has been "preserved" with period furnishings and personal belongings. While the interior may be cheesy to some, to those who know their Dominican history or even just love the book *In the Time of the Butterflies* by Julia Alvarez, the Mirabal home is tantamount to a pilgrimage spot despite its forced sentiment (the girls' dresses and their personal affects have been laid out as if they have just left). In the beautiful and meticulously kept garden are the graves of Las Mariposas (The Butterflies, their underground codename)— Patria, Minerva, and María Theresa. You can pay your respects to the martyred women.

Feria Artesanal

During the first week of August, a blazing hot time of year to be in these parts, hundreds of people gather their art and sell it at the Feria Artesanal. You will be able to purchase pottery and other Dominican handicrafts like woven baskets, carved figurines, and paintings.

Tours

Ecotourism and sustainable tourism are on the rise in the Dominican Republic, and in the land of coffee, there is no better combination than **The Coffee Route** (Calle Prof A Regalado 5, tel. 809/577-1475, www.larutadelcafedominicano.org). This is a cultural, educational, and ecological experience. You will walk (different degrees of difficulty) or ride on donkey back while observing coffee plantations, blooming tropical flora, and mountain scenery and enjoying the local hospitality. You will be escorted along the still-undiscovered-by-mass-tourism trail by expert ecological guides. You will stay in local homes and eat local food. You will visit not only coffee plantations, but also cocoa producers and other local cultivators. You will taste the Atabey (the Taíno word for "Mother Earth") and Jamao (located in Salcedo) coffee, visit local craftsmen, and dine at restaurants. It is a well-rounded and educational tour looking at the rich and the impact that coffee has had on the culture of the Dominican Republic. There are two routes to chose from and packages within each: the Route of Atabey (one day RD$1,910, three days RD$5,205) or the Route of Jamao (one day RD$1,745, three days RD$5435).

EL CIBAO

THE SOUTHWEST

Driving through this part of the country, your eyes are met with a spectacular panoply of change: cactus-dotted deserts, lush plantations, towering mountains and cliffs, thriving crops, white-pebbled beaches, and serene lakes. Not many tourists choose to come to this region because it doesn't offer the conventional beach vacation idyll or must-see sights. The majority of the Southwest's beaches are carpeted with smooth white rocks along a rough-water, deep shoreline instead of white sand and calm waters. And the closer you get to Haiti, the hotter the climate gets and the more impoverished the towns are. But what is attractive about the Southwest is its uniqueness. It is a perfect destination for visitors seeking an off-the-beaten-path experience where you'll encounter gorgeous coastline vistas, a surreal desert terrain, remote and private beaches, flamingo colonies and crocodiles lazing on a river bank, and an extra-strong welcome from people who are glad to have tourism come knocking at their door.

The Southwest's history, while venerated and celebrated, is not memorialized with museums and grandeur here, but rather, through silent remembrance of its people. It was once the home of the great Taíno cacique Guarokuiá (or Enriquillo, as he was renamed by the Spaniards and is historically referred to), who fought off the Spanish conquistadors through a series of battles for 14 years. Freedom fighter Máximo Gómez, who went on to liberate the republic's sister nation, Cuba, also hailed from here. The black shadow of self-indulgent opulence and egoism of brutal dictator General Rafael Leonidas Trujillo Molina, who killed

© ALICIA CHAVIER CAAMAÑO

HIGHLIGHTS

◖ **Reserva Antropológica El Pomier:** This anthropological reserve holds one of the most significant collections of rupestrian art found in the Caribbean. A series of caves features about 4,000 paintings and 5,000 rock drawings by the Taíno, Ingeri, and Carib people (page 253).

◖ **San Rafael:** Take a dip in the cold and refreshing waters of the *balnearios* San Rafael, then enjoy the breathtaking and photo-perfect views along this highway stretch of the Península de Pedernales, where cliff-top vistas with flowers bloom against the backdrop of white-stone beaches and the azure Caribbean Sea (page 269).

◖ **Parque Nacional Jaragua:** Take a boat trip to watch the flamingos and 130 other species of birds in their natural habitat of this protected lagoon (page 269).

◖ **Bahía de las Águilas:** Charter a boat from the fishers at the **Las Cuevas** village to one of the most pristine and definitely the most remote beach in the Dominican Republic (page 270).

◖ **Parque Nacional Isla Cabritos and Lago Enriquillo:** Visit the crocodiles and endangered iguanas at Lago Enriquillo, four times saltier than the sea and the lowest point in the Caribbean (page 272).

LOOK FOR ◖ TO FIND RECOMMENDED SIGHTS, ACTIVITIES, DINING, AND LODGING.

THE SOUTHWEST

thousands of people throughout his regime, has stained the otherwise lovely town where he was born, San Cristóbal.

There is a feeling of remoteness from the rest of the Dominican Republic here. It is unlike the rest of the country in geography and most definitely in number of tourism dollars. The southwestern region is a destination for the adventurous visitor, the ecoconscious tourist, and those who want to immerse themselves in the Dominican culture without being separated by the guarded walls of resort complexes.

PLANNING YOUR TIME

To visit the Southwest, you could cover some major attractions in just a few days. Perhaps take a three-day weekend away from the city to make your way over the Península de Pedernales or scope out a driving loop around Lago Enriquillo. Whichever direction, inland or coastal, the best town to look to for a home base is Barahona. It offers the best accommodations options and has some semblance of a nightlife, albeit small.

If you plan a day at the beach, make it Bahía de las Águilas and save a day for it. You'll want

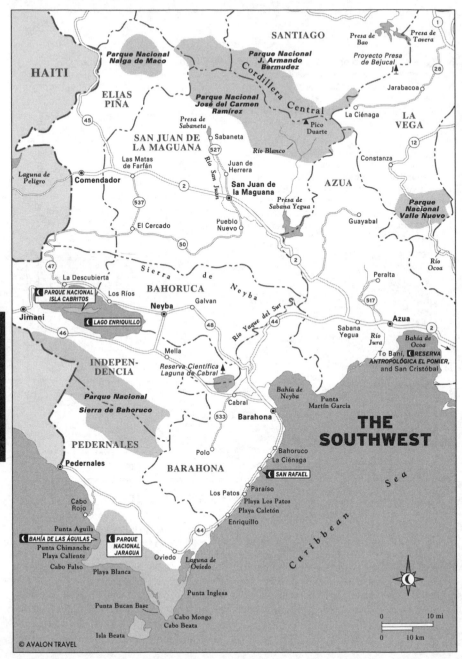

THE SOUTHWEST

to get there midmorning to have a day at the beach, so you'll have to spend your morning gathering provisions and securing the boat ride. The same is true for a loop around Lago Enriquillo, with the tour of the lake being only a couple of hours long.

West of Santo Domingo and the Interior

SAN CRISTÓBAL

Just 25 kilometers west of Santo Domingo is San Cristóbal, known infamously as the birthplace of the brutal dictator Rafael Leonidas Trujillo Molina, who ruled from 1930 until his assassination in 1961.

It is believed that the city was named after the nearby San Cristóbal fortress that Christopher Columbus had built on the Haina riverbank. But in 1934, Trujillo changed the name of the town to Ciudad Benemérita (Meritorious City), supposedly because it was the place where the first legal constitution of the Dominican Republic had been signed in the Palacio Municipal in 1844, but it probably had more to do with the fact that it was his birthplace. The name quickly reverted to San Cristóbal when Trujillo was killed and his regime overthrown.

Today's San Cristóbal is a good day trip from Santo Domingo and has the ghostly (or ghastly) memories of Trujillo's egoism and "hard-earned" (at the hands of the Dominican people that is) ostentatious wealth in the form of two of his old palaces. San Cristóbal, with a population near 170,000, buzzes like a mini Santo Domingo without its cosmopolitan feel. A good sampling of the pumping life and activity can be felt near the center, the Parque Colón, right by the cathedral. It is the gateway to the "Wild West" of the Dominican Republic, where the cacti start to dot the landscape and the ground becomes more arid. Although its vibe is busy like a city, it does not have the amenities of one and is, therefore, best for a day trip from Santo Domingo.

San Cristóbal has, a short distance north, a series of caves, **Cuevas El Pomier,** part of a series of interconnected caves, that contain a huge array of Taíno cave art and are home to thousands of bats.

Sights

Just west of town, on top of a hill, is **El Castillo del Cerro** (Castle on the Hill), one of Trujillo's houses—more of a palace really but it looks more like a giant post office. Trujillo had the six-story structure built in 1947 for US$3 million and never stayed one night in it when it got back to him that his confidants had criticized it. Trujillo quickly claimed that it was a gift from the townspeople. After Trujillo's death all five stories were looted, and today it sits like an opulently empty shell with some accents still clearly visible as testament to the lavish lifestyle he had: marble staircases, gold leafing, dining rooms, ballrooms with intricately painted ceilings, mosaic tiles, and multiple bedrooms and bathrooms. Trujillo commissioned José Vela Zanetti to paint murals in his opulent home. When the famous painter agreed, he went on to portray campesinos dancing with sad faces. This angered Trujillo (he had wanted them painted with happy faces, of course!) so much that the painter had to flee the country in fear of his life.

The second floor has a recreation room and library, on the third floor was where the dictator and his daughter had their living quarters, and the fifth floor was devoted entirely to Trujillo's beloved son, Ramfis. Perhaps the most surprising thing about El Castillo del Cerro is that it is not even a museum and yet you must wear long pants and sleeves and no sandals to be granted a tour. It simply is locked up and guarded by an armed guard who will open it up and show you around if you tip him. To get there, take Calle María Trinidad Sánchez to Avenida Luperón and take a left at the Isla gasoline station; veer right at the fork in the road, then left and up the hill. The tour is free.

© ANA CHAVIER CAAMAÑO

Iglesia Nuestra Señora de la Consolación, San Cristóbal

Casa de Caoba (Mahogany House), another of Trujillo's houses, was looted too after his death, and while it appears as though it was probably once a beautiful home, it was ransacked and sits empty. Not just empty but totally stripped and like a concrete ghost. This one is five kilometers north of town. Promises have been made off and on to restore it to its former glory, promises that have not been kept. This site could easily be skipped unless you are a hard-core Trujillo history buff. Casa de Caoba is not open to the public but sits on the opposite side of a chain-link fence. Visiting it is limited to looking at its skeletal remains from a short distance, unless you catch sight of the guard, in which case you can ask to be let in and shown around.

Iglesia Nuestra Señora de la Consolación (6–8 A.M. and 5:30–8 P.M. daily) was built on the Plaza Piedra Viva, where Trujillo's childhood home once stood and where he had originally intended to be buried (his remains are in France now). The church is a huge mustard-yellow and white structure that cost an exorbitant US$4 million to build back in 1946. Trujillo

spent government funds to build the church and the Plaza Piedra Viva. Inside the church is a large, truly beautiful mural from renowned Spanish muralist José Vela Zanetti.

Food

San Cristóbal is best left for a day trip. There are no satisfactory accommodation choices, but if it is a gastronomic tour of the Southwest that you are making, make sure not to miss **◖ Pastelería Chichita** (Calle General Leger 58, tel. 809/528-3012, 7:30 A.M.–midnight). This café-style restaurant has been around for over 50 years satisfying the people in San Cristóbal. Lately, the word of locals has spread and it has become a must-stop eatery with traditional Dominican favorites one would usually find at family celebrations: *pastelitos* and *empanadas, kipe, sancocho,* a truly killer *cosido* (RD$125), *arepitas,* fish, and *plátano.* They are most famous for their *pasteles en hojas,* which are similar to a tamale wrapped in a banana leaf; add a little catsup or hot sauce and they are a delectable treat.

Fela's Place (General Leger 55, tel. 809/288-2124, 8 A.M.–midnight) is a very informal place of cheap eats serving Dominican fare and specializing in chicken. San Cristóbal is known as the capital of the *pasteles en hoja,* a traditional dish made from plantain with meat or chicken sometimes added to the mixture that is then wrapped like a present in a banana leaf and boiled. Fela's is another of many of the good cheap-eat spots where you can get these little bundles for a quick and economical meal (about US$0.50 each), served with hot sauce on the side.

Information and Services

For health-related matters or emergencies, **Centro Médico Constitución** (Av. Constitución 61, tel. 809/288-2121) has a 24-hour emergency room.

The **Oficina de Turismo** (Av. Constitución, 9 A.M.–3 P.M. Mon.–Fri., tel. 809/528-1844) has limited information but a staff that is willing to help with any questions you may have.

For an ATM or money exchange, head to **Banco Popular** (Av. Constitución 97, tel. 809/528-4335, www.bpd.com.do, 8 A.M.–5 P.M. Mon.–Fri., 9 A.M.–1 P.M. Sat.) on Parque Colón.

Getting There and Around

San Cristóbal is 25 kilometers west of Santo Domingo and can be accessed easily by driving Highway 2, or you can catch a *guagua* from Parque Enriquillo in Santo Domingo. In San Cristóbal, you can catch a *guagua* back to Santo Domingo about every half hour or so from the Parque Central. If you're headed toward Barahona in the west, you'll need to go out to the main highway to flag down a *guagua*. There is no major bus terminal.

Taxis and *guaguas* are readily available in San Cristóbal near Parque Independencia.

AROUND SAN CRISTÓBAL

The area of San Cristóbal makes for a good day trip if you are staying in Santo Domingo. Spending a couple of hours in the town itself sightseeing is good enough, but then you should venture out and go to either the Reserva Antropológica El Pomier or to one of the area's beaches for a relaxing afternoon. These are both great self-guided tours good for those who want to get away from the tourist clogged areas and fold themselves in with local culture.

◖ Reserva Antropológica El Pomier

In Reserva Antropológica El Pomier (15 kilometers north of San Cristóbal, 8 A.M.–5 P.M. daily) there is a series of 57 interconnecting caves, the most significant collection of rupestrian art found in the Caribbean. The drawings and carvings (the latter are found only in the front of the cave where the sunlight is) in this anthropological reserve are from not just the Taíno Indians, but the Igneri and Carib as well, and are estimated at as much as 2,000 years old. For the Caribbean, this is tantamount to what the pyramids of Egypt are for the Middle East. The caves contain over 4,000 paintings and 5,000 rock drawings. Cave One contains 590 pictograms alone. Most of the paintings depict animals and birds with some

that are believed to be representative of deities. The caves that will be open to the public (five total) are undergoing renovation complete with walkways and electric lighting for viewing. The caves are also home to thousands of bats. In 2009 the caves were closed to the public for said remodeling. However, there are always some unofficial "guides" (Spanish only) hanging around ready to take you through the first and easiest one if you tip them. It is an easy walk because so far, the walkways are smooth and wide giving you an easy stroll through a very dark cave. The electrical system was not working, so definitely take your own flashlight. This is a unique cave experience regardless. Claustrophobics may not have fun with the lights being out.

The best way to get to the caves is by taxi or *motoconcho,* but make sure the driver knows that you need a ride back so that they either wait for you or come back. If you decide to drive, follow Avenida Constitución (in front of the cathedral) all the way out of town. It will lead you past the Casa de Caoba. Keep going until you see a sign to turn left to the *cuevas* (before the La Toma turnoff) at the fork in the road.

Beaches

There are two good beaches near San Cristóbal, and both are a fun option for a day in the sun, especially if you are staying in Santo Domingo and need a break. Since most people in the capital who want a beach getaway head toward the east to Boca Chica and Juan Dolio, going west makes for a more authentic and unique day trip. If you need to take a *guagua* from San Cristóbal, regular service leaves from the Parque Central to both Najayo and Palenque beaches.

Playa Najayo is 14 kilometers south of San Cristóbal on Carretera Palenque and followed six kilometers farther along by **Playa Palenque.** These beaches are especially popular hangouts for local families on the weekends and holidays. It is customary to order drinks or food if you plan to park yourself at one of the tables. Even if you have brought your own cooler of drinks/food, don't be surprised if you are asked to place an order. The seafood is very

THE SOUTHWEST

fresh and fried perfectly. You can often get it in a combo plate with rice and *plátano frito* (fried plantains) on the side. Add an ice cold Presidente to that and you have a nice day at the beach!

BANÍ

After driving past plush fields of sugarcane that wave through the countryside, you'll reach the town of Baní. The saltpans of Las Salinas, south of the city, are what have given Baní its major economic lift. Keep your eye out for roadside stalls selling mangoes. The *mango banilejo* has turned Baní into the mango capital of the country, and it is making its way into the international market as well. While they might be the smallest mangoes you've encountered, they will be the sweetest you'll ever eat. Other crops in the area are coconut, yucca, plantains, and onions. *Chivos* (goats) are raised here.

A lovely, friendly, prosperous, and clean town, Baní has very few tourist curiosities but is a great place for travelers to stop for the night if they can't make it to their final destination. It was here that the Cuban liberation fighter, Máximo Gómez Báez, was born on November 18, 1836.

Baní is known as the "city of poets" and was named to honor the Taíno cacique Baní, who is said to have been a very wise man.

You'll need a little desire for adventure to come to this part of the country. Construction on the road from San Cristóbal–Baní has been a little paralyzed as of late, but if you have a fixed need for discovery, following the "Route of the Mango," as it has been dubbed, will pay off with many rich discoveries along the way.

Sights

The **Casa de Máximo Gómez** (8 A.M.–5 P.M., free) is Baní's main attraction, really more of a park placed on what was the location of Gómez's childhood home, with what is said to be one log of the home. There is a bust of him, the Dominican and Cuban flags, and a mural with scenes depicting his life. The **Museo Municipal** (Calle Sánchez 1, 8 A.M.–noon Mon.–Fri., free) is on the first floor of

the Palacio del Ayuntamiento facing the park and is rather uneventful.

Playa Baní, while challenging to get to, is worth the effort. Both fishing and windsurfing are fantastic here, but very undeveloped. You won't find the windsurfing schools and rentals like in Cabarete. Farther west along the coast, the sand dunes at **Las Calderas** and salt gardens at **Las Salinas** make for surreal yet beautiful views and great photo opportunities.

Plaza de Pilones is not exactly a sight per se, but more of a place to buy a necessary object for cooking Dominican fare. You have your choice of very small to gigantic mortar and pestle sets made with the wood from the *cambron* trees. The Taínos introduced them to the Spanish and they are now found in every kitchen in the Dominican Republic. No kitchen is complete without one. They are a good, authentic gift to take home with you. The more elaborately decorated ones tend to be Haitian; the Dominican ones are basic and sturdy. You can't make an authentic *mofongo* without one (a plantain dish served right in the *pilón*). Plaza de Pilones is an outdoor market on the left side of the highway outside of Baní traveling toward Ázua. There is a booth to buy snacks. Look for it after you have passed the Parador Cruz de Ocoa.

The **fiesta patronal** of Baní, held from June 15 to June 24, will give you a chance to see a unique folkloric dance called *sarandunga*, which is danced in celebration of San Juan Bautista. Despite the reverence expected in honoring Saint John the Baptist, the customary dance is overflowing with the distinctive Afro-Latin rhythms of the *tambor* and the *güira* drums and is a flirtatious circular game between a man and woman occasionally brushing shoulders.

Accommodations and Food

Most people simply pass through Baní. But if you find yourself needing a place to rest for the night, there are a couple of choices. If you are simply looking to replenish your car trip munchie-snacks while driving through Baní or are on a day trip, you have stumbled into

LA RUTA DEL MANGO (THE MANGO ROUTE)

Following the Mango Route (a full-circle driving route) you will travel through the Peravia province in the southwestern region of the Dominican Republic. Even though it is the third smallest province in the country it offers a great deal of biodiversity to the landscape, including the largest set of dunes in the Caribbean.

The name of the route refers to the fruit that identifies Baní, as it is the largest producer of mangoes in the country. Don't leave this province without trying some mango.

Peravia was an active hot spot in both the Restoration and Independence wars, and many presidents, historical figures, and authors have hailed from this area.

Your first stop (and potentially your last on the way back) is **Las Marías** (Paya, Carretera 2, no phone), just five kilometers before Baní. This eatery is famous for regional sweets like *flan de leche,* candies, and *dulce de leche.* **Paya** is the center for the production of candy and sweets made from coconut and figs. Each July, there is a traditional horse race dedicated to St. James that dates back to colonial times.

After Paya, continue on the same road to **Baní,** where you will stop at the **Casa de Máximo Gómez** (8 A.M.-5 P.M., free) and the **Museo Municipal** (Calle Sánchez 1, 8 A.M.-noon Mon.-Fri., free), in honor of the son of Baní, General Máximo Gómez, who became a freedom fighter for Cuban independence. Here you will see some photos, copies of documents, a chronology of his life, and the last remains of his childhood home.

Not far away is **La Catedral de Nuestra Señora de Regla** (Calle Sánchez and Calle Mella), which was renovated in 2008; its 50-year-old facade was given a facelift. Inside, the painter Jaime Colson began work on several frescoes. His project was taken over as part of the refurbishment, and behind there is now a plaza with murals dedicated to the founders of Baní.

Still in Baní, make your way to the **Villa Sombrero,** filled with endangered 150-year-old *guayacán* trees. Villa Sombrero is also home to the **Museo Histórico de la Familia Ortiz.** General Fausto Ortiz was a hero during the wars of Restoration and Independence. The museum has odd hours and was closed when we passed through, but Villa Sombrero is lovely enough for a shady respite from your travels. The museum is on a small irrigation canal that runs through town across from the Immaculate Conception School on Calle Hnos. Peña.

Taking the main road again, head toward the famous national shrine to see the stone temple in honor of St. Martin de Porres in the community of Las Tablas. To access it you will need to take the road that begins next to the Zona Franca Banileja. This is a place of religious pilgrimage on the third of November. There is also a subtropical dry forest here.

Return to the main road and follow the Ruta del Mango signs. Pass through **Matanzas** on the southern coast. Matanzas is known for the furniture they make – their *mecedoras* (rocking chairs) are famous. Salome Ureña lived here for a while and wrote some of her most celebrated works. You will reach the **Plaza de Maíz** (Corn Plaza), a great opportunity for a snack made from the plant.

You will reach a fork in the road. The **Cruce de Arroyo Hondo** delineates two paths: one way to Las Salinas and the other toward Palmar de Ocoa. Go toward **Las Salinas.**

Las Dunas de Las Calderas (16 km south of Baní on Carretera Las Calderas) awaits; you can explore the dunes, salt mines, and beaches. Make sure to take your camera as you explore. To reach the beaches of Las Salinas, take the trail next to the salt mines. This is one of the best locations in the nation for windsurfing.

If you are looking for a restaurant or a beach club, look no further than the **Salinas Hotel & Restaurant** (Las Salinas, Puerto Hermoso 7, tel. 809/866-8141). After a long day, this hotel may tempt you into staying the night before you make the return to Las Marías and end your trip with dessert.

THE SOUTHWEST

the town with the Dominican reputation for the best *colmados*. What does that mean? That means a lot for Dominicans. *Colmados* are not just corner stores, but they are places where Dominicans hang out and socialize. So for these to have a national reputation as being the most well-stocked and tidiest, well that just adds to Baní town pride!

Hotel Caribani (Calle Sánchez 12, tel. 809/522-3871, US$33 d fan only), one block from Parque Duarte, offers clean rooms with hot-water bathrooms, cable TV, and comfortable beds. It is a good location because there are many services close by. This is the best option in town. Also on-site is the restaurant **El Gran Artesa,** which serves Dominican and international food. It is probably the nicest dining option in town with buffet and à la carte service.

Restaurant y Pizzería Yari (Calle Sánchez, tel. 809/522-3717, 8 A.M.–11 P.M. daily, US$4–10), right next to Hotel Caribani, is a favorite and always reliable pizzeria of Baní. There is great service in the open-air casual dining room. It has more than pizza; many meat and seafood dishes tend to fare better than the pizza.

Parador Cruz de Ocoa (no phone, 6 A.M.–10 P.M.) is outside of Baní on the way to Ázua. It is a good place to stop to use a semi-clean public bathroom (take your own toilet paper if you have some), one of the last you'll find for a while if you're traveling west—they're better than some of the ones out there. There is a very large assortment of food in a cafeteria setup, ranging from *comida criolla* to pastry, beer to coffee. There is a clothing boutique adjacent to it. Buses often stop here to let their passengers get provisions and use the bathrooms.

Cafeteria Comedor Abuela is across the street from Parador Cruz de Ocoa and is well known with Dominicans that pass through here for its top-notch *dulce de leche,* a very sweet candy made of condensed milk with a fudge-like consistency. Comedor Abuela is another choice for a "just passing through" snack stop and has recently gotten a facelift, so now you can sit outside on some nice tables after

you get your food from the front counter on the side of the highway where they serve up the yummy food and sweets.

But the best and most famous "sweet spot" in Baní is **Las Marías** (Paya, Carretera 2, no phone), just five km before Baní. Even if you're not hungry, don't pass up the opportunity to stop in and get some traditional desserts to save for later. *Flan de leche, dulce de leche,* and pastes made from many different fruits such as guava, pineapple, figs, or oranges are also popular. Cookies, cakes, and other delectable candies are on the menu. Cashews are plentiful in this region and the sweets made from them are particularly good. Don't be shy; there is no such thing as an orderly queue in Las Marías. Just belly up to the counter and start ordering (or pointing to) what you want. They will tally it up and ring you up at another counter.

Information and Services

Banco León (Hwy. Sánchez at Calle Mella, tel. 809/522-4454, 8:15 A.M.–5 P.M. Mon.–Fri., 9 A.M.–1 P.M. Sat.) has a 24-hour ATM, or try **Banco Popular** (Av. M. Gomez, tel. 809/522-3889).

To get Internet and long distance calling services in one place, it's best to head to **Punto Flash** (Flash Point, Mella 44, tel. 809/522-2436), a cybercafé located near the park.

Getting There and Around

Guaguas to and from Santo Domingo (US$2.75) are based out of the terminal a half block away from Parque Central every 15 minutes.

At a terminal west of the park on Máximo Gómez, you can find the buses whizzing by headed for Barahona (US$4.50) from Santo Domingo every half hour to hour. The ride to Barahona is two hours.

There is no major bus company terminal in Baní.

Walking around in Baní is easy and quite pleasant as it is a very small and clean town. As always, though, there are *motoconchos* buzzing about if you'd like to flag one down to take you around town or to the beaches, although it's

© ANA CHAVIER CAAMAÑO

Las Salinas

not recommended since the road to the beach tends to be as smooth as a runway on Mars.

LAS SALINAS

This often-overlooked spot on the coast is a beautiful southwestern getaway 16 kilometers south of Baní on Carretera Las Calderas. Here you will find the **Dunas de las Calderas,** which stretch about 15 kilometers in a straight line from the town of Matanzas to Las Salinas at Puerto Hermoso. They are the largest sand dunes in the Antilles and were declared a national monument in 1996. Amid the brown sand dunes, you will find endemic flora like cacti, olive trees, and other plants that enjoy this arid environment. Gulls and pelicans are among the fauna that live here. This unforgettable land is a perfect backdrop for photographers looking for peaceful subject matter in a unique setting unlike any other Caribbean vacation.

Without a doubt, the best place to stay or grab a good meal is ◖ **Salinas Hotel & Restaurant** (Las Salinas, Puerto Hermoso 7, tel. 809/866-8141, hotel_salinas@hotmail. com, per person US$84 per day). Located in

Calderas Bay, this all-inclusive hotel is a splendid step up (way up) from what you will find in Baní. Standard rooms are comfortable (and quite large) and rich-rustic with dark woods and tile floors and ceiling fans. Best of all, most rooms are afforded phenomenal views from the balcony. If you are on a romantic vacation and can swing the extra cost, inquire about renting the large fourth floor suite, which actually sleeps four with one bed lofted (the other is in the main living space). Decorated all in white with windows galore and dark wood accents, it comes complete with treadmill, weight bench, dining area, and refrigerator. The crowning glory of this flat is the winding staircase leading up to a thatched roof lookout deck with panoramic views. The rates include all meals. The restaurant looks out over the bay and across to the mountains. Even if not staying here, you should come and feast on grilled seafood (US$20) or *lambí criolla* (US$7), octopus in vinaigrette (US$7.80), and pork chops (US$7). Outside of Cabarete, this is the best windsurfing spot in the nation. Bring your own equipment, though. The hotel has a large dock where sailboats are docked. You can charter one of these boats (US$40–55) to take you to see the nearby mangroves and the beach at Punta El Derrumbao.

The salt mines just beyond the village of Las Salinas are what define the area. Make sure to have your camera; this area is one of the most uniquely atmospheric in the whole southwest region.

ÁZUA DE COMPOSTELA

Although Ázua (as it is commonly referred) is a bustling and fairly large town, it doesn't have much to offer tourists and isn't as charming as Baní. It is an agricultural town that has a healthy watermelon and honeydew melon crop. Most who pass through simply use Ázua as a pit stop.

Even though there isn't much by way of tourism here, Ázua has an compelling history, having briefly been a home base for three infamous Spanish conquistadors.

Ázua was founded in 1504 by Diego Velásquez, who came to Hispaniola with Columbus in 1493 on Columbus's second voyage. He later was instrumental to the brutal conquering and governing of Cuba. At one time Ázua was also home to a notary public, Hernán Cortés, who fought alongside Velásquez in Cuba and was later key in the conquest of the Aztecs in what is now Mexico. And the third Spanish soldier, Juan Ponce de León, also lived in Ázua; that is, before he went off to look for the fountain of youth in what is present-day Florida. Ázua was demolished by fire three times by Haitian soldiers in 1805, 1844, and 1849.

Sights

Modern-day Ázua has missed its opportunity, unfortunately, to be a location of interest to tourists as there is only one small monument in the **Parque Central** commemorating a battle that took place 16 kilometers away at **Puerto Viejo,** where the great Taíno leader Enriquillo is said to be buried.

Playa Río Monte, while popular with locals, is not a very pretty beach. It has food stalls, is a rather stony beach, and is quite crowded on the weekends.

Playa Blanca is about a kilometer west of Playa Río Monte and has a sandier beach but is best for its vantage point; offshore, dolphins play and manta rays hang out skimming the surface for food. These beaches are in the **Bahía de Ocoa** and are reachable from a marked turnoff six kilometers off the main highway.

Accommodations and Food

Ázua is not a good place to stop for the night. It simply doesn't have adequate hotel accommodations. You should plan ahead carefully to at least make it to Baní instead.

Food is only somewhat easier to find in Ázua, and most of the restaurants are inexpensive and specialize in true Dominican fare.

El Meson Suizo (Calle 19 de Marzo 121, tel. 809/521-9821, US$5–11) serves both *comida criolla* and international dishes along with desserts and seafood fresh from the ocean in a pleasant atmosphere.

Restaurante Francia (Av. Francisco del Rosario Sánchez 104, tel. 809/521-2900, 8 A.M.–10 P.M. daily) will give you a good sampling of tasty Dominican traditions, especially their rendition of *la bandera.*

Quaint **Comedor Dilone** (Av. Francisco del Rosario Sánchez 77, tel. 809/521-3431, 8:30 A.M.–11 P.M. daily) is especially affordable.

Information and Services

For an ATM open 24 hours, go to **Banco Progreso** (Av. Duarte at 19 de Marzo 1, tel. 809/521-2592, 8:30 A.M.–4 P.M. Mon.–Fri., 9 A.M.–1 P.M. Sat.) or **Banco Popular** (Av. Duarte, tel. 809/521-3400).

For any pharmaceutical needs you're bound to find what you need at **Farmacia Ramírez** (Calle Emilio Prud'homme 46-A, 8 A.M.–10 P.M.) and **Farmacia Frank** (Calle Emilio Prud'homme 70, tel. 809/521-3280).

Getting There and Around

Azua is located 100 kilometers west of Santo Domingo and 47 kilometers east of Barahona on Carretera 2. *Guagua* departures to and arrivals

© ANA CHAVIER CAAMAÑO

roadside veggies, Ázua

from Santo Domingo (US$3) occur every 15 minutes from the corner of Calle Duarte and Miguel Angel Garrido 5 A.M.–6 P.M. You can also catch a *guagua* to San Juan de la Maguana and Barahona every hour.

Caribe Tours (N.S. Fátima, tel. 809/521-5088, www.caribetours.com.do) buses run between Santo Domingo and Barahona, making a pit stop in Ázua. The stop is near the Parque Central, with buses departing from 7:15 A.M. until 6:25 P.M.

Walking in Ázua is easy because of its small size. *Motoconchos* are easily found. They usually all hang out together in front of *colmados* (corner stores).

SAN JUAN DE LA MAGUANA

With a dual-purpose name, San Juan (named for Saint John the Baptist) de la Maguana (named for a Taíno tribe) honors both of its heritages. This is an old town, simply referred to as San Juan, that was founded in the 1500s by the Spanish in what was an area populated by the indigenous Taíno around the time of the Spanish invasion.

This town was home to Cacique Enriquillo and his wife. The Battle of Santomé occurred here between Haitian and Dominican armies on December 22, 1855, sealing Dominican independence. This is also the birthplace of Colonel Francisco Alberto Caamaño Deño, in 1928 who was the hero of the Constitutional Revolution in April 1965.

San Juan is a pleasant town that has added much to Dominican history but has only one historical semi-tourist sight to show for it. It does, however, have some interesting festivals that are fun to see if you're in the area while they are happening. The rest of the year, life in San Juan seems to move slowly, like the heat across the desert.

El Corral de los Indios

El Corral de los Indios (free) is 10–15 minutes outside of town (about seven kilometers), with an unfortunate name more befitting of a place to keep animals. A more appropriate name for an ancient Taíno site thought to be a gathering point for games and rituals would be the Plaza Ceremonial Indígena. Archaeologists

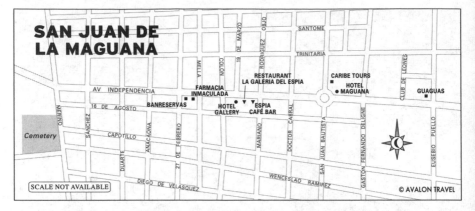

SAN JUAN DE LA MAGUANA

SCALE NOT AVAILABLE

© AVALON TRAVEL

believe that at one time, there was a circle of rocks surrounding the field; only a few rocks are left, including one large one in the center. In 2005, a government official was making an assessment in order to restore it for tourist purposes. To get to El Corral de los Indios, follow Calle Independencia westbound to Avenida Anacaona and turn north onto Juan Herrera. Good signage will point you to the field.

Entertainment and Festivals

Adjacent to the Hotel Gallery and Restaurant La Galeria del Espia, **Espia Café Bar** (Calle Independencia 7, tel. 809/557-5069, 8 P.M.– until people leave) is a lively and popular bar that has karaoke and dancing. It is an informal bar and a lot of fun.

La Fiesta del Espírito Santo, held around the first Sunday of June, is a procession from the town of El Batey to San Juan. This religious celebration includes carrying a religious icon to drums and chanting. It is a showcase of the Haitian and remaining Taíno influences in the culture of this region. The festival culminates in the plaza of San Juan for another full day.

On June 24, **Día de San Juan,** the town honors its patron saint, John the Baptist, ending a two-week celebration. Two weeks earlier food stands set up, dancing and music in the streets begins, and the festival balloons until the final blowout on the 24th, when a live band plays at the archway entrance to town.

Accommodations and Food

Hotel Gallery (Calle Independencia 5 and Monsenor Merino, tel. 809/557-1007 or 809/557-2317, US$25 d) has good service, and even though the 12 rooms are small and boxy, they are clean and have air-conditioning, which is a huge plus in this hot region. Rooms come in single, double, or triple. Suites are available that are more like a double room with a king-size bed and a full bed, along with a small refrigerator. In addition to air-conditioning, all have phone, TV, and a private bathroom. The restaurant serves good Dominican and Mexican food, and room service is available. This is a good value; it's owned by the same proprietors as the adjacent Restaurant La Galeria del Espia and the Espia Café Bar.

Hotel Maguana (Calle Independencia 72, tel. 809/557-2244, US$30 d) has been a mainstay of San Juan since 1947. The rooms are spacious and clean with comfortable beds, but you won't always get a window, so be sure to ask for it, otherwise it can get a bit stuffy. All rooms have a private hot-water bath. The Trujillo suite is by far the most roomy, but don't expect the luxury that he would've demanded. Those days are gone.

⟨ Restaurant La Galeria del Espia (Calle Independencia, tel. 809/557-2704, 1:30–4 P.M. and 6:30 P.M.–3 A.M., US$4–7), directly adjacent to the Hotel Gallery, is owned by a Dominican and his Mexican wife and serves authentic dishes from each country, like *chivo*

SAN JUAN DE LA MAGUANA AND THE TAÍNO *BATEYES*

Founded in the early 16th century, shortly after Christopher Columbus's "discovery" of the west, San Juan de la Maguana is one of the oldest cities in the Dominican Republic. But long before the Spaniards set foot on the island, which Columbus would call Hispaniola, the Taíno walked its earth. However, less than 100 years after Spain staked its claim, the island's entire population of Taínos was destroyed.

Archaeologists, sociologists, and anthropologists have since been able to learn a great deal about the Taíno culture. Much attention has been paid to the cave art discovered in many areas of the island and its spiritual significance to the lives of the Taíno. Also of great religious importance, and the subject of much research, are *bateyes*, or paved courtyards surrounded by large stone blocks and often centrally located in the villages. One particular *batey* – La Corral de los Indios de Chacuey, which is in San Juan de la Maguana – has been the focus of much study and speculation about Taíno life.

The Taíno lived in villages throughout the Dominican Republic – it is thought that the populations of these communities ranged from single families to upwards of 3,000 people. The *batey* was likely used for many purposes, both social and ceremonial, including markets, dances, ritual celebrations known as *areítos*, and ritual ball games.

In the ball game, very similar to soccer, the players were not permitted to use their hands but could use their feet, legs, hips, heads, and bodies to hit the ball, which was made out of a tough and heavy combination of rubber and fiber. It is believed that this game was played for more than just fun, as it seemed to be quite dangerous. Teams probably consisted of anywhere from 10 to 30 people. The Taíno may have believed that winning the game meant children and harvest would prosper. And, as the Taíno seemed to have been a mostly peaceful folk who did not believe in confrontation, it is possible the game was played, in part, to work out or avoid disagreements that might occur within the tribe or between tribes.

The word *batey* also means a modern-day set of barracks for migrant sugar workers. These "homes" are often windowless, one-room squares and are set on the land of the sugarcane fields and the sugar mill. *Batayeros*, whether Haitian or Dominican by nationality, are stigmatized as Haitian and are therefore socially undesirable in the Dominican Republic. There is a great deal of prejudice against Haitians in the Dominican Republic and especially against migrant workers. The *batey* way of life is hard; they live in unbelievably substandard conditions and do the backbreaking work of cutting cane for about 14 hours a day.

guisado and enchiladas. It has a nice atmosphere, clean with wonderful service and a big drink menu and wine list. The odd hours speak to how late-going the adjacent Espia Café Bar can run.

Information and Services
Farmacia Inmaculada (Calle Independencia 45 at 27 de Febrero, tel. 809/527-2801, 8 A.M.–10 P.M.) has a decent selection of medications (probably the best you'll find in the area).

BanReservas (Calle Independencia 47 at 27 de Febrero, tel. 809/557-2430, 8 A.M.–5 P.M. Mon.–Fri., 9 A.M.–1 P.M. Sat.) has a 24-hour ATM, or try **Banco León** (Av. Independencia 9, tel. 809/557-6094), by Calle Mariano Rodríguez.

There is a **Verizon Centro de Comunicaciones** (Calle 16 de Agosto, 8 A.M.–10 P.M.) for any long-distance calls you may need to make.

Getting There and Around
Driving into town on the Carretera Sánchez, it changes into two one-way streets, Calle Independencia (westbound traffic) and Calle 16 de Agosto (eastbound traffic). These are the main drags, and most commercial necessities and hotels are on or very near these streets.

Caribe Tours (Calle Dr. Cabral 29, tel.

809/557-4520) has buses for Santo Domingo (US$6.75) leaving at 6:45 A.M., 10 A.M., 1:45 P.M., and 5:15 P.M. from its depot which is near the Hotel Maguana. The Santo Domingo trip takes 2 hours. For a bus to Barahona, you'll need to take one to Ázua (US$2.25) (which takes one hour) and transfer there. Caribe Tours has buses leaving Santo Domingo 6:30 A.M., 10:15 A.M., 2 P.M., and 10 P.M.

To catch a *guagua* bound for Santo Domingo, head toward the Parque Central on the Calle Independencia. These minibuses leave and arrive three blocks east of the main archway into town on the eastern side. They depart for Santo Domingo every 20 minutes 4 A.M.–6 P.M.

Taxis and *motoconchos* can be found hanging around at the Parque Central.

Driving to Santo Domingo will take about two hours by car along the Carretera Sánchez (Carretera 2); you will pass through Ázua and Baní on your way to the capital.

COMENDADOR DEL REY OR ELÍAS PIÑA

This is the town of many names: Locals refer to it as Comendador, others call it Elías Piña, and it has had even more names in the past. About the only reason any visitors head to this town is to go to the Haitian Market or cross over into Haiti. It is not a good place to stay overnight.

Haitian Market

This is very easy to find so long as you stay on the main road as you enter town. Just keep driving and you'll run into it. Just as the market goes in Dajabón, so does this one. Twice a week (Monday and Friday), Haitian and Dominican merchants (mostly women) put their wares onto blankets on the street and shield themselves from the sun with whatever is handy. You won't find tourist souvenirs like the ones in gift shops, but more the likes of pots and pans, housewares, clothes, and produce all for very cheap. Sometimes you'll find sunglasses and pirated DVDs. They expect you to haggle, and there are many schools of thought on whether haggling in a third world country is worth it, or even the right thing to do. Go with your natural instincts. If you feel the price the merchant has asked you to pay is fair, then pay it. If the sport of haggling interests you, play along. Just remember, these prices are already knocked down a considerable amount to begin with and then marked up for tourists. You do the math.

Getting There and Around

You'll find *guaguas* at their terminal on 27 de Febrero at the Parque Central. Buses to Santo Domingo leave every 30 minutes for US$8. If you're going to Barahona, you'll need to board an Ázua bus and exchange there. Going to San Juan de la Maguana is only US$2.50.

Crossing the border to Haiti is a bit different here than in Dajabón. At the **Dominican immigration office** (8 A.M.–6 P.M.) they will stamp your passport (make sure you have it on you) and you'll likely be asked to pay US$25 to cross over, the official amount that should include your re-entry fee at the same gates. When you cross over, take a taxi about 2.5 kilometers to the Haitian immigration office, where you'll pay US$10 to enter Haiti. Don't be surprised if you are asked for an extra US$10 when you come back to the Dominican Republic. They shouldn't be asking for more money but sometimes it is easier to just pay the money than to argue. So make sure to have some small American bills if crossing into Haiti is part of your plan in order to do this. That is, unless they ask for a ridiculous amount of money.

Taxis and *motoconchos* usually hang around near the Dominican immigration office.

Península de Pedernales

The Península de Pedernales has been called the Dominican Republic's best-kept secret. But how can it be a secret if the Ministry of Tourism and guidebooks (like Moon!) have been blabbing about its beauty and attributes for years? The Península de Pedernales is the last place you should go if you want all-inclusive resorts, shopping till you drop or casino-lit nights. But, it is the first place to go to be embraced by what is left of the true Dominican experience. Here you will find hospitable locals, beaches with Dominican families relaxing and endangered species roaming freely. The true traveler is in search of the "real" Dominicans as if they are endangered species themselves. This is the region of the Dominican Republic where one can feel warm hospitality from locals as warm as the Caribbean sun. At the same time, travelers are able to disappear into fold of authentic Dominican society free from mass tourism.

The Península de Pedernales is as gorgeous for its realness as it is for its physical beauty and natural diversity. It makes up the southernmost shoreline along the Caribbean and contains three national parks, attracting more ecotourists every year. Some unique natural attractions are here: Bahía de Las Águilas, Laguna Oviedo, Parques Nacionales Jaragua y Sierra de Bahoruco, Lago Enriquillo, the Larimar Mines, and Hoyo del Pelempito, for starters.

BARAHONA

Driving Highway 44 along the coast, the road begins to wind and climb while delivering picturesque vistas of red rock mountains dropping into the coast of the intensely blue Caribbean Sea. Then with the emergence of the **Bahía de Neyba** before you, green fields of sugarcane and bananas begin to brighten the view.

Barahona sits in the western edge of the bay and is the last big town you'll encounter in the southwestern Dominican Republic. With all the beauty surrounding, one has to wonder why tourists haven't been flocking here all along. It is virtually undiscovered. Barahona has a satisfactory variety of accommodation and food choices (it's known as the town of the *plátano*) and a location on a breathtaking coastline within proximity of a number of activities for day trips, so it is a good place, the perfect place, to set up base camp if you want to explore the Península de Pedernales.

While the surrounding area of Barahona is beautiful, the town itself is a little drab. It was founded in 1802 by the Haitian liberation fighter Toussaint L'Ouverture, when the export of wood was a major source of revenue. Then, with Trujillo in power, it became a major sugarcane producer when he had fields planted to make money for himself and his family. Today, the sugarcane gives money to the city, but there is also coffee, bauxite, and gypsum production.

There are no sights whatsoever in Barahona proper, and the public beach of Barahona isn't nice at all, but there are a number of locations within a short drive for some fun day trips, like the Larimar Mines and various *balnearios* (freshwater swimming holes).

Tours

Although the idea of the Southwest being undiscovered by mass tourism is a tantalizing idea, it can also make it a bit challenging when trying to plan excursions. Never fear; contact **EcoTour Barahona** (Paraíso, Carretera Enriquillo 7, second floor, tel. 809/243-1190, www.ecotour-repdom.com). This experienced company offers many options for discovering the splendor of the Southwest. Ecotour choices (one-day, US$65–140, including lunch) are popular and range from choices like a day at Bahía de Las Águilas, Lago Enriquillo, Laguna Oviedo, Cachote, Isla Beate (expensive but worth it!), and the Larimar Mines. Other options include eco-holidays (4–7 days), eco-adventures (multiday, spendy activities by land or sea or both), and eco-treks (cacao, coffee, or horseback). The guides speak three languages.

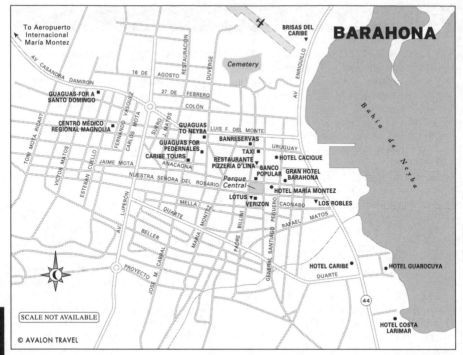

Thank goodness for **Tody Tours** (Santo Domingo, tel. 809/686-0882, www.todytours.com), because if it wasn't for Kate Wallace—owner, bird specialist, and local guide—people would continue to say that the Dominican Republic is no place for a bird watcher! Birders everywhere are flocking to her (okay, that was a bad joke) to help them find and appreciate the endemic species of the island of Hispaniola. The company is run out of the capital, but tours are given in the Southwest with a week's notice. The tours are US$200 per day for four people plus expenses. Tody Tours makes all arrangements for accommodations, food, and transportation.

Entertainment and Events

At night, most of Barahona's young people hang out along the Malecón, flirting, spinning around on their mopeds, and playing loud music.

Los Robles (Av. Enriquillo and Nuestra Sra. del Rosario, tel. 809/524-1629, 9 A.M.–2 A.M.) is a good spot for a beer. You can sit on the outdoor patio or go inside to the brand-new disco and dance to some salsa, merengue, and *bachata*. It's a happening spot.

Lotus (Calle Padre Billini at Nuestra Sra. del Rosario, 7:30 P.M.–2 A.M. Wed.–Sun., US$1), across from the Parque Central, has been a main dance club in Barahona for years. It's a good (not seedy) place to go to have fun.

Barahona's **Carnaval** is celebrated in February with the rest of the Dominican Republic (specific date varies). In July, the **Festival de Atabales** is a celebration and an educational opportunity to see the amalgamation of musical instruments that have come together from the mix of cultures making up the fabric of the Barahona area. The African heritage of the slaves that were brought during the Spanish colonial era is evident in the dance's movements and the accompanying instrument's rhythms. This festival is a genuine Dominican treasure that celebrates Afro-Caribbean heritage.

Accommodations

Barahona is a rather popular spot for Dominicans needing respite from the city for the weekend.

Hotel María Montez (Calle Jaime Mota 48, tel. 809/524-6503, US$25 d) was named after the famous Hollywood actress from the 1940s who was born in Barahona. The hotel was built in 2000 and is in a quiet neighborhood. There are shared balconies on each of the three floors where you can enjoy the crisp night air. There was talk of creating a fourth level for a restaurant. All the rooms are similar in size, very clean and comfortable with private bathrooms. All have air-conditioning and cable TV—no phones yet but there is a pay phone in the lobby that you can use. There's a generator for extra power. The owner, Doña Gladys, is very hospitable and friendly. Parking is available. When we passed through, the sign was down but hopefully it will be back up by the time you read this.

Hotel Cacique (Av. José Francisco Peña Gómez 2, tel. 809/524-4620, US$11 d) is an amazingly cheap budget option one block away from the Malecón. There are 16 clean rooms with cable TV, air-conditioning, fan, and private hot-water bathrooms. While this is cheap, the comfort that you'll get at a hotel for just a little more money might be worth the good night's sleep, because you might not get one on these mattresses.

Gran Hotel Barahona (Jaime Mota 5, tel. 809/524-5353, US$35 d) offers 39 clean rooms with hot-water bathrooms and cable TV. This is a good choice for location's sake, near Parque Central—so restaurants, banks, and other services are near.

Hotel Caribe (Av. Enriquillo 27 and Duarte, tel. 809/524-4111, US$ 30 d), although not as nice as some of the others, does include breakfast in the rate Tuesday–Friday (excluding holidays). The 31 rooms have air-conditioning, telephones, hot-water bathrooms, and TV in each. The restaurant is right next door and is called La Rocca. Hotel Caribe is across from Hotel and Casino Guarocuya.

One of the first hotels in Barahona, **Hotel Guarocuya** (Av. Enriquillo, tel. 809/524-2121, US$30) is showing its age. Once the holiday spot of Trujillo himself, unfortunately it looks like it could have already had its glory days and is now resigned to settling into a gloomy old age. It is right on the oceanfront, so the rooms facing the water have great views. All rooms have air-conditioning, cable TV, and telephone. The restaurant is open at 7 A.M. Julio Felix is a bird-watching guide based out of this hotel (Spanish only) and can take you on a one-day excursion (US$70) to see some of the island's endemic species.

❮ **Hotel Costa Larimar** (Av. Enriquillo 6, tel. 809/524-5111, www.costalarimar.com, US$80 d includes breakfast) is Barahona's rather limp attempt at an all-inclusive hotel. The rooms are spacious and have comfortable beds, ceiling fans, working but very loud air-conditioning, and private baths. The windows are nice, but not all of them open to let in fresh air. There is a big pool with a good-sized bar next to it where meals are served along with drinks at night, and sometimes there's live music or karaoke. Although some call it the five-star hotel of Barahona, one should seriously ponder how many stars are possible on that scale. The beachfront was rather a letdown. But if you're looking for a good room in a hotel that has a pool, this might be your only choice in the town of Barahona. They offer all-inclusive (US$20 per person), but don't bother. The town offers better food options and the hotel restaurant isn't that great.

Food

❮ **Los Robles** (Av. Enriquillo and Nuestra Sra. del Rosario, tel. 809/524-1629, 9 A.M.–2 A.M. daily, US$5–15) is for sure the most popular spot in town to dine. There is a lot of action at this corner at night, the food is good, and the prices are, too. It's on an outdoor patio with a thatched-roof bar and a jukebox that pumps out very loud Latin tunes. For a quieter meal, head

THE SOUTHWEST

to the back garden area where the picnic tables are set up next to an aviary and a pond that has turtles in it. There is also a "take-it-to-go" shack in the back where you can get sandwiches. The pizza is wonderful, as is the *mofongo;* there is a big menu to choose from for international and Dominican fare, including grilled meats and seafood. They deliver. After dinner, head to the disco of the same name in the building in the back. It is a small dance floor, but they play great music and it's very air-conditioned.

Restaurante Pizzería D'Lina (Calle 30 de Mayo at Calle Anacaona, tel. 809/524-3681, US$2–15) has a very loyal following. Pizza is good; there is also seafood, *comida criolla,* appetizers, and sandwiches (the *cubano* was excellent). With so many other restaurants around this area, this one still stands ahead of the others. It has outdoor seating.

Seafood is a specialty at **(Brisas del Caribe** (Av. Enriquillo 1, tel. 809/524-2794, 8 A.M.–11 P.M. Wed.–Mon., closed Tues., US$8–20), an upper-crust yet informal restaurant. Enjoy super-fresh lobster, shrimp, sea bass, and many more types of fish. Try anything *a la plancha* and you won't go wrong. It's right on Barahona's Malecón with a view of the sea. Yet another reason to not choose an all-inclusive hotel. The staff is impeccably trained to offer phenomenal service.

Information and Services

The **Oficina de Turismo** and **Politur** (Calle Batey Central, tel. 809/524-3573) are in the same building on the Malecón as you drive into town from the north.

Centro Médico Regional Magnolia (Av. Uruguay at Francisco Vásquez, tel. 809/524-2470) has a 24-hour emergency room.

Try **Verizon** (Calle Luperón and Calle Padre Bellini, 8 A.M.–10 P.M. daily) for long-distance and computer needs. You'll find another **Verizon** on Calle Nuestro Señora del Rosario across from the Parque Central.

Banco Popular (Calle Jaime Mota at Calle Padre Bellini, tel. 809/521-2102, 9 A.M.–3 P.M. Mon.–Fri.) has a 24-hour ATM and is located at Parque Central.

BanReservas (Av. Uruguay at Padre Bellini, tel. 809/524-4006, 8 A.M.–5 P.M. Mon.–Fri. and 9 A.M.–1 P.M. Sat.) has a 24-hour ATM as well.

Getting There

At **Aeropuerto Internacional María Montez** (Hwy. 44, tel. 809/524-4144), **Caribair** (tel. 809/567-7050) has small planes commuting from Santo Domingo on Monday, Friday, and Sunday, departing at 8:30 A.M. and returning at 5 P.M.; there are also regular flights on the weekend to Haiti from Barahona. The charter company, **Aerodomca** (tel. 809/567-1984, www.aerodom.com), can get you there, but there are no regular commercial flights.

Caribe Tours (Calle Anacaona, tel. 809/524-2313, www.caribetours.com.do) has direct service to Ázua (1 hour, US$2.15) and Santo Domingo (3.5 hours, US$6.70) from Barahona. If you are going to either of these cities direct, this is the most luxurious option. You will appreciate the air-conditioning that *guaguas* don't have, especially in this part of the country.

Caribe buses leave Santo Domingo (27 de Febrero, Santo Domingo, tel. 809/221-4422) bound toward Barahona at 6:15 A.M., 9:45 A.M., 1:45 P.M., and 5:15 P.M.

The direct buses from Santo Domingo (US$5.50, express US$6, 3.5 hours) pick up and drop off at the **Sindicato de Transporte** (Av. Luis Delmonte between Matos and Suero, tel. 809/524-2419), a fancy term for *guagua* station. It is across from the archway entrance into the city and has service starting at 6:25 A.M., 7:30 A.M., and 9 A.M. and every hour afterward until 6 P.M. Reservations are accepted.

Other *guaguas* leave from on or near the corner of Avenida Luis Delmonte and Calle Padre Billini. For San Juan de la Maguana, take the Santo Domingo (non-express, 1.5 hours) *guagua* and let them know where you are going so they let you off at the right connection point. From this popular connection point (known as Cruce del Quince) you will need to take a westbound bus toward San Juan (US$3).

Guaguas for the western border, Jimaní

(US$3.70, 45 min.–1 hour), and Pedernales (US$5, 2 hours) leave between every hour 7 A.M.–3 P.M. For *guaguas* to La Descubierta and Lago Enriquillo (US$3, 45 min.) transfer in Neyba (US$2.40, 1.5–2 hours).

Driving to Barahona from Santo Domingo, you will follow the Carretera 2, passing San Cristóbal, Baní (here you will need to make a right turn to stay on Carretera 2). Continue through Ázua until you reach the San Juan de la Maguana junction. Here you will switch over to Carretera 44, traveling gradually southwest until you reach the town of Barahona. Carretera 44 is the Peninsula de Pedernales' coastal road, eventually culminating at the Dominican-Haitian border town, Pedernales.

Getting Around

There are plenty of *motoconchos* and taxis twirling around Barahona, and they can be found at the Parque Central or along Avenida Luis Delmonte. Remember, there are no security checks done on these buzzing little devils, so hire at your own risk. Barahona is a rather sprawling city, but walking around the center part is easy.

Taxi Sindicato de Transporte (Calle Uruguay 119, tel. 809/524-3003), the local taxi union, will get you anywhere you need to be. This is for sure the best option for nighttime travel.

AROUND BARAHONA

Driving west of Barahona on Carretera 44, you will see some of the country's most pristine coastline. Often called the Larimar Coast, it is still largely undiscovered by mass tourism and is a favorite vacationing spot for Dominicans. To drive from Barahona to Pedernales takes about a half a day. There are many places to stop and take photos of the dramatic coast, take a dip in a natural spring, head to the beach, or visit the Larimar Mines.

Playa Quemaito

This beach, popular with Dominican families, lives up to its name in that it is a hot little beach. *Quemar* means "to burn" and the beach

gets its name from the warmth of its waters and rocky beach. The water here is shallower than at nearby **San Rafael** beach. There are *frituras* (food vendors selling fried food) where you can get typical beach food, mostly fish and other *yaniqueques* (fried bread) or even fried sweet potatoes for very cheap.

The Larimar Mines

The Larimar Mines (Mon.–Fri., closed when it rains, free), high up in the lush mountains, are open for viewing, and the drive there is gorgeous. A craftsman from Santo Domingo named the semiprecious blue pectolyte after his daughter Larissa and the Spanish word for "sea," *mar*. Today, larimar is found in two mines in the Bahoruco Mountain Range, 10 kilometers from Barahona. They are the only mines in the world. These open-cast mines are where the semiprecious mineral is dug. The Dominican Republic is the only place where larimar is mined; it is then mostly used for jewelry. It is mined by hand, and the men will sell you uncut stones by weight for around US$5–10. Remember that larimar's blue color is enhanced when wet, which is why some will try to sell you pieces that are in jars filled with water. You'll need a four-wheel-drive to get to the mines. Just south of Las Filipinas village (about 14 kilometers south of Barahona), turn right onto a dirt road for 15 kilometers into the hills. Follow this rough road to Las Chupaderos and the mine is at the end of the road. Tours are available with the **EcoTour Barahona** company by Safari truck. They will take you on a visit to the mines complete with lunch and a visit to the beach and natural swimming pools (US$70).

Bahoruco and La Ciénaga

Located 17 kilometers south of Barahona are the twin towns of Bahoruco and La Ciénaga. Although there aren't really any sights here (Bahoruco Beach is not even particularly stunning) or services, there are a few nice places to stay and the people are very nice and known for their very blue eyes.

 Casa Bonita (Carretera de la Costa, Km 16, tel. 809/476-5059, Sun.–Thurs. US$130, Fri. and Sat. US$170) is the

THE SOUTHWEST

© ANA CHAVIER CAAMAÑO

Playa Quemaito

Southwest's prettiest hotel without a doubt, and one of our favorite hotels in the country. Set high on a hill overlooking Bahoruco and the Caribbean Sea, it is a charming find. This one-time private summer house of the Schiffino family, designed by renowned architect José Horacio "Sancocho" Marranzini, was opened to the public in 1991. In 2006, they made major renovations with architect Rafel Selman to make it the boutique hotel you find today complete with infinity pool. Today, it is owned by the third generation of Schiffinos. There are 12 thatch-roofed cabins decorated in a sleek, modern-tropical motif. The high, sloped ceilings of the cabins swoop along with the lush, mountainside views you will appreciate from your private balcony. Tranquility and high-style comfort abound. All rooms have air-conditioning, hot water bath, hair dryer, wine cooler, iPod-ready clock radios, and private balconies. The restaurant serves a Caribbean fusion menu made with fresh local ingredients and meals are served alfresco in an elegant poolside environment with panoramic views of the ocean and mountains. This is a small, quiet hotel. Sunsets here are torturously romantic.

French-owned **Hotel-Restaurant Playazul** (Carretera Barahona–Paraíso Km 7, tel. 809/204-5375, US$55–65) offers spectacular views peering down to the sea from poolside. Beach access is done via a series of steps leading down from the hill. Standard rooms have twin comfortable beds, cable TV, air-conditioning, and hot-water bathrooms.

ApartHotel Pontevedra (Carretera Barahona–Pedernales Km 15, El Arroyo, tel. 809/341-8462, www.pontevedracaribe.com, US$69 d includes breakfast and dinner) is just before the turnoff for the larimar mines, so if you see that sign, you've gone too far. The large swim-up pool overlooks the crashing surf of the Caribbean. This sounds great, doesn't it? However, the poolside is rather scruffy, and there are no loungers. The resort offers 16 bare-bones minimum apartments, all with air-conditioning, seating area, kitchenettes and eating area. The on-site restaurant is not great (US$7–15), but it does have a glorious view of the Caribbean sunset.

Coral Sol Resort (La Ciénaga, tel. 809/233-4882, www.coralsolresort.com, US$55 d) is on the southern end of the two towns. The turnoff is well marked by a sign off the main highway just after you think you've passed it all. The 10 cabins are roomy and clean. Each has two beds and two bathrooms. The beach is the typical pebbly kind that you find in this area of the coast, but pleasant. Breakfast and dinner are included in the rate. It's not as charming as Casa Bonita, but it's a nice place to stay.

(San Rafael

After just a short three kilometers south of Bahoruco and La Ciénaga, you'll reach San Rafael. Its beach has forceful waves and is therefore not advisable to swim in, although it is a popular gathering point for Dominicans on the weekends. The things to see here are the *balnearios* (swimming holes) and magnificent vista points on either side of the town.

Balneario La Virgen (8 A.M.–6 P.M., free), right off the main highway, is cleaned often and very cold—but that is the beauty and the experience of swimming in a *balneario.* There is food and drink available in a shack next to this tiered pool. One tier is more for children since it is shallower, and it can get crowded and loud.

Villa Miriam (8 A.M.–6 P.M. daily, US$1.75) is off the highway up a steep road. It is a formed set of several pools and one regular pool. Since this one isn't free, it isn't as popular, but it is quieter and less crowded.

The *mirador* (viewpoint) up the hill from the *balnearios* has a breathtaking panoramic view of the southern coast of the Dominican Republic. The cliffs have blooming azaleas in fire red and orange, set against the blue of the Caribbean Sea; it makes for phenomenal photos.

Los Patos, several kilometers south of Paraíso, has a white-rock beach that is not very safe to swim in as the coastline is incredibly deep. But the adjacent **Balneario Los Patos,** where the Río Los Patos meets the sea, is a great place to swim. Its water is crystal clear and frigid with lots of room to splash around. It can get crowded on the weekends,

but if you come midweek, it should be relatively empty. There are public bathrooms by the pool. The food vendors have gotten together to form an association, and they clean and care for the area because it's the bread and butter of a very poor area. Seafood and drinks are for sale in many booths. They say they can fit 1,000 cars in the parking lot, but that is highly doubtful.

Nearby, the town of **Paraíso** has only one decent hotel (within town) and a pretty beach. But there are no services save for a **Western Union** (Calle Ana Irma Tejada at Calle Arzobispo Nouel) and a typical *colmado* on the same corner where you can buy food like cheese, sausage, bread, and liquor.

Hotel Paraíso (Av. Gregorio Luperón and Calle Doña Chin, tel. 809/243-1080, www. hotelparaisodr.com, US$21 d fan only) is a family-owned hotel that has very friendly service, spacious rooms with air-conditioning (for an extra few dollars) and cable TV. They are clean. You're not getting a spectacular hotel, but a good one for the area. Find this hotel on the Carretera at kilometer 34.

The beach can be litter-filled in some spots near town, but for the better part, go out past the hotel and you'll find the white-stoned beach in much better shape than the one in town.

L'Hotelito Oasi Italiana (Los Patos, Calle Jose Carrasco, tel. 829/918-6969, www.lospatos.it, US$36), the Italian-owned small hotel, has comfortable rooms, although not stellar accommodations. The poolside comes with a hot tub and is attractive for dozing on loungers. But it is the restaurant that has put this hotel on the map (technically in Los Patos, Carretera Km 37). Its truly scrumptious food and welcoming hospitality reign supreme here, with the ocean vista as your backdrop.

Guaguas stop in Paraíso at Calle Enriquillo from both directions.

(PARQUE NACIONAL JARAGUA

Jaragua National Park (8 A.M.–5 P.M., US$1.50 entrance) is named after a Taíno chief and is the largest park in the nation. In it is a combination of terrestrial, coastal, and marine environments including two continental islands, **Isla Baeta** and **Alto Vela.** Its 1,400-square-kilometer expanse includes scrub in a subtropical dry and a thorny forest. The high temperatures and low precipitation associated with that type of environment make the area dominated by different types of cactus. But in addition, you'll see cedar, mahogany, oak, and even grapes.

The park protects flocks of flamingos who spend much of the year on the 27-kilometer surface area shore of **Laguna de Oviedo,** with hyper-saline waters, where you can also find egrets and black-crowned tanagers, all of which are a part of the 130-some species of birds found in the park. The ricord iguana and rhinoceros iguana, which are endemic to Hispaniola, also call this park home.

For a tour of the park, ask for a guide at the entrance, which is in a well-marked turn-off from Highway 44 just north of the town of Oviedo. The guide will take you by boat for a 2–3 hour ride through the lagoon at Oviedo, showing you the flamingos, three islands, and a cave containing Taíno artwork. Although the cost of the tour was quoted at US$60, this price fluctuates and is easily bargained down.

EcoTour Barahona (tel. 809/243-1101, www.ecotour-repdom.com, US$70) arranges excursions to Laguna Oviedo, picking you up at your hotel. You'll have lunch on Iguana Island. This excursion requires quite a bit of walking so wear good shoes.

Birds are better viewed earlier in the day. This is a very sunny and hot area. Bring bug spray, sunscreen, and a hat.

This park makes for a good day trip when you use Barahona as your base. *Guaguas* will drop you off at the entrance. It is best to drive, though, so as not to risk missing the last *guagua* at 4 P.M. You don't want to miss it since there are no hotels nearby.

If you are driving the Carretera Oviedo–Pedernales highway, be on the lookout at kilometer 16 for three Ecological Wells. These small fresh-water lakes are crystal clear and are a good remedy for the scorching heat of the area. Two are embedded into the rocks and are accessible for tourists to swim in, although there is no tourist infrastructure at these pools, just an all-natural dipping opportunity.

◖ BAHÍA DE LAS ÁGUILAS

This is the most pristine beach in the entire Dominican Republic. It is also one of the hardest to get to, in the middle of nowhere. Getting there is half the adventure, but the payoff is out of this world.

To get to it, first you must travel along the road to Pedernales, but turn off about 12 kilometers before Pedernales at Cabo Rojo (Red Cape), where the land is literally red and surreal against the larimar-blue water of its shallow beach. From the highway, take the marked turnoff for Cabo Rojo, which curves around near where a large American bauxite mining facility has trucks speeding over the road (be very careful). Follow the sign directing you to veer left to Bahía de las Águilas. You'll end up in a tiny fishing community called Las Cuevas (The Caves). Up until a couple of years ago, the people of Las Cuevas had their homes inside the caves of the cliffs in an effort to stay cool in the oppressive heat of the area. They are very friendly, and at a small Ministry of Environment shack you can arrange for a fisherman to take you and your party to the remote beach. Standard cost to enter the park is US$1.50 per person. The beach is completely unspoiled with absolutely no facilities, so make sure to take plenty of water and munchies and return to Las Cuevas with your garbage to help maintain its pristine state for the next visitor.

Rancho Típico (tel. 809/753-8058), in Las Cuevas, is a restaurant/bar serving fresh seafood and beverages as well as a place to hire a boat captain to take you to Bahía de las Águilas. Typical price is US$45 to take up to six people on the boat ride. The price goes down per person the more you have in your party. They will arrange with you how long you would like to stay and come back to pick you up.

EcoTour Barahona (tel. 809/243-1101, www.ecotour-repdom.com, US$70) arranges excursions complete with transportation from your hotel if making the drive seems a bit daunting. They provide lunch and will take you snorkeling as well.

You can camp on Bahía de las Águilas, but keep in mind, your tent will be your only shelter. Abide by the rules of responsible ecotravel: leave no footprint. The threat of commercial development looms constantly, but preservationists thankfully fight against it. Visit it before the big hotels succeed in their encroachment.

PARQUE NACIONAL SIERRA DE BAHORUCO

This national park (8 A.M.–5 P.M. daily, US$1.50) covers over 800 square kilometers of protected and mostly mountainous land. This hard-to-traverse park is home to 1,268 different plant species including 166 orchid species, nearly 55 percent of the total found in the Dominican Republic. The vegetation survives in a variety of climates from dry forest at sea level to humid rainforest up in the mountains. The pines, broad-leafed forest, and mixed forest are home to 49 species of birds, including the Hispaniolan lizard cuckoo, Hispaniolan trogon, the stolid flycatcher, and the white-necked crow.

It was here in these mountains that the great Taíno chief Enriquillo led battles in defiance to the Spanish encroachment. For nearly 14 years, the natives kept the conquistadors at bay, and in 1533, the Spanish decided to back down and made peace with the cacique, making him, to this day, a celebrated figure in the history of the republic.

Without a motorcycle or four-wheel-drive, this park is virtually impossible to explore, making camping impossible as well.

From Highway 44, at the Cabo Rojo intersection, turn north (away from Bahía de las Águilas) and drive for about an hour. Or if you're coming from Barahona, take Highway 46 to Duverge, where you'll then turn south on a pretty terrible road to Puerto Escondido; the ranger station is on the first right. There are no guides at this park.

A day trip to this area is best (if Barahona is your base camp). There are no hotels.

El Hoyo de Pelempito

The "hole" of Pelempito is actually the greatest geologic depression in the whole country, over 1,000 meters in depth, which was brought about by the collapse of a huge coral shelf millions of years ago. Bird watchers will find a variety of a little over 100 species, five of which are in danger of extinction. Also on the endangered list living here are the solenodon and the hutia, both endemic to the island.

Even if hunting for a sighting of rare mammals is not top on your list of must-dos, the scenery alone will be satisfying enough. Take a walk through the pine forest. At 1,165 meters, there is a panoramic view on the edge of "the hole" from a lookout. El Hoyo de Pelempito is on the southern edge of the Sierra de Bahoruco. You need to turn off 12 kilometers east of Pedernales (opposite the road to Bahía de las Águilas). Halfway up the mountain, you will find the ranger station (no phone, US$1.50). Wear warm layers (since temperatures can dip down to 0 degrees Celsius), comfortable walking shoes, sunblock, and bug repellent. Take plenty of drinking water and remember to pack out what you take in. You'll want to drive a four-wheel-drive. Even though the road to get to the turnoff is well paved, the 30-kilometer stretch up the mountain is bumpier. Don't forget your camera!

Visitors can spend the night in El Hoyo by requesting special permission from the Sub-Ministry of Protected Areas at the Ministry of the Environment and Natural Resources (tel. 809/472-7170, www.medioambiente.gov.do).

LAGO ENRIQUILLO LOOP ROAD

This area of the Dominican Republic has the most unique terrain in the entire country, not what you'd expect to see on a Caribbean vacation. Countless varieties of cacti dot the countryside, crocodiles lie around in the estuaries of rivers, flamingos flock on the salty shores of Lago Enriquillo, and iguanas saunter around like house cats on sedatives. It's a truly distinctive experience. The near-desert environment also brings heat. The heat in this part of the country is intense, so it is best to travel in a rented car with air-conditioning in good working order. And don't forget to take water with you.

As for the entire peninsula, Barahona has your best options for accommodations. From there, travel northwest on Highway 46 (a well-paved road, surprisingly!) until you come to Cabral, about 30 kilometers west of Barahona.

For a strange encounter with mystery (or just plain scientific reasons), follow signs from Cabral to the town of Polo and to a place called **Polo Magnético.** Along this drive your car will feel very heavy like you're going uphill, even though the ground is flat. When you reach the Polo Magnético, a spot where the road appears to rise, roll an item along the ground and watch it as it appears to roll uphill in a strange optical illusion. Slip your car into neutral (but stay in there ready to brake!) and feel the car independently pick up speed uphill.

If you're in the area on the first weekend in June, look for the **Festival de Café Orgánico de Polo** (tel. 809/227-0012 or 809/687-2148, www.festicafe.org) held in Polo. It was established in 2004 as a sociocultural event for organic farmers from Polo and the surrounding communities of the Bahoruco mountains and throughout the Southwest to celebrate harvest and make their products known. This weekend marks the end of the coffee-growing season with live merengue, *bachata,* coffee tours, lots of coffee drinks, dancing, an arts and crafts fair, and games for kids.

Back on the Highway 46, you may run into soldiers who are trying to hitch rides from their military posts. They tend to wait near the speed bumps so that they can say where they need to go when you slow down. Generally they are harmless and very respectful. You are not obligated to give them a lift; it is all just a courteous exchange. If you have a truck and signal them to get in, they'll automatically hop into the back and tap on the side of the truck when they're ready to get out.

◖ Parque Nacional Isla Cabritos and Lago Enriquillo

This national park (7 A.M.–5 P.M., US$1.50) encompasses Isla Cabritos, which is an island in the center of the 200-square-kilometer **Lago Enriquillo,** the enormous saltwater lake that is famous for being the lowest part (below sea level) in all of the Caribbean. The lake's water is four times saltier than the ocean and was created when gradual tectonic movements cut it off from the ocean. On the beaches of the lake and the island within, you can find ancient seashells and coral fragments.

If you want to see the island, you'll have to have a guide. The entrance to the park is east of La Descubierta and you'll see the kiosk for the entrance from the road. Plenty of parking is available. Tours cost US$35 for a boatload of 1–8 people. You'll get a two-hour ride out to see the island and the crocodiles and flamingos that inhabit the area. Since it's so miserably hot here most of the time, you'll need sunscreen and a hat, and take water with you on the boat.

One of the most interesting features of the park is its animals. Numerous reptile species including endangered rhinoceros and ricord iguanas and a very large American crocodile population live around the lake. Entrance into the park to see the iguanas and just view the lake is US$0.40, and a nice shady path leads down to the water's edge. Here the iguanas heavily pepper the walkways and get surprisingly close; they can be rather big.

In the park, there is a *balneario* for a very frigid dip after a sweltering day of exploration.

Las Caritas is next to Lago Enriquillo and is a free look at some Taíno art in a shallow cave on the north side of the highway. It's visible from the road and you'll have to hike up to see it up close. It's not a very easy hike. You'll need good shoes for both this and the Lago Enriquillo visit.

The best way to get to this park is by your own vehicle. Taking a *guagua* from Barahona will mean making a transfer in Nagua and switching to the line that will bring you to

© ANA CHAVIER CAAMAÑO

iguana at Lago Enriquillo

Lago Enriquillo. Just let the drivers in Nagua know that is your destination.

The tour company **EcoTour Barahona** (tel. 809/243-1190, www.eco-repdom.com, US$75) has a tour including a boat tour of Lago Enriquillo, a visit to Isla Cabrito, lunch, a visit to Las Caritas, a visit to a Haitian marketplace, and a dip in a natural swimming pool.

JIMANÍ

Jimaní is the most trafficked route to Haiti through an authorized crossing point. It is a sprawling town that was once even larger, until the rains and flooding of the 2004 hurricane season wiped out over 600 of its inhabitants. The empty shells of ruined homes still sit as a ghostly reminder on the way into town. The only reason to visit this town is to access the crossing point to Haiti, which has the market just behind the border gates in what is called Malpaso but is more commonly referred to as "no-man's land."

Crossing into Haiti, you'll need to present your passport and pay US$10 for a Dominican departure tax, a US$10 Haitian entry fee, and a US$10 entry fee when you come back through. The immigration office is open 8 A.M.–6 P.M. At the **market** you'll find household goods, pirated music and movies, clothing, and some random objects.

Accommodations and Food

The **Hotel Jimaní** (Calle 19 de Marzo 2, tel. 809/248-3139, US$25 d) is a decent place to get a night's sleep and a meal. It's not much on the outside, but this ugly duckling has rooms that are actually rather comfortable, with cable TV and a private bathroom (cold water). The restaurant serves all meals in a limited fashion, but it's food. It's not the Ritz, not even remotely, but if you're in a pinch you don't have much choice all the way out here, so you're going to have to cowboy up and do this thing the southwestern way.

Getting There and Around

Caribe Tours has bus service that goes from Santo Domingo to Port-au-Prince and makes a stop in Jimaní. Otherwise, *guaguas* serve this area from Santo Domingo (US$9) every half hour to 45 minutes and from Barahona (US$4.25) every 45 minutes from the corner of 27 de Febrero and 19 de Marzo.

On your way from Jimaní to Neyba, it might be refreshing to jump into some ice-cold water. **Las Varias Balneario** in the town of La Descubierta has a nice river-fed swimming hole where they also have food and drink. It is popular with families. It is a nice break on what will most likely be a hot day of driving. There are bathrooms here, albeit nightmarish. If you can, wait until Neyba.

NEYBA

It might be quite a stretch to call this the Napa Valley of the Dominican Republic, but Neyba is indeed wine country. Locals sell big jugs of the often sour wine made from regional grapes not only in the town of Neyba, but on road side stands along the *carreteras* of this region. Neyba has a nice Parque Central and is a small town with no sights, but it makes for a good spot to stop for a bite to eat on your loop around Lago Enriquillo. The Parque Central also serves as a pit stop for *guaguas*.

Accommodations and Food

Hotel Restaurant Babey (Calle Apolinar, US$10 d), across from the Parque Central, offers small rooms with fan or air-conditioning (you'll pay extra). It's rather clean and very basic. The restaurant, which is down a long corridor from the sidewalk, serves *comida criolla* at very low prices. The dish of the day (rice and beans and some kind of meat) is about US$2.

BACKGROUND

The Land

GEOGRAPHY

The Dominican Republic's geographical differences are reflected in its diverse landscape, where the roaring surf and sultry heat of the coastlines seem a world apart from the temperately cooler mountains in the center of the country. Here, tropical forests coexist with fertile valleys rife with rivers and fresh springs, only to collide with cactus-dotted semi-arid deserts. The highest point in the Caribbean tapers into the lowest point in the Caribbean. And all of this is on the 48,734-square-kilometer section of Hispaniola that the Dominican Republic occupies.

The island of Hispaniola is positioned in the middle of the Caribbean with the Bahamas to the north, Cuba and Jamaica to the west, Puerto Rico and the Leeward Islands to the east, and South America to the south. The Atlantic Ocean crashes into the northern coast and the southern shore is bathed by the Caribbean Sea. The Dominican Republic occupies two-thirds of Hispaniola, separated from neighboring Haiti by a 388-kilometer border.

Mountains and valleys are natural demarcations dividing the country into northern, central, and southwestern portions. In the northern region, plains hug the coastline from Monte Cristi to Nagua and then rise dramatically to

© ANA CHAVIER CAAMAÑO

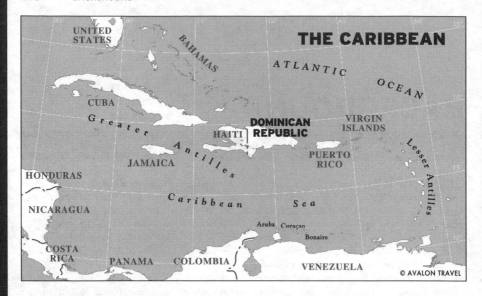

form the **Cordillera Septentrional** (Northern Mountain Range), situated just south of the plains and parallel to the ocean. The range's southern face then drops down into the **Valle del Cibao** (Cibao Valley). This valley scoops its path from the northwest corner of the country and stretches all the way to the Bahía de Samaná (Bay of Samaná). The connection of **La Península de Samaná** (Peninsula of Samaná) to the mainland is a swampy area—perfect for growing rice—which then rises up to lushly vegetated mountains up to 600 meters high.

The central region mainly consists of the **Cordillera Central** (Central Range), the nation's spinal column. It begins at 2,000 meters near the Haitian border, rises to the highest point of 3,087 meters at **Pico Duarte** (Duarte Peak), curves southward by the **Valle de Constanza** (Constanza Valley), and finally dips its southern portion, the Sierra de Ocoa, into the Caribbean Sea. The Cordillera Central extends its reach with the Sierra de Yamasá through to the Cordillera Oriental. Just south of these ranges are the Caribbean coastal plains, which extend out from the mouth of the Ocoa River in the midwest to the eastern end of the

island. These plains contain limestone terraces that rise to 100–120 meters at the northern edge. The Valle de San Juan (in the west) extends 100 kilometers from the Haitian border to meet up with the Bahía de Ocoa.

In the southwest corner of the country, the Sierra de Neyba extends from the Haitian border to the Yaque del Sur River, with peaks up to 2,000 meters high. On the eastern side of the river is the Sierra de Martín García. The Hoya de Enriquillo is a basin from the Haitian border to the Bahía de Neyba and from the Sierra de Neyba to the Sierra de Bahoruco, a ridge that extends from the Haitian border to the Caribbean Sea.

The Dominican Republic enjoys a diverse topography in its 30 provinces, of lowlands and highlands, rivers and lakes, and includes some offshore islands as well. The islands of Saona, off the southeastern coast, and Beata, south of the Península de Pedernales, are the largest.

Even though the beaches make up only a small portion of the country's 1,633-kilometer coastline and an even smaller portion of what the Dominican Republic has to offer visitors, they are (and justifiably so) the main reason people take their vacations here. Also a part of the coastline are limestone cliffs that reveal cozy coves with small, tucked-away beaches.

Rivers and Lakes

The Dominican Republic has rivers in both the mountains and the plains. The **Yaque del Norte** is the longest river in the country, at 296 kilometers long, and is used for much of the adventure tourism in the central highlands. It rushes and curves through dramatic cliffs and mountains from its home near Pico Duarte in a northerly direction to its emptying point at the Bahía de Monte Cristi. The Río Yuna flows east, serving the Vega Real, and empties in the Bahía de Samaná. Together, these two drain the Valle del Cibao.

In the Valle de San Juan de la Maguana, the Yaque del Sur forms in the southern slopes of the Cordillera Central and flows to the Bahía de Neyba by Barahona, and the Río Artibonito crosses over into Haiti. Much of this water is used for irrigation in the otherwise very dry landscape of the southwestern region.

The Ríos Magua, Soco, Chavón, and Ozama drain the eastern portion of the country.

The very fertile and vegetated landscape of the rest of the nation begins to dwindle in the far western half of the country, where the closer you get to the Haitian border, the more the landscape is characterized by dry scrub and cacti. The Neyba Valley is home to Lago Enriquillo, which is the lowest point in the Caribbean and was once a strait of the Caribbean Sea. The lake has a high level of evaporation, but on average it is 40 meters below sea level and is four times saltier than the ocean. Its drainage basin is made of 10 minor rivers.

CLIMATE

For the most part, the Dominican Republic has a tropical climate. The average annual temperature is 25°C (77°F), and the weather is warm and sunny for a majority of the year.

The seasons have only slight variations. The winter season (November–April) is when humidity is minimal with temperatures lower in the evening than they are in the summer nights.

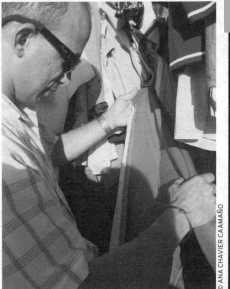

It gets cold in the mountains. Bring a jacket or buy one here.

© ANA CHAVIER CAAMAÑO

Coastal areas have temps around 20°C (68°F) in the evening, and in the interior mountain areas, it is much cooler, sometimes dropping below freezing, allowing for a rare frost on the peaks of the mountains. The summer starts in May and goes until October with average daily highs around 31°C (87°F) around the coast, dropping about 10 degrees at night—but the humidity makes it seem hotter.

Whatever the season, the towns of the Cordillera Central enjoy a "perpetual spring" as opposed to the desert region of the Southwest, where temperatures can rise above 40°C (104°F). The cool temperatures draw the city folk to the mountains during the hotter months on the perimeter of the island.

October through April is the rainiest time for the northern region; in general the west gets the least precipitation, and the south gets the rain heaviest between May and November. Most of the time, the rain falls (150 centimeters on average for the whole country) with excited short bursts, book-ended by sunshine, resulting in quite a pleasant break in the otherwise near perfection of the weather—*near* being the key word. Abnormalities are inevitable, such as overcast skies (marring a sun worshipper's beach vacation) or perhaps unexpected rains (ruining a windsurfer's paradise). But for the most part, it is blue skies and sunshine.

The El Cibao region is fortunate in that it has healthy land and sea breezes that sweep up from the sea to cool the air during the day and then move out again at night, taking the hot air with them.

Hurricanes

The Dominican Republic is prone to tropical cyclones (tropical depressions, storms, and hurricanes), and a majority of them strike the southern part of the country. Hurricane season lasts from the beginning of June to the end of November, but most hit during August or September. Coming all the way from the coast of Africa, hurricanes usually start as tropical depressions that build up their ferocity as they cruise across the Atlantic Ocean, eating up all the warm moist air they can gobble up to fuel their speed as they careen toward the Caribbean islands, producing winds in excess of 200 kilometers per hour and with rainfall sometimes greater than 50 centimeters in a 24-hour period.

In 1998, Hurricane Georges plowed over the Dominican Republic, killing about 300 people. It caused gigantic agricultural losses of staple crops like rice, plantain, and cassava, and caused severe structural damage, leaving thousands homeless. Many people were without electricity for months, and food supplies were minimal after the hurricane.

Even though the Dominican Republic seems to be smack-dab in the middle of a hurricane bowling alley, the chances of getting caught in one are minimal. If you are, though, head inland and stay away from the ocean. It's best to go to a major city so that there are adequate emergency services and shelters. If you're in or near a resort when a hurricane hits, listen to management; they have procedures for evacuation and shelter. Mudslides are a major result of storms in the Dominican Republic, so stay away from all rivers, lakes, and hillsides.

Flora

The Dominican Republic's biodiversity yields a huge assortment of plants and flowers. If you're vacationing only in the metropolitan area of Santo Domingo, the best way to see the full scope of the environment's capabilities is by visiting the Jardín Botánico Nacional in Santo Domingo. But if you're going to the countryside, beaches, mountains, or desert, you'll quickly learn that the Dominican Republic is truly a rich country when it comes to vegetation. No matter what the season, something seems to be blooming, growing, or adding fragrance to the air.

There are over 5,600 species of plants found in the 20 different zones, which is unique for a Caribbean island, and 30 percent of the plants found here are endemic to the Dominican Republic.

TREES

The national tree, whose flower is also the national flower, is the West Indian mahogany. It is a medium-sized semi-evergreen tree that can stand about 9–11 meters tall and is native to the island of Hispaniola. Wood from the mahogany tree was used to build the first cathedral in the New World. Other trees that are native to the Dominican Republic include the ceiba (silk cotton tree), known for its massive stature and long life (up to 300 years!); the Dominican magnolia; the *mamón;* and the *bija* tree. In the semi-arid desert, cacti and agave dominate the terrain. When the Spanish came, they introduced many trees, including the coral tree, the African tulip, and the poinciana.

Perhaps the most prevalent vegetation zone found in the country is the subtropical forest.

No true tropical rainforest is found here because rainfall isn't sufficient and, unfortunately, because many of the types of trees found in that sort of environment were hacked away. The subtropical forest is found in the Santo Domingo lowland, in the valleys of the northwest (including Valle del Cibao), and on the Península de Samaná.

Main species of trees found in these moist subtropical forests are royal palms and mahogany. Also found are the nonindigenous capa trees, the jagua palm, lancewood, ground oak, and the yellowwood. The cashew tree (*Anacardium occidentale*) is also found and flowers with the cashew apple (pseudofruit), which looks like a little red, yellow, or orange boxing glove and whose taste punches you in the mouth with bitterness—not too appealing, but when the nut is roasted it is very good. These tasty snacks are often sold in jars along the countryside highways.

As you pass the landscape of the country, it would be nearly impossible to miss that the scores of hills, lowlands, riverbeds, and shorelines are brimming with palms. The coconut palms (imported from Africa) that line the beaches of the Atlantic and Caribbean are the postcard views that most see of the Dominican Republic palm varieties. However, there are other varieties. While the coconut is mostly found along shorelines, the royal palm, or *Roystonea boringuena* (highly regarded as a national symbol, even appearing on the coat of arms), needs deeper soil and more moisture; it grows in clumps everywhere but high elevations. The sabal palm is found in regions with either environment. Other types of palm, like the cana, guano, and yarey, are all native to Hispaniola and are still used for making things like brooms and furniture.

Subhumid forests have semi-evergreen trees that lose their leaves during the three-month dry season, making for a rather bare landscape, but for the most part they are green leafy regions. An unexpected meeting between palms and coniferous (cone-bearing) trees characterizes the mountain forests. The Reserva Científica Valle Nuevo protects the virgin woodland from forestation and is the perfect place for an afternoon walk while checking out the variety of flora.

Mangroves are woody trees that grow in coastal and estuary areas like those of the Parque Nacional Los Haitises and the Parque Nacional Jaragua. They grow in areas where they are protected from direct wave action and are essential in the protection of the island from strong storms, tides, and erosion because their roots stabilize the sand and mud. The relationship between the mangroves and marine life is very important. They provide a stable home and act as a nursery for fishes, crustaceans, and shellfish. Inside a mangrove's safe structure, the survival rate of offspring increases. Additionally, they provide food for many varieties of marine life, and animals such as sea birds also seek shelter inside the mangroves, using both the roots and branches as nesting areas.

FLOWERS AND FRUIT

Plants here are affected by elevation and rainfall, and because of the wide spectrum of geographical variables in the Dominican Republic, there is a bewildering array of plants and flowers.

The country is gorged with pineapples, grapefruit, papayas, mangoes, guavas, passionfruit, bananas, and melons. Let us not forget coffee and sugarcane. Breakfast tables have never been this happy. In the morning, start your day with a common breakfast of a milkshake made with fresh *lechosa* (papaya) and mango.

Along the city streets and across the country, fruit and vegetable markets overflow with produce like avocados, *plátanos* (plantains), sugarcane, eggplants, herbs, onions, and cassava.

Tree ferns, orchids, bromeliads, and epiphytes are found in abundance in the humid forests. It is estimated that more than 300 varieties of orchids grow in the Dominican Republic. The Jardín Botánico Nacional in Santo Domingo displays 67 of them. In fact, in the forested highlands of the Sierra de Bahoruco (in the deep southwest of the

Península de Pedernales) more than 50 percent of all native orchids are found.

Taínos cultivated the indigenous crops long before the Spanish showed up. They were fairly skilled farmers who grew the *higüero* (calabash) tree for food. They then used the dried gourds to make masks and containers. They also grew papaya and the *yuca* (cassava) plant that played a major role in their diet and still does to most Dominicans. *Yuca* is one of the most important ingredients for *sancocho,* a traditional Dominican stew.

Fauna

Because the island of Hispaniola was never joined to a continent, it doesn't have many land animals. Most of the mammals that you see today were introduced by the Europeans who made the journey. Out of the nearly 500 vertebrate species of animals, 140 are various reptiles, 60 are amphibians, and 20 are land mammals. The rest are birds, marine mammals, and bats.

LAND MAMMALS

Before Christopher Columbus and his men showed up, there were an estimated 20 native mammals. Now, there are only two and they are hanging on for dear life. If you see one in its natural habitat, consider yourself lucky; they are rare and tend to hide out.

The **solenodon** is a primitive shrew-like creature about 30 centimeters long with a tail up to 25 centimeters. These insectivores are stout and have an unusually long snout. They're not the cutest kids on the playground (think "rat meets anteater"), with long bristly faces and small eyes. They have brown fur but naked tails and huge feet that have long, clawed toes. They have a "Bless his heart, he's

© SAMUEL KRUCKER

Most of the mammals in the DR are non-native.

so ugly, he's cute" look about them. Still, they are survivors and have been in existence for 30 million years feeding on insects and worms. It's taken scientists a long time to get to know the solenodon, partly because they are nocturnal, burrowing in trees and caves during the day. When they do come out, they scuttle about in a serpentine pattern. Their grooved incisors make them even more inaccessible; poison runs from a gland at the base of each, fatally wounding any would-be captor in the wild. However, this mean bite was no match for the bigger animals (especially the mongoose) that were introduced. Solenodons are slow, clumsy runners and are not agile. They have had a hard time surviving.

The **hutia,** yet another small rodent, shares many similarities with the solenodon. They both live in tree trunks and caves and are nocturnal. The hutia is, for the most part, an herbivore. It resembles a prairie dog and likes to climb trees.

Instead of native animals, most visitors will notice a remarkable overabundance of stray dogs, cats, and chickens.

MARINE MAMMALS

If the Dominican Republic coastal waters were a Broadway play, the **humpback whales** and manatees would have stars on their doors. These top-billed actors draw audiences from all over the world.

Each winter some 3,000 humpback whales migrate all the way from the frigid waters of the arctic circle to mate and calve in the balmy tropical waters off the coast of the Dominican Republic, with the Bahía de Samaná acting as a kind of nursery. Peak "show time" for this event is in January and February. This is a world-renowned venue for viewing these magnificent creatures as they lumber through the water and sometimes breech right before the gape-mouthed camera-clad tourists. It is one of the most glorious spectacles, natural or otherwise, in the country.

This species of whale can grow to be 12–15 meters and weigh up to 60 tons. They are named for the way that they come above the water's surface with an arched back. As they cut across the water's surface, you'll be able to see the signature knobby heads, white flippers, two blowholes, and large tails. For their entire time in the tropics, humpbacks do not eat a single thing. While in the arctic circle they build up their 15–20 centimeters of fat to sustain them on their journey and for the rest of the time they're in the tropics.

The endangered **West Indian manatee** can sometimes be found in the shallow waters of slow-moving rivers, estuaries, bays, canals, and coastal areas. Nicknamed "sea cows," these are very gentle and slow-moving animals that "graze" on plants at the ocean floor. In fact, everything about them is slow. They spend their days feeding and resting at the water's bottom or surface, only coming up for a breath every 3–5 minutes. Females cannot reproduce until they are 5 years old, and males mature at 9–11 years old; gestation is 13 months, and a calf is born every 2–5 years. It's not a hurried lifestyle—perhaps this is why they can live up to 60 years old. Manatees have no known natural enemies, unless you count human interaction. Unfortunately, hunting and tour-boat excursions (ironically, to appreciate the mammals) have caused a decline in manatee numbers.

The reefs of the Dominican Republic create a wonderful habitat for a wide variety of sea life, including four kinds of **sea turtles:** the green sea turtle (the kind hunted to make soup), the leatherback (the largest living turtle), the loggerhead (found in lagoons and bays), and the hawksbill. These beautiful creatures can grow up to two meters long and come ashore at night by the Parque Nacional Jaragua from May to October to lay eggs in the sand. Of these four, the hawksbill's survival is in the most jeopardy because of its attractive shell, which is sold widely in the form of belts, jewelry, and other decorative items.

CORAL REEFS

While diving and snorkeling are two of the most popular activities for tourists vacationing in the Dominican Republic, it might be good to get a handle on some basic knowledge before

ENDANGERED SPECIES

The Dominican Republic, with its diverse flora and fauna, is home to a number of endangered animal species. There are three classifications of threatened species, each with its own criteria, which are based on the amount of population reduction in the last 10 years or over the last three generations – whichever is longer – or the projected reduction over the next 10 years or three generations. Also taken into account is the "extent of occurrence" or "occupancy" over a given area. Current population of the species is also a factor in categorizing the extent of the threat. Throughout the country, national parks that have been designated conservation lands are home to these threatened species.

"Critically endangered" refers to animals whose populations have been, or are projected to become, reduced by 80 percent over the 10-year/three-generation margins. These species contain fewer than 250 adults with an estimated decline in population of 25 percent over three years or one generation (again, whichever is longer), or only 50 or fewer mature individuals are known to exist.

For species in the "endangered" category, the numbers of reduction drop to 50 percent over the same past or future time periods. The mature individual number rises to 2,500 with a projected consistent drop of at least 20 percent over the next five years or two generations, or the known existence of fewer than 250 adults.

Those on the "vulnerable" list have a suspected reduction of 20 percent in the past 10 years or three generations, or in the next 10 years or three generations. The population would contain no more than 10,000 mature individuals and hold an estimation of a 10 percent decline in numbers within 10 years or three generations. Another possibility is that the population just flat out numbers fewer than 1,000 mature individuals.

As of 2004, the Puerto Rican hutia, a gerbil-like rodent that with a bit of luck can be spotted in the Parque Nacional del Este, is on the critically endangered list. The Haitian solenodon is an endangered species. Its characteristics include a small body and a long snout. Like the hutia, the solenodon resides in the Parque Nacional del Este. Among the Dominican species that fall under the category of vulnerable are the American manatee, the humpback whale, and the Hispaniolan hutia.

Other threatened or endangered species that occupy the Dominican Republic, or its surrounding waters, are the West Indian manatee and the bottlenose dolphin, both of which can be spotted along the coasts of national parks or in the Bahía de Samaná. There are thousands of species of birds that live on the island, and among those that are endemic to the country are the white-crowned quail-dove, bay-breasted cuckoo, and the hawk buteo. The rhinoceros iguana, endemic to the Dominican Republic, can be found throughout the country in the drier areas of the national parks.

---

paddling out to see the splendid colors, to make sure to preserve the delicate ecosystem.

There are three types of coral reefs: the fringe, the barrier, and the atoll. The fringe is a great place for beginners, since it is close to (and connected to) the mainland and therefore tends to be in shallower waters. It has a good variety of coral species.

Just past the fringe reef you'll come to the barrier reef, where the sea life is dialed up a notch from the fringe reef. The type of barrier reef commonly found here is the bank/barrier reef, which is smaller than a barrier reef found in the Pacific Ocean. You'll need transportation to get out to a bank/barrier reef as there are hundreds of meters between it and the shore.

Charles Darwin reasoned that an atoll came to be from a fringing coral reef surrounding a volcanic island that eventually grew upward as the island began to sink, turning the fringe reef into a barrier reef. In time, the old volcano fell below the surface of the ocean and the barrier reef remained, thereby graduating to atoll status. This type of reef is rare in the Caribbean and the closest one to the Dominican Republic is in Belize.

There are two types of coral: hard and soft. While it would seem that the hard corals are the skeleton of the reef and the soft corals merely decorate it, that is not the case. In fact, the creation of a coral reef is very much a team effort. While the hard corals do indeed form the skeletal portion, many types of algae act as the mortar to help bind and solidify the frame. Then crustaceans, mollusks, sponges, urchins, and soft corals all come in to anchor the reef. And just as in a community, there are the vandals. Let's cut the snails, crabs, and parrotfish a little more slack, though; they are, after all, surviving off of the reef.

Scuba diving and snorkeling are vastly popular activities, but so much "flipper traffic" has done tremendous damage to the reefs. Make sure that you follow the simple and very important rules while visiting their habitat: Don't stand on it or touch it. Be careful with your fins; while kicking you can easily accidentally do a lot of damage. And above all, don't take a piece as a memento, even though it is very tempting. Many of the coral reefs have suffered as a result of the tourism industry, which includes individuals who harvest the reefs to make jewelry to sell on the beaches and in the markets.

BIRDS

The Dominican Republic isn't traditionally thought of as a bird-watching destination. But that is changing because, in fact, its environment is a bird's paradise and a bird-watcher's dream. There are 300 recorded bird species, including 27 endemics and a number of Caribbean specifics as well as "vacationing" birds from North America. Species to look for are the Hispaniolan parrot, the Hispaniolan woodpecker, the Hispaniolan trogon, and the Hispaniolan parakeet. Also on the island are owls, egrets, herons, pelicans, parrots, parakeets, and flamingos, just to name a few. The national bird is the **palmchat,** which nests in the royal palms within the coastal plains.

© SAMUEL KRUCKER

sea bird in Los Haitises

The Sierra de Bahoruco has one of the highest bird densities of the Caribbean and is the only place in the Dominican Republic where you have even a slim chance of seeing 26 out of the 27 endemics. You'll have to go to the mountains to see the white-necked crow or a warbler.

REPTILES AND AMPHIBIANS

While there are snakes and frogs on the island, they are greatly outnumbered by the more than 20 species of lizards.

Lago Enriquillo, with its dry, rocky ground, is the preferred location for the **rhinoceros iguana.** This species of iguana is so named because of the small horns on the males' snouts and their gray color, which make them look like rhinoceroses. A full-grown rhinoceros iguana can be over a meter in length. Although they may look scary, they are indeed rather shy and are herbivores. **Ricord iguanas**

are also found at Lago Enriquillo and live only in the Dominican Republic. These red-eyed creatures are omnivorous and can live more than 30 years.

The olive-brown **American crocodile** also makes its home in Lago Enriquillo. In fact it has gotten so comfortable in the Dominican Republic that it represents one of the largest wildlife crocodile populations in the world. With Lago Enriquillo four times saltier than the sea, the crocs tend to lurk near the river inlets to try to catch some fresh water. However, with the diversion of these rivers (for irrigation purposes) the crocodile babies are suffering, since they have not yet developed their tolerance to the briny stew. The average male can grow to be four meters long. The crocodiles mainly feed on fish, turtles, and occasionally goats. They are protected under Dominican law, and the best time to go to Lago Enriquillo to see them is in the early morning or late afternoon.

Environmental Issues

When Columbus arrived, the forests of the island were plush and vibrant. Over the centuries, it is estimated that nearly two-thirds of those original forests have vanished. Illegal forestation, fires, mass farming without forethought as to how to replenish soils after failed crops, and pollution caused an immense amount of destruction. Over time, fertile and pine-covered hillsides increasingly vanished. In the 1970s, environmentalists warned that by 1990, a majority of the native forest would be destroyed, much like what had begun to occur in Haiti. With that, the Dominican government finally stood up and began an active move toward conservation. Today great amounts of land throughout the country are being protected as national parks.

However, there is still quite a lot going on in the environment. A growing tourism industry picks up more momentum with each year, and the mad rush to create more services, resorts, and activities is only now beginning to be

monitored. Thankfully, many ecosavvy travelers have become attracted to the Dominican Republic as a destination. They are not just lying on the beaches anymore. Instead, more visitors are headed inland to raft the rivers and climb the mountains of the central highlands. They are taking boats through mangroves and diving to see the coral beds that fringe the island. While tourism is good for the economy, all of this nature appreciation can take a toll on the environment. An already fragile ecosystem can be crushed under the pressure of so much traffic. Although government programs exist for the protection of these ecosystems, they remain grossly underfunded.

NATIONAL PARKS

In an effort to preserve the ecosystems of the Dominican Republic, 16 national parks, nine natural monuments, and six scientific reserves have been created.

In the center of the country, the northern

ECOTOURISM

Tourism is no doubt a major industry in the Dominican Republic, which receives around three million visitors a year. Although this boosts the economy significantly, creating jobs for local people and generating a good amount of revenue, relying so heavily upon tourism can exacerbate the strain on the country's natural resources. While it may not be so easy being green, through the collaborative efforts of businesses, government, and communities, the possibilities for sustainability are being fully realized around the country.

The Dominican Republic's Dirección Nacional de Parques has designated conservation areas in the form of six scientific reserves, nine natural monuments, and 16 national parks *(parques nacional)*. Its main objective is to conserve natural resources and ecological inheritances for future generations. Also under protection are a number of panoramic routes and ecological and recreational areas.

Sustainable tourism and ecotourism are movements that seek to support the tourist industry through reducing the negative impact on the environment, and by preserving the integrity of the communities in which tourist accommodations and attractions are located. This includes, in some cases, not just maintaining the communities and economy, but actually pumping new life into them by providing local residents with greater opportunities for a higher standard of living, including educational programs.

Some tour operators, like Iguana Mama and Tequia Experiences, are starting to incorporate this new conscientiousness into their businesses by showing their customers the Dominican Republic that exists outside the all-inclusive resorts that have become so popular. They do this by providing background into the natural history of the country, as well as through fostering interactions between their customers and local folks. Hotels are also starting to get in on the action. Punta Cana Resort and Club is considered the model of the success that can result when private businesses, government, local communities, and educational institutions work together for the good of the country.

---

slopes of the Cordillera Central are protected lands of the **Parque Nacional Armando Bermúdez,** which was founded in 1956 and is home to Pico Duarte at 3,087 meters high. Sliding down the southern slopes is the **Parque Nacional José del Carmen Ramírez,** founded two years later. Together they were created in an effort to protect the remaining pine forests of the Cordillera Central.

The **Parque Nacional Sierra de Bahoruco,** in the Southwest, is a forest highland that receives a good deal of rain due to its height compared to the surrounding arid countryside. Almost 52 percent of orchids in the Dominican Republic are found here.

Located on the southern tip of the Península de Pedernales, including the Isla Beata, are the (for the most part) dry forests of **Parque Nacional Jaragua.** Many bird species (flamingos included!) enjoy the habitat created here

by mangroves, beaches, and lagoons along the fringes of this park.

The country's second smallest park is that of **Parque Nacional Isla Cabritos.** It is an island in Lago Enriquillo and ranges 4–40 meters below sea level. Perhaps the most fascinating thing about this park is that it has one of the largest populations of the American crocodile and endemic iguanas.

On the eastern shore, tangled in mangroves and swamp land, is the **Parque Nacional Los Haitises,** which forms the southern coast of the Bahía de Samaná. Here, rock formations jut out into the water and caves are homes to bats.

Isla Saona and a portion of the southern coast just below San Rafael de Yuma make up the **Parque Nacional del Este.** The mainland part is made up of limestone terraces and is a dry and hot environment.

In the upper northwest corner of the country is the **Parque Nacional Monte Cristi.** It comprises a land portion that is subtropical dry forest with cliffs dropping dramatically into the sea (like El Morro at 239 meters above sea level), numerous coastal lagoons, and a collection of small islands (Los Cayos de Siete Hermanos).

Parque Nacional Submarino La Caleta, just east of Santo Domingo, is the country's smallest national park, weighing in at just 10 square kilometers. Its offshore coral reef (and its shipwreck) gets top billing in this park, which is frequented by divers exploring its marine life.

ETHICAL ECOTRAVEL

What is this "eco" that is getting thrown around everywhere? The term "ecotourism" was coined in the 1980s and was meant to describe responsible tourism in natural areas (like national parks and forests), making sure to conserve the environment and improve the well-being of local people. Emphasis has been put on areas where the flora, fauna, and culture are the primary attractions. Besides simply paying attention to the environmental and cultural factors of an area, it means that the businesses touting the ecofriendly claims should be taking initiative to promote recycling, energy efficiency, water re-use, and economic opportunities for local communities. Unfortunately, the prefix "eco" has become a sort of marketing gimmick in the tourism industry lately, and the Dominican Republic is guilty of it, too. Be wary of establishments that claim ecofriendliness while behaving in environmentally and socially irresponsible ways. For instance, simply placing a resort in a beautiful landscape does not make it ecofriendly.

Tourists with the best of intentions in seeing the Dominican Republic in an ecoconscious manner can actually do more damage than they realize if they don't adhere to some basic practices. Just going there and spending your money doesn't quite do it. If you really want to help out in an effective way for the Dominicans and their natural environment, there are a few ways to go about it.

Giving Dominican-owned independent businesses your money rather than big corporations helps keep the money in the Dominican economy rather than being sent overseas. Many all-inclusive resorts are foreign owned (mainly Spanish, French, and American). Dominican-owned establishments are relatively rare or short-lived ventures (sad but true). One great Dominican-owned choice is the **Paraíso Caño Hondo** resort in Sabana de la Mar, where you can also book tours of the Parque Nacional Los Haitises.

Consider planning your trip for a lower tourist season. In the case of the Dominican Republic, this means *not* December–March. This will minimize congestion in small towns and spread the influx of tourist money more evenly throughout the year, especially for those mom-and-pop organizations whose livelihoods depend on foreign money. Also, visiting in smaller groups (like 4–6 people) is much less shocking to the cultural environment.

Spending the night out in wilderness is a great idea, but make sure to set up camp in designated areas or on durable surfaces like rock, gravel, and dry grasses. Use existing trails for hiking and don't venture from the trail. Build fires only where it is permitted and burn everything down to ash.

If you're visiting an area that is pristine, it's best to try to inhabit areas that have not been visited so that you don't help to create campsites and trails. Right now Bahía de las Águilas (Bay of the Eagles) is pristine. In 2006, a French development company was proposing building four 70-room hotels along its untouched shoreline. Environmentalist groups like the Coalition for the Defense of the Protected Areas are fighting hard to create other options for true ecofriendly establishments for the area's incredibly fragile ecosystem.

Whatever you take into a natural area, bring it back with you when you exit. Packing out all trash, leftover food, toilet paper, hygiene products, and litter is a small task that has a huge impact on the ecosystem. Dig holes for solid human waste (15–20 centimeters deep and at least 60 meters from any water, camp, or trail). While most Dominicans living in the country have no objections to washing themselves and their clothing in rivers, streams, or lakes, it is not good for the environment. Carry water 60 meters away from the source and use biodegradable soap. The philosophy, "When in Rome…" should not apply here.

Marveling at the rich culture and historical artifacts is part of the fun. But don't touch them or take them! Hard to believe and sad examples of people not adhering to this rule are the Taíno drawings found in some caves that have been completely ruined by graffiti. This goes for plant life too. While the country is dazzling with phenomenally beautiful orchid species, picking them is not cool; in fact it's against the law.

Appreciate the wildlife from a distance and don't feed animals. While there aren't many big mammals in the Dominican Republic, you should never approach or follow any if you see them. The same etiquette applies while diving: If a big sea turtle swims past, don't chase it down—just appreciate it as it passes.

Be courteous to other visitors and they will more than likely be courteous to you. Hiking Pico Duarte can be a very populated venture. Yield to others on the trail and you'll avoid confrontations, which have been known to occur. Keep noise levels down. Everyone is there to hear nature, not you.

History

INDIGENOUS PEOPLE
Pre-Columbian Amerindians

Time didn't start with the arrival of Christopher Columbus. For at least 5,000 years before his appearance Amerindians had settled throughout the Caribbean and eventually on the island he later named Hispaniola. First was a group called the Ciboney. Two tribes immigrated after them from South America, one from the Yucatán (the Caribs) and the second from a tribe in the Amazon (the Arawaks), who became the ancestors to the Taíno people, the tribe that ultimately welcomed Columbus.

The Arawaks were skilled seafarers who built long canoes able to carry 50–80 people in order to hunt for a new land to call home. Moving north through the Caribbean, they settled on various islands, scattering themselves around. They were an agricultural and fishing society, so they tended to live near the coasts, eating sea turtles, manatees, and fish. They planted vegetables like cassava, yams, sweet potatoes, and gourds; harvested fruits; and hunted animals like iguanas and birds. They were smart traders and often went from island to island trading what they had.

Hot on their heels were the Caribs, thought to be an extremely aggressive bunch, especially against the Taínos. They attacked them often, killing most men and enslaving the rest. The Caribs and the Arawaks had similar languages, but their social and political organizations were different enough to refer to them as separate nations.

Although the Arawaks were highly organized and smart, they were not warlike and were no match for the tyrannical Caribs, so they escaped and found themselves face to face with the Ciboney on the island of Hispaniola. The Ciboney were engulfed as slaves into what was, by then, Taíno life.

The Taínos

After the Arawaks made their home (over the stretch of about a thousand years) in what is modern-day Dominican Republic, their farming and gathering society evolved into a highly organized one with complex agriculture, art, politics, leisure activities, and rituals. From about A.D. 900 until 1492, the nation lived a blissfully happy existence. Conflicts were resolved peacefully through a game called *batu,*

LAS MARIPOSAS

The rise of Rafael Trujillo to the Dominican presidency in 1930, followed by his subsequent destruction of his supposedly beloved country, led to a growing discordance between the Dominican people and their government. The economy suffered greatly as Trujillo's own wealth flourished. People started living in fear of Trujillo and his secret police – the Servicio de Inteligencia Militar (Military Intelligence Service) or SIM – who would descend upon any individual who gave off even the slightest hint of dissent. But in addition to those who lived in fear of the dictator were those who lived in defiance of him, and among them were the Mirabal sisters – namely Patria, Minerva, and María Teresa – who, in their strength and determination to help their country break free from such a repressive and dangerous regime, became known as Las Mariposas (The Butterflies).

The Mirabal sisters grew up in a well-to-do family. They were educated and strong-willed. Patria was the oldest, born in 1924, on February 27, the anniversary of the Dominican Republic's independence from Haiti. Dede, who was not directly involved in the anti-Trujillo movement of which the others became an active part, was born on February 29, 1925. Minerva was born on March 12, 1926, and María Teresa, the youngest, on October 15, 1936.

Minerva was the first of the sisters to get involved in the resistance. She studied law at the University of Santo Domingo, where she met her husband, Manuel Aurelio Tavares Justo. On January 14, 1959, the Dominican Liberation Movement, which consisted of exiled Dominicans, tried to take down the Dominican government. This attempt, which became known as the Luperion Invasion, was thwarted by Trujillo's military. However, it did spawn the Movement of the Fourteenth of January, an underground anti-Trujillo coalition, of which Minerva's husband became the president. Patria, the most religious of the sisters, and María Teresa, who was an aspiring mathematician, followed their sister into action, and together the three became widely known and admired throughout the country.

The sisters' steadfast opposition to Trujillo led to the dictator lashing out against them (as he did against anyone whom he felt was a threat to his rule). Early on, their family's possessions were confiscated by the government; Trujillo ordered Minerva kicked out of the university because of a paper she wrote in which she detailed what was wrong with the way the country was being run – she included several suggestions for improvement. (She eventually returned to school.) Over the years, the sisters

like soccer. They lived communally in *bohios* (round structures that held 10–15 families) and sometimes practiced polygamy. For the most part they were an agricultural society but hunted and fished as well, using nets made of hemp, cotton, or palm. They used words like *barbacoa, hamaca,* and *tobacco,* words that have been incorporated into modern Spanish and English. In their own language, their name, *taíno,* meant "good" or "noble."

They had large settlements of about 1,000 people, and each had a cacique who acted as a shaman-like priest and a law-maker, and he (or she; though rare, it was not unheard of to have a woman be a cacique) was born into the role. There was a second level to politics—the council of elders. All settlements were part of a larger district, of which there were five at the time of Spanish arrival. These districts' caciques were headed up by the most important regional cacique.

The Taínos were a religious people, and this is the most well-understood aspect of their culture. At the center of their dogma were the ideas of respecting life and worship of ancestors and the dead. They referred to spiritual beings as *zemís* and often depicted them in their art as turtles, snakes, and abstract faces. Some of their ceremonies involved a hallucinogenic snuff called *cahoba,* which they prepared from the beans of a tree. Inducing vomiting with ornately designed spatulas was a way to cleanse and other members of their family – including their mother, father, and husbands – were arrested and sent to prisons, some known for torturing their inmates, where they would be held for up to months at a time. Still, the women did not back down. And in the meantime, the rest of the country was growing more and more disillusioned with Trujillo.

In a final effort to rid his country of the rising influence of the Mirabal sisters, Trujillo ordered several of his men to silence the women for good. On November 25, 1960, the sisters were on their way back home to Salcedo after a visit to Patria's and Minerva's imprisoned husbands. Their car was stopped by Trujillo's devoted thugs, and the three women, along with their driver, Rufino de la Cruz, were ordered out of the car. They were taken into a nearby sugarcane field, where they were beaten and killed.

The killers returned the bodies to the car and pushed the vehicle off a cliff.

Despite the attempt to make their deaths appear accidental, when word got out that Las Mariposas were dead, the Dominican people were not fooled. They knew Trujillo was behind the women's demise. Now, the influence of Las Mariposas was more powerful than ever. Discontent and rage among the Dominicans was at its apex. Six months after Trujillo had ordered Patria, Minerva, and María Teresa killed, the dictator was assassinated at the hands of his own countrymen.

Today, Las Mariposas live on. In Santo Domingo, an obelisk that Trujillo had originally commissioned in honor of himself has been dedicated to the women and repainted to depict their likenesses. It is entitled *The Song to Liberty*. In Ojos de Agua, just outside the city of Salcedo, Dede has created a museum out of the last home the sisters had shared, to honor the three women's memory. Patria, Minerva, María Teresa, and Minerva's husband, Manuel, are all buried on the property, which is open to the public. Throughout the town, murals are painted in honor of the women, with either their faces or images of butterflies to signify their underground code name, Las Mariposas.

In 1995, Julia Alvarez wrote a fictionalized account of the Mirabal sisters. The title of the novel is *In the Time of the Butterflies,* and in 2001 it was made into a major motion picture of the same name. Now, the entire world commemorates Las Mariposas; November 25 – the anniversary of the women's deaths – has been designated International Day Against Violence Toward Women.

---

themselves of any corporeal impurities to symbolize their spiritual purging before the ritual of receiving a communal bread or other rituals.

Although they had no written language, they created extensive cave drawings and petroglyphs in various caves around the island that depicted much of their culture, beliefs, and events. One such drawing in the Parque Nacional del Este is said to depict the trade agreement between a Spanish galleon and a Taíno community.

Tobacco is perhaps their most notable contribution to the Spanish, which they rolled and smoked much like the cigars of the Dominican Republic today.

Whatever discord there was in Taíno life, there was no misery compared to what was about to happen. There is much controversy regarding how many Taínos were living on Hispaniola when Columbus arrived. Figures are all over the map and range from 200,000 all the way up to eight million, although an estimate closer to one million is more likely. Regardless of how many there were, they knew no disease like the horrible smallpox "gift" that the Spanish brought. By 1530, the numbers had shrunk to an estimated 3,000, due to disease, suicide to escape slavery, or genocide.

COLONIALISM
Columbus Arrives
Christopher Columbus, sailing for the Spanish

throne, was expecting to reach Japan and instead stumbled across modern-day Cuba and the Bahamas. But when gold was not to be found on the Bahamian island of Guanahaní, he redirected and found what he dubbed "La Isla Española." After he ran the *Santa María* into a coral reef, it was the Taíno who helped the Spanish salvage every last board and nail so that they could build their fort, named for the day they landed: Christmas Village, or Villa La Navidad. The Taíno generosity and hospitality didn't stop there. They gave the sailors gold as gifts and helped them to build their new home. Columbus wrote to the Spanish crown about the glorious world he'd "discovered," exclaiming that there was gold to be had practically for nothing and remarking how gentle and wonderful the "Indians" were.

Soon after he arrived and set up camp at La Navidad, Columbus felt so confident that he left the settlement to go back to Spain with the understanding that some of his men would hold down the fort. What happened when he left was the bloody beginning to a long story of genocide and slavery. When Columbus returned two years later, he found La Navidad burned to the ground; his men had either died or abandoned their posts, setting sail again in their insatiable hunger for the gold they had been promised. Columbus grew bitter and moved his fort 110 kilometers east, where he built a settlement and named it La Isabela, after the queen of Spain. But this was an unlucky venue as well. Plagued with disease and death, it was abandoned five years later and moved south to the east side of the Río Ozama and eventually to the west bank of the river, where it is now called the Ciudad Colonial, or Santo Domingo.

Genocide of the Taínos

With the establishment of the first settlements of the New World came the establishment of the genocide of the Taíno people. They were forced to work in mines, were horribly mistreated, and died of disease or accidents; many committed suicide rather than continue their new lives at the hands of the Spanish.

In addition to being overworked in the mines, they were murdered. Governor Nicolás de Ovando, who came to Santo Domingo and began building it up with stately buildings and homes, pampering the colonists with beautiful surroundings, took the exploitation of the Taínos to a whole new level. He instituted a system of slavery called *encomienda,* in which entire Taíno villages along with their caciques were forced into a type of feudal serfdom. Determined to squash the Taínos, de Ovando devised a horrible plan. In 1503, he invited the female cacique, Anacaona (the widow of the revered cacique Caonabo who died while in Spanish captivity), to a "meeting" along with 80 other caciques. As Anacaona looked on, de Ovando ordered that all the tribal leaders be burned alive because he suspected them of conspiracy. A horrified Anacaona fled but was eventually captured by de Ovando and hung.

Diego Columbus (Christopher's oldest son) arrived with a sense of entitlement; he was appointed governor (1508–1515) of Santo Domingo and then viceroy of the Indies (1520–1524). He set up his friends and supporters with the best digs and slaves, and started one of the first sugar plantations on the island. Like de Ovando, he beautified the city even more and laid the foundation for the first cathedral in the New World. This was the era of the "firsts"—the first cathedral, the first hospital, and even the first mint. It seemed that Santo Domingo was to be a place of great wealth and power.

But outside the walls of the rich gem, Santo Domingo, lay the outback of Hispaniola, completely ignored by Diego and his cronies, as they let smallpox nearly wipe out the entire Taíno population. That resulted in a severe shortage of slaves.

THE SLAVE TRADE

The Spanish saw the potential for a "cash cow" in Europeans' insatiable need for the sweet stuff, so it was the development of the sugar industry that fueled the slave trade. But with the Taíno population dwindling, the Spanish turned to Africa and began importing slaves. In 1522, the first slave revolt took place, right on Diego Columbus's plantation. Unfortunately, the slaves were horribly massacred. Nearly a half million slaves were brought to Hispaniola between 1520 and 1801. They made the trip in the bellies of galleons, chained together for a horrendous three-month voyage to the Caribbean—a trip that would leave many dead before arrival. Then they had to suffer the incomparable horrors of slavery, being denied their culture and identities, all for the gain of European wealth.

The slave trade was a triangle, literally. Boats set out from various European ports toward Africa's west coast with goods they would use in a trade for people. Once they loaded their slaves onto the ships, they would journey to the Caribbean, where the ones who survived were sold. The ships then returned to Europe with sugar, coffee, tobacco, rum, and rice, all produced by slave labor.

Spanish fortunes were made through the sugar and triangular trade industry, and England and France got jealous. As pirates and buccaneers got wind of the riches, they went with the blessings of (and sometimes funded by) their countries to impede the successes of the industry. One famous incident was when Sir Francis Drake and his 18 ships of men, sent by England, took over Santo Domingo and held it for ransom for a month. When the Spanish finally paid, he looted and burned the entire city before leaving.

The French, on the other hand, in a bold move sent over 13,000 men (farmers and African slaves) to populate the poorly guarded western half of the island. Eventually, the population of their colonies greatly outnumbered that of the Spanish side, making the Spanish incredibly uneasy; in fear of losing control of the rest of the island they agreed to a border treaty called the Treaty of Ryswick (1697), which officially ceded the western portion of Hispaniola to France. It was named Saint-Domingue and the Spanish side was named Santo Domingo. The border that was created is more or less the same today.

THE TUG OF WAR

By 1789 Saint-Domingue was a very wealthy colony, heavily coveted by England, which then overtook Port-au-Prince. It was in this moment of unrest in 1793 that the slaves, led by a brilliant ex-slave, Toussaint L'Ouverture, allied with the Spanish to revolt against the French. But when the French government made a counteroffer to the slaves that slavery would be abolished if they joined again with the French to defeat the encroaching British forces, Toussaint returned to the French side along with his army.

With the French, Toussaint and his men successfully defeated both British and Spanish forces. The British finally withdrew from the island entirely in 1798, and in 1801 Toussaint (without direction from the French government) took control of Santo Domingo for the French Republic. In 1802, Napoleon's French Imperialist forces invaded to try to reinstate the pre-revolutionary climate. Toussaint was eventually captured by the French and sent to Paris, where he died of pneumonia in 1803.

The revolutionary war continued under Toussaint's successor, Jean Jacques Dessalines, and in 1804 Haiti won its independence. It was the second independent country and the first black republic in the New World.

While the French were forced out of the western side of the island, they remained present in Santo Domingo until 1809, when they finally returned it to Spanish control. At that point the colony of Santo Domingo declared its independence and requested to join the Gran Colombia Federation, a South American anticolonial movement run by Simón Bólivar. But that request was never realized because Haiti jumped in and invaded in 1822 and stayed for 22 years under the Haitian president Jean-Pierre Boyer. The 22-year Haitian occupation is a sore spot between Dominicans and Haitians even to this day. Boyer was a hardhanded leader who expressed outrage and discontent toward the former Spanish colony.

On February 27, 1844, Juan Pablo Duarte, with the help of his separatist movement, La

EL JEFE AND THE RÍO MASACRE

One of the most notorious, devastating events in Dominican history was the slaughter of tens of thousands of Haitians at the aptly named Massacre River. The river seems to have derived its name from a battle back in the colonial period, when a number of French buccaneers lost their lives at the hands of the Spanish. In October of 1937, its waters ran red once again.

The man who ordered the massacre was Dominican president Rafael Trujillo, also known as El Jefe (The Boss). In an effort to "whiten" the Dominican population, known as *blanquismo*, Trujillo ordered soldiers to kill any Haitian attempting to cross over the border into the Dominican Republic. The soldiers tried to distinguish the Haitians from the Dominicans by telling anyone who crossed their paths to say the Spanish word for parsley – *perejil*. The soldiers' thinking – or, rather, Trujillo's – was that those from the wrong side of the border, coming from a French background, would be unable to pronounce the trilled "r" in the word. Of course, this theory was rather faulty in that many Haitians, having grown up in such proximity to the Spanish-speaking Dominican Republic, could pronounce the word "properly." Still, in the end, this did not save most of them.

It is thought that Trujillo admired Adolf Hitler and was heavily influenced by what he was trying to accomplish in Europe at the time. In fact, not long before the slaughter began, Trujillo played host to a delegation of Nazis. Paradoxically, after receiving loads of criticism for his murderous attempt to cleanse his country of Haitians, Trujillo invited 100,000 Jews fleeing Hitler to settle in the Dominican Republic. And while this was a blatant attempt to clear his reputation and current standing as a murderer of thousands, it is also thought that by inviting these Europeans to take refuge in his country, Trujillo was in fact trying to further his campaign to whiten at least the eastern two-thirds of Hispaniola.

Despite the amount of disgust and mortification the world felt toward him at the time, Trujillo remained in power until 1961, when he was assassinated by a group of wealthy Dominicans who had had enough of his destructive leadership. Through his efforts at ethnic cleansing, Trujillo succeeded only in befouling his name and his memory. To this day, and no doubt far into the future, the anniversary of Trujillo's assassination is celebrated as a national holiday in the Dominican Republic.

Filantrópica (The Philanthropy), captured Santo Domingo at the Puerto del Conde and claimed independence. Duarte, who was widely supported to be the president of the new republic, was then forced into exile by Pedro Santana, who led the troops that were in favor of returning to Spanish rule. Two decades of Spanish rule ensued.

Finally, in 1865, independence fighters reclaimed control in what is now called La Guerra de la Restauración (The War of the Restoration). And on March 3, 1865, the queen of Spain finally withdrew all her soldiers from the island.

The new rulers soon encountered internal strife and within six months they were ousted from power. The Dominican Republic fell into the era of *caudillos*, strongmen who ruled areas as if they were personal fiefdoms complete with armies made up of local peasants. These men were more concerned with getting rich in their own area than for the betterment of the country as a whole. To keep the people in line, their armies strong and themselves in power, they used fear as a tool by keeping the constant threat of a Haitian invasion. The oldest political trick in the book.

During the age of the *caudillos*, leadership of the country was a tennis match switch-up of civil war between the armies of General Pedro Santana and General Buenaventura Báez, fighting back and forth for control of the government. The Dominican economy was devastated by Santana and Báez printing pesos and the civil war. Currency was worthless. Baez went into exile and Santana declared himself president and pleaded for Spanish annexation. The Dominican Republic was annexed to Spain once again in 1861 and they immediately began to phase out the Dominican governing leaders. The Dominican populace felt the sting as their rights began to gradually slip away, and as a result rebel forces kicked off La Guerra de la Restauración (The War of Restoration) in February 1863. The Dominican rebels succeed in showing the Spaniards the way off the island in July 1865.

Enter the second wave of *caudillos*. After the War of Restoration, many were grappling for control of areas and depending on various natural resources like mahogany, tobacco, farming, and cattle ranching. Between 1865 to 1870 there were 20 changes in government, but in 1869 Buenaventura Báez became president again and he tried to sell the Dominican Republic to the United States for US$150,000. Even though U.S. President Ulysses S. Grant was all for it, and Presidente Báez signed the treaty, the agreement was defeated in the U.S. Senate.

In 1882, General Ulysses Heureux (known as Lilí) began his brutal dictatorship. He had borrowed a lot of money from the United States and Europe to finance his army (as well as to bulk up the sugar industry), but he ground the Dominican economy into a pulp and brutalized the people so harshly that he was assassinated in 1899. This caused constant rock and sway of individuals coming into power and overthrowing one another, causing general chaos and corruption in the Caribbean nation and turning the heads of the Americans, who had great interest in the sugar industry. The U.S. took control of the Dominican customs houses and demanded payment of the loans. After two years, the debt was reduced to a treaty, which helped the Dominican Republic get back on its shaky economic feet, thanks in part to the booming sugar industry.

In 1914, U.S. President Woodrow Wilson demanded that the two bickering (and fighting) sides, the *Horacistas* (supporters of Horacio Vásquez) and the *Jimenistas* (supporters of Juan Isidro Jimenes) stop and pick a president of the country. To press the point, U.S. military landed in Santo Domingo in 1916 and stayed until 1924, eventually taking over complete control. They disbanded the Dominican army, allowed all incoming American products to come through customs tax-free, created a domineering National Police Force, disarmed the people, and installed a puppet government, who answered to the U.S. Marine commanders. They also organized a tax system, built highways, improved education, and organized other institutional reforms.

TRUJILLO DICTATORSHIP

After the American occupation ended, the Dominican Republic saw a short period of hopeful growth. And then Rafael Leonidas Trujillo reared his head.

Trujillo had joined the National Guard when the Americans were occupying the country and was trained by the United States Marines to "maintain order" once they vacated. In reality though, the training just ignited his greed and obsessive need for power. Having risen through the ranks, he held a sham election in 1930 and, as the only candidate, "won" the presidency. Very quickly, the Dominican people were introduced to the first true totalitarian (and egomaniacal) dictator in the Caribbean. He changed the name of Santo Domingo to Ciudad Trujillo and renamed the highest mountain Pico Trujillo. By 1934 he was the richest man on the island, having seized sugar plantations and ranches for himself. Tying his personal wealth to the wealth of the country, he set it up so that the country flourished, even achieving the support of the United States. The economy soared, as did agricultural production, as did industrial progress, as did his own personal spending; he even built homes that he never lived in.

And the high cost was being paid by the people in the currency of repression. Under Trujillo, all households had to have portraits or plaques stating their allegiance to "El Jefe" (The Boss), children recited daily prayers for him, and anyone who was thought to be against him could suffer torture or death. His secret police would follow and question, perhaps even jail, anyone they wanted. Trujillo trusted no one, and spies were everywhere.

Trujillo was obsessed with creating "whiteness" in the Dominican Republic. *Blanquismo,* as it was called, was the driving force behind his order to massacre around 20,000 dark-skinned Haitian sugarcane workers in a river now named Río Masacre (Massacre River), although he claimed it was a response to the Haitian government's support of exiled Dominicans who were plotting against him. In a mad dash to clean up his image, he promptly invited Jewish immigrants to relocate and escape the horrors of Hitler. This act and the anticommunist policies he adopted put him in the good graces of the U.S. government, but that relationship would eventually be his demise.

With Trujillo's blatant attempt on the life of the Venezuelan president, Rómulo Betancourt, and his murder of the revolutionary Mirabal sisters, resentment grew, and he was assassinated by members of his own regime on May 30, 1961. It is widely believed that the CIA in the United States provided the weapons to his assassins in fear of having "another Cuba" on their hands.

After his death, Ciudad Trujillo and Pico Trujillo, along with a host of other places, reverted to their original titles, Santo Domingo and Pico Duarte.

POST-TRUJILLO

After Trujillo's death, Joaquín Balaguer was president. But it was not a presidency that was supported by the people. He was merely a puppet. Soon, a council took control until elections could be held, at which point the first free elections in the Dominican Republic in years took place and Juan Bosch Gaviño won the presidency. A liberal man, he was a scholar and had a soft spot for workers and students. He enacted many liberal concepts, like separation of church and state, and wanted very much to instill economic and social justice. He went so far as to give Trujillo's estates to peasants (what was left of them after Trujillo's family took off with a majority of the money).

After only seven months in office, Bosch was ousted by conservatives. Eventually a civilian triumvirate ruled the nation and did away with his constitution (saying Bosch's ideas were outlawed), declaring it nonexistent.

But Bosch, with the aid of a group called the Constitutionalists, started plotting for his return.

U.S. Intervention

The United States decided to back the conservatives, but even that didn't deter the Constitutionalists, who, on April 24, 1965, led by Col. Francisco Caamaño Deño, rose up against the triumvirate to restore Bosch's office. They seized the National Palace and radio stations, asking people to take to the streets and demand Bosch's return. Lawlessness ensued; both sides were heavily armed.

Twenty-three thousand U.S. Marines were sent by Lyndon Johnson, ordered to restore peace and elections. Balaguer eventually was put back into power (no doubt with bribes) and won the elections again in 1970 and 1974. He lost in subsequent elections but won yet again, in 1986. In that term, he supported the need for a healthy tourism industry, set up the industrial free zones, and basically spent a lot of public money. Food and power were in short supply. And still, in 1990, he ran again. He won the 1994 election (by this time totally blind and 86 years old), but under pressure from the military, he cut his term short.

Dominican Republic Today

In 1996, Leonel Fernández (born and raised in the U.S.) won the presidency over José Francisco Peña Gómez (a liberal), and he brought a change of economic growth. But with the dawn of the new millennium came Hipólito Mejía, who promptly sank the peso to a hurtful RD$52 to the U.S. dollar.

In 2004, Fernández won again, defeating the incumbent Mejía. His win was likely in direct reaction to the severe economic crisis that was the signature of Mejía's presidency, when food costs quadrupled and debt doubled and unemployment soared. It was a significant election in that it was the first time Dominicans abroad were allowed to vote in the national election.

President Fernández won a third term in office in May of 2008. Nevertheless, many Dominicans would argue that he has a fixation on technological development for the nation that sometimes is to the detriment of basic needs such as adequate health care. Around 40,000 people carry the HIV-AIDS virus, and most don't know of their condition; 75 percent of the people carrying this virus are from the poorest populations. Yet, 2.2 million (23.8 percent) Dominicans have Internet access, and 56 percent of the population have cell phones, and Fernández controversially allocated US$700 million for Santo Domingo's new Metro system.

Certainly the global economic crisis made 2008 a challenging and difficult year, but, looking to the future of the Dominican Republic, familiar challenges of the past continue to plague the president, and he continues to plead with the nation to have confidence that his government will find solutions for issues such as the ever-present energy crisis, crime, and food production while hopefully increasing economic growth and attracting investments.

Government and Economy

GOVERNMENT

The Dominican Republic has a democracy with executive, legislative, and judicial branches. The executive power is the president, who appoints a cabinet, is the commander-in-chief of the armed forces, and executes laws passed by the legislative branch. The president and vice president both hold four-year terms.

The National Congress consists of the Senate (32 members) and the Chamber of Deputies (150 members). The judicial system has a Supreme Court consisting of nine judges elected by the Senate.

The three main political parties in the Dominican Republic are the PRD (Partido Revolucionario Dominicana or the Dominican Revolutionary Party), the DLP (Partido de la Liberación Dominicana or Dominican Liberation Party), and the PRSC (Partido Reformista Social Cristiano or the Social Christian Reformist Party). The current president, Leonel Fernández, is a member of the DLP.

With one of the first free elections occurring in 2004, a new generation of "clean" politics has the opportunity to strengthen. But corruption, which has always been a problem, is not gone yet. With each election, government workers fear for their jobs, since most who gain power reward their supporters and oust the previous staffs, and this goes through all levels of government, not just the top seats.

ECONOMY

In 2003, a major banking scandal tipped the economy on its ear, ending in the collapse of the bank Baninter. Confidence in the government's ability to handle the economy plummeted, hitting rock bottom along with the peso. As the peso lay cold on the economic floor, then-president Mejía's spending and borrowing habits (US$1.1 billion) added even more insult to injury and brought the inflation rate to around 25 percent—prices rose and wages didn't—and the poor got even poorer.

The Dominican Republic has long been dependent on agriculture (especially sugar) for the economy, but it is no longer a one-trick pony as the cigar production industry has stepped up its game.

But for exporting, mining (gold, silver, ferronickel, and bauxite) is number one, with agriculture behind it. Dominicans living abroad—sending money home—are huge supporters of the economy, offering about US$3 billion a year.

Perhaps more controversial are the manufacturing plants called industrial free zones (like the one in San Pedro de Macorís) that were set up to specifically make goods for the U.S. market. These plants offer tax concessions and supply extremely cheap labor under harsh conditions. In 2005, under the Bush administration, the CAFTA-DR agreement was signed between the United States and Costa Rica, El Salvador, Guatemala, Honduras, Nicaragua, and the Dominican Republic, in the hopes of strengthening and developing economic relations and encouraging trade between the countries by reducing and eliminating barriers of trade in goods and services. Major opponents to this bill say that the supposed benefits of globalization don't make it down to the citizens (doing the work) with proper work environment guidelines and benefits.

A huge boom in tourism helped what seemed to be an ongoing economic sinkhole. Since the 1960s, tourism had been gaining on sugar, which was the main provider for the nation's economy. But now, tourism brings in the most foreign currency (about US$2 billion each year) and has created many jobs (about 150,000), but not nearly enough. About half of the Dominican Republic's population lives in poverty and about a third of the people don't have secure jobs. The inequality between rich and poor is obtrusive. And so it goes; the middle class (what little one there is left after the recent economic turbulence) holds on feebly.

Tourism

It's unclear why the Dominican Republic arrived so late to the tourism game. Perhaps it was a controlling dictator who didn't like foreigners in his own backyard, or perhaps it was the political and civil unrest of the 1960s. Whatever the reason, tourism did begin to take hold later on, but then 9/11 happened in the United States and people stopped traveling for a little while. As tourists started arriving again, it was the American contingent that picked up because of the United States' proximity to the Dominican Republic. Vacationing closer to home became very desirable to Americans, and

the Dominican Republic was benefiting and continues to do so.

The Dominican Republic tourist industry has traditionally focused on budget travel, with special attention to the all-inclusive scene. Tourism is highly concentrated in the complexes along the coasts, which are mostly foreign owned. This type of vacation caters to the sun-worshipping visitors who rarely leave the confines of the resort's walls. When they do, it is most often only to go to the metropolitan area of Santo Domingo. For a very long time, budget travel was the only game in town, but in 2008, the tourism industry's tides turned toward courting a new batch of travelers with high demands for Shangri-La-type resorts. These resorts have high-style decor, butlers, non-buffet restaurants, private pools, and VIP areas. But with the struggling U.S. economy affecting the world economy, it remains to be seen just how successful that switch will be. No matter what the fad du jour, the Dominican Republic is still the budget travel capital of the Caribbean, relying on its excellent geographic location—proximity to the United States and Canada—and plenty of options for savings and fun.

The potential for ecotourism has risen dramatically over the years. Born to oppose the practices of mega-resort complexes (which mistreat the environment with their pesticides to kill mosquitoes and their blind eye toward the ecosystem), ecotourism, with its emphasis on environmental sensitivity, has inadvertently shined a spotlight on the center of the country, where adventure sports are really taking off and becoming a viable competitor for the "best-kept secret in the Caribbean."

Agriculture

The real face of the Dominican Republic is the one of its countryside, where the produce grows and where the sugarcane waves through the breeze in magnificent green fields. Agriculture was the supporting structure of Dominican economy for centuries. In the 1960s, it encompassed about 60 percent of the labor force and yielded about 80 percent of exports. By the 1980s those numbers dramatically dropped. Even sugar production dropped down the list of important economic producers. In large part, the transformation paralleled the trend of the population moving to more urban areas. At the same time, the United States reduced its call for sugar quotas, thereby depressing the production of the crop, which was the backbone of the economy for a very long time.

Culture

Take one small island in the heart of the Caribbean and divide it in two. On the larger part, remove all organic Taíno (set aside, you'll need it later as a garnish), then immediately add Spanish with a twist of French, English, and a huge dose of African, then add a dash of American and the constant press of Haitian influence, and season with culture, food, people, race relations, music, literature, poetry, politics, war, various occupations, genocide, and the slave trade. Steep inside of a pressure cooker, adding at least one devastating natural event each year. After 500 years you will have the rich multicultural soup that is the Dominican Republic. It is in this way that the Dominican Republic has become the proverbial *carnaval* of culture that we know today.

Despite the fact that this nation has such a memory of tyranny and fear as the genocide of the Taínos on their historical welcome mat, it is often said that the Dominican people are some of the friendliest and most hospitable in the world. In fact, most discussions about Dominicans begin this way because it is so true. They are fierce believers in making a visitor feel welcome and included in the Dominican experience. The Dominican experience is to walk lightly through life with a smile for everyone to see and a polite demeanor. Whether you are purchasing something from

© ANA CHAVIER CAAMAÑO

typical clapboard home

a stranger or talking with someone you know, polite behavior is to chitchat for a bit first and be complimentary. In other words, don't be in too much of a hurry to have people flit in and out of your life; everyone is important enough to have an interaction with, even if just for the duration of buying a bottle of water.

The Dominican psyche is to always have a song in your head and to sing it out loud no matter who is around. It is to have a sense of humor about their own world and the world outside of the Dominican Republic. Laughing is a big part of life. At the same time, there is a very strong sense of pride in their culture and nationality. This is evident in Dominican expats in other countries. When they find each other amid the sea of other Latinos, they are instant friends.

Family is a thick bond that goes beyond blood. Loyalty to those they care about is a more accurate statement. It is perhaps the most welcoming sensation to be invited into a Dominican home and made to feel included with such honest warmth. Families stick together in times of sickness and financial stress, and the closeness is not a class issue. This trust crosses all levels of socio-economic strata. The trust of a family member is something that Dominicans do not take lightly.

But it would be overly romantic to say that there aren't some fissures of discontent or discord running through the cultural fabric. Race relations are just one sore spot and by far the worst. There is a great deal of emphasis put on color and how one fits on that spectrum, and it is strongly tied to class. This is especially obvious when it comes to Haitian/Dominican relations.

While Dominicans are hospitable and loving people, they are for the most part quite conservative. The day-to-day male chauvinism and homophobia can be quite unsettling to an outsider but is incredibly normal there.

THE PEOPLE

It is difficult to talk about race and class separately in the Dominican Republic. Dominicans see skin color as a definite line between upper

FAMOUS DOMINICANS

- Moisés Alou – baseball player
- Julia Alvarez – writer
- Ashanti – R&B singer
- Robinson Cano – baseball player
- Oscar de la Renta – fashion designer
- Junot Díaz – writer
- D.M.C. – rapper
- Juan Luis Guerra – musician
- Juan Marichal – baseball player
- María Montez – actress
- Michelle Rodríguez – actress
- Porfirio Rubirosa – racecar driver and playboy
- Zoë Saldaña – actress
- Arlenis Sosa – fashion model
- Sammy Sosa – baseball player

and lower class. Perhaps this is an inherited outlook from centuries of ingrained thought passed on from Taíno/Spanish and Spanish/Haitian relations.

Most light-skinned Dominicans (about 70 percent of the entire population) refer to themselves as *blanco* or white but are usually of "mixed heritage," showing more European features than African or indigenous ones. There are other terms to define color: *Indio claro* and *Indio oscuro*. The first is used to describe a whiter and the second a blacker skin tone and the terms are meant to hint at Taíno blood. This is a near impossibility since barely any Taínos survived the Spanish onslaught. *Negro* simply means black and refers to those who are of pure African descent.

The wide ethnic variety is largely due to

the various waves of different immigrants to come through here—Jewish, Middle Eastern, African, Spanish, Japanese, German, Italian, English, and other Caribbean islanders, to name just a few. Of course the Haitians have the longest history as immigrants to the Dominican Republic. Thousands of Haitians live and work in the sugarcane fields and live in poverty-stricken conditions despite their great contribution to the Dominican workforce and economy. They are often mistreated and discriminated against.

All you need to do to see the class differential is to take a drive through the country or cities. Luxury cars and shopping malls contrast with dirt roads and poor wages. Look into the faces and you'll see the color distinctions. The whiter the skin, the higher the class. Although most Dominicans don't like to say that there is indeed racism and classism, the Dominican Republic is a nation fragmented along the color lines of its people. A very small percentage of people (5 percent at best) enjoy wealth, status, and power, whereas 80 percent live in poverty. But living in the pressure of the middle (as all middle children do) is the growing and struggling-to-hang-on middle class (roughly 15 percent).

RELIGION
More than 90 percent of Dominicans practice Roman Catholicism, the official religion of the Dominican Republic. However, it is not as strictly adhered to today as it once was. And few practice a pure form of Catholicism. Instead they often practice the symbolic gestures of it.

Folk religions and beliefs are practiced (as is Vodou), but they often are in more closed circles and private spheres since they are berated as "evil." *Curanderos* are a kind of folk healer that many seek out for healing herbs and incantations for the purpose of healing. At many open markets, you will see various herbs and candles being sold for just this purpose.

During World War II, a few Jewish families were invited by Trujillo to immigrate to the North Coast. They were given land to farm and stayed for a short while, but after suffering anti-Semitic ridicule, many left after a few years. Some 20 families remain and maintain a synagogue in the town of Sosúa.

GENDER ROLES
Like many Latin American countries, the Dominican Republic exhibits a strong, male-oriented culture, much of which was inherited from Spanish colonialists. Latino machismo, an exaggerated sense of masculine power, is very prevalent here. Dominican men carry the hefty reputation of being womanizers. Performing acts that flaunt sexual prowess is central to the macho attitude. Leering, bold comments, gestures, and the ever-so-infamous hissing noise made toward women of all ages and types that pass by are just some of the ways they flaunt their colors. Simply ignoring them will usually stop the behavior. The more you engage with them, the more they keep at it. It is not so much meant as a direct pass as it is about proving importance to themselves and other men and to make themselves feel secure.

While women in the Dominican Republic have made gigantic strides toward equality, there is still work to be done. Today, women make up a majority of high school and college graduates and are increasing the likelihood of getting jobs and pay equal to those of men. Slaying the machismo dragon is a hard battle, but one that Dominican women are more than ready for. Still, they play the game as hard as men do with a flirtatious nature.

On the home front, women are usually in charge of organizing and maintaining all family rituals and events, while men maintain the traditional role of being "head of the household" and the figure of authority. One of the foundations of Dominican culture is their sense of family, and women are what hold that together.

While many Dominican men are worried about proving their sexual prowess, many Dominican women are very concerned with their physical appearance. A great amount of pressure is put on women of all ages to be thin, and women spend hours on their hair, straightening it to look more "European" or desirable to men.

More than 90 percent of Dominicans are Roman Catholic.

LANGUAGE

The official language of the Dominican Republic is Spanish, although in the coastal tourist areas, English, French, Italian, and German are all spoken. Dominican Spanish is a far cry from the official Spanish of Spain. Less formal and laced with innuendo and colloquialisms, it is a hard form of Spanish to get hold of, especially when Dominicans drop S's off the ends of words. But Dominicans are usually very happy to know that a foreigner wants to learn their language and are very patient listeners and teachers. Most are willing to walk you through whatever you're trying to say and correct you politely when you make an error. They may even be eager to learn a few words in your language in exchange.

Dominican Spanish is filled with riddles and limericks used to describe even the most mundane of occurrences. It is a sort of oral tradition passed down for generations. If you are faced with an expression and you don't understand it, politely ask for an explanation. Although the translation might not be as funny in your language, it is probably a laugh-riot in Spanish, so try to conjure a giggle.

Music and Dance

Merengue and *bachata* are the soundtrack to everyday life in the Dominican Republic. But unlike the music in a movie, which fades into the background setting the mood, this music takes over the scene. A merengue band greets you at the airport the moment you get off the plane, music blasts from the stereo of your taxi, and your driver shouts over it. *Bachata* issues from the radios at the *colmados* that you pass on the highways. Music is everywhere in the Dominican Republic, and Dominicans know a lot about it. They are quick to tell you who the singers or musicians are.

The happy sounds of these forms are what hook you, but both merengue and *bachata* are tightly connected to the Dominicans' national identity. Lyrics have deep social meaning and encompass love, humor, and politics. Dominicans take great pride in both merengue and *bachata* while claiming affinity for one or the other, but it is safe to say that these soundtracks have deeply impacted the collective imagination of the nation and have affected each and every artist at some point in their artistic endeavors.

Merengue is usually composed in 2/4 time, and there are three different styles: *perico ripiao,* more commonly called *merengue típico; merengue de orquesta;* and *merengue de guitarra.* They are rhythmically similar, but what makes them different are their instruments and repertoire.

Perico ripiao literally means "ripped parrot." The term has been linked to the name of a brothel in Santiago in the 1930s. The suggestive name became connected to the style of music played there. While originally starting in the Cibao region, *merengue típico* is often considered the "country music" of the merengue genre. Instruments began with only a Spanish guitar and a *marímbulla* ("thumb piano") and evolved into *merengue típico,* which replaced the guitar with the accordion (brought to the Dominican Republic by Germans in the 19th century) and incorporated the *güira* (a long cylindrical metal scraper believed to be of Taíno

origins) and the *tambora* (a two-headed drum of African origins). As *típico* evolved over the 1900s, *merengueros* began adding instruments like the saxophone, the electric bass, and the bass drum (played by the *güirero,* keeping the band at five men. One of the most famous musicians of the *típico* style is Luis Kalaff, who was honored in 2008 by the governor of New York with the prestigious Bobby Capo Lifetime Achievement Award for the annual Hispanic Heritage Month. However labeled, *merengue típico* plays an important role in Dominican music history and modern social culture. Today you can find *perico ripiao* bands at family functions, roaming neighborhoods on Christmas and New Year's Eve, and playing for tourists in many of the popular hot spots.

Merengue orquesta developed in the 1930s and is the "big band" of the merengue genre. It was derived for the ballrooms and dancehalls of the social elite as well as the middle class. While *típico*'s strength is improvisation and pushes the accordion into the forefront of the arrangements, the *orquesta* relies heavily on horns, replacing the accordion altogether. Johnny Ventura and Wilfrido Vargas were two highly stylized musicians of the 1960s who brought a flashy new sound and look to merengue. Think Motown meets merengue.

With the arrival of Juan Luis Guerra onto the musical scene in the 1980s and 1990s, the sound of merengue changed to mix with more modern arrangements influenced by jazz and pop and with a return to some *típico* styling. Merengue crossed into other genres as the new century arrived. New fusions surfaced like merenhouse, merenhiphop, and merenrap. Fulanito (a Dominican-American group), Sandy y Papo, and the group Sancocho are just a few examples of these bands who thought outside of the box.

Bachata is a guitar-based form of music that comes from the Cuban bolero. Dominican radio stations didn't start playing it until the 1960s, and even then its rotation was very

DOMINICAN FESTIVALS AND EVENTS

While **Carnaval (February,** various dates) lasts all of February throughout the Dominican Republic, it all climaxes with a pre-Lenten celebration in Santo Domingo. Representative *diablos* come from each town to create a colorful parade of masks and costumes. Floats and dancers parade down the Malecón, culminating in a riotous party that lasts until dawn.

Semana Santa (dates vary; usually in **April**) is the holy week for both Christianity and Vodou leading up to Easter Sunday. The party stretches all across the nation with loud music, dancing, and barbecues. Hate crowds but want to see Santo Domingo? This is a great time to visit the capital city. The metropolis is a ghost town with many locals going on vacation to beach resorts and mountain retreats.

Bookworms amble through the gates of the Plaza de la Cultura Juan Pablo Duarte annually to attend the **Feria Internacional del Libro Santo Domingo** (Santo Domingo International Book Fair, **April-May**), which lasts two weeks. The cultural event is 12 years running and has over 650 international and national exhibitions from more than 20 countries, boasts over 40 pavilions, and is one of the most well-attended fairs in the country.

The **Santo Domingo Jazz Festival** (every Thursday in **June,** www.casadeteatro.com) is a jazz aficionado's dream. Every June, Casa de Teatro, a small theater in the Colonial Zone, hosts performers from around the world. The 2009 festival boasted a hot lineup from the Dominican Republic, the United States, Argentina, Cuba, Spain, and France in an outdoor concert series bursting with melodies, changing tempos and rhythms, and passionate improvisations.

The **Feria Internacional de Arte** (FIART, May, www.fiart.com.do) was new to the Dominican Republic in 2009. This annual festival in Santo Domingo has more than 35 participating art galleries.

The festival of **Espíritu Santo** (first or second week in **June**) is celebrated all over the island, but the most amazing festivities are in Santo Domingo's Villa Mella. Listen to the playing of African congo drums and watch the religious processions.

Santo Domingo Jazz Festival (Thursdays in **June and July,** www.casadeteatro.com).

The **Merengue Festival (July** in Santo Domingo, **October** in Puerto Plata; dates vary slightly each year) takes place along the Malecón in both cities with amateur DJs spinning merengue all along the seaside. Live music is played and beer is sold to huge crowds of dancers. These festivals are both national favorites.

Día de Restauración (August 16) celebrates the Dominican Republic's independence from Spain (Restoration Day) with parties all over the nation. In Santo Domingo, it is celebrated around Plaza España.

The **Dominican Republic Jazz Festival (November,** www.drjazzfestival.com) takes place in the small town of Cabarete, on the Atlantic. The festival is internationally known and gives participants music, dancing, and events under the stars.

On **New Year's Eve (December 31)** the year is sent out with a bang and a large party on the Malecón (of course), with more than 250,000 people dancing in the streets to the tunes of multiple live bands. Plan way ahead for this holiday. The hotels near the Malecón book up fast with locals as it is next to impossible to get a taxi.

---

limited because it was born of the lower class neighborhoods and the countryside and was therefore associated with backwardness by the upper class of society. As it was relegated to the barrios and the brothels, the themes began to tell the stories of the prostitutes and the poor. The songs were packed with jilted lovers, workers ripped off by the government, and the troubles of the barrio residents—all told in colorful language and with sexual double entendre.

Its instruments are a lead guitar, rhythm guitar, electric bass guitar, bongos (or instead sometimes the tambora drum), and the *güira* (or maracas). The influence of merengue can be heard in the rhythm and guitar

FROM THE BARRIO TO THE BIG LEAGUES

Baseball is not just a game in the Dominican Republic; it is part of the cultural landscape. It is a place where big dreams that have turned to reality for so many have become a solid ray of hope for many of getting out of poverty. Baseball is practically a lucrative export. Dominicans in Major League Baseball in the United States in 2008 made up the largest minority in the game. In fact, the mecca of baseball, San Pedro de Macorís, has produced more professional players per capita than any city, anywhere.

Baseball fans who come to vacation here October through January are landing smack dab in the middle of the Liga de Invierno (Winter League), which consists of 50 games. The winner will go to the Caribbean World Series and will play against other Latin American countries. Watching a game, you could catch a glimpse of the next big major league star; even some of the current American major league stars who call the Dominican Republic home will come here to play in these games to hone their skills since this season runs after the major league season ends. Two dozen major league teams have training camps here.

The Dominican Republic has six professional baseball teams: Licey and Escojido (both of Santo Domingo); Las Águilas (from Santiago); Las Estrellas (from San Pedro de Macorís); Gigantes (from San Francisco de Macorís), and the Azucareros (Toros) del Este (La Romana).

Even the most uneventful or low scoring game has a party in the stands. There are dancers on top of the dugout and a band roaming through the bleachers.

lines, and many artists cross over between the two genres, like Juan Luis Guerra. While many music critics dispute whether Guerra fits into this category of music or not, it is undeniable that his widely sold album, named *Bachata Rose,* increased awareness of *bachata* on a world music stage. This crossover made *bachata* a more accepted form of music not only throughout the country, but all around the world.

A few *bachata* giants are José Manuel Calderón (the first recorded *bachata* song), Raulín Rodríguez, Joe Veras and Antony Santos, Aventura, Frank Reyes, Yoskar Sarante, Monchy & Alexandra, and Luis Vargas.

Even though merengue and *bachata* are the national music genres, other forms exist. There is salsa aplenty and reggaeton, too; everything from alternative and pop to jazz and classical can be heard in cafés and cars rolling down the street. There are festivals for merengue and even a successful annual **Dominican Republic Jazz Festival** held in Cabarete.

But dancing is a must for Dominicans. When it comes to rhythm, there is an old saying that Dominican children can dance before they can walk. The danceable music is their birthright. At any gathering you will find the intoxicating music; there is no defense, you will eventually find yourself tapping your feet and getting up to dance. The "Cuban motion" (figure eight hip motion) and fast foot action necessary to execute both *bachata* and merengue dances seems to be an innate motion for a Dominican. If you are not a dancer, they will be very puzzled by this. Dancing is directly equal to enjoying life to its fullest.

Art and Artists

One of the few positive things that Trujillo's regime did for his country was to open **La Escuela Nacional de Bellas Artes** (The National School of Fine Arts) in 1942 in the Palacio de Bellas Artes in Santo Domingo. Trujillo invited important and talented Spanish artists like José Gausaches (painter), Jose Vela Zanetti (painter and muralist), Eugenio Fernández Granell, and Manolo Pascual to create works for the presidential palace and teach students. Their presence had an impact on the generations of artists in the mid-20th century, and they left their mark on many public buildings and churches.

From the 1960s to the 1970s, the Trujillo assassination, the short Bosch presidency, and the Civil War gave way to a decade of artists with political art in mind and brought about a movement combining poetry with painting. During this time, the poetry and paintings were equally as valuable, often being a part of (if not embedded in) the same piece. Some artists who came to the stage during that time were Ramón Oviedo and Cándido Bído, Elsa Núñez, and José Cestero. Many of their works depicted peasants, street people, and topics of everyday politics and alienation.

In the 1970s and 1980s there was an energetic rocking back and forth between neorealism and abstract. Expressionism, surrealism, sculptures that were also paintings, multimedia, installations, and performance art were all explored. Dominican artists living abroad came home to create during this decade. Some of these artists were: Alberto Bass (the first to produce photorealism in the Dominican Republic), Dionisio Blanco, Joaquín Ciprián (metal sculptor), Jose García Cordero (gets his inspiration from dreams and relies on the viewer's ability to respond to symbolic metaphor), Alonso Guadalupe, José Miura, Manuel Montilla, José Perdomo, Alberto Ulloa, and Fernando Ureña Rib.

From the 1990s to current day, many artists have been competing in regular biennial competitions and have highly individual styles. A few notable names are Belkis Ramírez, Tony Capellán (mixed media), José García Cordero, Martin Lopez, Marcos Lora Read, Jorge Pineda, Raul Recio, Freddy Rodríguez, Bismark Victoria, and Amaya Salazar.

Fashion Design and Architecture

Oscar de la Renta was born in Santo Domingo and moved to Spain when he was 18. Although he never went to fashion school, he began his career as a fashion illustrator for Cristobal Balenciaga in Madrid, where he learned the techniques of fashion design. In Paris he was a couture assistant for Antonio Castillo, and then he worked with Elizabeth Arden in New York, who put Oscar's name on the label. In 1965, Oscar finally began his own design house and started his own ready-to-wear label. It was marked by Caribbean-bright colors and crossed with his European-trained eye for embellishments.

At **Altos de Chavon School of Design** in La Romana, students can study fashion design, graphic design, interior design, and fine arts/illustration. The school is associated with the Parsons School of Design in New York. **Dominicanamoda** (www.dominicanamoda.com) is a high fashion show held in October in Santo Domingo, with 23 runway passes showcasing new-to-market Dominican designers, well-known Dominican designers, and designers from abroad. This highly successful event has been running since 2006 and includes presentations from countries like Argentina, Chile, Colombia, Ecuador, and Venezuela. It is also a benefit for local charity groups.

Architecture styles in the Dominican Republic are as varied as the terrain. The city of Santo Domingo was a walled city when it was first founded (1503) by Nicolás de Ovando with a grid plan layout inside. All important buildings were constructed according to the Spanish design of the time and around the main plaza, Plaza Colón. Most buildings in Santo Domingo at that time were built in Isabelline Gothic style (such as the cathedral). But look elsewhere both in the capital and on the rest of the island and you will find Victorian (late and gingerbread), Modern and Art Deco styles. Perhaps the most memorable for a visitor will be the clapboard homes in multiple colors.

Literature and Film

Political oppression fueled writers from the days of Spanish settlement on the island of Hispaniola back in the 1400s. Literature in the Dominican Republic began as a form of protest against the government and its abuses of the Taíno people and the land—as was the case for Bartolomé de la Casas in his *Historia de las Indias.* His writings were a first-hand account of the atrocities and a plea to the Spanish rulers to stop the inhumane treatment of the Taíno people.

From the 1400s to the 21st century, the Dominican Republic's literary landscape has been one of a nation both reconciling with a tumultuous political history and trying to grasp an image of its own national identity. The Dominican Republic has undergone not only Spanish rule, but also French and English. African influence has superimposed itself onto the culture by way of the slave trade. Haitian influence comes by way of invasion, annexation, and sharing an island. The Trujillo years, from 1930 to 1961, intensely influenced all aspects of Dominican day-to-day life and, therefore, its literature during the decades he was in power and to this day.

Early female poets were Leonor de Ovando (the first poet in America), Manuela Aybar, Josepha Antonia Perdomo, and Salomé Ureña de Henríquez. Ureña is a celebrated nationalist, poet, and revered teacher who launched the first teacher training school, a superior education center for women in the 1880s. Her style is mostly neoclassical poetry. Another lasting work from this time is by the poet José Joaquín Pérez, who penned a collection of poems called *Fantasías Indíginas* (Indian Fantasies) about encounters between *conquistadores* and Taínos.

Trujillo's impact on poetry and literature has had a lasting effect. During his time of rule, he had an oppressive hand in sanctioning only the type of poetry that he approved of. However, this meant that a few underground movements of new poets and writers, including La Poesia Sorpredida, were bubbling under the surface waiting to burst forth with new styles, ways of thinking, and words when the time was right. And they did just that. They blatantly confronted issues of racism and classism throughout the country. The Sorpredida voices were surrealists who used dream-like imagery and were: Franklin Mieses Burgos, Freddy Gatón Arce, Aída Cartagena Portalataín, Manuel Rueda, Manuel Valerio, and Antonio Fernández Spencer. Juan Bosch Gaviño, president of the Dominican Republic in 1963, was one of the most influential essayists, novelists, and short story writers of 20th-century Dominican literary history. His writing has inspired new writers to either emulate him or rebel against his traditional topic: the problems of the lower-class citizens.

Some notable Dominican writers who have emigrated to the United States are Julia Alvarez and Junot Díaz. Alvarez's *How the Garcia Girls Lost Their Accents* is a story about a family leaving the Dominican Republic during the time of Trujillo and the subsequent acculturation of the Garcia girls in the United States. Her book *In the Time of the Butterflies* is an award-winning novel that fictionalizes the lives of the Mirabal sisters—three Dominican women involved in a plot to overthrow Trujillo. Díaz's novel, *The Brief Wondrous Life of Oscar Wao,* won the 2008 Pulitzer Prize.

FILM

Although the Dominican Republic itself doesn't have a strong film industry, it is striving to foster growth in the industry. In 2008, the country hosted the second **Dominican Republic Global Film Festival.** Films were screened in 10 venues, in Puerto Plata, Nagua, Santiago, Higüey, and Santo Domingo, over the course of five days. Its mission was to bring world dramatic and documentary cinema to the Dominican Republic and hopefully create a cinematic presence in the country as a location for the business.

Hollywood has passed through to make more than 60 films or TV shows either partially or in full. Some of the better known titles are: *The Godfather: Part II* (1974, Francis Ford Coppola); *Apocalypse Now* (1979, Francis Ford Coppola); *Jurassic Park* (1993, Steven Spielberg), shot at the Salto Jimenoa Uno near Jarabacoa; *The Lost City* (2005, Andy Garcia); *Miami Vice* (2006, Michael Mann); *The Good Shepherd* (a 2006 spy film by directed by Robert DeNiro); and *Sugar* (2008, Anna Boden and Ryan Fleck), an independent film that received much critical acclaim at the 2008 Sundance Film Festival, about a baseball player from the Dominican Republic who tries to make it in the minor leagues in America.

A couple of Dominican-made films have seen some success in recent years: *Sanky Panky* (2007, directed by José Enrique Pintor) and *Yuniol (2)* (2007, directed by Alfonso Rodríguez).

ESSENTIALS

Getting There

BY AIR

The Dominican Republic is fortunate enough to have 10 international airports. **Aeropuerto Internacional Las Américas** (SDQ, Santo Domingo, tel. 809/549-0081) is considered the main international airport on the island. **Aeropuerto Internacional Punta Cana** (PUJ, Punta Cana/Bávaro, tel. 809/959-2473) serves the busy tourist area known as the Costa de Coco. **Aeropuerto Internacional Gregorio Luperón** (POP, Puerto Plata/Playa Dorada, tel. 809/586-1992) is the main airport for the Costa de Ambar's Playa Dorada and Puerto Plata resort areas. **Aeropuerto Internacional Cibao** (STI, Santiago, tel. 809/581-8072) serves Santiago and the interior or the Cibao region. **Aeropuerto Internacional La Romana** (LRM, La Romana/Casa de Campo, tel. 809/689-1548) serves La Romana and the Casa de Campo resort complex specifically. **Aeropuerto Internacional Arroyo Barril** (ABA, Samaná Península, tel. 809/248-2718) and **Aeropuerto Internacional El Portillo** (EPS, Las Terrenas, tel. 809/248-2289) are mostly for small aircraft during whale-watching season (January–March). **Aeropuerto Internacional El Catey** (AZS, Samaná, tel. 809/338-0094) is the newest airport on the island and accepts flights from Europe and Puerto Rico. **Aeropuerto La Isabella** (JBQ,

© ALICIA CHAVIER CAAMANO

Stay safe; always ask for a life vest in a boat or ferry.

Higuero, tel. 809/567-3900) is a domestic airport, and **Aeropuerto Internacional Maria Montez** (BRX, Barahona, tel. 809/524-4144) isn't open for commercial passenger flights.

Some airlines that fly to the Dominican Republic include: **American Airlines** (tel. 809/542-5151, www.aa.com), **Air Canada** (tel. 809/541-2929, www.aircanada.ca), **Continental Airlines** (tel. 809/262-1060, www.continental.com), **Delta** (tel. 809/200-9191, www.delta.com), and **Jet Blue** (tel. 809/549-1793, www.jetblue.com).

The Internet is the best place to look for affordable flights to the Dominican Republic. There are often deals depending on what time of the year it is, what day you fly, and how long you stay.

If you want to look into all-inclusive resort vacations, check online or with a travel agent, as they have package deals where you pay one lump sum that includes air, hotel, food, drink, and often transportation from the airport.

BY FERRY

Ferries del Caribe (Santo Domingo port, tel. 809/688-4400; Puerto Rico port, tel. 787/832-4400) is the only ferry company that can get you to the Dominican Republic. It is based in Puerto Rico and offers thrice-weekly service. All are overnight trips. If you can swing the cost, getting a private cabin is the way to go; that way you can sleep for the 12-hour boat ride rather than sit in an airplane-style seat while crossing the ocean (see the *Santo Domingo* chapter for more information).

Getting Around

BY AIR

Since the Dominican Republic is a very small country, most people either take the bus or drive wherever they need to go. But if you want to wing it, literally, there are a few domestic air charters available. Most flights cost under US$100. Two such companies are: **Aerodomca** (tel. 809/567-1195, www.aerodomca.com) and **Caribair** (tel. 809/826-4444, www.caribair.com. do). Both companies fly to many cities within the Dominican Republic as well as to other Caribbean islands. If you would like to charter a private plane, would like to set up a special air excursion, or need a helicopter ambulance (here's hoping you don't need that!), **Air Century** (tel. 809/426-4222, www.aircentury.com) offers those services. **Take Off** (tel. 809/552-1333, www.takeoffweb.com) offers daily flights within the Dominican Republic as well as shuttle service to/from airports and area hotels.

BUSES AND *GUAGUAS*

The first type of service is a first-class bus. Much like the Greyhound buses in the United States, these are modern and have the big comfortable seats with toilets on board. Some even have movies playing on small TVs. These buses are one of the best options for transportation if you want to move around the country. The country is so small that most trips are under four hours. There are a few bus companies, but only two truly good options. These top companies stand out above the others because of their affordability, reliability, and cleanliness. They are: **Caribe Tours** (tel. 809/221-4422), perhaps the best one with the most departure times, and **Metro Tours** (tel. 809/566-7126), which has similar service at less frequent intervals. Most tickets cost US$3–10.

Another option is to take a *guagua*. *Guaguas* are the true Dominican transportation system (aside from the *motoconcho*). This can be a fun way to meet the locals or a nerve-wracking experience. They are minivan-sized buses that can hold up to 30 people. To flag one down (which is the way you do it), just stand on the side of the road for the direction that you want to travel in and wave it down, or wait to find out what the *cobrador* (charger) says. He is the man who hangs out the side of the bus and takes the fares and says the destination of the *guagua*. They rarely display destination signs, so don't feel bad if you have to flag down a couple before getting the right one. As always, most Dominicans are happy to help if you have questions. The typical fare for a ride is US$2.

THE FREEDOM OF THE OPEN DOMINICAN ROAD: SCARY OR THRILLING?

Motorcycle enthusiasts everywhere agree that feeling the air rush all around you and the road thrumming beneath you makes exploration by car pale miserably in comparison. There is something infinitely sexier about motorcycle travel, especially if you are hugging the hot Caribbean curves of a road lined with palms, destined for a beach hideaway.

Dominican highways are dangerous, no doubt about it. Say this to a motorcycle fanatic, though, and you are met with a "And your point is?" stare. This notion is only fodder for excitement to these thrill seekers. Luckily for them, more and more adventure tour companies are picking up on this trend and offering motorcycle adventures. One such company sets up one- to seven-day tours and can even arrange for custom tour packages. All arrangements are made with them: **MotoCaribe Adventure Tours** (U.S. tel. 877/668-6386, D.R. tel. 809/574-6507, www. motocaribe.com).

Try to have the exact change. They may not offer change for you if you don't ask.

RENTAL CARS

Renting a car can be a fantastic way to experience and see the real Dominican Republic for yourself. Many international companies have offices in Santo Domingo, at major airports, and in high tourist areas like Punta Cana and Puerto Plata. Avis, Hertz, Alamo, and Dollar are just a few examples. Before renting a car in the Dominican Republic, check with your credit card company to see if you are automatically covered for international rentals. If not, getting the optional car insurance through your chosen rental agency can be expensive but worth it considering the road conditions, lack of rules being obeyed by other drivers, and potential for accidents.

Renting a car, even if it might not fit within your vacation budget, might be an expense worth the trouble if what you want to do is travel to a remote part of the island where public transportation becomes less easily accessible, like Bahía de las Águilas on the Península de Pedernales in the Southwest. Try to reserve a four-wheel-drive over the Internet before you arrive if you plan to drive outside of the cities. You'll be so happy you did (you'll be so surprised how often roads can sometimes just end).

Driving Conditions

Driving here can be downright scary. If you don't have experience driving in fast conditions with quick reflexes, perhaps you should consider the bus. Road conditions can change quickly; there are often pedestrians on the sides of the roads and crossing very busy thoroughfares.

But, if you really want to try it, you're in for a fun experience. Some words of advice: Keep your eyes peeled for potholes and random speed bumps, known as *policía acostada* (sleeping policemen), in the middle of the highway. Always drive defensively. Trucks, *motoconchos,* and other cars do not follow very many rules—you have to be ready for anything. Just because there is a red light does *not* mean they will stop.

Try to run with the pack; otherwise, you might cause a pileup.

PÚBLICOS

These jalopies are found in the bigger cities. They are usually minivans, trucks, or regular cars, and they pick passengers up along main drags. Similar to *guaguas, públicos* can be hailed from anywhere. They will usually slow down enough for you to gesture. If you don't, they'll zoom past you quickly. They don't have signs (although technically they're supposed to), and the fare is usually US$0.30. Often, drivers cram them to the breaking point with as many passengers as the car can physically hold with the doors shut (sometimes even that is tested!). Hold your purse here—pick-pocketing can occur when it gets full. But if no one else is in the car, you might end up paying taxi rates unless you specify that you want *servicio público*.

MOTOCONCHOS AND MOTORCYCLES

Motoconchos are a cheap and easy-to-find transportation option. These mopeds can

Motoconcho ride or portable phone booth?

© SAMUEL KRUCKER

usually be found around main town squares or tourist-frequented areas. Flag them down and secure a price before hopping on. Never expect a helmet to be offered up—they won't have them. Beware: The drivers can be downright maniacal. While very dangerous for trips on the highway, they are undeniably cheap and easy to find in small towns. They are more suitable for short distances, and you can always request that the driver go slowly. They are used to this request from the tourists. Samaná's multiperson version of the *motoconcho* is considered safer than the more common one-passenger type because it is more like a carriage that is pulled by a motorcycle and is therefore slower-going and more visible to other motorists.

As if driving isn't scary enough in the Dominican Republic, motorcycles are becoming more popular. But on the plus side, on a bigger motorcycle (as opposed to a *motoconcho*), you will be louder and bigger than the *motoconchos* and, therefore, more easily seen by the car drivers. Hopefully, that will make your experience safer.

Many of the same rental agencies that rent cars also rent motorcycles. However, there are more and more specialty excursion outfitters, such as **MotoCaribe Adventure Tours** (U.S. tel. 877/668-6386, www.motocaribe.com). They offer guided one-, four-, and seven-day trips through the country on Suzuki V-Strom 650s. Nevertheless, motorcycle riding in the Dominican Republic should be left to highly experienced riders. Beginners should never dare to start on these roads.

Visas and Officialdom

All tourists will need a passport to enter the Dominican Republic. You will also be required to purchase a US$10 tourist card to enter the country via one of the airports, so make sure you take exact change. Check to see if your passport is valid and that you have sufficient room for an entrance and exit stamp prior to departure.

Tourist cards can be purchased in your arrival airport and allow you to stay for 30 days. Once you get off the airplane, you will be led (or just follow the crowd) to the immigration room. Here there will be a window where you need to get in line and purchase a card. Fill it out (make sure to have a pen with you) and then get in the appropriate line in front of the immigration officers. They'll check your passport and approve your visit for however many days you say you'll be there. By the time all of this business is taken care of, your luggage will most likely meet you in customs. Usually it's quite painless, and they don't tear your luggage apart unless you're carrying a lot.

If you decide to stay longer than a 30-day period, you'll need to visit the **Migration**

Department in Santo Domingo (Centro de los Héroes, Autopista 30 de Mayo, tel. 809/508-2555, open 8 A.M.–3 P.M. Mon.–Fri.) and request an extension, or you can pay a scaled charge at the airport upon departure from the Dominican Republic.

For those who fly into the Dominican Republic, departure tax is charged upon leaving. The cost is US$20 and must be paid before leaving the airport.

Those who use a visa to enter the country and overstay the legal period will be charged a fee. This fee starts at RD$60 and depends on the length of the stay.

Traveling with Children

Children under the age of 13 who are traveling with a parent or legal guardian are not required to have a passport but should carry a birth certificate. Children traveling with non-parents should have a passport. No special letter of authorization is required for children traveling with non-parents, so long as they return with the same adults they arrived with. However, get in touch with the Dominican Republic consulate or embassy to confirm the situation has not changed.

The all-inclusive resort can be a fix-it trick for the parent who needs a vacation. As you are researching your trip, make sure to find out if the resort you chose has a Kids' Club or children-specific activities. Often they will have babysitters or fun activities that occupy the little ones while parents are getting to have their vacation too, like a nap by the ocean. In addition to diversion, these complexes offer food variety that will satisfy even the pickiest and have sweet treats to spoil them that they will love, like make-your-own-ice-cream-sundae bars. It is a vacation, after all. Most of these resorts come equipped with a medical unit for simple medical needs like sunburns, food poisoning, and fever.

The rest of the nation can be a little challenging for families only in the sense that there aren't a lot of kid-specific activities to chose from. Santo Domingo can be a frenetic experience for some toddlers who get cranky with a lot of activity, but at the same time, it can offer a great deal of historical, cultural, and art learning opportunities for the curious youngster.

As always, it is best to travel with basic necessities. Don't forget plenty of sunscreen that is waterproof. Also bring allergy medications, diaper rash ointment, bandages, and antibiotic ointment.

Traveling with Pets

If you are traveling with your cat or dog, you must bring a veterinarian's certificate of vaccination against rabies, which has to have been issued within 30 days of entry into the Dominican Republic. You are also required to bring a veterinarian's certificate of health, issued within 14 days prior to entry. For further details on traveling with a pet check out www.dominicanrepublic.com or www.hispaniola.com under Travel or Tourism.

Conduct and Customs

Dominicans are incredibly fun-loving people. While not stuffy by any means, they do adhere to codes of behavior that are rooted in politeness. It is a very important aspect of Dominican culture. For instance, it is considered impolite to get right down to business with someone, which tends to be the American way. Instead, if you don't speak Spanish, a nice smile with a *buenos días* is a good way to start a conversation. If you speak Spanish, you might even venture forth into a small dialogue about something pleasant (like what a nice day it is) before you go into what you are about to ask of them. This is the same for telephone etiquette.

The Spanish words *por favor* (please) and *gracias* (thank you) go a long way toward bridging cultures and making new friends. When faced with street or beach vendors, if you're not interested in what they're selling, politely say *no, gracias*. They will try again and again, but just keep a smile and say *no, gracias*.

Capturing the Dominican culture can be a lot of fun for photographers, but always keep in mind that taking a photo without permission is not respectful. It is culturally acceptable to ask permission first and then offer a tip if they let you. Most young people will be happy to pose and will be very smiley for your photos, but it's best to ask first.

While Dominican vendors expect you to haggle, already hiking prices up for the challenge, don't take advantage of it. It is tempting to haggle in flea markets and with vendors for the lowest of the low prices. But just keep in mind that it is their livelihood. Paying a fair price is a respectful thing to do. The same thing goes for the service industries. If you get good service somewhere, let them know you appreciated it and tip well. Ten percent of a bill is considered a generous gratuity.

Dominicans are famous for being very hospitable people. They are excited to show their

WEDDING CELEBRATIONS IN PARADISE: IDEAS AND MUST-DOS FOR YOUR I-DOS

How does a wedding in paradise sound? On the beach? Amidst 15th-century buildings in the colonial city of Santo Domingo? The Dominican Republic offers wildly romantic venues for beginning your life together. Major resorts and hotels throughout the Dominican Republic have experts on staff to coordinate a flawless wedding that will give you and your guests lifetime memories.

Most wedding packages include the following: judge, license, flowers, music, cake, champagne, and special touches for the bridal accommodations. Here are some more tips for a carefree wedding celebration:

1. Start planning your wedding at least six months in advance. This way you are sure to get better deals than a last-minute booking; vacancies are more likely, and most hotels prefer at least a three-month leeway to make all necessary arrangements. If you choose a wedding on the beach or under the stars, what will you do if it rains? Religious ceremonies take longer to prepare.

2. Research venue options by visiting their websites. Often, venues will provide complimentary wedding services, but they have other wedding packages for additional cost that offer options above and beyond bare essentials for your stay, wedding, and honeymoon (e.g., religious ceremonies, couple's massage, breakfast in bed, pre-wedding day breakfasts, or spa treatments for the wedding party).

3. Ask if the hotel has a photographer/ videographer on staff. If not, can they recommend one?

4. Do you need a translator? Ask if the hotel has someone who can translate the ceremony if need be.

5. Consider decorations. When arranging for decorations and cake toppers, ask what the staff can do. Tropical flowers are an easy and low-cost choice. Orchids are abundant in the Dominican Republic. How about seashells? If you have a cake in mind, send a photo of your dream cake and see if they can copy it.

6. What will you wear? When choosing attire for your ceremony, keep in mind the Caribbean climate. Sleeveless dresses are great, but consider the fabric. And what will the groom wear? Does he want to be in a full tuxedo under the blazing sun, or are there other options? If you plan a wedding right on the beach, remember that a dress with a train will not stay white.

7. Plan on being at the resort or hotel at least three work days in advance. This is best for any last-minute arrangements. Use the time to ready yourself for any guests that will join you. Perhaps put together a welcome basket with local fare or might-need items like suntan lotion or disposable cameras, for their room upon check-in. Or simply work on getting the perfect tan for your wedding.

WHAT YOU'LL NEED FOR MARRIAGE PAPERWORK

- Passport

- Original birth certificate

- Single status affidavit in Spanish

- Divorce act in Spanish. Legal transcripts of the single status affidavit and divorce act can be prepared at the Dominican consulate nearest to you.

- Two witnesses. If they are not Dominican, they will need to bring their passports.

You will receive the wedding certificate from the justice of the peace.

CUSTOM WEDDINGS

Do you want someone else to do all this legwork for you so you can just show up and have it all happen? Richard Weber at **Tours, Trips, Treks and Travel** (Cabarete, tel. 809/867-8884, www.4domrep.com) can make your dream wedding happen in the tropics. Dream big; it's okay. Richard is a miracle worker who uses all his Dominican Republic knowledge and contacts to get the job done so you can have all of the memories but none of the headaches.

culture and country to newcomers who want to learn. They don't mind answering questions at all when asked politely. They might even offer to show you around or help you beyond what you had asked.

The Dominican Republic is notorious for fantastic music, great festivals, and all-night dancing. It is also famous for rum drinks. However, partying to Dominicans doesn't mean excessive drunkenness. In fact, it is highly frowned upon.

Tips for Travelers

ACCESS FOR TRAVELERS WITH DISABILITIES

By law, resorts and hotels on beach properties cannot exceed three floors. This isn't a disability-friendly law, but it does, by default, make navigation over the resort grounds a bit easier since most restaurants and facilities will be on the ground floor. Make sure to request a room on the ground floor, in case there is no elevator. Many of the all-inclusive resorts have rooms for travelers with disabilities. However, outside of the all-inclusive resorts, the Dominican Republic isn't exactly an easy place to get around, so expect some logistical glitches. It's best to check with a travel agent prior to booking. Your agent should make the right reservations at the right hotels.

WOMEN TRAVELING ALONE

It's generally safe for women to travel in the Dominican Republic. However, women traveling alone are best off playing it safe and doing any trekking during the day and on public transportation so that they are not alone. You might be given some grief and opposition if you tell a Dominican (male or female) that you wish to travel throughout the country alone. It is not seen as "right" for women to "have" to travel alone. The major thing you will come face to face with is the machismo of Dominican men in the form of whistling and ogling. They mean no harm and it is a completely normal interaction for them even though it might startle a newcomer. Just be smart about whom you talk to and whom you decide to befriend.

GIVING BACK: VOLUNTEER TOURISM

You've done the all-inclusive resort, the spa getaway, and the city shopping spree. But sometimes, you wonder if there is more to vacationing than just making it through the buffet line for the fifth night in a row while wondering if you will fit into your bikini by the time you leave. Maybe you want to show thanks for your good fortune, or perhaps you want to learn about the community you are visiting and at the same time give back to them. Well, this is what volunteer tourism is all about. You will contribute to the local economy in a bigger way than buying a trinket that will just sit on a shelf at home.

Voluntourism is the best way to augment your vacation in the Dominican Republic. Lots of companies are jumping on the bandwagon of voluntourism, so do your homework before you sign on to any one company. Reputable companies should be able to produce a list of past participants and their contacts.

While voluntourism isn't free, it shouldn't be expensive to help others, either. You should expect to pay for housing, meals, and some other costs, but the expenses shouldn't be exorbitant.

If you are concerned about not getting enough rest and relaxation from the stresses in your regular life, consider mixing a shorter stint as a volunteer with a fun vacation for yourself, and your vacation will be a well-rounded one.

SUSTAINABLE AND RESPONSIBLE TRAVEL

Reducing the impact on the country that you travel in is a responsible way to visit a new culture. To make a positive impact as you travel, help conserve natural resources and support the local culture and economy. Here are just a few ideas on how you can do that.

Learn at least a few courtesy words in Spanish. Although the Dominican people are very hospitable and many know English, it is very appreciated (and the polite thing to do) when you try to speak Spanish.

Visit during a local festival. Not only is this great fun, but it is a wonderful way to learn about the culture through music, history, dance, art, and crafts. Dominicans can throw a party!

Avoid buying food in containers to go and instead eat inside the restaurant. This will minimize your waste on the road. It can be hard to be in a country that hasn't fully grasped the idea of recycling and where you see garbage strewn. So if you see trash, pick some up and put it in a bin.

Shut off your lights, air-conditioning, fan, TV, computer, and radio when you leave your hotel room. The Dominican Republic is notorious for electricity shortages. Help 'em out.

Better yet, pick a hotel that is environmentally aware and practices energy-saving tactics too. Find one at www.environmentallyfriendlyhotels.com

When shopping: Support the local artists by buying their hand-made products. Say *"no gracias"* to mass production. Where is the personality in that? Know what is endangered. In the Dominican Republic, watch out for red coral and tortoiseshell anything! Check out www.traffic.org for up-to-date information.

Use public transportation instead of renting a car. Dominican highways and streets are dangerous to drive on anyway, so let a local do it for you and you'll be supporting the economy at the same time.

When choosing a beach, go to a Blue Flag beach. Communities that have earned this moniker for their *playas* have been practicing responsible environmental policies. There are seven in the Dominican Republic and they are named at www.blueflag.org.

Hey, Wanderer, stay on that trail! When hiking, it may be tempting to venture off, but you could be seriously damaging some land or treading on and destroying flora and frightening fauna.

Choose Dominican-owned businesses, restaurants, and hotels as often as you can. If you are cooking for yourself, shop at the local farmers market. The produce on the island is gorgeous, fresh, and cheap. However, when buying seafood, limit what you buy to fish and shellfish that are in great abundance in the ocean.

Shop in the *colmados* (corner stores). It supports the true Dominican workhorses of the nation. Have a *fria* (beer) and a sandwich there, and listen to music; they are the keepers of the culture and hold the mood of the country in their hands. Whatever you do, support them by spending some money there. Buy a telephone card, gum, or some *platanitos* (plantain chips).

Perhaps most important: Respect the culture you are in and their traditions and customs. Things that are not normal in your culture are commonplace here and vice versa. Respecting the Dominican way of life for the short time you are visiting is responsible travel. You wouldn't want someone to come to your house and sneer at you, would you?

Using common sense is always a good idea. Don't wear flashy jewelry—you don't want to attract attention for a robbery—and dress conservatively when traveling alone. If you carry a purse, don't carry all your money in it. Separate your cash, credit cards, and bank cards so they aren't all in one spot.

SENIOR TRAVELERS

The days of senior travelers content to sit for their entire trip on a lawn chair in the shade with a book are all but gone. Older travelers are finding a lot more pep in their worldly steps as they globe-trot and aren't content to sit around as much (okay, so taking a load off for a bit is a much-deserved break, of course). In the Dominican Republic, there are oodles of things for the energetic to do.

Seniors on a budget may want to consider the all-inclusive resort. They offer comfort, security, cleanliness, and luxury at an unbeatable bargain price, and excursions can be booked right at the front desk if you should choose to have some adventure at the last minute.

Enjoying your golden years golfing will be purely divine in the Dominican Republic. The nation was voted Golf Destination of the Year by the International Association of Golf Tour Operators for its 2009 celebrations. Many of the all-inclusive resorts and major hotels can organize tee times at any course.

GAY AND LESBIAN TRAVELERS

There have been positive strides made in the gay and lesbian community of the Dominican Republic recently: Gay bars are able to have a longer shelf-life than before without being forced to close their doors; the first all-gay, all-inclusive resort opened up on the Península de Samaná; and the first gay pride parade was held July 1, 2001, in Santo Domingo to little opposition.

Still, homosexuality is relatively taboo, while not intolerable to most, and just isn't something that can be openly shown. If you're traveling with your partner (or you meet someone there), showing affection, even holding hands in public, is not acceptable.

For gay and lesbian nightlife options, Santo Domingo has the best scene. Many of the bars are in the Ciudad Colonial. Check out www.monaga.com/casamonaga.htm and www.santo-domingo-gay-tourism.com/ for some info on where to go. Some venues can be more discreet than others.

Health and Safety

BEFORE YOU GO
Vaccinations and Medications

For those who take prescription medications, it is important to bring enough for the duration of your trip—and perhaps even a little extra—as there is no guarantee specific types will be available. Also, pack medication in carry-on luggage to ensure it does not get lost if there are complications with the airline. If you will be traveling with children who are prone to childhood illnesses such as ear infections, be sure to bring along the appropriate antibiotics.

Vaccinations for typhoid and hepatitis A are important for both adults and children. Check with your doctor at least eight weeks in advance to make sure the timing of the vaccinations is appropriate. Updates of routine immunizations (for children in particular) such as tetanus, polio, diphtheria, measles/mumps, and varicella are highly recommended. Also speak to your doctor about malaria and diarrhea medications.

Internet Information

Consult the **World Health Organization (WHO)** website (www.who.int/ith/) for any information on your destination. Look for its book, called *International Travel and Health.* Also, **MD Travel Health** (www.mdtravelhealth.com) has a Dominican Republic page that is updated regularly.

STAYING HEALTHY
Bottled Water

Drink only bottled water in the Dominican Republic. Even brush your teeth with it. It's better safe than sorry. Fortunately, most restaurants, resorts, and hotels now use bottled water even for their ice cubes, but if you're not certain, ask for no ice in your drinks.

Most all-inclusive resorts (and some smaller hotels) have small refrigerators in the rooms. If they provide water for you, drink it only if the seal isn't broken. If they don't provide it, go buy some at the local *colmado* (corner store); you'll need it, especially for all those hot days spent in the sun. Don't forget to hydrate yourself with pure water. Nothing keeps away the stomach-yuckies like flushing your system with tons of water.

Sunstroke

Many folks who get a form of heatstroke think that they've gotten food poisoning, when really, they are just starved for water. Most vacationers tend to overdo the sun exposure in the first days, drinking alcohol and sweating more body moisture than they're used to. The key, once again, is to drink lots of water. Use sunscreen of at least SPF 30 and take a hat or seek out some shade under a nice palm. Oh, and lots of water. If you do get burned, get some aloe to *gently* rub on your skin, and take it easy. Oh, and drink water.

Traveler's Diarrhea

The only way to avoid this is to avoid tap water and to avoid fresh fruits and vegetables (if they're raw). You can tell it is simple "traveler's diarrhea" if there are no other symptoms like fever.

If you get diarrhea just let it pass. Your body is trying to tell you that something is wrong. Taking Imodium should only be for emergency situations, like the plane trip home or salsa dancing. Drink lots of fluids that replace the electrolytes you're losing with fluids. A few loose stools is normal; if it's more than five a day, you should take an antibiotic. If you develop a bloody stool or a fever, see a doctor.

Hepatitis A and B

Hepatitis A is a viral infection that attacks the liver and is passed via contaminated food, water, ice, or another infected person. Symptoms may include fever, jaundice, malaise, nausea, vomiting, and abdominal pain. There is no treatment for hepatitis A, but most cases will resolve themselves. Occasionally, though, it can cause severe liver damage. Ask your doctor for the vaccine against hepatitis A. It is not a safe vaccine for pregnant women or children under two, but it's very safe and effective for everyone else.

Hepatitis B also affects the liver but is transmitted sexually or through infected blood (like via a blood transfusion). Getting vaccinated against it is important for those who will be traveling longer than six months.

Dengue Fever

Dengue fever is a viral infection specific to the Caribbean that is transmitted by a certain type of mosquito. These mosquitoes bite during the daytime and like to hang out wherever humans are, in stagnant water containers like jars or cisterns. Symptoms feel flu-like and include joint pain, muscle aches, headache, nausea, and vomiting and a rash to follow. Most cases will only last a couple of days. There is no treatment. But you can take acetaminophen like Tylenol and drink lots of fluids. There is no vaccine. Protect yourself from mosquito bites for prevention.

Malaria

Malaria is also transmitted by mosquitos; these usually attack around dawn and dusk. Symptoms include a high spiked fever, with chills, sweats, headache, body aches, weakness, vomiting, and diarrhea. Severe cases can lead to complications in the central nervous system, including seizures, confusion, coma, and death. Ask your doctor about malaria pills; they are sometimes recommended for areas in the Dominican Republic (mostly near the Haitian border, but also in Punta Cana). If your doctor prescribes malaria pills for you, continue taking them four weeks after you've returned from your vacation.

Women's Health

The Dominican Republic has all of the women's sanitary products you may need. Although the exact brand might not be available, pads, tampons, and panty liners all are readily available at the big supermarkets, pharmacies, and corner stores.

Small Necessities

Bring a small medical kit with Band-Aids/gauze, rehydration salt packets, duct tape for blisters, tweezers, antiseptic cream, strong sunblock, aloe for sunburns, antibiotics, Imodium (just in case), Tylenol, birth control, condoms, and anti-fungal cream. And by all means, throw in a roll of toilet paper. Traveling through the Dominican Republic, you never know what kind of bathroom you'll get.

HEALTH AND EMERGENCIES

In case of a crime emergency, find your nearest Politur office. This is a specifically appointed outfit of police to serve the tourists. Politur officers are appointed in their jobs because they are able to speak a language other than Spanish. For any other emergency, call 911.

Health Emergencies and Clinics

Foreigners seeking medical attention are advised to go to **Clínica Abreu** (Santo Domingo, Calle Beller 42 at Av. Independencia, tel. 809/688-4411) or **Clínica Gómez Patiño** (Santo Domingo, 701 Independencia, tel. 809/685-9131). These clinics are high cost, but the level of care is good and they have 24-hour emergency rooms.

While this may sound strange, calling a taxi might get you to an emergency room quicker than calling an ambulance. A company like **Techni-Taxi** (Santo Domingo, tel. 809/566-0109) is a good one to call. They will have one at your door in usually 3–5 minutes. Obviously, only call for a taxi if you think you won't be needing medical care on the way to the clinic.

Insurance

Check with your health insurance provider to make sure you are covered while traveling abroad. Don't forget to carry proof of your health insurance with you. Another option is to get traveler's insurance. If you are booking your trip through a travel agent, ask for some suggestions. Policies can get you some short-term coverage for medical, evacuation, flight accident, and life insurance. Do an Internet search for providers in your area.

Information and Services

MONEY, EXCHANGE RATE, AND ATMS

The monetary unit of the Dominican Republic is the Dominican peso. Most banks in the main towns have ATMs that dispense pesos. Go to the big banks like Banco Popular, BanReservas, ScotiaBank, and Banco León. Always choose an ATM in a well-populated and safe part of town.

Items marked in stores are priced in pesos, but you can always ask if they'll take your currency. Before you do this, you should know the daily exchange rate, which is published in the newspaper every day. Because the exchange rate fluctuates frequently, the prices presented in this book are in U.S. dollars. A recent example of an exchange rate is US$1–RD$35.13. In general, it is best to exchange your money in the large commercial banks as opposed to with the moneychangers who approach you.

Although debit cards are becoming more common, it is still primarily a paper money exchange. Credit cards are widely accepted in bigger venues, especially where tourists go. Traveler's checks are almost obsolete but can be exchanged at almost any bank or exchange booth. Most hotels and other tourist spots will list prices in U.S. dollars as well as pesos in the current exchange rate.

COMMUNICATIONS

Without a doubt, the easiest and most readily accessible way to make a **long-distance call** is by using a Verizon Comunicard. You can buy them at hotels, gift shops, corner stores, pharmacies—everywhere, it seems. All you do is follow the directions on the back of the card and it is a prepaid long-distance phone call.

If you are going to be staying in the Dominican Republic for an extended amount of time and

© SAMUEL KRUCKER

Dominican pesos

have an old cell phone to spare, take it with you. You can then take it to any Verizon office and they will activate it for you for a small fee. You can then receive phone calls on it and buy phone cards to use from it. It is a very convenient way to communicate, probably the most cost effective if you're staying for a while. Placing long-distance calls in the Dominican Republic is easy. What looks like the area code (809) is actually the Dominican country code and doesn't need to be dialed before a phone number within the country. If a Dominican phone number is 809/555-0012, then while in the country you only need to dial 555-0012. Calling from the U.S. or Canada, you would dial 1-809/555-0012.

Verizon also happens to be the country's number one **Internet access** provider. Most bigger towns, especially ones that are frequented by tourists, have a Verizon office. Cybercafés are becoming more and more popular and are in towns such as Santo Domingo, Puerto Plata, Bayahibe, Boca Chica, Cabarete, Bávaro, and Las Terrenas.

For excellent Internet sources for all things Dominican (news, travel information, business, tourism, sports, message boards, directories, exchange rate, weather) in English, go to www.dr1.com or www.dominicantoday.com. These are both fantastic English-language, Dominican reference websites.

There are two main **newspapers**—*Listin Diario* (www.listin.com.do) and *El Caribe* (www. elcaribecdn.com). Others include: *Hoy* (www. hoy.com.do), *El Nacional* (www.elnacional.com. do), and *Diario Libre* (www.diariolibre.com).

The **postal** system in the Dominican Republic is a completely useless organization, not to be trusted with any important documents or packages. However, most hotel front desks will mail things for you. For really reliable service pay extra for FedEx (tel. 809/565-3636) or DHL Dominicana (tel. 809/543-7888).

MAPS AND TOURIST INFORMATION
The national tourist office, **Secretaría de Estado de Turismo** (Ministry of Tourism,

TIPPING AND TAXES

Restaurants: There's a 16 percent sales tax on food and drink items, plus a 10 percent service charge added to checks. It's also a good idea to tip an extra 5-10 percent if you liked the service. Pay with cash whenever possible and try to have small bills for tipping. You may find service in the Dominican Republic infuriatingly slow compared to what you are used to. Try to remember that there is a more laid-back approach to time here. Of course, if you find service that really makes you happy, reward it well. Tips are shared with the entire staff.

Shopping: Shops add a 16 percent sales tax for products and services.

Hotels: A 26 percent sales tax will be added to the bill. It is customary to tip the bellhop US$1-2 per bag and leave around US$1-2 per day for maid service.

Departure tax: You pay US$20 upon leaving the country.

Oficinas Gubernmentales, Bloque D, Av. Mexico, 30 de Marzo, tel. 809/221-4660, www.godominicanrepublic.com), is an administrative office where you will most likely need an appointment to talk to anyone.

Specific tourist offices (*oficinas de turismo*) for each region in the book are in that destination's chapter. Go to those offices if you want information regarding the region you are visiting. They may or may not be of any help. Sometimes they just have brochures to hand you, other times they are very chatty and have a wealth of information. Always cross-reference material that they give you with other information you get elsewhere.

FOOD

If you're staying in an all-inclusive resort, your meals will be included into your package deal. While that will feel great for the first few days, you may get the itch for something else and want to venture out. Or, if you are staying in an independent hotel, you may find that meals can differ in their prices big time depending on what area of town you are in. Trying moving away from the main tourist areas, sometimes even just a couple of blocks, and you will find the prices drop dramatically.

Most restaurants will have a variety of things to offer (especially in the tourist areas), with prices ranging US$6–US$17. Pizza and sandwiches are at the low end of the scale, and pricey seafood and steak sit at the higher end.

A plate of *la bandera dominicana,* rice and beans and chicken with some plantains, will run you about US$2–5 depending on the area.

ACCOMMODATIONS

The Dominican Republic offers an unbelievable array of choices for not only the traveler looking for bargains, but also for the traveler who wants to travel relatively on impulse, especially in the low season. The high season requires a little more planning, but deals still abound, especially when you look for deals on the Internet. Prices given in this book are all based on double occupancy for the high season.

The **all-inclusive resort** has been the poster child for Dominican tourism for decades and for good reason. They have been quite successful with travelers who are seeking luxury at a reasonable price. They are lining the coasts and taking up prime beachfront property. All-inclusives are great for people who live hectic lives at home and want the kind of vacation where they can leave "it" all up to someone else. All meals are planned and served in multiple restaurants on location. You don't have to carry any money, you could nap all day and no one would look down their nose at you except to ask you if you want another drink. It is the ultimate in lazy vacations on dry land. Yet, there is a lot to do if you want it. Dance lessons, aerobics, beach volleyball, pool games, excursions, even shopping. When you book a room at one of these resorts, you can expect quite uniformly that the room will have a private bathroom, a TV with lots of channels (in English), hot water, air-conditioning, a balcony (be careful; not all have views), and a mini-refrigerator (the contents of which will cost you extra).

The downside to all-inclusive resorts is that if you never leave the complex, you won't feel the pulse of the island and will probably never see the real Dominican Republic.

Camping

Dominicans will give you a wrinkled nose when you tell them you are going camping.

"*¿Afuera?*" Sleeping outside on purpose is not a popular activity for most Dominicans. That being said, there are a few cabins that are free (first-come, first-served) en route to Pico Duarte. Elsewhere on the island, it is not recommended that you just plop a tent down wherever you choose. You should always ask the owner of the land if it is permissible to sleep there before doing so. If you aren't certain who the owner is, find the nearest Politúr office and ask where the best place is to camp.

RESOURCES

Glossary

apagón power failure

avenida avenue

bachata a type of music and dance (like Dominican country music)

bahía bay

balnearios freshwater swimming holes

bandera dominicana rice and beans and meat dish with fried plantains (literally, the Dominican flag)

barca a big boat

bizcocho cake

bohío thatch hut

botánica a shop where religious and Santeria articles are found

bulto luggage

calle street

campesino a country peasant

campo the countryside

Carnaval pre-Lenten celebration

carretera highway

carroza a horse-drawn wagon

caretas masks; like Carnaval masks

casa house

casabe traditional bread made from yucca plant

casa de cambio money exchange business

catedral cathedral

cerveza beer

civiles civilians; traditional Carnaval character

chicharrones deep-fried meat

chichi baby

chivo goat

colmado small grocery store

Colón, Cristóbal Christopher Columbus

comedor a small restaurant serving Dominican-style food

comida criolla Dominican-style food (literally, Creole food)

conuco a traditional Dominican farm

cuba libre rum and Coke

cueva a cave

fiesta patronal patron saint festival

fortaleza fort

freidurías fried food vendors

fucú an item of bad luck

gallera cock-fighting ring

gomero tire repair shop

guagua small public bus

hostal inn

iglesia church

jeepeta an SUV-type vehicle

la frontera the Haitian border

lago lake

lambí conch (type of seafood)

larimar a semiprecious blue stone found only in the southwestern Dominican Republic

lavanderóa Laundromat

lechón piglet; traditional Carnaval character

longaniza sausage

malecón any boulevard that runs along the ocean

Mamajuana a traditional aphrodisiac drink

mantecado made with lard or butter

mercado market

merengue type of music and dance

mofongo a mashed plantain dish

monasterio monastery

motoconcho motorcycle taxi

museo museum

oficina de turismo tourism office

oro gold

paella seafood and rice dish

palacio palace
parada a stop
parque park
parque central central park or town plaza
pastelito meat- or cheese-filled pastry
pensión inn
pepin a duck-like Carnaval character with spiked horns
peso the monetary unit of the Dominican Republic
plata silver
plátano plantain
playa beach

públicos privately owned cars, trucks, or mini-vans that act as shared taxis, picking up passengers on city streets for a small fee
Presidente a very popular brand of beer
puerta door
puerto port
ruinas ruins
Taíno Amerindian indigenous people
toros bulls; a traditional Carnaval character
vejiga inflated animal bladder; traditional Carnaval prop
yaniqueques johnnycakes; fried bread
yuca yucca plant

Spanish Phrasebook

Your Dominican Republic adventure will be more fun if you use a little Spanish. Dominican folks, although they may smile at your funny accent, will appreciate your halting efforts to break the ice and transform yourself from a foreigner to a potential friend.

Spanish commonly uses 30 letters – the familiar English 26, plus four straightforward additions: ch, ll, ñ, and rr, which are explained in "Consonants," below.

PRONUNCIATION

Once you learn them, Spanish pronunciation rules – in contrast to English – don't change. Spanish vowels generally sound softer than in English. (*Note:* The capitalized syllables below receive stronger accents.)

Vowels

a like ah, as in "hah": *agua* AH-gooah (water), *pan* PAHN (bread), and *casa* CAH-sah (house)

e like ay, as in "may:" *mesa* MAY-sah (table), *tela* TAY-lah (cloth), and *de* DAY (of, from)

i like ee, as in "need": *diez* dee-AYZ (ten), *comida* ko-MEE-dah (meal), and *fin* FEEN (end)

o like oh, as in "go": *peso* PAY-soh (weight), *ocho* OH-choh (eight), and *poco* POH-koh (a bit)

u like oo, as in "cool": *uno* OO-noh (one),

cuarto KOOAHR-toh (room), and *usted* oos-TAYD (you); when it follows a "q" the **u** is silent; when it follows an "h" or has an umlaut, it's pronounced like "w"

Consonants

b, d, f, k, l, m, n, p, q, s, t, v, w, x, y, z, and ch
pronounced almost as in English; **h** occurs, but is silent – not pronounced at all.

c like k as in "keep": *cuarto* KOOAR-toh (room), Tepic tay-PEEK (capital of Nayarit state); when it precedes "e" or "i," pronounce **c** like s, as in "sit": *cerveza* sayr-VAY-sah (beer), *encima* ayn-SEE-mah (atop).

g like g as in "gift" when it precedes "a," "o," "u," or a consonant: *gato* GAH-toh (cat), *hago* AH-goh (I do, make); otherwise, pronounce **g** like h as in "hat": *giro* HEE-roh (money order), *gente* HAYN-tay (people)

j like h, as in "has": *Jueves* HOOAY-vays (Thursday), *mejor* may-HOR (better)

ll like y, as in "yes": *toalla* toh-AH-yah (towel), *ellos* AY-yohs (they, them)

ñ like ny, as in "canyon": *año* AH-nyo (year), *señor* SAY-nyor (Mr., sir)

r is lightly trilled, with tongue at the roof of your mouth like a very light English d, as in "ready": *pero* PAY-doh (but), *tres* TDAYS (three), *cuatro* KOOAH-tdoh (four).

rr like a Spanish r, but with much more emphasis and trill. Let your tongue flap. Practice with *burro* (donkey), *carretera* (highway), and Carrillo (proper name), then really let go with *ferrocarril* (railroad).

Note: The single small but common exception to all of the above is the pronunciation of Spanish **y** when it's being used as the Spanish word for "and," as in "Ron y Kathy." In such case, pronounce it like the English ee, as in "keep": Ron "ee" Kathy (Ron and Kathy).

Accent

The rule for accent, the relative stress given to syllables within a given word, is straightforward. If a word ends in a vowel, an n, or an s, accent the next-to-last syllable; if not, accent the last syllable.

Pronounce *gracias* GRAH-seeahs (thank you), *orden* OHR-dayn (order), and *carretera* kah-ray-TAY-rah (highway) with stress on the next-to-last syllable.

Otherwise, accent the last syllable: *venir* vay-NEER (to come), *ferrocarril* fay-roh-cah-REEL (railroad), and *edad* ay-DAHD (age).

Exceptions to the accent rule are always marked with an accent sign: (á, é, í, ó, or ú), such as *teléfono* tay-LAY-foh-noh (telephone), *jabón* hah-BON (soap), and *rápido* RAH-pee-doh (rapid).

BASIC AND COURTEOUS EXPRESSIONS

Most Spanish-speaking people consider formalities important. Whenever approaching anyone for information or some other reason, do not forget the appropriate salutation – good morning, good evening, etc. Standing alone, the greeting *hola* (hello) can sound brusque.

Hello. *Hola.*
Good morning. *Buenos días.*
Good afternoon. *Buenas tardes.*
Good evening. *Buenas noches.*
How are you? *¿Cómo está usted?*
Very well, thank you. *Muy bien, gracias.*
Okay; good. *Bien.*
Not okay; bad. *Mal or feo.*
So-so. *Más o menos.*

And you? *¿Y usted?*
Thank you. *Gracias.*
Thank you very much. *Muchas gracias.*
You're very kind. *Muy amable.*
You're welcome. *De nada.*
Goodbye. *Adios.*
See you later. *Hasta luego.*
please *por favor*
yes *sí*
no *no*
I don't know. *No sé.*
Just a moment, please. *Momentito, por favor.*
Excuse me, please (when you're trying to get attention). *Disculpe or Con permiso.*
Excuse me (when you've made a boo-boo). *Lo siento.*
Pleased to meet you. *Mucho gusto.*
How do you say...in Spanish? *¿Cómo se dice...en español?*
What is your name? *¿Cómo se llama usted?*
Do you speak English? *¿Habla usted inglés?*
Is English spoken here? (Does anyone here speak English?) *¿Se habla inglés?*
I don't speak Spanish well. *No hablo bien el español.*
I don't understand. *No entiendo.*
How do you say...in Spanish? *¿Cómo se dice...en español?*
My name is . . . *Me llamo . . .*
Would you like . . . *¿Quisiera usted . . .*
Let's go to . . . *Vamos a . . .*

TERMS OF ADDRESS

When in doubt, use the formal *usted* (you) as a form of address.

I *yo*
you (formal) *usted*
you (familiar) *tu*
he/him *él*
she/her *ella*
we/us *nosotros*
you (plural) *ustedes*
they/them *ellos* (all males or mixed gender); *ellas* (all females)
Mr., sir *señor*
Mrs., madam *señora*
miss, young lady *señorita*

wife *esposa*
husband *esposo*
friend *amigo* (male); *amiga* (female)
sweetheart *novio* (male); *novia* (female)
son; daughter *hijo; hija*
brother; sister *hermano; hermana*
father; mother *padre; madre*
grandfather; grandmother *abuelo; abuela*

TRANSPORTATION
Where is . . . ? *¿Dónde está . . . ?*
How far is it to . . . ? *¿A cuánto está . . . ?*
from...to . . . *de...a . . .*
How many blocks? *¿Cuántas cuadras?*
Where (Which) is the way to . . . ? *¿Dónde está el camino a . . . ?*
the bus station *la terminal de autobuses*
the bus stop *la parada de autobuses*
Where is this bus going? *¿Adónde va este autobús?*
the taxi stand *la parada de taxis*
the train station *la estación de ferrocarril*
the boat *el barco*
the launch *lancha; tiburonera*
the dock *el muelle*
the airport *el aeropuerto*
I'd like a ticket to . . . *Quisiera un boleto a . . .*
first (second) class *primera (segunda) clase*
roundtrip *ida y vuelta*
reservation *reservación*
baggage *equipaje*
Stop here, please. *Pare aquí, por favor.*
the entrance *la entrada*
the exit *la salida*
the ticket office *la oficina de boletos*
(very) near; far *(muy) cerca; lejos*
to; toward *a*
by; through *por*
from *de*
the right *la derecha*
the left *la izquierda*
straight ahead *derecho; directo*
in front *en frente*
beside *al lado*
behind *atrás*
the corner *la esquina*
the stoplight *la semáforo*
a turn *una vuelta*

right here *aquí*
somewhere around here *por acá*
right there *allí*
somewhere around there *por allá*
road *el camino*
street; boulevard *calle; bulevar*
block *la cuadra*
highway *carretera*
kilometer *kilómetro*
bridge; toll *puente; cuota*
address *dirección*
north; south *norte; sur*
east; west *oriente (este); poniente (oeste)*

ACCOMMODATIONS
hotel *hotel*
Is there a room? *¿Hay cuarto?*
May I (may we) see it? *¿Puedo (podemos) verlo?*
What is the rate? *¿Cuál es el precio?*
Is that your best rate? *¿Es su mejor precio?*
Is there something cheaper? *¿Hay algo más económico?*
a single room *un cuarto sencillo*
a double room *un cuarto doble*
double bed *cama matrimonial*
twin beds *camas gemelas*
with private bath *con baño*
hot water *agua caliente*
shower *ducha*
towels *toallas*
soap *jabón*
toilet paper *papel higiénico*
blanket *frazada; manta*
sheets *sábanas*
air-conditioned *aire acondicionado*
fan *abanico; ventilador*
key *llave*
manager *gerente*

FOOD
I'm hungry *Tengo hambre.*
I'm thirsty. *Tengo sed.*
menu *carta; menú*
order *orden*
glass *vaso*
fork *tenedor*
knife *cuchillo*

spoon *cuchara*
napkin *servilleta*
soft drink *refresco*
coffee *café*
tea *té*
drinking water *agua pura; agua potable*
bottled carbonated water *agua mineral*
bottled uncarbonated water *agua sin gas*
beer *cerveza*
wine *vino*
milk *leche*
juice *jugo*
cream *crema*
sugar *azúcar*
cheese *queso*
snack *antojo; botana*
breakfast *desayuno*
lunch *almuerzo*
daily lunch special *comida corrida* (or *el menú del día* depending on region)
dinner *comida* (often eaten in late afternoon); *cena* (a late-night snack)
the check *la cuenta*
eggs *huevos*
bread *pan*
salad *ensalada*
fruit *fruta*
mango *mango*
watermelon *sandía*
papaya *papaya*
banana *plátano*
apple *manzana*
orange *naranja*
lime *limón*
fish *pescado*
shellfish *mariscos*
shrimp *camarones*
meat (without) *(sin) carne*
chicken *pollo*
pork *puerco*
beef; steak *res; bistec*
bacon; ham *tocino; jamón*
fried *frito*
roasted *asada*
barbecue; barbecued *barbacoa; al carbón*

SHOPPING
money *dinero*

money-exchange bureau *casa de cambio*
I would like to exchange traveler's checks. *Quisiera cambiar cheques de viajero.*
What is the exchange rate? *¿Cuál es el tipo de cambio?*
How much is the commission? *¿Cuánto cuesta la comisión?*
Do you accept credit cards? *¿Aceptan tarjetas de crédito?*
money order *giro*
How much does it cost? *¿Cuánto cuesta?*
What is your final price? *¿Cuál es su último precio?*
expensive *caro*
cheap *barato; económico*
more *más*
less *menos*
a little *un poco*
too much *demasiado*

HEALTH
Help me please. *Ayúdeme por favor.*
I am ill. *Estoy enfermo.*
Call a doctor. *Llame un doctor.*
Take me to . . . *Lléveme a . . .*
hospital *hospital; sanatorio*
drugstore *farmacia*
pain *dolor*
fever *fiebre*
headache *dolor de cabeza*
stomach ache *dolor de estómago*
burn *quemadura*
cramp *calambre*
nausea *náusea*
vomiting *vomitar*
medicine *medicina*
antibiotic *antibiótico*
pill; tablet *pastilla*
aspirin *aspirina*
ointment; cream *pomada; crema*
bandage *venda*
cotton *algodón*
sanitary napkins use brand name, e.g., Kotex
birth control pills *pastillas anticonceptivas*
contraceptive foam *espuma anticonceptiva*
condoms *preservativos; condones*

toothbrush *cepilla dental*
dental floss *hilo dental*
toothpaste *crema dental*
dentist *dentista*
toothache *dolor de muelas*

POST OFFICE AND COMMUNICATIONS

long-distance telephone *teléfono larga distancia*
I would like to call . . . *Quisiera llamar a . . .*
collect *por cobrar*
station to station *a quien contesta*
person to person *persona a persona*
credit card *tarjeta de crédito*
post office *correo*
general delivery *lista de correo*
letter *carta*
stamp *estampilla, timbre*
postcard *tarjeta*
aerogram *aerograma*
air mail *correo aereo*
registered *registrado*
money order *giro*
package; box *paquete; caja*
string; tape *cuerda; cinta*

AT THE BORDER

border *frontera*
customs *aduana*
immigration *migración*
tourist card *tarjeta de turista*
inspection *inspección; revisión*
passport *pasaporte*
profession *profesión*
marital status *estado civil*
single *soltero*
married; divorced *casado; divorciado*
widowed *viudado*
insurance *seguros*
title *título*
driver's license *licencia de manejar*

AT THE GAS STATION

gas station *gasolinera*
gasoline *gasolina*
unleaded *sin plomo*
full, please *lleno, por favor*

tire *llanta*
tire repair shop *vulcanizadora*
air *aire*
water *agua*
oil (change) *aceite (cambio)*
grease *grasa*
My...doesn't work. *Mi...no sirve.*
battery *batería*
radiator *radiador*
alternator *alternador*
generator *generador*
tow truck *grúa*
repair shop *taller mecánico*
tune-up *afinación*
auto parts store *refaccionería*

VERBS

Verbs are the key to getting along in Spanish. They employ mostly predictable forms and come in three classes, which end in *ar, er,* and *ir,* respectively:

to buy *comprar*
I buy, you (he, she, it) buys *compro, compra*
we buy, you (they) buy *compramos, compran*

to eat *comer*
I eat, you (he, she, it) eats *como, come*
we eat, you (they) eat *comemos, comen*

to climb *subir*
I climb, you (he, she, it) climbs *subo, sube*
we climb, you (they) climb *subimos, suben*

Here are more (with irregularities indicated):

to do or make *hacer* (regular except for *hago,* I do or make)
to go *ir* (very irregular: *voy, va, vamos, van*)
to go (walk) *andar*
to love *amar*
to work *trabajar*
to want *desear, querer*
to need *necesitar*
to read *leer*
to write *escribir*
to repair *reparar*

to stop *parar*
to get off (the bus) *bajar*
to arrive *llegar*
to stay (remain) *quedar*
to stay (lodge) *hospedar*
to leave *salir* (regular except for *salgo*, I leave)
to look at *mirar*
to look for *buscar*
to give *dar* (regular except for *doy*, I give)
to carry *llevar*
to have *tener* (irregular but important: *tengo, tiene, tenemos, tienen*)
to come *venir* (similarly irregular: *vengo, viene, venimos, vienen*)

Spanish has two forms of "to be":

to be *estar* (regular except for *estoy*, I am)
to be *ser* (very irregular: *soy, es, somos, son*)

Use *estar* when speaking of location or a temporary state of being: "I am at home." *"Estoy en casa."* "I'm sick." *"Estoy enfermo."* Use *ser* for a permanent state of being: "I am a doctor." *"Soy doctora."*

NUMBERS
zero *cero*
one *uno*
two *dos*
three *tres*
four *cuatro*
five *cinco*
six *seis*
seven *siete*
eight *ocho*
nine *nueve*
10 *diez*
11 *once*
12 *doce*
13 *trece*
14 *catorce*
15 *quince*
16 *dieciseis*
17 *diecisiete*
18 *dieciocho*
19 *diecinueve*
20 *veinte*
21 *veinte y uno* or *veintiuno*
30 *treinta*
40 *cuarenta*
50 *cincuenta*
60 *sesenta*
70 *setenta*
80 *ochenta*
90 *noventa*
100 *ciento*
101 *ciento y uno* or *cientiuno*
200 *doscientos*
500 *quinientos*
1,000 *mil*
10,000 *diez mil*
100,000 *cien mil*
1,000,000 *millón*
one half *medio*
one third *un tercio*
one fourth *un cuarto*

TIME
What time is it? *¿Qué hora es?*
It's one o'clock. *Es la una.*
It's three in the afternoon. *Son las tres de la tarde.*
It's 4 A.M. *Son las cuatro de la mañana.*
six-thirty *seis y media*
a quarter till eleven *un cuarto para las once*
a quarter past five *las cinco y cuarto*
an hour *una hora*

DAYS AND MONTHS
Monday *lunes*
Tuesday *martes*
Wednesday *miércoles*
Thursday *jueves*
Friday *viernes*
Saturday *sábado*
Sunday *domingo*
today *hoy*
tomorrow *mañana*
yesterday *ayer*
January *enero*
February *febrero*
March *marzo*
April *abril*
May *mayo*

June *junio*
July *julio*
August *agosto*
September *septiembre*
October *octubre*
November *noviembre*
December *diciembre*
a week *una semana*

a month *un mes*
after *después*
before *antes*

(Courtesy of Bruce Whipperman, author of *Moon Pacific Mexico*.)

Suggested Reading

FICTION

Alvarez, Julia. *A Cafecito Story*. White River Junction, VT: Chelsea Green Publishing Company, 2001. A parable about people participating in sustainability: growing coffee, caring for land, consumerism, and impacting tourism.

Alvarez, Julia. *How the Garcia Girls Lost Their Accents*. Chapel Hill, NC: Algonquin Books, 1994. Alvarez paints a beautiful and honest portrait of a Dominican family and their struggle and desire to Americanize. The details of Dominican society, the immigrant views, and the first-generation rebellion stories are both subtly written and profoundly present.

Alvarez, Julia. *In the Time of the Butterflies*. Chapel Hill, NC: Algonquin Books, 1994. The award-winning, historical fiction novel about the Mirabal sisters, who died for the underground movement to overthrow Trujillo.

Bierhorst, John. *Latin American Folktales: Stories from Hispanic and Indian Traditions*. New York, NY: Pantheon Books, 2003. A wonderful collection of Latin American folktales, including some early colonial tales.

Danticat, Edwidge. *The Farming of the Bones*. New York: Soho, 1999. Set in the Dominican Republic of 1937, this is a historical fiction tale of the Haitian experience in the Dominican Republic under the brutal tyranny of Trujillo.

Díaz, Junot. *The Brief Wondrous Life of Oscar Wao*. New York: Riverhead Books, 2007. The celebrated first novel from Díaz, about a geeked-out Dominican-American comic book lover, won the author the Pulitzer Prize. Street lingo meets lyrical prose with a seamless beauty to create a work of art. It's a spot-on representation of this country's oral history.

Díaz, Junot. *Drown*. New York: Penguin Putnam, 2000. A collection of 10 short stories set in the Dominican Republic and in America brimming with sensory accuracy, complex characters, and evocative language.

Vargas Llosa, Mario. *The Feast of the Goat*. New York, NY: Farrar, Straus and Giroux, 2001. A historical fiction about the final days and assassination of Trujillo. A Spanish film company made the novel into a film in 2005 with the Spanish name *La Fiesta del Chivo*, starring Isabella Rossellini.

HISTORY

Cambeira, Alan. *Quisqueya la Bella: The Dominican Republic in Historical and Cultural Perspective (Perspectives on Latin America and the Caribbean)*. Armonk, NY: M.E. Sharpe, Inc., 1996. A look at pre-Columbian Hispaniola, the various peoples and cultures that have occupied the island, and modern-day Dominican Republic.

Chester, Eric Thomas. *Rag-Tags, Scum, Riff-Raff, and Commies: The U.S. Intervention in the Dominican Republic, 1965–1966.* New York: New York University Press, 2001. A historical look at U.S. and Latin American relations with a focus on the events of the 1965 U.S. invasion of the Dominican Republic using recently declassified intelligence documents.

Diederich, Bernard. *Trujillo: The Death of the Dictator.* Princeton, NJ: Markus Wiener Publishers, 2000. A look at how Trujillo was assassinated and how his politics shaped the country and its people for decades even after his death.

Hall, Michael R. *Sugar and Power in the Dominican Republic: Eisenhower, Kennedy, and the Trujillos.* Westport, CT: Greenwood Press, 2000. An examination of the sugar industry in the Dominican Republic, the effect it had on U.S.–Dominican relations, and how leaders of both countries manipulated one another through the industry.

Kelsey, Harry. *Sir Francis Drake: The Queen's Pirate.* London: Yale University Press, 2000. Brave explorer or ruthless pirate? Depends on who you ask. In Sir Francis Drake's exploits through the Caribbean, he repeatedly sacked Spanish ships and ports (like Santo Domingo), yet was rewarded by the queen of England and quite admired by his countrymen (but hated by his shipmates). This biography offers the potent opinion that the history books didn't get it right, suggesting that Drake was a very selfish and often cowardly man.

Lowenthal, Abraham F. *The Dominican Intervention.* Baltimore, MD: The Johns Hopkins University Press, 1972. A good resource for data, politics, origins, and understanding of the American "intervention" in the Dominican Republic using over 100 personal interviews and classified documents.

Matibag, Eugenio. *Haitian-Dominican Counterpoint.* New York: Palgrave Macmillan, 2002. The complicated history of the Haitian–Dominican border and relations. Cultural differences and likenesses are also examined.

Wucker, Michele. *Why the Cocks Fight: Dominicans, Haitians, and the Fight for Hispaniola.* New York: Hill and Wang, 2000. This book looks at the overexaggerated differences between Haitian and Dominican cultures and tries to examine what is truly at the center of so much tumult.

Taíno History

Alegria, Ricardo, and José Arrom. *Taíno: Pre-Columbian Art and Culture from the Caribbean.* New York: Monacelli, 1998. It didn't take even 100 years for Columbus's men to wipe out the Taíno civilization, but some of their art, language, and cultural practices survive in modern societies throughout the Caribbean.

Deagan, Kathleen, and José María Cruxent. *Columbus's Outpost among the Taínos: Spain and America at La Isabela, 1493–1498.* London: Yale University Press, 2002. The authors studied the settlement of La Isabela for 10 years, along with scores of colonial-era documents. They draw conclusions about the reasons why Columbus failed at La Isabela.

Rouse, Irving. *The Taínos: Rise and Decline of the People Who Greeted Columbus.* New Haven, CT: Yale University Press, 1993. Thirty-five years of archaeological research went into this author's examination of Taíno society.

CULTURE

Gonzalez, Clara. *Aunt Clara's Dominican Cookbook.* New York: Lunch Club Press, 2005. Learn to make a killer *sancocho* for your next celebration! A must-have cookbook for good, basic Dominican fare.

Klein, Alan. *Sugarball: The American Game, the Dominican Dream.* London: Yale University Press, 1993. This book outlines the history, growth, and obsession of baseball in the Dominican Republic and how it has affected the country's relations with the United States.

Lipsitz, George. *Footsteps in the Dark.* Minneapolis: University of Minnesota Press, 2007. While this is a broad look at all music genres, there is a very good chapter on merengue and the hidden history of the Dominican migration.

Pacini Hernandez, Deborah. *Bachata: A Social History of Dominican Popular Music.* Philadelphia, PA: Temple University Press, 1995. Often called the country music or blues of the Dominican Republic, *bachata* emerged in the 1960s and has been enjoying a resurgence since Juan Luis Guerra won a Latin Grammy award in 1992. This book examines the culture and politics of *bachata* as a stand-alone medium and in relationship to merengue.

Ruck, Rob. *The Tropic of Baseball: Baseball in the Dominican Republic.* Lincoln, NE: University of Nebraska Press, 1999. The history and present state of Dominican baseball, its impact on the country's collective dream, and its effect on society as a whole.

Sellers, Julie A. *Merengue and Dominican Identity: Music as National Unifier.* Jefferson, NC: McFarland & Company, 2004. Music and dance is the unifying thread that connects all Dominicans, whether at home or abroad. Book and CD edition.

ECOLOGY

Bond, James. *A Field Guide to the Birds of the West Indies.* New York: Houghton Mifflin, 1999. This is a very thorough catalog of more than 400 birds in the West Indies.

Latta, Steven, et al. *Birds of the Dominican Republic and Haiti.* Princeton, NJ: Princeton University Press, 2006. This is an indispensable guide when bird-watching in the Dominican Republic.

Poinar, George O., and Roberta Poinar. *The Amber Forest: A Reconstruction of a Vanished World.* Princeton, NJ: Princeton University Press, 1999. The resin of the algorrobo tree created a sap 15–45 million years ago. The authors of this book use their knowledge of amber today to recreate what the Dominican ecosystem would've been like back when the sap still flowed.

Spalding, Mark. *A Guide to the Coral Reefs of the Caribbean.* Berkeley, CA: University of California Press, 2004. This guide is endorsed by the United Nations Environment Programme (UNEP) and the World Wildlife Fund (WWF) for those who not only want to explore the reefs of the Caribbean, but who also want to protect them.

ADVENTURE

Bory, Marc. *Kitesurfing.* Paris: Fitway Publishing, 2005. A guide to help you become a real kitesurfing fanatic.

Boyce, Jeremy. *The Ultimate Book of Power Kiting and Kiteboarding.* Augusta, GA: The Lyons Press, 2004. A good resource for learning how to buy a kite, care for the equipment, and how to use it.

Leubben, Craig. *Rock Climbing: Mastering Basic Skills.* Seattle, WA: Mountaineers Books, 2004. Plenty of how-to tips on the technique, movement, and strength required when learning how to rock climb. Photos and graphics further illustrate the necessary skills for the novice.

Internet Resources

Active Cabarete
www.activecabarete.com
Look here for any information on water sports, accommodations, upcoming events, restaurants, bars, and general services for Cabarete, a water-sports hot spot.

Cabarete Kiteboarding
www.cabaretekiteboarding.com
This site has lots of great info on kiteboarding schools, lodging (hotels and other options), weather, and water conditions.

Caribe Tours
http://caribetours.com.do
While this bus company's site is only in Spanish, navigating through it is simple and you'll find addresses to the bus stations in the country as well as departure times from Santo Domingo to the rest of the towns *(Horarios desde Santo Domingo)* and to Santo Domingo from the other towns *(Horarios desde el interior).*

The Dominican Batey
www.dominicanbatey.org
A great site dedicated to educating people on the state of migrant sugarcane workers, culture, and life in the *bateyes* of the Dominican Republic.

DR1
www.dr1.com
DR1 is the best online English-language source for Dominican news, travel information, weather, currency exchange rates, and just about anything you might need to know. There is even a forum to post questions or talk to other English speakers about the country.

DR Pure: Adventure in the Dominican Republic
www.drpure.com
This website gives loads of information on the adventure options in the Dominican Republic, where you can do them, in addition to some handy general information.

Embassy of the Dominican Republic in the United States of America
www.domrep.org
The embassy site has information on tourism, airlines that service the Dominican Republic, immigration, and even what you'll need to get a quick Dominican divorce.

Golf Dominican Republic
www.punta-cana-golf.com
While the website sounds like it has info only on golfing in Punta Cana, there are links to other regions in the Dominican Republic, complete with information on greens fees, course designers' names, hours, and even which hole is the most challenging.

Hispaniola.com
www.hispaniola.com
This is another good website for travel and tourism information, including helpful information on where to stay.

Iguana Mama
www.iguanamama.com
Iguana Mama is perhaps the most respected, safest, and most well-organized adventure travel tour company; it's located in Cabarete.

Ministry of Tourism
www.godominicanrepublic.com
This site offers information not only about the Dominican Republic in general, but also about transportation, shopping, visa regulations, what you'll need to get married, and events calendars.

Samana.net
www.samana.net

Try this site for all information about the Península de Samaná (including the towns of Las Galeras, Las Terrenas, and Samaná)—accommodations, restaurants, and visitors guides.

Tours, Trips, Treks & Travel
www.4tdomrep.com

This tour company offers treks to lesser-known areas and interesting packages like educational tours or exciting helicopter trips. They also do custom wedding package trips.

Index

List of Maps

Acknowledgments

Thank you to the people of the Dominican Republic.

Thanks to Dr. Luis Simo, Doña Tatis de Olmos, Carlos Bautista, and Daniel and everyone from the Ministry of Tourism for all their hard work and hospitality during my visit and research.

Thank you to my *entire* families Chavier and Caamaño for helping me and housing me during my research. I love you all.

Mom and Dad. Thank you for sharing your knowledge of the country and for helping me in so many ways. The time that we have spent together while researching these books are some of my most cherished memories in the Dominican Republic.

Alicia and Sam: Having you in Santo Domingo made it a party! Who else would have *chimichurri* on speed dial?! Thank you for sharing your photography and hard work back home too.

Thank you to the entire staff at Avalon Travel. Especially my editor Tiffany Watson, photo editor Kathryn Osgood, and map editor Mike Morgenfeld. I appreciate everyone's hard work.

I would also like to thank the following people for their help or encouragement along the way: Terry Minkler, San Manh, and the volunteers of Just Dance Ballroom and Clay Stiles.

I have special gratitude for Sabrina Smith. Thank you, for being cheerleader and supporter to a travel writer, for patience with dirty dishes around deadlines, for unconditional love, for a tear-inducing sense of humor, and for help with maps!

Thanks to everyone who supported and encouraged me or to whom I had the pleasure of meeting along the way. Save the next *bachata* for me!

www.moon.com

DESTINATIONS | ACTIVITIES | BLOGS | MAPS | BOOKS

MOON.COM is all new, and ready to help plan your next trip! Filled with fresh trip ideas and strategies, author interviews, informative blogs, a detailed map library, and descriptions of all the Moon guidebooks, Moon.com is all you need to get out and explore the world—or even places in your own backyard. As always, when you travel with Moon, expect an experience that is uncommon and truly unique.

MAP SYMBOLS

▭ Expressway	**C** Highlight	✗ Airfield	♩ Golf Course
Primary Road	○ City/Town	✈ Airport	**P** Parking Area
Secondary Road	◉ State Capital	▲ Mountain	⚎ Archaeological Site
Unpaved Road	⊛ National Capital	✛ Unique Natural Feature	♦ Church
Trail	★ Point of Interest		⛽ Gas Station
Ferry	• Accommodation	⌇ Waterfall	Glacier
Railroad	▾ Restaurant/Bar	♠ Park	Mangrove
Pedestrian Walkway	▪ Other Location	**T** Trailhead	Reef
Stairs	Λ Campground	⛷ Skiing Area	Swamp

CONVERSION TABLES

°C = (°F - 32) / 1.8
°F = (°C x 1.8) + 32
1 inch = 2.54 centimeters (cm)
1 foot = 0.304 meters (m)
1 yard = 0.914 meters
1 mile = 1.6093 kilometers (km)
1 km = 0.6214 miles
1 fathom = 1.8288 m
1 chain = 20.1168 m
1 furlong = 201.168 m
1 acre = 0.4047 hectares
1 sq km = 100 hectares
1 sq mile = 2.59 square km
1 ounce = 28.35 grams
1 pound = 0.4536 kilograms
1 short ton = 0.90718 metric ton
1 short ton = 2,000 pounds
1 long ton = 1.016 metric tons
1 long ton = 2,240 pounds
1 metric ton = 1,000 kilograms
1 quart = 0.94635 liters
1 US gallon = 3.7854 liters
1 Imperial gallon = 4.5459 liters
1 nautical mile = 1.852 km

°FAHRENHEIT / °CELSIUS thermometer scale:
230 — 110
220
210 — 100 WATER BOILS
200
190 — 90
180 — 80
170
160 — 70
150
140 — 60
130
120 — 50
110
100 — 40
90 — 30
80
70 — 20
60
50 — 10
40
30 — 0 WATER FREEZES
20
10 — -10
0
-10 — -20
-20 — -30
-30
-40 — -40

Clock face: 12/24, 1/13, 2/14, 3/15, 4/16, 5/17, 6/18, 7/19, 8/20, 9/21, 10/22, 11/23

INCH ruler: 0 1 2 3 4

CM ruler: 0 1 2 3 4 5 6 7 8 9 10

MOON DOMINICAN REPUBLIC

Avalon Travel
a member of the Perseus Books Group
1700 Fourth Street
Berkeley, CA 94710, USA
www.moon.com

Editor: Tiffany Watson
Series Manager: Kathryn Ettinger
Copy Editor: Deana Shields
Graphics Coordinator: Kathryn Osgood
Production Coordinator: Darren Alessi
Cover Designer: Kathryn Osgood
Map Editor: Mike Morgenfeld
Cartographers: Chris Markiewicz, Kat Bennett
Indexer: Deana Shields

ISBN: 978-1-59880-253-5
ISSN: 1092-3349

Printing History
1st Edition – 1997
4th Edition – January 2010
5 4 3 2 1

Some photos and illustrations are used by permission
and are the property of the original copyright
owners.

Front cover photo: Boy swinging on tree, Caribbean,
Dominican Republic, Samana Peninsula, Las Terrenas
© Angelo Cavalli
Title page photo: © Ana Chavier Caamaño
Interior color photos: © Ana Chavier Caamaño except
pages 7 (upper left), 10, 14, 18, 20 © Alicia Chavier
Caamaño; pages 12, 15 © Samuel Krucker

Printed in Canada by Friesens Corp.

KEEPING CURRENT

If you have a favorite gem you'd like to see included in the next edition, or see anything
that needs updating, clarification, or correction, please drop us a line. Send your
comments via email to feedback@moon.com, or use the address above.